A Military History of
Modern South Africa

A Military History of Modern South Africa

Ian van der Waag

CASEMATE

Philadelphia & Oxford

To Adam and Michaela

First published in South Africa in 2015 by Jonathan Ball Publishers

Published in the United States of America and Great Britain in 2018 by
CASEMATE PUBLISHERS
1950 Lawrence Road, Havertown, PA 19083, USA
and
The Old Music Hall, 106–108 Cowley Road, Oxford OX4 1JE, UK

Hardcover Edition: ISBN 978-1-61200-582-9
Digital Edition: ISBN 978-1-61200-583-6

A CIP record for this book is available from the British Library

Printed and bound in the United States of America

For a complete list of Casemate titles, please contact:

CASEMATE PUBLISHERS (US)
Telephone (610) 853-9131
Fax (610) 853-9146
Email: casemate@casematepublishers.com
www.casematepublishers.com

CASEMATE PUBLISHERS (UK)
Telephone (01865) 241249
Email: casemate-uk@casematepublishers.co.uk
www.casematepublishers.co.uk

Set in10.5/14pt Minion Pro

Contents

Maps

Figures

Tables

Abbreviations

ACF	Active Citizen Force
Apla	Azanian People's Liberation Army
BDF	Bophuthatswana Defence Force
CAHT	Cape Auxiliary Horse Transport
CCF	Cape Colonial Forces (pre-1910)
CF	Citizen Force (from 1957)
CGF	Coast Garrison Force
CGS	Chief of the General Staff
CPR	Certified Personnel Register
DCGS	Deputy Chief of the General Staff
DRA	Defence Rifle Association(s)
EEF	Egyptian Expeditionary Force
FEAF	Far East Air Forces (USAF)
FTF	Full-Time Force
GOC	general officer commanding
MK	Umkhonto we Sizwe
MPLA	Movimento Popular de Libertção de Angola
NPKF	National Peacekeeping Force
NSF	non-statutory forces
OAU	Organization of African Unity
PF	Permanent Force (from 1957)
Renamo	Resistência Nacional Moçambicana
RNVR	Royal Naval Volunteer Reserve
SAAC	South African Aviation Corps
SAAF	South African Air Force
SAC	South African Constabulary
SADF	South African Defence Force
SAEC	South African Engineer Corps

SAFA	South African Field Artillery
SAMC	South African Medical Corps
SAMR	South African Mounted Riflemen
SANDF	South African National Defence Force
SANF	South African Naval Forces
SANLC	South African Native Labour Contingent
SANS	South African Naval Service
SAP	South African Police
SAPF	South African Permanent Force
SAR&H	South African Railways & Harbours
SDF	Seaward Defence Force
SDUs	self-defence units
SSB	Special Service Battalion
SWAP	South West Africa Police
Swapo	South West Africa People's Organization
SWATF	South West Africa Territorial Force
TBVC	Transkei, Bophuthatswana, Venda and Ciskei (forces)
TDF	Transkei Defence Force
UDF	Union Defence Force (Union Defence Forces until 1921)
Unita	União Nacional para a Independência Total de Angola
Untag	United Nations Transition Assistance Group
VDF	Venda Defence Force
ZAR	Zuid-Afrikaansche Republiek (Transvaal)

Introduction

Twentieth-century South Africa saw continuous, often rapid and fundamental socio-economic and political change. The century started with a brief but total war. Less than ten years later, a triumphant Britain, with beneficence not unmixed with self-interest, brought the conquered Boer republics and the Cape and Natal colonies together into the Union of South Africa. The Union Defence Force (UDF), from 1957 the South African Defence Force (SADF), was deployed during most of the major wars of the century as well as a number of internal and regional struggles: the two world wars, Korea, uprising and rebellion on the part of Afrikaner and black nationalists, and industrial unrest chiefly on the Witwatersrand. The century ended as it started, with another war. But this was a limited war, a flashpoint of the Cold War, which embraced more than just the subcontinent and lasted a long, thirty years. The outcome of this regional conflict included the final withdrawal of foreign troops from southern Africa, the withdrawal of South African forces from Angola and Namibia, and the transfer of political power in South Africa away from a white elite to a broad-based democracy. This period of about one hundred years is packed full of episode and personality.

History, as we are so often vividly reminded, is a complex business and happens on a broad front. Writing, on the other hand, is a linear development and no historian can possibly get *the whole* of his history between the covers of a single book. 'Every history', Georg Iggers reminds us, 'can only present a partial reconstruction of the past.'[1] However, while this book addresses the various wars and campaigns in which South Africa was involved, the narrative is more ranging than the utilitarian and antiquarian approaches of more traditional accounts. This book is not an encyclopaedia of South Africa's battles and military events (this has been attempted by others[2]) or, at the other end of the spectrum, of how South Africa's wars have been commemorated and memorialised.[3] In this regard, I have taken my inspiration from a number of eminent military historians who have, in many ways, set the yardstick with their histories of the armed forces of their respective nations. They have produced deeper, wider-ranging narratives, but have succeeded in retaining enough of the mêlée and the noise of battle and the smell of cordite to satisfy most battle enthusiasts.[4] I hope to have achieved the same.

This book is the first study of the South African armed forces as an institution and of the multilayered and complex roles that these forces played in the wars, rebellions, uprisings and protests of the period. It deals in the first instance with the evolution of South African defence policy, the development and shaping of the armed forces and the people who served in these forces and commanded them. I have been aware throughout of Michael Howard's call for width, depth and context, and have attempted to place the narrative within the broader national past.[5]

My approach is therefore at three levels. The first is at the defence policy level and deals with the politico-strategic landscape, the national threat assessment, strategy formulation and force design. The questions are ranging and by no means limited to the evolution of South African strategy, the interrelationship between policy, strategy and foreign affairs, the relationship between the civil and military authorities – particularly during wartime – inter-service competition and cooperation, and the relationship between South African policy and strategy and that of the country's allies, most notably Britain, during the period until 1961. Interestingly, the threat perceptions changed little over this period. There was always a non-African power, able to project force intercontinentally; this was, at various times, Germany (1910s and 1930s), France (1920s), Italy (1930s) and, after the Second World War, the USSR and possibly even the UK and (more unlikely) India. There was also the threat of landward invasion from continental Africa, first in the form of a colonial power with imperial objectives, and then (from 1920) the possibility of an African revolt against colonial rule; in the post-war years, it meant a possible Pan-African army formed by a coalition of newly liberated states. The third threat, amply recognised from 1906, was that of an internal uprising. By the 1960s these possibilities were feared, particularly if an internal uprising was supported by the concerted action of a world superpower and a coalition of African states.

The second level of analysis involves the deployment of the armed forces and their performance in the campaigns fought. This book arose in part out of my experience of teaching the military history of South Africa at the South African Military Academy, which revealed the need for a study in one volume spanning South Africa's involvement in the major conflicts of the twentieth century – a study of where South Africans fought and why, and of the impact of those wars and conflicts on domestic politics, on South African society and on the economy. In some ways South Africa is unique, for it was involved in three total wars during this period – the Second Anglo-Boer War and the two world wars. These conflicts form the foundation for what came later, for the Cold War in southern Africa and the proliferation of interconnecting conflicts in the region between 1960 and 1990, and for state formation between 1975 and 1994. These events form the core of a key historical period in the making of modern South Africa; a hundred years from now, historians may very well group together the wars of the late nineteenth century, the Second Anglo-Boer War, the Afrikaner rebellion, the campaign in German South West Africa and the armed struggle against apartheid as the 'Wars of South African Unification'.

At a third level, a number of broad themes investigate the impact of defence policy on the armed forces and on South Africa's development internally as well as on its relations with other states. The first armed forces for South Africa, as a political entity, were established from 1 July 1912, bringing together the armed forces of the four colonies that entered the Union of South Africa on 31 May 1910. Ten years before, the officers and men who were to integrate into the new Union Defence Force had been at war, cousin fighting cousin, and sometimes brother against brother. This war, a total war in every respect, and the first total war of the twentieth century, is therefore the logical place for this study to start. However, as the difficult integration of 1912 shows, the UDF was not a national institution in a true sense. It lacked broad-based acceptance, which opened a trans-national debate on the development of a *South African* defence policy and the definition of what might be described as a *South African* way of war. This debate was led first by Afrikaner nationalists, some of whom came out in open rebellion in 1914, and then toward the end of the century by a growing and more voluble black opposition to the apartheid state.

This debate leads directly to the question of military culture, which, to quote Williamson Murray, 'might best be described as the sum of the intellectual, professional, and traditional values of an officer corps; it plays a central role in how that officer corps assesses the external environment and how it analyzes the possible response that it might make to "the threat".'[6] Military culture, traditionally elitist, is influenced by a complex of intersecting and interacting factors and in South Africa has, for all the obvious reasons, been the focus of competing interests based in large part on military competition and contested histories. Military culture is important, for it is a crucial indicator of how armed forces think, how they prepare for war, and how those wars are fought. This line of investigation goes further and questions the historical and organisational continuity between the Union Defence Force, the South African Defence Force and the South African National Defence Force, and recognises the roles played by the armed forces and military structures of competing political organisations in a fractured society.

The study of South Africa's military experience has tended to follow parallel paths. The military historians have tended to focus almost solely on the UDF and the SADF, while social and protest historians and sociologists have investigated the history of the armed struggle and of MK and Apla. These historians have also tended not to engage with each other's work. This book is a modest attempt to connect these paths and recognise that the histories of these organisations, although in contest with each other for practically all of their past, need now to be woven into the new, single historical tapestry of the SANDF. Military culture is dynamic in concept, and a distinctive South African approach, which now imbues the SANDF, has developed over the past centuries, from a variety of influences. These strands, drawn from Western, African and revolutionary sources, came together at the end of the twentieth century.[7]

We need to study the military history of South Africa in width, depth and context. The military has played far too important a role in society for it to be neglected as the substance of an academic backwater. But to do so at all adequately we need to be rid of the myths that swamp discussion and cloud understanding. As Richard Bosworth has argued in relation to the Second World War, 'the initial traumatic effect of the war was to "freeze time" and thus to provide a simple historical explanation about what had recently happened. Eventually, however, a thaw occurs.'[8]

My principal debt, as is the case for all archives-driven research, is to those individuals who left first-hand accounts or created a correspondence, which has been fortuitously kept, of the events covered by this book. For without them this book could never have been written. They include active participants, sometimes casual observers, and the clerks of, especially, the Department of Defence during times of war as much as the more leisured periods of peace. These historical actors range down the tiers of society, from the corridors of power to the lowest-ranking Springbok soldier in the field or clerk at Defence

Headquarters. The first tier includes Jan Smuts, who stands centrally for much of the first half of the twentieth century and is well buttressed by the papers of a succession of South African politicians and British High Commissioners. Many first- and second-tier actors, and several from the third tier, left papers and, for the first part of our period, were also responsible for cranking out the enormous volume of official paperwork through a number of government departments. Providentially, the official record is occasionally also supplemented by private papers generated towards the bottom of the social-military pyramid, giving something of a view 'from the bottom'. All are now dead. Their accounts and the details of their documentary residue may be found in my list of Sources.

The research for this book was conducted over an extended period on three continents and took me on a rewarding adventure through many libraries, archival repositories and record offices, where, in every case, I was ably assisted by a range of historians, archivists, librarians and research officers. They include Louise Jooste, Steve de Agrela, Evert Kleynhans and Gerald Prinsloo at the SANDF Documentation Centre in Pretoria; Amy Hurst of the Royal Marines Archives, Eastney Barracks, Portsmouth, UK; Alison McCann at the West Sussex Record Office in Chichester; Joyce Purnell at Hagley Hall, West Midlands; Lesley Hart and her staff in the Special Collections Department of the University of Cape Town Libraries; Louise Fourie, Special Collections, JS Gericke Library, Stellenbosch University; Marie Coetzee, Archives and Special Collections, University of South Africa; Carol Archibald at the William Cullen Library (University of the Witwatersrand); Annette Kelner of the Ferdinand Postma Library, North-West University, Potchefstroom; Mark Coghlan, Natal Carbineers Archives, Pietermaritzburg; and the many others who assisted me at the Military Academy Library in Saldanha, the Bodleian Library and the Rhodes House Library in Oxford, the British Library in London, the National Library of Scotland, the South African National Museum of Military History, the Worcestershire Record Office, the Omar N Bradley Special Collections Library of the Thayer Library at the US Military Academy, West Point, Ridgeway Hall and the US Army Heritage and Education Centre outside Carlisle, Pennsylvania, the National Archives of South Africa in Pretoria and Cape Town, and the National Archives of the United Kingdom at Kew, London. I gratefully acknowledge permission to use and quote from papers in their possession. A special thanks in this regard is accorded to the Rt Hon Viscount Cobham for access to the Hagley Hall Archives, to the Rt Hon Lord

Egremont and Leconfield for access to the Hugh Wyndham Papers, and to Mr John Maxse for access to the Maxse Papers.

I have previously published some of the ideas contained in this book. This has been in other forms, chiefly as articles in the journals *War in History*, *Historia* and *Scientia Militaria*. In most instances, these ideas have been subjected to further research, reconsidered and reworked, the refreshed ideas being incorporated into this publication. In all cases I am grateful to the editors of these journals and special collections and to the copyright holders.

My heartfelt thanks also to the historians and other scholars upon whose scholarship many of my conclusions rest. The references only hint at the richness of the available work. Friends and colleagues have given advice and encouragement, especially Jeffrey Grey (who first suggested that I write a military history of South Africa), Kent Fedorowich, Andrew Stewart, Ross Anderson, Donal Lowry and Fransjohan Pretorius. My colleagues at Stellenbosch University, on both the Saldanha and Stellenbosch campuses, and in particular Deon Visser, Fankie Monama, Sandra Swart, Albert Grundlingh, Bill Nasson, Wessel Visser and Anton Ehlers, have all offered encouragement and inspiration along the way. Sam Tshehla, our Dean of Military Science, places a high premium on research production and fosters a laudable flexible-time arrangement for researchers who, due to pressures of the lecture roster, cannot leave the lecture halls and seminar rooms unattended. My neighbour, Polla Smit, took care of my house and my hounds when I did manage to get away.

Students past and present, particularly Evert Kleynhans, David Katz, Will Gordon, Tony Garcia, Victor Moukambi, Gustav Bentz, Tjaard Barnard, Herman Warden, Richard Gueli, Andries Fokkens, Clifton Nkadimeng and Rassie Nortier, challenged me and helped shape my thoughts in various ways over many years. I must also mention Thibault Frizac, Hervé de Bentôt, Philippe-Edouard Rendu and Adrien Bresch, all graduate students of the French military academy at Saint-Cyr who, over a number of years, spent their international semester with us and enriched our discussion of South Africa's military past.

The team at Jonathan Ball have been nothing short of fantastic. I should like to thank (again) Jeremy Boraine, the publishing director, who has been patient and understanding; Ceri Prenter, the production manager; and Alfred LeMaitre, who has been a careful and considerate editor, offering useful advice of all kinds along the way and noting many errors of fact that slipped my attention. Having said that, any remaining errors are of course mine alone.

To my family, my gratitude is due, as always. My late father, although an accountant and businessman by profession, instilled a deep sense of history and a love of the finer things in life. In this he was ably assisted by my mother, who since his passing more than twenty years ago has been the ballast in the life of our wider family. Of my siblings, I must thank Patrick and Jose and Emil, remarkable people who give and care, in reality without measure. The bulk of this book was written during a difficult time and it is dedicated, for all of the reasons, to Adam and Michaela, two of the very best.

CHAPTER ONE

South Africa, 1899–1902:
The Last Gentleman's War?

The Anglo-Boer War, fought more than a century ago, has a fixed place in modern historical memory ... Some part of that interest is certainly lingering popular nostalgia for a long-gone era, an imagined time before the advent of modern, industrial-scale mass slaughter, when men were supposed to have fought more honourably, or at least more politely ... an image in which plodding but hardy British regiments fought clean and courageous engagements with decent Boer citizen commandos.[1]

– Bill Nasson, historian, 2010, on the imagery of the war

Individual bravery, of the kind which takes no heed of personal risk, reckless heroic dash, they have not, nor do they pretend to have. Their system is entirely otherwise. They do not seek fighting for fighting's sake. They do not like exposing themselves to risk and danger. Their caution and their care for personal safety are such that, judged by the standard of other people's conduct in similar positions, they are frequently considered to be wanting in personal courage.[2]

– Sir Percy Fitzpatrick, writer and politician, 1899, on the Boer forces

At 5.50 am on 20 October 1899, a shot from a Krupp gun on Talana Hill entered the British camp at Dundee. The shell landed with a thunderous roar near the tent of Major General Sir William Penn Symons, sending dirt showering across the camp. A reality dawned. The shells that now streaked across the morning sky, shattering the pre-dawn stillness of the small Natal town, announced the arrival of a Boer army. Symons, who had, some hours before, carelessly disregarded the Boer van as nothing but a small raiding party, now realised his mistake. The British war machine swung into action. Officers and NCOs barked commands, whistles sounded and the troops of the 18th Hussars, three batteries of field artillery and four infantry battalions assembled rapidly to dislodge the Boers from the hill. The Second Anglo-Boer War, triggered when a Pretoria ultimatum expired on 11 October, had started in earnest.

Opinions as to what – or, perhaps more importantly, who – caused the war were many. Decades of escalating tension between Britain and the two small Boer republics – the Zuid-Afrikaansche Republiek (ZAR), or Transvaal, and the Orange Free State – had reached flashpoint at the time of the Jameson Raid in December 1895. By 22 September 1899, a wide-scale war in South Africa had become inevitable. Thoughtful explanations include the financial and moneyed interests of empire-builders like Cecil John Rhodes, the aggressive manoeuvring of Alfred Milner, the British High Commissioner in South Africa, in pursuit of British supremacy in southern Africa, and the position of the so-called *Uitlander* population on the Witwatersrand and in the towns of the Transvaal republic, as well as the tenacity of the Boers in the maintenance of their independence and way of life. For some, Milner had brought the war on; for others, it was the recklessness of Transvaal president Paul Kruger and his Volksraad (parliament). Whatever the causes, no one could foresee what the war would be like. Most hoped optimistically for a short war. But, instead, a modern war was fought over three long years. Both the British and the Boers fought for unlimited objectives – the British for supremacy, the Boers for greater independence – and a compromise was seemingly impossible. No short, restrained war would convince either side to yield. Few Boers shared General JH de la Rey's concerns regarding the nature and impact of a war with Britain. While most Boers looked forward to a second Majuba – the British defeat that brought to a conclusion the First Anglo-Boer War, or Transvaal War, of 1880–1881 – the British predicted a swift and easy victory.[3] But only a prolonged and brutal struggle would resolve the issue one way or the other.

The Second Anglo-Boer War was one of the crucial events in South African history and has been the subject of much research and reassessment. The battle for the naming of the war reflects the tremendous impact it had; the 'South African War', the 'Second War of Independence', the 'English War' and the 'Boer War' all insufficiently express the complexities. The Anglo-Boer War, perhaps too simplistically, is taken from the two main belligerents and is problematic. Firstly, it excludes the 'other' parties: the Cape Afrikaners, Australians,

New Zealanders, Dutch, Belgians, Austrians, Russians, Germans, Frenchmen, Canadians, the Englishmen of Natal and the Cape, the *Uitlanders* and, of course, the thousands upon thousands of black South Africans.[4] Furthermore, it was not the second conflict between Boer and Briton. Enumerating the events culminating at Slagtersnek (1815), Boomplaats (1848) and the Transvaal War of 1880–1881, the war that erupted in 1899 must number as the fourth Anglo-Boer War. The 'Three Years' War', General CR de Wet's terminology, is vague yet perhaps the best of a poor list.[5] In South Africa, each of these terms is politically loaded. Yet, as General JC Smuts pointed out, this was in many respects a total war, among the first of the twentieth-century mould, and for this reason its ramifications for South Africa's development were profound.[6] Unsurprisingly, the war, the nature of the Boer armies and the way in which they held the world's greatest superpower at bay, and for almost three years, was also of close interest to other powers with colonial interests in Africa.[7] This chapter addresses these concerns.

The geopolitical landscape and the rival strategies

As the crisis had mounted, the various players – President Paul Kruger in Pretoria, President MT Steyn in Bloemfontein, the British government in London and Milner at the Cape – had considered their strategic options. Britain's initial policy objective, to bring the Transvaal republic into the Empire by conquest and subjugation if necessary, required offensive operations and complete military victory. For the Boer republics, needing only to defend themselves, a stalemated war that eroded British determination and brought foreign assistance would suffice. Thus the strategic equation was simply stated. Britain had to conquer the republics before the Boers convinced the British populace and the British government that they were unconquerable; the Transvaal had succeeded in doing this in 1880–1881. In the meantime, the strategists for the opposing armies considered the geography, domestic and international politics and public opinion, the perceived intentions of the enemy, resources, including the nature and size of military forces, and the logistics of a campaign in southern Africa.

The topography and geography of South Africa presented a number of military challenges for the British. The general physical features of the operational theatre comprise a coastal region, rising gradually to an upland country,

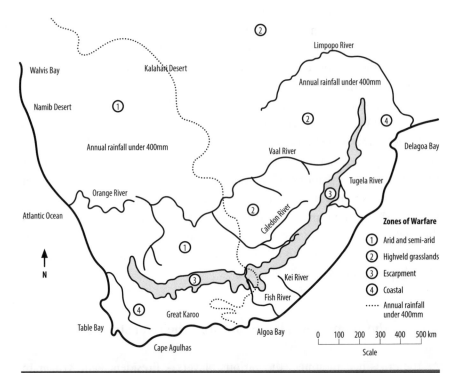

Map 1: **The four environments for war and politics in southern Africa**

Source: I van der Waag, 'Water and the ecology of warfare in southern Africa', in JWN Tempelhoff, ed,
African Water Histories: Transdisciplinary discourses (North-West University, Vanderbijlpark, 2005), p 124.

narrow on the east and west coasts, with terraced country or a gradual slope running up to the escarpment at which the great plateau starts. An interior tableland (the *veld* or veldt), some 1 000 to 2 500 metres above sea level, was flat or undulating and broken only here and there by solitary rounded hills (*koppies*). The veld sloped down gradually from east to west; all the major rivers flowed across the plateau to the Atlantic, where there were no ports of consequence for the British forces to utilise. An escarpment, which marks the transition, sometimes gradual, but generally abrupt, between the coastal region and the veld, commences near the Tropic of Capricorn in the northeast and runs parallel to the coast. As it passes southward, the mountains gradually become more precipitous until they rise to a height of 3 482 metres in the Drakensberg, in what was then Natal. From the southwestern end of the Drakensberg, the escarpment takes a westerly course and runs along ranges of mountains such as the Stormberg, the Sneeuberg, the Nieuveld and the

Kornsberg, where for a time it merges in the parallel ranges north of Cape Town.[8]

Terrain and logistical difficulties constrained military operations. While South Africa possessed a number of good anchorages and harbours, all of which (Cape Town, Port Elizabeth, East London, Saldanha Bay and Durban) were situated within the Cape and Natal colonies, there were few navigable rivers, and the only river of consequence, the Orange, flowed east-west. There was no inland water transportation. British troops would encounter problems the moment they left the coast. Rail appeared to be a panacea. Yet, from a military point of view, rail had many shortcomings, all of which would be highlighted during the coming war. While ramified rail networks had developed in Europe, rail was far less extensive at the imperial peripheries. In southern Africa, the main western line from Cape Town, via Kimberley and Mafeking, to Salisbury in Rhodesia, crossed at Orange River Bridge, near Hopetown. Surprisingly, the Boers' strategic vision did not stretch to seizing this bridge or destroying it and more of the railway, which would have forced the British to undertake expensive repairs. Likewise at Springfontein, where the lines coming up from the three main Cape harbours converge onto a single track into Bloemfontein, and where the congestion during the war was considerable. In December 1900, General Sir Redvers Buller suggested that a lateral line be constructed linking the western line to Bloemfontein, but Lord Roberts, the commander-in-chief of the imperial troops in South Africa from 1900, would have none of it. The success of any British operation depended on the single-track railway lines from the ports of the Cape and Natal colonies. A third line, opened in 1895, connected the Transvaal to the port of Lourenço Marques in Portuguese East Africa (Mozambique).

Although rail was the strategic key to all communications, the paucity of railways limited strategic options. Troops and supplies could be moved relatively easily to the railhead, but the effort required to progress beyond that point was immense. Moreover, railways predetermined the lines of advance, so sacrificing surprise, were vulnerable to enemy action, as the British would experience in South Africa from 1900, and required significant manpower to protect and maintain.[9]

The dual problems of transport and supply would dog the British columns. London tried to meet the dramatic shortage of horses in southern Africa by importing animals from the United Kingdom, Australasia and North and South America. Global variation in horseflesh, as Sandra Swart has argued, brought unanticipated difficulties, in variegated types of forage and riding habits, for example, while privation, combat stress and compromised immunity brought susceptibility to diseases.[10] Buller had reason for his frequent complaints about the quality of horses and their shortage.[11] Colonel (later General Sir) Frederick Maxse admitted, in June 1900, that the British had 'not yet learned the secret of mobility in the field of action'.[12] British operations were, as a result, limited at first to the area traversed by rail and, more so, by the lack of transport animals.

Four main theatres were evident as the strategists surveyed the prospective front lines, which stretched from the western and southern reaches of the highveld to the lowveld of the eastern Transvaal, an arc spanning more than 1 500 kilometres. The western theatre, extending from the Orange River to the town of Mafeking, consisted of two sub-theatres: the districts of Kimberley and Mafeking. This was not bountiful country. An invasion would be difficult for the British, despite an adequate railway running up from Cape Town into British Bechuanaland (Botswana). In many ways, this was a strategic dead end, forcing the British to channel deeper into the arid and semi-arid regions of western highveld and further and further away from their bases and depots. Here, on the plateau, the few rivers were of no value for transportation but excellent for defence against an army approaching from the south.

Lying between the east coast of Natal and the Drakensberg escarpment, the eastern theatre also had two sub-theatres: the Natal front itself and the lowveld border with Portuguese East Africa. Here geography again favoured the Boer republics. An invading British army would have the benefit of the railway line running up from Durban to the Witwatersrand. The Boers, however, would be able to use the rivers and mountains, in increasing measure as the advance moved inland and the country became more broken, to harry the British advance.

The third theatre was the northern region of the eastern Cape, stretching from the main railway line to Basutoland (Lesotho). This too was a vast area, and included several main junctions that connected Cape Town to the Orange Free State capital of Bloemfontein and linked the harbours of Port Elizabeth and East London to the western theatre. Control of the rail junctions at Noupoort, Middelburg and Stormberg would either facilitate the arrival of British supply and reinforcement or sever lateral communication between the western and southern theatres. Nonetheless, both the British and the Boers reckoned the southern theatre to be secondary in importance to the western and eastern theatres.

The fourth theatre, a northern front, centred on operations from Rhodesia, was opened later in the war and was conducted largely by troops from Australia.[13]

The four theatres covered an area approximately thirteen times the size of England, encompassing both Boer republics and the British colonies and territories of the Cape, Natal, Bechuanaland and Rhodesia. The sheer size of the operational area, and the relatively small forces employed, would result in a war mainly of movement, something for which Britain was ill-prepared. The difficulties of containing enveloped Boer formations could be surmounted only by drastic increases in troop strength and by the employment of harsh counter-guerrilla strategies.

The climate also favoured the Boers. The veld, on account of its height and remoteness from the sea, is subject to marked variations between winter and summer. These extremes of heat and cold, and the variation between veld and coast, are shown in Table 1.1. The timing of the Kruger ultimatum at the start of the South African summer was therefore crucial to the Boers. Much of the coastal region, through which the British troops had perforce to move, burns up almost to a desert during the hotter months. The moment the British broke through the escarpment and moved beyond Ceres, they would be exposed to severe heat, lack of water and a countryside with little to live on – perhaps only some sheep, goats and ostriches.

Table 1.1: **Comparison of average high temperatures (°C)**			
	East Coast **(Durban)**	**Veld** **(Bloemfontein)**	**West Coast** **(Cape Town)**
January (summer)	28	31	26.1
July (winter)	23	17	17.5
Variation in average temperature	5	14	8.6

Farther inland, beyond the escarpment, the veld (where the Boer republics lay) receives summer rains. Growth at the start of the war would therefore have been luxuriant, with ample food and fodder, and plentiful animal and water resources. In winter the picture changes drastically, with only coarse grasses surviving in scattered tufts. The State Secretary of the ZAR, Francis Reitz, could say with some satisfaction, in late August 1899, that food sufficient for six to eight months had also been laid up in storage and that there would be no shortages of meat or flour.[14] He and other government officials expected the war to be over by the end of summer. Yet, despite low income and dependence upon imports for manufactured goods, the two republics seem to have experienced few problems regarding food supply.

The Boer strategists attempted to make the most of the geography. They realised that the British would roll up the railway line to Bloemfontein, conduct holding actions elsewhere and, if at all possible, avoid an advance through Natal and, particularly, that colony's mountainous northern apex. Through skilful distraction, they would divert British energy to the defence of Ladysmith, Kimberley and Mafeking, draw the imperial regiments into the semi-desert hinterland of the Cape and strike at the enemy's logistic lines. A similar strategy, albeit on a smaller scale, had found success in 1881. Few British commanders, excluding Buller himself, who had seen action during the First Anglo-Boer War, and Major General Sir William Butler, who had served in South Africa and had written a biography of Major General Sir George Colley (the British commander who fell at Majuba), were acquainted with the dangers of pushing troops into northern Natal or understood the realities of fighting in South Africa.[15]

The opposing sides stepped up their preparations through September 1899 in anticipation of the outbreak of hostilities. The British tried to gain time through further talks, while they awaited the arrival of reinforcements from India. Jan Christiaan Smuts, the youthful Attorney General of the ZAR, read the British posture correctly and designed possibly the only realistic strategy for Kruger and his government. The Boer republics would have to take the offensive immediately, well before the arrival of reinforcements bolstered the British forces already in South Africa. This would allow farming to continue and would not empty the treasury, while steps had to be taken to produce arms and ammunition locally. Smuts convinced Kruger that they should act before the arrival of Buller and the reinforcements from Britain. Kruger telegraphed President MT Steyn along these lines. But Steyn, hoping against hope, decided to make one last effort to avoid hostilities. Acting with the consent of his Volksraad, Steyn attempted vainly to convince Milner to stop the arrival of the reinforcements. Valuable time was wasted from 27 September to 9 October. Milner, who wanted the war and had worked hard to build the crisis, would have nothing of it. Eventually, Steyn realised this and recognised the necessity of acting immediately. Smuts' strategy of driving to the sea, of isolating or defeating the British garrisons and of contesting the arrival of reinforcements came to nought, largely due to poor generalship, the indiscipline of the burghers on commando and the grit of the British soldiers they encountered. Moreover, the Boers had changed. These were not the same men who had fought in 1881; many were urbanised and lacked experience from a young age with horse and rifle.

The Transvaal government, with the consent of its Orange Free State allies, delivered an ultimatum to the British Resident in Johannesburg, Conyngham Greene, on 9 October 1899. Recognising the threat posed by the movement of British troops to the borders and the pending arrival of reinforcements from India, they demanded a peaceful resolution to the crisis, the withdrawal of British troops from the borders, the withdrawal of British reinforcements that had arrived in South Africa since 1 June 1899, and the recall to India of the British troops still at sea. Should a satisfactory answer not be received before 5 pm on 11 October, a state of war would exist.

Boer and Briton

Britain also underestimated the enemy. In October 1900, after a year of operations, Milner expressed his disillusionment to the Colonial Secretary, Joseph Chamberlain: 'I am fairly taken aback at the vitality and ubiquity of the enemy, the staleness and dissatisfaction of our men, and the aimlessness and inconsequence of our present operations.'[16] When the declaration of war came in October 1899, Britain did not expect serious resistance from the two tiny agrarian republics. Overconfidence led the British to underestimate the military potential of their opponents.[17] Yet there is something feigned in Milner's expression of surprise. As British proconsul in southern Africa, and the person ultimately responsible for Britain's deception, he had 'always regarded war with the Republics as a very formidable war indeed'.[18] With the possible exceptions of Buller and Butler, Milner, more than anyone else, 'believed in the Boer's capacity for war'.[19] He knew the true size of the Boer arsenal and of what the republican forces were capable. He, furthermore, not only had timely warning of ZAR preparations[20] but also knew the fundamentals of the Boer campaign plan – and as early as June 1899.[21] These were details, it would seem, he failed to pass on to the War Office.

As Thomas Pakenham has shown, Milner had been less than frank with his principals in London. The War Office, in *Military Notes on the Dutch Republics*, expected the Boers to limit themselves to a raiding strategy conducted by no more than 2 000 to 3 000 men, and then, after a serious defeat, to surrender. British soldiers 'asserted over and over again that the death of a few hundred of their comrades would be enough to scatter the commandoes [sic] to their farms'.[22] The intelligence department correctly predicted the coalition of the two republics but underestimated the number of rifles by at least 10 000. Major General Sir John Ardagh's *Military Notes* estimated that 26 500 ZAR burghers were liable for military service. However, as the War Office appreciated, these figures were untrustworthy, and any estimate 'should rather be too high than too low'.[23] The inability of the ZAR government to conduct an accurate census worked against Britain's war preparations, and London remained unable to gauge figures with reasonable precision.[24] The total number of burghers liable for service (ages 18 to 34) in the ZAR was eventually estimated at 14 391, those between the ages 34 to 50 at 7 242, and those aged below 18 and above 50 at 4 666.[25]

Table 1.2: **The republican forces**	
Commandants	41
Field Cornets	140
Assistant Field Cornets	99
Troops	
South African Republic (Transvaal)	32 353
Republic of the Orange Free State	22 314
Agterryers ('After-riders' or servants)	±10 000
Foreign corps	±2 000
Total	**± 66 667**

This figure of 26 299 was too low. The armed forces of the two Boer republics, including roughly 2 000 foreign volunteers, numbered as many as 66 667 (*see* Table 1.2), although this was only about one tenth the size of the British Army.[26] At the outbreak of war, the Boers outnumbered British forces in South Africa by four to one. Had they maximised the benefits of this initial numerical advantage, their knowledge of the country and their superior mobility, they might very well have swept the British to the coast, occupied the harbours, contested the landing of reinforcements and undermined the resolve of the British Parliament.[27] But caution and ineptitude prevailed, and the moment was lost.

Milner had different figures, and he had failed to pass on cardinal intelligence gained by Conyngham Greene in Pretoria. 'A middle-aged man in a hurry',[28] he could not afford to be frank; he wanted to reshape the subcontinent, and for this he needed a war.[29] While Milner believed that the power of the Boers could be broken, he also believed that the war would be fierce yet short. As the man on the spot, Milner had not underestimated the military power of the republics, but, like most others, had 'overestimated the competence of the British Army'.[30]

Moreover, as to the 'vitality and ubiquity of the enemy', the British should have been familiar with the Boer military system. The common pattern for colonial warfare – serious defeat followed by British adaptation to local circumstances – should have been unnecessary. The British had faced the Boers on a number of previous occasions, most notably at Boomplaats (1848) and in the various battles of the First Anglo-Boer War.[31] Furthermore, during the nineteenth century, many British regiments had fought against the Xhosa – in no less than seven of the nine eastern Cape frontier wars – and so gained field experience in South Africa.[32] Yet the colony's soldier-settlers, 'many ... who had fought and hunted side by side with the Boers ... all asserted that the Boers could not shoot, and were wanting in every military quality except cunning and endurance'. This was probably based upon 'personal dislike and racial feeling'.[33] Thus, although having had ample opportunity to study the Boer military system, the British thought that their defeat at Majuba, no matter how humiliating, had been a fluke. Despite Butler's study of Colley's actions in 1881, it seemed that no 'lessons' had been learned.

Although by 1899 the military system of the Boer republics had reached a peak of sophistication, the majority of burghers remained members of the commando system. While the officers of the two republics – even the generals – were elected, they were in other respects little different from their British counterparts. At the outbreak of the war, the officers of the ZAR belonged, almost without exception, to the ruling oligarchy, and many of the generals were related through ties of kinship and economic interests.[34] Through the hustling of voters and the mobilisation of dependants, the notables saw to the 'election' of their relatives to the leadership of the commandos and wards: commandants were elected for a term of five years, field cornets for three years. The exercise of patronage undermined morale and esprit de corps.[35] Moreover, the election of officers, of course, did not always lead to creative strategy and tactics, or to effective command. The very wealthy, or the most popular, are seldom military geniuses. Some of the best Boer generals, including Christiaan de Wet, started the war as ordinary burghers. Boer veterans wore no medals or uniforms, and their status was signalled by a white beard. It was age, often in combination with family credentials, that brought respect, not – as Louis Botha and Christiaan de Wet experienced – a youthful genius for innovation.[36] According to Smuts, De Wet's 'active genius was thwarted at every stage by the stupidity of his superiors and the insubordination of his undisciplined men'.[37]

High-level leadership can make a difference in war. General Piet Joubert, the Commandant General of the Transvaal, was a powerful man. An elected official, he was both Minister for Defence and commander-in-chief in the field, but he also fixed the prices of commodities, acted as a general broker in the ivory trade and controlled the distribution of arms and ammunition, which brought him into conflict with the president's cartel.[38] In 1894, the powers of the Commandant General were limited and his term of office reduced from ten to five years. Although popular, Joubert, who had led the Transvaal to victory in 1880–1881, was in 1899 no paragon of good generalship. He was unable to innovate and adapt to new technology and, on the eve of the war, gave 'the impression of being bewildered at the heavy responsibility' that rested upon him. Deneys Reitz thought him 'unequal to the burden [and] unfit to lead armies'.[39]

Ineffective, even counterproductive, leadership was only part of the problem. Contemporary observers recognised that undisciplined troops severely affected the conduct of operations. Discipline was generally bad. Officers who could not stamp their authority and attain respect through force of personality experienced tremendous problems. In fact, most officers, particularly in the beginning, encountered problems in command and control.[40] Even the charismatic Christiaan de Wet was no exception.[41] The State Artillery Corps and the ZARPs – referred to as 'the disciplined force of Transvaal'[42] – also reported severe disciplinary problems.[43] There are many references to generals and commandants having to use force (De Wet carried a whip) to keep the burghers at the front or to enforce obedience. One must doubt De Kiewiet's description of the commando (although dating from a different era) as 'the sum of individual willingness'[44] and Charles Townshend's belief that they were 'held together by voluntary co-operation'.[45] The weakest feature of the commandos was indiscipline: the burghers disliked being organised, and their officers could never count on all the men on the muster roll being present to go into action.

The burghers were untrained in matters military. Discipline and blind obedience to orders were foreign concepts to them. Townshend has stated that 'the Boer forces had always been at best (or worst) semi-regular armies ... loosely organized in "commandos" rather than conventional military structures'.[46] Although this facilitated the transition to guerrilla warfare, following the defeat of the main Boer field armies, it certainly complicated the opening phases of the war. While one must agree with Preston et al that 'the Boers were hardy farmers who were excellent marksmen', one must question the too-generous statement that the Boers 'were not hampered by traditional military concepts and methods'.[47] Training in the art of war, and perhaps even the study of military history, might have produced quite different results. Not every Boer general was a De Wet, a Smuts or a De la Rey.

Although the republics had not faced a European enemy since the Transvaal had humiliated the British at Majuba, they had amassed considerable experience in the so-called native wars. Moreover, the Transvaal and Orange Free State forces had been built up after the Jameson Raid. Attempts were made to modernise their arsenals. Some 30 000 modern Mauser rifles were imported from Germany. The State Artillery Corps was expanded and equipped with ordnance from Creusot in France, from Krupp in Germany and from Maxim-Nordenfelt in Britain. By 1899, it comprised four batteries of field artillery (Creusot and Krupp), four of siege artillery (Creusot Long Toms), 12 of pom-poms (Maxim-Nordenfelt), a number of hand Maxims and some antiquated guns. The republics were dependent upon imported weaponry and their artillery corps was weak and small by Western standards. A ring of fortresses was created on the Rand and around Pretoria, but these, home of much of the artillery, flew in the face of the Boer way of war, which was predicated on mobility and low-level initiative. The fortresses were the visible sign of how static Boer strategic thinking had become. Nonetheless, on the eve of the war, the Boer armies were the most modern in South Africa, and the 54 000 armed burghers, who could mobilise within a week, outnumbered the British troops on the subcontinent by four to one.

The officers and men of the two republics, and principally the State Artillery, also had significant contact with European officers, particularly French and German artillerists, instructors who may have shared the 'lessons' of the Franco-Prussian War (1870–1871) – of cover, and fire and movement – with the Boers. The republics might have done more to recruit foreign veterans, with their valuable experience of European wars, and ensure the return of South Africans living abroad. Offers of military hardware and expertise, from hot-air balloonists, German, French, Austrian and Dutch officers, medical doctors and artillery officers, met with a less than warm reception.[48] Some talent was recruited before the war, especially from Germany and Austria, to assist particularly with the republican artilleries.[49] Germans laid the foundations for the Transvaal State Artillery and a Hollander established its Field Telegraph Section, while a veteran of the Franco-Prussian War, Major RFW Albrecht, founded the State Artillery of the Orange Free State. Captain Adolf Zboril, an Austrian artillery officer, was second-in-command of the Transvaal artillery before the war. As the only officer with training in the Western way of war, he tried to improve the unit's organisation and efficiency. This reorganisation gathered pace following the appointment of Adolf Schiel, a former Prussian hussar, as Zboril's lieutenant. Zboril could, however, not convince Joubert, the Commandant General, 'of the importance of a modern and efficient artillery force – and despairingly, devoted more time to his remarkably beautiful wife than to the artillery'.[50]

Although some 2 000 foreigners fought with the Boer commandos, the two republics failed to exploit the knowledge and experience of foreign soldiers. Many of the foreigners, as veterans of the Franco-Prussian War, were familiar with the latest military technology, but foreign ideas on its application – particularly the rifle, but also artillery – fell on deaf ears. However, their impact was lessened by the inaction of the Boer governments, together with xenophobia and hatred for *Uitlanders*, which brought suspicion and increasing Boer control.[51] The development of doctrine and training may also have been compromised by the rivalry between the Austrian Zboril and the Prussian Schiel.[52]

The British were nonetheless surprised by the strength of the republican artillery. The British had not shared in the recent experience in European warfare, in which the rifle and the defence had come to the fore, and few officers attempted to keep pace with developments where Britain was not involved.[53] Boer tactics, more sophisticated than they had been in 1881, surprised the British and Lieutenant Colonel ES May, Professor of Military Art and History at the Royal Military College, Camberley, had reason to commence his *Retrospect on the South African War* (1901) with

> There has probably never been a more striking example of a foe being underrated than has been given to the world of late in South Africa ... each and every one of [our] assertions has been shown to have been untrustworthy, and every cannon by which the potential strength of our opponents was gauged may be shown to have been misapplied.

The British had nothing but contempt for the farmers against whom they fought. Some, as Sir Percy Fitzpatrick noted, thought Boer military power 'the biggest unpricked bubble in the world'.[54] While the Boer republics lacked a military force in the conventional sense, and their generals and commandants possessed a coherent grasp of neither strategy nor tactics, they did have modern rifles and their men were hardy, expert marksmen and admirable horsemen. Although the commandos at the best of times held to the loosest of discipline, they knew the veld and had the toughness born of farming a harsh land. The lack of conventional military forces induced overconfidence in a well-disciplined and organised British Army, few of whose generals understood South African conditions. How could a country of backwoodsmen, whose entire population was no more than that of an average British town, stand against the British Empire?[55]

The British Army and the armed forces of both Boer republics went through an extensive rearmament programme during the last three decades of the century. The armies of both belligerents introduced breech-loading rifles that enhanced rates of fire and allowed soldiers to fire from a prone position. Other innovations – a bolt mechanism and magazine, smaller-calibre ammunition and smokeless propellants – enabled infantry to maintain rapid, aimed fire without powder smoke obscuring their field of vision. The artillery of both armies had also converted to breech-loading ordnance and adopted a smokeless propellant that had been available since the early 1890s.[56] But how effective were these rifles? A comparison between the Mauser – chief weapon of the Boer commando – and the standard British Lee-Metford is revealing. Mauser rifles and cartridges were lighter. They could fire further and at a greater speed, and their magazines, accommodating five cartridges, were filled by means of a loading strip. The magazine of the Lee-Metford, on the other hand, could accommodate ten cartridges, but these had to be loaded individually. The deadly effect of the Mauser in the hands of the burghers eventually forced the British to alter their tactics.

However, not all burghers carried the Mauser. Many, and particularly Free Staters, still used the cumbersome, outdated Martini-Henry. According to a veteran: 'Enkele dra nog Martini-Henry gewere en gaan gebuk onder die gewig van die swaar loodkoeëls, waarvan nie baie nodig is om 'n pond gewig op te maak nie' (Some still carry Martini-Henry rifles and labour under the weight of the heavy bullets, of which not many make up a pound in weight).[57] The burghers expressed a strong preference for the Mauser, and in Krugersdorp they refused to accept anything else.[58] However, the older generals, familiar with the Martini-Henry, did not trust the newer technology. In 1896, Piet Joubert, in a less than lucid moment, placed an order for antiquated, and by then much-maligned, Martini-Henrys.[59]

Most burghers were excellent marksmen. Their ability to estimate distance resulted in deadly accurate fire. The British regiments, on the other hand, still fired in volleys at the command of officers who also determined the distances, without actually aiming at a particular target. This was perhaps the reason why Boer veterans believed British fire at close quarters to be less accurate than at 600–1 000 yards (548–914 metres).[60] Although experiencing an initial difficulty in judging distance, the musketry of British troops improved after 1900. To say that all burghers were excellent marksmen is also an oversimplification. Although some (perhaps most) attended the annual *wapenschauw* (literally, 'weapon show'), no structured military training took place in either of the republics.[61] Burghers living on farms and in rural areas grew up with a rifle in the hand and were masters at bushcraft. Those living in the towns, on the other hand, had no better acquaintance with either rifle or bush than had the average British soldier.[62] This may perhaps explain the poor showing of the Johannesburg Commando under General JHM Kock at Elandslaagte on 21 October 1899. Urbanisation, the accumulation of wealth and a generally easier life certainly impacted negatively upon Boer musketry and fieldcraft. The requisitions for supply submitted by the logistics commissioners at the front also present an interesting picture. Many commandos spent the first months of the war ordering extra bedding – pillows, mattresses and blankets – cutlery and crockery.[63] Ardagh's *Military Notes* were perhaps correct; the burgher of 1899 was possibly not as hardened, nor as rough and ready, as his counterpart in 1881.[64]

Doctrinally, the British and republican armies were poorly prepared. Despite having enormous resources for making war, the British soon found that 'technology and organisation were only adjuncts to, not substitutes for, inventive operational solutions', and that they could not always press what should have been their strong suit – technology. Their firepower, which normally gave them 'an important, but by no means decisive, advantage' in colonial warfare was somewhat counterweighted by the artilleries of the two republics.[65] European rivalries played a role in arming the Boers with modern weapons, comparable to those in the British arsenal. Of the two republics, the Transvaal, with approximately 450 well-trained artillerists in the State Artillery Corps, had the better artillery. Their guns were of heavier calibre than even those of the enemy, and comprised 12– and 15–pounders, Krupp guns, a few old Armstrongs and the quick-firing Maxim-Nordenfelts, in addition to the heavy Creusots (Long Toms).[66] The British, however, had guns in greater numbers, and the impact of these increased following the fall of Pretoria and the loss to the Boers of the workshops there. The remoteness of some battlefields also made artillery a liability. The use of larger guns, such as the Creusot 75mm, could be maximised only if the battlefield was accessible and the enemy was willing to fight on the defensive. The 155mm Long Toms, which remained underutilised, even wasted, had to be sacrificed early in the war in view of their bulkiness and relative immobility.

Britain had strategic reach. It could project manpower and firepower and institute a naval blockade to halt the passage of arms and ammunition to the republics. Already in August 1899, consignments from the Creusot works in eastern France and the Deutsche Waffen und Munitionsfabriken at Karlsruhe were stopped from leaving the docks at Lourenço Marques, following British pressure.[67] War materiel had to be sent under the guise of machinery.[68] The landlocked republics, in turn, could not interfere with British sea communications. Moreover, Britain's industrial superiority was unchallengeable and the military potential of the Empire enormous. But London would require time to convert war-making potential into actual military power. The Boers hoped that a brief war would render Britain's advantages superfluous.

Although facing long odds, the Boer cause was not hopeless. One of the great uncertainties was the role the Cape Afrikaners would play. Another was a possible, although always unlikely, foreign intervention. The Boers looked to Germany, and possibly France and Russia, but, in the end, with the exception of the foreign corps and a number of ambulances, little real military assistance arrived. During the last days of peace, the burghers, called up by their field cornets and commandants, moved up to the frontiers. The main Transvaal force drew up to the Natal border where the British thrust was again expected, while the main Free State force deployed to the western front for the investment of Kimberley. By 11 October, when the ultimatum expired, the majority of the Boers, if not ready, were armed and eager.

The Boer offensive and the battles of the frontiers

The broad course of the war and its three main phases are now well documented. The war commenced with a conventional phase, lasting from the outbreak of hostilities to the last set-piece battles fought at Bergendal (or Dalmanutha to the British) in late August and Spitzkop in early September 1900. It ended with a guerrilla phase, characterised by Boer insurgency and British counterinsurgency, conducted from September 1900 to the end of the war on 31 May 1902. The period from March to August 1900 may arguably be regarded as a transition phase.[69]

On the western front, the first shots of the war were fired by De la Rey when his commando neutralised an armoured train near Kraaipan. The railway was severed to the north and south of Mafeking. The Boers expected Mafeking to surrender quickly, but here the British put up a dogged resistance and a siege commenced. General Koos Snyman, in command of the investment, showed little initiative and frittered away the time of several thousand burghers, so preventing a sizable portion of the Transvaal forces from engaging on the more important fronts. The commander on the western front, Piet Cronjé, the Majuba legend and a strong Krugerite, was highly regarded among the rank and file. Joubert and De la Rey did not share this admiration: Cronjé had a penchant for siege warfare. Yet, 'considering Cronjé's reputation, Kruger decided it was prudent to give him a high-profile command with De la Rey appointed as his second-in-command to exercise control over him'.[70] De la Rey had an impossible task, and, according to Jan Smuts, De la Rey and Cronjé's other subordinates had to suffer their commander's 'arrogant stupidity'.[71] This stupidity led to the costly siege of Mafeking (De la Rey had advised Cronjé to avoid the town and move south immediately) and was displayed again during the battles against the British relief forces at the Modder River, and at the disastrous battle at Paardeberg, where Cronjé himself was besieged.

In Natal, the Free State commandos occupied the Drakensberg passes, while a force under Joubert occupied Newcastle on 15 October. Further north, the main Transvaal force of the eastern front divided, with a column under General Johannes Kock moving towards Elandslaagte to cut off the forward British garrison at Dundee, while the commandos under generals Lukas Meyer and Daniel 'Maroola' Erasmus moved towards that town to inflict a blow on Symons' troops. On 19 October, Meyer and Erasmus had occupied Impati and Talana, the features dominating the town of Dundee. Symons moved recklessly against Talana to dislodge Meyer, which he did after an artillery bombardment and infantry charge. The losses were heavy. A troop of cavalry was captured, and the impetuous Symons died later from wounds sustained in the battle. Colonel JH Yule, Symons' second-in-command, with his force severely mauled and thinking a Boer attack imminent, decided to retreat toward the main British position at Ladysmith. This he was able to do because Kock's force had suffered a crushing defeat at Elandslaagte on 21 October.

Elements of the Boer strategy reflected a surprising Napoleonic influence, the vehicle of which is difficult to ascertain. This may have resulted from the reading of military history and works on military theory – several Boer leaders had quite extensive libraries – or reflected something of the impact of the European volunteers. Deneys Reitz referred to the division of the Transvaal army into corps for easier passage through the Drakensberg: this would be speedier and would make for easier foraging.[72] The army converged for the battle at Dundee, and linked up with the Free Staters under General Marthinus Prinsloo for the assault on Ladysmith. However, the over-cautious Erasmus sat on Mount Impati to the north of Dundee while Meyer attacked from the east. Kock now positioned himself between Ladysmith and Dundee. Recognising the threat this move posed, the British commander in Ladysmith, Sir George White, sent cavalry, infantry and three artillery batteries under the command of John French to dislodge Kock's forces from the crest at Elandslaagte. Here the Boer positions were first softened up by artillery fire, and the infantry was sent forward in the late afternoon. Kock's Transvalers were overwhelmed, their retreat cut to ribbons by the British lancers. Kock himself, mortally wounded, was captured. This was a severe blow for the Boers. While Kock faced annihilation at Elandslaagte alone, Erasmus' force looted Dundee.[73] It would seem as if personality – and possibly poor functional demarcation – prevented several mobile, strategically dispersed forces from cooperating against a relatively immobile, concentrated enemy. This lack of cooperation between Boer generals marked the entire conventional phase of the war. These strategic blunders were costly, denying the Boers the decisive victory they sought at the start.

White was forced to concentrate the remaining British troops, some 10 000 men, in Ladysmith. He would not withdraw to the south, which would have meant the surrender of northern Natal, but instead consolidated his position, prepared the town's defences and piled up supplies. He decided on one final attempt to inflict a defeat on the approaching Boer forces before an investment began. On 30 October, he attacked the Boer positions on the high ground to the north of Ladysmith. The Boer forces were deployed in a half-moon shape, with Meyer's force on the left flank and Erasmus' in the middle, at Pepworth Hill, and Schalk Burger between them. The Boer right flank was formed by a Free State commando, although a considerable gap lay between them and Erasmus. Joubert had his headquarters at Modderspruit, a few kilometres behind this position. The opposing forces on the day were approximately equal in strength, although White could place 42 guns in the field against Joubert's 12. White planned to attack the Boer left and then, when the Boers had had enough, to send his cavalry around their flank. The previous night White had sent Colonel Carleton with two infantry regiments to Nicholson's Neck in the west as a diversion. The main British attack failed and White was forced back into Ladysmith, while Carleton's force was defeated resoundingly by the Free Staters under Acting Commandant CR de Wet.

Joubert's failure to capitalise on this success made many Boers bitter. They watched in disbelief as he allowed the British to withdraw. Reitz heard Christiaan de Wet mutter, 'Los jou ruiters; los jou ruiters' (release your horsemen; release your horsemen). Yet Joubert, not exploiting the victory, gave his staff, jocularly called 'the Royal Family', a lesson in theology: 'When God holds out a finger, don't take the whole hand.' This might have been sound catechism, as one burgher, Isaac Malherbe, pointed out, but was not good war-making.[74] Reitz, writing in 1903, believed that Joubert was not taken seriously after his failure to exploit the victory at Pepworth Hill. The siege of Ladysmith had begun.

From this point, the Boers largely lost the initiative on the eastern front. The Tugela (Thukela) River was reached on 27 November and, positioning themselves astride the railway to the north of Colenso, the Boers dug in to wait for the British relief column. Having lost the strategic initiative, they hoped to maximise the advantages of a tactical defence and so prolong the war. The conflict settled down, and there was little activity bar a raid the British conducted on the northern front with the assistance of two Batswana chiefs, Kgama and Lentswe, at Derdepoort in the district of Rustenburg. Several burghers were killed, ending any notion that this would be a white man's war. An expedition the following month punished Kgama's people severely.[75]

During the last days of October, Boer forces occupied Vryburg, Taung and Fourteen Streams in the Cape Colony and the railway was cut north and south of Kimberley. The railway north of the Orange River, with the exception of short portions near the invested towns of Kimberley and Mafeking, was in Boer hands. Many Cape burghers in these northern districts joined the commandos. The isolation of Kimberley was completed on 3 November. The Free State commandos crossed the fords of the Orange River and entered the northern districts of what is now the Eastern Cape, where they were joined by many Cape burghers. The Free Staters surprisingly failed to occupy the rail junction at Noupoort, and they withdrew to the north when troops under John French arrived in force. The junction at Stormberg, vacated by the British, was occupied, while Cape Afrikaners throughout these districts joined the commandos.

This was the rather dark strategic position when General Sir Redvers Buller, the new British commander-in-chief, arrived in South Africa on 31 October. Buller, responding to urgent appeals to relieve the besieged towns and drive the Boers back, was forced to abandon the original British strategy of rolling up the railway from Cape Town to Bloemfontein and Pretoria. The appeals of Cecil John Rhodes, trumpeted by telegraph and newspaper from Kimberley, were the loudest. But Buller hurried to Natal, where the danger was greatest, while he dispatched generals William Gatacre and John French to the north-eastern Cape, to shore up the British position in the Stormberg and around Colesberg, and General Methuen, in command of a division, up the railway from Cape Town toward Kimberley.

Methuen, on 23 November, was the first into action. This was a small encounter at Belmont, where a mixed force under Prinsloo and De la Rey barred the railway. Methuen drove the Boers from their positions at Belmont and later from Graspan. Falling back to the north, the Boers dug themselves in on the banks of the Modder River near its confluence with the Riet. There, under the command of Cronjé, they withstood a major attack by Methuen on 28 November. Methuen commanded superior numbers of artillery and troops, but preparatory bombardments and the charge of the Guards Brigade, in too-closed formation, failed to push the Boers from their well-prepared positions on the river. The British casualties were many, but Cronjé, misjudging the situation quite entirely, abandoned the Modder River line and, falling back a few kilometres to the north, formed a new line at Magersfontein.

Methuen could not attain surprise. His route followed the railway line and his approach was necessarily observed. On the afternoon of 10 December, his artillery needlessly bombarded the hills near Scholtznek. Cronjé, with his Potchefstroomers in the middle of the Boer position on Magersfontein Hill, was prepared. During the night, Brigadier General Andrew Wauchope and his Highland Brigade moved forward with a view to storming the Boer positions at first light. Because of poor reconnaissance and a catalogue of battlefield mistakes, the British, at daybreak, still unaware of the precise position of the Boer trenches, encountered devastatingly accurate fire from the Boer Mausers. Hundreds died, more were pinned down, unable to move, and pestered by heat and insects. Artillery fire covered the retreat. After suffering some 1 000 casualties, Methuen fell back to the Modder River. The battle at Magersfontein, a resounding Boer victory, spelled the end of Methuen's attempt to relieve Kimberley from the south.

At the same time, the British suffered defeat in the Stormberg, where Gatacre, having courageously established his headquarters well forward at the end of November, decided to launch a surprise night attack on the Boer positions there. In so doing, he hoped to occupy the mountain, an important feature, and the railroad junction, which would open communications with French at Noupoort. A victory would also dampen local enthusiasm for the republics. During the night of 9 December Gatacre led some 3 000 men in an attack on the Free Staters, but, losing their way in the dark, the British force failed dismally. Gatacre lost 100 men killed and seven times that number captured. Within two days, the British forces on both Cape fronts had suffered major reverses, the seriousness of which, and concomitant loss of British prestige, fed an incipient insurgency in the Cape country districts.

During this same week, a third and possibly more important disaster unfolded on the Natal front, where a young General Louis Botha, having assumed command of the Boer forces, prepared to face Buller and the forces dispatched for the relief of Ladysmith. Botha's forces dug in along the northern banks of the Tugela, with Colenso at their centre and their far left flank on Spioenkop. Buller enjoyed several advantages. He had more artillery and his 30 000 men outnumbered Botha's 5 000 by a factor of six. Moreover, he could select the point of attack, while Botha, although having the advantage offered by terrain, had to defend the full length of the line and could not concentrate his forces. Buller attacked on 15 December, but was driven back at Colenso, losing two batteries of field guns and presenting the British with their third defeat in what became known as 'Black Week'.

The Boers, occupying the highveld grasslands, enjoyed the natural advantages of the central position, terrain and climate. Yet by remaining largely on the defensive they did not exploit these advantages. The imperial forces had perforce to operate on external lines, a factor that complicated logistics and harmed cooperation between the British columns under Buller, Gatacre and Methuen. The British forces were vulnerable and could be attacked piece-meal, leading to a position that was 'humiliating and unpleasant to the last degree'.[76] The Boers were wise to contest the convergence of the British col-umns, but, instead of first massing against one force, destroying it and then massing against the next, several concurrent operations were conducted: for example, at Kimberley, Ladysmith and Mafeking. Furthermore, although the Boer forces were to converge on the battlefield, late arrivals and the inability to seize the moment limited their strategic gains.[77] Nowhere could they attain a numerical advantage, and so British arms came to dominate the conventional battles and engagements of the war.

The British invasion of the republics

The combination of rifle and horse made the Boer commando almost invin-cible against African opponents armed largely with assegai and knobker-rie. As a general tactic, the Boers rode to within range of an African enemy, fired, reloaded and returned to within range and repeated this as necessary. African armies had little chance of coming close enough to use their weapons. Moreover, most African formations were tightly bunched, so enabling maxi-mum effect from concentrated fire.[78] When it halted, the commando always fortified its position in the form of the laager. Boer tactics aimed to draw the enemy close to the laager and so derive maximum use of the commando's firepower. Against the British, however, this did not work. The Boers had to keep moving, denying pitched battle and operating against British weakness. Bombardment by British artillery – as General Piet Cronjé was to experience – made life in the laager none too comfortable.

Colonel Maxse noted on 3 June 1900: 'We hope to march [to Pretoria] start-ing tomorrow or next day and from what one hears I don't suppose a very protracted resistance will be offered in Kruger's absence.'[79] He could not have been more wrong.

In the darker, earlier days of the war, Milner viewed the 'colossal arma-ments of the S.A.R., [and] could not but anticipate a terrible struggle'.[80] A year later, the situation had changed drastically. The republics had a limited infra-structure and little logistical support to keep their weapons in service. For the first year, maintenance of guns and the manufacture of shells took place in

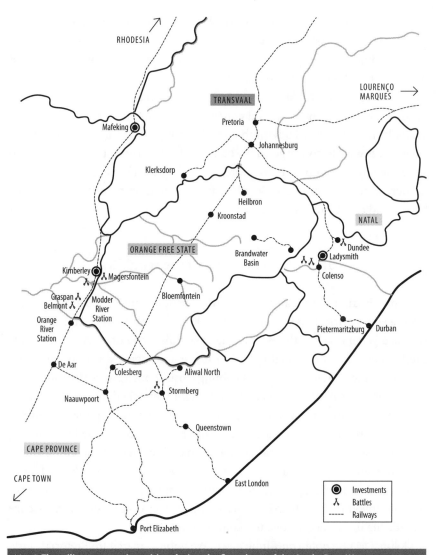

Map 2: The military-strategic position during the first phase of the Anglo-Boer War

Pretoria. By December 1899, the government stocks of rifles were diminishing, and the Boer victories of that month created grave concern that ammunition supplies would be exhausted. Thriftiness in battle was coupled with return of cartridges to Pretoria for reloading at the South African Explosives Factory. The workshops of the Netherlands-South African Railway Company (NZASM) repaired defective guns, while the engineering firm of Grunberg and Léon ensured a supply of artillery ammunition – perhaps as much as 200 Krupp shells per day. Local manufacture and repair ended following the fall of Pretoria in June 1900.[81]

The flow of consumables – spares, ammunition, fuel, clothing and food – to the republican armies was difficult at the best of times. Much could not be produced locally and had to be imported. Communication with the outside world, from whom promised support never came, was erratic and dependent upon the Portuguese authorities in Lourenço Marques. These shortcomings seriously diminished Boer combat capability.

Because they were fighting over their own country, the Boers had few problems with supply. The government of the ZAR was satisfied that sufficient food, particularly meat and flour, was held in storage.[82] As a result of its many wars, the Transvaal had developed an efficient logistical system. Yet despite this, the commandos experienced shortages of food right from the start.[83] Logistics broke down after the burghers had consumed their own supplies. The meat was of poor quality and in small quantity. The *boere beskuit* (rusks) were likewise inferior and in short supply.[84] Faced with these conditions, alternative means had to be sought: at Belmont, for example, supplies were bought, some goods were looted, and the burghers also did some 'drinking at the Bar'.[85] The commissariat depots disappeared with the start of the guerrilla phase of the war.

With overwhelming numbers of men and materiel being brought to bear by Britain, the Boers were by March 1900 falling back on all fronts. This was the start of the war's transitional phase. Boer strategy had been based on numerous past successes against African polities and had been adopted without any real discussion or understanding of the nature of the British forces or the type of war they were to fight. The Boers prepared for a limited war, but what Milner and Kruger brought on was total war. If the British arrived in South Africa with the wrong force, then the Boers, disregarding cooler counsel, certainly set about with the wrong strategy. Personality and other conflicts often prevented the Boers' mobile, strategically dispersed forces from cooperating against a relatively immobile, concentrated enemy. Yet, while the lack of cooperation between Boer generals marked the entire conventional phase of the war, this fragmentation, which increased as the war progressed, was an essential ingredient for guerrilla activities, which increased after the British had defeated the two republics.

The Boers were courageous but ignorant. However, as Fitzpatrick noted,

'Individual bravery, of the kind which takes no heed of personal risk, reckless heroic dash, they have not, nor do they pretend to have'.[86] The methods of Boer warfare differed vastly from those of the British. They did not seek pitched battle and disliked exposure to risk and danger. Caring first and foremost for personal safety, they were cautious, at times overly cautious. They would select positions carefully and utilise the advantages presented by modern firepower and the defence. They were not expected to sacrifice life needlessly or attempt, against the odds, to recover lost positions or overcome a superior enemy where these advantages were not present. However, while their conspicuous personal daring was not proverbial, they were, as Fitzpatrick noted, young and old, men and women, prepared to answer the call to defend their independence, and without hesitation.

As the clouds of war cast their long shadows over southern Africa, the republics had entered a defensive pact in 1897. Although their Calvinist faith was a common denominator, the Boers were not a united people with a common vision. Friction between the Transvalers and Free Staters became more pronounced as the war progressed. Furthermore, as has already been noted, class differences existed in both republics. Traditional Afrikaner historians have emphasised the lack of social distinction within the republican military systems, basing their argument upon the practice of officer election and the accessibility of officers to the ordinary burghers.[87] While the builders of Afrikaner nationalism stressed this equality, other historians, chiefly neo-Marxists, have questioned it.[88] Voting was not secret and *bywoners* (tenants) were pressed to elect their landlords, or at least the foremost landowner of the district, to the position of field cornet.[89] And while ordinary burghers did have immediate and personal access to their officers,[90] the evidence suggests that this was the access *bywoners* would normally enjoy when presenting personal problems or grievances to landowners.

Stan Trapido has argued that 'the weakening of client-patron relationships and … growing, but regionally uneven, impoverishment might have led to intra-Afrikaner class conflict'.[91] Boer society was divided, politically and economically, and, in the Transvaal, Kruger and his cronies no doubt realised that a long war, won or lost, would inevitably change the little republic. During the war, it would seem as if there was a drift of landless *bywoners* to the British side; many became *hensoppers* (or 'joiners', literally 'hands-uppers') for they too wished to overthrow an ostensibly corrupt, land-based oligarchy.[92] The *bywoner* had nothing to fight for. As land became commercially viable before the war, the *bywoner* had become an encumbrance. His status declined and his tenure became more precarious, for the war provided the opportunity for many landlords to refuse to resume patronage for those *bywoners* who had left the land to serve with the commandos.[93] Having lost their movable property, mostly livestock, in the first months of the war, these *bywoners* may have tended to opt out of the war. But here much research needs to be done.

In Britain, the early enthusiasm for war was more noticeable among the middling classes. As Rex Pope has argued, jingoistic music-hall songs were 'commercial products for, not of, their working-class audiences'.[94] Despite the seeming popularity of these patriotic songs, the disruption of pro-Boer meetings and the Conservative government's success in the 1900 'khaki' election, there is little evidence of strong, broad-based popular support for the war. The working classes entered the armed forces for the want of employment, not because they embraced notions of imperial vision. Moreover, the 'spontaneous rejoicing' connected to the key battles, and, in particular, the reliefs of Kimberley, Ladysmith and Mafeking, represented a national sigh of relief. Significant portions of the working classes, influenced increasingly by syndicalism, viewed the war as a capitalist venture. Many were, unsurprisingly, pro-Boer. Longer-term voting patterns, the disorganisation of the Liberal Party and local issues also go a long way in explaining the Conservative and Liberal Unionist victory at the polls in 1900.

Throughout the war, the growing pace of surrenders and defections took its toll on morale. The unnecessary surrenders of Cronjé, early in 1900, and of Marthinus Prinsloo, in July of that year, broke not only the spirit of Joubert but also of the republican cause. 'What a shock it was to see him [General Joubert] only a few months later, grey-headed, with care-worn features and hollow cheeks. His heart was broken then, after Cronjé had blundered by allowing himself with close on 4 000 men to be captured, thereby breaking the spirit of nearly all and well-nigh ruining our cause.'[95] Both Smuts and De Wet realised that the republican forces had to be 'purged by these losses and defections' in order for the war to continue.[96]

But, just as Boer national resolve seemed to be crumbling, that of the British Empire seemingly rallied. The great hope of the republicans was a true people's war – a rising of the whole Afrikaner population, including the Cape Dutch. This, their only realistic chance of success, might have swept the British out of southern Africa. Many of the most ambitious guerrilla operations were designed to inspire such a rising, but it never came. In its absence, the Boer commandos were effectively confined to defensive operations and, although the guerrilla war lasted nearly four times as long as the conventional phase, many (if not most) Boers recognised the futility of their struggle against an empire with immeasurable war potential and seemingly limitless military capacity.[97] According to De Wet:

> We knew, I need scarcely say, that humanly speaking ultimate victory for us was out of the question – that had been clear from the very beginning. For how could our diminutive army hope to stand against the overwhelming numbers at the enemy's command.[98]

But there were other factors that impacted upon Boer morale. Relations between the Boers and the foreigners, who from June 1899 had volunteered to help oppose British aggrandisement,[99] were less than cordial. There was a good measure of mutual distrust, perhaps cultural contempt. As Fransjohan Pretorius has argued, the clash between the educated, largely urban, middle-class foreign volunteers and the 'rustic, patriarchal and conservative' Boers was to be expected.[100] This was not a new thing. Kruger's erudite Dutch officials were ridiculed and criticised.[101] They had, it was thought, 'no knowledge of the Afrikaners' language or morality and were unsuited to his style of warfare'.[102] Joubert had complained that he was continually harried by these foreigners with requests for accommodation, food, transport and arms.[103] The archival evidence, which seems to point to the opposite, would show this to be a little unfair.[104]

The change in Boer strategy

Although the war began disastrously for Britain, the Boers were administratively weak and incapable of a major offensive. Unable to convert tactical success into strategic victory, the republics could not stand up to the growing stream of men and equipment that Britain poured into the country. There were no great battles; the war was characterised by a series of ambuscades, skirmishes and sieges. The final regular battle was fought on 8 September 1900 at Spitzkop. Having lost all hope of winning the war, the Boers harassed the British with guerrilla tactics, denying pitched battle and concentrating, whenever possible, against British weaknesses.

In June 1900, only days after the flight of President Kruger and two days before the surrender of Pretoria, Colonel Maxse confided to his sister what most British soldiers thought. He did not expect a protracted resistance, but rather the exile of Kruger and the disintegration of the Boer armies, which were already in the process of collapse. This had been the prediction for the outcome of the war, and any close examination of the Boer administration could lead to no other conclusion. Although the Boers had managed to divert British energy to the relief of Ladysmith, Kimberley and Mafeking, drawing the imperial regiments into the semi-desert hinterland of the Cape and the northern districts of Natal, the British continued to pour men and materiel into the theatre and soon the Boer forces were falling back on all fronts. By September 1900, the unprofessional Boer high command, found wanting by the realities of war, had been replaced by a younger, better educated and disciplined cadre of commanders, who adopted a guerrilla strategy, which, as Maud Lyttelton, the perceptive niece of one of Britain's more successful Anglo-Boer War generals, noted in January 1901, tied up many thousands of British troops and delayed the outcome of the war, which was perhaps always inevitable, by twenty months. Lord Roberts' arrival in England was, she thought, 'somewhat befogged [for] he's not coming with a victorious army & flags flying behind him. The thought of all our bored troops plodding after de Wet out there takes the glamour off badly.'[105]

During the latter half of 1900, the Boer armies were transformed and a new strategy was adopted. The decision to adopt guerrilla tactics altered the nature of the conflict. The commandos would no longer be geographic entities, but would follow men who had earned respect in the field. The new leaders met at Cypherfontein, a Transvaal farm, at the end of October 1900.

Some of these men had realised that the only course open to them was guerrilla warfare. Of this kind of war they were not ignorant, several African leaders having conducted guerrilla campaigns against them, but now they were the guerrillas. Although aware of the possibilities, they were uncomfortable with this role reversal.[106] Yet, as De Wet had proved, they had much in their favour, including accurate knowledge of the countryside, which, if used carefully, could enable them to refuse battle.[107] And, if cornered, having good rifles, they could momentarily maximise the power of the defence. The Boer logistics system, rooted in access to the land, was still excellent; supplies could be supplemented by raiding British convoys.[108] Furthermore, guerrillas could pounce on British foragers and stragglers and so concentrate their weaker forces against smaller units of the enemy.

Yet, most of all, the Boers had the political goodwill and backing of their people, who, on the land, could provide them with food and good intelligence. There were dangers too. Some commandos might be unable, or perhaps unwilling, to refuse battle. And here there was something of a double dilemma. The Boer leadership had to bolster morale by achieving some military success, yet they and their forces, without heavy ordnance, could not always maximise the power of the defence even when concentrating in fortified positions. This was becoming more difficult, particularly after the loss of their last artillery. Yet, by concentrating their forces, weaker in armament, against surprised, numerically weaker imperial and colonial forces, such a raiding strategy might work.[109]

The very nature of the Boer commandos facilitated their transition to a guerrilla force. The majority of Boers lived in the country, surviving in relative isolation with the constant threat of attack by wild animals or African warriors. In a constant state of preparedness, they acquired essential survival skills from an early age. These hardy people, excellent marksmen, with an intimate knowledge of their own country, were a stubborn foe – even for a nation with the resources of Britain. They had a natural sense of minor tactics and, although nearly all were mounted, they fought on foot. Although incapable of conducting major operations, the Boers made excellent raiders.[110]

In fact, the successes of Christiaan de Wet, who had conducted a guerrilla war with great success in the Orange Free State since March 1900, gave much encouragement. That June, he cut the railway line to Pretoria, capturing £100 000 of stores and some 700 prisoners.[111] One British officer complained that 'De Wet knows all about movements of [British] troops' and that this intelligence was often only a few hours old.[112] De Wet had captured Broadwood's guns at Sannah's Post (30 March) and defeated the Royal Irish Rifles at Reddersburg (5 April). Moreover, he captured and held for 27 days the waterworks of the city of Bloemfontein, forcing the British garrison to resort to insanitary water resources, eventually doubling the typhoid mortality rate.

The British practice of farm burning, begun by Lord Roberts, impelled back into the field many burghers who had drifted to their farms during the first phase of the war.[113] The burned-out homesteads and blackened veld seemingly absolved them of their oaths of neutrality.

With the possibilities now apparent, the Boer leaders struck out from Cypherfontein, resolved eventually to take the war into the Cape and Natal colonies. Here, for political reasons, the British were unable to burn farms.

Jan Smuts, who, having studied at Cambridge, was familiar with the British mindset, believed too that there would eventually be a divergence between the methods followed by General Herbert Kitchener – who succeeded Lord Roberts as commander-in-chief in November 1900 – and British public opinion.

Apart from 'surviving' – the main task of the guerrilla – the Boer generals exploited opportunity. The commandos conducted raids against weak detachments of the occupying forces (in December 1900 Smuts and De la Rey inflicted a blow to Clements' column at Nooitgedacht[114]) and at railways and other logistical objectives. The Boers, almost invariably mounted, cut British railway lines more than 250 times in twelve months. Their increasing military proactivity was, as Geoffrey Robinson of the South Africa Department at the Colonial Office in London tells us, marked by 'floods of telegrams … [in one day] we sent off 10 to Capetown alone – recalling the balmy days of Sep '99'.[115]

The poor performance of the old leadership created an opening for a cohort of able younger men more deserving of the rank of general. The four geniuses of the war – Botha, Smuts, De la Rey and De Wet – all 'started and remained in a subordinate position until it was too late'. They could only push to the front rank after the death of Joubert, the surrenders of Cronjé, Piet de Wet and Marthinus Prinsloo, the disgrace of Hendrik Schoeman – who 'represented in his person a whole vanished or vanishing order of things, both political and military' – and, most importantly, the exile of Kruger. Nonetheless, by this time it was too late. Bloemfontein had fallen and the entire Boer campaign was being steadily rolled back. The nepotism of the republican governments and the incompetence and arrogance of the military leadership created a situation that by late 1900 was past redemption.[116]

The very nature of the Boer commandos – of the land, flexible, ill-disciplined – facilitated their transition to a guerrilla force. The disintegration of the Boer high command in 1900, and the coagulation of burghers around men who had proved themselves in battle, placed in the field what seemed a new force, ably led and conducting a strategy to which the British now had to adapt. Moreover, the Boers gained an advantage, while the British fumbled to find a counter-strategy. The Boers, by avoiding battle, and so reducing Britain's technological advantage, now controlled the strategic pace of the war.[117]

There are, in the primary sources generated by British junior officers, numerous references to a lack of understanding of the new war. Men like Beresford Gibbs and Jack Lyttelton did not recognise the purpose of the Boer commando. Gibbs complained that his outfit 'always seem[ed] to miss the big fights'. The Boers would neither attack nor present themselves for a decisive fight; as a result, the British became tied up in garrison duty. With the Boers not having 'the slightest intent of ever surrendering' Gibbs despaired that 'the war [would] go on till they [were] all wiped out'.[118] Trained primarily in conventional methods, such officers had little understanding of battle avoidance and harassment, or that simply remaining alive was the most important thing – undermining as it did both morale in Britain and British attempts at political pacification in South Africa. Milner, the British proconsul in southern Africa, had to admit in March 1901 that the 'Government [was] more or less a farce, with the country swarming with brigands and nothing but the railway line and a few towns really in our possession'.[119]

The Boers were victorious in many of the ensuing skirmishes and actions. Executing a fine Fabian strategy, they dispersed into the hinterland, refused battle and counterattacked only when the invaders least expected combat. In concentrating against weaker elements of the invader, the Boers managed to inflict several defeats. Yet, forced to flee in the face of larger numbers, they were not able to protect their settlements, which were devastated and their harvests and herds appropriated by the British. The British resolved to attack Boer logistics, to exile people, to destroy their homesteads and food supplies, and to capture their livestock. They developed, after some falling about, an effective counter-guerrilla strategy.

Following the capture of the two republican capitals in 1900, the British formed several new-breed regiments of irregulars, whose purpose was suppression rather than conquest. One of these was Steinaecker's Horse, which was raised to close the frontier between the Transvaal and Mozambique. In the lowveld they built and occupied a line of fortifications, stretching from Swaziland to the Letaba area of the present Kruger National Park. Drawing on local intelligence gathered by a good network of African spies, they ranged the countryside from these forts. However, exploiting their remoteness from the rest of the British army in South Africa (a remoteness both geographical and organisational), they involved themselves in the illegal hunting of game, at least some looting, and probably some gun-running in this borderland, as much as prosecuting the war. General Ben Viljoen, their primary opposition in the lowveld, thought the irregulars nothing more than a ragtag lot of vagabonds, desperate men drawn from all corners of the empire.

The British counterinsurgency strategy: logistics, blockhouses, mobile columns, camps

The change in Boer strategy gave the political aspect increasing importance, and Milner, taking this as his cue for increased intervention in military affairs, pressed Roberts and Kitchener for a change in British strategy. Milner argued, in a letter to the former and in conversation with the latter, that the holding and governing of secured, demarcated districts was preferable to the ranging of much larger areas. The country, he went on, could not be occupied by relatively static operations, securing only certain positions. The abandonment of localities once taken only encouraged the Boers. Mobile forces were needed to operate between military posts, secure the countryside, occupy localities effectively and instil confidence in the local population, who might thus be encouraged to join the British.[120] Milner hoped to establish a nucleus in Johannesburg, where ordinary industry could continue and spread out to the surrounding districts.

This strategy, one from the inside out, was endorsed by Joseph Chamberlain, who suggested that the refugees who hailed from Johannesburg be allowed to return to the Rand on condition that they enlist for service, allowing the mines to be reopened and protected. Chamberlain proposed similar nuclei at Bloemfontein and Pretoria, with mobile forces available for pursuit and 'inferior troops' entrenched and fortified on the lines of communication, 'each separate body being able to hold its own for a given period of a week or a fortnight against any assault'. Chamberlain, at first somewhat hesitant to give his views, was 'dying to hear' that some sort of civil administration had commenced 'anywhere in the two Colonies'. He distrusted military administration and acerbically noted to Milner that it was 'calculated to increase the number of our enemies and to exacerbate their hostile feelings'.[121]

Chamberlain's views on military operations were precisely those of Milner. Both doubted the abilities of the soldiers, and Milner went so far as to declare that he was 'now sufficiently profane to doubt the existence of some occult military science, putting to shame the amateur view of common-sense'. Milner and Kitchener had a special telephone line between their houses on which, according to Kitchener, they conversed on all subjects.[122] Yet, while Kitchener kept his plans to himself, both Milner and Chamberlain knew that his scheme for ending the war was not theirs. Milner's experience in South Africa was such that, on questions of military policy, 'the civilians in South Africa have generally been more in the right than the soldiers'. The latter were better left to sort out the purely technical matters, such as armament and tactics, leaving strategy to the civilians.[123]

Milner thought Kitchener 'a man of great ability, unconventional mind and strong will', and, although Kitchener's strategy was not his, he did not doubt that Kitchener had a plan to end the war. Even an inferior plan, if carried out consistently, was better than none. Nevertheless, it cut Milner 'to his heart' to see places abandoned that had been held for months, like Jagersfontein and Smithfield, and the small nucleus of people who had accepted British rule obliged to take refuge, with much loss and suffering, in refugee camps. 'As far as the bulk of the country is concerned,' he lamented, 'we are further off than ever from protected areas.'[124] Maxse noted that 'stationary posts won't really defend any line and they leave the whole surrounding country open to Boer raiders. What we want is a mobile column, and no one knows it better than headquarters, but we simply have not got one until remounts reach us!'[125]

Britain, conducting the greatest of its colonial campaigns, had to change to a severe logistical strategy and commit overwhelming resources to contain the mobile, independent commandos. Milner, referring to the counterinsurgency campaign, rightly remarked to Chamberlain that 'the fight is now mainly over supplies'.[126] Frustrated at there being no centre of gravity at which to strike, the British attempted to deny the commandos their source of physical and emotional succour: their farms were burned and their families[127] herded into concentration camps. In Lord Wolseley's words: 'Your first object should be the capture of whatever they prize most, and the destruction or deprivation of which will probably bring the war most rapidly to a conclusion.'[128]

British troops burned farms and crops and drove off livestock; the women, children and older menfolk of the two republics were taken into so-called concentration camps. This included Boers as well as blacks, indeed all those who rendered (or were suspected of rendering) assistance of any kind to the commandos in the field. In the camps, a combination of indifference and incompetence resulted in the deaths of 27 927 Boers and 14 154 black South Africans.[129]

The denuding of the countryside had two aims: the supply of imperial forces and the denial of supplies to the enemy. Roberts gave instructions on 7 December 1900:

> The Commander-in-Chief has noticed that, after the passage through a dis-
> trict of a column of troops, the food supplies therein do not appear to have
> sensibly diminished. The Commander-in-Chief knows how difficult it is to
> collect supplies over a scattered area, and at the same time defend a long
> column and complete a long march before nightfall, but he urges on officers
> commanding the columns that they should fully recognise the necessity of
> denuding the country of supplies and livestock, in order to secure the two-
> fold advantages of denying subsistence, and of being able to feed their own
> columns to the fullest extent from the country.[130]

Friendly civilians, the so-called *hensoppers*, together with women and children, were brought into concentration camps to protect them from the full
effect of this extreme application of a logistic strategy. However, given the high
number of deaths in the British camps, one must necessarily question whether
the British drew any political advantage at all by 'shielding [their] supporters
from the effects of the programme of terror implicit in such a logistic strategy'
by concentrating them in these supposed places of refuge.[131]

Yet, the British columns scouring the country remained uncoordinated, and
(returning to the imperially minded Maud Lyttelton) 'the thought of all our
bored troops plodding after de Wet out there' certainly took 'the glamour
off badly' for many Britons.[132] By April 1901, Kitchener was no longer content
to simply 'hustle' the enemy. The monthly bag (of killed, captured and surrendered) was rising (*see* Table 1.3), but would not bring a quick end to the war.
And so Kitchener resolved to trap the enemy using a systematic and coordinated
strategy, for which he required two things: good intelligence and mobility.
Surveying and mapping, in combination with the use of the so-called National
Scouts, helped with the first.[133] For the second, he selected the best men and
the best commanders for the columns to hunt and trap the Boers. They were
the counterparts of the new breed of Boer generals, and several – Julian Byng,
Edmund Allenby and Douglas Haig – later became British field marshals.[134]
The essential element of Kitchener's attrition strategy was the British cavalry,
which were now, more rightly, mounted infantry. Operating in extended lines,
they drove the Boer guerrillas against fixed lines of barbed wire and blockhouses. The Boers, forced to abandon their cumbersome wagons, livestock
and dismounted soldiers, were ultimately reduced to near starvation.[135]

Table 1.3: Boers 'bagged', January to July 1901	
Month (1901)	**Numbers**
January	859
February	1 772
March	1 472
April	2 437
May	2 585
June	2 277
July	1 820

Source: Thomas Pakenham, *The Boer War*, pp 499, 512.

Blockhouses

To inhibit the movement of the commandos, the British built vast networks of barbed-wire entanglements, stretching for some 8 000 kilometres and guarded by approximately 9 000 blockhouses, cutting much of the highveld into squares. Mobile columns assisted in the capture of burghers by sweeping them against the blockhouse lines, which in some cases were connected by rail and equipped with searchlights that swept the veld on dark nights. Gustav Preller recorded that, on his journey as a POW from Ermelo to Standerton, he counted no less than 180 blockhouses, each with entrenched campsites. John Buchan, who landed at Cape Town in early October 1901 and made his way north to join Milner's personal staff, tells us that

> Schoeper [sic] and Smuts were supposed to be lying about 100 miles up the line so we went very slowly. It was funny to see the soldiers in the block-houses along the line turning out to meet the train with fixed bayonets, and the Kaffir [sic] scouts and the watch-fires.

The letters of Jack Lyttelton, who arrived in South Africa in January 1901 and seemingly enjoyed his life in the army and his time in Africa, provide a good loophole through which to study the life of a blockhouse garrison. A nephew of General Neville Lyttelton, he first commanded a fort and three blockhouses on the hills to the north of Kroonstad. Over the next two months he 'changed [his] country residence' twice, moving first to Doornkop and then to No 41

Blockhouse of the Kroonstad-Lindley-Bethlehem line, which, as he noted proudly, had seen more fighting than any other place between Kroonstad and Lindley since the line had been built. At both places he was well positioned to observe the movement of commandos as well as the tactical execution of Kitchener's counterinsurgency strategy.

Drives: mobile columns and armoured trains

Kitchener, whom the Bishop of Pretoria thought 'very pleasant and ... little ... bothered with the tremendous burden' he had on his shoulders, spent hours poring over maps and monitoring the minor sweeps and major drives of his columns. These operations varied in size according to the terrain and reputation of the Boer general in the field. In early 1902 there were seven columns chasing De Wet and his commandos in the northern Orange Free State. The elusive De Wet escaped yet again to one of his hiding places, but the drive was otherwise 'wonderfully successful'. Some 19 000 mounted soldiers lined out from Heilbron to Lindley and ranged over the veld, driving into the corner formed by the main line and the Wolverhoek–Heilbron railway blockhouse line. The drive lasted four days (Wednesday 4 February to Saturday 7 February) and led to the capture of 500 Boers and three commandants. Jack Lyttelton, some of whose command strengthened the railway, describes the sweep:

> The line started after several independent movements between Frankfurt and Lindley, and drove due west with blockhouses on each flank. When the right reached Heilbron, the left was pushed forward, to within 15 miles of Kroonstadt [sic], where it met with some resistance, but still advancing struck the mainline at America Station. So from now the triangle was America, Heilbron with Wolverhoek Junction at the peak, and the line advancing almost due north ... A line of mounted men, their right on the railway, and stretching away to the horizon, advancing at a slow canter, with the wretched band of terrified Boers hussled [sic] along in front, with 5 armoured trains keeping pace with them and helping them along with a liberal hail of bullets and 6–pounder shells, it must have been a perfectly wonderful sight. They made a sort of stand outside Wolverhoek, but of course had no chance at all, and all soon surrendered ... From the moment that the left hit the main line our direct interest in the drive was over as we couldn't

see any more but we wait in anticipation for this next one. Since Saturday
this place has been as thick as bees as 5 columns came in here to recoup.

Faced with such operations the Boers had two choices: either break out at
considerable risk or be captured. De Wet broke through the blockhouse line
on 6 February, and then crossed over again to collect his stores, which had
been mislaid on the north side. He negotiated the lines by rushing a herd of
bullocks at the wire, carrying all before them and allowing De Wet and his
men to gallop through after them. Although another drive was in the offing
and De Wet's capture confidently expected, Lyttelton surmised that he would
'probably get through somewhere'. Such operations eroded guerrilla strength
and, the British hoped, would end for the moment at least the 'rushing [of]
convoys'. An armoured wagon was placed between blockhouses 41 and 42 after
De Wet got through on 6 February, to prevent him doing it again. This was 'a
case of locking the stable door etc'.

At the beginning of March, De Wet attempted to break through the lines
at the place where Lyttelton's company was garrisoned. The attack, expected
between blockhouses 21 and 25, took place at blockhouses 27 and 28. That the
attack – conducted by De Wet in person – failed no doubt boosted morale.
Forced to stay where he was, De Wet went into one of his 'tight places', out
of which, as Lyttelton reminded his readers on the family estate at Hagley in
Worcestershire, 'he has a wonderful knack of getting'. Having lost neither a
single burgher nor a single ox, De Wet later suggested that 'the policy of the
blockhouse might equally well have been called the policy of the blockhead'.
Yet, the blockhouse lines often saw action and, by maximising the possession
of terrain, in combination with the columns of mounted infantry and armoured
trains, contributed to the eventual British success. On 23 February a commando
attempting to break through Rimmington's Vrede blockhouse line, by driving a
herd of cattle before them, was repulsed, and on 27 February some 600 of them
were 'bagged' near Vrede, a date, one of Milner's private secretaries noted, 'now
of many anniversaries'. From the Middelburg district came the news that Colonel
Park had almost captured the Boer provisional government, who, the previous
Saturday, had tried to cross the railway north of Pretoria in an attempt to join
De la Rey, but had been repulsed by three armoured trains dispatched for that
purpose. The news of the commandos, repulsed and 'touring about the country
in rather a defenceless condition', was enough to get 'everybody's pecker up'.

Although Kitchener's army was 250 000 strong, only 156 000 of them were 'effective' militarily, and only half the latter number were actually available for pursuit. While the commandos raided the rail network, blowing up trains and causing general irritation, and sometimes even casualties, the main guerrilla threat was to the now-empty veld. Attacks on the railways declined toward the end of 1901. The train bringing Jack Lyttelton into the Free State in January 1902 was sniped at between Norvals Pont and Bloemfontein. Yet, as he noted to his sister, the Boers

> never managed to hit the carriages and I personally never woke up while the sniping was going on. On Wednesday night heavy firing was heard quite close to us, but it must have been our blockhouses shooting at a party of [B]oers trying to cross the line. The carriage we travelled in was perforated with 4 bullets, tho' not when we were in it, probably about a year ago when the line was in such a bad state. It is the only one I have seen with bullet marks on it.

This certainly testifies to improving British security. As the blockhouse grid grew, the number of attacks on, and crossings of, the railway lines decreased (*see* Figure 1.1). Yet, occasionally, British columns were caught by surprise. Brigadier General HG Dixon received a drubbing at Vlakfontein, near Naauwpoort, and, with Kritzinger's raid into the Cape Colony, the spirit of militant republicanism rode through the colony once more. On 11 October 1901, two years after the start of the war, Merriman noted that 'parties of Boers are within 60 miles of Cape Town, apparently raiding at will'. The result was a confused situation of military stalemate, 'of concentration camps and systematic devastation, of invasion, rebellion and intensified martial law in the Cape Colony'. Although weak and unable to deal a decisive military blow, the Boer raiders caused much inconvenience, and Kritzinger forced the British to line the railway at Hanover Road.

By August 1901 there were 93 940 whites and 24 457 blacks in the 'camps of refuge', where, catastrophically, each month the deaths rose (*see* Table 1.4). The rising clamour of humanitarians, outraged at conditions in the camps, and the enormous amount (£1 250 000 per week) spent to keep 250 000 British and colonial troops in South Africa – and their seeming inability to crush an estimated 18 000 Boers – brought London to the conclusion that an ultimatum must be given to Kitchener: either end the war by September or adopt Milner's policy. Kitchener's problem, of course, was that there were too few Boers and they were too scattered. And the result was there: by July, the number of Boers 'bagged' had fallen for the second month (*see* Table 1.3).[136]

Table 1.4: **Camp deaths, May to July 1901**	
Month	**Numbers**
May	550
June	782
July	1 675

Source: Thomas Pakenham, *The Boer War*, p 510.

In the end, the combination of blockhouses and the denuding of the country, together with the adoption by Kitchener of the strategy proposed by Milner, proved the turning point in the guerrilla war. Protected areas, centred at first on Pretoria, Johannesburg and Bloemfontein, were gradually expanded as the country, now compartmentalised by the blockhouse lines, was cleared of guerrilla activity and civilian life returned to normal. By the end of 1901,

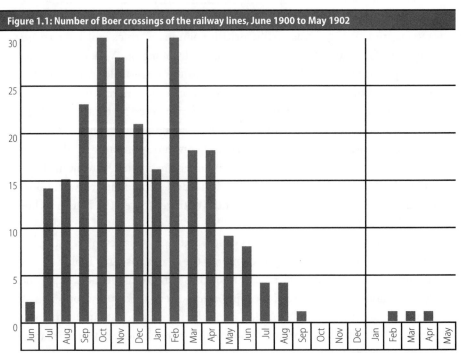

Figure 1.1: Number of Boer crossings of the railway lines, June 1900 to May 1902

Source: J Hattingh and A Wessels, *Britse Fortifikasies* in die *Anglo-Boereoorlog*, (Oorlogsmuseum van did Boererepublieke, Bloemfontein, 1997), p 140.

only three main centres of resistance remained. Here the lines were rapidly extended and the commandos, forced into ever-shrinking areas, faced three options: attempt to break through the lines, infiltrate back through the sweeps of the mounted troops or surrender and be added to the 'bag'.[137]

Boer tactics

The Boers, harassed by mobile columns and confined by fortifications, and lacking heavy artillery, were forced to adopt other means to counter British sweeps or to break through the lines. One way was to harass the British garrisons, both in the towns and along the railways and blockhouse lines. In April 1902, 150 Boers appeared on a ridge outside Kroonstad and were only moved after the British directed fire from 5.2-inch howitzers at their position. On this occasion the Boers killed a native scout and wounded another. When not on duty, Lyttelton and his company would fish or swim in the Vals River, where they were sniped at. Boer snipers normally approached the lines on nights 'pitch black and very fine and quiet'.[138] Lyttelton tells us that

> the Boers would crawl up to within 50 yards of a blockhouse[,] make themselves comfortable behind some rocks and begin sniping the sentry; of course the men inside the blockhouse begin shooting all round a few hundred rounds, during which time the Boer sits snugly behind his rock and when the firing stops, begins again hurrying off at dawn. Neither of them blockhouse or [B]oer ever hit a man doing this so it doesn't matter much, and helps to keep the sentry awake.[139]

In so doing, the Boers harassed enemy troops, gave themselves something to do and picked up some enemy kills along the way. 'Lying awake from 9 till 3 am waiting for the firing from the blockhouses on each side of you to stop, does not give you an angelic temper on the following day, but I suppose it is excellent practice'.[140] The value of such practice must of course be questioned. On the night of 4 March 1902, a party of Boer snipers got inside the square of blockhouses, formed by a twist in the line, where Lyttelton was positioned. The result was that five blockhouses amused themselves by either shooting at the other blockhouses or into the hospital, where the staff and patients had to lie below the sangar walls for safety.[141]

The troops in the blockhouses could fire at a terrific rate. The fusillades opened from the lines after dark, but expected Boer attacks seldom materialised. Jack Lyttelton complained in a letter to his sister:

> We 'rattle' a good deal on our side but the answering rattle of the enemy is mainly lacking ... A great deal of banging is now going on from 31–32 blockhouses and they have got the Maxim out. I am just going out to see what's up – same old game, a few snipers in the valley, and a lot of fuss to try [and] slaughter them. It is now 8.30 and pitch dark, and also begun to rain again, so I trust they don't come this way as it will mean getting soaked.[142]

Despite Lyttelton's discretion on this occasion, his company he thought easily held the record for ammunition expenditure. In one week they fired off close on 20 000 rounds. Vast numbers of animals were slaughtered in the process. One night a young colt broke loose from a convoy and at around midnight tripped the fuse wire near Lyttelton's blockhouse. A 25–pound (11.3 kilograms) dynamite mine was set off, which shook the surrounding blockhouses like an earthquake. The colt, unhurt by the explosion, succumbed shortly after 'to a marauding bullet, from a vigilant sentry'. It was, Lyttelton noted, 'exceeding[ly] dangerous to approach the part of the blockhouse line garrisoned by I Company'.[143]

The carnage – 'transport mules [and other animals] promptly added to the bag'[144] – was prodigious along the railway and blockhouse networks. The railway north of the Orange River was littered, on either side, with the carcasses and skeletons of oxen and horses. The stench was dreadful and presented the occupants of the line with the dangers of rinderpest and enteric fever. As a result, the British had to go to some lengths to dispose of the carcasses.[145]

Morale

Gradually, the British realised that the Boers were not on the point of surrender. Morale slumped within the ranks and even affected a number of senior commanders. Pretoria in October 1900, as Milner himself noted, was awful and crammed full of '*tired* and grumbling warriors'.[146] In November 1900, at variance with Milner and his methods, Kitchener too was canvassing support for a move to India.[147] In England, the politicians, nursing their constituencies, lost stomach for a war that was becoming increasingly total. And the Boer generals, at first reviled as uneducated frontiersmen, were increasingly admired in the capitals of Europe for the stiff fight they put up. Maud Lyttelton, seemingly, had a collection of Boer photographs, and her brother Jack thought 'the cheek of those fellows is simply wonderful'.[148]

Yet, for the soldiers in the line there were pressures from home. Lyttelton, hearing an officer suddenly laugh when reading his mail, asked him what ailed. He answered, 'I have just heard from a fellow in England who writes that he supposes the war is really over, and we shall be going back soon.' This officer was in command of the most troublesome section of the defences of Kroonstad and, Lyttelton thought, probably had had not three consecutive nights without being disturbed by snipers. Things were far from being kept dull, but such absurd ideas, which reflected a lack of understanding back in England, did nothing to boost sagging morale.[149]

When the war ended, with the signature of the Treaty of Vereeniging on 31 May 1902, there were 18 000 Boers still in the field. This surprised Milner's staff, and at least one of them thought that they had in fact 'finished the war very quickly'.[150] Congratulations for Milner's role in the peace negotiations streamed in. George Goschen, former First Lord of the Admiralty, thought that Milner and Kitchener 'had done splendid construction work in the negotiations, that though they had made one or two points rather clearer, the merit of the form [and] substance belonged entirely to you two'. Goschen was delighted with the phrase 'our lawful Sovereign' in Article 1 of the treaty. Thanks to them, 'altogether the surrender [was] complete'. However, as Goschen recognised, only then did the worst of Milner's troubles begin.[151]

Political warfare

Milner had realised from the start that the war would first have to be won militarily, and then, after a peace was signed, politically. The ravages of total war had to be repaired: in places, whole towns had been destroyed, some 30 000 farmhouses had been burned, and more than 250 000 refugees had been displaced. The repatriation and resettlement of refugees was an urgent priority; in late 1902 Boers, were returning from the camps to the Transvaal at a rate of some 3 500 per week.[152]

Although the political and psychological dimensions of reconstruction were important from the start, key Britons, including Milner and Lord Selborne (who succeeded Milner as High Commissioner), were unwilling to 'sacrifice strategy to political considerations'.[153] Yet, after the war it was the British administration that had to manage the repair of the ravages of total war, which involved more than rebuilding towns and farmhouses and resettling a traumatised population. The gold mines were returned to production. Municipalities were created for the first time in the hope, as expressed by Lionel Curtis, Milner's secretary, that 'everything that helps towards good Government will tend to the happiness of this most ill-starred people'.[154] Progressive agriculture was introduced and the country restocked with horses, cattle and sheep. Some farmers received grants, others compensation. Land was purchased for new settlers, who, Milner hoped, would form 'a useful element' in the agricultural population. An agricultural research station was set up at Potchefstroom. Breeding programmes were run in Standerton, a district earmarked as a future centre for the horse industry.[155] Government departments were recreated; some that had existed before 1899 received an overhaul, while others were built from scratch. The Boer defence structures, chiefly the commandos of the two former republics, disappeared altogether. Milner was resolute that 'the old condition of things should not be reproduced in which the race division coincided almost completely with a division of interests, the whole country population being virtually Boer, while the bulk of the industrial and commercial population was British'.[156] He explained to John Hanbury-Williams, his military secretary, late in 1900:

> The majority of the agricultural population will always be Dutch. This does not matter, provided there are some strong English districts and that, in most districts, there are a sufficient number of British to hold their own ... The only way to achieve this is by large purchase of land on the part of the Government with a view to resettling ... suitable settlers ... Men will-ing to risk some capital of their own should be preferred, and they should be planted on large or middle-sized farms ... Our great hope is in getting a considerable number – several thousands – of settlers of a *superior class*, and placing them in districts where there is already a British nucleus ... Well-selected settlers will flourish there and raise large families.[157]

Yet much of this effort failed. The Milner government was autocratic, and its members had only contempt for everything not English. Most of all, they failed to see that good governance did not necessarily win hearts and minds.[158] The 'new settlers' – the overwhelming majority with no independent finance or prior farming experience – were placed on isolated farms among a resurgent Boer population. Mutual support was difficult; a British presence could not easily form in small localities and the consolidation of sentiment 'in the general interests of the Empire' was not possible.[159] Sensing a threat to their interests and future political power, Boer magnates – many of whom, like Louis Botha, Christiaan Beyers and Coen Brits, retained considerable political ambition – held on to their enormous estates,[160] closed ranks and denied, or attempted to deny, British access to the platteland. They, like Milner, realised that the Boer system would survive if the new settlers remained politically insignificant when the Transvaal obtained self-government.

A new Afrikaner nationalism, now embracing the Cape and Natal colonies as well, was fanned by the experiences of the war, a process in which history and memory were major incendiaries. Such a development had been foreseen by Joseph Chamberlain in 1896:

> A war in South Africa ... would be a long war, a bitter war, and a costly war; and it would leave behind it the embers of a strife which I believe generations could hardly be long enough to extinguish.[161]

For this reason, Milner insisted on keeping a substantial imperial garrison in South Africa after 1902. He was convinced that the British should continue

Month	Boer POWs	Output of gold (ounces)	British refugees returning	Civil traffic on railways (tons)	Transvaal revenue	Total for last quarter
Nov 01	22 512	39 075	2 626		£95 491	
Dec 01	24 224	52 897	4 752	9 370	£97 943	£282 799
Jan 02	25 207	70 340	5 492	12 830	£161 664	
Feb 02	26 537	81 405	6 581	12 420	£86 684	
Mar 02	28 713	104 127	6 833	19 800	£116 000	£364 348
Apr 02	29 356	119 588	5 805	19 470	£179 104	
May 02		138 602	4 865	19 230	£171 117	

Table 1.5: **The reconstruction of the Transvaal**

Source: Milner to Chamberlain, 31 January 1902, 22 March 1902, 12 May 1902, 19 June 1902, BPP: Cd. 1663–1902, Further Correspondence relating to Affairs in South Africa.

for some time to hold Pretoria, Johannesburg and Bloemfontein in considerable strength.[162] Noting that many of 'our best Colonial loyalists have been the descendants of the officers or soldiers, or have been in the army themselves long ago', he hoped to couple this to programmes of army training and of military settlement. And, in the process, he dreamed of 'killing two birds with one stone'. By establishing the equivalent of an Aldershot or a Curragh in the Cape Colony, he could in a small way alleviate some of the overcrowding in Britain and at the same time boost the 'British' population of the Colony, which in another generation would be loyal.[163]

However, Milner was soon concerned by reductions in size of the imperial garrison, a large proportion of whom might eventually have settled in South Africa, adding valuably to the British population.[164] The adequate defence 'of our great central positions' troubled him in particular. The constant whittling away and eroding of the potential for offensive action would result in a perfectly useless force, '[f]or a few scattered and immobile garrisons would be an absolute danger, and merely so many temptations to would-be rebels, as, in case of any widespread rising, they would either have to be withdrawn or relieved'.[165]

By degrees, as the country settled down and a police force (the South African Constabulary, thought by Jack Lyttelton to be 'Wormwood Scrubs turned loose') was established for the former Boer republics, reductions in the number of troops were made.[166] This was hastened, too, by the raising of the Transvaal Volunteers, which incorporated some of the irregular formations that had served with the British in the war and formed the nucleus for the local defence force of the new colony.[167]

However, in 1905 a new government in London moved from the strategy of victory to one of containment. Responsible government was granted to both former republics. Afrikaner nationalism resurged, and the Het Volk (The People) party obtained an absolute majority in the new Transvaal legislative assembly in the elections of February 1907. This was followed that November by an even larger victory for the Orangia Unie in the Orange River Colony, while in the Cape Colony Jameson's Progressive government fell within three months. Jameson was replaced by John X Merriman, a sworn foe of Milnerism.

A total political metamorphosis occurred in British South Africa between 1907 and 1908. Economic depression, combined with drought and pestilence, brought much misery, while the idea that Britain might exact a war tax from South Africa – to pay for the war Britain had fought in South Africa – fuelled popular resentment. Eventually, London, and British minions in South Africa, unable to contain the floods of feeling and fearful of a rising tide of Afrikaner nationalism, backed down., Although London had won the war, it had lost face.

The butcher's bill

The war to destroy the independence of the two Boer republics cost Britain 97 477 casualties, of whom 7 091 were killed in action or died later from wounds, and £223 million. The cost to the Boers totalled 3 990 killed and a further 1 081 killed by disease, in addition to the camp deaths and incalculable economic losses. Yet these statistics misrepresent the physical and psychological impact of the war. With a long history of foreign wars, it was easy for the British to 'forget' the pain of a war soon dwarfed by the losses sustained in the First World War. British casualties of the Anglo-Boer War became more insignificant than the lesser numbers held in the collective Afrikaner mind. Boer war poets, most notably perhaps Jan FE Cilliers (1865–1940), have vividly captured something of the loneliness, the gloom and the devastation faced by the thousands of exiles returning after Vereeniging to burned farms, empty lives and the loss of family. Although Boer society had engaged in numerous conflicts since the founding of a permanent European settlement at the Cape in 1652 – not all perhaps classifiable as wars – for the Boers none other had the demographic and psychological impact of the Second Anglo-Boer War.

The nature and size of the operational area played havoc with the medical arrangements. The British lines of communication extended 1 800 kilometres from north to south and 1 000 kilometres from west to east. During the guerrilla war, the often small, mobile counterinsurgency units ranged over extensive areas, mostly without medical support. Transport, always scarce and vulnerable, remained disorganised, placing enormous pressures on medical supply and replacement medical personnel. The poor road infrastructure resulted in overturned ambulance carts and an uncomfortable ride for the wounded to the nearest railway station.

The Royal Army Medical Corps (RAMC) had been founded in 1898, and, at the start of the war, was critically short of medical resources, and particularly of personnel. Eventually some 850 medical officers staffed seven stationary hospitals and three general hospitals, located throughout South Africa, all along the major lines of rail communication. A further 2 280 other ranks were assigned to the hospitals or served as stretcher-bearers and first-line medical aiders. This number proved inadequate, forcing the British Army to contract 700 civilian doctors. By May 1902 more than 8 500 personnel were serving with the RAMC in South Africa, in 151 regimental medical units, 19 bearer companies, 28 field hospitals, five sanitary disease hospitals, 16 general hospitals, three hospital trains, two hospital ships and three advanced and two base medical supply depots. In all, there were 21 000 hospital beds in South Africa for British soldiers, who were cared for by some 800 nurses.[168]

At the start of the twentieth century, medical science stood at the threshold of extraordinary advances. This was especially so in the fields of surgery and disease prevention. However, in 1899, military health care still left much to be desired, and the military medical organisations were still unsophisticated. The British Army did not take military medicine seriously, yet (this was to come with the First World War). In many instances, the Boer armies, and the foreign ambulances that assisted the republican forces, suffered the same shortages in medical knowledge, medical supply and medical personnel. The opposing armies were largely unprepared and ill-equipped to save lives, patch the men up and return them to the battlefield.

The toll of combat fatalities was perhaps surprisingly light: 7 091 British soldiers and 3 990 Boers killed in action. Disease, as in so many wars, was the main killer, accounting for some 16 000 Tommies. Typhoid and dysentery were the main causes of death. Gabriel and Metz note that, over the duration of the thirty–month war, only 22 000 British soldiers were treated for wounds, injury and accident, whereas more than 74 000 suffered from enteric disease and dysentery, while more than 8 000 died from enteric fever. The British military hospital in Bloemfontein treated no fewer than 5 000 disease cases during November 1900. During that month, the Bloemfontein hospital suffered 40 disease-related deaths per day. In April 1901, the colonial troops[169] in South Africa suffered 385 casualties, almost 52 per cent having contracted acute infection or fever, while only four patients were released from medical care during this period (*see* Figure 1.2).[170] Fevers and infections accounted for the majority of imperial and colonial casualties for much of the war. The figures for the Boers were probably similar.

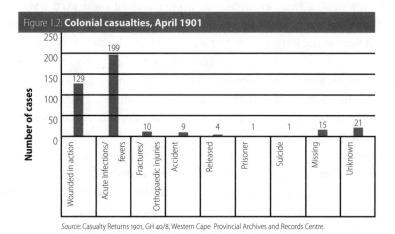

Figure 1.2: **Colonial casualties, April 1901**

Source: Casualty Returns 1901, GH 40/8, Western Cape Provincial Archives and Records Centre.

Conclusion

Superior technology provided British forces with a tactical advantage in battle, but, as was all too often the case, the Boers enjoyed the strategic advantage and could control the tempo of the war by maximising their knowledge of the terrain and climate, refusing battle and adopting guerrilla strategies.[171]

The war began disastrously for Britain. Before the long-drawn-out negotiations had quite played out, the Boers launched an already-delayed, pre-emptive strike against British forces in the Cape and Natal colonies. Their vigour and the distance of the conflict from Europe taxed British resources, as they had not been so burdened since the time of Napoleon. Although excellent marksmen, horsemen and fieldcraftsmen, the Boers were unable to resist the growing stream of men and equipment that Britain poured into the country. The last set-piece battle was fought on 8 September 1900 at Spitzkop, and the British achieved their main objective, the re-annexation of the Transvaal, during the following month. The Boer armies, the very nature of which facilitated their transition to a guerrilla force, underwent a transformation during the last half of 1900. There were no great battles; the remainder of the war was characterised by a series of ambuscades, skirmishes and minor sieges.

In the end, the South African War, the greatest of British colonial campaigns, was won militarily only through a severe logistic strategy and overwhelming resources. The last of the Boer republics were drawn into the British fold, 'vital imperial interests' were saved and British supremacy in southern Africa was, for the moment at least, ensured. Yet, Milner, having conducted a war with little feeling for the political dimension and the winning of hearts and minds, ensured that, in the longer term, the war would be won politically by a resurgent Afrikaner nationalism. Moreover, Milner had gathered around him an administration for the conquered republics comprising ambitious young men, all fired with the spirit of empire, who, almost without exception, were out of touch with the people of the new colonies. Yet, they attempted to recast the subcontinent in a British mould.

The political aspect had, of course, always been of the utmost importance. The country could only be secured for the Empire by gaining possession of the towns and districts and winning over the population. This the Milner administration failed to do. The lessons of the Second Anglo-Boer War were well caught by Patrick Duncan, another of Milner's administrators, in a letter to the journalist Leo Amery in 1904:

> It seems to me that we must ride one of the horses. One is the principle that we have to hold this place by force. The other is the principle that we can only hold this place by bringing the Boers into political life on other than race and *native* lines. If we are riding the first we are not nearly thorough enough. Nothing less than 20 years of Alsace Lorraine government will be of any use to us. But we are really trying to ride the second with one leg on the first.[172]

CHAPTER TWO

Integration and Union, 1902–1914

The unification of the South African colonies in 1910 was the artificial creation of a new State. As such it involved the throwing together of four territories which differed from one another in political and cultural background, economic condition and geographical environment. But even as an artificial construction the new State opened the way for the fusion of those diverse interests and embodied the expectation of a common future. In 1910 this was merely an ideal to be realised in time to come.[1]

— DW Krüger, historian, 1969, on the South Africa Act (1909)

It is really all very wonderful: All these men, who were at daggers drawn not seven years ago, all uniting now with the big end of unification in view.[2]

— William Carter, Archbishop of Cape Town, 1909, on Union

I seem to have lived in a bath of human blood ever since I can remember! The only thing we need such a defense [sic] force for, is to kill other South Africans. Our position, the nature of our country, the distance from its real base of supplies of any attacking country – even Germany – makes us perfectly safe if we are united.[3]

— Olive Schreiner, writer, 1912, on the need for a national defence force

The peace signed at Vereeniging in May 1902 ushered in a new era for South Africa, a geographic expression for a kaleidoscopic assortment of British colonies, Boer republics and recently conquered African kingdoms and chiefdoms. Britain, now supreme, refashioned the former republics as the Transvaal and Orange River colonies. New institutions were created, new laws were enacted, and Britons were settled to 'leaven' the platteland. An army of occupation, commanded from the Castle in Cape Town, garrisoned the major towns. The armed forces of the Cape and Natal colonies were redesigned largely for post-war duties of pacification, while new military structures were created in the Transvaal and Orange River colonies to meet a variety of perceived threats.

While much had changed, the structure of South African society, much as Lord Milner had feared, remained essentially unaltered. A new Boer leadership had emerged during the war, which, sensing the threat to their landed power after 1902, closed ranks and denied the British access to rural society.[4] Louis Botha, the former Commandant General of the ZAR, became the chief pillar of republican identity in the Transvaal, where Afrikaner society was organised soon after 1902 under the cover of agricultural societies. Milner's loss of control over the countryside was signalled by the formation of a People's Congress on 24 May 1904.[5] In January 1905, this Congress became Het Volk (The People) with an elaborate organisation comprising a network of committees. This was the old commando system writ in other terms: ward committees elected by the people, district committees elected by the ward committees, and all falling under an all-powerful head committee chaired by Botha.[6] London had cause for concern; several prominent Britons doubted the completeness of their military victory. This chapter addresses these concerns, the associated strategic problems and the policies that, with a good deal of fiscal realism, led to the unification of the four self-governing colonies in 1910 and the creation of a unified, national military force in 1912.

Empire, military organisation and the threat perception

The imperial powers developed a military concept for the occupation and, where necessary, the pacification of their variegated possessions. A vast literature, embracing the fashionable ideas of the Victorian soldier-theorist Colonel Charles Callwell, adopted the concept of 'small wars', a term applied to a variety of scenarios. Callwell, in fact, enumerated seven categories of potential enemies, ranging from well-structured armies to guerrillas and irregular cavalry.[7] Small wars, whether in the form of the pacification of simmering discontent or the crushing of outright rebellion, inevitably accompanied colonial enterprise. This history has not been neglected – certainly not in South Africa – and there is no doubt that our knowledge of small wars, and, more particularly, certain specific small wars, has advanced enormously over the past few decades. This was, of course, aided first by the 'new social history' of the 1960s and 1970s and, more recently, by the growing interest in asymmetrical conflict. The confluence of social protest and popular unrest with grassroots anonymity, black liberation and anti-colonialism appealed particularly to the technical and political interests of the 'new social historians' and the post-colonialists that followed.

New interest in South African protest history cannot but point in the direction of Bambatha (c. 1865–1906), who, although a relatively minor Zulu chief, embodied the spirit of black protest in early twentieth-century South Africa.[8] Incidents similar to the Bambatha rebellion of 1906 occurred elsewhere in the British Empire, and indeed in other empires at this time. The focus of imperial and colonial studies has shifted away from London, Paris and Lisbon to their imperial peripheries, to such disparate locations as Delhi, Dublin and Durban. Yet, too many studies focus solely on a particular place and disregard happenings in Europe or elsewhere in the colonial empires. The Bambatha rebellion, as it is historicised, and similar movements elsewhere were all manifestations of both popular discontent and thinking on imperial policing. Some ideas originated locally, others emanated from London or Paris or Lisbon or Berlin and washed out into the empires.

At the turn of the century, a number of military men in South Africa contributed to this debate on colonial discontent and imperial policing. They included Colonel HT Lukin (1860–1925), Commandant of the Cape Colonial Forces, Brigadier General George Aston (1861–1938) – a South African on Lord Methuen's staff – Major Percy Silburn (1876–1929) of the Natal Militia and Lieutenant Colonel Hugh Wyndham (1877–1963), the commander of the Southern Mounted Rifles of the Transvaal Volunteers. Between them, they captured in print much of the thinking of the time in terms of the threat perception and the concomitant strategy.[9]

South Africa, they argued, faced a peculiar tripartite problem. The first of these was seaborne assault. Compared to Australia and Canada, for instance, South Africa was favourably situated with regard to the possible seizure of its ports. Its immediate neighbours had no navies. The country could expect to have to deal with aggression by only one or two European powers, a challenge to which the Royal Navy would be more than equal. The landing of a raiding party or the temporary seizure of a port was therefore the only contingency considered. There were small numbers of naval volunteers in Natal and at the

Cape: the Natal Naval Volunteers had been formed in Durban in 1885, and the Cape Naval Volunteers established in Cape Town in 1905. In exchange for British naval protection, the Cape and Natal colonies made annual cash contributions, amounting to £50 000 and £35 000, respectively, towards the cost of maintaining the Royal Navy presence. These contributions were combined after Union (1910) and an annual contribution of £85 000 was made until 1922, when the Union government finally followed the example set by Australia and Canada, and accepted the principle of a South African navy, although an embryonic South African navy would only be formed in January 1940.[10] For the moment, the Royal Navy remained 'the policeman on the beat.'[11]

The second scenario, invasion from neighbouring territories – brought on, possibly, by a war between Britain and a European power that maintained an African army – was also regarded lightly. The frontier regions were undeveloped and, in the case of German South West Africa, deserts provided a seemingly impenetrable barrier (Kemp's march across the Kalahari in 1914 would prove the strategists wrong).[12] The worst, but least likely, contingency – never constant and seldom real – was a war between Britain and an imperial power, especially one opposing Britain in Africa. If the enemy was Germany or Portugal, the war would probably include an overland invasion from South West Africa (Namibia) or Portuguese East Africa (Mozambique), the sparking of an Afrikaner rebellion and, in the case of Germany, a limited naval campaign in the Southern Ocean. A war with France or Belgium would involve the same problems, less the landward invasion, but with the possible addition of an African rising. South Africa differed from the other self-governing dominions, for it had European powers within marching distance of its land borders and with easy access to its ports. The Royal Navy's presence at Simon's Town, a second-class naval base, was both a consolation and a political conundrum.[13]

Internal unrest, whether black or white, rural or urban, was the third contingency. If this coincided with a seaborne assault or a landward invasion, or both, a crisis of disastrous proportions would be forecast. Whatever advantage geography may have provided against a landward invasion, the opposite was true for internal rebellion. Because of the uncoordinated nature of black resistance, the government felt forced to maintain a presence in most districts. The Bambatha rebellion had shown that just the threat of uprisings elsewhere was enough to prevent a concentration of government forces. The problem of defence, invoking Wyndham, was 'one of remarkable complexity and magnitude'. Three requirements had to be met if South African defence was to be sound in terms of internal security. Rebellions, he observed, 'start suddenly and unexpectedly by the murder of outlying farmers', whom, he thought, would benefit from the protection offered by loopholed buildings erected on every farm in exposed districts. The first call was therefore for fixed defences, a system whereby farmers in outlying localities would be ready for emergencies and able to defend themselves and their families until they could be relieved and offensive action taken. Such action, he argued secondly, had to be short, sharp and decisive. Flying columns had to be organised, equipped and trained in peacetime and be ready at a moment's notice to take the field. Such a force had to have the power and mobility of the queen in chess, able to be moved where and when needed and 'not tied by the leg to local defence'.[14] An inter-colonial mobile force at least 20 000 strong, of all arms, was thought necessary. A permanent force of this size was desirable, but, as it was not viable financially, the armed forces had to consist of volunteers – a system of mixed blessing.[15] Moreover, the declining number of imperial troops in South Africa had to be balanced by the growth of volunteer organisations in the armed forces of the four colonies.

In 1906, alarmed at the seriousness of the Bambatha rebellion, the Cape government requested an inter-colonial conference to discuss military cooperation in South Africa. This was convened in Johannesburg on 21 January 1907. Although closer military cooperation was deemed desirable, no formal inter-colonial agreement was signed. An advisory conference of the colonial military chiefs met in Durban on 19 October 1908. They drafted suggestions for their governments on matters such as the organisation of permanent and part-time forces, uniform organisation and training, and standardised combat dress, and prepared several emergency schemes. The plans drafted by the colonial staffs were coded alphabetically, Plan Z being a lightning strike against the Portuguese and the seizure of the port of Lourenço Marques.[16] The initial successes achieved by Bambatha provided the impetus for the troops in South Africa, both imperial and colonial, to undergo training in asymmetrical warfare – conflict in which the military power and resources of the opposing forces differ in quality and quantity, each belligerent attempting to exploit their own advantages as well as their opponent's characteristic weaknesses. In September 1907, the Transvaal Volunteers deployed with the imperial garrison in Pretoria. Lukin's pamphlet, *Savage Warfare*, published too late for effect against Bambatha, was studied and its lessons put into practice in the field.[17] There was some resistance: Wyndham, clearly not a convert at that point – his essays would appear two years later – complained that the week of his attachment would 'be dull if they devote the whole of the five days to it'.[18]

The oldest local military force was the Cape Colonial Forces (CCF), which, although constituted as such in 1855, had a history dating back to the seventeenth century.[19] The Cape, lying astride sea communications with the East, was also a base for imperial troops. The strength of the latter was always subject to changing policy in London, the recurring dread of imperial expense and fiscal retrenchment at the Treasury.[20] The numbers of imperial troops, which had gradually diminished in most of the self-governing colonies from 1870, were again after 1902 in rapid decline, receding in the Cape from a pre-war figure of 3 740 (March 1899) to 1 453 in March 1910. Similar reductions were also seen in the other colonies during this period. The CCF had a permanent element in the form of the Cape Mounted Riflemen, a mounted force of five regiments, numbering together some 600 troopers, in addition to a battery of artillery and some auxiliary troops. Part-time volunteers served throughout the colony in much-decorated infantry regiments, field and coastal artillery regiments, the naval reserve and the Cape Medical Corps. They numbered a further 3 500 in 1910, a number that doubled when cadets were included.[21] However, the Duke of Connaught, Inspector General of the British Army, questioning their training and practical value, felt in 1906 that the volunteers in the CCF were 'too much for show'.[22]

The Natal Volunteers were formed in 1855 by suspicious and ever-vigilant settlers fearful of their powerful Zulu neighbours, with the object of protecting themselves from internal rebellion and, if the need arose, of deploying with imperial troops. Having received a thorough drubbing during the Anglo-Zulu War (1879), they served with more distinction against the Boers in 1899–1902. The force was reconstituted as the Natal Militia in 1903, under the command of colonial, not imperial, officers – first Colonel Henry Bru-du-Wold, and then, from 1908, Colonel Sir Duncan McKenzie, the former commander of the Natal Carbineers. Having but a small permanent element, the majority of its 2 000 men were volunteers in the infantry regiments, the Natal Field Artillery and a small number of auxiliary troops. After 1907, defence spending was reduced, together with the numbers of active volunteers; they numbered some 2 580 at the end of 1909. A permanent corps, although provided for in the Natal Militia Act, never developed. The officers enjoyed only local experience and the overwhelming majority lacked professional training; in 1909, Captain WEC Tanner became the first Natal officer to enter the Staff College.[23]

During the Bambatha rebellion, the Natal Defence Scheme had sprung into action, but, with the Natal forces proving quite unequal to the task of suppressing the uprising, an appeal had to be made to the other colonies, to which the Transvaal responded in strength.

Pacification of the highveld and creation of the Transvaal Volunteers

The Transvaal Volunteers, of more recent vintage, were created in October 1902 as part of Milner's greater plan for the pacification and resettlement of the highveld.[24] The years immediately following the Second Anglo-Boer War were turbulent ones. British supremacy in southern Africa had been confirmed, but societal relations in the former republics had changed. After 1902, Africans armed briefly during the war, chiefly by the British, refused to provide labour on pre-war terms. Moreover, their wartime participation had unhinged traditional patterns of deference. The war had brought opportunity: some Africans had occupied Boer farms; others enjoyed possession of Boer cattle. They were unwilling to return either, let alone to resume a life of servitude. The Boers, seeking renewed control over black labour, the return of land and livestock, and an end to cattle rustling, organised themselves into agricultural societies and embryonic political movements; as has already been noted, a People's Congress met in May 1904, and this led to the formation, in January 1905, of Het Volk (The People).

The war introduced a new struggle in the Transvaal, involving the rise of a nascent Afrikaner nationalism and the emergence of a new leadership, invigorated rather than broken by the war. Through show of arms and the collusion of some English farmers, the so-called veldtocracy coerced African labour and retook land and cattle, sometimes with, but often without, the assistance of the colonial state. The magistracy and the South African Constabulary (SAC), a paramilitary police force established in 1900 to police the rural districts of the former republics, found themselves in a complex and frustrating position. Sometimes the SAC had to defuse conflict between themselves and Africans (some of whom may have been former comrades-in-arms), sometimes between themselves and the Boers, and often between Boers and Africans. In some districts, Africans forcibly resisted. Black labour was gradually subordinated through the complete disarming of Africans – some 10 000 firearms were confiscated in the eastern Transvaal – and the resuscitation of the republican squatter laws (enforced by the resident magistrates and native commissioners, and backed by the SAC and sometimes by the Transvaal Volunteers).[25] However, between the Treaty of Vereeniging and the Act of Union, rural insecurity increased dramatically on the highveld. One resident magistrate, complaining bitterly of the 'very uncongenial' atmosphere, wished 'to leave this awful service [and] this country'.[26]

As we have seen, Milner was troubled by concerns over rural insecurity and the defence of 'our great central position', together with post-war reductions in the size of the imperial garrison. Not only did he hope to retain the soldiers for future settlement but also, more immediately, the constant whittling away of this force would result in a small number of scattered, immobile garrisons that would be a temptation to would-be rebels and would, in the event of a wide-spread rising, have to be withdrawn or relieved.[27] The answer to this dilemma, a problem that had led to the defeat of British arms by the Boers in 1881, was found, firstly, in the location of the imperial troops remaining in South Africa and the creation of a geography of loyalism – a heartland on the highveld – and, secondly, in the restructuring of the *Uitlander* regiments formed during the Anglo-Boer War into a Transvaal defence force.[28]

Milner's heartland embraced Johannesburg, the centre of wealth, the adjoining districts of Middelburg and Standerton in the Transvaal and Harrismith and Kroonstad across the Vaal River in the Orange River Colony.[29] In these districts, which had been relatively untouched by the war, the garrison towns would create opportunities for British troops to rub shoulders with Boers who, it was thought, were less bitter and would be more amenable to British settlement.[30] Moreover, soldiers were attractive settlers: not only would they enhance efforts to develop the economic potential of newly acquired territory, but also they were trained and disciplined and could bolster colonial defences and improve regional security if settled in borderlands.[31] In this way a heartland would be secured. In the event of war, British forces would seek to hold this heartland, together with the lines of communication to the coast, until the arrival of reinforcements from Britain and India. In time of peace, they hoped that a general sense of content-ment and pro-Britishness would radiate from it.[32]

The second answer to Milner's dilemma was the restructuring of the *Uitlander* regiments and the creation of an entirely new military system for the Transvaal, which took place in October 1902. The Transvaal Volunteers, as the new outfit was called, was organised according to the British tradi-tion of voluntary service and was, to some extent at least, a continuation of the voluntary organisation created by the *Uitlanders*, a portion of whom had joined irregular mounted units during the Anglo-Boer War. These units now formed the nucleus of the local defence force, which was tasked with keeping the Boers and Africans in check, thereby making possible a smaller imperial garrison.[33] Milner, moreover, hoped to achieve good cooperation between the local colonial forces in South Africa under some kind of federal structure, and to develop some 'organic connection' between them and the imperial forces. Overlapping would be reduced, cooperation and economy established, and the imperial government might even 'have a call on some proportion' of the force in case of an emergency.[34]

However, the reorganisation of the volunteer regiments and their structuring as the Transvaal Volunteers reflected mounting apprehension among so-called Greater Britons[35] over the adequacy of the military establishment for the defence of expanding British interests in South Africa, and for the creation and maintenance of political equilibrium. Created at a critical juncture, the Volunteers represented an attempt at the fostering of unity, albeit of a peculiarly British variety, and reflected the need for a fundamental overhaul of the military establishment. Britons in the newly annexed colony were made to understand the advantages that a better-oriented military policy held for them, as a group and as individuals, and Boers were encouraged in this view too. The military restructuring and the establishment of settlers' unions and agricultural cooperatives represented something of a national united front against the veldtocracy, which sought to exclude Britons from life on the platteland. The Volunteers presented a stark contrast to the quasi-feudal commandos of the Boer republics, whose military system lent itself to intermittent quarrels between Boers and other local notables, and served to foster local rather than national loyalty.

Long confronted with a restive Boer population, British authorities were faced with a real dilemma, for the creation of the Volunteers opened the troublesome question of Boer admission into the force. On the one hand, the Boers were now British subjects, deserving equal rights and liable for equal service. On the other hand, both Milner and Joseph Chamberlain, the British Colonial Secretary, were not prepared to rearm the Boers and take them up into the new defence structures. Both men, all too aware that the war had forged a new Boer leadership based on ability and no longer simply on kinship, were convinced that the Boers would again attempt to shake off British suzerainty at the earliest opportunity.[36] The burghers had been partially disarmed after the war, but Boer admission to the new voluntary force would imply an immediate re-arming, improved training (the Boers had been noted for their indiscipline and individualism) and, potentially, access to positions of command. But, as British subjects, the Boers could not be excluded. Milner found a compromise: admit Boers, but make the organisation of the force as British as possible and keep the financial contribution of the government small, so that the burden would have to be carried by the volunteers themselves. By making enlistment unattractive, Milner and Chamberlain aspired to limit the interest of the Boers, if drawn, for at least several years.

At the beginning of 1905, partly in answer to the concerns raised by Milner during the previous year, the Transvaal Volunteers converted to a district-based organisation, so eliminating overlapping areas of recruitment and establishing a 'British' military presence in the platteland. Several regiments were reconstituted, others raised for the first time. Local British notables were appointed to these regimental commands and charged with the proper arming, supply and training of the volunteers. They could look to each other for their social connections and business deals, the command of the local regiments and the guidance of a range of local initiatives. But, as a group, they were also always aware of alternative nodes of power in their districts.[37]

Regimental enrolment books are often inaccurate and incomplete, making comparison and statistical analysis difficult. Nonetheless, the enrolment books of the Southern Mounted Rifles, for example, show that farmers represented a majority (435) of the social composition of the regiment. Of the volunteers enrolled, 153 (or some 20.8 per cent) specified work identifying them as townsmen; the largest single category here was for clerks (16). To keep its horses, and therefore its troopers, in the field for as long as possible, the regiment benefited from having two saddlers, a farrier and two shoeing smiths, and two veterinary surgeons in addition to ten professional transport riders, a gunsmith and a bootmaker. By 1911, the regiment was also overwhelmingly 'British', with some 531 men describing themselves as such. A further ten were 'English', three 'Irish', one 'Scotch' and one 'Colonial New Zealand'. There were 69 'Dutch' and five 'British Dutch', categories replaced from 1908 by 'Africander' of whom there were 20. There were a further 67 'British Subjects', three 'South Africans' and five 'Colonials', one of whom had served in the Boer forces. Of the four attorneys in the regiment, an Oosthuizen from Piet Retief described himself as 'British' and Arnt Leonard Reitz, the son of Paul Kruger's State Secretary, gave himself as a 'British attorney'.[38] Such were the complexities of British identity.

Perhaps the Volunteers became, even if only in measure, a vehicle that defined a British national identity in the colonial Transvaal.

British settlers, encouraged by rumoured African risings, rushed to the colours. But the numbers also suggest that some Afrikaners in exposed, isolated areas, particularly on the always-insecure borders with Swaziland and Zululand, did the same. Some sub-units were predominantly Afrikaans; in 1906 in the Bethal troop of the Southern Mounted Rifles, 'all except four [were] Boers'.[39] Many of these men were republicans blooded during the countless 'native' campaigns and the 1899–1902 war, and they accepted the command of British officers, some still relatively young and inexperienced, with difficulty. Acts of insubordination were not uncommon and often less than subtle. Jan Kemp, a former Boer general serving in the Piet Retief troop of the Eastern Rifles, caused disciplinary problems, eroded the commander's authority and refused to turn out whenever the commander attended a deployment.[40]

Such men, discharged dishonourably from the Volunteers, found a new home in the commandos, now called rifle clubs, which were revived by Louis Botha in 1907 following the granting of self-government to the Transvaal. Boers flocked to these rifle clubs, which were instilled with republican traditions and where there were positions of command for those disappointed with the Volunteers. Joseph Alberts was elected field cornet for the Waterval ward of Standerton district in January 1908; he and his cousins, Commandant Claassen and Commandant PSG Botha, later led the two Standerton commandos in the campaign in South West Africa during the First World War. An analysis of the muster rolls reveals a strong pattern of kinship, with a large number of Bothas, Brits's and Breytenbachs.[41] This was probably a trend in other district and town commandos of the Transvaal and Orange River colonies too. The tool for Boer militarisation of a district would not be the volunteer regiment, but rather their shunning of what was now accepted to be an institution riddled with imperially minded Britons determined to maintain a presence on the platteland. The Transvaal now had two military forces. Having lost political support, the Transvaal Volunteers went into decline until the remaining elements were subsumed into the Union Defence Force (UDF), established in July 1912.[42] The Volunteers' most 'British' officers were forced to retire.

Unsurprisingly, the Volunteers experienced difficulty in enrolling reserves.[43] In June 1907, the total approved strength of the Transvaal Volunteers was 11 457, while the actual strength was only 6 619. At the time of the reorganisation of the Volunteers, in mid-1907, the mounted regiments were at only 57.5 per cent of approved strength. The rural regiments were considerably worse off, with the Western Rifles being at only 23.4 per cent of approved establishment. Wyndham's Eastern Rifles was placed comparatively well, at 63.3 per cent. This difference may be attributed to the long-term political impact of the Anglo-Boer War and the greater devastation and bitterness that conflict brought to the western Transvaal.[44] An analysis of the numbers and the locations of volunteers does suggest a geography of loyalism.

It would seem as if the Southern Mounted Rifles and other regiments of the Transvaal Volunteers cemented the small, often isolated pockets of British settlers and formed a British presence in remote localities. Drawing on historical English experience, EP Thompson has suggested that volunteers were the militant expression of a threatened section of society, chiefly the upper and middling classes.[45] Yet, in the colonial Transvaal, to a large extent at least, whites of all classes wanted to preserve the existing political and social structure. There is little doubt that military training and socialisation fostered individual Boer-British relations and most probably consolidated, as Milner had hoped, at least some sentiment 'in the general interests of the Empire'.[46] The Volunteers were, therefore, in measure a vehicle for white nation-building. Yet, clearly, bare numbers of volunteers is too simplistic a measure of loyalism and colonial nationalism.[47]

The colonial armed forces were a relatively small component of the armed forces of the British Empire, and, as such, formed part of wider imperial military policy and planning. The colonial commandants were requested regularly to take part in the drawing-up of local defence schemes. In 1908, the British commander-in-chief requested Colonel PS Beves, the Inspector of the Transvaal Volunteers, to prepare two plans: one for internal security (general African 'unrest') and the other to meet an external threat, and particularly with regard to German South West Africa in the event of war with Germany.[48] In his introduction to the first scheme, entitled 'Simultaneous Trouble with the natives in all the self-governing colonies', Beves thought it impossible to predict an area of greatest potential trouble, but highlighted the Witwatersrand, the western Transvaal and the region north and east of Pietersburg. Beves planned two mounted columns, to be drawn from the Transvaal Volunteers. Yet, except for minor operations within the borders of British South Africa,[49] the imperial defence staff knew they did not have sufficient troops, and so, from 1902, they had turned their attention to the creation of a manpower mobilisation system that reconciled projected wartime force estimates with the often whimsical, seldom extravagant notions of British imperial and South African politicians, administrators and officials.

Knowing how tenuous their hold on South Africa was after 1902, and recognising the potential for future challenge, the British courted the Afrikaners, granting self-government within the empire to the former Boer republics and then, encouraged by economic and defence considerations, facilitating the political union of the four colonies of the Cape, Natal, Transvaal and Orange River. The Union of South Africa came into being on 31 May 1910, as an autonomous, self-governing Dominion of the British Empire. The South African Party, led by Louis Botha and Jan Smuts, swept to power in elections held in September that year. Support for the Unionist Party, the 'British' party, was confined to the Witwatersrand and the large cities of the Cape Province. Natal went to local independents.

The forging of a new, white South African society was built on a consensus that the sectarian interests of the English and Afrikaans communities had to be finely balanced and the 'happiness' of their subject peoples carefully managed.[50] Military necessity had encouraged political union. The threat of 'native' risings, and the Bambatha rebellion of 1906, had led to defence talks between the staffs of the four colonies. Although the Bambatha rebellion was easily suppressed, it revealed all the flaws of colonial defence policy and the institutional weaknesses of the colonial militias. Greater inter-colonial military cooperation had followed, and, after a sequence of military conferences, a platform was established for the creation of a regional military force, which became the UDF in July 1912.[51]

The imperial conference system was developed for the exchange of information and ideas across the Empire and, holding the promise of possible cooperation, on problems common to the Empire as a whole. The system had been regularised in 1907, when it was decided that conferences would be held every four years in London, with more frequent specialist conferences as necessary. The British and Dominion governments met on an equal footing. In fact, Botha, like Canada's Wilfrid Laurier, had accepted cooperation only after receiving assurances that there would be no erosion of Dominion autonomy. In this way, the various governments could formulate policy where cooperation was needed and the Dominions would be made to feel more strongly the advantages offered by the British connection. In practice, the conference system matured in the defence sphere, seeing the growth of a Dominions Department, initially as a section of the Colonial Office, as well as the creation of an Imperial General Staff to promote the uniformity of military organisation, training and planning for wartime cooperation. The Asquith government, in power since April 1908, lured the cash-strapped Dominions 'to tighten the imperial relationship through closer cooperation for defence'.[52] Addressing the 1911 Imperial Conference, Asquith defined 'the nature of the imperial organisation in terms of what it stood for, namely, the combination of complete local autonomy with unity, in the form of loyalty to a common head, begetting spontaneous cooperation for common purses, and the rule of law'.[53] But Dominion independence was still incomplete, for the decisions for war and peace were not shared; the corresponding obligation to support mutual decisions, by arms if necessary, was precisely what the Dominions wished to evade. Moreover, a share in foreign policy, which has always been interrelated with the matter of defence, inferred an obligation to contribute fully to the cost of the British armed forces, something the Dominions were equally eager to avoid. Still requiring imperial protection and unable to stand fully on their own feet, the Dominions were in 1911 content to defer the question. In short, 'they could not afford to be too independent'.[54]

The politics of military integration: the forging of the Union Defence Force

The Union of South Africa was an artificial state combining the four self-governing British colonies in southern Africa. These colonies, themselves relatively new, differed markedly from each other in politics and culture, in economic wellbeing and in geography. But the Union was an ideal that, although overshadowed in 1910 by history and bitter memory, would, it was hoped, be realised at some future date. As DW Krüger has noted, the South Africans of 1910 had 'brought with them into Union not only their unified hopes for future political peace and happiness after a war which had divided them as never before, but also their different memories of a separate past'. Each former colony (now a province) entered the Union somewhat hesitantly, determined wherever possible to preserve its own identity. Similarly, the colonial politicians and soldiers brought their own hopes and aspirations, fears and mental reservations. Unsurprisingly, Union politics was for many years conditioned by provincial interests, the intentions of individual statesmen and the heritage of a heated past. Significantly, the 'compromise' enabled the two northern provinces, the former Boer republics, to imbue the wider Union with their republican ideals and practice of racial inequality.[55] As Bill Nasson has argued, the political exclusion of the black majority was easily shrugged off, for the Union 'would serve Britain's long-term economic, political and strategic needs by stimulating more rapid economic development and by nurturing Anglo-Afrikaner reconciliation and accommodation'. Moreover, the possibility of creating a 'Greater South Africa', through the inclusion of Bechuanaland, Basutoland and Swaziland, and possibly Southern Rhodesia and Barotseland, was not ruled out. However this proved delusional, as did Smuts' dream of adding German South West Africa and Portuguese East Africa as part of the spoils of war.[56]

The Union Defence Force (UDF) was, in turn, a compromise between the determination of English-speakers to maintain the British military connection and the desire of Afrikaner nationalists for a restoration of Boer political and military traditions. It was self-evident that, despite the appeals of Olive Schreiner and others, the new South African state was to be militaristic, if not well armed. The Union Defence Force, which combined the Cape Colonial Forces, the Natal Militia and the Transvaal Volunteers with the resurrected commandos of the former republics, was thought by politicians across party lines to be both natural and inevitable. But it was less evident how exactly members of four disparate forces, representing at least three military traditions, and speaking and protecting two languages, were to combine into the new defence structures.

This conundrum faced Smuts, the Minister of Defence, who, like his early rivals JBM Hertzog and CF Beyers, had seen service in the Boer armies, when they had commanded fronts and planned strategy against the British. Smuts, who recognised that the future of the UDF lay not in the recreation of the Boer forces nor in the sole efforts of former Boer commanders, appreciated the need for a modern defence force based on Western methods. He was undoubtedly the overwhelming influence behind the UDF and relied, at times heavily, upon carefully selected staff officers, of whom the foremost – Tim Lukin, Roland Bourne and Jack Collyer – were his former enemies. Always expedient, Smuts recruited talented men – well trained, experienced and battle-hardened – even if they came from former colonial or British regiments.[57] But this, and Smuts' easy erudition, was not well received in the backveld.[58]

Smuts, an eager minister, had to move cautiously to avoid any 'appearance of compulsion or militarism on the European model'.[59] MT Steyn, the former president of the Orange Free State, for example, remained concerned that the new force, and the school cadet system especially, would create a spirit of militarism, and that the lines between the imperial forces and the Union forces would be blurred. The Afrikaners were not alone. John X Merriman, Cape politician and elder statesman, was concerned that South Africa 'not be led into militarism and to any unwise pledges of sharing in the quarrels in [the] inciting [of] which we have not been consulted'.[60] His vision for a small force, having good organisation and excellent supply but with 'not too much discipline', was countered by the Unionists, who demanded a force sufficient not only for internal defence but also able, in concert with British forces, to repel the attack of a European enemy elsewhere in British Africa.

Opposing his own party, Smuts introduced the South Africa Defence Bill in February 1912. An avalanche of criticism and high levels of discontent in the country districts of, particularly, the Transvaal followed.[61] There remained, as Hugh Wyndham noted, 'a great deal of suspicion of its provisions amongst the old-fashioned Boer population', and mostly regarding the principle of compulsory training.[62] Petitions were considered, and the Military Code and Rules of Procedure, as provisionally adopted from the British Army Act, were consulted. In the face of severe opposition, the Bill was passed into law as the South Africa Defence Act (13 of 1912) in April of that year.[63] As a party, only the Unionists were satisfied, for the Bill stressed the importance of defence as an imperial matter.[64] However, this legislation contained the seeds of its own near-destruction. 'South Africa', as used in the Act, was a geographical expression left purposely undefined by Smuts, although he had assured the Governor General that 'it would surely cover any part of the continent of Africa South of the equator'.[65]

However inadequate the UDF was, it represented a fundamental change in South African military policy. The Defence Act recognised a dependence on the Royal Navy to protect South Africa from foreign invasion, and there were now coastal defences backed by military forces in the interior. But few thought the UDF would undertake military tasks beyond 'South Africa', and so the UDF remained essentially a colonial constabulary and coast-defence organisation, with few sharing Smuts' vision for a more balanced, modern force capable of engaging a modern enemy.

The Defence Act was promulgated on 14 June 1912 in the face of severe Afrikaner opposition, and its provisions were implemented systematically. A Council of Defence was appointed on 22 June. The Department of Defence was established on 1 July as a separate department of state. (Until then, defence matters had been conducted by a branch of the Department of the Interior.) On the same day, the militia, volunteer and cadet headquarter staffs in the Cape, Natal and Transvaal provinces were abolished – there was no defence organisation in the Orange Free State, although a Volunteer Corps Ordinance had been passed in 1905 – and replaced by three separate and independent executive commands. These were the Citizen Force Command, the Permanent Force Command and the Cadet Command. The total strength of the militia and volunteers in the various provinces as at 31 December 1912 was 9 081. On that date 65 per cent of that number, or 5 937 militiamen and volunteers, signified their willingness to transfer to the Active Citizen Force (ACF) on its formation on 1 July 1913 (see Table 2.1). There were high levels of anxiety in some established colonial regiments, and not without cause. Some of the Cape, Natal and Transvaal units were incorporated into the ACF, most keeping their old names in whole or in part. Some were closed; others were amalgamated. The two wings of the Natal Carbineers, for example, were made into separate regiments and, for the moment, designated the 1st and 2nd Mounted Rifles. The addition, in brackets, of the words 'Natal Carbineers' assuaged feelings and preserved continuity.[66]

Table 2.1: **Numbers of militiamen and volunteers transferred from the colonial forces to the Active Citizen Force**

| Force | Strength at 31 December 1912 | Transferred to Active Citizen Force | | | | | |
| | | With old units | | To new units | | Total | |
		Officers	Other ranks	Officers	Other ranks	Officers	Other ranks
Cape Volunteers	3 096	132	1 948	8	133	140	2 081
Natal Militia	2 449	121	1 285	21	176	142	1 461
Transvaal Volunteers	3 536	87	1 065	87	874	174	1 939
Total	**9 081**	**340**	**4 298**	**116**	**1 183**	**456**	**5 481**

Source: UG 61 – 1913. Annual Reports, Department of Defence, 1913.

The UDF, in terms of the Defence Act, was created for the defence of 'South Africa', and it encompassed the traditional cornerstones of South African military policy, namely, citizen soldiers, a small permanent force, a small local division of the Royal Naval Volunteer Reserve, which was stationed at the major ports only, and very thinly spread coastal fortifications. However, several factors affected the UDF and undermined its standing as a reliable, well-equipped and deployable defence force.

Firstly, there was the matter of military culture. The UDF remained an unhappy marriage between the British and Boer military value systems. A Defence Council, essentially a safety mechanism for the protection of language interests, was created.[67] But many Afrikaners could not endure the 'melting pot' of the new defence force, and appealed to old patrons for personal support or, eventually, followed them into rebellion in 1914.[68] Several explanations, chiefly from the Afrikaner nationalist perspective, have been advanced for the alleged heavy British imprint on the UDF. These range from the length of Britain's presence in southern Africa and its pre-eminent position after 1902, to the blaming of Smuts and Botha for their abandonment of the *volk* and their embracing of empire.[69] Yet, while each of these explanations has merit, they remain, even collectively, inadequate. Historians generally have not assessed the role of the individuals behind the establishment of the UDF, the nature of that force and the specific purposes for which it was designed. The UDF was a consensus, a product of a combination of systems, but nonetheless a thoughtful combination, one (hopefully) of 'proper conception'.[70]

Secondly, there was the apparent need, even at the cost of military effectiveness, to balance language and sectarian interests. This is evident from the start. The parliamentary select committee on defence, to which the Bill was referred in March 1912, comprised nine members (four Afrikaners and five English-speakers), with a political division of four Unionists, four members of the 'Dutch' party, and one Labourite, and was representative of force of origin and province.[71] Even the specialists interviewed by the committee represented the British-colonial and Boer military systems in almost perfect equity. A prosopographical study of the South African high command during this period shows, moreover, that the split between the language groups was exceptionally fine (*see* Table 2.2). The drive for language equity was seemingly the preferred way for finding a consensus in a difficult environment characterised by competing military traditions and language preferences.[72]

Thirdly, and relating to the matter of equity, was the appointment of the high command. This was a difficult political decision, and, when the various arms of the UDF came into being in 1913, the whole was placed under a divided command (*see* Table 2.3) to protect sectarian interests and also diminish the possibility of a coup. The two most important positions were filled by HT Lukin, the former Commandant of the CCF, and the staunchly republican former

Table 2.2: Composition of the Union general staff: career point and language		
Category	English	Afrikaans
1912–20	8	11
1920–30	2	3
1930–40	4	1
1940–50	17	15
Total	**31**	**30**

Source: I van der Waag, 'Smuts' generals: towards a first portrait of the South African high command, 1912–48', War in History, 18(1) January 2011, p 51.

Boer general CF Beyers. Lukin's was arguably the more important post in the new structure; he had to create an atmosphere in the Permanent Force that was congenial to both English- and Afrikaans-speaking South Africans, which he achieved to a remarkable degree. The Battle of Delville Wood (July 1916) and its post-war constructions provided glue to unite vast swathes of white South African society. As Rassie Nortier has shown, Lukin's fairness, impartiality and professionalism endeared him to his men and assisted in the merging of the South African English and Afrikaner worlds, to the extent that the Labour Party considered him a political asset.[73]

Table 2.3: The executive command of the Union Defence Force, 1912		
Commander	Appointment (1912)	Former post
Brig Gen HT Lukin	Inspector General of the SA Permanent Force	Commandant General of the Cape Colonial Forces
Brig Gen CF Beyers	Commandant General of the Citizen Force	Former Boer general
Col PS Beves	Commandant of Cadets	Inspector of the Transvaal Volunteers

The fourth factor involved the military factions created before 1912 in the struggle for military power and the rush for the available posts in the new structures. Beyers, the Commandant General of the Citizen Force, was cut from different cloth to Lukin. He and several other high-ranking officers openly provided organisationally for their clients and political followers, with Beyers even emptying the citizen regiments of their more 'British' officers.[74] This sort of thing, as Charles Leonard had complained, worked towards 'permanent alienation instead of reconciliation'[75] and affected materially the unity of the UDF. Wyndham, pushed out of the Citizen Force in 1912, had noted somewhat prophetically two years earlier that Beyers was 'a very violent Boer', capable of making 'very racial speeches' and that if he were made 'Minister of Defence, or Commandant General, [this] would lead to the dismemberment of any defence force that we may possess at present or in the future'.[76] The UDF failed to employ officers with the appropriate military training and education. This led to appointments based upon criteria other than merit, and to the establishment of organisational fiefdoms, which stunted development and war planning, and created distrust, even fission, in the new structures.

The fifth factor that undermined the UDF was the presence of two British commands in South Africa. These were the cause of political mischief on both sides, and pressed Pretoria to 'demonstrate independence'. The British Army command at the Castle, in Cape Town, and the Royal Navy base at Simon's Town presented problems that were both political and military. They were necessary for the adequate defence of South Africa, but were simultaneously a visible sign of South Africa's constitutional and military dependence. South Africa's answer, to invoke a later British High Commissioner, Sir William Clark, was 'to devise some difference of method so as demonstrate South Africa's independence'.[77] Unsurprisingly, relations between South African officials and their British counterparts were often difficult, and reached several nadirs during the First World War and then during the 1930s. Smuts and his generals, for example, did not bother to consult the imperial commander in South Africa when war erupted in 1914, which incensed Major General CW Thompson and his naval counterpart in Simon's Town, who commanded the Royal Navy's Cape of Good Hope Station. Often, Anglo-South African cooperation was a matter of personality.[78] Imperial distrust of certain South African officers, exacerbated by Beyers' Macbeth-like hesitation, was confirmed by the outbreak of rebellion in 1914. Similar friction arose during the build-up to the outbreak of war in 1939, when the South African government seemingly refused to cooperate with the British admiral in Simon's Town and in 1940, much to the chagrin of local Royal Navy men, manufactured conditions that enabled Pretoria to create its own navy.[79]

Following the Swiss example as far as conscription was concerned, the military and paramilitary forces of the four colonies were absorbed into the Union Defence Force, which comprised six separate forces (see Figure 2.1): the South African Permanent Force (SAPF), the Active Citizen Force (ACF), the Coast Garrison Force (CGF), the rifle associations (or resurrected commandos), the South Africa Division of the Royal Naval Volunteer Reserve (RNVR) and the Cadet Corps.

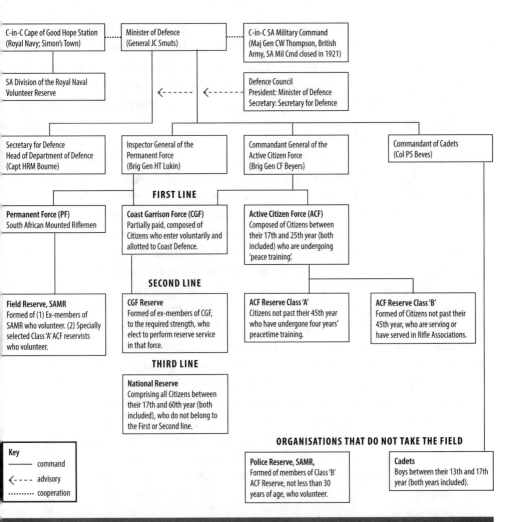

Figure 2.1: **The organisation of the Union Defence Force, 1912**

Note: The Police Reserve, SAMR, would occupy areas normally policed by the SAMR, when the SAMR took the field.

The South African Permanent Force (SAPF), comprising the five regiments of the South African Mounted Riflemen (SAMR), was organised along the lines of the old Cape Mounted Riflemen and had both police and defence duties. Representing the sum of the standing army, the SAMR troopers were to be 'thoroughly good horsemen and riders, good shots, thoroughly dependable men; [and] men thoroughly fit for field service.'[80] The Active Citizen Force (ACF), the mainstay of the system, comprised townsmen organised into infantry battalions and countrymen in mounted infantry regiments. The ACF, the receptacle for most of the old volunteer and militia regiments, was kept up to strength through qualified conscription and trained continuously over four years, with 30 days' continuous and non-continuous training each year. The Coast Garrison Force (CGF) was home to the Cape and Durban garrison artillery and the Cape Fortress Engineers.

The question of a South African navy triggered an acute political debate. While all political parties recognised the need for a naval presence in South African waters, they could not agree on its character. Roland Bourne, the Secretary for Defence, opined that the available finances would determine this: a South African navy would for many years be beyond the resources of the Union, and he supported the idea of continued contribution to maintain the Royal Navy presence.[81] The ever-practical Merriman saw the contribution to the fleet as an insurance premium for South Africa's seaborne trade. He believed the development of independent navies, as was happening in Canada and Australia, would mean disruption and spell disaster.[82] The nationalists saw any naval contribution as a form of imperial tribute and an emblem of ultra-jingo imperialism, although President Steyn did prefer Merriman's idea of an insurance premium, which was 'a more business-like proposal than a blind contribution'.[83] The South Africa Division of the Royal Naval Volunteer Reserve (RNVR), formed through the amalgamation of the Natal Naval Volunteers with the Cape Naval Volunteers, was located primarily in Durban and Cape Town, but had a presence even in the smaller ports. This outfit was to be mobilised in the event of war and placed under the command of the British admiral in Simon's Town: at the outbreak of war in 1914, the Division provided 12 officers and 267 ratings to the British Admiralty for the defence of ports and for service on British warships.

The Rifle Associations were designed specifically to expose a vast number of the male white population to military training. Their membership was largely rural and, as resurrected 'commandos' – the chief symbol of Afrikaner nationalism – they provided the focus of the main controversy. The 'Dutch' party (the Afrikaner Nationalists and the more nationalist-inclined members of Botha's governing party) hoped to continue the old republican tradition of the commandos as a people's army, and received support from unexpected quarters, including some Unionists. The commandos had developed from the early eighteenth century to protect home and hearth and could easily be transformed into a third-line reserve, ideal for internal security. Moreover, the commandos, or

Rifle Associations, as they were now called, presented an excellent opportunity for citizens who did not undergo military training to learn musketry skills.[84] However, many realised, as no doubt did Smuts, that the Rifle Associations, with their early-modern structure, would have little ability to counter a large, sophisticated, external threat. The extension of the cadet system, from some English-medium schools to the education system nationally, rankled with the nationalists, who feared the regimentalisation of the Afrikaner youth and the fostering of 'an unhealthy kind of European militarism, an overbearing state culture alien to the personal loyalty traditions of Boer men'.[85]

Military service in these structures was confined to white men, and specific procedures were adopted by district staff officers in connection with the registration and attestation of citizens deemed to be not 'of European descent'. Black South Africans were precluded from service in terms of the Defence Act, but in times of emergency could be attested by special parliamentary authorisation.[86]

These forces were organised in three lines of defence. The trained citizen force, of a size and so organised that a 'formidable and effective army can be put into the field', constituted the first line of defence. This had to be reinforced by trained citizen reserves, or the second line of defence. In an extreme emergency, all able-bodied citizens would be brought into service as a National Reserve, which constituted the third line. The first line was supplemented in two important ways: by providing for a small nucleus of permanent forces (a special striking force) and by making special provision for the defence of South African ports.[87]

While the outcomes may have brought some alignment with British organisation, training and equipment, Britons, or even people of British descent, did not dominate the process. In fact, difficult as it was, the UDF achieved a surprising, near-perfect balance between language and provincial interests. This stands in sharp contrast to the literature. According to Louise Jooste, the officer corps, and the command posts in particular, were held principally (*hoofsaaklik*) by English-speakers and only over the ensuing three decades was some form of

Line of defence	Landward threat	Seaborne threat	Internal threat
1st	Active Citizen Force	Coast Garrison Force	Permanent Force (SAMR)
2nd	ACF Reserve, Class 'A' and Class 'B'	CGF Reserve	Field Reserve (SAMR)
3rd	National Reserve		

Table 2.4: **The threat perception and the design of the Union Defence Force, 1911**

balance effected.[88] John Lambert, in a probing article on South African identity, supports this notion of a 'British' high command.[89] Yet, the figures show quite the opposite. Over the first two decades, Afrikaners were in the majority, and it was the numbers of English-speakers that gradually increased – not the opposite. And, what is more, a remarkable 'racial' parity was achieved and at all levels, over the four decades – the split is 31 to 30 (*see* Table 2.2).

Moreover, when a group of 51 officers from the former British colonies and Boer republics was nominated for the first course at the newly established Military School in Bloemfontein, they were in almost equal numbers: the English-Afrikaans split was 25 to 26. These officers – later dubbed the 'fathers' of the Union Defence Force – were posted to the new headquarters in Pretoria and as the district staff officers of the 13 military districts. The group included men like WEC Tanner from Natal, ET Thackeray from the Transvaal Volunteers, AH Nussey, a Free State-born Englishman who had served under De Wet during the Anglo-Boer War, former Boer generals SG (Manie) Maritz, Ben Bouwer and Jan Kemp, and half a dozen officers of the Cape Mounted Riflemen. This was the politics of consensus and 'representivity' seemingly at its best.[90]

In Bloemfontein, the group lived and received instruction in the Old Government House. Here they came under the command of a watchful George Aston, who, one of the 51 later noted, 'thought only in global terms', and Major JJ Collyer, who, having served as a trooper in the Cape Mounted Riflemen, had climbed steadily in the Cape Colonial Forces. This was a remarkable group of men, practically all of whom had been at war with each other less than a decade before. A young Piet van der Byl, one of the two exceptions in this instance, writing in 1971, felt that a 'climate of goodwill and friendliness' reigned.[91] Aston, far less flattering, noted at the time that 'they all came with a sort of official veneer of goodwill to each other but were really like a lot of dogs smelling round each other and ready to snarl and bite at the first chance'.[92] Certainly for men like Ben Bouwer, Manie Maritz, Jan Kemp and Jack Pienaar, integration presented opportunity. Kemp records that, in their rooms at night, they fantasised about a time when, as commanders of their respective military districts, they would have the opportunity to take revenge upon 'the robber empire'.[93]

A Defence Council was created to advise the Minister of Defence on every proposal involving the exercise by the Governor General of the powers vested in him under the provisions of the South Africa Defence Act. The Governor General could also consult the council in relation to the general or special defence requirements of the Union, whether arising from normal or abnormal conditions, affecting the peace and security of South Africa. There were four members, appointed by the Governor General – two English and two Afrikaans – and representing the four provinces (*see* Table 2.5). The Minister of Defence was ex officio President of the council,[94] and the capable Roland Bourne served as its secretary. The Defence Council could summon specialists to join its deliberations and give advice. Essentially, it was a safety mechanism for the protection of language and provincial interests, and was to function for five years from the commencement of the Defence Act, a period that was renewable. Lacking real power, the Council met on only 13 occasions between 1912 and July 1918 – surprisingly few considering the passage of the First World War.

Table 2.5: Defence councillors, representing provincial and language interests, 1912–1924	
Defence councillors appointed in 1912	Successors
Col CP Crewe (Cape)	Succeeded by Lt Col HA Wyndham (1918) and then Maj Gen Sir HT Lukin (1924)
Brig Gen D McKenzie (Natal)	Represented Natal to his death
Gen CR de Wet (OFS)	Succeeded by Brig Gen LAS Lemmer (1914)
Gen SW Burger (Tvl)	Succeeded by Brig Gen Manie Botha, nephew of General Louis Botha (1918)

Within a year of its founding, the UDF faced its first test. There had been no major labour disputes before the Anglo-Boer War; in fact, no labour organisation existed until the formation of a union in 1892 to resist the employment of black convict labour in the mines. The convicts did not arrive and the union soon dissolved. However, a strong miners' organisation was established soon after the resumption of mining in 1901, and in May 1907 a strike was called to resist changes in working conditions. Smuts, then Colonial Secretary of the Transvaal, called in imperial troops to protect scab labour and mining property, and the strike failed to achieve its object.[95] But in July 1913 labour discontent came to a head in a general strike that spread from New Kleinfontein on the East Rand. The strike became increasingly violent and culminated in acts of sabotage, arson and bloodshed in Johannesburg on 4 and 5 July. Gunsmiths' shops were looted by rioters, who now sniped at the soldiers – mostly imperial troops – and police were called in to clear the streets. Nineteen rioters were killed and some 150 members of the security forces were wounded, some seriously.[96] Botha and Smuts brokered a settlement. But

Smuts, determined not to have to rely on imperial troops, was loath to be caught off guard a second time.

A second, more serious strike began on 7 January 1914. Soldiers were posted to key points and special constables were sworn in. The strike leaders were arrested for sedition, just as the defence force, on its first real deployment, swung into action. Hundreds of troopers, mostly men of the old commandos under De la Rey, arrived to guard the mines and mine owners. The Transvaal Federation of Trades called a general strike on 13 January. The movement was promptly crushed, the closing scene taking the form of a siege on 15 January of the Johannesburg Trades Hall, where the executive of the federation and a body of supporters had barricaded themselves. Those inside surrendered without resistance. During the night of 26 January, nine strike leaders who were not of South African birth were deported to Britain. Smuts' action triggered an outcry, but the defence force had passed its first test, seemingly with flying colours, and Botha's position was strengthened by the prompt action of his government, both of which, it was expected, would lead to the improvement of Anglo-Afrikaner relations. And, a satisfied Mary Drew noted, this was not due to the threat of a 'black peril'.[97]

Yet, despite the extraordinary measures taken to protect sectarian interests, the UDF remained a contested space of competing interests, personal rivalries and remarkable 'middle grounds', where military cultures clashed and mingled, and harmony and shared understanding was often exaggerated. Some individuals enjoyed multiple, layered identities and, sharing transnational genealogical connections, moved consummately on the imperial military landscape during the early twentieth century. One such individual was Brigadier General George Aston, who was born at the Cape, his mother coming from a celebrated Afrikaner family. Having joined the Royal Marine Artillery in 1879, Aston returned to South Africa in 1899 and then again in 1908, as Lord Methuen's chief of staff. He led the British expedition to Dunkirk and Ostend in 1914 and retired three years later, as a major general, having commanded the Royal Marine Artillery Division.[98] Another was Piet van der Byl, also of Cape Afrikaner background, who studied at Pembroke College and rowed for Cambridge. He was brought to Smuts' notice by Lord Methuen and offered a place in the new Permanent Force. Van der Byl was in Pretoria in August 1914, when the British garrison was withdrawn for war service in Europe, and later (in 1971) recalled his mixed feelings at the time; the British withdrawal was, on the one hand, the departure of an army of occupation, and yet, on the other hand, he felt a tremendous loss of friendship. It was 'the end of a period that would never recur'.[99]

Within the defence force, discontent bubbled continuously to the surface and trouble, during the immediate pre-war years, was never far off. There was much suspicion, 'amongst the old-fashioned Boer population', regarding the principle of compulsory training.[100] The Botha government was embarrassed continuously by headlines such as 'No Dutch No Drill' (*Volkstem*), which undermined cohesion and fostered distrust. This suited the Hertzogites, the supporters of former Justice minister JBM Hertzog, who broke with Botha to form the National Party in January 1914.[101] Smuts acted in the face of rank insubordination as well as a need to husband public opinion. May 1914 saw the transfer of Jack Pienaar, whose divisive presence on the highveld, it was thought, would lead to numerous resignations.[102] And all the while, the quotas of Dutch and English officers had to be balanced at General Headquarters and throughout the military districts of the Union. Yet even Smuts was surprised at the regularity with which he had to cajole Beyers, who seemingly still had trouble with the language issue. As late as 9 May 1914, Smuts had cause to remind Beyers, the Commandant General, that he (Beyers) was to satisfy the expectations of the government in the exercise of his duties in the language matter.[103]

The modernising role played by the Union Defence Force in early twentieth-century South Africa angered traditionalists among the Boer elite. They felt, and perhaps had reason to feel, that the new military structures eroded the personal attachment between themselves and their traditional support bases. The 1912 Defence Act undoubtedly provided for a modernised military along Western lines – the subordination of the armed forces to the civil authority, rigid discipline and chains of command, a rudimentary general staff structure – but this the traditionalists, appealing to an anti-British ultra-nationalism, sold as 'British' rather than as modern or Western.[104] At first they advised Afrikaner men not to sign the UDF attestation forms, instilling a fear that they would be bound 'entirely as soldiers of the British Government', something the rural elite could not afford and would not permit. In 1915, Captain Hendrik Watkins, Kemp's staff adjutant, told the court of inquiry into the 1914 rebellion that De la Rey himself had

> declared [in conversation with him] that we were trying to make British soldiers of the people, and said that if he wanted to call *his commandos*

together, for instance, the men would be all tied up under these undertak-
ings they were asked to sign, and *he* would not be able to get them.[105]

In 1914, seizing the opportunity presented by the war in Europe, the traditional elite called upon the commandos to defend, through armed protest, the
traditional social order and therefore their political and military influence.
Some Dutch-speaking South Africans, on the other hand, despite the sense
of a declining personal influence in the new dispensation, supported South
Africa's First World War effort, but purely out of personal loyalty to Louis
Botha.[106] The rebellion of 1914–1915 was in many ways the swan song of the traditional Boer commando, with its loyalty to a lineage head and not the state.

Conclusion

British South Africa never developed a large standing army. It was opposed
by liberals, as it had been in Britain, on the grounds of cost. Moreover, the
idea of a standing army was regarded with suspicion by the Boers, on political
grounds, and by the Africans, against whom standing forces were putatively
aimed. There were general, ongoing reductions in the size of the British garrisons in South Africa between 1902 and the last major withdrawal in 1914; the
South African Military Command closed on 1 December 1921. Local colonial
forces assumed responsibility for defence in 1909, reflecting traditional and
conflicting attitudes, Boer and British, towards the military participation of
the colonial society.

South Africa's military forces, colonial and varied, existed from 1900 on a political landscape that was subject to rapid and dramatic change. Several interrelated
factors shaped this environment. First and foremost was the military geography
of South Africa and its relatively isolated position at the southern end of the
African continent, seemingly far from the discord of Europe and Asia. Moreover,
South Africans presumed that, in the event of war, the Royal Navy would counter
any seaborne threat, while imperial troops would assist local forces in repelling
any land-based enemy. South Africa had at this point in Britain and its empire
not simply an ally, but a professed protector that was then the world superpower.

Secondly, South Africa had its own fault lines, which were immediately sus-
ceptible to the grinding of geopolitical fault lines in Europe. The presence of a
German colonial army in South West Africa, and the warm relations between

the Germans and a significant number of Afrikaners, cast this into dramatic relief. The Second Anglo-Boer War had been a total war, one that cast long, historical shadows, and, although the military conflict ended in 1902, for many Afrikaners, brought unwillingly into the British fold, their struggle against 'the English' ended only in 1961, when South Africa withdrew from the Commonwealth.[107] Britain's claim to protect small nations would, in 1914, have seemed dubious to many South Africans. Moreover, from 1902, the likelihood of a war between the great powers was increasing. Imperial rivalries, particularly in Africa, and the competition for resources necessary to fuel European industry and manufacture the weapons of industrialised warfare, threatened to make the next war both global and expensive. The European situation impacted on South Africa, despite its relative geographic isolation and apparent strategic safety.

Thirdly, there was a widespread anti-military sentiment, particularly though not exclusively among Afrikaners, who remained for much of the twentieth century distrustful of the British and of British institutions and baulked at the military institutions the British created. Many Britons misread the situation quite entirely: '[T]he backveld Boer', Maud Wyndham informed her father, 'likes to sit on his stoep in safety & see the English soldiers standing guard & buying their produce.'[108] But this was an anti-militarism of a peculiarly anti-British nature that permeated the collective mind of a people fashioned by the traditions of small wars and irregular forces and determined to regain their lost independence. Afrikaner domination of the South African political establishment from 1907 virtually ensured that compulsory peacetime military training, at least along British lines, would not be adopted.

Louis Botha, as the first prime minister of a united South Africa, had to balance the demands of English-speaking South Africa with the armed opposition of fellow Afrikaners, many of whom demanded the restoration of the *status quo ante bellum*. Rejecting the new South Africa and a common South Africanism, and feeling alienated within the new state structures, Afrikaners drifted in increasing numbers to Hertzog and the National Party. Hertzog's actions, aimed at the reorganisation of the political landscape on the national issue, was sure, many British South Africans felt, to lead to another South African war. Wyndham, then the Union shadow Minister of Defence, noted that 'wars, whether industrial or civil [were then] quite the fashion'.[109]

A new country had come into being on 31 May 1910, forging together four territories that had been at war with each other only eight years before. On 1 July

1912, a new, supposedly all-inclusive defence force was established, bringing the armed forces and militias of the four incorporated territories together into one military organisation. The Union Defence Force (UDF) was at once a contested space of competing interests, personal rivalries and remarkable 'middle grounds', where military cultures clashed and mingled, and harmony and shared understanding was often exaggerated. The mould was broken in August 1914 as the ailments, all neatly concealed, led inescapably to military disaster. 'The outbreak of the general European war', as DW Krüger has argued, 'came at a most inopportune moment for South Africa. It came too soon after the unification experiment because the people were not yet united ... It came too soon after the political break in the ranks of Afrikanerdom, and it even came too soon after the South African War ... South Africa faced the world crisis not as a united nation, but as one divided against itself.'[110]

CHAPTER THREE

The First World War, 1914–1918

In Pretoria we heard this terrible news – or perhaps I should say what may be terrible. I know very little of European politics – but it is difficult to understand why because Austria has a grievance against Servia [sic], there should be the probability of a Great European War – and why we should be dragged into it – for my part, after what I have seen of the French in Madagascar, I wish that we had an 'entente cordiale' with Germany rather than with France.[1]

– William Carter, Archbishop of Cape Town, on the impending outbreak of war, 1914

This sentiment, expressed by the Anglican prelate in Cape Town on the events leading up to the First World War, was typical. Few South Africans, in July and August of 1914, understood how an assassination in an obscure Balkan town could lead to a war into which Britain and, by extension, South Africa – still hard at work removing the traces of another devastating war – could be drawn. A complex chain of events led to a global conflagration that pitted two hostile European power blocs against each other. Vienna and Belgrade tumbled immediately into a diplomatic contretemps. Austria-Hungary declared war against Serbia on 28 June 1914. A complicated system of alliances was activated and, over the ensuing days, other powers entered the conflict. Soon Germany, Austria-Hungary and Turkey were at war with Britain, Russia, France and even Japan. Italy entered the war in May 1915, the United States in April 1917.

The Union of South Africa's decision on the nature and level of its participation in the First World War was difficult. A new country had come into being in 1910, forging together four disparate territories that had been at war with each other only eight years before. In 1912, a new, supposedly all-inclusive defence force had been established, bringing the armed forces and militias of the four incorporated territories together into one military organisation. As we have seen in Chapter Two, the Union Defence Force (UDF) represented a remarkable 'middle ground'. However, the UDF floundered in August 1914 as its underlying ailments, all neatly concealed, led inescapably to military disaster.

South Africa's military task was complicated. The UDF was little more than two years old and South Africa, as John Buchan reminds us, had 'foes within and without her gates' and its task, 'of all the nations of the British Commonwealth … [was] at the outbreak of war the most intricate'.[2] On 4 August 1914, South Africa duly offered to take care of its own defence, freeing imperial troops for deployment to France; these regiments formed part of the 7th Division and fought at Ypres.[3] The defences of South Africa were now for the first time manned solely by the new UDF, some of whom, disliking the tedium of garrison duties and the manning of home defences, were anxious to form a South African expeditionary force. Failing this, many left to join the British Army.[4]

For the fledgling UDF, a series of complex and divergent campaigns commenced with the attempt to neutralise the radio stations in the German colony of South West Africa. This campaign was suddenly suspended while attention was diverted to the Afrikaner rebellion. When this was put down, the South West Africa campaign recommenced. An infantry brigade helped quash the Senussi incursion into Egypt before being practically annihilated a few months later at Delville Wood in France. The brigade, accompanied to the Western Front by a field ambulance and a general hospital, had to be reconstructed more than once. Two brigades of heavy artillery, a signal company, a railway company, an Auxiliary Horse Transport Company and the South African Native Labour Contingent (SANLC) also served in France, but not in association with each other or the infantry brigade. A large South African force broke German resistance in East Africa, while a brigade of field artillery and later the Cape Corps served in Egypt and Palestine. Numerous South Africans were recruited into the Royal Flying Corps (RFC) and then the Royal Air Force (RAF). Some 6 500 South Africans volunteered for service in imperial units. And, all the while, the conquered territory of South West Africa was garrisoned by occupation troops, who, in the words of the official historians, had 'a successful little native campaign of their own'.[5]

The politics of participation

Despite the fine talk regarding the unification of South Africa (1910) and the supposed confluence of the 'white' sectors – English and Afrikaans – into a new South Africanism, South Africa was not a united country in 1914. There was no South African nation, and no consensus on the war. Even the nomenclature differed. For English South Africans, following the British trend, it was the 'Great War'.[6] For the clerks in the Defence department it was the 'European Crisis'; for their counterparts in the prime minister's office in 1914, it was 'the German South West Expedition', almost as if these two events could be separated.[7] For FS Malan, the Education minister, it was, in August 1914, 'die Brits-Duitse-oorlog' (the Anglo-German War),[8] a description supported by MT Steyn, the former Orange Free State president, who, writing to Smuts on 31 July 1914, reckoned that 'the troubles in England are the result of the South African War. One sees still more. This war has driven England out of her splendid isolation into her "ententes" and her yellow alliances and today she has fallen foul of Continental entanglements. The mills of Providence grind slowly indeed!'[9] The republican Boers had hoped for this in 1900. Now, fourteen years later, it had happened, and there was, to the mind of Afrikaner nationalists, no reason whatever to assist Britain. They might, as Steyn was suggesting, rather seize the moment offered by Providence. The whole war issue was engulfed by the battle between Afrikaners and English South Africans for the meaning of white South Africanism.[10]

The newspaper-reading public in South Africa, and elsewhere in the British world, expected an enormous naval engagement in the North Sea shortly after the outbreak of war. This was in part connected to the assumption that the war would be short. The expectation was so great that many rumours, entirely without substance, flew about, and grand tales of supposed naval victories in the North Sea and English Channel circulated widely. Censorship was implemented. But Johannesburg society revelled for two days in news of the defeat of the German fleet in the North Sea, following a fierce engagement on the Dogger Bank, the firing being heard even at South Shields. When the reports from Europe were published, it turned out that there had been no sea battle at all.[11]

Unsurprisingly, Prime Minister Louis Botha battled to achieve, and then to maintain, consensus in his Cabinet. Faced with potential defections and the growing rift in Afrikanerdom, his first wartime ministry was unstable, and his second ministry, formed after the October 1915 election, could only govern with Unionist support, though not in formal coalition (*see* Table 3.1). Nationally, Botha found himself between two camps: a 'British' sector, wanting to involve South Africa fully in the war, and an Afrikaner camp, wanting South Africa to remain neutral. The first considered it South Africa's duty, as a loyal Dominion of the Empire, to freely support the British war effort with a South African expeditionary force. Their newspapers, anti-German and stirred by popular imperialism, were full of news from the fronts in Europe. Patriotic fervour spilled over;[12] meetings were held at political and social clubs around the country, where speeches were made in French and English. In Johannesburg, demonstrators caused damage to the German Club, a round of popular agitation that flared up again the following year at the time of the sinking of the *Lusitania*.[13] Some called for the re-garrisoning of the old Anglo-Boer War blockhouse lines, although to what end was unclear.[14] To Afrikaner nationalists, this display of British nationalism, and the very idea of joining the fight against Germany, was anathema. Botha had hoped to unite the country behind the war effort, and so cement long-term bonds. This was, as Frans Malan noted, 'wonderful politics' and Botha succeeded to a surprising degree in quietening the voices of radical labour and African nationalists, both eager to exact political concessions in exchange for their support of the war. However, as Malan predicted, by committing South Africa to the war, Botha ran 'the danger of losing the sentiment of the [Afrikaner] people'.[15] The war and the questions it opened fuelled Afrikaner nationalism.

The South African and British governments were concerned that the war would increase disquiet among the black peoples of South Africa and the wider Empire. They believed the UDF able to suppress any risings, but issued a statement appealing to all black South Africans, disenfranchised and barred from military service, to show their customary loyalty and continue with their daily routines. The South African Native National Congress (SANNC), forerunner of the African National Congress (ANC), which happened to be meeting in Bloemfontein at the beginning of August, passed a resolution of loyalty, pledging to suspend criticism of the government as well as agitation against the 1913 Natives' Land Act. Albert Nzula, the first black secretary general of the Communist Party of South Africa (CPSA), would later maintain that this promise of loyalty by the SANNC was the 'first act of betrayal [by the] chiefs and petit bourgeois native good boys [which undermined the] liberationist struggles of the native people'.[16]

Table 3.1: **The position of parties in the House of Assembly, 1910 and 1915**						
	1910			**1915**		
Party	**Seats**	**Votes**	**Percentage**	**Seats**	**Votes**	**Percentage**
Labour	3	11 549	10.9	4	25 690	9.8
Labour – GM				–	802	0.3
Independent	12	19 563	18.5	5	10 911	4.2
Independent Lab	1	815	0.8			
Independent SAP	1	3 430	3.2			
Independent UP	2	*				
National Party				27	78 184	29.9
SAP	66	30 052	28.4	54	93 482	35.8
Socialist	–	448	0.4			
Unionist	36	39 766	37.6	40	48 034	18.4

* The Independent Unionists were uncontested in two seats in the Cape Province.

South Africa, at the outbreak of war, offered to take care of its own defence. This freed the majority of imperial troops stationed in the Union for service in Europe. Their duties, largely of a garrison nature, were assumed by members of the UDF, and 'the stigma of having an armed garrison of British troops on her soil [was] removed'.[17] Some soldiers feared that garrison duties and the manning of home defences would be rather dull, while many Unionists were anxious to form a South African expeditionary force or to join an imperial outfit. Others, like Hugh Wyndham, the shadow Defence minister, who would in 1916 produce the first draft of the official history, felt that the dispatch to some distant shore of much of the UDF, still inexperienced and possibly needed locally for the suppression of internal unrest or to deal with the German troops stationed in neighbouring South West Africa, would be nothing short of madness.[18]

Botha's real dilemma came on 7 August, when the British government asked whether South Africa would invade South West Africa and capture a local network of wireless stations, at Windhoek, Swakopmund and Lüderitzbucht. Lying astride the sea route to the East, these stations numbered among many imperial concerns at the start of the war. The station at Windhoek could communicate with stations in Togoland, Cameroon and Tanganyika, and, in favourable weather conditions, directly with Nauen, outside Berlin, and with German ships on the high seas. The seizure, London proposed, of 'such part of German South West Africa as would give them command of Swakopmund, Lüderitzbucht and the wireless stations there or in the interior, we should feel that this was a great and urgent Imperial service'.[19] The UDF, scarcely embarked on the organisation for homeland defence, the monitoring of the Germans across the Orange and the maintenance of a strike force in the event of an African rising or industrial unrest, had now to prepare for a campaign outside Union borders. After considerable deliberation in a divided Cabinet, South Africa acquiesced on 10 August and steps were taken to organise and equip an 'adequate force to provide for contingencies'.[20] However, parliamentary approval would have to be acquired and only volunteers used.[21] Although appreciating South Africa's political and military difficulties, London pushed Pretoria toward an early expedition.[22]

Broad-based public opinion stood in sharp contrast to the parliamentary division approving the war plans. Botha and Smuts, egged on by the English-speaking community, embraced the comfortable notion that their Afrikaner compatriots welcomed with equal enthusiasm the opportunities for nation-building and patriotism presented by the war.[23] Yet, far from nation-building and the creation of some common 'feeling', the war presented, for what Bill Nasson has termed 'the non-loyalist strata of Afrikaner society', unique opportunities for party politicking, with the far right hoping to seize the chance to restore a Boer republic.[24]

Jan Smuts, a very keen Defence minister, began mobilisation immediately, even before parliamentary approval. The South African public witnessed the movement of troops but, with a blanket of censorship thrown over the press, knew little of the government's plans. Rumours abounded, some emanating from the Union Buildings, that the government had 'important and effective plans for doing their share'.[25] This riled the nationalists, whose worst suspicions were confirmed on 9 September, when Botha and Smuts addressed a special session of Parliament just as, in France, the German spearheads were being pushed back across the Marne.[26] The House divided 92 for and 12 against a motion justified by defence and not conquest, and, with Senate approval following shortly afterwards, South Africa officially entered the war on 14 September. Less than a fortnight later, at Sandfontein, German troops surprised and defeated the van of an invading South African column.[27]

A bad beginning: gambits and crises

Geography, predictably, shaped the general strategic direction of the South African invasion of South West Africa. The German territory was bounded to the south by the Orange River. The eastern boundary was a longitudinal line running through Nakob, where there had been a minor border incident on 21 August, and from there north into the vast expanse of the Kalahari Desert.[28] The coastline formed the western boundary, where the only places of any consequence were Lüderitzbucht (occupied by South Africa on 19 September), Walvis Bay (a South African enclave) and Swakopmund (bombarded and then occupied ahead of the second invasion). A railway line ran from Tsumeb and Grootfontein in the north to Kalkfontein in the south, some 120 kilometres from the Orange River. This main north-south line was linked to the coast by a line running due west (380 kilometres) from Seeheim to Lüderitzbucht; some 585 kilometres to the north there was a line running 200 kilometres from Karibib to Swakopmund. The terrain traversed by the lines linking Lüderitzbucht and Swakopmund with the north-south line was, for more than 80 kilometres at least, in each case open desert, marked by some of the world's largest sand dunes.[29] The Germans used these features – the waterless, desolate and inhospitable landscape, together with the railway network – to design a classic defensive strategy. As the engagements at Sandfontein, Gibeon, Riet Pforte and Trekkoppies showed, when the conditions were favourable 'they put up a very good fight indeed'.[30]

The *Schutztruppen* (protection troops), the local German forces in South West Africa, were on their own from the moment war erupted. They could expect little support from the mother country, for German shipping would have to risk facing the Royal Navy. The Schutztruppen, comprising volunteers and a local levy, numbered 140 officers and some 2 000 other ranks, in addition to some 2 500 reservists, and were organised into eight mounted companies, a camel corps, four field batteries and a small air wing. The Schutztruppen were supplemented by 1 500 German police and perhaps 200 South African rebels.[31] The commander, Colonel Joachim von Heydebreck, was dismissed by South African intelligence as 'a martinet of the old school, fond of red tape and pipe clay', an unpopular commander who ran the risk 'of being shot by his own men if ever he [took] the field'.[32] They thought more of his second-in-command, Major Viktor Franke, a tough disciplinarian, full of dash and initiative, although a heavy drinker and addicted to morphia and opium.[33] The permanent German forces in South West Africa were well trained and experienced in colonial warfare, the reservists reasonably so, and all were under one, undivided command. At the start of the campaign, the Schutztruppen enjoyed better organisation and an advantage in artillery and machine guns.[34]

In January 1914, the Colonial Department in Berlin had instructed the local commanders that, in the event of war, they were to take defensive measures only. Accordingly, the staff in Windhuk (now Windhoek), under Von Heydebreck, planned to make the most of the geography, the advantages of the central position and a good, if limited, rail network. The Schutztruppen were entrenched at Windhuk and Keetmanshoop and astride each of the two lateral railroads. Von Heydebreck's aircraft and scout corps would monitor South African movements. From his strongpoints, he could raid the South African lines of communication and spheres of operation. In case of a closer investment, which would be difficult for the South Africans because of the scarcity of water, the Schutztruppen would assume a purely passive defence and attempt to hold out for as long as possible. The South Africans would be forced to advance along a limited number of clearly defined routes, determined by the physical features of the land and the presence of water sufficient for troops and animals.[35]

The South African strategists had good information, sources that had informed the War Office's official 'Military Report on GSWA 1913',[36] and the obstacles facing an invading South African force were well known. Captain Johann Leipoldt, a surveyor by profession, who had worked on Smuts' strategic concept for the campaign, was himself a Namakwalander. Yet, despite the physical obstacles, the South African leadership appeared to approach the campaign with growing confidence, satisfied in their knowledge of the geography and in their presumed ability to mobilise perhaps as many as 100 000 men. Commentators in 1914 shared reservations regarding the efficiency of the South African forces: the UDF was organised under a divided command, had no coherent general staff, and experienced a dearth of trained staff officers and critical shortages of arms and munitions.

Moreover, the strategy, devised by Smuts, for a direct march on Windhoek with diversions in the south, was changed on the eve of the expedition. As a preliminary move, he had deployed a force under Brigadier General HT Lukin to Steinkopf near the Orange River, while the railway was extended north from Prieska. Seaborne elements were mobilised in Cape Town, where they awaited a Royal Navy escort for the assault on Swakopmund and Lüderitzbucht. Smuts awaited parliamentary approval for his plans, but these were now modified.[37] Fate seemed to conspire against him. Firstly, while the Royal Navy could bombard the two German ports, it could provide transport and escort vessels to Lüderitzbucht only. Secondly, there was a serious lack of vehicles and equipment and a severe shortage of munitions, which would arrive over the ensuing weeks from Australia and India.[38] Although expressing appreciation for these difficulties, London continued to push Pretoria toward an early, somewhat abbreviated expedition.[39]

In the end, Smuts acquired a plan, adopted at a meeting of the principal officers, who assembled at Defence Headquarters on 21 August, with which he was in fundamental disagreement. The object of the impending operations in South West Africa, the plan said, was 'to gain complete possession of the Territory'.[40] Events now prescribed a smaller arc of operations extending only around the southern extremities of the German territory. Yet, importantly, the South Africans, having abandoned the direct approach, would still be operating on exterior lines. CF Beyers, Commandant General of the Citizen Force, had helped shape this plan, but, saying he had another pressing appointment, had left the meeting early.[41]

Command of the expeditionary force would be given to Beyers, with the subordinate commanders appointed from the Permanent Force and volunteer regiments. A column of 1 200 riflemen and six guns under Colonel PS Beves ('C' Force) was to occupy Lüderitzbucht and capture the wireless infrastructure there, while the station and other facilities at Swakopmund were to be destroyed by naval bombardment. A column of 1 800 riflemen, with eight guns, under HT Lukin ('A' Force) would land at Port Nolloth and, in a feint, draw pressure from the Lüderitzbucht expeditionary force. A column of 1 000 men under Lieutenant Colonel Manie Maritz ('B' Force) would threaten the eastern frontier of South West Africa from Upington. When these forces reached their objectives they would be deployed along an arc of some 900 kilometres, with lateral communications dependent upon dispatch riders. The entire operation was planned, and the columns coordinated, from Pretoria, which was 800 kilometres distant from 'B' Force and 1 600 kilometres from 'C' Force. Communications were made difficult by a system of hastily arranged telegraphs and made worse by the divided command. As Brigadier General JJ Collyer noted in the official history, the entire South African operation depended upon 'proper coordination and careful timing'. The German forces were capable of rapid concentration and could easily gain local superiority.

Clearly, the advance of one South African force without the others would court disaster.[42]

Beyers resigned on 15 September, the day after the resolution for war was passed in the Senate. Other senior officers, including Jan Kemp, also resigned, 'showing', as a quietly alarmed John X Merriman noted, 'a very curious sense of military duty'.[43] A hunt for two local murderers, which ousted the war as the leading news story for a few days, led to the killings of several policemen, the suicides of both murderers, the fatal shooting (in error) of General De la Rey, the opening of the Afrikaner rebellion and the treason of several senior officers, including Beyers and Kemp, and soon Maritz.

New appointments were made rapidly at Defence Headquarters, while Beves occupied Lüderitzbucht on 18 September and Swakopmund was subjected to naval bombardment.[44] Urged on by Pretoria, troops from Lukin's 'A' Force, under the command of Lieutenant Colonel Reginald Grant, occupied the waterholes at Sandfontein, some 40 kilometres into German territory. They were surrounded and, after an all-day battle on 26 September, forced to surrender. Some 3 000 shells are said to have fallen on their position, changing the shape of the koppie on which they sought shelter. The South African casualties numbered 67, some 22 per cent of Grant's force, of whom 16 were killed or died later of wounds. The Germans suffered 60 casualties, including 14 dead. This was a bad beginning for the campaign.

Heydebreck had used his strengths, good intelligence and interior lines, to advantage and had been able to concentrate 2 000 troops against Grant's 300. The unfolding rebellion in South Africa was equally important, for Maritz, the commander of 'B' Force and who was privy to the details of the campaign plan, had shared information with the German command.[45] Maritz not only refused to reinforce Lukin, when requested to do so, but also seemingly knew of the impending German envelopment. Maritz had said that the UDF would have little hope of defeating the Schutztruppen, which he thought better trained and better equipped. He ensured that the defeat at Sandfontein would, for the moment at least, prove his point.[46] Here was the military setback that government supporters had feared. An anxious Merriman observed, the day after Beyers' resignation, that, 'if we have anything like a reverse we may have [in South Africa] something like a revolution'.[47]

Emotions had been stirred since the decision in Parliament to invade South West Africa, and were intensified by the death of General De la Rey. Nationalist leaders called meetings to protest against the government's war policy. The situation rapidly got out of hand when armed men arrived at these meetings, and inflammatory speeches were made. No sooner had news arrived of the reverse at Sandfontein than a number of prominent military officers, including Beyers, Maritz and Kemp, went into rebellion. Thousands of their followers joined their protest.

There is a growing literature on the Afrikaner rebellion and its causes. Most scholars now agree that, although the material culture of the new South African state and of the UDF, with its beardless, khaki-wearing, disciplined soldiery, was important, the origins of rebel discontent were more complex and lie largely in networks of kinship and the politics of post-Anglo-Boer War poverty.[48] Economic pressures had undermined the white poor and, unable to secure credit, including tangible aid from the state, they were disillusioned, bitter and volatile.[49] Scores of Afrikaans servicemen resigned from the Union forces in mid-September.[50] Beyers, Kemp and De Wet took the field. Maritz proclaimed a republic at the beginning of October 1914.

It was on Louis Botha that the success or failure of the rebellion and of the campaign in South West Africa now hinged, and he acted immediately. Botha was the key to government success. Smuts simply did not have the same influence as Botha: the former's roots were in the Boland and, as Carter noted, he was 'too clever for them and does not suffer fools gladly'.[51] The burghers of the Transvaal followed Botha personally. Former Boer general Coen Brits sent the following telegram in response to Botha's request for support: 'My men are ready; who do we fight – the English or the Germans?'[52] Martial law was proclaimed on 12 October, while most of the military sections, until then dispersed about the Union, were centralised during October at Defence Headquarters, established in the old Artillery Barracks in Potgieter Street, Pretoria. This building complex, vacated recently by imperial troops, provided the UDF with a central node from which to coordinate the war effort.[53]

The government forces achieved rapid success. The rebellion, poorly planned, poorly coordinated and led by an indecisive leadership, was suppressed by measures put in place largely by Smuts. The government forces were well led by Botha. Smuts had secured the railroads and mobilised loyalists, many of whom answered the call to follow Botha personally. Moreover, having secured ammunition supplies, Smuts used the rail network and motorised transport to outflank and outgun the rebels. Deneys Reitz, hearing how Brits had used motor vehicles to corner and capture De Wet, felt 'almost sorry, for it spelt the end of our picturesque South African commando system'.[54] Most of the government troops were burghers, much like their kinsmen in revolt. When the government forces entered the Free State town of Reitz, the inhabitants, many of them strongly pro-rebel and believing that Botha was leading an imperial army from overseas, had expected to see British soldiers. An elderly woman is reputed to have rushed into the street, but, seeing only ordinary burghers, exclaimed: 'But, where are the bloody English?' To this a young government scout, Afrikaans like her, retorted: 'Old lady, we are the bloody English!'[55]

By the end of November, the rebels had been scattered and only mopping-up operations were necessary. The rebellion was over by January 1915. Beyers, suffering a major heart attack, drowned in the Vaal River while attempting to escape. He was a tragic figure, hesitant and unsure from the start, caught as he was between traditional values and the professional code of the new defence structures.[56] Of the rebels, a total of 7 119 men were from the Free State, 2 998 from the Transvaal, 590 from the Cape, and 4 from Natal. More than half of them were captured, the remainder surrendering following the proclamation of an amnesty. In all, 286 were tried by the Special Treason Courts, of whom 281 were convicted. Captured rebel leaders received prison sentences and fines, all paid for by public subscription. Captain Josef Fourie, who took up arms without resigning his commission, was executed. The total of 10 711 rebels (Figure 3.1) excluded the 970 members of Maritz's force, against whom special action was taken.

The parliamentary session of 1915 was comparatively brief. The finances of the country were arranged and several war bills passed.[57] But the House was also inundated with oratory on the rebellion and the associated Indemnity Bill, debates that exacerbated the bitterness of the Nationalists and produced the final break between Botha and the far right. New issues arose during the succeeding war years: the Nationalists would base their attacks on Botha on the question of soldiers' overseas pay, the conduct of the campaign in Tanganyika, the export of food and agricultural products to Britain at fixed rates, and the employment of black South African troops, particularly in Europe.

For the moment, Botha continued to hope for rapprochement, but this was made difficult by the Unionists and complicated further by the general election of October 1915.[58] The electoral result, a severe disappointment to Botha, was such that he, most reluctantly, could only remain in office with the parliamentary support of the Unionists. Divisions were worse than ever. Moreover, the Unionists, although giving Botha a majority in the House of Assembly, felt excluded from real government. They were drawn, in some degree, into wartime decision support and even military office, but there was

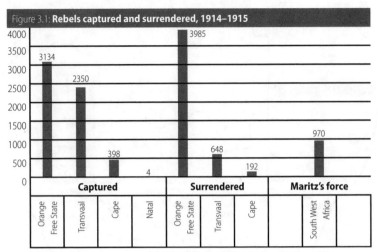

Figure 3.1: **Rebels captured and surrendered, 1914–1915**

Note: The middle column enumerates rebels who surrendered under the amnesty proclamation or who subsequently were permitted to return to their homes and against whom no action was taken. The first column enumerates rebels who were captured in the field or who surrendered after the amnesty proclamation. *Source:* statistics drawn from PMK, box 108, PM 920 Innocence Commission, SANDF Documentation Centre.

no war government or government of national unity. The Nationalists, in turn, would have no part in the war effort, and on this they were joined at times by what remained of the Labour Party. Botha, like the official opposition, realised that good war news would solidify the country, undermine the belief in nationalist quarters that Britain was going to be defeated, and so build a larger measure of national unity.

The setback at Sandfontein highlighted several deficiencies. Smuts, the 'super-minister', had been dangerously overconfident and trusted too much in the superior numbers of the UDF. Inevitably perhaps, a month passed before Parliament sat, which caused much speculation and further uncertainty. While blame is difficult to apportion for the setback, and Maritz bears more blame than most, there can be no doubt that the mobilisation and deployment of the UDF had been compromised by poor military organisation and planning, a lack of munitions, poor naval cooperation and genuine confusion resulting from the lack of a central staff and command organisation, and, seemingly, no contingency plans. Lukin's hasty move across the Orange, an initial intelligence failure at Defence Headquarters and the unfolding Afrikaner rebellion made the situation fatal. If indeed the first invasion 'fell only just short of disaster',[59] then the second, launched in December 1914, would be undertaken by a South African army of an entirely different nature.

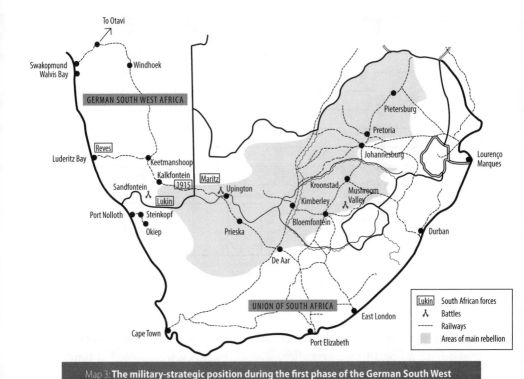

Map 3: **The military-strategic position during the first phase of the German South West Africa Campaign and the Afrikaner Rebellion**

Military reform and the second invasion of South West Africa

By early December 1914, the strategic landscape had improved. With the rebellion at an end and with Von Spee's naval squadron no longer a threat to Cape waters, Botha and Smuts could focus on German South West Africa once again.[60] Botha assumed overall command as the commander-in-chief in the field, a new position created especially for him.[61] There would henceforth be a single strategic direction, with political and military authority combined in his person. JJ Collyer was appointed as chief staff officer to Botha and placed in charge of the administration of the campaign: admired by his staff for his sense of space and time on campaign, he later became the first Union Chief of the General Staff, in June 1917.[62] Colonel PCB Skinner was on loan from the British Army. Brigadier General Sir Duncan McKenzie was a gentleman farmer, who, through years of active social campaigning, had come to the command of

Table 3.2: **The change in the South African general staff**					
Force of origin			**Age**		
	1914	**1914–1918**		**1914**	**1914–1918**
ZAR Forces	4	12	30s	1	7
OFS Forces	1	2	40s	3	8
Transvaal Volunteers	1	2	50s	6	7
Cape Colonial Forces	3	3	60s	1	1
Natal Militia	1	2			
British Army	1	1			
SA Police		1			
Total	**11**	**23**	**Total**	**11**	**23**

Source: I van der Waag, 'The battle of Sandfontein, 26 September 1914: South African military reform and the German South-West Africa campaign, 1914–1915', *First World War Studies*, 4(2) October 2013, p 156.

the Natal Militia. The remaining force commanders for the second invasion were all Afrikaners, who had served with the Boer forces during the war of 1899–1902. Botha, abandoning the policy of language equity and provincial representation for the remainder of the campaign, appointed trusted former republican officers, who were younger, and whose numbers increased from five in August 1914 to 14 by November 1918 (*see* Table 3.2).

Smuts, who had assumed direct command of the Citizen Force following Beyers' resignation, now also reverted to his original plan. Walvis Bay and Swakopmund would be used as advance bases for a direct advance on Windhoek. With coordinated attacks along four axes, German use of interior lines would be limited. The South Africans aimed now to envelop the German forces and, if necessary, destroy them in the field, before the enemy initiated a guerrilla campaign.

Walvis Bay was developed as the advanced base for Northern Force and the primary attack. Northern Force, the largest of the invading columns, was a whole new deployment and comprised more than 20 000 troops, approximately half of them burgher commandos, under the command of Botha himself. Reinforcements were also dispatched to the three columns poised to the south of the German territory: Southern Force (Colonel JL van Deventer) increased fourfold, Eastern Force (Colonel CAL Berrangé) more than doubled and Central Force (McKenzie) grew fivefold.

The support services also grew exponentially. In March 1915, Northern

Force, then comprising three infantry brigades, one mounted brigade and seven guns, was further reinforced, and the organisation provided for line of communication and special troops to protect the railways, whose path did not always coincide with either the line of communication or the intended direction of advance. Field troops now included one squadron of armoured cars and six aeroplanes of the South African Aviation Corps (SAAC).[63] The first air operations, flown by Captain Kenneth van der Spuy, commenced out of Karibib toward the end of May in support of Northern Force and included reconnaissance missions and bombing raids.[64] The presence of line of communications troops, and of engineering, medical and transport and logistics units, gave the Union army a modern appearance.

Possibly the most important duty of the new South African Engineer Corps (SAEC) was the provision of drinking water, which presented severe problems along all lines of advance and remained the chief anxiety for much of the campaign. The water situation had been made worse by the Germans, who destroyed condensers and blew up wells and boreholes as they withdrew. All of these had to be reopened.[65] In some cases, water resources had been poisoned. Condensers were erected at the beachheads (Lüderitz, Walvis Bay and Swakopmund) and the supply was augmented by ship-borne water from Cape Town.[66] Boreholes were sunk for the four routes of march and hydrants used to convey water by gravitation from boreholes into large storage tanks and specially erected concrete reservoirs (each containing 100 000 gallons). From here, water was piped to camps and down the lines to blockhouses protecting the railway.[67] Animal water transport was abandoned and supply was taken by train.[68] For much of the campaign, there was some fear that the German air force would bomb the boreholes and reservoirs.[69]

Table 3.3: **The four forces in the field, 15 March 1915**					
	Northern Force	**Central Force**	**Southern Force**	**Eastern Force**	**Total**
Artillery	741	575	117	40	1 473
Mounted	12 773	3 858	8 438	2 016	27 085
Infantry	5 864	5 583			11 447
Administrative	1 491	855	631	420	3 397
Total	**20 869**	**10 871**	**9 186**	**2 476**	**43 402**

Source: Adapted from [HA Wyndham], 1916.

There had been, during the first invasion, some difficulty supplying the three forces with rations.[70] Moreover, the Germans quarantined the operational area, driving cattle ahead of their withdrawal and denuding the countryside of meat on the hoof. South African logisticians had no contingency plan, and cattle had to be hurriedly acquired, often commandeered, and rangers hastily appointed. Smuts persuaded the British authorities to loan the South African Garrison Institutes (SAGI), the British canteen system in South Africa, to the UDF for deployment into South West Africa, and branches of the SAGI were opened with each of the four columns.[71] Nevertheless, with the men on half rations at times, there were the inevitable reports of looting. German civilians complained of this at the time of the Riet Pforte battles. Botha appointed a board of inquiry, which encouraged Major Toby Taylor of the Transvaal Horse Artillery to write a script for a short theatrical production dubbed 'Ali Botha and the Pforte Thieves'.[72]

The Medical Department, established only seven months before the outbreak of hostilities, underwent similar reorganisation. Assistant Deputy Directors Medical Services (ADDMSs) were appointed for each of the invading columns. Hospitals were established at Lüderitzbucht, Swakopmund, Karibib, Windhoek and elsewhere, often moving into German infrastructure. Some 25 367 patients were treated in hospital. South African troops suffered only 295 deaths during the campaign: 122 were killed in action or died subsequently of wounds; 58 were killed by accident; and 115 died from disease or illness. Almost overnight an effective medical organisation had been established, capable of deployment in a rugged area of poor roads and great distances.[73]

Smuts had desired a modern military for the Union, a vision that had been compromised by the consensus politics of 1912.[74] From late 1914, with many of the dissenting voices now quieted, he moved ahead and laid the essentials of a modern military organisation. The unification of the command and the development of a general staff and an administration, together with the deployment of more troops, properly equipped and supported, were the elements of success. By mid-1915, Botha's columns, overcoming the physical constraints of the campaign, strategically enveloped the German forces and forced their surrender at Otavifontein, on 8 July 1915. As Collyer records, 'only 24 days of actual movement by the forces under General Botha were necessary to carry them from Swakopmund to Riet and Windhoek, and thence to Tsumeb and Otavifontein, a distance in no instance less than 400 miles'.[75] The record march of the entire campaign was executed by the left wing of the 2nd Mounted Brigade, which, after a 40–mile march in just 14 hours, marched a further 76 miles in 22 hours. Their war diary records their move from Swakopmund at 6 pm on 18 March, arrival at Husab at 8 am on the following day (40 miles in 14 hours). They then left Husab at 8 pm on 19 March and arrived at Jakalswater at 5 am on 20 March, where they were in action for three hours, but had to return to Husab on the same day for water. This was a remarkable feat. The mobility and manoeuvre of the South West African campaign would stand in sharp contrast to the conditions South African troops would encounter in France from mid-1916. If organisational reform had followed from the experiences of 1914, then the tactical reforms of 1916 came as a result of the bitter experience of the malarial jungles of Tanganyika and the trenches of the Western Front.

German forces in South West Africa surrendered unconditionally on 9 July 1915. Ten days later, Beves, now a brigadier general, was appointed military governor and commanding officer in the conquered territory. On 30 October, the first position expired, and a civilian official, EHL (Sir Howard) Gorges, was appointed as the first administrator of South West Africa. Gorges served until 1920. Martial law was lifted with effect from 31 December 1920 and the territory was from that time administered by South Africa under a mandate of the League of Nations.

Raising and dispatch of expeditionary forces

With the 1915 election over and his political position stabilised, Botha, urged on by the Unionists and loyalist Afrikaners, who were concerned that South Africa was not doing enough, turned to the wider war. South Africa was exporting steel and war-related materials to Britain, Russia, France, Italy and Japan, but Botha, seeing that South Africa's economic wellbeing was tied to the fortunes of the British Empire, felt obliged to do more than simply support the wider British war effort through South African trade and industry.[76]

A new realism was now dawning too. For the British sector, the early war enthusiasm, experienced by many Afrikaners as ultra-jingoistic, had gone, while many Afrikaners, of the non-loyal type, came to accept that the war would not provide the much-wanted opportunity to fix old grudges with Britain. Moreover, many South Africans, men like Lieutenant Cyril

Newton-Thompson, having left to join the British armed forces, were already serving on the Western Front, and there had been some talk of recruiting men in South Africa for a 'New Army'.[77]

At the end of June 1915, before the end of the campaign in South West Africa, Britain approached South Africa on the question of a South African expeditionary force for France. John Buchan, perhaps succumbing to South African nation-building and sensing the need to boost the popular image of Botha and Smuts after 1918, credits them with initiating the proposal.[78] This immediately encountered difficulty, as South Africa was not prepared to discuss 'the contingent question' until the campaign in South West Africa was over. Moreover, with an election coming up, it was not advisable to ask Parliament[79] to vote the money for another campaign, which would raise 'acute political controversies … with results which [Smuts forecast] might be most undesirable'.[80] Lord Buxton, the Governor General, agreed and so Britain left the question for a time. But, on the day of the German surrender, Buxton was pushing his ministers again: 'Now,' he wrote to Smuts, 'that this affair [in German South West Africa] is over I suppose South Africa will break out in a new place – I wonder where?'[81]

These questions – whether another expeditionary force would be raised and where it would serve – elicited mixed feelings in South Africa. Merriman, for one, felt that South Africa had already made its great sacrifice in German South West Africa.[82] Moreover, this campaign had been fought to ensure the security of the country's own borders. The theatres now proposed for South African involvement – East Africa and France – were far from the Union, geographically speaking. And, creating further ambiguity, the South Africa Defence Act (13 of 1912) authorised deployment of the UDF only in 'South Africa' and for the immediate defence of the Union. For this reason, only volunteers could be deployed further afield. However, from September 1914 many South Africans had left to enlist as individuals in the British Army, and more could be expected to leave. It seemed a pity that these men, willing to serve in Europe, were not fighting as South Africans. Moreover, as the Minister of Finance, DP Graaff, acknowledged, Pretoria was under increasing pressure and they would have to do something 'to meet the demands of those who are anxious to see a contingent depart'. In fact, Pretoria, recognising that the conclusion of the South West African campaign would produce a large number of unemployed men, was quite happy 'to have [these men] at the front than on our hands'.[83] For these reasons, the Cabinet decided to send another contingent. But where was this 'second little bit' to be sent?

Two theatres were proposed. The first was the main battleground in northern France, where the other Dominions were already well represented; the other was German East Africa (Tanganyika). The latter, supposedly 'more in our line' than a European campaign, was supported by a wide number of Britons and South Africans. A small contingent in France would not only be 'swallowed up in the enormous armies' and lose their identity, but also South African troops had neither the training nor the campaign experience to fit them for the Western Front, whereas in Tanganyika, South Africa would have its own 'show' once again and 'they could fight in their own way'.[84] Smuts liked the idea of Tanganyika too. He agreed with the military arguments, the promise of mobility – South Africa's strong suit – in which mounted infantry could play a role, but recognised, too, that, if South Africa conquered the territory, some sort of exchange with the Portuguese might consolidate territories south of the Zambezi and Kunene rivers.[85]

However, Britain had requested specifically an infantry contingent for the Somme sector of operations. So, when Pretoria responded to London's call, the government expressed its 'readiness to render all the assistance in their power in prosecuting the war in Europe and elsewhere'.[86] In doing so, Pretoria hoped to satisfy the British request as well as their own sub-imperial goals. In pursuance of this dual policy, Pretoria agreed to send a contingent to Europe, to be composed of the volunteers they expected in large numbers, perhaps sufficient to form a second and even a third brigade. In fact, with the South West African campaign at an end, Smuts was confident that South Africa would be able to raise three infantry brigades, which offered the prospect of forming a South African division.[87]

However, Smuts was to be disappointed. The recruitment drive opened on 21 July 1915, in time to draw the troops returning victorious from South West Africa.[88] A call was made for heavy artillery as well as infantry,[89] although the War Office had asked specifically for infantry. As expected, there was a flurry of interest, particularly from inhabitants of British blood.[90] Men rushed again to the colours. Some, like Louis Matthews, writing once the brigade had been formed, was 'afraid of being left in the cold'.[91] However, in view of the small white population and the complexity of South Africa's other tasks, including the pending deployment to Tanganyika, it was agreed that South Africa could not raise and maintain in France much more than a brigade.[92] On 10 August 1915, Botha informed Buxton that the South African contingent would

Table 3.4: **Composition of 1st South African Infantry Brigade, with battalions representing the main political divisions in South Africa**		
Regiment	**Source**	**Commander**
1st SA Infantry	Cape Province	Lt Col FS Dawson (4th SAMR)
2nd SA Infantry	Natal and Orange Free State	Lt Col WEC Tanner (District Staff Officer, Pietermaritzburg)
3rd SA Infantry	Transvaal and Rhodesia	Lt Col ET Thackeray (District Staff Officer, Kimberley)
4th SA Infantry	South African Scottish	Lt Col FA Jones (District Staff Officer, Johannesburg)

comprise one infantry brigade, one signals company, one field ambulance and one general hospital, in addition to five batteries of heavy artillery and some, if not the whole, of the personnel for five four-gun batteries (13–pounder quick-firing) of field artillery and some aviation personnel, together with aircraft and spares. Botha, however, noted rather ominously that reinforcement could prove difficult.[93]

The force was established in accordance with the war establishments fixed for the New Army[94] and the British government assumed liability for pay – an issue soon to have political consequences.[95] The four battalions, designated the 1st South African Infantry Brigade, were, as shown in Table 3.4, 'designed to represent the main divisions of the Union, and recruits were given the option of joining the regiment affiliated to their own province'.[96] This formed part of a difficult but broad-front attempt to gain language equity and balance sectarian interests. In East Africa and France, where Smuts himself and Lukin were to command, respectively, the former represented the Afrikaans sector, and the latter the English. Moreover, with only about 15 per cent of the original brigade being Afrikaans-speaking, the bulk of the contingent that went to France was English. As Ian Uys has shown, by the end of the war 'the portion of Afrikaners had increased from 15 to 30 per cent'.[97] Buchan has suggested that the Afrikaners, renowned as light cavalrymen and having enhanced this reputation in the South West African campaign, were not expected to be attracted to British-style infantry warfare, and so they were by preference destined for Tanganyika.[98]

For those leaving the Union, their military experience was quite irrelevant to the tasks at hand in Tanganyika and France. The Union Defence Force, although still in embryo in 1914, was not inexperienced. But this experience was all South African, and almost exclusively of the small-war variety. As we have seen, the UDF was a rather difficult marriage of four disparate forces, representing at least three military traditions and speaking two languages. Sectarian interest was very strong, and this did not facilitate organisational design and effective command. To make matters worse, there was little respect and equally little cooperation between the South African Department of Defence and the local British military authorities. Smuts and his generals did not bother to consult, to any real extent, Major General CW Thompson, the representative of the British regular army in Cape Town. Over the following years, relations between the Castle and Defence Headquarters in Pretoria declined further, reaching a nadir in 1917 with the recall of Brigadier General AEJ Cavendish.

The 1st South African Infantry Brigade was placed under the command of HT Lukin, a seasoned campaigner in South Africa since the time of the Anglo-Zulu War (1879). Both Botha and Smuts had had their doubts about Lukin, which they had raised during the campaign in South West Africa.[99] They thought him ill-suited to a mobile role and perhaps too wedded to the British way of doing things. They felt he lacked the necessary African zest, and thought him better suited to warfare in Europe. Moreover, when rumours surfaced that Smuts might be offered the command in Tanganyika, the idea of having a general officer representing the 'English' interest seemed a good one. Sending Lukin to France would satisfy English South African opinion. Douglas Haig, who had encountered Lukin during the Anglo-Boer War, thought him a commander of 'great ability' and, in 1918, declared that he viewed him as 'one of the most reliable Divisional Commanders in France'.[100]

Of the battalion commanders, only WEC Tanner was South African-born, but all, like Lukin, had small-war experience. FS Dawson had spent some time as a planter in British Honduras before 1899, while Thackeray, at about the same time, had had an interlude as a cowboy in the American West. All had seen service in South Africa during the Anglo-Boer War. Dawson, born in Sussex, and Thackeray, in Middlesex, had entered the South African structures through the South African Constabulary. All had served in German South West Africa, with Jones having been brigade major in the 1st Infantry Brigade.[101]

German East Africa, 1915–1918

The East African campaign was the most expensive of the four African campaigns of the Great War and lasted until news was received of the armistice signed in France. Operations had commenced, under British command, on 8 August 1914, with the bombardment of Dar es Salaam. British forces in East Africa remained on the defensive, awaiting reinforcements and parrying the initial limited German offensives. However, when reinforcements arrived, mostly from India, British ambitions for a quick victory were dealt a severe blow when their assault force was soundly defeated at Tanga in early November 1914.[102] British prestige had already slumped with the sinking of HMS *Pegasus*, near Zanzibar, by the German cruiser *Königsberg*, on 20 September. The British effort was dogged by poor leadership and low morale, and the troops lacked adequate preparation and proper training. Other setbacks followed throughout 1915.

Steps were taken in late 1915 to wrest the initiative back from Lieutenant Colonel Paul von Lettow-Vorbeck, the German commander, but, as Ross Anderson, who has without doubt produced the best history of the campaign, notes, the real change came in early 1916 with the arrival of Smuts and the South African troops. Smuts' force comprised two infantry brigades, one mounted brigade, an unbrigaded mounted regiment and a Cape Corps battalion, together with artillery and supporting services.[103] These men, representing a total strength of some 18 700, were all Imperial Service units, raised on a volunteer basis, as the Defence Act protected members of the UDF from being compelled to serve unless in direct defence of the Union itself.[104] The 5th Battery, SAMR, was the only Permanent Force unit to serve in East Africa, though with volunteer personnel.

The SAAC had been disbanded after the South West African campaign, but the majority of the pilots volunteered for further service in England, where they were to form the nucleus of No 26 (South African) Squadron of the RFC. However, after being brought up to strength by further recruits from the Union, No 26 Squadron was dispatched to East Africa in December 1915 with BE 2e and Henri Farman aircraft to carry out reconnaissance, bombing and communication missions in support of Smuts' operations. The squadron was recalled to the United Kingdom in June 1918 and disbanded the following month.[105]

Smuts assumed command of the imperial forces in East Africa, at the request of the British government, and gradually South Africa came to dominate in-theatre troop strengths. The first drafts left South Africa in December 1915. By the end of the war, 47 521 white and some 18 000 black South Africans had volunteered and served in East Africa. The campaign against the able Lettow-Vorbeck and his elusive forces proved long and arduous. Smuts' force, together with a force under Brigadier General JL van Deventer, nevertheless succeeded in advancing southwards into Tanganyika, gaining territory without coming to blows with the Germans, while a mostly British force under Brigadier General Edward Northey attempted to cut off Von Lettow-Vorbeck's retreat east of Lake Nyasa. By January 1917, when Smuts left for London to join the Imperial War Cabinet, the German army was depleted but still very much undefeated. The campaign entered a guerrilla phase and the British commenced a programme of 'Africanisation', in the belief that black troops would withstand the regional disease ecology better than white troops. More than 12 000 South African troops were repatriated to the Union, many of them physical wrecks. They were, Collyer reminds us, 'in varying stages of exhaustion, ravaged by tropical disease, emaciated by illness and want of proper food, and generally in a condition which made hospital treatment, in some cases literally for years, essential'.[106] Van Deventer, however, remained in overall command in East Africa until Von Lettow-Vorbeck, by then in Northern Rhodesia, finally surrendered on 25 November 1918. More than 2 000 South Africans died during the campaign. There are no records of the German losses, while the numbers of African porters lost to enemy fire and disease are estimated to run into the hundreds of thousands.

This campaign was entirely different from that fought in German South West Africa. Firstly, Von Lettow-Vorbeck was a professional soldier, well trained, brave, determined, charismatic and prepared to lead from the front. He spared neither his troops nor himself. Recognising that the fate of the German colonies would be decided in Europe, Von Lettow-Vorbeck used his army of some 3 000 Germans and 11 000 Askaris, his African troops, to prevent far larger numbers of Allied troops from participating in the main theatres of war and, along the way, to cause them losses. At their peak, the total ration strength of the 'British' forces, imperial, Dominion and colonial, in East Africa in 1916 numbered 98 580.[107]

Secondly, Tanganyika was ill-suited to the type of campaigning at which Botha and Smuts excelled. The terrain and vegetation – thick bush and, in places, jungle – prevented wide, sweeping movements of mounted troops. Being equatorial, it was also very humid. Rainfall was plentiful, vegetation thrived and the countryside teemed with animals. The wastage of manpower, from malaria, tick-bite fever, dysentery and hookworm, was appalling, to which might be added the lesser ills of heat rashes, veld sores, malnutrition and the jigger flea. In December 1916, the number of British troops hospitalised for one week was a staggering 10 700: by contrast, battle deaths for the entire four-year campaign numbered just 3 443.[108] Dysentery and malaria were the principal diseases. The South African uniform – short trousers and short-sleeved shirt – afforded little protection from the sun or from mosquitoes. During the rains, animal and mechanical transport quickly became bogged down. Moreover, tsetse fly killed livestock, horses and draught animals. Various equine sicknesses decimated the horse transport: troopers were issued with arsenic for their horses and quinine for themselves.[109] Piet van der Byl, Smuts' staff captain in Tanganyika, had between eight and ten horses die under him in less than a year.[110] The campaign, in the words of the British official medical history, became 'more and more a campaign against climate, geographical conditions and disease'.[111] Colonial campaigns remained severe tests of nature and of sheer physical endurance, with fatigue and disease claiming more soldier deaths than battle.[112]

Thirdly, the nature of the armies differed. The African campaigns of the Great War were but a continuation of earlier colonial campaigning. The colonial forces were variegated, comprising small numbers of white officers and troops, larger number of black troops, and vast numbers of porters, who, suffering terribly, carried tons of ammunitions and rations through vast, often inhospitable areas. In East Africa, the British force was much larger than the German, and the Royal Navy controlled the seas. Von Lettow-Vorbeck never had more than 14 000 troops at his call, while his adversaries had almost 100 000, drawn from India, South Africa, East and West Africa, the Belgian Congo and Portuguese East Africa. However, enjoying the advantage of internal lines, Von Lettow-Vorbeck fought in the foothills of Kilimanjaro, threatened British rail communications in Kenya and Uganda, and later took the war deep into the jungles of Tanganyika, exposing his enemy to the problems of lengthening lines of communication, erratic supply and constant guerrilla activity.[113]

But Smuts faced other difficulties too. While his army was disparate, the professional British and Indian Army officers, all white, considered Smuts an amateur. This was particularly so in camp, where, Van der Byl reminds us, Smuts encountered 'some of the senior British "dug-outs", who had not been very successful elsewhere'.[114] Smuts was unorthodox, leaving his base to reconnoitre personally – much as Von Lettow-Vorbeck did – and at times well in advance of his forces. His coolness in battle and the excellent press he received, particularly in London, did not go down well, and the malice and personal jealousies of some of his British staffers have resounded loudly in the historiography.

At home, the Nationalists and government backbenchers, and some Unionists, attacked Botha on the matter of raising and deploying black and coloured South African troops, particularly in Europe.[115] This was contrary to policy, although the 1912 Defence Act provided for special enlistment during emergencies. The Cape Corps was raised in August 1915, comprising coloured volunteers only, for duty in East Africa. This was done to 'save' white troops, who were thought to be ineffective in tropical climates, but the coloured men suffered the same extremes and experienced similar casualty levels from illness and disease. The Indian stretcher-bearers and medical orderlies who served in East Africa with the South African Medical Corps fared the same. However, the deployment of coloured, Indian and black men in East Africa in non-combatant roles did not cause the controversy; the combatant roles performed by the coloured men of the Cape Corps did.

The Middle East: Egypt and Palestine

The 1st South African Infantry Brigade, which had been earmarked for service with British forces in France, arrived in the United Kingdom from September 1915 for training, but was soon diverted to assist British troops in the defence of Egypt and the Suez Canal. The entry into the war of the Ottoman Empire, as an ally of Germany and Austria-Hungary, in November 1914, and the promotion of a militant, anti-colonial Islam, threatened British, Italian and French interests in the eastern Mediterranean basin and the passage of vital oil supplies from the Middle East. Turkish forces attacked the Suez Canal in February 1915, but a defensive line formed in Sinai held through 1915 and early 1916, while British and Australian forces suffered reverses against the Turks at the Dardanelles and in Mesopotamia.

A now largely forgotten phase of the Egyptian campaign was the intervention of Sayyid Ahmed as-Sharif as-Senussi, the emir of Cyrenaica and Tripolitania. In November 1915, encouraged by the Sultan in Istanbul, the emir and his horsemen invaded Egypt and took Sollum, forcing British forces to withdraw to Mersa Matruh and giving German submarines a port on the North African coast. The Grand Senussi exercised great influence over the peoples of the oases. The threat was taken seriously: the British position in Egypt was now threatened on both the western and eastern flanks.[116] Reinforcements, including Lukin's brigade, were sent to shore up the defences.[117]

Arriving at Alexandria in January 1916, the 1st SA Infantry Brigade was ordered into action, and two companies of 2nd SA Infantry Regiment were despatched by sea to Mersa Matruh, from where they moved inland to join Major General A Wallace's Western Frontier Force. They came into contact with the Senussi at Halazin on 23 January. Lukin and his brigade headquarters, with 1st SA Infantry Regiment, moved to Mersa Matruh by sea at the beginning of February. Further reinforced over the following weeks, the brigade moved forward to Agheila and on 25 February reached Aqqaqir. There they made contact with the Senussi forces and, on the following day, attacked and defeated them. The Turkish commander, Gaafer Pasha, was captured. The Senussi elements escaping from the battlefield were run down over the following days by a flying column of six Rolls-Royce armoured cars, under the command of the Duke of Westminster. Sollum was retaken on 14 March and the 1st SA Infantry Brigade left for France and the trenches of the Western Front.[118]

Although the campaign on Egypt's western front had been won for the moment – the Senussi would conduct an irregular war well into 1917 – the war against the Ottoman Empire was far from over, and several other South African formations and units served against the Turks in Palestine, firstly under General Sir Archibald Murray, who commanded primarily from Cairo, and then from June 1917 under Edmund Allenby. The Egyptian Expeditionary Force (EEF), created in 1916, varied by nationality and formation. Australia, providing the bulk of the cavalry, fought in every major engagement of the campaign. South Africa did not. The Palestine campaign has therefore remained a little-studied portion of the Union experience in the Great War. Although fought over three years, it remained a small campaign for South Africa, in stark contrast to the deployment to France and the Battle of Delville Wood, which, described by Liddell Hart as 'the bloodiest battle-hell of 1916', dominates South African memory of the war.[119]

Relatively little has been written on the batteries of South African artillery deployed to Palestine during the summer of 1916, or of the Cape Corps battalion that arrived in theatre in 1918. The Allied need for artillery led to the formation of the South African Field Artillery (SAFA) Brigade, manned by some 650 volunteers from the Cape Field Artillery, the Natal Field Artillery and the Transvaal Horse Artillery. The brigade initially comprised three batteries of four 13-pounder guns. But, attached to the 75th (British) Division, the organisation and ordnance changed to two batteries of six 18-pounders in August 1917. A third battery, C Battery, with four 4.5-inch howitzers, was added in April 1918. The SAFA Brigade took part in the third battle for Gaza and the advance on Jerusalem at the end of 1917, and then the advance up the coast to the Megiddo battles of 1918.[120] The two South African elements in Palestine, the SAFA Brigade and the Cape Corps battalion, linked up only toward the end of the campaign.[121]

The 1st Battalion Cape Corps, having earned its stripes in Tanganyika, was moved to the front in July 1918, after a short period of desert training. The battalion was attached to 160th Brigade of 53rd Division in time for the main Allied offensive. Over the following months, the EEF drove the Ottoman army from Palestine and Syria, the Cape Corps earning imperishable glory in September 1918 at the battle of Square Hill; Smuts lauded them later, saying: 'You fought as bravely and as well as any other unit of the British Army, and established a brilliant record for your Corps.'[122] This accolade was a remarkable tribute from a man who, in 1914, had made some caustic comments about the value of 'coloured' troops.[123]

The Palestine campaign's sweeping cavalry operations, operational movement and tactical mobility, and the relatively low casualty rates, seemed the very opposite of conditions on the Western Front. However, as Jean Bou argues, this is an oversimplification for a campaign that revealed all of the developments of modern warfare, including the use of all-arms formations, massive bombardment, creeping artillery fire and chemical weapons.[124]

The Imperial War Cabinet, convinced that the surest path to victory lay in the defeat of Berlin's weaker allies, had sought for greater effort to be exerted on other fronts. Lloyd George, as Secretary of State for War, losing confidence in Murray, sought commanders with more dash. Smuts, in London as an additional member of the War Cabinet, was offered the command of the EEF, but refused, doubting that the resources for a decisive victory would be made available. Allenby was appointed in June 1917. But the general war situation looked bleak. The defeat of Russia had freed German troops for service in France, while American troops, it was thought, would not arrive on the Western Front in strength before mid-1918, allowing Germany one last main effort. However, Ottoman power had also weakened considerably from early 1917. The War

Cabinet, sensing an opportunity, sent Smuts to Palestine to discuss the strategic situation with Allenby and then report to London on the requirements for a successful advance to Damascus and Aleppo and, hopefully, a rapid victory in the eastern Mediterranean theatre. Smuts' proposals regarding large-scale reinforcement, in cavalry, infantry and air power, associated with a campaign of rapid manoeuvre, were approved, with minor amendment.[125]

Smuts did not have an easy time in London. He was feted and lionised, but was simultaneously the object of some distrust and much jealousy. Brigadier General Alfred Cavendish, the chief of the South African Military Command, in November 1917 described the South African general as 'that modern miracle' who 'for [the] beaten enemy … had a very nasty knack of asserting himself at times'.[126] Cavendish was recalled for having made these remarks and his career was effectively terminated.

France: mud and trenches

If North Africa is the forgotten campaign of the Great War, then France and the Western Front, where the opposing armies had settled down to a static war by the end of 1914, was the converse. Massed armies, industrialisation and the associated technological changes, particularly in the steel, engineering and chemical industries, had dramatically increased the potential for waging war. Infantrymen armed with rapid-fire rifles and improved machine guns took position in often-elaborate trench systems. Yet the development of heavier artillery, the high-explosive shell and toxic gases, together with the new technologies of radio and aircraft, could not bring a breakthrough on the Western Front. Technological change had given decisive advantage to the defence.[127]

Against this background, the mobilisation and training of the 1st South African Infantry Brigade, first in Potchefstroom and later in Britain, and then the brigade's diversion to Egypt for the campaign against the Senussi, had caused concern in South Africa. After succumbing to the early wave of war enthusiasm, most Anglo-South Africans had, by mid-1915, settled into a new realism. The accounts of the fighting in Europe were terrible. Archbishop Carter admitted that he did not understand how men could stand the brutality of it all. Yet, while he recognised that there were most probably 'worse things to come', he embraced the notion that the war was being fought for civilisation and justice and that, for these reasons, despite the horror, it was also 'all splendid'.[128] Soldiers, unsurprisingly, had other ideas. Cyril Newton-Thompson, the young South African serving with the Royal Horse Artillery in France, derided the generals, the politicians, a gullible public – in fact, everything about the war. At the start of the Battle of the Somme, he told his girlfriend that any gains would be more than offset by the losses, which would be appalling:

> The soldiers will have gone to their last long rest recking [sic] little of why it all was, except that they thought our cause the better, and it will be left to the historian and especially the student of military history to determine whether in the great offensive of June-July-August 1916 the game was worth the candle.[129]

As the elements of the South African expeditionary force approached the Western Front, the South African Parliament was prorogued after a most unwarlike session.[130] Debates over miners' phthisis and the university question seemed very South African, narrow and unimportant, against the backdrop of a global war and the vital imperial issues with which the conflict was seemingly associated.[131] Moreover, the political and military situation had not improved. Amid nationalist rhetoric and rumours of another rebellion, the silence from German East Africa seemed ominous. If the campaign seemed to be stalling there, at least the news from France was more encouraging, and, with the arrival of the South African expeditionary force, eyes were firmly fixed on the Western Front.[132]

The 1st South African Infantry Brigade arrived in Marseille from 20 April 1916 and entrained via Lyon to Versailles and then continued on to Abbeville.[133] They arrived at Hazebrouck on 23 April, where, for the first time, they experienced the artillery and aircraft activity then characteristic of the Western Front.[134] Over the next days, the regiments were kitted out (they found that 'the gas helmets already in possession' were 'the wrong pattern and unserviceable'). Much training was done, specifically in bayonet and trench fighting, bombing, attacking from trenches and 'moving up over ground swept by long range artillery fire to reinforce our own front line'.[135] The brigade, having moved to Le Bizet, was strafed for the first time on 20 May and was shelled repeatedly during the following days,[136] experiencing their first 8-inch shellfire on 23 May.[137] The brigade, having replaced 28 Brigade in the 9th (Scottish) Division, moved, 'often a very trying journey through the mud', to Grovetown

Valley on 30 June.[138] The South Africans, forming part of the corps reserve of General Sir Henry Rawlinson's Fourth Army, missed the bloody offensive on 1 July, the first day of the Battle of the Somme.[139]

Two medical outfits accompanied the brigade: a field ambulance and a general hospital.[140] The 1st SA Field Ambulance moved to France in April 1916, following the conclusion of the Senussi campaign in Egypt. The ambulance comprised three sections each, with three medical officers and 60 other ranks: A Section was the headquarters unit under the unit commander, while B and C sections were each under the command of a major. The sections were divided into tent and bearer subsections or divisions. The bearer divisions were placed with the brigade, while the tent divisions were grouped into a dressing station for wounded able to march the approximately six kilometres from the front line, a main dressing station (at the divisional headquarters) some 15 kilometres from the front line, and a corps rest area, some 22 kilometres from the front, where recuperating patients and the war-weary were taken up for final recovery. During the first phase of the Battle of the Somme this was at Chateau Corbie. Casualty evacuation was in the form of a chain; wounded able to march and bearer casualties were taken by regimental bearers (responsible for field dressing) to the regimental medical post. Wounded able to march were taken from here to the dressing stations, where they were further cared for by the staff of the Field Ambulance. Serious casualties were conveyed to 1st SA General Hospital, by either car or barge.[141]

The South African General Hospital had a staff of 21 officers, two warrant officers, 43 nursing sisters and 142 other ranks, of whom Major William Lennox Gordon and Sergeant Major Alex Knox have left small but rich collections of private papers.[142] Knox, on arriving at the port of Le Havre, noted what he termed 'several quaint customs of [the] French': 'Traffic on right of road, open sanitary conveniences, dirty aspect of town, absence of proper drainage systems.'[143] At the rest camp, they were accommodated in 'Bell tents on boards with only one blanket.'[144] Abbeville, as Knox diarised, was an important railhead and the advanced base on the lines of communication in the Somme valley. It was also a quaint town with a 'nice old abbey which shewed [sic] marks of bombardment of war of 1570/1571 still on walls'. The hospital was 'camped on [a] site adjoining No 2 Stationary Hospital just outside town itself on Doullens-Amiens Road to Arras. Hospital very much worked since rush of July 1st.'[145] The Field Ambulance was stationed there, temporarily only, Knox thought, to relieve pressure on No 2 Stationary Hospital, on a 'very small piece of ground pitched up against large cornfield no chance of expansion'. Temporary buildings were erected for the operating theatre and kitchens, with everything else in tents.[146] The personnel underwent training on the nature of static warfare and the handling of casualties exposed to gas and braced themselves for the impending flood of patients that would follow the coming offensive on the Somme.[147]

A considerable number of the artillerymen serving with the five South African heavy batteries had served in German South West Africa. They mobilised for service in France as the 71st, 72nd, 73rd, 74th and 75th Siege Batteries, Royal Garrison Artillery. In April 1916, a sixth battery, the 125th, was formed. Two further batteries, the 542nd and the 496th, were formed early in 1918 but were broken up when they arrived on the Western Front and their guns and personnel distributed among the other South African batteries. Also in 1918, the South African batteries were consolidated into two South African brigades of heavy artillery.[148] However, as the historian of 72nd Siege Battery noted, despite a 'wonderful keenness' displayed by all ranks, their 'training facilities were not of the best, for the guns at the disposal of the batteries were by no means up to date and new methods of warfare, suitable to the changed conditions on the Western front, were constantly being brought out'. Moreover, on arrival in Britain, it was suddenly announced that the batteries would be siege batteries, armed with 9.2–inch howitzers, 'a new weapon then under construction', and affiliated to the Royal Garrison Artillery.[149] This, Ernest Lane, one of the officers, thought a mistake:

> The greatest asset a South African has is his mobility and power to trek around, and they should have given us animal traction guns which are easier to learn how to handle, and then sent us off to some of the more distant and warmer scenes of war, whereas now we are siege artillery, tractor-drawn, with 9.2–inch howitzers that require the highest technical knowledge, and are likely to get to Flanders, where all the men will get horribly tucked up with cold.[150]

However, despite such gloomy forecasts, the batteries not only performed well but enjoyed a life far more pleasant than that experienced by the brigade. The 73rd Siege Battery, for example, was, in July 1916, 'comfortably billeted in farm buildings, while the guns were sited for camouflage purposes under fruit trees in an orchard' and 'at this time the surrounding country and village behind the lines showed little signs of war'. The battery's historian records that 'everything was fresh and green', a countryside that was beautiful and to be enjoyed, 'and the general consensus of opinion throughout the Battery was that the war – to quote the popular expression – was "a good war"'.[151] However, as the 73rd's historian noted, 'conditions gradually became harder'.[152]

The much-expected Allied offensive commenced in the Somme sector on 1 July. The South Africans all along the British sector of the line witnessed something of the opening of the offensive, and were eager recipients of early news passed back from fellow South Africans or captured Germans.[153] Before midday on 1 July, the first prisoners arrived in batches of 50 in Grovetown Valley. One prisoner told Captain Harry Bamford, of the 2nd South African Infantry (2 SAI), that the attack had been expected for the past four days. Their officers had told them that the Scottish divisions of the British Army were in front of them and that these divisions 'took no prisoners'. As a consequence, they had had no sleep for four days and nights![154] The massive bombardments, according to Bamford, were 'as intense an artillery bombardment as has ever been heard during the whole war on any front'.[155] And, with 'dead Bosches [Germans] … lying everywhere in their trenches and the ground beyond', the news was 'extremely good', and the South Africans were, Bamford records, 'anxious to be sent forward'.[156] Forming part of the XIII Corps Reserve, they were eager to be in the thick of the action. Back in South Africa, a news-hungry public, aware that the great offensive had commenced, eagerly awaited the first reports.[157]

The South African brigade moved forward on 3 July and entered the trenches on the edge of Bernafay Wood on 8 July. Here it was first blooded: the casualties since 1 July approached 1 000 and included Lieutenant Colonel FA Jones, the commander of the 4th South African Infantry Regiment (4 SAI). With Rawlinson's offensive against the German second line about to commence, Furse's 9th Division was tasked with the capture of Waterlot Farm, the village of Longueval and Delville Wood (*see* Map 4). The attack commenced on 14 July. The Springboks were initially held in reserve and entered the fray over the following days. The 1st South African Infantry Regiment (1 SAI), tasked with the clearance of Longueval, and two companies of 4 SAI, responsible for the clearance of Waterlot Farm, were the first in. They were ill-prepared for street fighting in Longueval, characterised by small-group action, close-quarter fighting and the flushing-out of German soldiers from positions of concealment, which, easily bypassed, became places for counterattack.

In the meantime, the remainder of the brigade moved up from Montauban

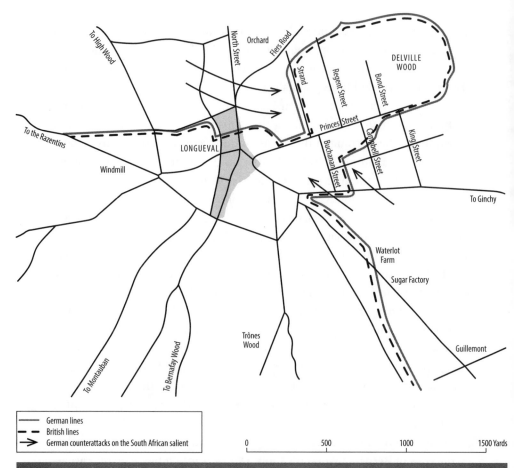

Map 4: **Longueval and Delville Wood – the situation on the evening of 17 July 1916**

in preparation for the impending attack on Delville Wood. Initial German resistance in the Wood was slight and, at first, the primary problem facing the Springboks was the 'profligate undergrowth and tangle of trees and branches brought down by artillery fire'.[158] Notwithstanding, by 2 pm on 15 July Delville Wood was in South African hands. But, in taking the Wood, the brigade had moved into a trap, for no sooner had they reached the northern edge than Germans began a fierce bombardment of the entire wood, a salient which had to be held in strength or lost.[159]

The new warfare, enormously destructive of life, exposed soldiers, and especially a vulnerable infantry, to appalling casualties. From 8 July, during the battles for Bernafay Wood and Trones Wood, and then for Longueval and Delville

Table 3.5: The killed and missing of the 1st South African Infantry Brigade, 14–20 July 1916								
Regiment	Total	14 July	15 July	16 July	17 July	18 July	19 July	20 July
1st SAI	192	13	2	27	26	114	5	5
2nd SAI	177	3	35	14	21	82	19	3
3rd SAI	145	1	29	33	20	32	17	13
4th SAI	156	1	28	40	27	32	25	3
Total	670	18	94	114	94	260	66	24
Percentage	100	3	14	17	14	39	10	3

Source: Ian Uys, *Rollcall: the Delville Wood story*, p 195.

Wood, casualties increased to the extent that the planned pattern of medical evacuation disintegrated. Casualties were heavy, and the bearers faced an enormous task in carrying wounded to the forward dressing station at Bernafay Wood. Staff Sergeant Walsh, of the bearer section, collected a Distinguished Conduct Medal. The movement of casualties from the dressing stations to the hospital was also no easy task; patients were dispatched by train, motor vehicle and, for the most serious cases, by barge on the Somme River.[160]

Table 3.5 shows that 39 per cent of the casualties occurred on a single day, 18 July, when, due to the arrival of large convoys of wounded, No 2 Stationary Hospital became more of a clearing station.[161] Over the following days, as the casualties among the South African infantry and South African Field Artillery increased, life at the South African hospital at Abbeville became more hectic. The hospital, now a receptacle for overflow from the nearby British hospital, as well as for cases that arrived directly, faced several difficulties. The first of these was dealing with the British hospital system, and the second was the weather. Having just taken up 243 new cases on 24 July, Knox records:

> Unsatisfactory methods by which these people kept their books made it extremely difficult at first to find out where we were. Everything in state of chaos. Temporary tents and operating theatres fixed up. Everything made exceedingly difficult and unpleasant by appearance of drizzling rain which left everything in about 3 inches of mud.[162]

Knox was 'fed up with [the] unsatisfactory way patients were left to the mercy of a willing and efficient but ill-equipped staff'.[163] The nature of the cases presented a third range of challenges. On 24 July, the South African hospital lost two patients from gas gangrene following gunshot wounds, all 'fearful wounds'

Table 3.6: Through-flow of patients at the South African General Hospital, Abbeville, July 1916					
Date	Incoming sick	Incoming wounded	Surgery performed	Further evacuation	Number of deaths daily
23 July				118	
24 July	140	103			
25 July	54			118	
26 July					
27 July		43			10
28 July	10	53	57*	143	

* Among these were many amputations resulting from gas gangrene caused by corrosive shells and gas shells.
Source: Diary, July 1916, NASAP: A164 Sergeant Major Alex J Knox Collection.

Knox thought.[164] The range of injuries varied from serious bullet and shell wounds to gassing and shell shock.[165] The following day was 'absolute hell'. The medical officers were pushed to the limit in the operating tents, as were the orderlies in the wards and the bearer division, which, under Major Pringle, worked hard conveying casualties to the field ambulance and on to the hospital.[166] Knox, an administration sergeant major, on some days spent a few hours in the theatre when not engaged in the evacuation of patients to England and elsewhere. His diary gives an impression of the work of the hospital, although accurate data cannot be compiled from it. Nonetheless, with 243 new patients on 24 July and the evacuation of 118 on 23 July and the same number two days later (*see* Table 3.6), the activity must have been frenzied.

The medical officers and orderlies were the first to hear of the 'terrible suffering of the Brigade in the Wood. Roll call only revealed 80 of each regiment, percentage of officers killed very large.'[167] As shown in Table 3.7, all of the officers of the 2nd and 3rd regiments became casualties, a record, Buchan noted, that equalled that of the 1st Coldstream and the 2nd Royal Scots Fusiliers at the First Battle of Ypres.[168] When Major WL Gordon paid a visit to the 1st Regiment on 16 August 1916, he found few of the friends he had made earlier in Egypt and France:

> There were not many of the men I knew. Most of the officers have been wounded. English and Tempany have both commissions. Tempany is wounded & English is away. Brown was killed, he had his commission for only a few minutes as he got it in the field.[169]

Regiment	On 14 July		On 20 July		Casualties between 14 and 20 July		Percentage of casualties	
	Officers	Ranks	Officers	Ranks	Officers	Ranks	Officers	Ranks
1st SAI	31	748	8	213	23	535	74	71.5
2nd SAI	26	669	2*	185	26	484	100	72
3rd SAI	29	847	1	104	28	743	96.5	88
4th SAI	27	672	7	183	20	489	74	73
Machine Gun Company	8	96	–	17	8	79	100	82
Totals	**121**	**3032**	**18**	**702**	**105**	**2330**	**87.5**	**77**

Table 3.7: **South African casualties at Longueval and Delville Wood, 14–20 July 1916 (fighting strength less all detached men)**

* These two officers were wounded but returned to duty.
Note: A considerable number of officers and other ranks who were slightly wounded in Bernafay Wood and the trenches between Maricourt and Montauban returned to duty within a few days and were killed or wounded in the later fighting. These Lukin showed only once as casualties.
Source: Schedule B to Despatch No III by Brig Gen HT Lukin, 14 August 1916, SANDF Documentation Centre: WO1DA, box 5, South African Infantry Brigade Headquarters, July 1916, Operations on the Somme.

The 1st SA Infantry Brigade and its field ambulance were withdrawn from the Longueval sector of the Somme front on 20 July. The nature of the war on the Western Front, which, though seemingly static, included the shifting of military units up and down the front and into reserve and back again, makes the South African deployment in France seem complicated. The artillery batteries were also sometimes withdrawn, only to be moved back into the line, sometimes at the same place, a few days or a few weeks later. However, two events loom large in the South African experience of the Somme campaign, marked purely by the intensity of the experience and the scale of the human losses. They are Delville Wood, where, between 1 July and 20 July, the South Africans suffered 3 155 casualties, and Butte de Warlencourt, where, that October, the brigade sustained a further 1 150 casualties (*see* Figure 3.2). In sum, the campaigns in Egypt and France claimed 4 454 South African lives and more than 10 000 wounded.

With the Allies attacking on all fronts, and the Russian advance supposedly going 'on and on like a song from Boris Godunov',[170] Germany's defeat must have seemed inevitable. At last, the South Africans were doing something, or were about to do something, and as part of an attack that, it seemed, would not 'fizzle out in a week'.[171] Moreover, the first newspaper reports, listing Allied successes, had an immediate effect in South Africa. Even *De Burger*

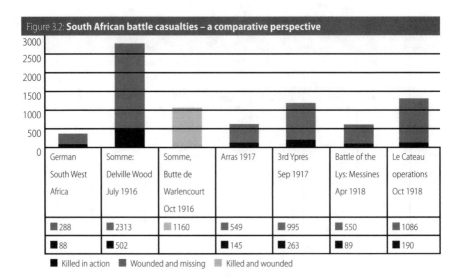

Figure 3.2: **South African battle casualties – a comparative perspective**

	German South West Africa	Somme: Delville Wood July 1916	Somme, Butte de Warlencourt Oct 1916	Arras 1917	3rd Ypres Sep 1917	Battle of the Lys: Messines Apr 1918	Le Cateau operations Oct 1918
Killed in action / Wounded and missing	■ 288	■ 2313	■ 1160	■ 549	■ 995	■ 550	■ 1086
	■ 88	■ 502		■ 145	■ 263	■ 89	■ 190

■ Killed in action ■ Wounded and missing ■ Killed and wounded

broadcast the news of South African success. The South African contingent, it proclaimed, had captured Delville Wood, 'een van de belangrijkste centra is van de vijand in deze streek' (one of the most important positions of the enemy in this region). Moreover, noting the casualties, *De Burger*, using considerable licence, praised the troops:

> de manschappen zich van hun taak hadden gekweten op een wijze, waar-over Zuid-Afrika inderdaad trots kan zijn. Toen het ogenblik aanbrak, dat zij over de verschansingen heen moesten springen en de zone binnengaan, welke door de machinegeweren bestreken werd, was er met een die aar-zelde. Er had slechts weinig handeschudden plaats voor de sprong, en toen weergalmde de zuidafrikaanse oorlogskreet. Enige minute later worstelden zij met de Hunnen op leven en dood, gebruik makende van de bajonet, de kolf en de sable, maar zij gingen vooruit over duitse lijken heen, over gebro-ken versperrigen, slagijzers en zo voort … roemrijke aandeel …[172]

(The men acquitted their task in a way in which South Africa can be justly proud. When the moment came, they went 'over the top' into a no-man's land and into the fire of enemy machine guns. Some shook hands before the jump, and then resounded the South African war cry. Moments later they were in a life and death struggle with the Huns, making use of the bayonet, the rifle

butt, and sword, but they continue forward over the German dead, over the
obstacles, the iron traps and so forth … a glorious part they played …)

The good war news bolstered British prestige and that of the Botha government, and so quietened Boer dissatisfaction. JBM Hertzog even published a
letter in the press, calling for restraint among the extremists in his party. Other
Nationalist leaders followed suit, expressing their intention of adhering to constitutional means in addressing grievances. English South Africans believed that
nationalists around the Empire were more careful, as a consequence of the
fate of Irish nationalists in the wake of the Easter Rising in Dublin. Yet, Maud
Wyndham felt it 'so different being away from it all'.[173] She wanted to be in the
midst of events, nursing soldiers in France or doing war work in London, where
she could hear 'everything rather than being in [South Africa] missing things,
even croaks and grumbles [which] I suppose go on all the time even now when
the news is so good – or at any rate veering slowly but surely in our favour'.[174]
Nonetheless, through July 1916, she thought the war news cheering, 'as progress
really seems steady on our side all round'. It made a great difference to read the
papers then. Formerly the allies 'were forever "retreating to straighten our line" or
to "consolidate our position"'.[175] Not for a moment doubting Germany's eventual
defeat, Mrs Wyndham dreaded 'all the unhappiness every hour' brought.[176]
However, no matter how terrible, she felt that at least they now had something
'to show for [the losses]'.[177]

The heavy casualties sustained by the brigade during July made the recruitment of reinforcements a 'most pressing necessity'.[178] In fact, on 4 July 1916,
before the brigade had entered the front line, the Army Council had raised
the matter of recruitment to fill the coming losses. A monthly intake of 10 per
cent of establishment was suggested.[179] Botha postponed his answer. He left for
German East Africa on 11 July to consult with Smuts.[180] By early August, when
he still had not replied, London probed Pretoria again.[181] Roland Bourne, the
civilian head of the Department of Defence, doubted whether they would be
able to recruit much more than Smuts' requirements for East Africa. However,
recognising that the brigade's situation was grave, owing to the very heavy casualties, Bourne suggested that they would soon know whether the East Africa
campaign was likely to be prolonged. If so, on Botha's return, they would make
a special recruiting effort, which, if successful, might even produce some 500
to 1 000 recruits for France, in addition to meeting the need for troops in
Tanganyika.[182]

Yet Botha, persistently unrealistic, still hoped to supply a complete division, with reserves, for France. An early end to the Tanganyika campaign would release men for Europe. Buxton, however, shared Bourne's caution. The Governor General warned Botha that, if South Africa was to field a division, he would need, in addition to the brigade already in France, a further 28 000 recruits over the next six months. Furthermore, as Buxton noted, mounted troops, even with the experience of the Afrikaner rebellion and the campaigns in South West Africa and Tanganyika, would not be of much use in France. A South African infantry division was, therefore, out of the question, and all that could be done to increase South African visibility in France would be to brigade the multifarious South African units together in the same division.[183]

Botha returned from Tanganyika knowing that the campaign there was not at an end. He knew, too, that there was 'no reasonable prospect of reopening recruiting for the 1st South African Infantry Brigade with any chance of success, and at the same time of keeping pace with the requirements of Union Imperial Service Infantry Units in East Africa for reinforcements to replace wastage.'[184] He faced two choices: await a successful conclusion to the campaign in Tanganyika before reopening the recruitment drives and then raise the additional units, allowing for the formation of a complete South African division;[185] or, recruit concurrently for both Smuts and Lukin. Botha, wanting to cover both his sub-imperial and prestige objectives, opted for the second.

Two recruiting campaigns started on 1 September. However, amid an outcry over pay[186] and complaints regarding the irregularity of supply in Tanganyika, far fewer recruits came forward than were expected. Following Botha's appeal of 17 August, 2 084 recruits were obtained, but only 146 were destined for the brigade in France. This fell far short of the 600 that was the minimum draft requirement. Yet, the Union Cabinet thought the general result of the appeal neither unsatisfactory nor surprising. The recruits had gravitated to East Africa for two reasons: they 'felt that the first call on them was for the arduous campaign close to their gates' and the fact that East Africa offered a better rate of pay. Although recruitment for the brigade in France was of the utmost importance, only 100 infantrymen left for Europe that October. The ministers requested the Army Council to 'understand the position' and the 'difficult circumstances' under which these arrangements were made.[187]

By September 1916, the offensive on the Somme had clearly petered out. Together with the mixed reports from German East Africa, where the progress was slow and the complaints many, this did much to undermine Botha's position at home. The failure of the recruitment drives was a symptom of this unpopularity. Keen to fill the drafts, some recruiting centres seemingly relaxed the race attestation policy, and possibly quite unconsciously. In September 1917 unofficial complaints from the front line in France arrived in Pretoria that a number of 'coloured men' had been attested and sent with the reinforcements for the 1st SA Infantry Brigade. The government, facing declining numbers of volunteers, found itself in a dilemma. Botha and Smuts appreciated the military service rendered by 'coloured' troops and were keen not to alienate this loyal sector of the community. Moreover, some of these men had already served in German South West Africa, and with merit: a certain Hulley had served with Hartigan's Horse and then with the SAMR and 9th SA Horse, attaining the rank of platoon sergeant.[188] But the Botha government was equally keen not to cause resentment among white troops, or to risk media exposure and the political capital the nationalists would no doubt make.[189] That October, the commander of the brigade's 2nd Reserve Battalion, in England, reported that 17 coloured men had arrived at Woking with the latest draft: the number gradually climbed over the ensuing weeks. These men were given the option of transferring to the Cape Auxiliary Horse Transport (CAHT) companies or of returning to the Union for discharge. All but two decided to return to South Africa rather than be transferred to CAHT companies. The gravity of the mistake was recognised immediately; the men would return with legitimate grievance and affect recruitment adversely. Smuts intervened, and the men were allowed to remain with the brigade and deploy to France. Action was taken to avoid the inclusion of 'coloured men' in future drafts. Greater cooperation between the attesting officers and the medical officers, who physically inspected recruits, was called for in cases of 'doubtful descent'. But the Union Defence Force had, by 1917, albeit by accident, its first mixed combat units.[190]

In early September 1916, faced with critical shortages of manpower in France, Whitehall asked Pretoria to enlist large numbers of black South Africans in labour battalions. The South African Native Labour Contingent (SANLC), although recruited and administered by the Department of Native Affairs, had a military organisation. By November, 4 000 men had been sent to Europe and further drafts followed throughout 1917.[191] In the end, more than 25 000 black men enlisted, some seeking adventure, others hoping to prove their loyalty to King and country. All would inevitably be disappointed by the meagre post-war returns. In France, they served in the harbours, most notably at Le Havre, Rouen and Dieppe, on the railways and in the shunting yards of

Picardy, and in quarrying stone, cutting trees and building roads, keeping the arteries of the war on the Western Front open. Their deployment to France evoked even greater criticism from Botha's opponents, who feared that these men would return to the Union experienced, emboldened and unwilling to conform once again to segregated South African society. As a result, the men of the SANLC were housed in compounds reminiscent of the mining compounds in South Africa, separated from contact with the women of France and the mix of foreign influences.[192]

On 21 February 1917, tragedy struck the SANLC and South African society. The transport ship SS *Mendi*, conveying 882 members of the SANLC to France, was struck by another troopship, the SS *Darrow*, off the Isle of Wight. The *Mendi* was lost, together with 615 men of the SANLC; just 267 were saved. According to legend, the men showed the utmost discipline and, facing certain death in the waters of the English Channel, are said to have performed a final dance on the deck before the *Mendi* disappeared beneath the waters. In an unusual gesture for the time, the South African Parliament adopted a motion of sympathy and all members rose to pay their respects to the dead black men. Grief poured out across the country, but some saw the death of the men as having wider import. The newspaper *Abantu-Batho* announced that 'they have died to set us free'.[193] This was wishful thinking, but the legend has since been embraced with sorrow and pride and is marked in various ways in post-apartheid South Africa and by the South African National Defence Force (SANDF).[194]

For white South Africa, the focus of commemoration has always been, most specifically, Delville Wood. This tradition commenced on 18 July 1917, when a large crowd gathered at the City Hall in Cape Town to mark the first Delville Wood Day. The tribute, offered 'to the memory of the noble band of South Africans who ... made the supreme sacrifice at Delville Wood under circumstances which have won imperishable glory for their country', was, as the *Cape Times* reported, 'most impressive ... and in every respect ... worthy of the great anniversary that it marked'.[195] And it was a great anniversary for several reasons. First, although the engagement was only an episode in the war on the Western Front, it signified far more than that to the South Africa of the day. Delville Wood was, according to John X Merriman, former Cape prime minister, 'the first stiff fight' in which the newborn UDF 'met under the most extreme conditions of modern warfare' and where they showed 'themselves not unequal to the dreadful task'. The Somme battlefield, and Delville Wood

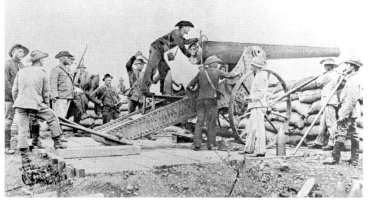

TOP: The dual problem of transport and supply: a Boer laager with wagons.
SOURCE: SANDF DOCUMENTATION CENTRE, NO 700000285.

MIDDLE: Boer artillerymen fire a Creusot gun during the siege of Kimberley: the use of larger ordnance could be maximised only if the battlefield was accessible and the enemy was willing or forced to fight on the defensive.
SOURCE: SANDF DOCUMENTATION CENTRE, NO 700000422.

BOTTOM: The British Guards Brigade enters Bloemfontein, following the relief of Kimberley and the battles of Modder River, Magersfontein and Paardeberg. The British came to realise that the centre of gravity of the Boer republics lay not in the towns but with the commandos.
SOURCE: SANDF DOCUMENTATION CENTRE, NO 700000465.

TOP: President MT Steyn (seated, centre) and his staff take an operational pause en route from Hectorspruit to Pilgrim's Rest in the Transvaal.
SOURCE: SANDF DOCUMENTATION CENTRE, NO 700010275.

MIDDLE: Christiaan de Wet, the elusive Boer pimpernel, in more leisured times.
SOURCE: SANDF DOCUMENTATION CENTRE, NO 761000406.

BOTTOM: Peace feelers: General Louis Botha and British counterparts at the Middelburg conference. Front row (left to right): Nicolaas de Wet, Louis Botha, Lord Kitchener, Colonel Hamilton; back row (left to right): Colonel Henderson, Van Velden, Major Watson, Fraser, Maxwell, De Jager.
SOURCE: SANDF DOCUMENTATION CENTRE, NO 771003262.

TOP: Farm burning: 'Your first object should be the capture of whatever they prize most, and the destruction or deprivation of which will probably bring the war most rapidly to a conclusion.' Kitchener's scorched-earth policy also absolved many surrendered Boers of their oaths of neutrality and impelled back into the field many of those who had drifted to their farms during the first phase of the war.
SOURCE: SANDF DOCUMENTATION CENTRE, NO 781000179.

MIDDLE: Deneys Reitz, trusted confidant of Jan Smuts, on commando during the Anglo-Boer War.
SOURCE: SANDF DOCUMENTATION CENTRE, NO 791000334.

BOTTOM: The Nkandla Forest, site of the main Zulu stand during the 1906 Bambatha rebellion in Natal.
SOURCE: SANDF DOCUMENTATION CENTRE, NO 761002487.

TOP: A Daniël Boonzaaier cartoon (circa 1912) on the nature of the new Union Defence Force, portrayed as eminently foreign to the youth of South Africa.
SOURCE: UNIVERSITY OF SOUTH AFRICA LIBRARIES, ARCHIVES AND MANUSCRIPTS DEPARTMENT.

MIDDLE: The Military School, Bloemfontein, established for the education and further training of Union officers, became a hotbed of disaffection.
SOURCE: SANDF DOCUMENTATION CENTRE, NO 781002190.

BOTTOM: Union officers in 1912: within two years they were at war with each other. In front are shown (from left to right) Jan Kemp, Christiaan Beyers and George Brand. In back (from left to right) are HCW Grothaus, Manie Maritz, FS van Manen, Ben Bouwer and Jack Pienaar.
SOURCE: SANDF DOCUMENTATION CENTRE, NO 781005733.

TOP: General Louis Botha, first prime minister of the Union of South Africa and general officer commanding the South African troops in the field in 1914: in July 1915 he presented the hard-pressed Allies with a much-needed campaign victory after Union troops invaded and took over German South West Africa.
SOURCE: SANDF DOCUMENTATION CENTRE, NO 700000126.

MIDDLE: General Louis Botha and his staff at Mushroom Valley where he defeated De Wet and ended the Afrikaner rebellion in the Orange Free State.
SOURCE: SANDF DOCUMENTATION CENTRE, NO 761002481.

BOTTOM: South African troops with German captives, during the UDF's lightning campaign in South West Africa.
SOURCE: SANDF DOCUMENTATION CENTRE, NO 771000469.

TOP: South African machine gunners
in Tanganyika, 1916: the East African
campaign presented a new set of
challenges in terms of terrain and the
maintenance of personnel and supply.
SOURCE: SANDF DOCUMENTATION CENTRE, NO
771003975.

MIDDLE: Waiting to advance: South
African infantry on the Somme front
in France.
SOURCE: SANDF DOCUMENTATION CENTRE, NO
200300698.

BOTTOM: Delville Wood: 'the bloodiest
battle-hell of 1916', according to Liddell
Hart, dominated South African memory
of the First World War.
SOURCE: NATIONAL LIBRARY OF SCOTLAND,
NO 74300984.

TOP: For members of the South African Native Labour Contingent (SANLC), the appalling conditions in France were reminiscent of mine compounds on the Rand. The transport ship SS *Mendi*, which sank off of the Isle of Wight on 21 February 1917, became an important alternative site of memory.
SOURCE: NATIONAL LIBRARY OF SCOTLAND, NO 7440897.

MIDDLE: The South African General Hospital in France: South African military casualties on the Western Front were more than 25 per cent of force strength, the highest of any of the country's campaigns.
SOURCE: SANDF DOCUMENTATION CENTRE, NO 781004262.

BOTTOM: A Daniël Boonzaaier cartoon of HT Lukin, in gladiatorial attire, on the Western Front, a place portrayed in the Afrikaner press as foreign to South Africa and the South African way of war.
SOURCE: UNIVERSITY OF SOUTH AFRICA LIBRARIES, ARCHIVES AND MANUSCRIPTS DEPARTMENT.

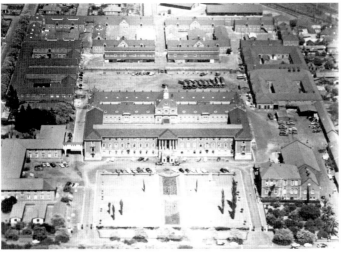

TOP: Troops were deployed on the streets of Johannesburg against striking mineworkers during the Rand Revolt, 1922. Smuts was unafraid to use the military internally, despite the criticism this drew.
SOURCE: SANDF DOCUMENTATION CENTRE, NO 991000973.

MIDDLE: The Defence Headquarters complex in Potgieter Street, Pretoria. The British government presented the ZAR State Artillery Barracks to the Union government for a wartime defence headquarters. The transfer was made permanent in 1921 and the new front wing of three floors was added from 1924.
SOURCE: SANDF DOCUMENTATION CENTRE, NO 781002910.

BOTTOM: The Ipumbu revolt in South West Africa, suppressed by the UDF in 1931, highlighted both the advantages and disadvantages of the application of armoured cars in African theatres.
SOURCE: SANDF DOCUMENTATION CENTRE, NO 991002085.

specifically, was, moreover, a sacred place where South Africans had stood together, and with the rest of the British world, against German militarism. And therefore, although 'only an episode in the great strife', it defined not only the grittiness of the South African soldier, but also the Union's place in the world and as part of the Allied coalition. It was, Merriman continued, South Africa's Thermopylae, its Morgarten.[196]

This line has been assumed, both by soldiers and historians, with the result that Delville Wood, South Africa's special part in the Battle of the Somme, looms large in South African military history. Contemporary soldiers played the first part in this construction,[197] which was used by the politicians and nation-builders of pre-1994 white South Africa. And, in a book published in 2006, Delville Wood is, yet again, billed as one of the 'seven battles that shaped South Africa'.[198]

These constructions, and the complicated nature of the South African deployment in the Western theatre, divergent and often unconnected, have slanted the historical record. Several South African units and formations served in France during the Battle of the Somme. The 1st SA Infantry Brigade formed the core of this presence, but did not fight in the vicinity of the five batteries of heavy artillery or the signal company or, of course, the South African General Hospital stationed near Abbeville. Besides, there were South Africans in many British battalions and regiments and in the Royal Flying Corps.[199]

However, the focus of the historian of South Africa's part in the campaign has always been with the infantry brigade, which was not only the most visible South African contribution 'to the main battle-ground' but also, to quote Buchan, claimed 'to have had no superior and not many equals'.[200] More recently, these studies, often simply chronicling events, have been supplemented by studies of the activities of the SANLC, which arrived in France in late 1916, too late for the Battle of the Somme.[201] During the past decade, much new work has been done in exploring both 'identity' and the meaning of the battle to a modern, collective new South Africanism.[202]

Apart from the South Africans who served with No 26 Squadron, several hundred South Africans volunteered for service with other RFC squadrons. Among them were Captain Alistair Miller, Andrew Weatherby Beauchamp-Proctor and Pierre van Ryneveld. Their numbers increased drastically from early 1918, when, following the spring German offensives, volunteers from around the Empire were sought. Piet van der Byl, at 29 almost too old for a pilot, and suffering from

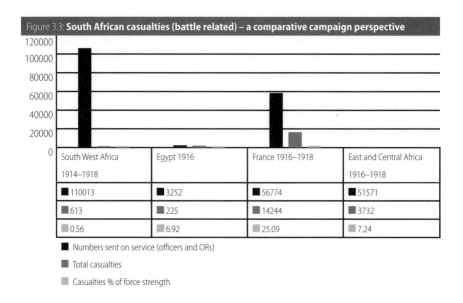

Figure 3.3: **South African casualties (battle related) – a comparative campaign perspective**

	South West Africa 1914–1918	Egypt 1916	France 1916–1918	East and Central Africa 1916–1918
■	110013	3252	56774	51571
■	613	225	14244	3732
▨	0.56	6.92	25.09	7.24

■ Numbers sent on service (officers and ORs)

■ Total casualties

▨ Casualties % of force strength

East African fever, possibly malaria, found himself at Upavon, the RAF's Central Flying School (the RFC became the RAF in April that year). There he immediately linked up with another South African, 'Duke' Meintjies, and a Rhodesian, Major 'Zulu' Lloyd, who was in command. The air force provided a welcoming home for young men eager to do their part, but also independent-minded, perhaps casual in dress, somewhat untidy in appearance and 'allergic to discipline of the barrack-square type'. They were rushed through training at an appalling rate to meet the need for more and more pilots.[203]

The war highlighted a number of deficiencies in the UDF, which during the war years underwent a number of organisational changes. On 2 August 1915 Brigadier General JJ Collyer's post of Staff Officer, General Staff Duties, was redesignated Chief Staff Officer, General Staff Duties and Adjutant General. The officer in charge of the Administrative Section became Quartermaster General and the head of the Medical Services Section became Director of Medical Services on 14 March 1916. On 4 June 1917 the post of Chief Staff Officer, General Staff Duties and Adjutant General was again altered, to become the Chief of the General Staff and Adjutant General, a post Collyer retained until retirement in March 1920, although the functions of the Adjutant General were separated from those of the General Staff Section on 28 May 1918. Until May 1918, all defence policy had been directed by the Defence minister through his civilian Secretary for Defence. Henceforth the Chief of the General Staff assumed responsibility for the coordination of all military staff work at Defence Headquarters and for the communication of the minister's wishes. Under him, the CGS had four sections: the General Staff Section, the Adjutant General, the Medical Services and the Quartermaster General.

For the Allied powers, the ostensible victors of the First World War, victory was bittersweet. For South Africa, this was little different. Although South Africa emerged physically unscathed, the price tag, in money and human sacrifice, had been high. The war cost South Africa some £31.5 million.[204] A total of 254 666 South Africans of all races served in uniform, comprising 146 897 whites, 25 000 coloureds and Indians, and 82 769 blacks. Of these 8 325 whites, 893 coloureds and Indians, and 3 136 blacks were killed in action or died on service. More than 30 000 South Africans experienced the horror of trench warfare on the Western Front, the accompanying devastation and the shocking casualty levels. Although South African casualties were comparatively low when compared with the other Dominions, most of the 7 241 killed had died on the Western Front. For South Africa, a country accustomed to limited wars and low casualties, such losses were unacceptable.

A number of South Africans went on from Europe to serve with the White Russian forces in the Russian Civil War (1918–1920). This is another little-studied aspect of the Union's Great War. Some autobiographical material and letters do exist, some of which appeared in *The Nongqai* between 1918 and 1920.[205] Although the exact number is unknown, as some men enlisted from the British forces – and for them there are no personnel cards at the SANDF Documentation Centre – their calibre was remarkable. Two won the VC and most of the others were also decorated. Distributed over the front, they served with the Cossacks at the Dwina River and trained White mounted infantry. Kenneth van der Spuy, having flown for the RFC, the SAAC and the RAF, formed and commanded an air force component based at Archangel.[206]

The experience of war and rebellion meant that country's wartime leadership was largely discredited, with government and military leaders widely viewed with suspicion. This was, of course, not a uniquely South African phenomenon. Generals, across the board, were blamed for the costly failures of the war and for the apparent waste of human life in a succession of offensives that gained little. Many South Africans saw Delville Wood as an example of this callousness. The South African leadership, although praised in Britain for their stance in support of the war, was, at times, both for the British sector in

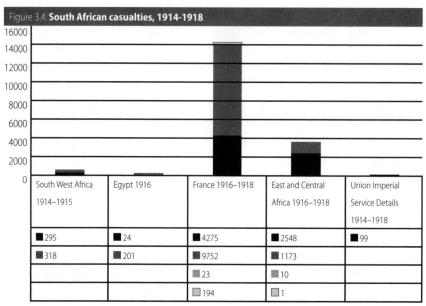

Figure 3.4: **South African casualties, 1914-1918**

	South West Africa 1914–1915	Egypt 1916	France 1916–1918	East and Central Africa 1916–1918	Union Imperial Service Details 1914–1918
Dead from all sources	295	24	4275	2548	99
Wounded	318	201	9752	1173	
Missing			23	10	
POWs			194	1	

Source: Adapted from *Statistics of the Military Effort of the British Empire during the Great War* (HMSO, London, 1922), p 772.

■ Dead from all sources ■ Wounded ▨ Missing ☐ POWs

South Africa and for the Afrikaner right, the object of amusement or scorn. Furthermore, the politicians were blamed for not facilitating a solution to the deadlock on the Western Front. The politicians, Cyril Newton-Thompson complained, were seemingly 'prepared to fight to the last drop of blood of the soldiers at the front'.[207] And they did not seem to have any answers to the problems, answers that soldiers at the front seemed to have had. To quote Newton-Thompson, who admitted he did 'not know enough about the interdependence of the German armies to know what effect our attack at the Somme has in helping the attack of our allies in other parts':

> The Allies must realise that if they are going to win this war (i.e. hands down) they must have roughly three men in the field to every two which the Germans and Austrians have and they must have three guns to every two German guns; and we must count three Italians as one man in reckoning our strength. If we settle down to this we shall win in the end. The hordes of Russia must be marshalled and discipline; the wavering Italians must be exhorted to action, and the drooping spirits of the French must be revived; above all John Bull must plunge deeper and deeper into debt and must be prepared to get over another

million of his stoutest sons killed and wounded in battle. Are we prepared to do all this? I wonder.[208]

The politicians were cast as callous, a true enemy of the soldiery, who fostered a collective victimhood. Emily Hobhouse blamed the politicians, 'who make troubles', for sending the troops in to be killed.[209] NW Nichol, voicing a popular sentiment, reckoned that 'there is no doubt the politicians ought to get it in the neck, it's an awful shame that the soldiers should be the only ones to suffer'.[210] The soldiers had been exposed to the brutality of warfare in Europe without proper training. There was a notion that colonial volunteers ought not to have been thrown into the line against German militarism.

South Africa went through several processes to arrive at the so-called lessons of the war. The first of these was conducted under HT Lukin and at the behest of Major General William Furse, the commander of the 9th (Scottish) Division, to which the South African brigade was attached in early 1916: 'The Division has done well in the recent fighting. We must now, while our several experiences are fresh in our memories, dig out and clarify by close discussion the lessons of the fighting so that we may do even better in the future.' Furse called for frankness and an inclusive process, based not on 'fault finding' but 'fact finding', so that 'the best way of dealing with similar situations in the future' could be discovered.[211] A list of 'subjects for enquiry' was distributed, and the South African report addressing numerous tactical matters, probably written by James Mitchell-Baker, the brigade major, was submitted by Lukin on 3 August 1916.[212] No doubt the report, as with hundreds of others generated between 1914 and 1918, influenced the growing insight that an abundance of artillery, of high-explosive shells, and skills needed to fight the new kind of war, were the keys to success.

As the Secretary for Defence, Sir Roland Bourne, declared in his official report on the war, published in 1921, this was a war on a scale not dreamed of in South Africa. In 1914 there had been no complete defence organisation. The normal function of a military organisation, Bourne argued, was to prepare in peacetime for the abnormal, namely, war. But, as he noted, in the Union they had of necessity to begin with the abnormal and, after almost ten years, could only move for the first time to the normal.[213] As will be seen in the next chapter, for South Africa the greatest impact of the Western Front experience was to be in the domain of foreign policy.

Conclusion

The First World War differed fundamentally from previous conflicts in terms of scope. Nations were fully mobilised, and the accompanying devastation and shocking casualty statistics were without parallel. For South Africa, attuned to small wars, limited 'native' campaigns, chiefly of pacification, and accustomed to low casualties, the change to total warfare and the experience of the Western Front was cataclysmic. The South African stand at Longueval and Delville Wood in 1916 lasted one week, from midday on 14 July to dusk on 20 July. This remained the most expensive week in South African military history until surpassed in 1942 by the surrender at Tobruk. The war, moreover, together with the rebellion and rumour of rebellion, had come at a political cost, increasing as it did popular suspicion of government, of leaders and of institutions like the military. It discredited Botha and Smuts, the wartime ministers, and, although temporarily aligning South Africa with the Allied powers, estranged Smuts and those of broader vision from the mass of Afrikaners.

Britain emerged from the conflict depleted and exhausted. This was the onset of retreat from empire, although much of Britain remained in denial until at least 1945. Paradoxically, the moment the Unionists chose to seize in order to draw South Africa closer to a so-called Greater Britain was, in the end, also the vehicle of imperial decline. In South Africa the nationalists, then largely still the Afrikaner far right, came out strong and ready to take power with Labour in 1924. The Great War opened a debate on participation in foreign wars, on the development, design and preparation of appropriate modern armed forces and on their use as foreign policy instruments in far-off theatres, on military planning and, as the Delville Wood and *Mendi* commemorations illustrate, on the interface between foreign campaigning and domestic politics.

CHAPTER FOUR

The Inter-war Years, 1919–1939

South Africa's military preparations in peace time were always on a modest scale. Often said to be too modest. The Union's general staff, in their reports to Parliament even before the war, complained that they were in the difficult position of being without a well-defined military policy. They complained of the poor condition of military equipment and about the financial limitations that, in effect, meant a poor combat effectiveness and military value of the defence force that existed in name only.[1]

— Frans Erasmus, circa 1950, excusing the poor state of the defence force

Thank God and the British Fleet
  For what I eat;
Thank God and the silent Navy
  For all this gravy;
Thank God and the Lower and Upper
  Decks for my Supper.[2]

— 'A very practical grace', 1 August 1919

The First World War ended on 11 November 1918 and the peace conference, arranged to settle the new world order, opened in Paris ten weeks later. All of the Allied and Associated powers, including the Union of South Africa, were present. South African generals Louis Botha and Jan Smuts argued for the mitigation of the sentence passed particularly against Germany, although both were equally determined to obtain possession of German South West Africa, a territory that Union troops had conquered and occupied in 1915, as well as a portion of Portuguese East Africa in exchange for a portion of German East Africa. However, Botha and Smuts left Paris with considerably less: a mandate was granted over South West Africa only.[3] Decades later, South Africa's trustee-ship over this territory would be disputed, leading to an extended bush war in Namibia and Angola (*see* Chapter Seven).

Botha returned to South Africa in July 1919, tired both physically and mentally. He died suddenly in August 1919, and Smuts, Minister of Defence and for so long heir apparent, became prime minister. Smuts set about rationalising the Union Defence Force from its war-inflated strength to more or less its pre-war status. 'An army', as a British general noted, 'is a depressing place after a great war.'[4] The period from 1918 was bleak for armed forces worldwide. Military innovation was difficult, and often the best personnel left the service. South Africa was no exception. The UDF was constrained almost immediately by influences that militated powerfully against development. Growing insecurity, following the rise of Hitler and the advent of Mussolini's African adventures, led again to a reshaping of defence policy during the 1930s. Yet, South Africa remained ill-prepared for the next war. This chapter investigates the difficult environment of the interwar years, analyses the reasons for the lack of military readiness in 1939 and explains these in terms of the politico-strategic context.

Defence policy, strategic calculations and threat perception

During the interwar period, reformers managed to institutionalise new ideas on warfare, but often in the face of a general staff and service organisations that did not always appreciate the potential of new forms of operations. This was done through the institutionalisation of the study of military history, and of the lessons of the last war, in service schools and colleges, through the writ-ing of doctrinal manuals, and through the creation of real operational units. As we have seen, for South Africa the process of deriving lessons had started during the war,[5] and it continued with a series of military publications between 1920 and 1939. These included several drill manuals and textbooks,[6] as well as the official history of the Great War, which appeared in 1924. The last-men-tioned, described later by Agar-Hamilton as having 'no outstanding merit',[7] was a tremendous disappointment to JJ Collyer, wartime chief of the General Staff, who had hoped for a utilitarian history that would draw lessons and provide instructional material.[8] Collyer, who was incidentally HT Lukin's brother-in-law, bridged the gap himself with two books, one on the South West Africa campaign (published 1937) and another on the East African campaign (published 1939).[9]

The First World War shattered any possibility for post-rebellion national reconciliation and left South Africans confused and deeply divided on the goals to be pursued and methods used. Even before it had ended, the traumatic experience of the war, combined with the apparent improvement of relations between Afrikaners and some English South Africans, and a growing preoccupation with domestic problems, produced a drastic re-ordering of national priorities. Smuts had placed foreign policy consistently near the top of the ranking of national concerns, but this was to change in the post-war period. By the time of JBM Hertzog's first term in government, foreign policy was well down on the list.[10]

Nowhere was the impact of the Western Front for South Africa greater than on the nation's foreign policy. In the very different climate of the mid-1920s, the debate over the war – that had not fully taken place at its end – assumed a central place in the larger, and at times quite vocal, debate over South African foreign policy. The basic issues remained. Firstly, there was the question of the morality of intervention. Ought South Africa to involve itself in foreign imperial wars? Closely associated with this was the aversion to technological warfare, for the *materielschlacht*.[11] Smuts himself wrote:

> There is much to make us profoundly sad and almost to despair of the future
> of the race when we see our greatest intellectual and scientific discoveries
> turned like so many daggers at the heart of civilization.[12]

The individual had to be recovered and returned to the centre stage, something, it seemed, that could be done more easily in Africa, where human skill seemed to count for more. This raises the second matter: the wisdom of the intervention. Europe, simply stated, was not the place for South African military ventures. The campaigns in German South West Africa and East Africa had been, as Buchan noted, 'frontier wars, fought for the immediate defence of her borders and her local interests'.[13] Sub-Saharan Africa was South Africa's backyard. Warfare in Europe had to be avoided, and after 1924, and the advent of the first Nationalist government, the UDF refocused on Africa, seemingly more suited to the South African way of war and where asymmetry would be to its advantage. France and the Western Front had been geographically foreign, the circumstances militarily unfamiliar.[14]

Immediately after the end of the First World War and the defeat of Germany, the only immediate threats to the security of the Union of South Africa were industrial trouble (which finally erupted in the form of the 1922 Rand Revolt) and African uprisings, with the latter holding the possibility of regional war. Although an intelligence sub-branch had been established at Defence Headquarters, Pretoria, in December 1917,[15] the War Office still supplied most of South Africa's strategic intelligence. Major Johann Leipoldt, the man posted to inaugurate this branch, was left to concentrate on the internal threat (the persistent rumours of 'native' unrest and industrial strikes) and the operations of enemy agents in neighbouring territories.[16] A full-time Intelligence Section was established at Defence Headquarters following the 1921 Imperial Conference, which conferred on South Africa the ultimate responsibility for the restoration of order in the event of an uprising in southern and central Africa.[17] The other possible danger to South Africa was a war between the United Kingdom and a European power that maintained a 'native' army in Africa. The problem of defence, therefore, no longer remained confined to African disturbances in the Union, but embraced happenings in the greater part of the continent.[18]

Geography and post-Versailles politics had combined to give South Africa reasonably safe and defensible borders. The 1922 Smuts-Churchill agreement left the Royal Navy responsible for the protection of the coastline, and, with Simon's Town now recognised as a British naval base, all of the reasonable risks of war seemed effectively covered. Germany had been driven out of Africa, South West Africa was in South African hands, Tanganyika had gone to Britain, and Portugal was a traditional and trusted ally. There was now no apparent danger of attack overland. In any case, the possible overland routes were limited, the potential European enemies geographically distant, and any potential African opponents at a technological disadvantage. The government of National Party leader JBM Hertzog, which came to power in a coalition with Labour in 1924, could, as a result, settle into an easy military economy. Hertzog, who remained in Tuynhuys until September 1939, would avoid foreign deployments, especially if these were 'outside Africa'.

The National Party, in opposition, equated military and industrial power with Smuts, holism and a so-called Greater Britain.[19] The war experience had provoked strong opposition to military intervention abroad, particularly in aid of Britain and in support of objects perceived to be British or imperial rather than South African.

The indifference and tendency toward withdrawal, so manifest immediately after the war, also declined in the following decades as the Nationalists grappled with the difficulty of having to marry ideology and reality. With time, three broad principles emerged. Firstly, the zone of deployment was definitely Africa, and the UDF would only be deployed for the immediate defence of South Africa, where it would enjoy the advantages of technological asymmetry. By implication, it also meant that the UDF would never again be deployed to Europe and that European-style warfare would be avoided. Secondly, the UDF would be a small force, but well-equipped for its purpose. There would be an emphasis on mounted infantry, and a small air force, but there would be little room for mechanisation, as the limited transport infrastructure in Africa pointed to little use for it. At the same time, the UDF would be sufficiently lethal to deal with internal conflict, and sufficiently potent not to run the risk of casualties. This would be seen clearly at Bulhoek and during the Bondelswarts uprising, the Rand Revolt of 1922 and the Ipumbu uprising of 1931, where the UDF, deployed in three of these cases to conduct punitive operations, had a great psychological advantage.

There were several constraints, however. For one, there was no common vision on who constituted the most likely enemy. Interestingly, the threat perceptions had changed little since the turn of the century. With the defeat of Germany, France was seen, during the 1920s, as the European power most capable of projecting force intercontinentally. During the 1930s, Italy and Germany were assessed as the greater threats. Nationalist politicians, and their supporters within the military, reckoned Britain a threat, either as a possible foe or as the mechanism through which South Africa would be dragged into another war.

There was also the threat of landward invasion from continental Africa, which might take the form of a colonial power with imperial objectives or the possibility of an African revolt against colonial rule sweeping south, possibly a mutiny by the Force Publique of the Belgian Congo.[20] Three assumptions underlay Nationalist policy: there would be time for mobilisation; the war would be mobile and in the African bush north of the border; and South African cities and town would be safe from air attack.[21] A third threat was that of an internal uprising by African nationalists or syndicalised labour within South Africa itself.

For the first contingency – the threat from a European power – there was the Royal Navy. But for the second and particularly the third contingency, South Africa, they argued, was vulnerable. In time, various measures would be taken to buttress the defence force, which had been stripped out for reasons of economic efficiency, and counterstrategies to meet each of the three contingencies were designed and, by degree, implemented. These measures, sometimes meaningful, but often feeble, included increased professionalism in the military, appointments based upon military merit rather than political affiliation, the search for alliances and re-equipment.

The 1930s brought several triggers for defence growth and a re-examination of defence policy. The first was the creation of the so-called Fusion government in 1933 and the appointment of Oswald Pirow as Defence minister. Second was the improving economy, which led to Pirow's five-year plans. The third was the Italian occupation of Abyssinia in 1936 and the sudden realisation that small advances would bring South Africa within striking range of Italian air bases. Moreover, Germany made diplomatic moves to recover its lost colonies. All the while, the Royal Navy was facing competition from the aggressive naval building programmes of Germany, the United States, Japan and Italy. The strategic landscape had changed suddenly, but the UDF, facing no immediate land-based threat, was designed to meet an enemy on African soil, somewhere near the equator, and in bush warfare.[22]

Demobilisation, rationalisation and reorganisation

After 1918, South Africa followed a policy of strict economy and retrenchment. Although the Active Citizen Force (ACF) regiments raised during the German South West Africa campaign were already demobilised in 1917,[23] most of the temporary wartime units were disbanded with effect from 31 December 1919. During this process, most of the volunteer units that had served so meritoriously during the First World War were disbanded or demobilised. Of the engineer units, only the Cape Fortress Engineers remained to maintain the defence electric lights (searchlights) and telephone equipment in the Cape Fortress.[24] By July 1919, the SAMC units of the Active Citizen Force had ceased to exist, the Medical Training School was closed and an ever-decreasing number of personnel were serving at the various hospitals in the Union and in South West Africa. As the demobilisation proceeded, the number of medical officers was further reduced until sufficient medical support remained for the requirements of only one or two mounted regiments.[25]

The Chief of the General Staff assumed the functions of the Commandant of Cadets in 1919, and three years later the work of the Secretary for Defence. The post of Inspector General was abolished on 30 November 1921, when the

Adjutant General took over the work of that section. The return of civilian rule to South West Africa also had its effect on the size of the Union Defence Force. Two mounted regiments of Military Constabulary, together with the Protectorate Garrison Regiment, were disbanded on 30 June 1920 and replaced by a civilian police force called the South West African Police.[26] The remainder of the troops arriving back in the Union were all demobilised. Yet, this process was barely over when new realities emerged.

In many ways, 1921 was a watershed year in the history of the UDF. Its importance was signalled by the final withdrawal of the imperial garrison from South Africa, the concomitant transfer of all War Office and certain Admiralty property in South Africa to the UDF during 1920 and 1921, and the 1921 Imperial Conference, which identified a range of threats to the security of the Union, including those which might jeopardise imperial interests locally and abroad. Such flashpoints were indeed witnessed in 1922.

The continued presence of a British garrison in South Africa was a politically loaded question and related to the whole issue of demobilisation. Smuts believed the return of an imperial garrison after the war to be unnecessary. After all, between 1914 and 1918, South Africa had proven itself not only loyal but also capable of defending itself. Furthermore, imperial defence had to be reconsidered in the light of the new conditions brought about by the war, and particularly by the defeat of Germany and the removal of the menace previously associated with the German colonies. An attack on the Cape defences was even more unlikely than it had been in 1914. Defensive measures against a seaborne attack were unwarranted, and, in view of the absence of an immediate external threat, Smuts believed that the return of the garrison to South Africa would be a clear indication that Britain did not fully trust the loyalty of its South African subjects.[27]

Toward the end of 1920, the decision, for so long pending, to withdraw the imperial garrison in its entirety, was finally taken in London and what was called the South African Military Command was closed on 1 December 1921.[28] As a result, most of the cantonments and defences belonging to the War Office and the Admiralty were handed over to the UDF. The poor state of many of these buildings and the need for an efficient maintenance organisation to undertake the work proved cardinal to the establishment of the South African Engineer Corps (SAEC) in 1923.[29]

After 1918, the only immediate threat to the security of South Africa was the internal unrest that manifested in periodic 'native uprisings' and the industrial trouble that finally erupted with force in January 1922. The former had occurred almost annually since the disturbances at Grahamstown in April 1917, and clearly underlined the important role the Defence Rifle Associations, and later the commandos, had to play in territorial defence when the Permanent and Citizen forces were otherwise deployed.[30]

Technology, military innovation and organisational politics

Black people lacked the means to oppose the growth and monopolisation of military power in South Africa by people of largely European descent. The Union Defence Force was all-white, and the more than 20 000 blacks who served in the Great War did so largely as unarmed labourers. The exception was the 18 000–strong Cape Corps, whose members had served meritoriously in East Africa and Palestine, and which was only disbanded in the face of political pressure.

Resistance to white rule was impaired not only by lack of access to modern weapons and training but also by cultural and historical differences. Despite white fears, the chance of a general rising was remote. Some members of the urbanised black elite subsequently went to the Soviet Union for training. Some, victims of the Stalinist purges of the 1930s, never returned. Albert Nzula, the first black secretary general of the Communist Party of South Africa (CPSA), dragged out of a meeting in Moscow by two Soviet agents and never seen again, was not the only case.[31] African traditional leaders, in awkward suspension between state responsibility and community support, did not cooperate militarily, and when one fell afoul of the law he almost invariably faced the state as an individual.[32]

When traditional or religious leaders challenged the state, the lack both of cooperation and modern weaponry brought a predictable result. With the Israelite Rebellion of May 1921, the Union faced one of the more serious 'disturbances' of the 1920s. The UDF provided half a battery of artillery, a medical officer, a motor ambulance and a stretcher party in support of the South African Police.[33] In the end, no use was made of the artillery, and the Israelite attack at Bulhoek was repulsed by rifle and machine-gun fire, with considerable loss to the Israelites: 167 dead, 132 wounded and some 100 captured.[34] The police casualties were one man stabbed in the stomach, one man cut over the hand and one horse killed.[35] Superior weapons clearly decided the day, with no use being made of the UDF.

The Bulhoek incident had, nonetheless, caught the security forces off guard.

The Department of Defence had made no budgetary provision for military emergencies, and certainly none for police duties.[36] In fact, in November 1920, as the problem at Bulhoek was developing, Brigadier General AJE (Andries) Brink, then Chief of the General Staff, submitted proposals to reorganise the Permanent Force and to replace the South African Mounted Riflemen (SAMR) with a combat-ready and mobile force of 2 500.[37] However, financial considerations scuttled the idea. In May 1921, the UDF could not provide military assistance to the police in excess of 150 to 200 SAMR details. Beyond this and a small garrison of SAMR, and 450 returned soldiers, the UDF had no troops available to assist the police in maintaining order. The troops at Cape Town could, in any case, not be removed from the Cape Peninsula except in the event of a very serious emergency. The only other option was to call out the Citizen Force by proclamation,[38] as happened in 1922 to quell the Rand Revolt.

By the early 1920s, two other threats to white South Africa had come to the fore. The first of these was Pan-Africanism, which presented the potential danger of a general African uprising against European rule. The second was a war between the United Kingdom and a European power that maintained a native army in Africa.

In terms of the second scenario, South Africa could find itself drawn into an African war involving the colonies of two or more European powers entangled in a war in Europe. Whereas South Africa, like other British territories on the continent, followed a policy of disarming all black Africans, the French, Belgian and Portuguese colonial administrations openly militarised vast numbers of their colonial subjects. By 1926, the Force Publique, the colonial gendarmerie of the Belgian Congo, numbered 16 650 troops under a white leadership of only 450.[39] (By comparison, there were only 168 Permanent Force officers in the entire UDF in 1923, and this included officers seconded from the imperial forces.)[40] The problem of defence, therefore, no longer remained confined to disturbances within the Union, but embraced happenings in the greater part of Africa.[41]

Furthermore, the British, tied down in various parts of the world, had become involved in a number of military operations that not only pressed the taxpayer but also stretched to the maximum the deployment of their overseas forces. Britain therefore planned to delegate certain of its military responsibilities to the Dominions during the 1921 Imperial Conference. Although the War Office did not expect a major war for the next five to ten years, it was anxious that each Dominion give an indication of the maximum strength they could send in an emergency. The various Dominions were equally reluctant to make unconditional commitments. The War Office, however, stressed that it was not intended that the Dominions should surrender in advance their discretion as to whether they would undertake any particular operation at any particular time, since their action would necessarily depend on the political circumstances when the emergency arose. Furthermore, time and geography could make Dominion contributions vital, as these troops, in some cases, could reach theatres of operation thousands of kilometres away from Europe, weeks before the arrival of British troops.

Although the chief concerns of the conference included the problem of the Anglo-Japanese alliance and relations between Britain and the Dominions, the question of imperial defence was the most vital. Previous attempts at imperial defence planning had failed. The Committee for Imperial Defence, formed in 1902 in the wake of the Anglo-Boer War, was purely advisory and achieved little. The Imperial General Staff had been established in 1907, but the Dominions had refused to make any definite commitments. In 1911, Canada and South Africa shot down a New Zealand-sponsored proposal for an imperial defence council, although this did not prevent Louis Botha from accepting a general's rank in the British Army a year later![42]

The conference also aimed to implement a number of general measures. These included the coordination of military thought throughout the Empire by means of regular liaison letters and exchanges of personnel for military courses. The standardisation of establishments and equipment, manpower distribution schemes, the supply of war materiel and the collection and coordination of intelligence were also discussed.[43] However, as Martin Kitchen has pointed out, 'to keep the Empire together Britain had to [be] tolerant and reasonable'.[44] The training of South Africans at Woolwich, Cranwell and Dartmouth had little impact. There were too few officers – the quotas could not be maintained because of problems in passing both the literacy and physical tests in South Africa[45] – and most of those who did come to the United Kingdom were subsequently seconded to British forces (*see* Figure 4.1). There were exceptions, most notably Dan Pienaar (1893–1942) and George Brink (1889–1971).

Major General Dan Pienaar, later the hero of the Abyssinian campaign (1940–1941) and commander of the 1st South African Infantry Division at the Battle of El Alamein, attended several arms courses in the United Kingdom and lectured in gunnery and mapping at the South African Military College in the 1920s.[46] Lieutenant General George Brink, the creator of the South African expeditionary force during the Second World War and first commander of the

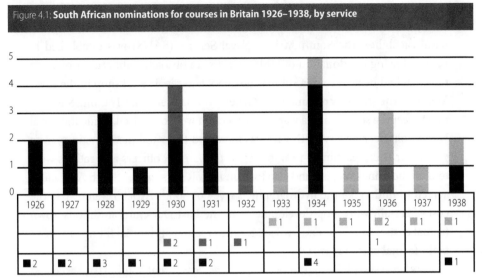

Figure 4.1: **South African nominations for courses in Britain 1926–1938, by service**

	1926	1927	1928	1929	1930	1931	1932	1933	1934	1935	1936	1937	1938
								▨1	▨1	▨1	▨2	▨1	▨1
				■2	■1	■1					1		
	■2	■2	■3	■1	■2	■2			■4				■1

Note: No nominations were made before 1926.
Source: Annual Reports of the Department of Defence, 1925–1939.
▨ RAF   ■ Royal Navy   ■ British Army

1st South African Infantry Division, was a classmate of Bernard Montgomery, Bernard Paget and Richard O'Connor and reckoned his time at the Staff College, Camberley, to have been of 'inestimable value'. Brink, his biographer tells us, 'was assiduous in assimilating data on military organisation and administration. He continued to study on his own. To the end of his life his reading, apart from newspapers and periodicals, consisted largely of political and military history.'[47] Brink became Chief Instructor, Tactics, at the Military College after the Rand Revolt, a position he held for nine years. There he influenced the Permanent Force and Active Citizen Force officers, from whose ranks the Second World War leadership was drawn. Under his guidance, junior officers studied the art of war at the tactical level, while senior officers deliberated on the command and logistics of larger formations. Commissioned by Defence minister Oswald Pirow, Brink went on a study visit to Europe in 1937. There he studied the British armed forces, those of France, Italy and potential enemies in Africa and, above all, Germany. Brink returned brimming with ideas to revitalise the UDF.[48] His zeal and progressive spirit are impressive, particularly when seen against the gloomy background of the era.

South Africa in 1921 recognised an obligation to contribute on a more equitable basis to the naval requirements of the Empire.[49] Until then the Union had maintained no permanent naval forces but made an annual cash contribution of £85 000 to the Admiralty. These now ceased and South Africa developed a naval capability. The South African Naval Service (SANS) was established in 1922, following the donation of HMS *Thames*, an obsolete light cruiser of 4 050 tons that had been used as a submarine depot and repair workshop in the River Medway. The ship was renamed the 'General Botha Memorial Training Ship'.[50] A minesweeping section and a war reserve section were organised, while the Royal Naval Volunteer Reserve (RNVR) was increased from 309 members in 1921, to 750 a year later, reaching a peak of 857 in 1933. SANS officers and ratings were to man the minesweepers and also to train RNVR personnel.[51] South Africa also agreed to undertake the hydrographic survey of South African waters, pay the cost of certain workshop developments in the East Dockyard at Simon's Town (actual cost of £192 188) and provide for the erection and initial filling of two oil tanks (actual cost £123 179).[52]

Another result of the 1921 Imperial Conference was that South Africa accepted the responsibility for colonial policing in southern and central Africa. The country could, it was thought, raise a force of sufficient strength to deal with any rising south of the Zambezi River, and, by the end of the conference, South Africa had in effect accepted ultimate responsibility for the restoration of order should local colonial forces fail.[53]

The air arm was considered most effective, for financial and moral reasons, and, despite the policy of strict economy that was applied immediately after the war, a South African Air Force (SAAF) was established.[54] Smuts had spent a good portion of 1917 in London, where he had drafted two reports on air warfare. In the second, more seminal, report he forecast the role for the new service:

> Unlike artillery, an air fleet can conduct extensive operations far from, and independent of, both armies and navies. As far as can be foreseen, there is absolutely no limit to the scale of its future use, and the day may not be far off when aerial operations, with their devastation of enemy lands and destruction of industrial and populous centres on a vast scale, may become the principal operations of war, to which the older forms of military and naval operations may become secondary and subordinate ...[55]

Smuts was a man for gadgets. He liked 'the big thing rather than the adequate but unspectacular'.[56] The report, with its fantastic concepts and particularly the idea of a separate, autonomous air force, was not well received. Animosity among anti-Boer British officers played a role. To many a British officer, South Africa was still perceived as the 'beaten enemy' of the Anglo-Boer War. Nevertheless, despite the opposition and the difficulties posed by climate, obsolete aircraft, inadequate logistic support and financial stringency, air policing was applied in South Africa and elsewhere to great effect throughout the inter-war era. And while vocal minorities denounced the application of air power, and particularly against tribesmen, as inhuman and unworthy of civilised nations, poor communications allowed the harsh effects of aerial bombardment in colonial contexts to continue for as long as it did.[57] The following decade saw South Africa still focusing on the cost-effective, and Britain upon what was considered more humane. In 1935, the Acting British High Commissioner, Edward Evans, declined a South African offer of a bomber for punitive use against the Khama regent at Serowe.[58] Whereas criticism of 'policing dissident tribesmen from the air [attracted] both operational and moral criticism' in the United Kingdom, and brought an expansion in the role of ground forces, this was not so in South Africa, where the air force retained its novel appeal and special claim on the budget, and had a loud voice in the person of its executive commander, Colonel Sir Pierre van Ryneveld.[59] The establishment of the SAAF and SANS was only made possible by the donation of equipment. The fledgling air force comprised two squadrons of three flights, each of six aircraft, with a depot and a repair and aircraft parts workshop. Van Ryneveld, the vainglorious airman knighted after his epic flight from London to Cape Town in February-March 1920, also headed the Air Service Section at Defence Headquarters.[60]

The added responsibilities brought about by the withdrawal of the imperial garrison and the assignment of responsibility for imperial policing placed the Union Defence Force in a dubious position. The tiny post-war defence force was now tasked with the entire defence of the Union, and with the suppression of any 'native insurrections' in the Portuguese colonies, Matebeleland, Mashonaland and in the High Commission territories of southern and central Africa – Swaziland, Basutoland, Bechuanaland and Barotseland.

This presented something of a predicament. The Bulhoek incident had revealed severe inadequacies in the UDF and, in 1921, there was no regular means of gauging the state of affairs to the north of the Union borders, beyond the information occasionally supplied by the Imperial Secretary. This immediately led to the re-establishment of an Intelligence branch within the office of the Chief of the General Staff on 1 September 1923, and closer liaison with the colonial administrations to the north.[61]

The intelligence situation at home was equally bad. The UDF lacked maps of more than half of the surface of South Africa itself. Good military maps existed only for the 'old trouble spots', including the Orange Free State, Basutoland and the Kalahari south of the Orange River to latitude 31 degrees. Moreover, no maps suitable for operations were available for practically the whole of the South African coast.[62] In January 1923, HMSAS *Protea* commenced survey operations at St Helena Bay. Strategically situated near Cape Town, this bay was identified as the most likely beachhead for an invasion force.[63] The situation in the interior was only slightly better. By 1921, Major JGW Leipoldt, a surveyor by profession, had surveyed the headwaters of the Okavango and Kwande rivers and the Lunge-Vungo River to within 160 kilometres of the Northern Rhodesian frontier, and was working on the Zambezi waterways. These surveys, although commissioned by the Department of Agriculture, were vitally important to the UDF and the planning for potential war against the Portuguese colonies.[64]

During the Rand Revolt of 1922, the Permanent Force proved totally inadequate to deal with the uprising of striking miners, and this necessitated the calling-up of not only the Citizen Force but also the Class A Reserve. Furthermore, when the alarm was received in Roberts Heights, there was 'utter confusion due to [the] lack of [a] Brigade headquarters to issue orders'.[65] The orderly officer issued the orders and valuable time was lost in dispatching orders to the individual artillery batteries of the SAMR. The crisis highlighted the need for a brigade headquarters with authority, continuously responsible for the training, administration and discipline of two or more units of the same arm of the service when stationed and working together.[66] The 1922 Defence Amendment Act provided for the formation of an Artillery Brigade Headquarters.

The nascent air arm was very much in line with the ideas mooted by Smuts and Trenchard regarding the use of air power in the policing of the colonies. It was economical in terms of both finances and manpower, but also held many other advantages. Air power was thought to be more humane and decisive, to elicit fear, and to be almost immune to ground attack at the time. The effect of air power was demonstrated in South West Africa in 1922, during the suppression of the Bondelswarts, after South African ground forces, including two field guns and 100 mounted troops, had failed to defeat Abraham Morris and his men at Haib. Morris, who had led a revolt in southern South West Africa against German rule, had served as a guide for Lukin's force in September 1914. Notwithstanding, he resisted South African occupation after 1915 and was considered to be 'the cleverest [and most dangerous] Native' in

Namaqualand.[67] He and his followers sought refuge in one of their traditional strongholds, the Fish River Canyon, which proved quite inaccessible to their pursuers. Eventually, two airmen, cooperating with the ground forces, forced a surrender within a matter of days. The ground forces were prone to ambush, constantly harassed by enemy raiders and held up in the mountain passes. Demonstration flights over Keetmanshoop put an end to further 'trouble' and the contingent returned to Pretoria as early as 3 July 1922.[68]

A more sophisticated defence force was required. The Rand Revolt and the Bondelswarts uprising had highlighted the importance of air power, with the latter seemingly emphasising the problems surrounding the deployment of ground troops in unfamiliar, broken terrain. The South Africa Defence Act, designed in 1912 as a temporary measure to bring four disparate colonial defence forces together, was accordingly amended in 1922. The amended Act provided for a total reorganisation of the Permanent Force, including the amalgamation of the five SAMR regiments into a single regiment of mounted riflemen. The various forces that constituted the UDF were brought under a single headquarters staff. Provision was also made for an instructional and administrative staff as well as specialised Permanent Force units. The latter included garrison and field artillery, regiments of mounted or dismounted riflemen, the South African Engineer Corps and the SAAF.[69]

Although the specialised units were 'reserved' for the support of infantry operations within South Africa, their value as suppliers of a nucleus of trained personnel for an expeditionary force was also recognised. In 1921, Britain had raised the question of Dominion support for its military efforts elsewhere in the world. As we have seen, this was a delicate issue in South Africa. The opposition National Party was vehemently opposed to the dispatch of a South African contingent overseas, but the UDF had by then withered from a strength of 254 666 during the First World War to a meagre 39 667.[70]

The 1921 Imperial Conference had spoken optimistically of 'a united understanding and common action in foreign policy' for the British Empire.[71] The world was notified that the Empire followed a combined foreign policy. However, a year after the conference, a series of events proved beyond all doubt that it was simply not possible to formulate one common policy for an entity subject to so many insecurities, stresses and variables as the British Empire.[72]

The war in Asia Minor, and the so-called Chanak crisis, underlined some of the flaws in the defence policy of the Empire. Britain had committed itself to provide support for Greece in the latter's war against Turkey. However, as a result of the demobilisation and rationalisation that had taken place after 1919, South Africa found itself to be without the necessary military infrastructure to act in concert with the imperial authorities should this be required. As the Permanent Force was not available for overseas service, such a contingent would be composed entirely of volunteers, many perhaps coming from the Active Citizen Force. Taking as a guide the numbers who had volunteered for service during the First World War, London estimated that South Africa could furnish a force of 25 000 men for service abroad. However, in the event of heavy casualties on the scale of the Western Front, the Union could not keep such a contingent in the field for more than a year. Based on previous experience, the minimum force that could be raised in response to any appeal for a contingent to serve overseas was 10 000, with a strong Native Labour Contingent.[73] No matter how willing, South Africa could barely provide the composite brigade considered 'a fair contribution' by the War Office.[74]

Smuts too did not want to risk a repeat of the Afrikaner rebellion, which had broken out in September 1914 on precisely this issue. Hertzog was firmly opposed to Britain's attempt to rescue Greece.[75] In a speech at Clanwilliam, Dr DF Malan (National Party MP for Calvinia) denied that South Africa had any agreement or obligation, legal or moral, to help Britain with her wars: 'Die Dardanelle is nie 'n druppel van ons bloed of 'n sjieling van ons geld wêrd nie, en Suidafrika behoort hom neutral te verklaar' (The Dardanelles are not worth a drop of our blood or a shilling from our treasure, and South Africa should maintain neutrality).[76] Over the following month, the National Party made use of every opportunity to again lay down their traditional policy of neutrality. On 22 September 1922, Tielman Roos (National Party MP for Lichtenburg) was quoted in the press:

> Ons is absoluut daarteen gekant om die Unie te stoot in die bynes van Eropese en Asiatiese politiek en oorloë. Dus sal die Nasionale Party veg teen die versending van 'n enkele Afrikaner-Engels- of Afrikaans-sprekende – en die uitgawe van 'n enkele pennie in verband daarmee. Ons mede-burgers van Engles, van Hollands en van ander afstamming, is vir ons te veel wêrd om hulle daar te verloor. Ons het hulle nodig om Suid-Afrika op te voer.[77]

> (We are absolutely opposed to pushing the Union into the beehive of European and Asian politics and wars. The National Party will therefore

fight against the dispatch of a single South African and the expense of a single penny in this connection.)

Fortunately for Smuts, the whole matter simply blew over. When the call came from London, he was away in Natal, remote from telegraph, telephone and wireless. In his absence, no decision could be taken, and upon his return the crisis at Chanak had dissipated. However, the war in Asia Minor highlighted the issue of Dominion participation in what nationalist elements described as 'Britain's wars'. The issue remained, for the moment, unresolved. And, in any case, in 1919, the War Office had turned down numerous offers made by South Africans willing to serve in Russia 'in view of [the impact of geography and] the time which will elapse before services could be utilized'.[78]

Politics: domestic and Commonwealth

The matter of imperial geography was a main concern of the 1923 Imperial Conference, held in London in October, which 'gave special attention to the question of Defence, and the manner in which co-operation and mutual assistance could best be effected after taking into account the political and geographical condition of the various parts of the Empire'.[79] The conference reiterated the necessity to provide for the adequate defence of both the territories and the trade of the countries making up the British Empire. However, it also recognised the onus of the parliaments of the several parts of the Empire to decide the nature and extent of any action that should be taken by them. A number of guiding principles were adopted: each portion of the Empire represented at the conference was primarily responsible for its own local defence; adequate provision had to made to guard maritime communications (the conference stressed the 'vital importance to the British Empire of safeguarding its overseas carrying trade against all forms of discrimination by foreign countries, whether open or disguised'[80]); naval bases had to provide repair and refuel capabilities, to ensure the mobility of British fleets and the maintenance of the minimum standard naval strength; and the development of air forces throughout the Empire was to be encouraged.[81]

Thus, from 1924, the role of the Active Citizen Force was restricted to combating African and other uprisings within the Union. These restrictions, together with economic considerations, led to the creation, late in 1924, of a special striking force, designated the South African Field Force, organised under one commander. Although small, and with only a small mechanised nucleus, this force was revolutionary, predating Britain's experimental mechanised force by more than two years.[82] Sadly, very few documents dealing with the South African Field Force are to be found at the SADF Archives, most of the records generated by the unit's commander having been destroyed following an archival appraisal in 1933.[83] We know nonetheless that the Field Force comprised two squadrons of the 1st Regiment, South African Mounted Riflemen (SAMR) and three batteries of the South African Field Artillery (SAFA),[84] with the 1st Regiment SAMR reorganised to include an Armoured Car Section of two cars (imported from the UK in 1925), each armed with two machine guns.[85] This special force could be dispatched at a moment's notice to any location within the country, to deal with disturbances in a quick and clinical manner. As events turned out, the force was not needed. The Rehoboth rebellion in April 1925 was put down with the aid of the SAAF, the only portion of the UDF employed to assist the South West Africa administration in quelling the disturbance.[86]

However, before Smuts could do very much, he lost the election held in June 1924 and the National Party came to power. This hastened the flight of talent from the UDF, an organisation now facing a dramatic reduction in defence expenditure. The new government's budget cuts allowed little opportunity for training, beyond that for regular officers, and provided for the purchase of essential equipment only. Promotion prospects evaporated and imaginative, progressive-minded officers, often beset by conservative or reactionary seniors, either left or lost their enthusiasm. Many left for the private sector, others for the British Army, although very much the same was happening elsewhere.[87]

The new prime minister, Hertzog, remained in office until the outbreak of the Second World War. His term of office was quieter than had been that of Smuts. Hertzog's government, initially a coalition with Labour, faced no industrial unrest, and there were few violent clashes between the security forces and black people during this period – apart from two incidents in South West Africa.

No further action was taken on the issues discussed at the 1923 Imperial Conference – coordination of the defence forces of the Empire, together with the maximum effort that could be expected from each Dominion in time of war. In 1926, when Britain conceded Dominion autonomy, these questions were still outstanding. The question of cooperation between the South African and Imperial general staffs in the design of a South African expeditionary force was not even brought before the South African Parliament.[88] For South Africa the answer was, for the moment, no.

During the National Party's first term of office (1924–1929), it built up a defence force that was 'calculated to protect South Africa's neutrality'[89] and little else. The new government resigned the responsibility for colonial policing in southern and central Africa. Colonel FHP Cresswell, the new Minister of Defence, set out his government's attitude to imperial defence at the 1926 Imperial Conference. The Union Defence Force was organised for the defence of South Africa in any part of southern Africa. There was no provision for war service outside southern Africa, and no South African citizen could be compelled to render personal war service outside these confines. Any assistance that might have been rendered by the Union in an 'Emergency of Empire' would have to be by means of volunteers, unless, of course, special legislation was passed authorising the deployment of the UDF beyond the borders of South Africa and other than in defence of the Union.

The policy regarding external aggression was quite distinct. In the event of South African involvement in a war outside the Union, the Active Citizen Force would not be sent. Special units would be recruited and would undergo a period of intensive training before proceeding to the theatre of war.[90] This had happened in 1914 and was to happen again in 1939. These units were rapidly dispensed with once the threat had disappeared. Although political motive is clearly discernible in the change of policy, financial considerations must not be forgotten. An expeditionary force was cheaper to raise and train from scratch than to maintain on a permanent footing.

The reservation of the Active Citizen Force for internal conflicts and local wars had a negative effect on the development of the UDF as a whole. Local wars, necessarily shorter in duration, held the prospect of a poorly equipped and numerically weak enemy. Strong, well-equipped specialised units were therefore not needed. Hence, official policy, together with the stringent financial situation, led to a long-term neglect of equipment, and this, in turn, had its effect on training.

From the mid-1920s the economic pinch was felt and the defence budget came under pressure as the UDF was made the target of further rationalisation. The original 15 military districts, controlled at the end of March 1926 by 12 district staff officers, were reduced in number to six districts or commands, and the title of 'District Staff Officer' was replaced by that of 'Officer Commanding Military District'.

The reorganisation of the Permanent Force necessitated the disbanding of the 1st Regiment, SAMR, and the transfer of its 138 ranks to the South African Police on 1 April 1926. The South African Field Force ceased to exist on 31 March 1926. The brigade headquarters of the South African Field Artillery was also disbanded and sections of artillery were distributed to various stations throughout the Union. The posts of Officer Commanding, South African Field Force, Officer Commanding Troops, Roberts Heights, and Officer Commanding Troops, Cape Peninsula Garrison, were abolished. The Commandant, South African Military College, Roberts Heights, was appointed Camp Commandant, Roberts Heights, and the duties of the Officer Commanding, Cape Peninsula Garrison, became the responsibility of the Officer Commanding No 1 Military District.[91] Yet, despite the cutbacks, 1926 saw the creation of three independent units: two infantry brigades and, in Natal, a mounted brigade.

The drastic measures of 1922 and 1926 left the Permanent Force strength at just 151 officers and 1 259 other ranks by 1927. However, rationalisation was not at an end, and the onset of the global economic slump had a severe effect upon the UDF. Difficult as the financial climate had been for the Union in the decade following 1918, the Great Depression placed even greater pressure on defence finances. With effect from 31 December 1929, no less than 49 Active Citizen Force units were disbanded, and between July 1930 and June 1934 continuous training for the Citizen Force ceased altogether. The Defence Rifle Associations (DRAs) did not manage to escape the austerity measures either, and in 1931 alone 54 DRAs were disbanded. The quantity of cartridges issued to DRA members was halved. This was a dangerous step. The DRAs were the second line in local defence and on a number of occasions had saved the situation when the Citizen Force had been deployed elsewhere.

As the Depression wore on, the need for further rationalisation in the Union Defence Force began to be felt and the decision to amalgamate various units of the Permanent and Coast Garrison forces was taken. By the middle of 1930, for example, the Permanent Force unit of the SA Engineers was attached to the South African Permanent Garrison Artillery (SAPGA) for disciplinary purposes. The unit, however, remained independent until 1 April 1931, when the SAEC personnel were all absorbed into the SAPGA. Had it not been for the Citizen Force field companies, the SAEC would have disappeared as a corps.

During the 1930/1931 financial year, defence expenditure was cut by £172 499. Another cut followed, so that, over a period of two years, military expenditure

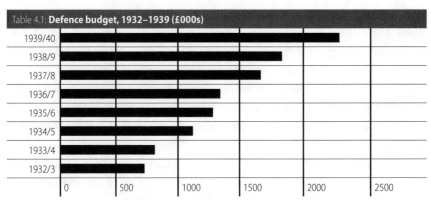

Table 4.1: **Defence budget, 1932–1939 (£000s)**

Year						
	0	500	1000	1500	2000	2500

Source: Votes and Proceedings of the House of Assembly, 1932–1940.

was reduced by £328 000. A nadir was reached in 1932, when Parliament voted only £736 831 for defence (*see* Table 4.1). In 1931, Major General AJE Brink reported on the difficult circumstances the UDF was facing: 'I much regret to report that the urgent necessity for economy which has curtailed the activities of most Departments of State has severely intervened with the training of Citizen Forces ... the Defence organization is called upon to curtail so large a portion of its activities.'[92]

From 1925, cuts to the military budget affected the efficiency of the UDF. There were no major acquisitions of weapon systems. The training programme of the Active Citizen Force, in particular, was affected by the lack of equipment. Citizen Force troops could not be fully armed and equipped with uniforms, while RNVR exercises ceased. Brink expressed the fear that, if the Depression continued much longer, the combat force on which the government had to rely would be insufficiently trained and inadequately equipped for an emergency.

His assessment proved accurate when, in July 1932, the Administrator of South West Africa approached the Defence department for assistance in dealing with Ipumbu, chief of the Kuambi people. The task force that was assembled comprised only three aircraft, equipped with seven 230lb bombs, two armoured cars dispatched from the Military College and a member of the Medical Corps. As it was, Ipumbu was deposed and the affair closed without loss of life. The Ipumbu expedition cost £3 316, in comparison to the £500 spent in the suppression of the Rehoboth rebellion in 1925.[93]

One of the more successful experiments in combating the social evils that followed the Great Depression was the establishment of the Special Service Battalion (SSB) at Roberts Heights on 1 May 1933. By 30 June 1934 the SSB had a strength of 1 929. Sections were later opened at Durban, Cape Town, Kimberley, Bloemfontein, Uitenhage, Port Elizabeth, Kroonstad and Harrismith. Designed to provide employment and training for the many white youths left destitute by the Great Depression, and instil in them a military fitness, pride and discipline that would serve them well in civilian society, the SSB was a great success. In later years, it became a valuable source of trained personnel for the UDF, other state departments and the state-controlled manufacturing sector.[94]

In addition to the SSB, a special short-service unit, consisting of 500 men, was given training for a period of three (later increased to six) months. This unit, the Pioneer Battalion, was established with effect from 1 January 1935 as a unit of the Permanent Force and played the same social role as that of the SSB, with the exception that the age limit was set between 18 and 30 years, and all candidates were to be unmarried. Unlike the SSB, no set standard of education was demanded. The recruits for the Pioneer Battalion were of a poorer, less-educated type, who all their lives were 'brought up in necessitous circumstances, badly fed, clothed, accommodated and not used to money'.[95] The UDF hoped to discipline them, and then to find them employment after the end of their period of service, so that they would become accustomed to regular income and strive for better prospects in life. The Pioneer Battalion, however, attracted 'really vicious types' and 'was very nearly a failure'.[96] Brink also recognised the danger that, after their service, members would return to their former environments, develop a spirit of dissatisfaction with the government and ultimately become a potential source of danger to the state.

Brink proved pretty much in touch with the situation. The Railway Board, in fact, undertook each year to find employment with the South African Railways and Harbours (SAR&H) for 500 members of the Pioneer Battalion. Many refused state employment, either with the railways or on other government schemes. Of the 66 details discharged during the first week of September 1935, only 12 accepted employment with the SAR&H. Four others went to work on the Vaal Dam Irrigation Works and a further three were placed in private employment. The remaining 47 refused either employment or re-engagement with the Special Service Battalion, and returned home to take up farming or eke out a private existence on their own. However, it is true that many of the 47 were under 21 years of age and not in possession of a Standard VI certificate, and therefore could not be considered for employment with the railways or enlistment with the SSB. All in all, the scheme was not the resounding success it was claimed to be.[97]

During the course of 1934, the South African economy began to show definite signs of an upward trend, so much so that a significant increase in the defence budget was approved for the first time since 1924. As a result, Brink could announce that the UDF would once again become a military organisation of modern standing.

Revised threat perception and policy change

After 1930, the international climate changed dramatically with the weakening of colonial authority in the French mandate territories and Gandhi's subtle acts of rebellion in India. France, perceived as a possible threat to British Africa in the 1920s, bound itself to Britain in the next decade in view of common colonial problems and a fear that a resurgent Germany would seek to regain some of its lost colonial possessions. Furthermore, international stability deteriorated rapidly with the decline of liberal democracy and the rise of authoritarianism in central and southern Europe.

The focus of British imperial defence, as a result, swung from the other colonial powers (France, Belgium and Portugal) to the Fascist powers. In fact, as early as 1926, the Intelligence Section in the office of the Chief of the General Staff, in collaboration with MI5, had became involved in the surveillance of German and Italian agents in southern Africa.[98]

In South Africa, with a recovering economy and a new coalition government in power, including both Hertzog and Smuts – who received the Justice portfolio – a number of changes were made with regard to the UDF. Defence minister Oswald Pirow, who described Hitler as 'perhaps the greatest man of the last thousand years',[99] began specialisation within the South African General Staff. General Andries Brink was appointed to the new post of General Officer Commanding the UDF and Secretary for Defence in 1933. The autocratic and stubborn Brigadier General (Sir Pierre) van Ryneveld, for whom the likes of George Brink had no affection or respect,[100] became the new Chief of the General Staff, while his old post (Director Air Services) was abolished and replaced by a smaller Directorate of Civil Aviation. In the same year, a Technical Services Directorate was established to relieve the Quartermaster General of all his technically oriented duties, and the General

Staff Section at Defence Headquarters passed under the control of the new Director of Military Operations and Training. These changes resulted in the formation of five major sections at Defence Headquarters under the overall control of the Chief of the General Staff: Director Military Operations and Training, Adjutant General, Quartermaster General, Director Technical Services and Director Medical Services.

These appointments proved to be a turning point in the history of the UDF. Pirow's first Defence budget, reflecting an improved economy and increasing security concerns, was a tremendous increase on the previous year, and military expenditure climbed steadily right up to the outbreak of the Second World War.[101] The guiding lights of this transformation were Pirow, Van Ryneveld and Brink. Only weeks after the formation of the new cabinet, it was Van Ryneveld who convinced Pirow of the need to expand the UDF. Although a direct attack on South Africa was improbable, there was the constant threat of internal unrest and the onerous imperial commitment. In the event of a world war, the defence of the Cape sea route would fall largely to South Africa, and the potential threats from the surrounding territories could not be ignored. Van Ryneveld grabbed at any argument for expansion, and particularly of the air force. Pirow was in agreement and made the issue his own. By 1934, Sir Maurice Hankey, Cabinet Secretary and secretary of the Committee for Imperial Defence, informed his prime minister, Ramsay Macdonald, that there was 'something of a military renaissance going on [in South Africa] under the impulse of Mr Pirow and General van Ryneveld'.[102]

After the 1933 Imperial Conference, South African forces were no longer confined to actions within the Union, and, as a result of this change in policy, the UDF was expanded. By the middle of 1934, and only a year after the inception of the coalition government, a major reorganisation had taken place. Coastal defences were considerably improved. The Coastal Artillery Brigade made its appearance in Cape Town, comprising various units across the country, including an armoured train, which was very much in keeping with the latest military thinking. Aircraft, from an expanded SAAF, were permanently stationed at the defended ports of Cape Town and Durban, to augment the fixed and movable armament. A coastal defence fighter-bomber squadron came into being in 1938, for the defence of the Cape Peninsula, including the Royal Navy base at Simon's Town.[103] The first three aircraft for this squadron, converted Ju 86s, arrived at Cape Town on 18 September 1939, from which point the squadron assisted the Royal Navy in the defence of the Cape sea route.[104]

The Active Citizen Force was increased by the addition of eight new infantry battalions, organised according to country districts, and a field organisation of six brigades was formed into 'forces' corresponding to divisions.[105] At Van Ryneveld's suggestion, the ACF was expanded to 12 urban and 12 rural regiments – divided linguistically on a 50–50 basis. Almost 400 Bren light machine guns were ordered from Britain in 1935. Two years later, only 15 had been delivered. Nonetheless, after five years, Pirow envisioned a trained and equipped PF and ACF of 56 000 and a national reserve of 100 000 men.[106]

However, the Admiralty was deeply concerned by the discontinuing of hydrographic survey work in South African waters. Much to their consternation, the survey vessel HMSAS *Protea* had been decommissioned on 1 May 1933.[107] A year later, the South African Naval Service was disbanded. The RNVR was increased in strength, reaching almost 1 000 in 1936, over six sub-divisions and three flotillas. But, as far as Britain was concerned, this was poor compensation. Britain was welcome to pay for its rule of the waves, but South Africa would focus on the protection of its harbours and shoreline. South Africa, on the other hand, wanted to invest more in coastal defence. The British view was that this was an over-investment.

The British saw other priorities, and the discrepancy caused problems. London believed that, in the matter of defence, 'it is essential to take into account the mentality of South African ministers and specially of Pirow'. The British High Commissioner in Pretoria warned London not to 'appear to belittle South Africa's place in the picture' of imperial defence and reminded them that 'the big thing rather than the adequate but unspectacular' appealed to Pirow, and apparently also to Smuts.[108] Vice Admiral Sir ERGR Evans of the Africa Station repeated these sentiments. Pirow was 'a man of action' with little use for half measures. Andries Brink was 'no lover of England or the Royal Navy' and was expected 'to support any suggestion for doing as little as possible', while Van Ryneveld, Evans opined, 'knows and cares little about the Navy, but is an enthusiastic airman. He will be only too ready to seize on any remark about mobility to press for an expansion of the Air Force to the exclusion of all else.'[109]

Nonetheless, Evans believed he 'had a great deal in common' with Pirow, his 'greatest friend in the Southern Hemisphere' whose 'company to me was like a glass of champagne after a successful Admiral's inspection'.[110] He was the first British admiral to write in Afrikaans, and Pirow could say with much justification in the House of Assembly that: 'Thanks to Admiral Evans, our relationship with the Africa Squadron is more cordial than it has been in our history.'[111]

Pirow's slide from favour was gradual. Eyebrows were raised during the Spanish Civil War, when he visited General Franco's headquarters instead of the Republican government, and, later, when he visited Hitler without disclosing the content of their discussions to the world.

Pirow's five-year plan, as far as the SAAF was concerned, included the training of a thousand pilots by flying clubs and schools throughout the Union by 1942, as well as the purchase of new aircraft, some of which were to be built under licence in South Africa. A new operational air station was built at a new site to the east of Zwartkop Air Station, home of the Central Flying School. The aerodrome, named Waterkloof Air Station, was opened on 1 August 1938.[112] Here one can clearly see the work of Van Ryneveld, the 'air-minded' Chief of the General Staff. Furthermore, after 1933 more than half of the South Africans sent to Britain for training were airmen, whereas in the preceding period none had been sent.

However, as far as an expeditionary force was concerned, Pirow stated that his government would not commit itself in advance: the circumstances of the emergency would determine South African participation. Pirow did, however, add that it was possible, even probable, to assume that the South African government would be willing to assist in the defence of British interests in East Africa, but then only if the white populations were threatened. Furthermore, most politicians and soldiers accepted that the defence of South Africa from overland attack 'should be undertaken as far to the north of her boundaries as her military strength and resources and the situation [would] permit'.[113] He emphasised that under no condition would the Union Defence Force be available for service outside Africa.[114]

This, however, was still an important concession on the part of the Hertzog government. South Africa's 'wartime frontier' had shifted to East Africa. No sooner had this new defence policy been laid down than it was put to the test following the Italian invasion of Abyssinia (Ethiopia) in October 1935.[115] On 4 February 1936, with war raging in Abyssinia, the government vocalised the policy as follows:

> the maintenance of international peace in such manner that the obligations which the Union assumed by becoming a member of the League of Nations will be loyally carried out, and the freedom and interests of the State will be faithfully and honourably safeguarded.[116]

Pirow, furthermore, was pressured to address the matter of South African participation in foreign wars per se. He told the House:

> We are not bound directly or indirectly to take part in any war, in Africa, or elsewhere. We shall not take part in a war except when the true interests of South Africa make such participation inevitable. We as a Government will not even take part in an apparently inevitable war except after the people of this country through their representatives in Parliament have with the greatest possible measure of unanimity, given us an unambiguous mandate to that effect.[117]

Concurrently, the South African General Staff appointed Major General JJ Collyer, who, in his retirement, was working on a history of the South West African campaign, to produce a textbook on the 'lessons' of the First World War. The book's East African focus was tacit proof of South Africa's recognition of its 'imperial obligations'. Aimed at instruction for officers at the Military College, Collyer hoped to prepare South African officers for service on 'the continent of Africa'.[118] Entitled *The South Africans with General Smuts in German East Africa*, the book appeared only months before the outbreak of the Second World War, too late to influence many of the officers who were sent to East Africa in 1940 and 1941. Many of Collyer's 'lessons', in particular those concerning air power and mechanical transport, were misinformed. However, they provide a rare insight into inter-war South African military thinking. Collyer, thought by some to be 'the Liddell Hart of South Africa',[119] pointed out, and quite rightly, that South Africa had not been prepared for war in 1914, and his first call was for the systematic collection and updating of information in sub-Saharan Africa and 'the teaching of experience', emphasising both the importance of military history and the collection of accurate military information. Foreknowledge would lessen the difficulty of gaining strategic surprise, shorten campaigning in tropical Africa, and so limit casualties. However, Collyer, a mounted infantryman with fifty years of service in Africa, was clearly not a man for modern devices. He highlighted the problems of air power rather than possibilities[120] and discounted the immediate value of mechanised transport in Africa. In his view, only mounted troops could be relied upon, and so provided unwittingly a theoretical basis for Pirow's 'bush cart' policy, as the opposition press termed the new focus on South Africa's immediate defence and the reduced need, argued by Pirow, for expensive armaments and weapons systems.[121] The type of operations that would be undertaken by South Africa in East Africa in 1940 and North Africa in 1941 were simply not contemplated, or indeed planned for, by a defence minister who focused almost exclusively on internal security.

Political opposition and mobilisation

Gradually, the Union Defence Force was dragged fully into the party political arena. The event that brought the situation to a head was the appointment of Andries Brink as Chief Commandant of Commandos on 31 March 1937.[122] Through no doing of his own, Brink had an association with the Jameson Raid. A year later, Frans Erasmus (GNP,[123] MP for Moorreesburg), the shadow Minister of Defence, lambasted Pirow for not modernising the commandos and for effectively splitting the Union Defence Force by placing it under two chiefs: Brink and Van Ryneveld. This, in Erasmus' mind, reduced the commandos to the 'second line of troops', whereas the National Party wished to continue the old republican tradition of the commandos, as a people's army of the first line. This had been cardinal to the two resolutions on defence that the Cape Congress of the National Party had passed in September 1923. Erasmus stated in 1938:

> I cannot use sufficiently strong language to express my disapproval of the Minister having brought about a split in the Defence Force. If a person is not suitable for his position, why then must you split up the Defence Force owing to a man who is unpopular with the Boer Commandos? Why do you not get rid of him?[124]

The opposition Purified National Party (GNP), in the person of NJ van der Merwe (MP for Winburg), believed that the money voted by Parliament for the Defence budget was not for the defence of South Africa, but for the defence of the Empire. It was, he said, in the interests of the country for the Union Defence Force to feel that it had the whole country behind it, and that the question of defence should not become a party political matter. He did not believe that the people as a whole stood behind the defence force, as it did not yet bear 'a truly people's national character amongst our public' and 'all we have to-day appears to be nothing else than an outward show, nothing else but window-dressing … When we go to Roberts Heights then we have a caricature of a miniature Aldershot.'[125]

The layout and colonial architecture of Roberts Heights lent a decidedly British atmosphere to the country's main military base. An attempt to dilute this atmosphere was taken in December 1938, when, in the heat of the celebrations marking the centenary of the Great Trek, General JCG Kemp, the old rebel leader, announced unexpectedly, and to the consternation of English-speakers, that Roberts Heights would henceforth be called 'Voortrekkerhoogte'.

Criticism also came from the Smuts supporters on the government benches. SF Waterson (MP for South Peninsula) questioned the Minister of Defence as to what the government was doing with regard to defence. Pirow had made two statements, one in 1934 and one in 1936, but had offered no additional information since then. His five-year plans would, after all, mature in 1939 and 1941, and he had given no progress reports on these.[126] What was more, according to Lieutenant General George Brink, 'by 1937 the Government had not informed the General Staff what its Defence policy was'.[127]

During 1938, Pirow was pressed to state for what contingencies the Defence department should plan, and on 7 September, in Parliament, he listed the factors that made South African participation in an international war unique. Firstly, there was the composition of the European (white) population, with neither section prepared to support a defence policy aimed exclusively at making soldiers out of the youth of the country. 'Any approach to our problem of national defence', he reassured Parliament, 'must be from a purely South African angle, and must take into consideration factors which are not found in any other portion of the Commonwealth, or which, if found, are of minor importance. The first of these factors is the comparison of our European population. With 60 per cent of the population Afrikaans-speaking no defence policy will command the support of the bulk of the people of the Union unless scope is explicitly confined to the protection of South Africa and her vital interests.'[128] Black South Africans were left out of the equation.

Furthermore, southern Africa could never become the main theatre of a major war. And, because of geography, a large-scale gas or air attack on the civilian population was not seriously considered. South Africa's manpower resources, when compared with those of even second-class powers, were very limited. Moreover, in spite of all its potential wealth, South Africa had much poverty, and there was a definite limit to what the country was prepared to spend on defence. However, as British defence planners recognised, South Africa's maximum effort would not have to be made until six months after the outbreak of hostilities, and this allowed for a period of intensive preparation. South Africa also faced the relative certainty that its troops would be called upon to fight a mobile war.[129] Precisely a year later, the country was at war with Germany.

For the official opposition, matters were not as cut and dried. Erasmus, the shadow Defence minister, used the opportunity to articulate the National Party's stance:

> At the moment my point is that we are in a comparatively safe position. South Africa has no enemies. The only danger we are in, and the only enemies that we have, are on account of our association with Great Britain ... The first way in which this association with Great Britain will involve us in a war is if we decide to take part in a war in which she is engaged.[130]

According to Erasmus, South Africa could also be drawn into a war in at least two other ways: in connection with the Smuts-Churchill Simon's Town Agreement and in the association of the Hertzog government with plans for the defence of colonial territories to the north of South Africa. The latter 'carried the implication of joint defence co-operation with the country [ie, Britain] whose territories they were'.[131] He went on:

> I hope that the Minister in future ... will keep his eyes less on the interests of England and the British interests at the Equator, and more on the interests of South Africa, for her self-defence. I hope that he will keep his eye more on our boundaries, not on the boundaries of Abyssinia, but the boundary of the Limpopo.[132]

The Purified National Party was not opposed to the expansion of the Union Defence Force. They were willing to vote money for the building-up of the UDF in the spirit of the Defence Act of 1912, that is, to enable South Africa to defend itself. In short, the Nationalists wanted to build up the UDF to protect South Africa's neutrality, not to take part in European wars.

Smuts, the Justice minister, stressed the contrary. In the event of a war against Germany or Italy, South Africa's first line of defence would lie outside the country. And when the war came, a new attestation form, requiring volunteers for service 'anywhere in Africa', was introduced. South Africa's 'wartime frontier' was Kenya, guarding against further Italian expansion in East Africa. Unsurprisingly, this was the first theatre to which South African troops were sent.

Many senior officers supported Smuts, who was a mentor to many of them, including Van Ryneveld. In fact, the relationship between Smuts and Van Ryneveld was described by the official historians of the Second World War as being 'an almost David and Jonathan association'.[133] Furthermore, conversations with military attachés, visits abroad (such as that undertaken by George Brink in 1937) and meetings with foreign counterparts, including the Chief of the Imperial General Staff (CIGS) and the British naval personnel at Simon's Town – Admiral Evans had a considerable influence upon George Brink, for example – convinced them that war was inevitable and that South Africa needed a modern defence force.[134]

Not all agreed on the potential enemy. Smuts and George Brink thought it would be Italy in Africa and possibly Germany in Europe. Van Ryneveld and 'most of his staff' were fixated on an Italian invasion of southern Africa, with the Italians possibly enjoying the cooperation of Britain's oldest ally, Portugal. Of particular danger was Italy's Cant Z 1007b three-engine medium bomber. This aircraft, with a range of over 2 000 kilometres, was capable of reaching the Witwatersrand from Madagascar.[135] The SAAF, as far as Sir Pierre was concerned, required fighters capable of mounting an adequate defence. An elaborate Z-plan was developed, in which South African forces would seize Lourenço Marques and so deny the enemy a base from which to strike at the industrial heartland of South Africa.[136]

Yet, of the issues highlighted during the first round of defence planning, in 1933, some had been addressed and others ignored. The latter related to South Africa's probable task, what forces would be required to cope with the task, how these forces were to be armed and equipped, and how they were to be trained.[137] As regards South Africa's probable task, Pirow took up a position somewhere between Erasmus and Smuts. South Africa would only go to war, he said, if it were vital for the protection of South African interests, and only if the people gave the South African Parliament an unambiguous mandate. South Africa would assist Britain if the latter were attacked by Germany, but would remain neutral should Britain and France declare war against Germany. This implied deployment in Africa at best. Nonetheless, South Africa's lack of response during the Munich Crisis (1938), while perhaps predictable, remained a severe disappointment in London. Hertzog had refused to issue the required proclamations for the RNVR. And, as a result, the British Admiral at Simon's Town decided, in the event of this happening again, to call up all retired Royal Navy and RNVR personnel in South Africa, irrespective of whether they were members of the South African Naval Service War Reserve.[138]

In a controversial book published in 1960, Eric Hartshorn, brigade major of the 1st South African Infantry Brigade Group and later commander of the 1st Transvaal Scottish, exposed a plot by a handful of ACF officers to take extreme steps in the event of Parliament's voting for neutrality. Convinced that the whole of the UDF would not fight should South Africa go to war, and having no confidence in 'the majority of Senior Regular Officers', they hatched a plan to mobilise the Witwatersrand Citizen Force and make for Natal. There was a similar plot in the SAAF. According to an anonymous squadron leader:

> We had every Nationalist supporter in the Air Force carefully marked ... We had all our aircraft ready with every scrap of ammunition that we could carry and we were going to fly every aircraft in South Africa to Rhodesia ... The few British fighters in Rhodesia were actually standing by to escort us in.[139]

The defence plan launched in the mid-1930s called for the raising of nine Citizen Force infantry brigades. By September 1939, these were made up by 26 infantry units as well as the Special Service Battalion. In addition to this infantry core, the provision consisted of three field artillery brigades and two field batteries, two medium batteries, two light batteries, an anti-aircraft and anti-tank battery, two artillery batteries for the Coast Garrison, seven heavy batteries of Coast Garrison artillery and various supporting elements – including the SAEC, SAMC and SACS. The 1st Field Survey Company (ACF) was established with effect from 1 April 1938.[140] Three more field companies, together with no less than 21 other ACF units, were established with effect from 1 April 1939,[141] and by September of that year there was a field company to support each of the nine infantry brigades.[142] However, many of these units were very understrength or existed only on paper.[143]

Despite the existence of a sizable and largely state-controlled industrial complex, poor planning and financial stringency during the inter-war years meant that the defence force had to be built up almost from scratch during the late 1930s. In May 1937, at the prodding of George Brink and others, Pirow set up a War Supplies Board under Colonel FRG Hoare, the Director of Technical Services. The board established a factory for the manufacture of small-arms ammunition, in collaboration with Imperial Chemical Industries (ICI), and this came into production at the end of 1938. Bren guns were adapted to fire grenades, and spare barrels for howitzers of varying calibre were manufactured.[144]

Following the vote for war in the House of Assembly on 6 September 1939 and his appointment as prime minister, Smuts immediately went about putting war supply on a businesslike footing. He became commander-in-chief with Van Ryneveld confirmed as his Chief of the General Staff. Collyer was recalled from retirement and appointed as Smuts' military secretary, while CH Blaine, appointed with the rank of brigadier, replaced Pirow's protégé as Secretary for Defence. Colonel Piet de Waal, a grandson of Louis Botha, became Director General of Operations and flew to Nairobi to ascertain what assistance South Africa could provide in the event of an Italian offensive. Smuts promised to have a brigade group ready for East Africa by June 1940. This was to include three infantry battalions (one of which was motorised), one artillery brigade, engineers, signals, medical, technical and 'Q' services, and line of communications personnel, together with three air force squadrons. A company of armoured cars would follow, once these had been produced in South Africa. The aircraft construction programme in the SAAF workshops included the Westland Wapiti, Avro Tutor and Hawker Hartebeest.[145]

Under the direction of the chairman of the Iron and Steel Corporation (Iscor), Dr HJ van der Bijl, materiel and equipment of all kinds was produced within a few months and largely from South African resources.[146] The engineering workshops of the gold mines and SAR&H became arsenals for war, and the Industrial Development Corporation (IDC) was established in 1940 to facilitate the development of new industrial enterprises.[147] Small arms ammunition, artillery shells, mortars and howitzers were produced, soon for export to other Allied countries thanks to the increased output of high-grade steel from Iscor.[148] In 1945, Iscor produced no less than 866 107 metric tons.[149] The production of trucks and armoured cars allowed the mechanisation of several units. By September 1940, the South African Ford plant alone had assembled 18 349 lorries, all for the war effort and some converted into mobile dental units, bath and laundry units, map printing vehicles and bacteriological laboratories.[150]

This was a remarkable achievement, all the more so as most of the skilled staff at Iscor, being German contract labour, was interned at the outbreak of hostilities. As-yet-untrained South Africans kept the works going. Then many of them were enlisted into the armed forces and were replaced by women and black workers. Van der Bijl and his executives are even reputed to have rolled up their sleeves and taken a turn in the works. Nonetheless, South African industry was much better equipped in 1939 to meet the challenges of war than it had been in 1914. Rapid expansion to meet wartime demand was proof of a broader base and greater maturity.[151]

The long-term lack of equipment between the world wars affected training. Only after the Munich Crisis did training assume a new urgency. In 1936, for example, Major Schoon of the South African Engineer Corps reported that 'the field companies held totally inadequate stores for their efficient training',[152] and, as a result, most sappers were simply trained as infantry.[153] This problem was not unique to the engineers. No medical training had taken place since the closure of the Medical Training School in 1919.[154] Furthermore, no physical training (PT) took place in the Union Defence Force between 1923, when the last British instructors left Roberts Heights, and 1937, when George Brink highlighted the omission. Pirow, having seen the emphasis placed by Germany and other European states upon physique, bought into the idea, although regular PT was only reintroduced in May 1939.[155] A vigorous recruiting programme yielded sufficient instructors to train the 137 000 recruits. Eventually, a quarter of a million white men were mobilised, together with several hundred thousand women and blacks, for the auxiliary services.

Pirow was a controversial minister. His German background and German wife (her parents had been interned in 1914), and his pro-German views, were the subject of numerous communications between the British High Commissioner and the Dominions Office, and between the Commander-in-Chief in Simon's Town and the Admiralty. He was seemingly the only South African minister to be monitored by the Security Service (MI5).[156] As a result of the Hertzog government's views on African defence and the likely theatre of war, the Union Defence Force, like many militaries in 1939, was not ready for the Second World War. Yet, castigated as the 'Little Hitler of South Africa', Pirow was lambasted in the months following the declaration of war as the pro-German, doing-nothing Defence minister.[157] A private in the Transvaal Scottish wrote: 'The only thing this particular Minister is known for is the equipping of the SA Army with "bushcarts". Some of these stand outside the military college at Roberts Heights as a remembrance of the futile work of an absolutely incompetent Minister.'[158]

This was a little unfair. South Africa's defences reached a peak in 1939 and were in a better state of preparation than at any other time in its peacetime history. Pirow can at most be blamed for doing little with regard to establishing an expeditionary force, something on which the Cabinet itself was divided.

Only in September 1938, at the time of the Munich Crisis, did the whole Cabinet subscribe to a defence policy. In the words of Pirow himself, South Africa

> would unhesitatingly support Britain in the – unlikely – event of her being attacked by Germany ... If, however, Britain and France were to declare war on Germany about happenings in Central or Eastern Europe, South Africa would remain neutral. In September 1938 ... General Smuts and the whole Cabinet, without exception, subscribed to this Policy. I reorganised the Defence Department to meet the above contingencies.[159]

Conclusion

The political debate during the inter-war period focused on the distribution of the burdens of defence, both across an increasingly moribund British Empire and within the Union of South Africa, where 'neutrality' was a rallying call for appeasers and pacifists, ever more militant Afrikaner nationalists and indeed anybody who bore a grudge against 'the British'. Such extraneous influences, together with a mix of institutional factors, brought military and intellectual 'rust-out' between 1918 and 1939, although indeed the UDF through this period had the appearance of greater professionalism and assumed an internal organisation and forms of behaviour typical of Western counterparts. Yet, like the rest of the British Commonwealth, much of the UDF's doctrine and tactical innovation did not keep pace with technological developments. Training and training facilities were inadequate and there was a shortage of uniforms and equipment. The army, despite constant undermining by the Afrikaner nationalist press, was still an honoured and respectable profession. Promising commanders studied tactics and strategy at the SA Military College, and the cream went on to British institutions, in some cases not to return.

The mechanisation of ground forces and the application of new technology for war contrasted sharply with developments in Europe. Although South Africa had the industrial capacity for the development of armour and mechanised forces, arguments based upon the nature of potential enemy forces, poor infrastructure and terrain inaccessibility, combined with government policy and financial stringency, resulted in nothing being done. As a result, when war came in 1939, an expeditionary force had to be prepared from scratch and the first South Africans to serve in the Second World War only left the country in July 1940.

CHAPTER FIVE

The Second World War, 1939–1945

The great hour had struck at last for Smuts. For the first time he was to have sufficient of the power he loved so much … Now his chance had come. He gained full control over the political and military machinery of his country and he made the utmost of the position he held. No longer young, he yet displayed remarkable energy and enterprise in his determination to lead the Union to victory by the side of her allies … The period from 1939 to 1945 was decidedly his.[1]

— DW Krüger, historian, 1969, on Smuts in 1939

Smuts himself, besides being prime minister, minister of external affairs, and minister of defence, also assumed control over the armed forces as commander-in-chief. With such a considerable concentration of political and military power in his hands, Smuts moved swiftly and decisively.[2]

— Albert Grundlingh, historian, 1993

Parliament sat on Monday 4 September 1939, following a morning meeting of the Hertzog Cabinet. The House was packed, as the press and public crammed the galleries. A vote was taken on the prime minister's neutrality motion, which was defeated by 80 votes to 67. Enthusiastic crowds greeted the news in Parliament Street. Sir Patrick Duncan, the Governor General, invited Smuts to form a government. Smuts held his first War Cabinet on 6 September. War was proclaimed against Germany and the first steps to move the country onto a war footing were taken. When the Cabinet met again three days later, Sir Nathan Clarke remarked somewhat ominously: 'We're in for a hell of a time! Make no mistake about it!'[3]

South Africa was certainly ill-prepared, and Hitler is reported to have laughed when news of the South African declaration came.[4] The Permanent and Active Citizen forces were severely understrength: the former comprised only 349 officers and 5 033 men, the latter 918 officers and 13 490 men. There were a further 122 000 men in the commandos, of whom only 18 000 were reasonably equipped. Being rurally based and overwhelmingly Afrikaans, many of these men did not support the war effort. Furthermore, training and training facilities were inadequate, there were shortages of uniforms and equipment and, like the rest of the British Empire, much of the UDF's doctrine had not kept pace with technological developments. As a result, when the war came in late 1939, the expeditionary forces that would be dispatched 'North' had to be prepared from scratch.

Politics, domestic and imperial

Smuts faced his difficult task with great enthusiasm. No general election had been called. He could not ascertain the relative strength of the parties. His parliamentary strength was not imposing – an effective majority of 17, including the three black representatives. He reconstituted the Cabinet, introducing yet again a neat language balance, half of the ministers being Afrikaans and half English. The Cabinet included Deneys Reitz and Colin Steyn, both sons of former republican presidents, and Jan Hofmeyr, as well as the Labourite Walter Madeley and Colonel Charles Stallard of Natal's Dominion Party. In general, the Cabinet was a strong team, although none of its members had the energy and capacity that Smuts revealed from the start. The British High Commissioner, Sir William Clark, summed up Smuts' position:

> In the meantime General Smuts with a small majority will have to proceed with a caution which is alien to his temperament, though it may well be that, if things go satisfactorily at the start, he may find the country increasingly behind him as time goes on, and, as I have hinted, I think it will help him if the new Nationalist Party commits itself too deeply to republicanism. Nevertheless, I regret his decision to allow Parliament to be prorogued without waiting to pass the emergency legislation which the previous Government already had on the stocks. His attitude, I am told, was that he could do whatever might be wanted and secure validating legislation later on. This seems to me to involve unnecessary risks of creating trouble,

especially for one who on his past record is apt to be accused of leaning towards dictatorial and undemocratic methods.[5]

South Africa's entry into the war marked the start of a new political struggle as the United Party broke up and a new political realignment took shape. While the primary confrontation was ostensibly between Smuts and his supporters on the one hand and the opponents of his war policy on the other, there was also a growing battle, within an increasingly fractured opposition, for the soul of the Afrikaner. Smuts commanded the support of the large cities, the Witwatersrand and the Cape Peninsula, as well as the province of Natal and the eastern Cape. The remainder of the country was divided in allegiance between JBM Hertzog and DF Malan. Yet, although Hertzog and Malan staged an impressive demonstration at the Voortrekker Monument, outside Pretoria, on 9 September, they remained divided. Hertzog resigned from the United Party in November 1939 and took his place on the opposition benches when Parliament met the following January. The leadership of the opposition was poor and remained divided and prone to increasing factionalism. Hertzog retired into the political wilderness, a broken man, unwilling to embrace the national brand of Malan.[6] Hertzog's lieutenant and former Defence minister, Oswald Pirow, who was castigated ruthlessly in Parliament, in the press and on the street for having equipped the defence force with 'bush carts', had done nothing. His image and prestige were irreparably damaged.[7]

Already in May 1939, Smuts had told the British High Commissioner that he still had some anxiety 'that there might even be some sort of a rising in the event of the Union joining in a British war'. This had surprised Clark. The situation seemed very different to 1914, when the Union was but four years old and the memories of the Anglo-Boer War were fresh. Moreover, in 1939 there seemed to be no prestigious leaders, of the likes of De la Rey and De Wet, and 'one hardly saw the present Nationalist leaders taking to the veld with horses and rifles'. But, as Smuts noted to Clark, he was less concerned about the parliamentary opposition than about the Ossewabrandwag (OB), or 'ox-wagon sentinels', a supposedly cultural organisation started in 1938. This, Smuts believed, was something more subversive, and more dangerous. Moreover, the members of the OB were also mostly members of the rifle associations and the commandos; they had rifles and ammunition. Smuts took no chances and, as Justice minister, he had had the OB very carefully watched by the police.[8]

However, although divided, the opposition would not allow Smuts to have his way easily. It was not clear how, when and where the UDF would be deployed. Smuts had undertaken not to send men 'overseas', but there was the continent of Africa. Germany no longer had colonies, but Italy, Germany's partner and ally – admittedly not in the war yet – had colonial interests in North and East Africa, from which Egypt and Kenya might be threatened.[9] Smuts argued that East Africa formed South Africa's front line. Others did not agree. Smuts wanted to send a field force to East Africa to assist in the defence of Kenya. For this, he would have to rely upon volunteers only, and they would have to sign a special oath. To distinguish them from other soldiers they would wear an orange tab (*rooilussie*) on the epaulette. This caused an unfortunate conflict within the armed forces between the 'red lice' (*rooi luise*) and those who refused to take the oath. Silent pressure no doubt accounted for some volunteers. Some servicemen refused the oath.[10]

In all, 342 792 full-time volunteers of all races served with the UDF during the Second World War. Of these, 217 122 were whites, 46 412 were coloureds and Indians, and 79 258 were blacks (*see* Table 5.1). In a segregated South Africa, the coloureds and Indians were enlisted into the Cape Corps (CC) and the Indian and Malay Corps (IMC), respectively, while blacks served in the Native Military Corps (NMC). These three units, all of whom served in non-combatant roles, were organised in what was termed the Non-European Army Services (NEAS). In addition, there were a further 63 341 servicemen in the part-time units. The English-Afrikaner language divide was still a basic partition in white society. The former seemingly fought for King and country; the latter, enlisting for reasons primarily economic, fought largely for a living.[11] There were, of course, many that broke this mould. Sir De Villiers Graaff, for example, was from a wealthy, anglicised, Cape Afrikaner family, who, having served in the 2nd SA Division, entered Parliament after the war and later led the United Party, on a ticket calling for the protection of ex-servicemen and at least a measure of social justice for South Africans generally grouped and labelled as 'non-white'.[12]

One of the government's first steps was the passage of the War Measures Act. Heavily contested by the opposition, this legislation ratified the emergency proclamations regarding the war and internal security arrangements and gave the government extensive emergency powers. Financial provisions were made, albeit at first on a very limited scale.[13]

The opposition disregarded an appeal from Smuts to shorten the parliamentary session, and thus Parliament was still in session when Hitler launched his

Table 5.1: **Whole-time volunteers, Union Defence Force, 1939–1945**				
Service	**White**	**Black** (NMC)	**Coloured and** Indian (CC & IMC)	**Total**
Land forces	132 194	77 239	45 015	**254 448**
SAAF	44 569	–	–	**44 569**
SANF	9 455	–	877	**10 332**
Women's Auxiliary Defence Corps	21 265	–	–	**21 265**
SA Military Nursing Service	3 710	–	–	**3 710**
ENSP*	5 929	2 019	520	**8 468**
Total	**217 122**	**79 258**	**46 412**	**342 792**

* The Essential Services Protection Corps (ESPC) was not strictly a military organisation. Members comprised whole-time civilian volunteers under military discipline and engaged in guard duties. They qualified for the Africa Service Medal.
Source: Union Office of Census and Statistics, Pretoria.

attack in the West in the spring of 1940. The fall of Denmark and Norway, of the Low Countries and of France followed in quick succession. The opposition stance remained fixed, regardless of the rough handling of the Netherlands at the hands of the Germans.[14] Their seeming indifference infuriated Smuts' supporters and alienated some of their own following. However, critically, the entry of Mussolini's Italy into the war, on 10 June, altered the strategic landscape materially. The war was brought much closer to the Union, and, dispensing doubt, Africa would yet again have its campaigns, although, unlike the First World War, the Second 'came to Africa piecemeal and with delay'.[15] Smuts had been justified, and Mussolini's actions had strengthened his hand. Using this platform, Smuts called for a wider and more active participation.

A house divided: subversion, propaganda and secret agents

South African participation in the Second World War was bitterly contested. The country was divided again, and the groups opposing the war effort were many, with some resorting to violence. There is thus a striking similarity in South Africa's experience of the two world wars. Belligerence was again contested in 1939, and again alternative centres of power formed within the country; a national rebellion loomed and significant elements of the police and even of the Union Defence Force held questionable loyalties. But in 1939 the position was arguably made more delicate by the presence of a variety of organisations, some political, others paramilitary, that opposed the Smuts government and the war policy.

The non-parliamentary disaffection, which favoured the Nazi cause more than the strict neutrality favoured by Malan's Nationalists, were highly vocal. With a ground swell of young student support and radical agitation, several extra-parliamentary authoritarian movements were formed, the most notable of which was the Ossewabrandwag (OB), a paramilitary, pro-Nazi organisation with links to Dr Luitpoldt Werz, the German consul in Lourenço Marques, and an Abwehr ring in Mozambique.[16] The OB, established initially to keep alive the ideals of the Great Trek and to stimulate Afrikaner culture, drew thousands of Afrikaners, including former soldiers who had left the armed forces to seek an extra-political means of ensuring Afrikaner unity and opposing the war effort.[17] The OB, Pirow tells us, 'deliberately launched a campaign of sabotage against the war effort. Its leader was the ex-Administrator of the Orange Free State, Dr Hans van Rensburg, one of the most brilliant of the younger Afrikaners. At one stage he completely eclipsed all the party leaders and had a greater personal following than Dr Malan.'[18] In pursuit of military objectives, the OB had contact with German agents in southern Africa as well as the Reich Chancellery.[19] There were clashes between OB members and soldiers on leave, and in some centres there were riots.[20] Notions were fostered that the Smuts government might be toppled and a new Afrikaner nationalist order might take power, a prospect that seemed strengthened by a German victory in Europe. Whereas the Afrikaner rebellion had been effectively quashed by December 1914, the threat of a similar uprising during the next war, although always probably unlikely, lasted until early 1944.

Another movement monitored by the police's Special Branch at this time was the Afrikaner Broederbond (AB). This was difficult, for the AB was secretive and associated closely with the National Party, the parliamentary opposition. Smuts described the Broederbond in 1944 as 'a dangerous, cunning, political, Fascist organisation of which no civil servant, if he is to retain his loyalty to the State and Administration, can be allowed to be a member'.[21] Members of the OB and AB were pushed out of the armed forces; members of the former eventually found a political home in the National Party. After the war, the Smuts government did not recognise the signs that the nationalist opposition was consolidating and gaining ground. The National Party, after an initial flirtation, distanced itself increasingly from fascism and began to act as a normal and responsible opposition, capable of forming an alternative government. They, however, retained a republican policy and strong stance in terms of the Indian and communist questions. In 1948 they swept to power, with a slender majority in the House of Assembly only.[22]

A considerable section of the population, mostly Afrikaans-speaking, was against Smuts' war policy from the start. Some were animated by genuine conviction, others by political considerations. Both groups, seeing the war as an opportunity of furthering the republican ideal, hoped that a German victory would enable them to realise their objective.[23] In a special intelligence operation conducted in early 1940, the German Foreign Ministry contacted the South African parliamentary opposition, via intermediaries, and offered, at the conclusion of an early peace with South Africa, to recognise the independence of the Union with the addition of the three High Commission territories of Swaziland, Basutoland and Bechuanaland, and Southern Rhodesia. Germany, of course, intended to take back South West Africa and also annex the South African enclave at Walvis Bay.[24] As the South African CGS, Sir Pierre van Ryneveld, noted in a memo to the CIGS in January 1942, 'there was plenty of material on which German propaganda could work, and the Germans, with their customary thoroughness, set upon this at long range by means of [Radio] Zeesen'.[25] The focus of the propaganda was predictably on the Afrikaner, the Afrikaner struggle against the British Empire, and a catalogue of 'crimes' committed by the British Empire, including, but not restricted to, the concentration camps of the Second Anglo-Boer War. German propaganda was the main subversive factor. Elements on the Rand were purportedly working to undermine the loyalty of miners and to gain control of the South African Mine Workers' Union.[26] Smuts warned the country in December 1941, that 'the internal danger in the Union was perhaps greater than the danger from without'.[27]

The attitudes of black South Africans were also diverse. Declarations of loyalty from political organisations, churches and the chiefs were invariably accompanied by calls for a more just political system. The African National Congress (ANC) was one such organisation, and called for the abolition of the pass laws and of discriminatory employment and trading regulations. Support for the war, it was hoped, might bring political and economic concessions. Others were perhaps more realistic and remained apathetic or, succumbing to Axis propaganda, became increasingly hostile to the war effort. The recruitment of blacks into the armed forces in non-combatant roles was also controversial, and the appalling conditions in which they often had to serve sometimes led to disgruntlement and misdemeanours, resulting in discharge from the service. This hastened political radicalisation, affected recruitment negatively and gave a platform to groups such as the ANC Youth League (formed in 1944) to criticise government policy.[28] Moreover, racial inequality persisted and would do so throughout the war and beyond. Santosh Kumar Das Gupta, a British Indian radio operator on the transport ship SS *Aust*, experienced this at first hand in Durban in December 1941. Gupta and a party of Indian soldiers were refused service at a public house and refused admittance to a cinema. Angered, they wrecked the front of the building by breaking all of the windows. Gupta's shipmates found 'the colour bar [to be] extremely rigid and distasteful.'[29]

Prior to the war, German propaganda took the fifth column form adapted in other countries. However, the Smuts government's steady policy of internment in time put an end to Nazi infiltration, including the pro-Nazi cell that formed under the supervision of Werz, and 'Germany was left with Zeesen as the spearhead of its attack'. Zeesen and the German shortwave broadcast service found ready success as long as Germany triumphed on the battlefields of Europe and Africa. However, as the tide turned against Germany, boisterousness and the outward signs of greater unity gave way to bewilderment and the return of disintegration among the opposition. Although Radio Zeesen continued to be the main vehicle of German propaganda, by 1942 it no longer had the same hold upon the anti-government factions in South Africa.[30] By 1944 the internal security position was sound, although this did not necessarily mean that Smuts had weaned more support from the anti-government forces. They were simply just quieter.

However, in 1939 no plans for effective intelligence and counter-espionage existed, the South African Police (SAP) being responsible for the monitoring of Nazi activities. Liaison was established between Military Intelligence, the SAP and the New Consolidated Goldfields and the Johannesburg Consolidated Investment Company Police, that is, the mine police. The Essential Services Protection Corps (ESPC), established with the proclamation of martial law in 1939, operated under Colonel FC Stallard. Enjoying the powers of special constables, the ESPC assisted the SAP in protecting key buildings and installations.[31] The Civilian Protective Services (CPS), resorting under the Department of the Interior, was created to assist local authorities with the organisation and coordination of measures for civilian protection.[32] Special provision was also made in the Defence budget to meet expenditure for intelligence purposes, and the intelligence service was extended to include paid agents 'specially selected to obtain information necessary for military purposes'.[33] By the end of 1940 the security machinery had been reorganised and modernised.

As the war progressed, evidence of treasonous activities on the part of a growing, but always small, number of South Africans came to the attention of the government. There were reports of German spies and agents, of chandlers supplying German submarines along the South African coast, of illegal wireless transmissions.[34] Setting aside hoax reports and tips from innocent if naive members of the population,[35] the Smuts government clamped down on the internal security situation through the implementation of a policy of internment for enemy nationals and South African subversive propagandists, and the rolling-out of a government information programme as an antidote to pro-Nazi propaganda.[36] Licences for private transmitters were cancelled, almost across the board, and volunteer listeners were organised to keep constant watch for illegal transmissions, despite a frustrating lack of shortwave direction-finding apparatus.[37] The intelligence function, under Colonel BW Thwaites, was upgraded in November 1939 and made responsible for civil security, local censorship and propaganda.[38] In February 1940, a Directorate of Military Intelligence was created, at first under Lieutenant Colonel HT Newman and then Professor EG Malherbe, in the office of the Director General of Operations, to manage all military intelligence and security of the armed forces. When the Union Defence Force went on active service, Malherbe's duties included censorship and propaganda in East Africa, North Africa and the Middle East, and in Italy.[39] Reports within South Africa and from Europe raised new anxieties about the loyalty of some civilians as well as of the troops.[40]

In order to facilitate coordination and dissemination, all information regarding internal security was centralised in the office of the Controller of Censorship (Colonel HJ Lenton), and an Intelligence Records and Clearance Bureau was established to operate under him. The Bureau itself did not undertake outside investigations of criminal, subversive or disloyal activities of individuals. The post and section of the Director of Intelligence was abolished in view of the fact that the Controller of Censorship had assumed all the internal security and intelligence work done in that section.[41] Apart from filling a much-wanted need in the Union's domestic intelligence organisation (military and internal security), the Bureau provided a link in the imperial chain of intelligence centres stretching from Singapore to Nairobi to London.[42]

An Information Office was created to interface with the press and to collect and disseminate information. There was a propaganda campaign to 'break down and destroy the pro-Nazi bias as a preliminary to the building up of goodwill towards the Allies and the Union Government'. Four kinds of Afrikaners were identified: (1) those that were convinced supporters of Smuts; (2) the waverers thought to be open to persuasion; (3) those convinced supporters of Malan, but who were open to argument and sentiment; and (4) those deemed so 'rabid' that they were thought to be impervious to propaganda.[43]

At the start of the war, the people classified by the government as extremely dangerous were interned. They included at first German and Italian reservists, a small number of South Africans of German descent and a handful of Abwehr agents, who had been monitored over the preceding months and years by MI5 and Special Branch. Moreover, the Germans were using Lourenço Marques 'as a post office and observation post', monitoring shipping and military activities in the Union and providing succour to the OB.[44] Smuts, in turn, monitored these German agents and the activities of South African dissidents and intensified the internment policy.[45]

The onset of war meant that plans drawn up by the British, South African and Rhodesian governments for the occupation of Angola and Mozambique, in the event of Portugal's becoming hostile, were dusted off and modified. There were four plans, given the code letters W (the occupation of southern Angola by South African forces), X (occupation of Angola north of the Benguela railroad railway by Rhodesian forces), Y (the capture of Beira, another Rhodesian affair) and Z. Plan Z, aimed at the southern half of Mozambique, was to be purely a South African affair and was almost implemented in June 1941, it having 'been decided that as soon as Italy came into the war, the plan to capture LM would be put into effect', but was stopped when the forces were at the border.[46] It had been feared 'that Nazi elements in Portuguese East Africa would rise and take control of the Lourenço Marques area, with consequent dislocation of the Union's sea communications. Thereupon raids into Union territory and even a German expeditionary force relying on the support of the disaffected areas in the Union were not considered impossible.'[47] That October, a motion was made at the United Party Congress, convened in Bloemfontein, calling for tentative proposals regarding a Federation of Southern African States. Smuts disapproved and the motion was withdrawn. He remarked: 'If we talk now of federation – of a Greater South Africa – we make people nervous. We do not want to take advantage of any state to the north because of the war. We just want to extend our friendship by developing trade, by giving them the same opportunities in the Union as they have given us in their territories.'[48]

Over the ensuing years, an increasing number of South Africans, chiefly Afrikaners, were interned. Their numbers may have reached 2 000. These internments aided anti-government propaganda considerably and 'may [well] have been the greatest single cause of dissatisfaction among Afrikaners during the war'. Moreover, the OB had established its own counterintelligence structure, both in the internment camps and without, to ferret out government spies. Significantly, Hendrik van den Bergh, the head of this structure, befriended by John Vorster in the Koffiefontein camp, would head the Bureau of State Security during the Vorster premiership in the 1970s.[49]

In addition to the OB, there were South Africans who actively collaborated with Germany during the war. Their number was always small but increased slightly through the war years.[50] They comprise a number of South Africa-born German agents who were earmarked for operations inside the Union, as well as Springbok soldiers canvassed in prisoner-of-war cages as stool pigeons and collaborators or, from 1944, for service in the British Free Corps (BFC), an SS unit that was to fight on the Eastern Front. As far as is known, the German agents were all rounded up by 1944, while the activities of the BFC group came to light from late 1944. A number of these men were investigated and some were arraigned in the immediate post-war years on charges of high treason.[51]

The mobilisation of the Union Defence Force

In spite of the divisions within the Union, Smuts immediately took the steps necessary to prepare for war. On 7 September Major General JJ Collyer, newly recalled from retirement to become Smuts' military secretary, compiled a report on the country's military position. The report was blunt and to the point: South Africa was entirely unprepared for war: 'An army without leadership, and effective staff supervision would merely be a rabble in the field even if its training were considerably better than that of the Union Defence Force is today.' And, as Collyer ominously noted, 'the present experience of Russia lends force to this observation'.[52] In the Soviet Union, half the officer corps – and probably more than 80 per cent of the high command – had perished in the purges of 1936 and 1937, severely compromising the country's armoured warfare capability, at the time the most advanced in the world. While South

Africa underwent no such violent purge or rapid loss of knowledge and experience, the net effect of the years of neglect had been the same.

As may be expected, the changes to the high command in 1939 were far more invasive than those of 1933. South Africa entered the Second World War lacking broad-based national support. Discontent seethed, particularly in rural districts where 'problems' were encountered within the burgher commandos and Defence Rifle Associations. Former Boer general Manie Maritz fanned a rebellious spirit in the Potgietersrus area.[53] And in the Transvaal several senior officers were charged with conduct prejudicial to good order and military discipline.[54] A general cleaning-out of the general staff was required, although there was a difference of opinion on how exactly this was to be achieved.

As part of a general reorganisation, with a view to placing the UDF on a war footing, Smuts vetted the entire general staff. A report, designated 'most secret', on the 'Security of our own forces' identified a number of general officers as politically suspect. Brigadier J Holthouse, who was director general of the SAAF from 13 September 1939 to 25 November 1940, was described as an 'admirer of Hitler and of Mr Pirow'.[55] The British, on the other hand, thought Holthouse loyal and rather questioned the loyalty of George Brink, whom they thought was in the pocket of OB leader Hans van Rensburg.[56] So there was no necessary agreement between GHQ[57] and the British authorities, both in London and Simon's Town.

The vetting process was complemented by a range of appointments, all politically reliable and tuned to satisfy sectarian interests. Smuts became commander-in-chief, with Van Ryneveld confirmed as his Chief of the General Staff and the dependable Collyer as his military secretary, while CH Blaine, transferred from the Justice department, was appointed with the rank of brigadier to replace AH Broeksma, Pirow's protégé, as Secretary for Defence. Major General Manie Botha, who had supported Smuts in Parliament in September 1939, was appointed as an honour to the Botha family (he was Louis Botha's nephew). His cousin, Brigadier Piet de Waal, a grandson of Louis Botha, was promoted to Director General of Operations and posted to Nairobi as plenipotentiary. General SJ Joubert was a grandson of Piet Joubert, the old Commandant General of the Transvaal.[58]

Changes were also made to the structure and composition of the high command on the grounds of competence. These changes, relating really to the quality of the leadership, were mostly more gradual. The six years under Pirow had brought a significant increase in the number of junior officers in the UDF: in all, their number increased from 100 in 1933 to 289 by 1939 (*see*

Table 5.2: **Permanent Force officers**		
Rank	1932–33	1938–39
Major general	1	1
Brigadier general	1	1
Colonels	4	5
Lieutenant colonels	9	16
Majors	16	37
Captains	45	93
Lieutenants and subalterns	55	196
Total	**131**	**349**

Source: 'UDF Summary – August 1938', f.67, Smuts Papers, vol 132, NASAP.

Table 5.2). However, the general and senior officers remained few in number, there was little opportunity for progression, and none had experience of commanding large formations in the field. As a group, the commanders and staff officers had no real knowledge of their duties in wartime, and no senior general staff officers for divisions and brigades had been named in peacetime. A careful and deliberate selection of the best men, not the politically reliable, was therefore as vital in 1939 as it had been in 1914. The general staff was the chief difficulty. Whereas the training of a general staff officer, as Collyer noted, is a matter of years, the staff course for ACF officers lasted just one month. A staff course for Permanent Force officers – abandoned before the war – used to last from three and half to four months, and courses of this duration were thought 'almost [a] waste of time'.[59]

Smuts' generals had little education, almost no training and no experience. Moreover, an emphasis on management and the good execution of clerical and desk tasks had led to considerable cerebral rust-out. George Baston, the British High Commission's confidential liaison in the South African Police, thought Brink 'by far the ablest soldier at General Headquarters'.[60] Yet, the greatest shortcoming was the broad lack of regimental experience, something that the perceptive Baston did not miss. He predicted that the UDF would be let down by its junior officers, who, he thought, were poorly selected and as poorly trained. The selection boards, under the influence of Broeksma and Van Rensburg, attached primary importance to the appointment of Afrikaners, and particularly of Afrikaners with a rather anti-British background. At the same time, promising 'British' material was often rejected due to the bilingualism requirement, which, he thought, 'for one reason or another seemed to bear much more heavily on them than on the Afrikaner candidates'.[61] Moreover young Afrikaner officers were thought avowed republicans, still permeated by the tradition of individualism, although not quite of the kind that imbued the leaders of the old Boer commandos. Not having been exposed to the conditions that formed the old leaders, the youngsters lacked self-control and experience. And this Collyer confirmed in his report to Smuts in September 1939.[62]

At the outbreak of war, the armed forces of the Union consisted of a Permanent Force of 349 officers and 5 033 men, and an Active Citizen Force of 918 officers and 12 572 men. Of the Permanent Force, 173 officers and 1 664 men formed the SAAF, 47 officers and 562 men were members of the South African Artillery, and 17 officers and 1 705 men formed the Special Service Battalion. The rest of the UDF were concerned principally with the supply services and in administering the ACF. The latter was roughly parallel to the Territorial Army in Britain, since membership, although nominally compulsory, was in effect restricted to volunteers from among the various age groups called up annually for compulsory registration. Members of the ACF were enrolled in units, some of which could show a history dating back to the middle of the nineteenth century, and were required to perform 1.5 to 4 hours of non-continuous training per week, and 15 days of continuous training, in camp, each year.[63]

The first priority was to organise for a greatly expanded UDF. On 22 September 1939, ACF units were authorised to accept volunteers for the duration of the war, and part-time training was intensified, while each unit was required to undergo a month's continuous training. On 16 February 1940, owing to objections that the Defence Act did not require the UDF to serve except in the defence of South Africa, and to the difficulty of defining the area involved, the ACF was reorganised on the basis of volunteers who undertook to serve anywhere in Africa.

The chief difficulty in the way of training was the shortage of equipment, and many substitutes and improvisations were devised. Although hampered initially by the chronic shortage of equipment, the rate of recruitment into the reorganised ACF proceeded very satisfactorily, and within a short period three complete divisions had been established. Meanwhile other units were formed, including the South African Tank Corps. The South African Artillery was enlarged and strengthened, and the auxiliary services were reorganised on something approaching a modern basis. On 20 May 1940, the 1st South African Infantry Brigade was mobilised for fulltime service, and, after a short period of training, left for East Africa on 16 July 1940. Later in the year an increasing number of units were called up and other brigades were formed. The 1st SA Divisional Headquarters, with Brigadier General George Brink commanding, left for East Africa during November. The 2nd SA Divisional Headquarters was formed on 23 October 1940, but the division did not leave the Union until June 1941 when it proceeded directly to Egypt. Major General IP de Villiers was appointed general officer commanding (GOC). The units remaining in the Union were organised for home defence and garrison duty as the 3rd South African Division, with Major General Manie Botha as GOC.[64]

Although the vast majority of South Africans who fought in the Second World War served with the ground forces, the other services made an important contribution to the UDF's total war effort. The outbreak of war had caught the SAAF quite unprepared for large-scale operational deployment despite the attempts at modernisation and expansion made in 1937 and 1938. In September 1939, there was no air war policy.[65] The 'front-line' operational strength consisted of four Hawker Hurricanes, one Bristol Blenheim and one Fairey Battle, while it also possessed 63 obsolete Hawker Hartbeest biplanes and a few equally obsolete Avro Tutors, Westland Wapitis, Hawker Harts, Hawker Hinds, Hawker Furies and Hawker Audaxes – a total of 104 serviceable but largely outdated aircraft. For personnel, the SAAF comprised a total full-time strength of 160 officers, 35 officer cadets and 1 400 other ranks. A growing number of these officers were 'amphigarious' – airman-artilleryman-infantryman. A side effect and a compromise of the Depression, they now formed a new elite.[66]

During the 1930s, the depressing economic environment and lack of opportunity in the UDF had induced a number of South Africans to leave the country to join the Royal Air Force. Their numbers increased after September 1939, with the result that South Africans served in practically all of the operations of the RAF. Twenty-one South African RAF pilots fought during the Battle of Britain, nine of whom were killed. One of the RAF's top-scoring fighter aces, Group Captain Adolphus 'Sailor' Malan, having found the navy 'starch-ridden' and not liking 'the caste system', had joined the RAF in 1936. 'I dare say that as a man from the Dominions I was to some extent favoured. The RAF liked chaps from the Empire.'[67] The air force, a service never short of publicity, headlined Malan's name and, over the next few years, no fewer than six portraits of Sailor were painted. One of these, done by John Mansbridge in 1940, was unveiled in Cape Town by Wilfred Brinton, the mayor. 'Surely the lead given by young

Malan', Brinton said, 'must call out to the Afrikaans-speaking people of this country, whatever their feelings must be. His example should send out an urge to all South Africans who have not yet joined up to do so.'[68] Pat Pattle, born in Butterworth in the eastern Cape, entered the RAF in 1936. He had been rejected by the SAAF and served a short stint in the SSB. Based at Amriya, Egypt, when the war broke out, Pattle served with the Desert Air Force in 1940 and was killed in April 1941 in the air battle over Athens during the German invasion of Greece. He remains the top-scoring Allied fighter pilot of the war.[69]

The SAAF's first priority was to train more personnel and acquire more aircraft. Within weeks of the outbreak of war, new flying schools were established at Pretoria, Germiston, Bloemfontein and Baragwanath, while a Training Command was established under Colonel WTB Tasker to oversee the SAAF's overall training programme. The real breakthrough came in August 1940, with the establishment of the Joint Air Training Scheme (JATS), in terms of which SAAF, RAF and other Allied air and ground crews, including Free Poles and Free French, were trained at 38 South Africa-based air schools. Under this scheme, the SAAF began to prosper, and by September 1941 the total number of military aircraft in the Union had increased to 1 709, while the personnel strength had leapt to 31 204, of whom 956 were pilots. The first air schools were sited at Cape Town, East London, Port Elizabeth, Kimberley, Oudtshoorn, Baragwanath and Randfontein. There were 29 air schools by the end of 1941, and by May 1945 the JATS had passed out a total of 33 347 aircrew – pilots, observers, navigators, bomb aimers, air gunners and wireless operators. Of these, 12 221 were SAAF.[70]

Home waters: the expansion of an air force and the creation of a navy

The Royal Navy prepared for possible war from mid-1939. Two threats were perceived in South African waters: an attack on Allied trade by enemy raiders, at first cruisers and then, from the spring of 1942, by U-boats and minelayers.[71] In June, Vice Admiral GH D'Oyly Lyon, the C-in-C South Atlantic, proceeded to Freetown to administer the wartime South Atlantic Station. He left the senior naval officer in Simon's Town, Captain Charles Stuart, to activate the Africa Station War Order in so far as it affected southern Africa and to mobilise the RNVR in South Africa.

The question of control over the naval forces in South Africa immediately came to the fore. Smuts was adamant that South Africa would take part in the war as an autonomous state and have full control over its coastal defences and defence force. British naval officials in Simon's Town, Freetown and London viewed Smuts' stance with some bitterness. Stuart felt that Smuts was using the war to wrest control of the naval reserves and of the shore and port defences from him. However, eager to keep South Africa in the war and, by extension, Smuts in government, London would do nothing to jeopardise either situation. The Admiralty was eventually forced to accept South Africa's assumption of full responsibility for the defence of South African ports and the South African coastline. This, as D'Oyly Lyon predicted, proved 'the thin edge of the wedge', the first of a sequence of steps leading to the establishment of a fully fledged South African navy and the eventual withdrawal, in 1957, of the Royal Navy from Simon's Town. Again, the answer to the call to arms had served as catalyst in the inexorable advance of Dominion nationalism.[72]

The new naval arm, the Seaward Defence Force (SDF), was created on 15 January 1940 to operate minesweeping and anti-submarine vessels, the floating portion of the examination service, the coastwatching service and booms and other underwater defences. The first task facing the SDF was to acquire ships and train men as rapidly as possible. Recruits came forward readily, principally volunteers from the RNVR (SA Division) and from civilian life. The only ships available were a certain number of trawlers and whalers; as many of these as possible were requisitioned and converted for war at South African ports by South African labour. In January 1940, the strength of the force was 74 officers and 358 men, having at their disposal 14 vessels ready for sea, some armed, some not.

A Combined Operations Headquarters was created in Cape Town to conduct the defence of the coast. In 1940, the British Naval Intelligence Centre was absorbed into this Headquarters, where intelligence matters – navy, army and air – were coordinated.[73] The coastal defences were upgraded. But matters were at first chaotic. Two 9.2–inch guns, intended for the defence of Halifax and Freetown, were diverted, at Smuts' insistence and with Churchill's assistance, to Cape Town. South Africa welcomed 'this proof of Commonwealth solidarity'.[74] Orders of aircraft proved more difficult. Smuts was prepared to extend SAAF training facilities to European British subjects in southern Africa and was willing to establish a South African Coastal Flight at Mombasa. But this necessitated an increase in the order for coastal bomber reconnaissance aircraft by seven, that is, a total of 61 instead of 54.[75] Moreover, although in dire need of aircraft, Smuts felt compelled to divert the 28 Gloster Gauntlet aircraft destined for South Africa to Finland. While Smuts took pleasure at sending 'this small assistance to Finland' in its hour of need, the non-delivery of aircraft was becoming a headache.[76] Britain's apparent inability to meet the need forced Smuts to look elsewhere; he turned to the United States.[77]

On the operational front, from the very outset of the war, the SAAF provided a valuable protection service for Allied shipping along South Africa's vulnerable coastline. At first, the obsolete Wapitis made routine patrols from the Cape, reaching no further than Hermanus and Saldanha Bay, while a flight of Hawker Furies made a pretence of protecting Durban. During September, the Junkers 86s bought for South African Airways went into service, converted by the addition of gun turrets and exterior bomb racks. Four new coastal squadrons were formed, one each at Cape Town, Durban, Port Elizabeth and Walvis Bay. Right from the start there were rumours of German raiders. Sorties were flown in combined operations with Royal Navy ships, some stationed at Simon's Town, in a hunt first for the cruiser *Admiral Graf Spee* in October and November 1939 and the interception of the steamer *Watussi* in December. The war had come to the Southern Ocean.[78] By the end of war, in August 1945, a total of some 15 000 coastal reconnaissance sorties had been flown by the SAAF.[79]

The greatly increased size of the UDF, not surprisingly, provided the impetus for a whole series of structural alterations in its high command. By November 1939 the Chief of the General Staff (CGS) headed a greatly expanded command structure. On the one hand he had the Director General Operations (DGO), responsible directly to him for all matters concerning operations, intelligence and coastal defence. On the other hand was the Deputy CGS, through whom the CGS controlled the various directorates. These were: the DCGS section itself, responsible for all training, mobilisation and signals; the Director General of Defence Rifle Associations; the Adjutant General and Director General of Reserves (AG and DGR), responsible for personnel, reserves, organisation and discipline; the Quartermaster General (QMG), responsible for supplies, quarters, transport of stores, veterinary services, works and fortifications; Director General Technical Services, responsible for technical stores, artisan training and workshops; Director General Air Services (DGAS), in charge of all air force organisation and training; and, finally, the Director General Medical Services.

By 1942, some minor changes had been made to the above command structure, with the Adjutant General and Director General of Reserves becoming simply AG again, and DGAS becoming Director General Air Force (DGAF). By this time the Director General Defence Rifle Associations had ceased to occupy a place in the command structure.

The Seaward Defence Force, at first disparaged in Royal Navy circles as the 'Seaweed Defence Force', was soon called upon to carry out the difficult and dangerous task of clearing an enemy minefield laid along the main shipping route off Cape Agulhas. The operation began in May 1940, and continued at intervals for over 18 months. However, SDF activities were not confined to South African waters. The Mine Clearance Flotilla also carried out operations with units of the Royal Navy from time to time in other areas, such as Madagascar and the Indian Ocean, and, in late 1940, in response to an urgent Admiralty request, four South African anti-submarine vessels left for the Mediterranean to join the Royal Navy operations there. The 22nd Anti-Submarine Flotilla, as it was designated, arrived in Alexandria on 11 January 1941 and was almost immediately put to work protecting the exposed sea route to Tobruk. The HMSAS *Southern Floe* sank on 11 February 1941 after striking a mine, leaving only one survivor. Despite the loss of a second ship, the minesweeper HMSAS *Parktown*, in an action off Tobruk on 21 June 1942, the number of South African ships in the Mediterranean increased steadily from 1942 onwards and reached a peak of four anti-submarine vessels, eight minesweepers and a salvage vessel (HMSAS *Gamtoos*).[80]

Japan's entry into the war on 7 December 1941 increased the threat to South African interests in the Indian Ocean and ushered in a number of changes. An American request for a concession to establish a naval base at Saldanha was turned down, but the SDF now established a presence at all South African harbours, including Saldanha Bay, and all now became defended ports. Moreover, on 1 August 1942, the Seaward Defence Force and the RNVR (SA Division) were amalgamated under the designation of the South African Naval Forces (SANF), and all officers and men of the latter body serving with the Royal Navy automatically became SANF-seconded personnel. This meant the virtual extinction of the RNVR in South Africa. The SANF – 'Saldanha And No Further' as some RN personnel teased – was tasked with the surveillance of the entrances to South African ports. However, it was soon called upon to provide a rescue service for the survivors of the merchant ships sunk in South African waters following the launch, from June 1942, of the German U-boat campaign in southern waters. Later, when the convoy system was introduced in 1943 between Durban and Cape Town, SANF anti-submarine vessels were detached to take part in escort duties in company with Royal Navy auxiliary trawlers and corvettes.[81]

In the Mediterranean, the SANF lost two further vessels during the course of operations in 1944 and 1945. These were the minesweepers HMSAS *Bever*, which was sunk by a mine off Crete on 30 November 1944, and HMSAS *Treern*, which hit a mine in the Aegean on 12 January 1945. The embryonic navy received a substantial material boost toward the end of the war after the Admiralty offered to supply it with three of the latest frigates. The first of these, HMSAS *Good Hope*, was commissioned in the United Kingdom on 9 November 1944 and the second (HMSAS *Natal*) on 1 March 1945. The third, HMSAS *Transvaal*, arrived in Cape Town on 28 July 1945. HMSAS *Natal* had the distinction of sinking a U-boat in British waters on 14 March while on its sea trials – the only ship on record in the Allied navies to have done this.[82] When the Second World War ended, the SANF had 1 436 officers and 8 896 other ranks on strength, including 2 937 personnel who had been seconded to the Royal Navy. The SANF's losses during the war totalled 338.

Production and consumption

The Union, if politically rocky and militarily understrength, was at least economically steady.[83] Between 1939 and 1945, war-related industrialisation and sharp increases in government revenues and expenditures transformed the South African economy (*see* Table 5.3). South Africa could finance its war effort with its gold. Able to expand gold production, despite ongoing labour shortages, the country was able to benefit from increases in the gold price over the war years and so largely cover the costs of the war. Debt could be reduced through foreign exchange earned through exports and the surplus of government revenue over expenditure: such surpluses were enjoyed in each of the war years. And so, as Nicoli Nattrass argues, 'while South Africa's allies were running large deficits and borrowing money (especially Britain), she was accumulating substantial gold reserves and repaying government and private debt'. 'No wonder', she argues, Finance minister Jan Hofmeyr could declare in his 1946/47 budget speech:

Table 5.3: War expenditure, September 1939 to 31 March 1945				
	Expenditure (in £)			
		On behalf of other governments		
Financial year	Union Defence Services	Direct disbursements	Sale of stores ex Defence stocks and miscellaneous services	Total
1939/40	5 191 901	–	–	**5 191 901**
1940/41	54 869 930	–	–	**54 869 930**
1941/42	70 330 260	3 785 786	10 072 288	**84 188 334**
1942/43	91 683 926	12 816 363	5 004 332	**109 504 621**
1943/44	97 589 567	15 992 458	13 875 254	**127 457 279**
1944/45	105 905 358	17 102 171	17 925 287	**140 932 816**
Total	**425 570 942**	**49 696 778**	**46 877 161**	**522 144 881**

Our territory has been spared the ravages of war. Our financial and bank-
ing structure has stood the strain. As a state, we have ceased to be a foreign
borrower. Our foreign exchange reserves are soundly invested in a sufficient gold reserve. Our ability to buy from the world the goods which we
do not produce at home is not limited, as is the case with so many war-torn
countries, by a lack of internationally acceptable money.[84]

The war, while redistributing assets to South Africa, also saw 'a major shift
of state economic support towards industry, a shift of manufacturing income
from profits to wages, and a substantial decrease in the gap between white and
black earnings'.[85]

South Africa was undoubtedly transformed by the Second World War.
While the Smuts government attempted to control war-induced, social, economic and political changes, the pressures soon became too great. Increasingly,
the government became reactive on all fronts at home. Smuts promised to
consult the trade union movement on all matters affecting workers' interests.
The South African Trade and Labour Council and the Federation of Labour
Unions urged him to accept a labour representative on the newly created War
Supplies Directorate. They urged also automatic increases in wages when the
cost of living increased due to the war.[86] Government plans were many, but few
of these were implemented. A Social and Economic Planning Commission

Table 5.3 **Continued**						
Provision (in £)						
Voted by Parliament		**Receipts**				
Revenue vote	**Loan vote**	**Standard stock capital**	**Contribution by SAR&H and Commerce and Industries**	**Sale of stores ex Defence stock to other departments**	**Payments by other governments**	**Total**
4 391 901	800 000	–	–	–	–	**5 191 901**
20 500 000	39 500 000	1 455 379	250 000		–	**61 705 379**
28 800 000	43 200 000	–	250 000	4 522 342*	9 194 712	**85 967 054**
43 500 000	52 500 000	–	250 000	2 295 134	13 629 173	**107 584 039**
52 500 000	50 000 000	–	550 000	2 623 541	23 635 453	**129 308 994**
51 250 000	50 000 000	–	790 000	4 567 967	35 426 427	**142 034 394**
200 941 901	**236 000 000**	**1 455 379**	**2 090 000**	**9 418 716**	**81 885 765**	**531 791 761**

* £3 663 362 cash receipts shown in the 1941/42 financial year were applicable to 1942/43.
Source: Union Office of Census and Statistics, Pretoria.

(SEPC) was instituted in 1942 to prepare and design strategies for the inevitable post-war reconstruction. Plans covering all conceivable aspects of South African social and economic life were drawn up, and often in the greatest detail. Almost none passed the planning stage.[87]

There were several reasons for the bureaucratic logjam; the first and foremost was the matter of wartime priority. Smuts' leading technocrat was Dr Hendrik van der Bijl, founder of the Iron and Steel Corporation (Iscor) and the Industrial Development Corporation (IDC) and first head of the Electricity Supply Commission (Eskom). Van der Bijl was a major proponent of state planning, state-driven industrialisation and government intervention. Van der Bijl had an able deputy in HJ van Eck, the first head of the IDC. Van Eck was appointed chairman of the SEPC in 1942. Capable, driven and with the highest levels of political backing, these men 'found themselves torn for the duration of the war between the short-term needs of the war effort and the implementation of the longer-term plans envisaged by the SEPC. Invariably, when choices had to be made, the former took precedence.'[88]

Secondly, there was little state coherence and agency among state departments and organs, which were in competition with each other for a limited pool of resources and hamstrung by conflicting jurisdictions, at all levels of government. The war had created rapid employment opportunity for many disempowered people. Yet, institutional paralysis, between government departments – Immigration, Native Affairs, Police, Justice and Social Welfare – and local government led to uncontrolled urbanisation. Socio-economic change, combined with high levels of underperforming policy and rising expectations, aroused black communities. The government's response, 'invariably reactive, groping and piecemeal', further inflamed feelings.[89] One result was the appearance of a major new political force, the ANC Youth League, formed in 1944. The Youth League, which enjoyed the backing of the black urban poor, would transform the ANC from a passive organisation to a direct challenge to the white state. However, there was, for the moment at least, no organised assault on the state. The leadership for this, versatile and charismatic, would emerge only in the 1950s and then as a reaction to the repressive social programme of apartheid.[90]

Nonetheless, the record in terms of war production, and the provision of a wide variety of supplies for the South African war machine and those of its allies, is impressive. Van der Bijl was appointed as Director General of War Supplies on 24 November 1939 to control the acquisition and production of all materials required for the efficient prosecution of the war. A War Supplies Committee, with Smuts as chairman, was created to liaise between War Supplies and the military-operational side of the Department of Defence. A Joint Supply Council, to advise on the relationship between the war and economic development, was added to the bureaucratic structures in September 1943. South Africa had never planned to equip itself for war production, but rather hoped to rely on the United Kingdom and United States for its armaments requirements. However, as the war increased in pace and impact, the Union was forced to develop local armaments industries, producing everything from ammunition, explosives and technical stores to armoured fighting vehicles and artillery, as well as clothing, blankets and other personal equipment.[91]

South Africa had at least six important foundations on which to build immediate war production. The first was an iron and steel industry and vast raw resources of iron ore of the purest grade. The second was the excellent quantities of coal and the electric power generated by Eskom. The third was the presence in South Africa of the two units of explosives production that proved capable of rapid expansion. Fourth was the state's Railways and Harbours Workshops, a ramified network of workshops on the mines, and the private engineering firms that had developed alongside the primary industries. Fifth, there was the structure of secondary industries (textiles, boots, food packing and canning), which had grown progressively since the First World War. Finally, these were all supported by a flow of raw materials, many supplied from local South African sources. The results were nothing short of extraordinary, as a growing flood of materiel, including arms, munitions and equipment, food supplies, and textiles, were produced for the use or consumption of South African and Allied forces on practically all fronts. This included 3.7 million shell bodies, 4.3 million shell cartridge cases, 2.6 million mortar bombs, almost half a million landmines, more than 12 million boots and shoes of varying kinds, 30 242 tons of vegetables, and almost 2.5 billion cigarettes.[92]

Eating may be a highly personal activity, but it is also about society and government and, importantly, about government regulation and intervention. The very act of eating, as two North American food historians argue, connects us to our histories, for 'food, economics, agriculture, and human empires are all strands of the same narrative'.[93] The Second World War forced these strands together. Food control measures were implemented within the Union, where both shortages and surpluses were experienced. State intervention stabilised producer prices and supported the general health of the agricultural sector, which might otherwise have suffered because of the war and because of unfavourable weather conditions. Farmers were subsidised, minimum producer prices were set, and a good portion of the harvest was marked for export and external processing. The poor local consumer paid the price. The many control and marketing boards were thought not to have the consumer's best interests at heart. Unsurprisingly, state intervention in agriculture was not well received by a public unwilling to make (further) sacrifices for the war effort. Food control impacted negatively on public opinion, and public opinion in turn influenced agricultural policy. As a result, the government decided not to implement a formal system of rationing, despite severe shortages of some foodstuffs. Any notion of an equitable distribution of food and commodities, given the Union's segregationist structures and uneven development, 'remained no more than a pipe dream'.[94]

Military operations in Africa, June 1940 to November 1942

As early as December 1939, Smuts had offered to move a South African brigade and several squadrons of the SAAF to Kenya, as a precautionary measure in the event of an Italian invasion from Abyssinia. London, not wanting to pre-empt any move by Mussolini or to provoke Italian resentment, turned down the offer firmly but politely, with the exception of four squadrons of the SAAF, which were moved to Kenya in May 1940.[95] Notwithstanding, Smuts contin-ued to prepare a Union expeditionary force, while London prepared plans for the concentration in Kenya of East and West African troops.[96] Smuts' oppor-tunity came in June 1940 when the Italians overran British Somaliland and advanced southwards into Kenya, taking the wider war into a new direction. The first major campaign in which South African troops became involved during the Second World War was, therefore, in East Africa. Immediately fol-lowing the Italian declaration of war, on 10 June, the small SAAF force in thea-tre attacked Italian bases; the Ju 86s of 12 Squadron bombed Moyale, on the Kenya-Abyssinia border.[97]

The preparation of the expeditionary force for East Africa had been, from the beginning, the most urgent task of the Union Defence Force. This had been considered South Africa's front line from at least 1935, and it was here that Smuts, increasingly confident, would exert South Africa's interests far beyond the Limpopo.[98] It was originally proposed that a force of one brigade with aux-iliary troops (headquarters troops, supply and artillery) should be organised. To this was soon added the fighter section of the SAAF, and such bombers as were not required for coastal reconnaissance purposes. These forces would, it was believed, amount in all to some 7 000 personnel, and it was provision-ally arranged in May that they should be transported to Kenya by the end of June to assist the hard-pressed British forces endeavouring to hold a 1 300–kilometre front against the advancing Italians. The Union government also undertook to supply 1 500 lorries, and the necessary personnel, to establish an overland supply service between Kenya and the Sudan.[99]

The advanced units of the 1st South African Infantry Division, the 1st SA Brigade under Brigadier DH (Dan) Pienaar, arrived in Kenya in June 1940, with the remainder of the division arriving by the first half of July.[100] The dan-ger of fifth column activity in the Union and other security considerations led the government to retain part of the forces intended for Kenya in the Union for a further few weeks. Some 12 000 personnel made up the Infantry Brigade Group and General Headquarters and Divisional Auxiliary Services.[101]

By December the complete 1st SA Division had set up its headquarters at Gilgil, northwest of Nairobi. The South Africans fell under the overall com-mand of Lieutenant General Alan Cunningham (GOC East Africa Force), and the 1st SA Division was allocated the Marsabit sector, consisting of more than 400 kilometres of inhospitable terrain stretching from the Sudanese border to the area of Moyale. In January 1941, 1st SA Division (less the 1st SA Brigade, which was attached to the 12th [African] Division) was ordered to advance across the Chalbi Desert to the Abyssinian frontier, with the object of outflanking the Italian positions on the Mega-Moyale escarpment. This advance met with immediate success, and on 18 February Mega was captured by 2nd and 5th South African brigades and some 1 000 prisoners were taken. 1st SA Division's successes prompted Cunningham to deploy 2nd Brigade into British Somaliland, while the Divisional Headquarters and 5th SA Brigade were dispatched to Egypt by sea, arriving at Omuruja on 4 May 1941. For its part, 2nd SA Brigade, proceeded to advance towards Abyssinia against relatively light opposition along the route Nanyuki, Nyeri, Garissa and Mogadishu before it too was ordered to Egypt towards the end of May.[102]

In the meantime, 1st SA Brigade had been ordered, along with the rest of the 12th (African) and 11th (African) divisions, to advance to the Juba River and then to the port of Kismayu. So successful was the operation, which commenced in February 1941, that the attack soon developed by stages into a triumphant advance on Addis Ababa, the capital of Abyssinia. By 22 February enemy resistance along the Juba River front had collapsed entirely and thousands of prisoners were taken. Thereafter, the combined British and South African forces broke through to Mogadishu and Harar, the latter being occupied on 26 March after major actions at Babile and Bisidimo. On 29 March, patrols of the 1st Transvaal Scottish, in the vanguard of the British/South African forces, entered Diredawa. Finally, on 5 April 1941, Addis Ababa was captured.[103]

After further operations in the vicinity of the capital and in Eritrea, in which 1st SA Brigade played a leading role, enemy resistance was finally broken, and on 19 May the Duke of Aosta, Viceroy of Italian East Africa, surrendered with 5 000 men, the remnant of the Italian army in Eritrea. Exhausted by its exertions in the rapid advance on Addis Ababa and subsequent operations in Eritrea, 1st SA Brigade was at this point rested prior to transfer to Egypt via the Eritrean port of Massawa.

However, despite the fall of Addis Ababa and the surrender of the Viceroy, Italian forces in the lakes region south of the capital and in the Gondar area refused to capitulate, and it was not until the end of November that the last Italian forces in East Africa finally surrendered, after a protracted campaign in mountainous terrain and difficult weather, and in a battlespace almost devoid of infrastructure. The 1st Natal Mounted Rifles, 1st Field Force Battalion and various South African artillery regiments, light tank and support units participated in these final operations with great distinction.[104] Against this background, the contribution of the various UDF support units to the final victory should not be underestimated. After all, the main problems of the campaign were administrative, technical and logistic, rather than of a purely military nature. In this respect, the sterling efforts of the UDF engineering, road construction, motor transport and medical support units in supporting the fighting units over vast distances deserve special mention. South African losses were relatively light, with 270 casualties, of whom 73 were killed. The campaign had been won, almost too easily. North Africa would be different.

It was in East Africa, however, that the SAAF's exploits began to hit the headlines in earnest. With a few squadrons, equipped with Gloster Gladiators, Hawker Hurricanes, Hawker Furies, Hawker Hartebeests and Ju 86s, the SAAF engaged with an Italian air component comprising nearly 300 modern aircraft. Nonetheless, by the end of the campaign, the SAAF pilots had accounted for 71 Italian aircraft in the air and many more on the ground. In addition, they had destroyed numerous railway targets, convoys and supply dumps in interdiction sorties in support of the ground forces. SAAF losses during the East African campaign were 79 pilots and aircrew killed and five missing.[105]

By mid-1941, with the East African campaign to all intents and purposes at an end, the UDF transferred its attention to the North African theatre, where it was planned to deploy two full divisions in support of British forces, who, having defeated the Italian forces under Marshal Rodolfo Graziani, were now confronted by General Erwin Rommel and his Afrika Korps. By the end of June 1941, 1st SA Division, fresh from the East African campaign, had been assembled at Mersa Matruh in Egypt, where it concentrated on improving the Matruh defences and on training in desert warfare tactics. Towards the end of June, 2nd SA Division moved to Egypt directly from the Union. At the beginning of August, the division was deployed to El Alamein, where it also busied itself in constructing a defensive position and in desert training.[106]

By November 1941, the British Eighth Army, to which the two South African divisions were attached, felt strong enough to launch an offensive against the German and Italian forces in Libya with the object of relieving the besieged garrison at Tobruk. To 1st SA Division was entrusted the task of advancing beyond Sidi Rezegh towards Tobruk in support of the British 7th Armoured

Division. As the South Africans were soon to discover, they now faced an enemy far more formidable and resolute than they had experienced in East Africa. After initial successes, the Eighth Army attack broke down, and, during fierce fighting on 22 and 23 November 1941, the 5th SA Infantry Brigade was overrun and annihilated by Rommel's armour at Sidi Rezegh. Between 28 November and 1 December, 1st SA Brigade, too, became involved in heavy fighting in the Sidi Rezegh area.[107] All of the South African war correspondents, bar one, eager to watch the battle and get a 'scoop', were captured and went into the bag.[108]

In the meantime, 2nd SA Division had been attached to XIII Corps, and, during December 1941 and January 1942, it played a dominant role in the successful capture of Bardia, Sollum and Halfaya. These three battles cost the South Africans approximately 500 casualties, but they took 14 000 German and Italian prisoners. The sustained pressure from the Eighth Army eventually forced Rommel to fall back on the Gazala Line and contact was re-established with the beleaguered garrison in Tobruk. Between January and March 1942 the two South African divisions were employed in helping to strengthen the Eighth Army's defensive positions in Libya against an expected German counteroffensive. First SA Division was allocated a front along the Gazala Line, while, at the end of March, 2nd SA Division (less 3rd SA Infantry Brigade) was moved to Tobruk to take over the fortress protecting the harbour town.[109]

On 26 May, Rommel launched his long-awaited counteroffensive, and, after decisively defeating the British armour in the defensive 'boxes' at Knightsbridge, El Aden and Bir Hacheim, his Afrika Corps and Italian allies succeeded in driving the Eighth Army into headlong retreat back towards the Egyptian frontier. While 1st SA Division succeeded in reaching the Egyptian frontier without serious casualties, a series of tactical blunders on the part of the Eighth Army commanders during continued heavy fighting in June saw the fortress of Tobruk cut off and isolated by Rommel's forces. On 21 June the Tobruk garrison under Major General HB Klopper was forced to surrender when German assault forces broke through the fortress perimeter. Altogether 10 722 South Africans were taken prisoner, along with the rest of the 35 000–strong garrison. This meant, in effect, that 2nd SA Division had ceased to exist. This disaster followed the one at Sidi Rezegh by only eight months. Taken alone, each was of enormous magnitude; together, their impact was devastating, most especially at a political level for Smuts and Churchill.[110] Yet, as David Katz has argued, remarkably, Sidi Rezegh and Tobruk are barely remembered, a consequence of the national amnesia that set in soon after the events themselves.[111]

While Smuts and Churchill put out fires at home, Rommel wasted little time in capitalising on his success at Tobruk, driving straight for Alexandria and capturing Mersa Matruh on 29 June. The Eighth Army, however, made a successful stand in its defensive positions at El Alamein during July and August, with the brigades of 1st SA Division performing particularly meritoriously.

By September, Rommel's offensive had broken down completely, owing to the exhaustion of his men and the lack of reinforcements, supplies and fuel. The lull in operations allowed the new Eighth Army commander, General Bernard Montgomery, sufficient time to plan and train for a major offensive. At 21.40 on the night of 23 October 1942, the final and decisive battle of El Alamein commenced with an artillery barrage on an unprecedented scale. South African artillery units alone fired 62 000 rounds of 25–pounder ammunition during the night. The massive artillery barrage cleared the way for a decisive infantry and armoured assault on the German positions around El Alamein, with 1st SA Division one of four attacking divisions. The Eighth Army's El Alamein offensive succeeded beyond expectations, and, by the beginning of November, Rommel's forces were in a headlong retreat from which they were never to recover. Tobruk was recaptured on 12 November, and by month's end the German forces had been cleared from Libya.

With its services no longer required in North Africa, 1st SA Division was returned to the Union at the beginning of 1943. The price of victory had been high, however. Total South African casualties in North Africa were 23 625, including 2 104 soldiers killed in action, 3 928 wounded and 14 147 taken prisoner.[112]

The SAAF fighter, bomber and reconnaissance squadrons encountered, in the form of the Luftwaffe, a more tenacious and skilled opponent in North Africa than they had done in East Africa. Despite the climate and conditions even worse than those experienced in East Africa, the SAAF squadrons played a major role in enabling the Allied Desert Air Force to attain total air superiority over Rommel's air component by the beginning of 1942. The SAAF's single most memorable feat in North Africa was probably the 'Boston shuttle service', during which 18 aircraft of 12 and 24 squadrons dropped hundreds of tons of bombs on the Afrika Korps during the 'Gazala Gallop', as it relentlessly pushed the Eighth Army back towards Egypt during the first half of 1942. It was largely due to these bombing raids – three a day for many weeks on

Table 5.4: **SAAF sorties in Middle East operations, April 1941 to May 1943**

	Jan	Feb	Mar	Apr	May	Jun	Jul	Aug	Sep	Oct	Nov	Dec	Total
1941	–	–	–	105	162	289	405	955	632	529	1 353	1 287	5 717
1942	600	128	1 029	1 163	1 755	2 413	3 788	1 496	1 488	3 001	1 732	884	19 477
1943	965	796	2 671	3 027	1 318*								8 777
Total													**33 971**

* Up to 12 May 1943.
Source: J Ambrose Brown, *Eagles Strike*, p 407.

end – that Rommel's advance finally ground to a halt near El Alamein in mid-1942. After the battle of El Alamein, too, the SAAF's North Africa squadrons played a vital role in harassing the retreating German forces. Between April 1941 and May 1943, the SAAF, with a maximum of 11 squadrons operational, flew 33 971 sorties and destroyed 342 enemy aircraft.[113]

The entry of Japan into the war rendered the defence of South Africa against a possible invasion a matter of some urgency. Moreover, the risks to shipping in the Mediterranean, due to Axis naval and air activity, especially following the fall of Greece and Crete, and the threat Rommel posed to the Suez Canal, increased the strategic importance of the Cape sea route immensely. As a result, in June 1942, the forces in the Union were reorganised into Inland Area (comprising Northern, Central and Witwatersrand commands, with headquarters at Johannesburg) and Coastal Area (comprising the Fortress commands of Cape, Outeniqua, Port Elizabeth, East London and Durban, with headquarters at Cape Town). Major General George Brink was appointed GOC, Inland Area, and Major General IP de Villiers became GOC, Coastal Area. The defences at Union ports were strengthened; nine heavy batteries were developed or graded at the principal ports; and air and sea patrols of the coastline were intensified. Full use was made of part-time units, particularly in the Coastal Area, while the remaining ACF units were organised as a Mobile Field Force, with headquarters at Ermelo in the eastern Transvaal. On 23 September 1942, military forces in Southern Rhodesia were brought under South African command. And, for a moment, it seemed as if Plan Z was back on the cards.[114]

However, while the Japanese made no attempt at air or land attack, the German submarine offensive began in South African waters in June 1942, leading to the sinking of nine merchant ships in just two days. This had been made possible through the use of supply submarines, or 'Milch Cows', which could deliver fuel, torpedoes, ammunition, fresh food and drinking water, and medical equipment at a range of 12 300 nautical miles. The aim of the German Naval Staff was to 'disperse the enemy's forces and, by compelling him to extend the convoy system over further vast areas of ocean, slow down the whole worldwide movement of Allied seaborne supplies.'[115] The secondary objective was to ease the strain on the U-boats north of the equator and to supplement the efforts of the Imperial Japanese Navy's submarines, although there were no German-Japanese 'combined' operations. A Combined Operations Headquarters was established in Cape Town in March 1943 to coordinate anti-submarine measures, which remained a problem for some months, and to protect the vital shipping passing the Cape.[116]

However, as the First Sea Lord argued, the increased numbers of sinkings by U-boats in the Mozambican Channel would not have been possible without help from agents in Lourenço Marques, and quite probably the Union, and the provision of supplies and secure bases in the Channel. Churchill was resolved that Smuts should not invade Mozambique, and instead, in addition to an official protest in Lisbon, agents from Special Operations Executive (SOE) were ordered to stop wireless transmissions by Axis agents. In May 1943, British agents kidnapped Alfredo Manna, an Italian diplomat who operated the shipping intelligence network from his consulate in Lourenço Marques in collaboration with Dr Werz. Other agents were caught in South Africa and Kenya in 1943, and the Portuguese finally ejected Werz and five of his associates from Mozambique in October 1944.[117]

South African forces also played an important if limited part in the British invasion of Madagascar in mid-1942, an operation designed to wrest the island from its Vichy occupiers and to forestall the possibility of a Japanese invasion. British forces first landed on Madagascar on 5 May 1942 and captured the naval base at Diego Suarez, on the northern tip of the island. On 25 June, the 7th South African Infantry Brigade landed at Diego Suarez. Commanded by Brigadier GT Senescall, the brigade comprised the 1st City Regiment, Pretoria Regiment, and Pretoria Highlanders, with 'A' Squadron of the 1st SA Armoured Car Commando, 6th Field Regiment, and 88th Field Company, South African Engineer Corps. Based at first at Sakaramy, where defensive positions were prepared, in September the South African brigade took part in a large-scale operation to clear Vichy forces from the southern half of the island. Little serious opposition was encountered, but the topographical and climatic conditions were arduous and malaria casualties high. The Vichy governor general,

Armand Annet, surrendered on 2 November 1942. South African troops returned to the Union on the first anniversary of the Japanese attack on Pearl Harbor, having sustained 18 casualties, of whom four were killed.[118]

The 1943 election and the politics of reorganisation

In early 1943, South Africa at war presented a very different picture to the year before. For one, the war situation began to improve and Rommel's retreat from Egypt and then Africa 'heralded the end of the wartime republican dream in South Africa'.[119] But there was also more austerity, with shortages of certain goods and concomitant rising costs. The nation began to feel the cost of the war and there was even some grumbling among the government's supporters. The parliamentary session opened on 16 January 1943 in the atmosphere of mistrust and irritation that commonly surrounds a dying parliament. The victory at El Alamein and the Allied landings in French North Africa had marked a turning point in the war, and the inauguration of the Allied offensive on land. For two and a half years, government supporters had been on the defensive against the gibes and sometimes pro-German tendencies of the opposition groups. In that long period, a series of setbacks to the Allied cause had imposed well-understood restraints on pro-war critics of the government. However, once the Allies had set their feet on the long road to victory, the opposition was rent by ideological confusion and the ambitions of rival leaders; government supporters, released at last from the inhibitions imposed by adversity, could savour the satisfaction of indulging their own grievances against the executive, and even their private feuds within the government coalition.[120]

Even the *Daily Dispatch* of East London declared that 'there is much criticism of the Government in the country, even among General Smuts's most loyal supporters, but when constituents pass on their grievances to their members of Parliament the latter find it impossible to pass them on to the Government'. The *Natal Witness* suggested that the prime minister 'had usurped powers far beyond the limits needful for the effective running of the war machine'. Parliament, it seemed, risked becoming a rubber stamp, and a great national leader, as Smuts was, could shift the balance of forces in the state. This was something Lord Harlech, the British High Commissioner, recognised. By 1943, Smuts dominated the political and military scene to the exclusion of any rival. On the government side, his authority was unchallenged and unchallengeable.

'In his shade', Harlech opined, 'other trees appear stunted and puny growths.' The Cabinet had no independent existence, its members' power had declined vis-à-vis the prime minister. Yet the Cabinet as a whole had increased its authority and function against the general body of Parliament.[121]

The general election was held on 17 July, and produced an outright majority for the government. While bolstered by his electoral victory, Smuts was less sure of the continued value of the Union Defence Force, which had suffered two severe defeats in North Africa and was having increasing difficulty in keeping establishments at full strength, as an instrument of government policy. A string of changes followed a new policy course. Announcing the formation of Inland Command and Coastal Command, he proposed to utilise the returned men of the 1st Division, who were acquainted with the latest forms of warfare in Libya, to form Inland Command. It would be a highly mobile force that could be moved anywhere in the Union where danger threatened.[122] The entry of Japan into the war had caused South Africa to be more careful and to look to its defences from a new angle. 'Nobody', Smuts said, 'knew where Japan would halt when she was already in the Indian Ocean. We are the gateway to India, which I look upon as the most important part of the Globe today.' He was, however, adamant that the men of 1st Division would not return until the Egyptian campaign was over: 'We do not desert our jobs. We finished Kenya and Abyssinia and we want to finish off Libya and Egypt. We want to finish Africa.'[123]

The Mobile Field Force, under Inland Command and based at Barberton, comprised 1st Armoured Brigade Group, which was virtually the old 1st South African Brigade, in addition to a reconnaissance capability, 2 Field Regiment, 1 Antitank Regiment, 1 Light Antiaircraft Regiment and 1 Field Park Company. The Brigade was equipped with armoured cars. The Defence Headquarters troops, attached to the Mobile Field Force, comprised 2 Medium and 1 Field regiments, and 2 Armoured Car Regiment. A 4th Division (part-time) comprised mines engineering and national volunteer brigades. No divisional HQ existed, the brigades coming directly under Inland Area. A 5th Division, comprising commandos, remained virtually a paper organisation. The coast defence units comprised fixed defences with three full-time battalions, a light antiaircraft regiment, a special labour battalion, and 13 part-time coast defence battalions. Moreover, there were in the Union eight Cape Coloured battalions, of which two were motorised, and the Native Military Corps, who were armed only with assegais and employed on guard duties.

Smuts also announced the formation of new tank divisions, manned by some of those returning from North Africa and equipped with the most modern weapons systems. Armour, Smuts announced, better suited the South African fighting tradition: 'The days of stationary warfare are past. We are once more engaged upon a warfare of surprises, tricks, ruses and all sorts of things which we practised and knew so well in the Boer War.'[124] In Libya there had been no front: '[It] is just a wide war dance between the two armies.' Movement was rapid, by day and night, surprising the enemy. The total approximate strength of 6th Division, a new armoured formation, including 40 per cent reserves for armoured units and 25 per cent reserves for other units, was 18 000. Of these, 30 per cent were coloured and employed mainly as cooks and batmen and, to a limited extent, as gun and ammunition bearers.[125] The government had decided on a policy of complete Europeanisation of the fighting components of 6th Armoured Division, which, as the British expected, involved a considerable drain on the military forces of the Union. Only General Service volunteers could be used, while Africa Service Personnel would be used as far as practicable on garrison duties in North Africa. As a result, the British defence authorities expected a contraction in South Africa's land force programme.[126]

British observers in the Union, while recognising that 6th Division would probably become a good fighting formation, with good morale, expressed their concern to the War Office of the level of discontent and dipping morale in Union, and particularly among units of the old 1st Division. There was the matter of inequalities of pay and allowances, on which a parliamentary select committee was appointed, but also of a failure on the part of the government to fully appreciate the factor of esprit de corps. The 1st Division, with its fine spirit, was, they thought, the greatest asset of the Union Defence Force. Shortsightedness had now thrown this away, and units had been 'broken up to unwarrantable degree'.[127]

Notwithstanding any discontent over this in the army, the United Party was strong and Smuts could appeal to the country with confidence. Not one to gamble, he had amended the electoral law to enable the soldiers on active service outside the borders of the Union to vote. Moreover, ahead of the election, Smuts had withdrawn 1st SA Division from North Africa for reorganisation and utilisation within the Union. It was a war election, a 'khaki' election, and one won overwhelmingly by Smuts. In the House of Assembly his following increased to 110, while the opposition dwindled to 43. No other party was determined to carry on with the war. While the public did not like food control, increased taxation or, indeed, the composition of the Cabinet, there was no satisfactory alternative. Facing a demand for reform, a restiveness and signs of a possible split in the United Party, the only way the government could remain in power was by doing its job properly. These views were expounded by Arthur Barlow ('Democracy is this country is, unfortunately, tottering'), while *Die Burger* warned of the increasing power in the hands of the Cabinet, and especially those of the prime minister, at the expense of Parliament. The growth of executive power, an unplanned consequence of the war, highlighted the need for a vigilant Parliament and a tenacious, watchdog press.[128] Yet, importantly, Malan and the nationalists hadn't done too badly in the election either, for Malan had managed to consolidate the opposition, eliminate many of the splinter groups on the right of the political spectrum and form a solid phalanx of vocal MPs.[129]

There was special interest when the new Parliament met on 22 January 1944. The apparent delay in summoning the members to Cape Town after the July election invoked criticism of Smuts and the Cabinet and stimulated a debate on the place of Parliament in the machinery of government. Moreover, the administration had reached new levels of unpopularity due to rapidly rising living costs, shortage of many household commodities and foodstuffs, defects in the food control organisation and a lack of housing. The only concession to the rising tide of protest had been a slight reshuffling, and renaming, of Cabinet portfolios. The war all of a sudden seemed farther away than ever. The tempo of the South African war effort was slowing down, and the removal of the Japanese threat to South Africa's security had freed people's minds for the contemplation of their private grievances. The opposition used the parliamentary session to express their discontent, while the more politically conscious sections of government supporters hoped that the Cabinet would announce plans to address some of the more immediate post-war problems that were looming into view.[130]

Military operations in Europe, April 1944 to May 1945

The last major theatre of operations in which South African land forces fought was Italy. Key to the South African role in the campaign was the formation, on 1 February 1943, of the 6th SA Armoured Division – the first-ever South African armoured division – under the command of Major General WH

Evered Poole. The division comprised 11th Armoured and 12th Motorised brigades and divisional troops. The 24th Guards Brigade was attached in Italy. Although few knew it at the time, the division had been formed specifically to take part in the planned invasion of Italy and contrived by Smuts to wangle tanks from the British. Moreover, pressed by a shortage of new recruits in the Union, an armoured division would free up valuable personnel for service elsewhere in the South African forces.[131]

After a few weeks of intensive training at Zonderwater, the division moved to Hay Paddock near Pietermaritzburg in early April to wait for a convoy north. On 18 and 19 April 1943, the division set sail for Egypt. On arrival at Suez, the division was transported to a camp established at Khatatba, some 100 kilometres from Cairo, and for the next twelve months underwent an exhaustive training programme designed to bring its various units to a peak of battle efficiency. The division crossed to Italy in April 1944 and concentrated in the Altamura-Matera-Gravina area, in Apulia. The conditions in Italy were very different from those that 1st and 2nd SA divisions had encountered in North Africa. The 6th would have to operate in mountainous country ideally suited to defensive warfare, and to attack positions manned by a skilful and stubborn enemy. Rain and mud in spring, and snow and intense cold in winter, would impede mobile warfare, while the geography offered little scope for turning movements. This type of war would make heavy demands on all arms, but particularly on the engineers.[132]

The division remained in the Matera area until late May, when it was ordered forward to Caserta and from there to the battlespace around Monte Cassino, arriving just too late to participate in one of the largest and most decisive battles of the campaign. Here, since January 1944, the US Fifth and British Eighth armies had been trying in vain to capture the German positions around Monte Cassino, an imposing peak in the southern Appenines that dominated access to the Liri Valley, the only viable route to Rome for the Allies. According to South African war correspondent Carel Birkby, Cassino made the earlier battles seem 'as nursery brawls'.[133]

The capture of Cassino, following a massive Allied offensive, opened the way to Rome, and the entire 6th SA Armoured Division, with 11th Armoured Brigade leading the way, was ordered forward to assist in the capture of the city. After a rapid advance against relatively light opposition, the South Africans entered Rome on 6 June. The fall of Rome, however, did not by any means signal the end of the fighting in Italy. In fact, the next two months were to see some of the sternest fighting of the campaign to date, as the Germans met an all-out Allied drive towards Florence with dogged resistance.[134] All along the way, the mountains cramped operations, and were 'the great natural enemy encircling us, always closing in on us, barring our way'.[135] The problem posed by geography was explained by Captain Uys Krige, one of the war correspondents captured at Sidi Rezegh, but who had managed to escape and, after briefly joining the partisans, rejoin the South African forces:[136]

> It is not surprising that the Eight Army's progress through Southern and Central Italy has been so slow. Anyone who has visited that part of Italy – if only on a perfunctory little tour of a few days – will testify to the manifold difficulties an invading army would have to contend with as soon as it had crossed the Foggia plains and come to grips, once again, with the Appenine mountain chain. Or rather mountain chains – for the Appenines, virtually splitting Italy in two from the Swiss Alps in the North right down to the tip of the peninsula's toe – except for a few gaps in this great natural barrier – is no single chain of mountains; but chain upon chain, range upon range; with no order or sequence or fixed pattern; as inextricably entangled, it seems at times, as the threads of a finely woven web.[137]

Eventually, after a long hard slog of eight weeks through Celleno, Orvieto, Chiuse, Sinalunga and finally along the divisional 'Green Route' through Radda, Mercatale and across the Greve River, the 6th SA Armoured Division entered Florence on 4 August in the vanguard of the Allied advance. Celleno was captured on 10 June after a particularly fierce battle in which the 11th SA Armoured Brigade performed heroically. It was a confident and vigorous action that went far to justify commander-in-chief Field Marshal Sir Harold Alexander's words the previous day: 'South Africans are the spearhead of the advance.'[138]

The capture of Florence afforded the division the opportunity for a well-earned six-week rest. The respite was used to good effect; all of the division's equipment and vehicles were stripped and overhauled. On 22 August, the division was put under US Fifth Army command (General Mark Clark) and became part of IV US Corps. But there remained much to be done. The Germans were still firmly entrenched along the Arno River and along the formidable Gothic Line, which extended from the Ligurian Sea to the Adriatic Sea. It was of this line that a German commentator had said in 1943: 'There is a line in Italy on which Germany will resist with all her might.' The task of pushing the Germans back on the Gothic Line beyond Pistoia was given to 6th SA Armoured Division. For this part of the campaign, the armoured units were used as mobile reserves reinforcing the division's 12th Motorised Brigade and 24th Guards Brigade. In fact, during the following months the armoured units were often forced to adopt the role of 'infantry', as much of the Gothic Line ran along the northern Appenine range and was quite unsuitable for tank warfare. In addition, the onset of winter and the accompanying bad weather further restricted the use of armour. Nevertheless, despite the topographical and climatological handicaps, the 6th SA Armoured Division acquitted itself admirably throughout the grim winter as the Allied forces gradually pushed the Gothic Line back up the Appenines. On 24 February 1945, the division was again relieved and moved to Lucca for a period of rest and reorganisation.[139]

By the end of winter, the Allied forces stood poised to make the decisive breakthrough, which would lead to the capture of Bologna, the crossing of the Po River and the eventual collapse of German resistance in northeastern Italy. The breakthrough came in mid-April, when the Allies launched a massive and decisive offensive against the German positions in the Monte Sole and Caprara areas. On 18 April the entire German front started to collapse. Only now, in the final weeks of the war, was 6th SA Armoured Division able to revert to its true armour role as the Allied forces exploited the German collapse and raced across the plains towards Venice in pursuit of the retreating Germans. By the beginning of May, German resistance in Italy had effectively ceased, and a last-minute dash by 6th SA Armoured Division to Milan proved unnecessary; on their arrival on 2 May the South Africans were informed of the unconditional surrender of all German forces in Italy.[140]

By the time the Italian campaign had begun in earnest, in the European spring of 1944, the SAAF had developed into a true air force. Increasingly, as the Allies began to withdraw aircrews for deployment in support of Operation Overlord, the SAAF assumed a dominant role in the Allied air operations over Italy. At this point the SAAF comprised no fewer than 35 operational squadrons with 33 types of aircraft, operated and maintained by some 45 000 men and women. Their most noteworthy achievement in the air operations over Europe was the efforts of No 2 SAAF Wing, operating from Celone and Foggia, to supply the Polish Home Army during the Warsaw Uprising, in August and September 1944. Night after night, the Liberators of 31 and 34 squadrons, together with RAF and Free Polish squadrons, winged their way over 2 800 kilometres of some of the most heavily defended German-occupied

Table 5.5: **The South African contribution to the 'Warsaw Concerto' in comparative perspective**

Squadron	Number aircraft	Success rate reaching Warsaw	Percentage of aircraft lost	Number of containers dropped	Percentage of containers dropped	Average number of containers dropped by each flight
31 SAAF	28	89.3%	30.8%	228	47%	8.14
34 SAAF	6	83.3%	33.3%	33	6.8%	5.5
148 RAF	27	37.0%	13.6%	80	16.5%	2.96
178 RAF	24	66.7%	19.0%	132	27.2%	5.5
1586 PF*	14	14.3%	50.0%	12	2.5%	0.86
Total	**99**	**58.6%**	**26.7%**	**485**	**100%**	**4.9**

* 1586 (Polish Special Duties) Flight.
Source: Adapted from PL Möller, 'The South African Air Force and the Warsaw Airlift of 1944', Historia, 45(1), 2000, pp 135–48.

territory in Europe before streaking in over Warsaw at 200 feet to drop their supplies. The cost to the SAAF of the abortive 'Warsaw Concerto' was tragically high in men and machines, but the daring and skill of the pilots involved nevertheless earned the SAAF the lasting respect and admiration of the Polish resistance fighters.[141]

With the war in Europe officially over, the first units of the 6th SA Armoured Division began returning home towards the end of May 1945. The total UDF battle casualties in Italy amounted to 5 176, of whom 753 were killed. By war's end, the SAAF had flown a total of 82 401 missions in all theatres and lost 2 420 of its members killed or missing.

Human impact of a total war: prisoners, partisans, pregnancies

For South Africa, the Second World War was a colossal experience, profoundly affecting servicemen and -women as well as the populations that stayed and fuelled the war at home.[142] At the most personal level, the war generated millions of prisoners of war (POWs). This had been foreseen, and London had approached the Dominions to assist with the detention of German internees and prisoners. However, before an agreement could be reached, the position was complicated by Italy's declaration of war, which placed pressure on the authorities to accommodate the German and Italian nationals alike. South

Table 5.6: Prisoners of war held in the Union, 1939–1945						
	1941	**1942**	**1943**	**1944**	**1945**	**1946**
Italians	57 067	70 445	62 570	39 139	28 255	27 898
Germans		2 006	2 000			
Vichy French			1 657			
Total	**57 067**	**72 451**	**66 227**	**39 139**	**28 255**	**27 898**

Source: Union Office of Census and Statistics, Pretoria.

Africa, like Canada, expressed reservations about political internees, but agreed to assist with the POWs. The latter could be taken as a sign of South Africa's contribution to Britain's war effort; civilian internees, on the other hand, taken from their homes and placed in the care of organisations without official existence, were quite another thing. Moreover, Smuts had had his own problems with civilian internees.[143]

The first campaigns in North Africa and East Africa produced a flood of Italian prisoners, and from 1941 thousands were transferred to Kenya and South Africa.[144] By the end of 1942, there were 70 445 Italian and 2 006 German POWs in South Africa (*see* Table 5.6). In addition there were a number of Vichy French prisoners. Several hundred Vichy merchant seamen had been picked up in Cape Town and Durban and detained by September 1942, and after the fall of Madagascar 1 657 Vichy prisoners were added to the total. The bulk of the Madagascar garrison, largely Malagasy and Senegalese troops, were repatriated to West Africa: Smuts was seemingly less than anxious to detain large numbers of African prisoners in the Union.[145]

The repatriation of prisoners during and after the war did not always run smoothly. Many had served on agricultural projects or national infrastructure developments, such as road and bridge building, where they had come into contact with the daughters of the farm or of the nearby towns. Many of these women carried the fruits of this fraternisation, leading to the same sorts of questions of nationality and residence in South Africa, or in Italy, that some returning Springbok servicemen faced.[146]

The backgrounds and experiences of South African servicemen were highly varied. The first to go served in East Africa and then North Africa, where they fought alongside a good many 'native', colonial troops, while those that went 'up north' after 1943 were possibly drawn largely from the middling classes and served in Italy, where the South African government would not send black

Table 5.7: **Casualties, Union Defence Force, 1939–1945**

Casualties	White	Coloured and Indian	Black	Total
Outside the Union				
Killed*	3 656	246	182	**4 084**
Died while POW	260	20	101	**381**
Accidentally killed	965	163	115	**1 243**
Died other causes	284	126	97	**507**
Wounded	7 444	470	223	**8 137**
Accidentally injured (major)	4 253	1 038	665	**5 956**
Prisoners of war	12 313	615	1 655	**14 583**
Total	**29 175**	**2 678**	**3 038**	**34 891**
Inside the Union				
Killed *	40			**40**
Accidentally killed	854	129	247	**1 230**
Died other causes	1 148	305	594	**2 047**
Total	**2 042**	**434**	**841**	**3 317**
Grand Total	**31 217**	**3 112**	**3 879**	**38 208**

* Killed in action, died of wounds, presumed dead.
Note: The figures exclude the 324 casualties of the SA Naval Forces, who were not classified by race.
Source: Union Office of Census and Statistics, Pretoria.

servicemen in numbers. In all, 9 532 South African servicemen and women lost their lives during the conflict due to enemy action, accident or disease. A further 8 137 were wounded. A total of 14 583 South African soldiers were captured and detained by the Italians or the Germans (*see* Table 5.7).

The overwhelming majority of South African POWs were captured in Libya, at Sidi Rezegh (November 1941) and Tobruk (June 1942), and included a small number of black and coloured troops at Sidi Rezegh and perhaps as many as 2 000 at Tobruk. As a disadvantaged group, black POWs suffered conditions far worse than those faced by their white compatriots. Several did not submit to their fate, but showed remarkable bravery and daring. Lance Corporal Job Masego and Sergeant Ruben Moloi received the Military Medal for their exploits while in captivity: Masego managed to sink a boat in Tobruk harbour.[147] Others, such as Privates Dube and Dlamini, actively collaborated with their captors, and both were among those tried for treason after the war.[148]

Karen Horn notes that POWs had three options for liberation: they could wait for repatriation, attempt to escape before an armistice, or join the mass escapes that followed the toppling of Mussolini. However, a fourth option, namely, to join the Germans, opened in 1943.[149] The Rome Organisation, the escape line operated by MI9, had, at the time of the liberation, the names of 3 925 escapers and evaders on its book; no less than 896, the second-largest category, were South African.[150] Many of these men assisted Italian partisans in their civil war against Mussolini and the German occupation.[151] The South African escapees and evaders, and even the 16 deserters[152] in Italy, despite regulations to the contrary, established social and familial relations with local civilians. This complicated the evacuation of South African personnel after the war. By July 1946, 306 Italian wives and 25 children were evacuated from Italy. The UDF Liaison Office in Cairo reckoned the totals would reach 572 wives and 30 children. Moreover, there was a total of 31 fiancées, a number of whom were reported to be pregnant.[153]

While South Africa did not suffer enemy bombardment or a direct attack, the population experienced the destructive and disruptive dimension of total war, which urged at least some South Africans toward the reconstruction of society and sometimes to the building of a society better than that of the previous. Sixty-three per cent of these servicemen were 'white', and form the focus of an innovative study by Neil Roos. Feeling that class and race, 'the binary categories conventionally used by social scientists to interrogate South African society', were inadequate, Roos sought a fresh approach. Invoking David Goldberg and others, he argues that there was an evolving consensus among white South Africans 'on the political and social primacy of their whiteness' and this, Roos contends, offers a better framework for the study of their history as both white men and as war veterans.[154] As such, he uses the 217 122 white soldiers as a lens through which to study popular whiteness in mid-twentieth-century South Africa. Bonds developed between them while on active service, some of which, he argues, stood the test of time. In East Africa, Egypt and Italy, the theatres where the majority served, they formed notions and held hopes for both a 'better world' as well as for 'some form of post-war social justice, an ideal', Roos notes, 'that was in segregated South African society heavy with ambiguity and contradiction'.[155]

Although shared expectations and experiences undoubtedly shaped these men, white South African servicemen were not uniform in outlook. They differed, sometimes vastly, in terms of their social origins, their wartime experiences and, by implication, their expectations and aspirations for the post-war world. Roos argues that those who enlisted first were poorer, the military being a receptacle for the white unemployed (a point, incidentally, that still requires statistical testing). Their hopes, for a better life and post-war prosperity and social justice, shaped too by the Army Education Scheme, were limited to a large extent as an aspiration for whites only. However, as Roos shows, such social justice was not always of a discriminatory nature. Men like Joe Slovo and Rusty Bernstein, who were prominent in the 'shift toward armed resistance in 1961', numbered among these veterans and in the 1950s featured in the anti-apartheid struggle of the Congress of Democrats movement.

Conclusion

In many ways, although South African society was fundamentally divided along national, race and class lines, the Union in 1945 seemingly survived the 'test' of war. The UDF had grown into a significant military force and, economically, South Africa had been able to finance its war effort with gold and was still able to repay government and private debt.[156]

Yet great changes were to follow the end of the Second World War: 1948 brought the rise to power of the National Party, and of the men who had largely refused to contribute, especially through personal service, in South Africa's war effort. The command structure of the UDF was torn down by a man who had no military experience and little military knowledge. From May 1948, Frans Erasmus, the controversial Defence minister, purged the officer corps again, disposed of all the vestiges of the UDF's colonial origins, and scrapped the last British emblematic connections. The purging of the best-trained and most educated officers drastically reduced the intellectual quality of the military leadership.[157] Rapidly, South Africa moved down the path to 'garrison statehood' and 'total strategy', while the heroes of the two world wars were relegated to the dustbin.

CHAPTER SIX

Change and Continuity:
The Early Cold War, 1945–1966

A poor country has limits on what it might spend on defence. But, in these dangerous times it would be mad for South Africa not to have a well-defined military policy and to leave its defence forces in a state of inefficiency.[1]

— Minister of Defence Frans Erasmus, circa 1950, on South African defence

[The Union Defence Force] is controlled by General du Toit and Mr Erasmus, neither of whom understands the issues involved but whose first concern it is to promote the cause of Afrikaner Nationalism.[2]

– Sir John H Le Rougetel, UK High Commissioner, Pretoria, February 1952

Our Land, Air and Naval Forces emerged from the last war with a reputation which enhanced our prestige in the eyes of the world. It makes one sad to feel that that reputation and prestige has been largely destroyed by a group of extremist politicians and that our once magnificent Defence organisation has become a political toy and seethes with discontent and frustration.[3]

– Lieutenant General George Brink, March 1952, on the state of the UDF

After 1945, the threat of nuclear holocaust and the realities of the post-war bipolar system galvanised the world, as the rivalry between the United States and Soviet Union developed into an intense global struggle defined by national interest and ideology. The experience of the Second World War led to the creation of two instruments intended to ensure collective security. The first was the United Nations (UN), which came into being on 26 June 1945 in San Francisco with the signing, by 46 nations, of the UN Charter. South Africa was a founder member of the UN, and Jan Smuts, who played an active role in San Francisco, had personally drafted the preamble to the Charter. The second was the regional military alliance, which was provided for by the UN Charter and was soon embodied in the North Atlantic Treaty Organisation (NATO), an anti-communist coalition of Western European and North American nations formed in 1949, and later the Warsaw Pact, the military alliance of the Soviet Union and its Eastern European satellites, formed in 1955.

The post-war division of Central Europe brought the crystallisation of a new front along the line dividing the American, British, French and Soviet zones of occupation in Germany. A communist coup in Prague in 1948 brought Czechoslovakia firmly into the Soviet orbit, and by 1949 the Western Allies had merged their zones of occupation into an emergent West German state. The Soviet Union took similar steps with regard to eastern Germany, which became the German Democratic Republic (GDR) in 1949. In 1948, the Soviet closure of overland communication between West Germany and the city of Berlin, some 150 kilometres inside the Soviet zone but under four-power occu-pation, triggered an international crisis that marked the beginning of the Cold War. The Western response, in the form of the Berlin Airlift, signalled the resolve of the United States and its allies to counteract the spread of Soviet influence.

The resulting 'Red Scare', similar in nature and scale to that of 1918–1921, was exacerbated by strikes and unrest in France and Italy, the 'loss' of Czechoslovakia and the communist takeover in China in 1949. There was a belief in a Moscow-orchestrated strategy of world domination.[4] The convic-tion that Soviet agents had infiltrated Western governments and organisa-tions was widespread. 'Communists', real and presumed, were purged from government and positions of influence. Communist parties were banned; the Communist Party of South Africa (CPSA) was suppressed in 1950.

The post-war period also saw the waning of European influence in the developing world, particularly in Africa and Asia. India gained its independ-ence in 1947, and Ghana, the first of a string of new states in Africa, became independent in 1957. Africa at first drew little superpower interest, but later became a tempting Cold War target, for its mineral wealth, strategic location and prized votes in the UN General Assembly.[5] Although the US and the Soviet Union offered very different forms of post-colonial political organisation,

Washington remained ambivalent and lacked a consistent policy on African liberation. The Algerian war of independence (1954–1962) and the Congo crisis (1960–1965) demonstrated Africa's vulnerability to Cold War competition, and, although the USSR was frustrated in both instances, Moscow remained determined to increase its involvement in Africa and to court newly emergent nations. From the late 1960s, Egypt received lavish Soviet military aid, and from 1975 Moscow took the side of Angola's MPLA and assisted in the airlift of 160 000 Cuban troops into that country.[6]

Time and space, the Union's traditional guardians, were transformed by the development of transcontinental flight and increasing sophistication in airpower and missile technology. A political scientist could state somewhat naively, and as late as 1955, that South Africa was the only member of the Commonwealth whose interests were 'not involved in some strategic area fronting the communist power bloc' and, as such, was 'curiously detached even from the "cold war"'.[7] If true, this situation changed rapidly. The rise of the Afro-Asian bloc at the UN, growing criticism of apartheid and South Africa's racial policy, and increasing distance between South Africa and other members of the Commonwealth created problems for Pretoria that did not lend themselves to quick solution. In time, Pretoria developed a foreign and defence policy separate from the rest of the Commonwealth, a process that culminated in London in 1960 when South Africa left the Commonwealth. This chapter analyses South Africa's changing defence policy, set against the background of the early Cold War, the attempts by an embattled South Africa to find security in a rapidly changing and increasingly hostile world, and the organisational changes wrought largely by Defence ministers Frans Erasmus (1948–1959) and Jim Fouché (1959–1966).

Defence policy, threat perceptions and counterstrategies

The Second World War brought material advantage to South Africa. Industry accelerated, new capital poured in and, with the trek to the cities, secondary industry expanded rapidly. The ports, Cape Town and Durban in particular, had been flooded with troops moving between theatres of war in Europe, the Middle East and Australasia,[8] bringing prosperity for shopkeepers and service industries. Black South Africans, a majority of some 9 million in 1945, even accessed new levels of wage-earning and semi-skilled employment. White unemployment, in the general ferment of expansion, fell to a record low. To many in rationed, war-torn Europe, the southern hemisphere was a beckoning paradise: some 48 000 Britons migrated to South Africa between 1946 and 1948.[9] But the war, and the subsequent collapse of empire, exposed an array of Cold War conflicts, some of which held the risk of wider wars. As Smuts noted in the Senate, 'an entirely new wind blows in the world today. This change is coming over the world and we feel the shock thereof.'[10]

Smuts' government faced two pressing military questions in 1945. The first and most immediate priority was to dismantle the enormous war machine, to repatriate and demobilise the thousands of volunteers who had enlisted, and to disband the numerous volunteer units that had been established for the duration of the war. A Ministry of Welfare and Demobilisation and a Directorate of Demobilisation had been created in April 1944 to manage the process of demobilisation and the high expectations of soldiers returning to civilian life. Harry Lawrence, the minister responsible, promised them that there would be 'no forgotten men.'[11] Yet, for many sevicemen, ideas of a post-war Utopia were dashed by seemingly inexplicable delays and apparent unfairness, all worsened by poor socio-economic conditions. Some found it impossible to return to their pre-war employment. Several town councils, including Pretoria, Bloemfontein and Brakpan, all firmly in Nationalist hands, barred returned soldiers from municipal employment. Although the attempts made by Lawrence and his team were admirable, the Smuts government clearly 'did not take into account the broader political, economic and social issues that influenced the promises they had made to the ex-soldiers'.[12] Belatedly, they realised that it was one thing to frame a policy document; implementation was quite another thing. As a result, demobilisation proceeded not without hitches and dashed expectations. Some returned soldiers found it difficult to adapt to a changed post-war South Africa. Their expectations plummeted, and, at the ballot box and elsewhere, anger was directed first at Smuts and then, after 1948, at the Nationalist government.

Shortly after the German surrender on 9 May 1945, reports were received in South Africa that among the papers scattered on the floors of Hitler's Chancellery, in Berlin, were letters relating to Union nationals. A special mission flew to Germany to collect and collate evidence of South Africans suspected of treasonable activity.[13] The leader of the official opposition, DF Malan, was himself investigated for supposed contacts with German agents in 1940.[14] Malan, however, was exonerated; others were convicted and imprisoned. Douglas Mardon, a Durbanite from a troubled background, was convicted of treason:

while a prisoner of war in Germany, he had joined the British Free Corps, a German unit formed to fight against the Red Army on the Eastern Front.[15] Those accused of treason were released when the Nationalists came to power in 1948.

The second pressing matter for the government involved the design of a new post-war defence policy. The changed international landscape, and the question as to where South African forces might serve in future, affected decisions on the nature and shape of the post-war UDF. The Second World War had marked the beginning of a new era. On the one hand, South African foreign policy could no longer remain tied to non-involvement and putative neutrality, and its defence policy to concepts of internal security and wartime mobilisation. However, the Union could also not afford to maintain a large permanent force, and so the numerical strength of the UDF was drastically reduced from 1946. The size of the army and air force shrank dramatically, and equipment came to consist largely of materiel handed over to South Africa by its allies. The navy was reduced to three Loch-class frigates, two boom-defence vessels, one minelayer and a small number of motor launches.

The design of the post-war UDF was predicated on three suppositions. Firstly, the security of the continent of Africa rested primarily with the colonial powers – Britain, France and Portugal. Secondly, South Africa could be expected to play a significant role in sub-equatorial Africa. Thirdly, the neglect of the armed forces during the inter-war years had been a mistake of near-calamitous proportions, as the disasters at Sidi Rezegh and Tobruk had borne out.[16]

Smuts, however, was careful not to repeat the mistake made after 1918 of allowing the UDF to run down completely in terms of manpower and armaments. Two complete divisions, 1st SA Infantry Division and 6th SA Armoured Division, consisting of 1st, 2nd, 3rd, 12th and 13th (Citizen Force) infantry brigades and the 11th (Permanent Force) Armoured Brigade, were planned and established with effect from 1 July 1948. But, with the exception of 11th Brigade, these units were all disbanded on 1 November 1949, following the advent of the Nationalist government and difficulties in enlisting volunteers for the Citizen Force brigades. The 11th Armoured Brigade would itself be disbanded on 1 October 1953. In any case, after Smuts lost the May 1948 general election, the decisions made in 1946 on defence policy and the nature and size of the UDF underwent dramatic redesign.

The National Party had also reconsidered defence policy in the light of the war and with a view to the threats perceived internally and externally. Importantly, the party recognised the need for a well-defined military policy in peacetime. The development of an alternative policy by the Nationalist government after 1948 came slowly and with much agonising, with Defence minister Frans Erasmus, lacking expertise yet scrutinised by other reactionary elements in his party, focusing on less-important political matters.[17]

Erasmus is a controversial figure and, there is a growing literature on him, although the only full, in-depth studies are dissertations produced by Louise Jooste and Roger Boulter.[18] Both agree that Erasmus had no military experience and little military knowledge, and that this did not deter him from launching a thorough transformation of the UDF. His 'first concern', to quote the British High Commissioner, was 'to promote the cause of Afrikaner Nationalism'.[19] The recasting of the defence force, on land, in the air and especially at sea, giving it 'a South African orientation', was considered the primary task. The defence force had to be 'entirely recreated' so that it received a definite South African character, and contributed to the development of a South African military tradition.[20] At a cultural and political level, this meant a reversion to not only the labels but also the traditions of the old Boer republics.

Erasmus sought an immediate shift in the composition of the General Staff. There was no longer room for the men with multiple, layered identities, who had moved with relative ease on the imperial military landscape. A large number of Smuts' generals were from the Cape landed gentry, descended partly from the eighteenth-century Dutch oligarchy and the influx of British officers after 1795, that first clustered around the Berghs, the Swellengrebels, the Blankenbergs and later the De Wets, Van Reenens and Cloetes. This observation, which requires closer study, is based on a survey conducted on the families that contributed senior and general officers during the age of Smuts.[21] General officers like George Aston, George Brand, Andries Brink, Pierre van Ryneveld, George Brink, Hendrik and Piet van der Byl and Evered Poole shared these genealogical linkages and could enjoy position and promotion within a wider 'British world' setting. Aston, South African-born and with an Afrikaner mother, became a British general officer; Smuts himself became a British field marshal.[22] This practice now ended, and these officers disappeared from the passages of Defence Headquarters. Erasmus, Boulter tells us, 'initiated a process of ridding the defence force of officers who he believed were associated with the government of the Anglophile Jan Smuts and replacing them with party supporters'.[23] Sir Pierre van Ryneveld, the Chief of the General Staff, was forced into a period of leave and then retirement. Evered Poole, his deputy and presumed successor, who had commanded the 6th South African Armoured Division in Italy with such success, was sent to Berlin as attaché. Also born in South Africa and with an Afrikaner mother, Poole was labelled 'English' and had to go. Piet de Waal, Louis Botha's grandson, was likewise permitted to take up a post of little significance and no power.[24]

The organisational and human transformation of the UDF from 1948 was enormous. Poole and many others like him were replaced by men who were ideologically strong and who were committed to the Nationalist agenda. These men were also less educated, had largely not had the benefit of international exposure, and had escaped the formative experiences of the Second World War. There was a shift in the composition of the General Staff from the Cape country districts to the towns of the Transvaal and Free State. Overnight, members of the Ossewabrandwag and the Afrikaner Broederbond entered the armed forces.[25] As an opposition United Party publicist noted, after the election in 1948, 'all pretensions were discarded and the Ossewabrandwag, Nationalist Party and Broederbond reunited quite openly. The doors of the jails were opened and the "true Afrikaners" were hailed as heroes.'[26] The defence force became a socio-economic escalator for a new crop of officers from the burgeoning urbanised Afrikaner middle class.[27] Instantaneously there was a new emphasis in the armed forces on Afrikaner identity, the military culture and traditions of the old Boer republics, and allegiance to the National Party. Afrikaner culture came to dominate the military – in language, symbols and nomenclature. The creation of service gymnasia and a military academy, for much of their history insular and pedestrian, provided the all-important independence from Britain in training.[28] The Broederbond programme, aimed at an independent South Africa based on the 'Afrikanerisation' of public life and the education of the youth in 'a Christian National sense', permeated these institutions.[29] Moreover, race and the classification of peoples as 'black', 'white' or 'coloured' came to signify primary identity. Access to military careers remained strictly reserved for 'whites'.

The Reverend Cecil Miles-Cadman was one of only a few English South Africans promoted and supported by Erasmus. Born in Suffolk in 1888, Cadman came to South Africa in 1922. He entered Parliament as a Labour MP in 1938 and saw service as a senior chaplain during the Second World War. He left the Labour Party in 1947, feeling 'that a strong Communistic influence was gaining control of it', and formed his own party, the 'Central Group', to fight the United Party in the election. This did not go very far; he did not split the

'English' vote as he aimed to do. After the election, the Nationalists rewarded him with a senatorship and promotion to the rank of colonel in the Reserve of Officers. On 13 September 1948, as the *Rand Daily Mail* noted caustically, 'in the Senate, Senator Colonel the Rev Miles-Cadman approved the transfer of General Poole to Berlin and defended the Minister of Defence – and the bush cart'.[30] Durbanites threatened to beat him up and haul out the tar and feathers should he ever return to Natal. A police guard was placed on his Durban house.[31] Miles-Cadman subsequently moved onto the military base at Voortrekkerhoogte with a promotion and greater sense of personal security.[32]

At first, Erasmus offered the position of Chief of the General Staff (CGS) to Len Beyers, a retired general officer and a nephew of CF Beyers, one of the key figures of the 1914 Afrikaner rebellion. Beyers, who had started his career in the Royal Scots Fusiliers, accepted the position on two conditions: firstly, that it would be of only short duration, and, secondly, that, while he would give his unequivocal support to the government, there would be no deviation from 'military principles' – in other words, no political interference.[33] This did not happen. Beyers resigned in disgust the following March. In April 1950 he shared his misgivings with the country:

> Without reference to me [Erasmus] created posts for the absorption of persons in who, irrespective of their unsuitability or otherwise, he personally reposed political confidence. Political ambitions and opinion not based on professional knowledge should not be allowed to intrude into the responsibility of command and the functions of the military organisations.[34]

The command and control was key to the organisational transformation of the armed forces. In 1948, the post of Deputy Chief of the General Staff (DCGS) was changed to that of Director General Land Forces (DGLF) and, three years later, the directors of the Land, Air and Naval Forces were redesignated as the Army, Air and Naval and Marine Chiefs of Staff. Operations, training, mobilisation, intelligence and general administration were responsibilities of these three service chiefs. The Adjutant General, Quartermaster General and Surgeon General retained responsibility in their specialised fields. An Inspector General was introduced into the General Staff in 1953, subordinate only to the CGS. In 1956, the post of CGS was redesignated Commandant General as part of a broader drive to Afrikanerise the entire rank system.

Rudolph Hiemstra, an air force officer who had refused to serve during the war, was Erasmus' right-hand man. As a student at the University of the Witwatersrand, he had battled with the tempo of study, was afraid to question his lecturers and baulked at the use of the English language. He joined the UDF in 1931 and, having completed his first courses and training as a pilot, was grounded in 1932 for reckless flying. Family intervention and the ear of the Minister of Defence ensured a further opportunity. He was in Britain for part of 1936, where he had to 'hold his tongue' in the officers' mess on the matter of the Spanish Civil War. His reading at this time was limited to stories of Afrikaner heroism and the works of Afrikaner nationalist historians. His reading on warfare was seemingly limited to the atrocities of 'the English' and the courage of the Afrikaner people.[35] Hiemstra had OB connections, but hid these and remained in the defence force.[36] He took exception to English-speakers in the armed forces and their 'minagtende houding' (contemptuous attitude) to Afrikaans. English had been the language of training until Oswald Pirow became Minister of Defence in 1933. Pirow had promulgated a policy of bilingualism, whereby English or Afrikaans would be used, in monthly rotation, for the purposes of all correspondence and verbal communication.

Political discrimination and billet-filling – the filling of posts with politically reliable types – led to declining military efficiency, and lassitude was the price of political meddling. The maintenance of the UDF as a credible military force was quite another matter, although Erasmus professed the need to also equip the UDF with weapons systems that were, in all respects, commensurate with modern conditions. However, the supersession, dismissal and degradation of the men who had played prominent and distinguished wartime roles led to a dearth of expertise at Defence Headquarters, ensuring an incoherent defence policy for much of the 1950s.[37]

The policy Erasmus framed was based on three premises. Firstly, there was recognition of South Africa's sovereign independence, its isolated geographical location and its unique defence needs, which freed the country from 'entanglement in British defence schemes'. Secondly, the Union could not be bound, directly or indirectly, to participate in any war, and the consequent policy of neutrality must be South Africa's first line of defence against attacks from outside. Unsurprisingly, the Nationalists sought full control over all of South Africa's ports and naval bases and a revision of the Smuts-Churchill agreement of 1922 regarding Simon's Town. Thirdly, the Union had to be responsible for its own defence, and the interests of South Africa had to be placed first.

'Each consideration of our defence,' Erasmus proclaimed, 'must be taken from a purely South African viewpoint.'[38]

The military threat appraisal indicated a number of potential contingencies, which, as it transpired, had changed little since the turn of the century. The UDF now had two tasks. The first of these was to prevent internal unrest and, where this arose, to protect people and property. This, it was thought, might take the form of unrest (onrus), violence (onluste) and minor incidents (opstootjies), as would 'inevitably arise'. The training of the South African Police was to be streamed with the training of the Permanent Force to make possible coordination of all the security forces in times of emergency. The second task was to guard the Union (and Protectorate) against external attack, which would be met on the northern borders (the bush zone from the Kunene River to Punda Maria) or along the 4 552–kilometre coastline.[39] There were still non-African powers able to project force intercontinentally. In the past, attention had focused on Germany (1910s and 1930s), France (1920s) and Italy (1930s). After the Second World War, attention turned to the Soviet Union, France and possibly the UK or even India. Until the 1950s, the perceived threat of landward invasion from continental Africa still took the form of a colonial power with imperial objectives or, more likely but still remote, the possibility of an African revolt against colonial rule sweeping south. From the 1960s, this threat transformed into a possible pan-African army drawn from a coalition of newly independent states. However, the greatest contingency white South Africa would have to face was a combination of these two: an internal uprising supported by the concerted action of a world superpower and a coalition of African states, however remote this may have been.[40]

The presence of the Royal Navy and, from 1955, the new Simon's Town Agreement played a big role in terms of organisation and counterstrategy to meet the second contingency. The Second World War had shown clearly the vital importance of the sea route around southern Africa. In the early 1950s, negotiations began with the United Kingdom to place the defence of this route on a firm basis. By this time, the strategic landscape, internationally, regionally and locally, was changing, and there were ever-present questions about defence funding and access to technology.[41] Apartheid South Africa was becoming increasingly isolated and herein was situated a new vulnerability. Under the terms of the Simon's Town Agreement, signed on 30 June 1955, the Simon's Town naval base was handed over to South Africa, which took place on 2 April 1957. The agreement gave the South African Navy total and permanent control of the base in exchange for certain privileges regarding its use by the Royal Navy. South Africa would also purchase a number of ships from the United Kingdom, including six (later reduced to four) Type 12 frigates, ten coastal minesweepers, and four seaward defence boats. This ushered in a period of unprecedented expansion and modernisation for the navy. One of the more surprising changes was the move of the Naval Chief of Staff and his headquarters from Simon's Town to Pretoria.

But, for the first and third contingencies, apartheid South Africa now stood alone. After 1948, the distance between London and Pretoria grew, at first gradually. South Africa had no security service and the United Kingdom, despite having no security liaison officer in the Union, was opposed to the creation of such a service. Sir Percy Sillitoe, the head of MI5, stated that 'the improper uses to which a Security Service might be put by the Nationalists might well include its employment against the Parliamentary Opposition and against those members of the British community out of sympathy with the Nationalist political programme. It would certainly be used to keep down the black races.'[42] When the Second Commonwealth Security Conference convened in London in 1951, South Africa's objection to the attendance of representatives from India, Pakistan and Ceylon (Sri Lanka) certainly did not alleviate fears or assuage Commonwealth relations.

The government hoped that South Africa's border and coastal defences, inadequate in 1950 to say the least, would make an enemy approach from the sea or over land difficult. The country's geography and relative physical isolation remained an asset, it was thought, despite the destructive possibilities of the atomic bomb, long-range submarines and transcontinental flight. Large-scale air attack was unlikely, and, moreover, even in the case of a limited raid, South Africa's towns and cities were far apart and, in the case of the Witwatersrand, could only be reached with difficulty. Attention therefore turned to the northern bush zone and to the sea. For these, South Africa required a defence force larger and better equipped than it had been before 1939.[43]

On paper, this seemed plausible. South Africa could not consider a large permanent force. Defence planning and force design had to be based on a small number of troops, whose lesser numbers could be offset by greater combat effectiveness and by being equipped in liberal measure with modern automatic weapons. The defence force had to be of modest size, but so organised and equipped that an effective armed force might be placed at any moment in the field and, highly specialised and easily mobilised, cause little disruption to the social and economic activity of the country. The troops had to be able to deploy and conduct a mobile war. Erasmus felt they should not be encumbered with the heavy weapons of foreign battlefields. As a first line of defence, the Union therefore required a combat-ready, modern, permanent force on land, at sea and particularly in the air, which had become the dominant factor in South African defence.[44]

South Africa's second line of defence was formed by the reserves of the three services. The third line of defence was the National Reserve, comprising all able-bodied white men between the ages of 45 and 60 years. While acknowledging that the modern way of war demanded mechanisation, Erasmus felt that, without doubt, South Africa's best reserve combat forces were situated in the traditional commando structures, particularly when it came to internal defence. Here he was correct. At the head of these structures was the Chief Commandant, who reported directly to the Minister of Defence and was responsible for all matters of policy regarding organisation, training and discipline of the commandos. The commando system, and the Defence Rifle Associations, had been neglected by the Hertzog and Smuts governments, and they had slowly expired from a lack of state support. Erasmus was determined to revive the old spirit of the commando and to restore the system that he felt best suited the traditions and history of Afrikanerdom. Recruitment into the defence force was restricted to whites, and a comprehensive training programme, providing physical exercise and gymnastic training, was implemented to prepare boys to enter the system for military training at the age of 17.[45]

Faced with increasing isolation, within the Commonwealth and at the United Nations, because of the policy of apartheid, South Africa searched for alliances, first within a proposed Africa Defence Organisation (ADO) and then within the Middle East Defence Organisation (MEDO).[46] Pretoria was forthcoming with assurances that, in the event of a war against communism, South Africa would assist in the defence of the Middle East. It would send to Egypt, as soon as possible after the outbreak of war, an armoured division and an air contribution. These commitments, although subject to South African domestic politics and the availability of equipment, far exceeded anything London expected to have been able to extract from a Nationalist government in Pretoria.[47] This was in itself of major political importance, and, for the first time, London could expect the principal political parties in South Africa to actively support a decision to participate in a war from the beginning.[48] Yet, there was some concern in London that South Africa, having committed to the defence of the Middle East, had done very little to prepare the UDF for the possibility of a war there. The only major acquisitions had been two comparatively modern destroyers, in 1950 and 1952, a small number of Centurion tanks in 1952, and two squadrons of F-86 Sabre jets in 1955, all as a consequence of its obligations to assist with the defence of the Cape sea route and of the gateways to Africa in the Middle East. These acquisitions had brought a small increase in military strength.[49] Nonetheless, the UDF deployed twice during this period, in Germany and Korea, in support of Western allies and for the protection of post-war occupation zones.

Deployment: Berlin and Korea

The Malan government assumed power on 4 June 1948. Three weeks later, the Soviet Union closed all road, rail and river access routes to Berlin. On 26 June, the three Western Powers flew in the first consignment of food, medicine and post into the beleaguered city. Every available transport aircraft was mobilised for an operation codenamed 'Plainfare' by the British and 'Vittles' by the Americans. A multinational Combined Air Lift Task Force (CALTF) was created under United States Air Force (USAF) command. Britain again turned to the Commonwealth for assistance. Searching for military security in Africa and eager to be identified as one of the anti-communist Western states, South Africa despatched ten aircrews for service with the RAF; two SAAF Dakota aircraft left Zwartkop Air Station on 22 and 23 September, with 11 pilots, 10 navigators and 10 wireless operators aboard.[50] The small contingent, commanded by Major DM van der Kaay, were kept together in order to preserve their service identity; they trained together at the RAF base at Bassingbourne, were stationed together in Lübeck and quartered together in RAF messes. Major General Evered Poole, then the head of the Union's military mission in Berlin, added his personal aircrew to the task force. In April 1949 the South African crews were relieved by a second draft of 30 airmen. Together they flew no less than 1 240 missions in RAF Dakotas, and, by 12 May 1949, when the blockade was lifted, the South Africans had airlifted 8 333 tons of supplies into West Berlin, in the most inclement weather conditions and under harassment from Soviet live-fire exercises close to the three air corridors. Operations continued until 23 September, to rebuild stockpiles in West Berlin, when the SAAF crews returned to the Union.[51]

A year later, the SAAF mobilised for service with the United Nations Forces (UNF) in Korea. On 25 June 1950, the army of North Korea crossed the 38th parallel – demarcating the Soviet and American occupation zones – in overwhelming force to attack the American-sponsored government of the Republic of Korea (South Korea). The UN Security Council immediately condemned the invasion and called for the cessation of hostilities and the immediate withdrawal of North Korean troops. This and a further call were ignored, and the Security Council adopted a resolution to send a military force to the aid of South Korea. The Western Powers responded quickly. A multinational task force was formed under American command and a United Nations banner. The US hoped that the forces assisting South Korea would be 'truly representative of the United Nations'.[52] A United Nations Command (UNC) was established, with General Douglas MacArthur as commander-in-chief of the UN forces. By 29 June, many UN member states, including members of the Commonwealth, had pledged support. However, the matter of South African participation was problematic.

The Malan government, contrary to the popular fiction that South Africa 'wasted little time in offering the service of No 2 Squadron to the UN Forces', was cautious, almost in the extreme. Since its founding in 1914, the National Party had opposed common action with the armed forces of the Empire and the Commonwealth. Furthermore, the Union Cabinet did not see Korea to be within South Africa's sphere of influence and believed that, in any case, the war could quite possibly be over before a South African force could be dispatched. Indeed, the North Korean advance was routed by October 1950. The foreign minister, Eric Louw, who was in London at the time, tested British feelings about the developing war. He sensed an absence of enthusiasm and a nervousness that the Korea issue would expand into another global conflict. London clearly also had reservations about the US posture, that the world 'would see Korea as a barometer of American intent to deal with Communist aggression' and that possibly even the future of the UN was at stake, and had insisted that Washington tone down its position over the disputed Chinese province of Formosa (Taiwan) and avoid reference to direct attacks on the Soviet Union.[53] Although London was adamant that the Soviet Union had to be admonished and that a second Munich could not be tolerated, they were ill at ease over the readiness of President Truman and his military advisers to countenance a nuclear strike.[54] Louw detected also a cynicism in London over the way in which Washington had pushed the UN to the foreground and tried to create the impression that it was the Security Council that was acting in Korea. He cautioned Malan that the Union should act not in haste but carefully, and not compromise itself to a particular path of action.[55] Moreover, Korea was geographically far removed from South Africa's security interests, which focused on a presumed threat from the disenfranchised black majority within the Union, and involvement there also held the prospect of heavy expense.[56]

At first, the Cabinet decided to support the UN morally only, and on 20 July 1950, almost a month after the crisis had started, issued a statement saying 'that it would be unrealistic and impracticable for South Africa to give direct military assistance in Korea.'[57] However, fear of communism, the deteriorating military situation in Korea, South Africa's search for security in Africa and a rapprochement with Washington led Pretoria to reverse its position. Following direct consultations with the US, the Cabinet decided on 4 August to send direct aid in the form of an air contingent. The matter, and the United Party noted the irony, was not put to a vote in Parliament.[58] The South African offer was gratefully accepted, although the UN Secretary General had specifically requested ground forces. The contingent, designated the SA Air Force Far East Contingent, consisted of an SAAF Liaison Headquarters and No 2 Squadron, SAAF, the 'Flying Cheetahs'. The SAAF Liaison Headquarters was established in Tokyo, at the headquarters of the USAF's Far East Air Forces (FEAF), with effect from 5 September 1950, with a view to facilitating communication between Pretoria and the squadron in Asia, and between the South African contingent and the UN forces. This headquarters, with the Senior Air Liaison Officer (SALO) in command, fell directly under the control of the Director General Air Force in Pretoria.[59]

Within a month of the decision to send forces to Korea, 2 Squadron was assembled at Waterkloof Air Station under the command of Commandant Servaas van Breda Theron, a veteran fighter pilot of the Second World War. On 26 September, the 49 officers and 157 other ranks of the initial draft embarked in Durban for Asia. No aircraft or air technical equipment accompanied them; all equipment was to be purchased from the United States once the personnel arrived in theatre.[60] Much to the annoyance of the British, Pretoria attached the South African squadron to the FEAF. Daily news bulletins, together with printed news acquired in Singapore and Hong Kong, raised the fear that the war would be over before the squadron arrived. However, upon arrival at the port of Kobe, Japan, on 1 November 1950, the squadron heard that the possibility of recall had vastly diminished as 'volunteers' of the People's Volunteer Army (PVA), dubbed the Chinese Communist Forces (CCF) by the West, had been identified at the front.[61]

The squadron disembarked at Yokohama on 5 November 1950, and proceeded to Johnson Air Base, near Tokyo, where they commenced operational training on F-51 Mustang fighters supplied by the USAF. However, the pressing war situation in Korea, worsening almost by the day as more and more of the CCF crossed the Yalu River into North Korea, demanded that 2 Squadron become operational at the earliest possible time.[62] On 16 November, five Mustangs and a detachment of ground personnel were flown in two C-47s to airfield K-9, near Pusan in South Korea, where they were attached to 6002nd Tactical Support Wing, USAF, for further operational training. From this airfield, the first SAAF combat sortie in Korea was flown three days later.

Frenzied activity followed for the detachment in Korea. The 18th Fighter-Bomber Wing, to which 2 Squadron was now attached, moved to airfield K-24, near Pyongyang, as the CCF poured over the Yalu to assist the defeated North Koreans. More and more SAAF pilots, flying in from Japan in haste, went into battle immediately. They were employed in close-support missions, in an all-out effort to stem the southward advance of the CCF. For the younger pilots in the squadron who had not seen service in the Second World War, they were acquiring experience the hard way. Airfield K-24 had a bumpy runway, there were no hangars, the living quarters were tents, and sanitary facilities were almost nonexistent. In winter, temperatures dropped far below those to which the South Africans were accustomed. As the tempo of the war increased, and the Chinese intervened on an increasing scale, it was apparent that K-24 was in imminent danger of falling into the hands of the enemy. Consequently, on 4 December 1950, K-24 was evacuated and the squadron moved south to airfield K-13, near the town of Suwon. From here the pilots continued to provide close support to the retreating UN forces by attacking enemy troops, trucks and supply lines.

In the meantime, arrangements had been made for the squadron to have a permanent base in South Korea, and, on 17 December 1950, all of the personnel remaining in Japan were flown over to airfield K-10, situated on a bay close to the town of Chinhae. Soon the advance detachment at K-13 was also evacuated to K-10 and the whole squadron was together once more. K-10 became the squadron's home for the next two years, right up to January 1953 when they were re-equipped with F-86 Sabre jet fighters.[63]

From K-10 the South African aircrews flew almost continuous close-support missions. The Mustangs operated to a depth of 150 kilometres beyond

Table 6.1: **Aircrew casualties, 2 Squadron, SAAF, September 1951 to September 1953, quarterly**								
	Sept 1951	Dec 1951	March 1952	June 1952	Sept 1952	Dec 1952	March 1953	June 1953	Sept 1953
Killed	2	2	3	0	0	1	0	0	0
Missing	8	5	4	2	2	1	0	0	2

the bomb line (the line beyond which, for political reasons, no bombing was to take place). Areas suspected of enemy activity were thoroughly reconnoitred by Mustangs operating in pairs, with one aircraft flying at 30 to 100 metres, checking every building, haystack, ravine, wooded area, road and railway, while the other pilot flew at about 300 metres to provide top cover. The pilots encountered an increasing amount of ground flak, which, together with interception by MiG-15s, brought concomitant losses (*see* Table 6.1). The 'Flying Cheetahs', while equipped with F-51 Mustangs, flew 10 373 sorties. Of the 95 Mustangs acquired from the Americans, no fewer than 74 were lost due to accident or enemy action, with 12 pilots killed in action, 30 reported missing and four wounded.

The US planned massive air operations against North Korean targets in South Korea, the destruction of which assisted the ground forces under MacArthur, as well as the destruction of industrial targets north of the 38th parallel and the reduction of the North's ability to wage war.[64] Abandoning the idea of a limited nuclear war, FEAF strategy was to gain control of the air, isolate the battlefield as far as possible and provide close air support to the UN ground forces.[65] Engagements were frequent and these brought inevitable losses. With near-total UN air superiority, the North Korean Air Force was soon unable to mount air attacks of any significance against FEAF or UN ground forces. By the spring of 1951, the CCF had been halted, and the North Korean army and the CCF were forced to abandon Seoul on 14 March. Although Pyongyang, buttressed by the CCF, launched a further major offensive that April, employing some 70 divisions in all, the UN air campaign was successful. Lieutenant General George Stratemeyer, the FEAF commander, ordered a concentrated air assault against the North's supply lines. By May, the Communist offensive had collapsed, and a month later the UN had recaptured all South Korean territory with the exception of Kaesong in the west.[66]

From the start of the war, it had been apparent that the fate of Korea would be decided on land, by ground forces supported by airpower. Initially, most of the 16 contributing nations had provided naval and air elements to the UN forces. Gradually, as the military situation worsened, brigades and individual battalions arrived in the theatre from all corners of the globe. The United Kingdom committed an infantry brigade on 2 August 1950 and a Commonwealth brigade, consisting of British, Australian and New Zealand elements, was formed a month later. Following pressure from Britain and India, the United States stepped back from the use of atomic weapons during the critical stage of the war, in November 1950. In exchange, Britain agreed to commit further ground forces to the campaign. Eventually, the presence of a British brigade, a Commonwealth brigade and a Canadian brigade group in Korea led to the formation of the 1st Commonwealth Division on 28 July 1951. Although the division had a truly Commonwealth flavour, there was one conspicuous absence. One of the 'Old Commonwealth' – the Union of South Africa – was not represented.

Thus far, South Africa had not contributed ground forces to the war. The SA Army had been entirely demobilised after 1945, and the government was unwilling to take the political risk of calling up the reserves. However, early in May 1951, as a sign of solidarity, the Union Cabinet was persuaded to dispatch five Land Force officers to the 1st Commonwealth Division, in musterings to be stipulated by the British commander. This was only a gesture, and, according to the War Office, 'such demonstrations of solidarity [were] more important than the actual strength of the forces deployed'.[67] The United Kingdom accepted the Union's gesture in this spirit. The five officers arrived in the theatre in February 1952 and were relieved a year later by a second draft of five. Of the ten, four served at the divisional headquarters, three as artillery officers, one as an infantry officer and the remaining two with the 1st Royal Tank Regiment.

If the Korean War ushered in a new era for the armed forces of the Commonwealth as a whole, it very much represented the close of a period in the history of the UDF. It was the last time the Union was to act in concert within the Commonwealth defence structure.

In 1951 and 1952, a number of changes to the South African dress code were implemented. The new air force blue uniforms replaced the former khaki, a highlight for the personnel who had been somewhat envious of the service dress worn by other air forces in the theatre.[68] The SAAF officers were also issued with the new five-pointed star, which replaced the British-style pip. This initially caused some confusion among US military personnel, and, it should be said, some humour, as the star was almost identical to those worn by American general officers.[69]

Early in 1953, 2 Squadron made its final move, to airfield K-55 near the village

Table 6.2: **Targets destroyed by 2 Squadron, SAAF, in Korea**		
	Destroyed	**Damaged**
Vehicles	615	276
Tanks	18	26
Field guns	160	61
Flak positions	120	27
Locomotives	4	7
Railway cars	200	353
Petrol and oil dumps	49	29
Other supply dumps	243	87
Bridges	46	106
Buildings	3 021	6 816

of Osan, some 65 kilometres south of Seoul, where a vast new base had been built, and was equipped for the remainder of the war with F-86 Sabre jets. After several weeks of conversion flying, the 'Flying Cheetahs' began operational sorties in the new aircraft in March 1953. The squadron's role became more varied and pilots swept the valleys of the Yalu and Chongchon rivers and patrolled the 39th parallel, engaging MiG-15s on several occasions. In April 1953, the squadron reverted to a ground-attack role, bombing and strafing enemy troops, supplies and installations, including attacks on the North Korean hydroelectric power complex. In May the NKPA and CCF launched a final offensive and the UN squadrons once again reverted to close-support missions. Offensive operations against the North ceased on 23 July 1953, and an armistice was signed four days later. By 29 October 1953, when the last South African draft left Korea, the 'Flying Cheetahs' had flown a total of 12 405 sorties, more than 1 694 on Sabres, and had lost just five of the jets.

In all, 826 members of the UDF served in Korea. Of these, 34 pilots were killed in action, eight pilots were captured, and two ground crew died. Prisoners of war were exchanged during Operation Big Switch.[70] The destruction wrought upon the enemy in bombing, rocketing and strafing attacks reached impressive proportions. Discounting all claims of probable damage, Table 6.2 shows the effect achieved by 2 Squadron against some typical targets.

When compared to the other members of the Commonwealth, South Africa's contribution was small, although this must be viewed in terms of the strength from which the force was drawn. The Union was not in a position to commit more than a squadron and a few army officers to a theatre far beyond its sphere of influence. The rotation of both pilots and ground crew continued regularly throughout the war. The pilots were returned to the Union after completing 75 operational sorties, while ground crew were relieved after a one-year tour. By the end of 1951, a steady stream of personnel arrived regularly in drafts from the Union. The supply of Second World War veterans, however, was drying up and they were soon replaced by younger Citizen Force volunteers.[71] There was growing concern that the only deployable portion of the UDF was in fact in Korea.

Erasmus and the SADF: force design and military capability

The state of the UDF, and questions over its efficiency, concerned many during the early Cold War period. The matter sounded, over and over, in the press from as early as 1950. Some of this may be found among the United Party Archives; there are several thick files of newspaper clippings, one for each year, bringing together editorial and public comment on Erasmus and the changes he brought to the defence force. In 1950, the Free State Congress of the United Party adopted a resolution demanding the replacement of Erasmus by 'somebody who knew more about defence'.[72] Retired generals joined the clamour, including George Brink (who had joined the Torch Commando, a veteran's movement mobilised in response to the government's attempts to remove coloureds in the Cape from the common voters' roll[73]), while HS Wakefield and Frank Theron took up the cudgels on behalf of servicemen, some of whom had been dismissed unfairly, others who had resigned in disgust; many felt that the honour of the UDF was at stake.[74] Theron appealed to Erasmus 'to lift Defence above party strife and to recreate national pride and confidence in the UDF by reconstitution of the Defence Council as a gesture of goodwill'.[75] Theron enjoyed a personal correspondence with the Chief of the Imperial General Staff, Field Marshal Sir John Harding, who was 'an Old "Desert Rat" friend', about the proposed ADO and the poor condition of the South African military.[76] The leader of the official opposition, Sir De Villiers Graaff, who had served as adjutant of Die Middellandse Regiment in the Western Desert, pressed the minister in Parliament on a range of matters. George Brink, initiating a renewed public debate in 1952, lamented the rapid loss of personnel and efficiency. The SAAF, South Africa's main striking force, Brink argued, was in a constant state of re-organisation. During the past eighteen months or so, a large number of officers, mostly well-trained and very efficient officers, have resigned from the Air Force. We were told recently that this is normal; but then we know that this spate of resignations in our Public Service has become normal only since 1948. Our Air Force is totally unready and hopelessly inadequate to meet any sudden emergency.[77]

There was no doubt that the efficiency of the South African forces was deteriorating seriously and rapidly. The United Kingdom, to which South Africa had made obligations in terms of the defence of the Middle East, shared these concerns. Sir John H Le Rougetel, the British High Commissioner in Pretoria, concerned that remarkably few practical steps had been taken towards putting the UDF in a position to implement these assurances, raised the matter with his principals in February 1952. He felt that, although South Africa might produce men for an armoured division able to take the field in the Middle East, there was no prospect of Pretoria reducing the mobilisation period from six months by September 1953, as they had been asked to do at the June 1951 meeting of Commonwealth Defence ministers. Moreover, Le Rougetel noted with grave concern that the South African Air Force, apart from the squadron in Korea and two training units in the Union, was dwindling rapidly and that the South African Navy was far from being an effective force.[78]

British officialdom attributed the inefficiency and slowness in preparing war plans for the Middle East to three things. First was the 'policy of political discrimination deliberately pursued by the present South African Government',[79] whereby efficient senior officers, who had commanded the South African forces during the Second World War, were 'eliminated and replaced by officers whose sentiments lie primarily with the [N]ational [P]arty and whose war careers were entirely undistinguished'. This destroyed morale, and even efficient officers not targeted by Erasmus were resigning of their own accord.[80] Second was the inertia at Defence Headquarters and the stifling control of Frans Erasmus and General CL (Matie) de Wet du Toit, the Chief of the General Staff, neither of whom, the Whitehall mandarins felt, understood the issues involved. Du Toit in particular, they thought, did not appreciate the problems of the SAAF and the navy, both of which, in terms of British thinking, ought to have had their own service chiefs directly responsible to the Defence minister, whose competence was also doubted. And, finally, as responsible South African officials, Erasmus and Du Toit delayed orders for military equipment. The British suspected that Du Toit did this either in the hope of obtaining better terms from the Americans or, in the event of war, on the assumption that Pretoria would 'get from us better equipment more cheaply'.[81]

London felt pressed to do something, but recognised that this would not be easy. Any formal approach would be ill-received and lead inevitably to further arguments about the Simon's Town naval base, a problem then 'lying happily dormant'.[82] But how to nudge Pretoria? On the one hand, Pretoria had committed readily to MEDO, which went beyond anything London expected from the Malan government. Moreover, South Africa's martial spirit was recognised; once in a war, South Africans 'make a first-rate effort and produce fighting units rapidly'.[83] In the past, South Africa had responded speedily and effectively, both in 1914 and 1939, although hampered on both occasions by strong resistance on the part of a substantial minority of its people. Moreover, political interference in the armed forces was, London opined, 'an endemic malady in South Africa'.[84] Smuts, during the Second World War, had carried further than was necessary or desirable his policy of filling senior appointments from among those who were known to be supporters of his own party. The British government could not make a frontal attack on the present policy governing promotions and appointments, since this would be resented as an intervention in a domestic matter. The utmost care was needed. There was no purpose in antagonising or setting out to secure the removal of Erasmus and Du Toit, the men who, whatever their faults, were 'at least the architects of the new South African policy based on firm commitments'.[85] Moreover, the next Defence minister, coming from among Erasmus' colleagues, would have as little knowledge of defence and, tied to the same political ideology, would probably act much as Erasmus had done. Yet, the increasing deterioration had to be tackled. Ominously, the Secretary of State for Commonwealth Relations noted that, should the deterioration continue, 'we shall be faced with the questions whether we can continue to hope for any effective help from South Africa in the Middle East in time of war and whether we can afford to supply equipment to South Africa if the probability is that the South African forces will not be in a state to use it effectively'.[86]

This was a delicate matter that had to be handled with the greatest care. A high-level approach was taken. Le Rougetel used every opportunity to bring Malan into consultation on defence issues and to make the South African prime minister personally aware of the difficulties and of London's 'grave anxieties'.[87] This approach met with some success. Some 200 Centurion tanks were acquired in 1952 and two squadrons of Sabre aircraft in 1955; these were destined for the armoured division and air force squadron that South Africa had promised for the defence of the Middle East, the 'gateway' to Africa. The acquisition of jet aircraft allowed a much higher functional load and new training obligations, as flight and ground staff had to develop new skill sets.

In the meantime, in January 1951, the South African Air Force and the South African Navy were reorganised as services separate from the SA Army, with their own service chiefs and training gymnasia. Concurrently the South African Naval Forces became the South African Navy. A South African Marine Corps was established on 1 July 1951, but was disestablished on 1 October 1955. Two comparatively modern destroyers were acquired in 1950 and 1952, harbingers of technological change for a comparatively unsophisticated small-craft navy.

Under the terms of the Simon's Town Agreement, South Africa had agreed to purchase additional ships from the United Kingdom. During the late 1950s and early 1960s, South Africa duly purchased five seaward defence boats, ten Ton-class coastal minesweepers, one Type 15 frigate (the SAS *Vrystaat*) and three Type 12 frigates (the President-class ships: the SAS *President Pretorius*, the SAS *President Kruger* and the SAS *President Steyn*). These ships, together with the previously acquired SAS *Jan van Riebeeck* and SAS *Simon van der Stel*, then formed the nucleus of the South African Navy, which was developed over the following years 'from its wartime role of coastal defence and appendage to a larger naval power into an independent naval force with its own [self-proclaimed] responsibility for the protection of an important sea trade route for the West'.[88]

Difficulties in obtaining sufficient volunteers to fill the ranks of the ACF in the post-war period led to the decision to introduce the ballot system of conscription in 1953. The 1912 Defence Act had provided for a system of selection by ballot to compel citizens to undergo military training, but the system had never been implemented, and, until 1952, the ACF had been comprised entirely of volunteers. The new system was designed to draw an equal number of citizens from each magisterial district. The length of ACF training was also increased to three months' continuous training during the first year and 21 days during each of the second, third and fourth years.[89]

Furthermore, a committee, under the chairmanship of Brigadier HB Klopper, was convened in 1953 to consider the reallocation and distribution of ACF units so as to create a more even geographical and language distribution in relation to the manpower made available by the introduction of the ballot system. The committee recommended that some English-medium units be converted to Afrikaans-medium units, while other regiments should be amal-gamated or contracted. Despite representations made by some of the units affected, the reorganisation went ahead with effect from 1 January 1954. The 2nd Regiment Botha, for example, which had played a distinguished part in the Second World War as a unit of the 1st Division in East Africa and Egypt, lost its identity and became Regiment Christiaan Beyers. This was a level insult to the men who had served beyond the Union borders. Two deputations, to the Northern Command and the Director General Land Forces, met with no success. And then, as if to add insult to injury, the command of the unit was given to a commando officer with no ACF or war experience, who superseded two substantive majors, both with distinguished war records.[90]

The considerable increase in the number of men balloted for training in some areas led, in 1956, to a further reorganisation. The defence force was accordingly reorganised to comprise 32 Afrikaans-medium units (including six field regiments, two medium regiments, three light anti-aircraft regiments, five infantry regiments, five tank units and four armoured car units) and 20 English-medium units (three field regiments, one medium regiment, one anti-aircraft regiment, ten infantry regiments, four tank units and one armoured car unit). The changes were implemented with effect from 22 September 1956. The next phase of the restructuring, which had been planned in 1958, was implemented by January 1959, and the third phase was completed in February of the following year. This reorganisation left the ACF with 51 regiments and two sub-units. Of these, 22 regiments and one sub-unit were Afrikaans-medium and 16 regiments and one sub-unit were English-medium, with the remaining units being dual-medium.

The period following the Korean War was marked by consolidation and a revision of legislation, leading to the passage of a new Defence Act in 1957.[91] This consolidated the provisions of the 1912 Defence Act and its amendments of 1922 and 1932. The new legislation also gave the defence force a more South African character. Firstly, the UDF was renamed the South African Defence Force (SADF) and the Active Citizen Force and South African Permanent Force were, at the same time, redesignated as the Citizen Force (CF) and Permanent Force (PF). Secondly, the commandos, which Erasmus believed to be South Africa's best reserve combat forces for internal defence, were revi-talised and incorporated into the new defence structures. And, thirdly, new uniforms and badges, rank insignia, and a new pantheon of decorations and medals, were instituted.[92] The Castle rank insignia replaced the crown with effect from 1 April 1957. This was based on the design of the Castle of Good Hope and was symbolic of the earliest European defence of the Cape. From the same date, the CGS became known as the Commandant General SADF, a designation indicating rank as well as appointment.[93]

As a consequence of these developments, the traditional Citizen Force regiments and units were forced to dispose of the last vestiges of their colonial origins, of their emblematic connections with Britain and the Royal Family, and of their affiliations with British regiments. This was said to make the defence force more 'South African', but, for many South Africans, and for many veterans of the world wars, this was nothing other than naked 'Afrikanerisation'.[94] Some of these changes were a consequence of the structural adjustments in the expanding defence structure of the later 1950s and the reincorporation of the commandos into the mainline defence force. However, Erasmus also took a close interest in the designations and titles of these regiments and introduced policy that threatened their nature and ethos. The changes at first affected Afrikaans-medium regiments; much to their annoyance, the CF regiments were forced to defer to commandos sharing the same or similar designation. As part of this process, Regiment De la Rey, which had seen meritorious wartime service, became Regiment Wes Transvaal. Likewise, Regiment Gideon Scheepers became Regiment Groot Karoo, and Regiment Hendrik Potgieter became Regiment Mooirivier. The English-medium regiments were not spared. Using the home language of the majority of servicemen in the particular unit as rule, a spate of name changes was enforced. Most notoriously, the Cape Field Artillery, the oldest CF unit in South Africa, became Regiment Tygerberg with effect from 1 January 1960. Other regiments having foreign names and connections with the British monarchy or with British regiments were unceremoniously stripped of these associations.[95] After Erasmus left office, several of these units, including the Cape Field Artillery, had some success in regaining their original designations.

The revitalisation of the SADF

Erasmus, while Defence minister, expended his energy in recasting the defence force, its structure and processes, ranks and insignia and emblems, in an Afrikaner mould. He was, as Boulter has shown, little more than a party official intent on ensuring that party principles resounded loudly in his particular department of government. Criticism of Erasmus, driven largely through the press, but voiced also in Parliament, escalated through the 1950s. 'English South Africa' lost confidence in the Defence minister and, more generally, in the defence force, as reports of inefficiency, poor management and political interference came increasingly to light. As we have seen, concerns were also raised by South Africa's allies. The change sought by South African and British military specialists came in December 1959, when JJ Fouché replaced Erasmus as Defence minister, on the eve of South Africa's departure from the British Commonwealth.

In the years ahead, defence policy would be influenced by changing threat perception, the failure of the search for alliance and the ever-present questions relating to defence funding and access to technology. The scrapping of plans for the creation of the pro-West ADO was followed by the commencement of an informal arms boycott in the 1960s (made mandatory by the United Nations in 1977) and the abrogation of the Simon's Town Agreement in the early 1970s. The changing politico-strategic environment of the 1950s and 1960s, and the attempts by an embattled South Africa to find security in a rapidly changing and increasingly hostile world, forced a reappraisal of policy.[96]

The military threat appraisal conducted in 1960 indicated a number of potential contingencies, all with a strong Cold War focus, and all stressing the possible role Africa could play in the Soviet strategy of world domination. The fear of rampant communism was used by the South African government to gain support in Western capitals, and particularly in Washington. 'An attack', political and ideological, and possibly military, it was forecast, 'would be concentrated against the White governments in Southern Africa'.[97] The leaders of some newly independent African states announced their intention of freeing the remaining peoples of Africa from the bondage of colonialism by moral force and, if necessary, military support.

The General Staff, now called the Supreme Command, arrived at the conclusion that it was of vital importance to enhance the military capability and state of readiness of the SADF, purportedly for defensive action. Planning started and preparations were made to enhance the manpower and armament requirements so that the SADF's combat readiness could be raised to such a level of efficiency so as to counter any act of aggression emanating from Africa.[98] Measures taken to beef up the defence force included the development of counterstrategies, increased professionalism in the military, appointments based upon military merit rather than political affiliation, the search for alliances and contracts, the re-equipping of the SADF with modern hardware and weapons systems and the mobilisation of consent within white South African society.[99]

Moreover, by the early 1960s it had become apparent that the entire nature of warfare was changing, moving away from conventional warfare to various forms of unconventional warfare and insurgency. This led to the establishment of six combat groups, with the specific task of countering insurgency. Each was an organic tactical organisation designed to wage combat independently. They comprised all arms, often including a reconnaissance capability, armour, mechanised infantry, self-propelled artillery, combat engineers, signals, medical services and supply and workshop sections. Mobile and geared to fight insurgencies, the first four of these groups (11, 12, 13 and 14 Combat groups) were established on 1 January 1961, while 15 and 16 Combat groups were established with effect from 1 April 1963. However, with the re-evaluation of the role of the commandos in terms of area defence, the combat groups were disbanded towards the end of the decade. This, in retrospect, was a short-sighted decision.

The Permanent Force was maintained essentially as a command structure and a training nucleus for the Citizen Force. Over the same period, the Citizen Force was also vastly expanded. However, the long period of inactivity and complicated and lengthy mobilisation procedures proved problematic. In an attempt to overcome this, a system of Full-Time Force (FTF) units was introduced in January 1962, whereby a certain number of units were placed on a more or less permanent state of readiness. The training period was extended from three months per year to nine months and the number of ballotees called up for training was considerably increased (see Table 6.3). The system would drastically change in 1968 with the introduction of National Service.[100]

As far as conventional forces were concerned, 7th South African Division and 17th, 18th and 19th brigades were established on 1 April 1965. However, the ambitious plans for the expansion of the SA Army ran into serious difficulty in the mid-1960s as a result of a shortage of manpower. The FTF organisation and 7th SA Division were disbanded in 1967, on the eve of the introduction of the new National Service system; 7th Division was eventually replaced by Army Task Force Headquarters and 16 Brigade. The recommendations of the Groenewoud Committee led to the introduction on 1 January 1968 of the National Service system, whereby all medically fit white male citizens were liable for military service in the year in which they turned 18.

Table 6.3: **Number of ballotees (to 1967) and of National Servicemen (from 1968)**	
Year	**Number**
1962	11 759
1963	14 570
1964	19 784
1965	19 513
1966	23 164
1967	22 583
1968	22 460
1969	25 439
1970	26 357

Source: Republic of South Africa, *Review of Defence and Armaments Production: Period 1960 to 1970* (Defence Headquarters, Pretoria, April 1971), p 6.

South Africa became a republic on 31 May 1961 and left the Commonwealth. Nonetheless, defence cooperation remained important to both South Africa and Britain – to South Africa for vital access to military hardware and to Britain for access to naval and air facilities. This mutual interest was shown in the series of CAPEX naval exercises conducted in the South Atlantic by ships of both countries' navies. Moreover, the continued threat of conflict in the Middle East encouraged Whitehall to recognise the value of the Cape sea route and the strategic air route over southern Africa. (In 1961, for example, Turkey had denied clearance to British aircraft during Operation Vantage, the British military effort to support Kuwait in its dispute with Iraq.) This, however, presented something of a dilemma. On the one hand, London needed access to South African naval and air facilities to project force throughout the South Atlantic and across the Indian Ocean. On the other hand, the arrangements in this regard, extended by mutual agreement after 1961, diminished goodwill in what Whitehall termed 'Black Africa'.[101] Growing international criticism of South Africa and the prospect of a UN-sponsored arms embargo were cause for concern, particularly if Pretoria insisted on continued arms sales and on assistance, in the form of a British expeditionary force, if attacked. Abandoning traditional association and taking a more realistic view of Africa, London decided unilaterally to terminate its agreements with the new republic rather than suffer the indignity of a probable South African abrogation.[102]

In the face of dwindling defence cooperation from London, and then the

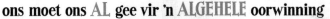

TOP: Springboks in Abyssinia, 1940: East Africa was considered by Jan Smuts to be South Africa's front line.
SOURCE: SANDF DOCUMENTATION CENTRE, NO 8510000142.

MIDDLE: South African graves on the battlefield at Sidi Rezegh, November 1941: facing an enemy far more formidable and resolute than they had experienced in East Africa, the 5th SA Infantry Brigade was overrun and annihilated by Axis armour.
SOURCE: SOUTH AFRICAN MUSEUM OF MILITARY HISTORY, NO E 395.

BOTTOM: Trek Saam! (Work Together!): from 1940 the Smuts government launched a wide-ranging information programme as an antidote to pro-Nazi propaganda.
SOURCE: SANDF DOCUMENTATION CENTRE POSTER COLLECTION.

TOP: During the campaign in Italy, a visiting Jan Smuts confers with Maj Gen Evered Poole, commander of 6th SA Armoured Division, in June 1944. Chief of Defence Staff Lt Gen Sir Pierre van Ryneveld, disliked by many of his subordinates, stands at rear.
SOURCE: SANDF DOCUMENTATION CENTRE, NO 700009554.

MIDDLE: HMSAS *Good Hope*, a Loch-class frigate, was South Africa's first major warship; the ship's company was the only South African naval outfit to qualify for the France and Germany Star.
SOURCE: SANDF DOCUMENTATION CENTRE.

BOTTOM: Sergeant Lucas Majosi distinguished himself at the Battle of El Alamein and became the only black soldier to receive the Distinguished Conduct Medal. Painting by Neville Lewis.
SOURCE: DITSONG SOUTH AFRICAN NATIONAL MUSEUM FOR MILITARY HISTORY, NO 1816.

TOP: A Sherman tank of 6th SA Armoured Division negotiates a mountain road in northern Italy during the closing phases of the war. The division was formed in 1943 and deployed to a country that was considered largely 'untankable'.
SOURCE: SOUTH AFRICAN MUSEUM OF MILITARY HISTORY, NO 1946.

MIDDLE: SAAF B-26 Marauder medium bombers in the air over Italy. The SAAF assumed a dominant role in air operations over Italy after the Allies withdrew aircrews in preparation for Operation Overlord.
SOURCE: SANDF DOCUMENTATION CENTRE, NO 700018516.

BOTTOM: A busy crossroads at Castiglione dei Pepoli, between Florence and Bologna: 6th SA Armoured Division occupied the Castiglione area in the winter of 1944-1945, during the struggle to breach the Gothic Line. Painting by Terence McCaw.
SOURCE: DITSONG SOUTH AFRICAN NATIONAL MUSEUM FOR MILITARY HISTORY, NO 1611.

TOP: Victory parade at Monza racing circuit, outside Milan, on 14 May 1945: the brass assembled included Commodore FC Sturrock (Minister of Defence and Transport), General Mark Clark (Commander 15th US Army Group), Lt Gen Sir Pierre van Ryneveld (South African Chief of the General Staff), Maj Gen Frank Theron (General Officer Administration, UDF, Middle East), and Maj Gen Evered Poole (Commander of the 6th SA Armoured Division).
SOURCE: SANDF DOCUMENTATION CENTRE, NO 851000730.

MIDDLE: An SAAF-crewed Dakota on the apron at Tempelhof Airport, West Berlin. The UDF deployed twice during the early Cold War, to Germany and Korea, in support of the Western Allies and the protection of postwar occupation zones.
SOURCE: SANDF DOCUMENTATION CENTRE, NO 991001456.

BOTTOM: Members of 2 Squadron, the 'Flying Cheetahs', examine a Japanese Okha rocket plane, while others service one of the squadron's Mustang fighters. South Africa used its deployment in Korea in support of the United Nations to acquire modern aircraft, specifically the F-86 Sabre jet, from the Americans.
SOURCE: SANDF DOCUMENTATION CENTRE, NO 761006474.

TOP: South Africa's initial, official response to the crisis in Korea was captured by Jock Leyden in a cartoon that appeared in *The Argus* on 2 August 1950. Generalissimo Erasmus did not escape attention. Note the ostrich desk ornament.

MIDDLE: The odd man out: Secretary for Defence HC Cuff (second from left) with Defence Minister FC Erasmus (far left) and generals Matie du Toit and RC Hiemstra (in uniform, at right) at Defence Headquarters in Pretoria. Cuff, appointed in 1946, was 'English' and the last of Smuts' senior appointments to remain in office.
SOURCE: SANDF DOCUMENTATION CENTRE, NO 700000117.

BOTTOM: Col Jan Breytenbach (centre) confers with his officers during Operation Reindeer, the SADF's airborne assault on the Swapo camp at Cassinga, in southern Angola, 4 May 1978.
SOURCE: SANDF DOCUMENTATION CENTRE.

A knocked-out T-62 tank in southern Angola: the lessons of Operation Savannah front-benched the SADF's re-equipment programme. SOURCE: SANDF DOCUMENTATION CENTRE, NO 991005784.

Troops boarding a Puma helicopter in southern Angola: the SADF adapted the Rhodesian 'fireforce' system to concentrate mobility and firepower in the open veld. SOURCE: SANDF DOCUMENTATION CENTRE, NO 991003765.

General Constand Viljoen (third from left) being briefed during a visit to 'the Border'.
SOURCE: SANDF DOCUMENTATION CENTRE, NO 851001273.

From 1976, the demands of the Border War led to the development of a range of infantry fighting vehicles (IFVs) and armoured personnel carriers (APCs), such as the Buffel and the Ratel, both of which are shown in this photo, which proved cardinal in the conversion of motorised infantry into mechanised infantry. SOURCE: SANDF DOCUMENTATION CENTRE, NO 8510011281.

TOP: The National Peacekeeping Force (NKPF) on deployment in a troubled township in 1994: patched together too hastily, the NPKF was a disaster.

RIGHT: A new national defence force: members of the SADF, the TBVC armed forces and MK and APLA cadres deployed together to honour Nelson Mandela, the new commander in chief, during the presidential inauguration in Pretoria in 1994.

implementation of the voluntary UN arms embargo by Britain and the United States, new sources of military equipment and technology transfer were found. In particular, from 1960, relations were strengthened with France; President Charles de Gaulle was eager to gain access to the minerals needed for France's nuclear programme. By 1964, Paris had become Pretoria's most important arms supplier. Licences were procured for the manufacture in South Africa of various weapons and weapons platforms, enabling Pretoria to further develop a growing arms industry. This military cooperation was broad-fronted and sustained until France implemented its first partial arms embargo in 1975 and then voted for the mandatory UN embargo two years later. But, by 1977, the South African weapons industry was well established, producing a range of vehicles and weapons systems based on French patents, including the Eland armoured car and the Impala fighter jet.[103] The first Dassault Mirage III CZ fighter arrived in South Africa in April 1963. On 9 November 1964, the Atlas Aircraft Corporation came into being, and, as little as two years later, the first Impala Mk 1 (MB326M) rolled off the production line. Over the ensuing years, the SAAF arsenal was complemented with Canberra light bombers, Buccaneer Mk 50 strike aircraft, Lockheed C-130B Hercules and Transall C-160Z transport aircraft and a number of combat helicopters. These aircraft were the last South Africa was able to procure internationally before the introduction of the total arms embargo. Thereafter all replacements had to be built locally.

Conclusion

If the first half of the twentieth century was the age of Smuts, the period after 1948 is less easy to define, dominated as it was by collectives of smaller figures. At the peak of the UDF's achievement, a man who had no military experience and little military knowledge tore down its command structure. From May 1948, Frans Erasmus, the controversial Nationalist Defence minister, purged the officer corps again, disposed of most of the remaining vestiges of the UDF's colonial origins and the last British emblematic connections. The departure of the best trained and most educated officers drastically reduced the intellectual quality of the military leadership. Closer analysis of intellectual quality may still tell us that Erasmus feared the most able as much as he did the most 'British'. The myth of an apolitical military was highlighted, as it would be again.

While the Erasmus ministry was an undoubted nadir, there were some positive developments during the 1950s, particularly in the technological domain. The Armour Corps was re-established with the acquisition of Centurion tanks in 1952. Entry into the Korean War, which proved less divisive than 1939, provided an opportunity for the Nationalist government, less than keen to be involved in a distant war of their own, to seek alternative alliances to that with the United Kingdom and to acquire jet aircraft and other technology from the United States.

Erasmus' departure was the necessary catalyst for the first of a series of efforts, almost all successful, to 'rehabilitate' the defence force. The new politico-strategic environment, and the need for South Africa to find security in a hostile world, forced a reappraisal. Great changes followed in 1961, under Defence minister JJ Fouché, and the advent of the republic. As we shall see in the following chapter, Black Consciousness and Pan-Africanism grew alongside, and in response to, the consolidation of Afrikaner political and military power. As South Africa moved down the path to 'garrison statehood' and 'total strategy', the liberation movements in southern Africa, invigorated, funded and supplied with arms by one or other party of the bipolar Cold War world, formed armed wings with the aim of overthrowing white rule on the subcontinent. The result was an interconnected series of wars fought in Rhodesia (now Zimbabwe), in the then Portuguese territories of Mozambique and Angola, and in the northern part of the territory of South West Africa (now Namibia), combined with an armed struggle against South Africa itself.

CHAPTER SEVEN

Hot War in Southern Africa, 1959–1989

The contestation over the meaning of the 'Border War' begins with the name itself. Naming (and more so, renaming) is a political act ... the very naming of this war denotes the conflict of ideologies inherent in its opposing forces.[1]

— Gary Baines, historian, 2014, on the naming of the war

The border is a geographic fact ... Whatever the interpretations of history, we know 'the border' was a long way from home, logistically and psychologically ... However, it can be argued that 'on the border' was more than a geographical concept. There were other borders in this war, other dividing lines, divisions and paradoxes.[2]

— David Williams, journalist, 2008, on the multiplicity of 'borders'

It's a nice story – what a shame nobody has written about it fully.[3]

— Fidel Castro, Cuban leader, in 2006, on the absence of a 'full history' of the Angolan conflict

The global influence of the Cold War was immense. For Africa, this ideological struggle between the Soviet Union and the United States and their allies brought a measure of stability to the raft of newly independent and impoverished states. While most remained beyond the reach of the main struggle between East and West, the former British and French colonies, benefiting from inherited institutions and continued relations with their former colonial masters, enjoyed relatively better internal stability. These states did not have the need – or perhaps the opportunity – to be courted by one or more of the new superpowers. For much of Anglophone and Francophone Africa, the influence of the Cold War would always be limited. However, different patterns emerged elsewhere, where exceptional local circumstances, such as the continued Portuguese colonial presence in Angola and Mozambique, South Africa's occupation of South West Africa (Namibia) and Ian Smith's unilateral declaration of independence for Rhodesia (Zimbabwe), drew these countries firmly into the struggle between East and West. Local nationalisms strengthened in Angola, Mozambique, Guinea-Bissau and Rhodesia. While Portugal, South Africa and Rhodesia looked to the West, the local insurgent groups turned primarily to the East Bloc for military and sometimes ideological succour.[4] The escalation of the struggle in the Portuguese colonies, against the background of the Cold War, made the inevitable independence of Angola and Mozambique far more difficult. Moreover, the politicisation of the armed forces and the militarisation of politics would become a further consequence for those countries most directly influenced by this ideological struggle.[5]

Portugal's decision, following the 1974 Carnation Revolution in Lisbon, to relinquish its colonies in Africa, and the contest in these territories for control of the post-independence state, is inextricably tied to the international contest over the future of South West Africa and the struggle for power in Rhodesia and in a post-apartheid South Africa. Although Namibian resistance to the South African occupation had started early – the protest of Mandume ya Ndemufayo had been crushed in 1917 – this received more focus and organisation in 1959 with the founding of the South West Africa National Union (Swanu) and the Ovamboland People's Organisation (OPO). The latter became the South West Africa People's Organisation (Swapo) in the following year.[6]

National resistance movements were also established in Angola and Mozambique, in Rhodesia, and in South Africa. These groups came, separately, to the conclusion that they could only achieve their objectives through violence. This led to a series of guerrilla campaigns in these states and territories. Each of these campaigns had its own characteristics, but, through common purpose, regional cooperation and the sharing of human and other resources, they became inextricably intertwined. These conflicts in southern Africa, embracing the liberation wars in Angola and Mozambique (1961–1975) and part of the post-independence civil wars in both countries,[7] the Rhodesian 'Bush War' (1964–1980),[8] South Africa's 'Border War' (1966–1989) and the 'armed struggle' for South Africa, can only be viewed as campaigns in a wider, thirty-year Southern African War lasting from approximately 1959 to 1989.[9] This wider conflict, as journalist Leopold Scholtz has noted, had three layers.

Firstly, there was a civil rights struggle against fundamentally unjust political systems, most notably against the South African policy of apartheid. Secondly, there were wars of national liberation, fought in Angola and Mozambique and for the independence of South West Africa. These first two layers, as Scholtz has argued, were imbued with an indigenous dynamic, but became tightly fused with a third layer, namely, the global, ideological struggle of the Cold War.[10] This thirty-year war, a proxy in the ideological struggle between the USA and USSR, was in many respects a war for the control of southern Africa (*see* Map 5).

However, for South Africa, involved in a low-level insurgency since 1960, the year 1966 was the watershed, with four particularly significant developments. Firstly, on 5 April, PW Botha, who would dominate South African military and political affairs until 1989, became Defence minister. Secondly, on 18 July, the International Court of Justice in The Hague ruled in South Africa's favour on the question of its continued mandate over South West Africa.[11] A number of African and Asian states took the matter to the UN General Assembly, which passed a resolution revoking South Africa's mandate over the former German colony. The resolution was impossible to implement and probably unconstitutional, and South Africa refused to recognise it. Thirdly, South African security forces attacked a guerrilla base at Ongulumbashe on 26 August, an event that marked the start of the 23–year Border War.[12] And fourthly, in September 1966, the Labour government in the UK announced its intention to withdraw altogether from the naval base at Simon's Town, purportedly as part of a cutback in defence costs. This encouraged South Africa's development of contacts outside the Commonwealth (which it had left in 1961), most notably with the United States and then with France and Israel.[13]

This chapter addresses the changing international landscape and threat perception, the implementation of what was termed the 'total strategy' and the rise of the garrison state, and the campaigns fought by South Africans in the neighbouring states.

The changing strategic landscape and threat perception

The steady rise of the National Party, from its beginnings in 1914 to the election victory of 1948 and the development of the policy of apartheid, is closely intertwined with the history of resistance in South Africa. Various groups,

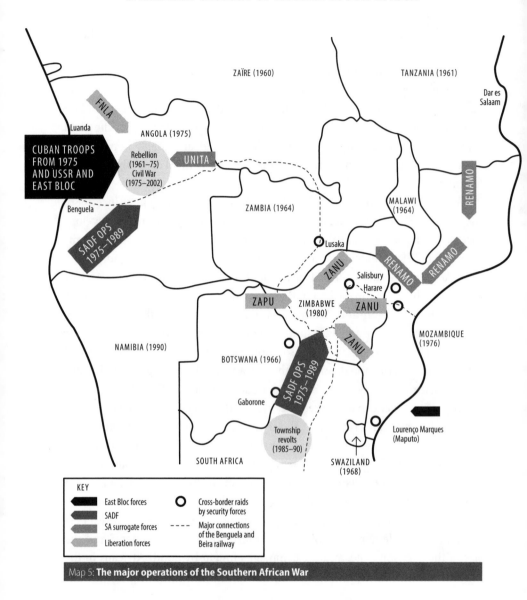

Map 5: **The major operations of the Southern African War**

including the African National Congress (ANC), the Pan Africanist Congress (PAC), the South African Indian Congress (SAIC) and the South African Communist Party (SACP), among others, mobilised to fight the imposition of segregationist legislation that gave substance to the policy of apartheid. A united front was presented in the 1950s by the Congress of Democrats who, through non-violent protest, launched the Defiance Campaign in 1952. A

'Congress of the People' met at Kliptown, outside Johannesburg, in 1955, when 'the ANC was effectively confirmed as first among equals within a movement structured as an alliance of interest groups' and the Freedom Charter was adopted as a founding manifesto of non-racial, democratic aspiration.[14] The government clamped down; organisations were banned and protestors jailed, while the shooting of 69 protestors at Sharpeville in March 1960 underlined the government's unwillingness to deviate from its policy programme.[15]

As a consequence, in June 1960, members of the ANC decided to give up non-violence and embark on an armed struggle against the government. Umkhonto we Sizwe (MK, 'Spear of the Nation') was formed the following year, as the armed wing of the ANC, and embarked on a sabotage campaign.[16] The campaign came to an abrupt halt after a spate of more than 200 incidents.[17] This was due partly to inexperience and partly to the presence of government agents and informers within the ranks of MK. In July 1963, the leadership of the ANC was arrested at a farmhouse at Rivonia, on the outskirts of Johannesburg. The subsequent trial and imprisonment of Nelson Mandela, who had been arrested near Howick the previous year, together with Walter Sisulu, Govan Mbeki and others, ended any significant internal resistance for nearly twenty years.[18]

In the meantime, South Africa was increasingly on the defensive internationally. At the United Nations (UN), the newly independent states of Africa and Asia, led at first by India, pressed the Western powers to take a stance against Pretoria's racial policies. Various resolutions, condemning apartheid and imposing a voluntary arms embargo, were passed by the Security Council in 1963. South Africa had left the Commonwealth in 1961, and was soon ostracised from other international bodies, including the Organisation of African Unity (OAU).[19] However, with the economy booming and black political dissent muted since the Rivonia trial, Pretoria felt sufficiently secure. Moreover, regionally, the Portuguese colonies and Ian Smith's Rhodesia 'served as a *cordon sanitaire* against the infection of independence fever'.[20]

But things changed rapidly from the mid-1970s. The sudden and complete collapse of Portuguese colonial rule, after almost half a millennium, following the April 1974 revolution, and the growing distance between Pretoria and its traditional allies, pointed to the constriction of the *cordon sanitaire*.[21] By the end of 1975, the South African Defence Force (SADF) had become entangled in a regional war, bringing it into conflict with the Soviet Union and its proxies. Moreover, and more importantly, from neighbouring Mozambique, following the rise to power of the Frente para Liberação de Moçambique (Frelimo), the ANC had direct access to a South African border little more than 400 kilometres from the financial and industrial centre of the country.

Encouraged by developments to the north, and pressed by an economic downturn, black South Africans once again took to the streets in protest. Violence erupted in Soweto on 16 June 1976, when a group of protesting students clashed with members of the South African Police (SAP). Sixty youngsters were killed, and disturbances spread to other parts of the country.

As a result of the Soweto uprising, three things happened: firstly, a new generation of more militant activists emerged, many of whom left South Africa to join the ANC-in-exile;[22] secondly, the ANC-in-exile, out of touch with grassroots domestic politics, had to quickly reassert its voice as the embodiment of the struggle; and thirdly, activists saw that domestic protests could galvanise international support and impact negatively upon the government. As Chris Alden notes, this third factor, internal pressure in the form of condemnation, sanctions and disinvestment from the country, 'increasingly became the focus of anti-apartheid activism and was to achieve crucial results by the mid-eighties'.[23]

The UN imposed a mandatory arms embargo in 1977. This, as Alden has noted, was 'the apogee of collective action in that forum against South Africa'. And further attempts to extend sanctions 'came up against a recalcitrant Western bloc'.[24] As a result, the anti-apartheid movement concentrated its efforts in other forums, primarily the Commonwealth, the European Community and a number of individual countries that gave succour through the provision of office space and broadcast facilities. The results were at first meagre, but were soon bolstered by two events. The first, discussed later in this chapter, was the expulsion of the ANC from Mozambique, Lesotho, Swaziland and Botswana. These insurgents, denied sanctuary in southern Africa and riven by internal dissension, sought alternative strategies, including the imposition of economic sanctions and disinvestment, and cultural and sporting boycotts. The second was the township revolt that began in 1985, which gave a major boost to these alternative strategies.

PW Botha, 'total strategy', and the shaping of defence policy

From the 1950s, defence policymakers and military personnel, in London and Washington as much as in Pretoria, perceived the threat of communism and communist-inspired insurgency in Africa.[25] The notion of a Soviet-orchestrated threat evolved gradually and was fed by Moscow's reiterated global ambitions and support for 'wars of national liberation', a multitude of pressures on the *cordon sanitaire*, the assistance rendered by East Bloc states to the insurgent movements in southern Africa, and the insurgents' rapid success in attaining power in Luanda and Maputo.[26] With the attack against South Africa seemingly occurring in almost every sphere – diplomatic, political, economic, military, social and cultural – the threat was articulated as a 'total onslaught'. A security policeman at the forefront of the counterinsurgency in the 1980s later described this total strategy as follows:

> Its underlying argument was that the country was the target of a Marxist-Leninist Total Onslaught. Only a Total Strategy – a co-ordination of the state's activities in the military, economic, psychological, political, diplomatic, cultural and ideological fields – would be strong enough to combat it.[27]
>
> The Total Strategy argument was that all of the country's internal problems could be blamed on an external onslaught, the ANC and other opponents of apartheid being merely the Soviet Union's [T]rojan horses. We were told that the enemy was 'everywhere' – in universities, trade unions and cultural organisations. They all harboured enemies of the state who were waging psychological and economic warfare against us.[28]

The Soviet Union was considered the orchestrator of global communism, and Pretoria believed that this would lead eventually to a direct conventional attack on South Africa. Defence minister PW Botha and Admiral HH Biermann, then Chief of the SADF, believed such an attack to be inevitable and that South Africa would ultimately be unable to withstand such an onslaught without the help of a superpower or, alternatively, direct access to a super weapon.[29]

In response, the SADF designed a comprehensive strategic doctrine, embodied in the 1977 White Paper on Defence, which 'called for the marshalling of all state resources to combat revolutionary warfare while simultaneously engaging in substantive domestic reforms'.[30] This strategic response was based in part on the work of André Beaufre, a French general who had seen service in Morocco, Indochina and Algeria and was considered an expert on counterrevolutionary warfare in the Third World,[31] as well as on ideas articulated by Sir Robert Thompson, who had played a key role in ending the

Malayan Emergency, the American political scientist Samuel P Huntington, and American colonel JJ McCuen, whose *The Art of Counter-revolutionary War: the strategy of counter-insurgency* (1966) was prescribed reading for South African military officers. Beaufre's ideas were introduced to the South African military in 1968 during a series of lectures by professors Deon Fourie and Ben Cockram. General Magnus Malan was present, and soon a following developed that included Lieutenant General CA Fraser (the commander Combined Combat Forces), Admiral Biermann and PW Botha. Beaufre, who visited South Africa in 1974, seemed to offer a comprehensive strategic answer to the problems South Africa faced. This doctrine formed the basis of the South African response during the Botha premiership.[32]

Portugal's rapid retreat from empire, and the move away from Prime Minister John Vorster's policy of détente, allowed the Department of Defence to gain ascendency over the departments of Foreign Affairs and Information.[33] Pretoria still hoped that informal military cooperation might underline South Africa's strategic value to the West and lead possibly to the elusive formal alliance. However, the cancellation of the Simon's Town Agreement by Britain's Labour government and Washington's withdrawal of support for the 1975 invasion of Angola, forced Pretoria to reassess.[34] 'One lesson in particular seems to have been drawn by the South African military establishment,' Chris Alden concludes, 'that the West could not be relied upon.'[35] As disillusionment grew in Pretoria, the government increasingly analysed events in terms of the 'total onslaught', thinking that led directly to a decision to embark upon a nuclear weapons programme as a deterrent strategy.[36] Project Coast, a sophisticated chemical and biological warfare (CBW) programme, was launched in 1981 or earlier.[37]

Total onslaught now became the hallmark of the threat assessment and was defined and published in the White Paper on Defence as the new 'Total National Strategy'. The White Paper defined total strategy as 'a comprehensive plan to utilize all the means available to a state according to an integrated pattern in order to achieve the national aims within the framework of the specific policies. A total national strategy is, therefore not confined to a particular sphere, but is applicable at all levels and to all functions of the state structure.'[38]

The State Security Council (SSC), established in 1972, became the wellspring of the total strategy. However, in order to accomplish the wide-ranging goals espoused by Beaufre, the full range of government departments and agencies had to be harnessed and coordinated. The security forces, in cooperation with other government departments, had to ensure a stable political climate, while the government implemented meaningful reforms designed to alienate the population from the insurgents. PW Botha, who became prime minister in September 1978, established a comprehensive state apparatus, called the National Security Management System (NSMS), which operated under his personal direction. This involved a network of more than 500 national, regional, district and local centres coordinated through 12 Joint Management Centres (JMCs), which gave the government an inside view of every region, city and township in the country. Every government department and institution took part in the NSMS, on a national level and at all other subordinate levels: 'The idea was to shorten and simplify the chain of command so that the SSC was in control of the country.'[39] On 15 August 1979, Botha released his 'Twelve Point Plan', explaining the direction the country would take in terms of security and government-led reform.[40]

In terms of Beaufreian thinking, the state adopted a strategic approach that embraced and coordinated actions in four principal areas, namely, politics, diplomacy, economics and military affairs. Beaufre, calling this blending 'total strategy', emphasised the need to sap the opponent's will to fight and stressed that, in the concept of manoeuvre, there were two 'modes of action' open to the state. The first was direct strategy, which was dominated by the military. The second, centring on non-military actions in the political, diplomatic and economic fields, was indirect strategy. Beaufre also differentiated between 'exterior manoeuvre', or the employment of indirect strategy in the fields of politics, diplomacy, economy and even the military to paralyse the opponent, and 'interior manoeuvre', or the subtle implementation of direct and indirect strategy in the region. The need to introduce domestic reforms in tandem with the security measures was considered to be of the utmost importance. Only the two together – the security measures creating a stable climate for political reform – could prevent internal conflict and avert an incipient state of revolution.[41]

Botha inherited a transforming defence force in 1966, a force that was undergoing measured expansion and modernisation. The high command was restructured in 1966, when the Supreme Command replaced the old General Staff. The Supreme Command, based on the principles of corporate leadership, now comprised the Commandant General (General RC Hiemstra), the GOC Joint Combat Forces, the Chief of the Army (Lieutenant General CA Fraser), the Chief of the Air Force (Lieutenant General HJ Martin), Commander

Maritime Defence and the Chief of the Navy (Vice Admiral HH Biermann). The civilian post of Secretary for Defence, constitutionally necessary but the focus of much ambiguity and clashing of personality, was abolished at the same time, and the Commandant General assumed full responsibility as head of department, while the Comptroller's branch was established to take over much of the administrative work of the old Secretariat.[42]

Further organisational change followed as the armed forces expanded. A fifth staff division was created as the office of the Chief of Defence Staff, who headed a coordinating staff group, while, in the supporting services, the Adjutant General was replaced by the Chief of Defence Force Administration, and the Quartermaster General was replaced by the Chief of Logistics Services. The posts of the service chiefs – army, air force, navy – were upgraded to lieutenant general and were provided with their own support staffs. The Chief of Defence Force Administration, tasked *inter alia* with personnel policy and the general administration of the department, was added to the advisory body to the Supreme Command. A Defence Staff Council replaced the Supreme Command in 1972, while, in 1975, an intermediate level of command was removed and the fighting services brought under the direct command of the Chief of the SADF when the posts of GOC Joint Combat Forces and Commander Maritime Defence were abolished.[43] In the same year, the office of Chief of Defence Force Administration was replaced by four staff divisions, namely, Personnel, Intelligence, Operations and Logistics.[44] Two further staff divisions – Finance and Planning – were added later.[45]

The pace of organisational change quickened with the perception of the increasing conventional and unconventional threat. In 1974, the army's conventional force was organised into two divisions: 7 SA Infantry Division, comprising 71, 72, 73 Motorised Brigades; and 8 SA Armoured Division, comprising 81 Armoured Brigade, 82 Mechanised Brigade and 84 Motorised Brigade. At the same time, alongside their conventional role, the Citizen Force and commandos were reorganised to conduct more effective counterinsurgency (COIN) operations. The planning and conduct of COIN operations was decentralised at territorial command level and, following the allocation of the area commandos and selected Citizen Force units to each territorial command, independent COIN forces were formed at a command level.[46]

The force size was dramatically increased and combat readiness and efficiency improved. A range of new Citizen Force units, numbering 51, had been established in cadre form with effect from 1 April 1965, and 16 of these had been

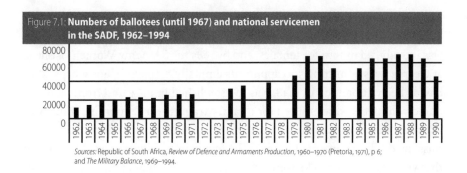

Figure 7.1: **Numbers of ballotees (until 1967) and national servicemen in the SADF, 1962–1994**

Sources: Republic of South Africa, *Review of Defence and Armaments Production*, 1960–1970 (Pretoria, 1971), p 6; and *The Military Balance*, 1969–1994.

converted to functioning units in 1966. However, expansion was thwarted by ongoing shortages of manpower. The ballot system, rigid, limited and unfair, was replaced by National Service from 1 January 1968, and all medically fit, white male citizens became eligible for military service in the year in which they turned 18.[47] Initial continuous training was extended in 1972 from a maximum of nine months to twelve months; at the same time, service in the Citizen Force was increased from four to ten years. A system of voluntary extension of National Service was introduced in 1974 to draw the manpower resources needed. But, despite these steps, the numbers were not forthcoming and compulsory National Service was extended in 1977 to 24 months. By 1990, 'some 600 000 white men had experienced extended military training, and 320 000 served in some way "on the border"'.[48]

Moreover, realising that an extended conventional campaign was impossible with existing National Service manpower, the SADF extended the call-up periods for the part-time units of the Citizen Force. These Citizen Force units, which had been mobilised for 14, 21 or at most 28 days of continuous training, were now called on for 90 consecutive days of operational duty. This was significant; the Citizen Force was now not only deployed operationally but the call to action was also extended to 'husbands and fathers, professional men, artisans, farmers and others playing a pivotal role in the country's economy'.[49]

Universal military service for white, male South Africans coincided with the world crusade against apartheid, the growing perception in Pretoria of a 'total onslaught' and the militarisation and polarisation of South African society. Resistance to conscription, often cast simply as a resented imposition, evolved gradually and, although always small, reached its peak in the difficult 1980s, when 'organisations such as the Conscientious Objectors Support Group (formed in 1980) and the End Conscription Campaign (formed in

1983) gave a more public "face" to the anti-conscription movement.[50]

Other sources of personnel were also tapped. A year of voluntary training was introduced in 1971 for females, and by 1985 the SA Army Women's College at George 'was admitting 500 applicants annually'.[51] The SA Cape Corps, after having been disbanded in 1948, was re-established in 1963, and from 1976 coloured volunteers were enlisted for infantry training for 12 months, which was extended in 1980 to 24 months. From their ranks the first 'non-white' commissioned officers emerged in 1975. The first black soldiers attested in April of that year. Although blacks were underrepresented when compared to whites and coloureds, the number of black uniformed personnel increased steadily through the 1980s. Several units, territorially based and associated with the 'homelands', were established from 1973 for black volunteers. These included 111 Battalion (Swazi), 113 Battalion (Shangaan), 115 Battalion (Ndebele), 116 Battalion (North Sotho) and 121 Battalion (Zulu). Other battalions were incorporated into the defence forces of the Transkei, Bophuthatswana, Venda and Ciskei, when these states received 'independence' from South Africa. The multi-ethnic 21 Battalion, formed first at Baviaanspoort, but moving to Lenz in 1975, became fully operational in 1987.[52]

The strategic and tactical conditions of the Angolan war

This transforming defence force, having assumed responsibility in 1973 for the defence of South West Africa (Namibia) from the SAP, was soon tested, first in operations against Swapo and then against forces of mixed provenance in southern Angola. South Africa's continued and contested occupation of Namibia had produced a guerrilla struggle in 1966. The opening of the Border War, coupled with sustained international pressure against the presence of South African troops, continually raised the stakes as well as the cost of an escalating conflict. Independence for Angola in 1975, and the intervention of the superpowers in the unfolding Angolan civil war, 'marked the elevation of the Namibian issue to that of a regional conflict with global security dimensions'.[53]

The liberation movements in Angola had divided along ethnic and ideological lines. The Movimento Popular de Libertção de Angola (MPLA) was largely a Marxist party founded by *mestiços* (mixed parentage) in Luanda, the capital. The União das Populações de Angola (UPA) was founded among the

Bakongo people and received support from Bakongo in neighbouring Zaïre. Its leader, Holden Roberto, was a kinsman of Mobutu Sese Seko, the Zaïrois president and army commander. The third group, the União Nacional para a Independência Total de Angola (Unita), was founded by Jonas Savimbi as a breakaway group from the UPA and drew support from the Chokwe and Ovimbundu peoples. The remainder of the Roberto group, amalgamating with other smaller groups, became the Frente Nacional de Libertação de Angola (FNLA) and set up a government-in-exile in Leopoldville (Kinshasa). The Frente para a Libertação do Enclave de Cabinda (FLEC) fought for the separate independence of the oil-rich exclave of Cabinda.[54]

The struggle for power and resources between these movements intensified as the Portuguese colonial empire collapsed, and their quest for foreign support set the stage for increased foreign intervention in the escalating civil war. When independence was achieved, on 11 November 1975, the MPLA, holding the colonial capital and much of the seaboard and bolstered by Soviet, Cuban and Portuguese support, was in the best position. The Soviet Union, reacting swiftly to the deteriorating situation, provided the MPLA with aircraft and tanks of varying kinds, multiple-rocket launchers, and instructors. Fidel Castro mounted a large-scale intervention, dubbed Operation Carlota, in which, by air and sea, 'complete tank units, a great deal of regular and anti-aircraft artillery, [and] armoured infantry units', together with some 36 000 soldiers, were sent to Angola.[55] The United States provided assistance, financial and military, to the FNLA, while South Africa supported Unita.

A growing refugee crisis and increasing East Bloc involvement led to more direct South African involvement. If Unita was defeated, 'the border war would escalate dramatically because for the first time Swapo would have a safe border directly opposite its main area of operations, central Ovamboland'.[56] SADF liaison officers were posted to the FNLA and the Unita headquarters at Nova Lisboa (renamed Huambo) in September 1975. South African instructors and some equipment followed as Angola descended into war.

The MPLA, bolstered by Moscow and Havana, took the offensive. Luanda and the coastal districts were cleared of the FNLA and Unita and a government, headed by the MPLA leader, Dr Agostinho Neto, was proclaimed. However, the three Fapla[57] columns converging on the Unita-held provincial capital of Huambo were repulsed on 5 October by Battle Group Foxtrot, a hastily assembled force comprising a reinforced SADF element and a company of Unita recruits. A second task force, codenamed Zulu, was formed as a SADF-Unita force and mounted an incursion deeper into Angola. This marked the start of Operation Savannah, a limited intervention by the SADF to prevent the Angolan conflict from spreading south across the Cunene River and into South West Africa.[58] The ports of Moçâmedes (Namibe from 1985), Benguela and Lobito were rapidly occupied, and Unita harassed and effectively closed the strategically important central railway line. However, in the north, the MPLA dealt a major blow to the FNLA and contained the FLEC incursions in Cabinda. The SADF element supporting the FNLA had to be evacuated by sea on 28 November. Luanda no longer faced a war on two fronts.[59]

In the south, the SADF advance soon outstripped supply and halted on the Queve River, where they encountered stiff resistance from the MPLA and the Cubans, who could now concentrate on Unita to the south. Unita was soon ejected from the various towns they occupied. Fapla was rapidly expanded to more than 45 000 troops, with the MPLA drawing increasingly on Cuba for support. Swapo's armed wing, the People's Liberation Army of Namibia (PLAN), now made common purpose with Fapla, but the two forces handicapped each other with continuous requests for assistance.

The campaign in Angola demanded determination and cold courage. According to official historian Warwick Dorning, 'Despite massive deliveries of sophisticated weaponry by the Soviets to the MPLA and the direct intervention of several thousand Cuban troops, the South African contingent in Angola – numbering no more than 2 000 – acquitted itself exceptionally well, scoring several major victories over the numerically superior and often better equipped Cuban/MPLA forces.'[60] However, the South Africans faced several unfavourable factors. The SADF had a much lower ratio of force to space.[61] This facilitated breakthroughs, but imposed severe logistical problems and made the envelopment and containment of enemy forces more difficult. Moreover, the climate and terrain added difficulties of their own. Angola has large rivers with many tributaries; there are five large basin systems, including those of the Congo and the Zambezi. The south, the focus of South Africa operations, is semi-arid, but, during the rainy season (February to April), large areas become flooded. Moreover, the poverty of the country, with a relatively low population density, meant fewer bridges and roads, more unpaved tracks, and less cleared growth and thicker vegetation.[62] Major General Roland de Vries, an advocate of mobility in bush warfare, records that the physical environment had an enormous impact on operations, even for the newer SADF equipment.

Tough though our Ratels and SAMILs were – and nobody knew more about building bush-proof vehicles than the South Africans – the bundu-bashing took its inevitable heavy toll … The short Mopani stumps played havoc with our tyres, and the Ratel crews spent many hours wrestling with their vehicles' huge wheels when one of them suffered a puncture and had to be swapped for a new one, and when the bell rang we had to be in position at the FUP, come hell or high water.[63]

These terrain conditions impaired, but did not preclude, the success of South African mobility and surprise. The SADF battle groups remained relatively mobile, and, in a series of remarkable advances, turned back the MPLA forces in southern Angola. John Stockwell, a CIA operator *in situ*, wrote of 'the most effective military strike force ever seen in black Africa, exploding through the MPLA-Cuban ranks in a blitzkrieg'.[64] The SADF's rapid advance caught the Fapla-Cuban forces off balance and they remained dislocated and unable to 'regroup and redeploy into well prepared defensive positions'.[65] The secret, they learned, lay in mobility and rapid, effective action.[66]

The opposing forces were also of vastly different strengths and natures. The SADF troops, perhaps as many as 3 000, served during Operation Savannah alongside several thousand Unita troops. However, most of the SADF were national servicemen, fresh out of school, 'not bush-savvy, and with just three months of basic training'. Such a national serviceman was thrown 'into the middle of a country that he did not know, people he did not understand and an enemy he had never seen'.[67] Scholtz attributes this mismatch to an inefficient personnel system, clumsy and unwieldy tactics and a good measure of disdain for a foe that avoided battle.[68]

Opposing the SADF, during Savannah and in following years, were some 45 000 Fapla troops, assisted by some 8 000 Swapo insurgents formed into seven field battalions (deployed chiefly against Unita and on railway security in central Angola), possibly as many as 3 000 MK cadres in addition to the Cuban deployment.[69] The numbers of Cuban troops and Soviet military advisers and the sophistication of East Bloc materiel grew steadily over the following years. The Cuban contingent numbered nearly 50 000 by 1988. Angola paid an estimated US$300 to US$400 million annually until the last of Castro's troops left Angola in 1991.[70]

The problems highlighted during Savannah persisted over the following years. The SADF had to rely increasingly on tactical skills to offset the numerical predominance of their opponents and the growing stream of personnel and materiel from the East Bloc, while deficits in materiel were offset in part also by the deficiencies in the Fapla-Cuban forces. Operation Carlota, Castro's deployment of troops to Angola in 1975, was a mission undertaken at the behest of a leader who craved recognition as leader of the Non-Aligned Movement.[71] The deployment, far beyond Cuba's 'geographical neighbourhood', was a remarkable feat, but it was troubled from the start and remained classified within Cuba until 2005.[72] The Cubans were mostly young, raw recruits, who received no mail from home. Under the supervision of political commissars, they lacked good officers, good rations and appropriate training. According to Boris Putilin, first secretary at the Soviet embassy in Brazzaville, they were unfit for regular warfare.[73] The number of Cuban dead is unknown, but is estimated to range from 3 000 to an incredible 10 000.[74] Ernesto C recalls:

> The longer we were there, the more I saw good comrades fall. There was no talk of ever leaving Angola. We began to feel somewhat depressed. Medical attention was always good. But our equipment began to break down, our clothes were not being replaced and our food supply was sometimes unpredictable ... we were never paid while serving in Angola.[75]

Facing falling morale, Castro became increasingly hesitant to fight, much to the frustration of General Kurochkin, the Soviet commander in Angola. Castro told Kurochkin: 'In your country the losses may be unnoticeable, but in our small country the human losses become known and have a great effect, therefore we are really trying to avoid losses in Angola.'[76] Kurochkin also questioned the values of the Fapla officers, their theft especially of foodstuffs, and the deep gulf that separated them from their troops. Doubt and distrust weakened cooperation between Cuba and the USSR and their allies in Angola. Castro needed Soviet hardware and at times used the non-arrival of equipment to blackmail Moscow with threats of a Cuba withdrawal.[77] Moreover, there was little love lost between Swapo and the Cubans, who did not have a high opinion of PLAN. Raul Castro felt that 'the Swapo men definitely did not fight and did not want to fight',[78] while Cuban general Leopoldo Cintras Frias ('Polo') believed that Swapo would lose any equipment donated by the USSR 'owing to the weak combat efficiency and low morale of Swapo fighters'.[79]

The SADF withdrew from Angola in February 1976 over concern for casualties, failed American promises of support and the fear of being drawn into a 'Vietnam situation'. A new strategy was devised to control the borders, to which the MPLA had rapidly advanced, to support Unita in southern Angola, and to win the insurgent war launched by PLAN in Namibia. The covert strategy included support for Unita and its transformation into an insurgent army. But the SADF had little influence among the people of Ovamboland, and Swapo, in broadening the geographical scope of war, 'could intimidate the local population by assassinating local pro-South African headmen and officials almost at will'.

By the end of 1977, the SADF was clearly losing the insurgent war in South West Africa, and a new approach based in part on Beaufre and the new security strategy, and in part on 'lessons' learned from Angola, Mozambique and Rhodesia, was implemented.[80] However, as Castro stressed, South Africa lacked a credible political programme.[81] An extensive programme of Communications Operations, or 'Compos', was implemented from 1976. The programme aimed 'to foster harmony between the Army and its units on the one hand and the population on the other. This applied especially to operational areas, since it is difficult to operate successfully in an environment where the locals are not friendly'.[82] However, while these programmes 'tended to prevent insurgency from starting in an area [they] were less successful in countering it if it had already commenced'.[83]

The changed conditions accelerated the process of doctrinal revision already under way, signalling a return to the mobile warfare typical of the traditional South African way of warfighting. The notion of a battle front and the quest for the elusive decisive battle was abandoned in favour of space and area combat. This concept of mobile warfare, according to General Constand Viljoen, was 'based on not to hold ground but to create the design of battle in such a way that you would lure the enemy into [a] killing ground and then [utilise] the superiority of firepower and movement, you would kill him completely'.[84] Mobility and superior firepower could now be coupled to great effect in small mobile operations marked by tactical surprise, infiltrations, raids and a mobile defence. In this way, the vast space and low population density of the operational area might be harnessed to execute envelopments of a more static, disorganised opponent.

The new doctrine was implemented from 1973. The same year, 1 SA Infantry Battalion had relocated from Oudtshoorn to Bloemfontein to enable cross-corps training with the armoured units based at Tempe. Savannah became the first practical test and, at an operational and tactical level, the new doctrine worked well. Attention also turned to training. Programmes developed for mechanised infantry training were accelerated after the first Ratel infantry fighting vehicles (IFVs) came into service in 1976, and were enriched by sending field officers on courses with the Israeli Defence Force (IDF) to study the mobile-mechanised wars of the Middle East.[85]

Existing organisations and structures were reorganised, while new formations, based on combat groups and combat teams, were organised at battalion (regiment) and company (squadron) level. These were composite units, based on the 'plug in' concept, and, drawn from the different corps, were shaped to provide a combined-arms force suitable to the objective. Battle Group Juliet evolved in 1979 into 61 Mechanised Battalion, comprising two infantry companies, one armour squadron, one artillery battery, an antitank platoon, a mortar platoon and a combat engineer troop. A permanent mechanised combat group, 61 Mech became 'arguably the most experienced conventional warfare unit in the army'.[86] General Jannie Geldenhuys, appointed GOC South West Africa Command in 1977, established the South West Africa Territorial Force (SWATF) together with several counterinsurgency battalions.[87] Several of these battalions were ethnically based, including the *flechas* (arrows) of 31 Battalion, expert at bushcraft and used in a reconnaissance role.[88] A new SADF unit, 32 Battalion, was created by Colonel Jan Breytenbach from largely former FNLA combatants, for deep-penetration tasks within Angola.[89] These units – 61 Mech and 32 Battalion – would bear the brunt of the fighting during the Border War.

Implementation of the new strategy meant increased mechanisation and motorisation, with an emphasis on the element of strategic mobility and tactical offence. But, in terms of materiel, the picture was quite bleak. The operations in Angola, despite the often impressive performance, highlighted deficiencies in the South African arsenal. Much of the weaponry and equipment dated from the Second World War. The arms boycotts, which had gained momentum since the early 1960s and would become mandatory in November 1977, had started to tell. The R1 rifle had replaced the Lee-Enfield, the 7.62mm light machine gun had replaced the Bren, and the 81mm mortar was on its way, but the infantry's Saracen armoured personnel carriers were by then twenty years old and the 6–pounder gun, which had seen fine service during the Second World War, was still the main antitank weapon. The artillery, including the 25–pounder and 155mm howitzer, was dated and badly outranged by the more modern artillery and rocket systems supplied by the Soviets. Their 122mm

Table 7.1: Comparison of South African and Angolan tanks at the start of the Angolan war			
	South Africa	Angola	
	Centurion	T-34	T-54/55
Weight (tons)	51	26.5	36
Speed (km/h)	35	53	48
Thickest armour (mm)	152	81	205
Main gun (mm)	105	76.2	100

rockets exceeded the range of the main gun on the Eland 90 armoured car by up to 8 000 metres.[90] The Centurion tank, bought from Britain in the 1950s as part of the MEDO agreement, of which some 141 were still in stock, was still the SADF's main battle tank, and these were supplemented by twenty Comet medium tanks and a small number of Shermans – all of Second World War vintage. The Centurions, carrying a main gun of 105mm, were heavier and considerably slower than the Soviet T-34s and T-54/55s they faced in Angola. Moreover, the new four-wheeled Eland armoured car, the locally-produced version of the French Panhard, had limited mobility in the Angolan bush and carried only 29 shells for its 90mm gun.[91]

The South African Air Force was reasonably well equipped at the start of the conflict, although the Dassault Mirage III aircraft (including 16 Mirage IIICZ interceptors and 17 Mirage IIIEZ ground-attack aircraft), which had been acquired from France during the 1960s, were inadequate. Their range was too limited for the southern African battlespace, which limited time for sorties to just 40 minutes. However, by 1975, these were being replaced with Mirage F1s (16 F1CZ interceptors and 32 F1AZ ground-attack fighters), which became operational during 1978. The new Mirage, which carried two 30mm guns, could fly at Mach 2.2 and had a range of 3 300 kilometres. These were supplemented by two light bomber squadrons (16 Buccaneers and 8 Canberras), forming a formidable airstrike capability. There were four helicopter squadrons: two with 20 Alouette IIIs each, one with 20 SA-330 Pumas, and one with 15 SA-321L Super Frelons, in addition to 7 Wasps assigned to the SA Navy. One squadron with Cessna 185A/D and A185E (replaced in 1975 with AM-3C) was assigned to the Army to provide tactical reconnaissance, while seven Shackletons and nine Piaggio P-166S Albatrosses formed two reconnaissance squadrons.[92] The Alouettes and, from 1977, the Pumas, as well as the Cessna 185 (Kiewiets) became critical elements in COIN operations. Despite having

Table 7.2: **Comparison of South African and Angolan air force fighters at the start of the Angolan war**			
	South Africa	**Angola**	
	Mirage F1	**MiG-17F**	**MiG-21**
Max speed (km/h)	2 338 (Mach 2.2)	1 145	2 175 (Mach 2.0)
Range (km)	3 300	2 060	1 210
Ceiling (m)	20 000	16 600	17 800
Main gun (mm)	2 x 30	1 x 37	1 x 23

four transport squadrons, flying seven Lockheed C-130B Hercules, 9 Transall C-190Z, 23 C-47, five DC-4, one Viscount 781 and four HS-125 Mercurius, the SAAF was ill-equipped 'to keep a large army on the move on the battlefield … this inability would prove a substantial limitation on the army's capability to strike deep into Angola for extended periods with large forces.'[93] The SAAF would become increasingly hard-pressed against a well-equipped opponent as the war in Angola extended into the 1980s.

The SADF experience in Angola in 1975 and 1976 and the mandatory arms embargo provided a dramatic boost to the South African armaments industry. The industry had started in earnest in the mid-1960s with the creation of the Armaments Production Board, the precursor of the Armaments Corporation of South Africa (Armscor). Growth, almost unparalleled in the history of armaments development, followed and Armscor grew rapidly from a producer of small arms and ammunition into a complex industry producing a range of sophisticated weaponry that was, at the time, equal or superior to comparable weaponry produced elsewhere in the world. The highlights were many. A range of infantry fighting vehicles (IFVs) and armoured personnel carriers (APCs) were developed, such as the Ratel, which proved cardinal in the conversion of motorised infantry into mechanised infantry. The Eland, having proved inadequate against the T-34 and T-54/55 tanks in theatre, was supplemented by the G5 and G6 155mm artillery pieces and the 127mm Valkiri rocket system. A range of Samil transport vehicles was developed for the Army. The Kukri heat-seeking missile system and Cheetah fighter aircraft were developed for the SAAF, while a missile strike craft was designed and developed for the Navy.[94] Operation Savannah had certainly front-benched the re-equipment programme. According to Magnus Malan,

Table 7.3: Improving South African land firepower during the Angolan war				
	1975 (1962)	**1982**	**1983**	**1987**
	Eland Mk 7	**Valkiri multiple-rocket launcher**	**G5 towed howitzer**	**G6 self-propelled howitzer**
Calibre (mm)	90	127	155	155
Rate of fire (rounds per min)		60	3	8
Max firing range (km)	4	36	39	39
Max operational range (km)	450	400		700
Max speed (km/h)	100	90		85

Ops Savannah bought us the time we needed after we'd discovered our equipment shortcomings and established our troops were good enough. It allowed us to reorganise and begin to work as a team, and it was one of the main reasons why we brought other population groups into the military. It brought a change in political outlook too.[95]

Internal security and a renewed armed struggle

After the Rivonia trial, South Africa showed almost no sign of dissent organised by the ANC or the PAC, both of which seemingly resigned themselves to exile and, in the case of the ANC, to support for the Zimbabwean African People's Union (Zapu) in its guerrilla campaign in Rhodesia.[96] However, the establishment of sympathetic governments in Luanda and Maputo after 1975 re-ignited the armed struggle.[97] Joint ANC-SACP study visits to Vietnam underlined the need for political mobilisation and institution-building to complement a military campaign. The classic four-stage path of revolutionary war was adopted by the Political-Military Strategy Commission of the ANC. South Africa was, they thought, on a continuum between stages one (political mobilisation) and two (armed propaganda – sabotage and terrorism). Calls were made to support existing anti-apartheid organisations, to promote the development of civic organisations and trade unions, and to establish youth and women's detachments, all of which could launch a series of campaigns in South Africa. Moreover, the commission promoted the development of an underground structure. This was to form a nucleus for the development of both alternative political structures and an internal armed force. In this way, it was hoped, the movement could progress to guerrilla warfare, the next stage in the revolution.[98]

There were soon tangible results. Sabotage and armed attacks increased from 13 in 1978 to 56 in 1983. Possibly the most dramatic was the attack on the Sasol storage tanks at Sasolburg, on 1 June 1980. A year later, there was an attack on power stations in the eastern Transvaal (July 1981), a rocket attack on the Voortrekkerhoogte military base outside Pretoria (August 1981) and a limpet mine attack at the Koeberg nuclear power station near Cape Town (December 1982). Throughout this period, attacks on police stations and other government offices increased markedly. Moreover, the movement's policy of avoiding civilian casualties was to some extent eschewed by the leadership in 1981, whereafter attacks on 'soft targets' increased.[99]

At the same time, active measures were taken to flush out government agents and informers, real or otherwise, inside South Africa and in the ANC camps and structures abroad. The first grievances, aired from 1979, related to the idea that the cadres were 'rotting' in the camps and were not sent on operations. These were followed by 'complaints and accusations that especially pointed at the command structures of the camps and the Security Department, as well as accusations of poor command and control in the forward areas'. A major purge, known as *Shishita*, the Bemba word for 'to sweep', followed, and a network of spies and *agents provocateurs* was allegedly uncovered. Those identified as dissidents were withdrawn to Angola, which some increasingly 'feared as a sort of Siberia', and detained at Camp 32, the Morris Seabelo Rehabilitation Centre (or 'Quatro').[100] There is little doubt that, in this way, political rivals within the liberation movements were eliminated and often in the most brutal fashion.[101]

Through the early 1980s the NSMS was transformed into an instrument of counterrevolutionary strategy and became fully operational in 1983, when the management centre system was extended down to municipal government level. At the same time, the SADF embarked on a civic action programme in the rural areas of South Africa, using national servicemen as teachers and medical conscripts, much as it was doing in South West Africa. A new raft of security legislation was enacted, to protect national key points and to staunch the flight of farmers from their lands in the vulnerable border areas.[102] The Public Safety

Act (1953) empowered the government to declare states of emergency, while the Internal Security Act (1982) consolidated earlier legislation, including the Suppression of Communism Act (1950), parts of the Riotous Assemblies Act (1956), the Unlawful Organisations Act (1960), and the Terrorism Act (1967), and allowed detention without trial, bannings and personal restrictions, and political trials.[103]

A range of 'covert and informal tools' supplemented these measures. The ideas of John McCuen, who emphasised counterterrorism and the elimination of revolutionaries, seemed to be eclipsing those of André Beaufre. A covert capacity for 'dirty tricks' was also created, involving the creation of vigilante groups and, later, special covert military and police units, drawn from personnel in the SAP, the SADF and other government structures. Several units were created, the most notorious being the Civil Cooperation Bureau (CCB), set up in April 1986, and the Directorate of Covert Collection (DCC) of Military Intelligence Division. A web of propaganda projects emanated from the SSC under the heading of strategic communication (Stratcom), and, it seems, from 1991, developed into a counterrevolutionary strategy unit (known as Trewits, from the Afrikaans acronym) of the Special Branch of the SAP. Then there were also the special sections of the Special Branch of the police, Section C being the ANC/PAC desk. The operational unit of Section C, based at Vlakplaas, outside Pretoria, was run by Eugene de Kock as 'a training centre and shelter for so-called "rehabilitated terrorists" who later became known as "askaris"'.[104]

Contacts between the SADF and the Rhodesian forces had developed during the 1960s and 1970s, and a particularly close relationship developed between the respective intelligence functions. The Rhodesians had been willing to experiment with 'new types of weapons', most notably chemical and biological agents. Moreover, South African participation in the Rhodesian Bush War, albeit limited, brought useful training opportunities and personal connections.[105] Burgess and Purkitt draw a straight line between the tactics used by the Selous Scouts and those employed by the SADF in Namibia and Angola, and, later, in South Africa. As they note, a number of members of the Rhodesian forces had been integrated into the SADF and SAP following the independence of Zimbabwe, and they served in units such as 5 Reconnaissance Regiment, the SAP's Koevoet unit and the Delta 40 unit of the South African Special Forces. The CCB, they argue,

employed many of these same tactics [use of chemical and biological agents] against political dissidents in the late 1980s and early 1990s. Toward the end of the apartheid era, the use of poisons against dissidents became routine CCB practice. By the time Eugene de Kock took charge of [section C1 of the CCB] in 1988, he had a working relationship and regular contacts with Dr Wouter Basson, the director of the CBW programme, known as Project Coast. Whenever the CCB wanted 'special tools' for interrogations or to eliminate political dissidents, Basson was available to supply custom-ised orders.[106]

The sophisticated CBW programme, developed to meet internal and exter-nal threats during the 1980s, surprised both South Africans and the world when the news broke during the hearings of the Truth and Reconciliation Commission (TRC). The stories of political assassinations, murder and torture of prisoners, biological engineering and behaviour manipulation riveted tel-evision audiences. Despite no training in covert activities, Dr Wouter Basson, a brigadier on the Surgeon General's staff and the director of Project Coast, became a master of deception, double-dealing and sanctions-busting, seem-ingly acquiring wives of convenience and becoming adept at smuggling and erecting front companies. These were real, unique glimpses into the macabre world of espionage, chemical and biological warfare, and medical research.[107]

Between 1979 and 1984, although the number of ANC infiltrations increased, South Africa remained essentially quiet. PW Botha was confident and unwill-ing to assume full powers in terms of the NSMS. Externally, however, a more active approach was adopted in three broad theatres – Namibia and Angola, the southern African region, and the international environment, while a fourth, clandestine, domain – nuclear strategy – increasingly became a feature of the total strategy.[108]

External security, 1978–1984: cross-border raids, envelopments

UN Security Council resolutions 385 (1977) and 435 (1978) mapped a path for Namibian independence, and Prime Minister John Vorster had given his assent to the latter. However, when PW Botha came to power in late 1978, there was a shift in government policy. While Botha followed the dual approach of pur-suing a counterinsurgency strategy in Namibia while simultaneously negoti-ating with the international community, he was willing at times to use the military option. As in South Africa, Pretoria's strategy came to rest on three pillars, namely, a counterinsurgency programme, a civic action programme and political reform. And, all the while, Pretoria used the instrument of direct and indirect strategy against Angola, Swapo's host.[109]

The SADF employed a classic counterinsurgency programme in Namibia. The development of local military capabilities, such as the SWATF, relieved the burden shouldered by the SADF as well as creating a nucleus for a post-independence defence force. Faced with growing defence expenditure and an escalating number of SADF troops 'on the border', Pretoria had good reason to expand the local defence contribution. Local recruitment was increased, and control of the SWATF was turned over to the authorities in Windhoek in 1980,[110] following the 1978 electoral victory by the Democratic Turnhalle Alliance (DTA). Specialist COIN units, such as 201 Battalion and 32 Battalion, operated on the border to intercept Swapo insurgents, while the military successes of Koevoet, a police COIN structure, won the unit praise and notoriety in equal measure. Koevoet became the most feared unit in the security forces.[111] At a tactical level, the Rhodesian 'fireforce' system, developed to offset the low number of security forces through a concentration of mobility and firepower, was adapted for the open veld and implemented.[112] Guerrillas, once located through aggressive infantry patrolling, would be attacked and pinned down, while a reaction force comprising paratroopers and an Alouette III helicopter, mounting a 20mm canon, would await the guerrillas as they fell back into a killing ground. Between 60 and 75 per cent of reconnaissance patrols resulted in 'contacts', and, over time, rendered a kill ratio of 3 900 insurgents for 167 security force members. Finally, a security zone, one kilometre wide, fenced and planted with landmines, was established on the Angolan border to impede the infiltration of Swapo insurgents.[113]

The Botha government, seeking to ensure a favourable outcome of the Namibian question, used carefully packaged incentives, such as financial and technical assistance for friendly states, and disincentives, such as economic disruption and destabilisation campaigns in neighbouring states hostile to Pretoria's interests. Here the focus was primarily on Zimbabwe, Mozambique and Angola. In the last-mentioned case, this involved military operations deep into that country. Following Operation Savannah, border tensions increased, with ongoing skirmishes between Swapo and the SADF. A range of measures, including a declaration of a state of emergency in the northern region of Namibia in early 1976 and the creation of the kilometre-wide buffer zone,

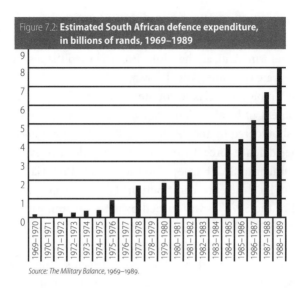

Figure 7.2: **Estimated South African defence expenditure, in billions of rands, 1969–1989**

Source: *The Military Balance*, 1969–1989.

did not seem to contain Swapo. It was reported that, in 1977, the SADF was intercepting Swapo guerrillas at the rate of 100 per month. By 1980 the annual operational casualty tally for the SADF was up to 100. Moreover, the build-up of Cuban troops in Angola was thought to be a precursor of a conventional attack on the SADF.[114]

Pretoria responded with a range of direct and indirect measures to counter these threats. These measures included the extension of the buffer zone into southern Angola, periodic cross-border raids into Angola and continued support for Unita. Several deep operations struck Swapo and, later, Fapla forces encamped in the Angolan bush and other priority military targets. Highly mobile SADF task forces launched a series of spectacular attacks between 1978 and 1983. The first, Operation Reindeer, was launched in May 1978 against a Swapo-Fapla camp at Cassinga, which was bombed and then attacked in a parachute drop.[115] The Cassinga raid has since become something of a historiographical controversy, with Swapo claiming that it was a refugee camp and that the 600 casualties were innocent civilians.[116] Other operations followed, but these were on a reduced scale. However, in May 1980, the SADF launched Operation Sceptic, a major raid against PLAN bases around Chifufua, some 100 kilometres inside Angola. This, together with a number of smaller raids or 'hot-pursuit operations' that followed, gave Unita, which had been badly mauled earlier in the year, the time and space to recover and then go on to

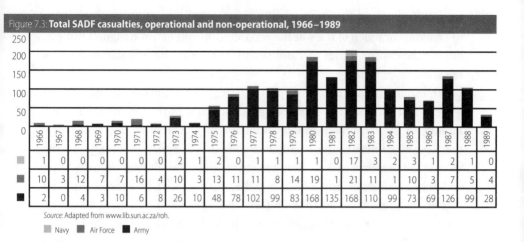

Figure 7.3: **Total SADF casualties, operational and non-operational, 1966–1989**

	1966	1967	1968	1969	1970	1971	1972	1973	1974	1975	1976	1977	1978	1979	1980	1981	1982	1983	1984	1985	1986	1987	1988	1989
Navy	1	0	0	0	0	0	0	2	1	2	0	1	1	1	1	0	17	3	2	3	1	2	1	0
Air Force	10	3	12	7	7	16	4	10	3	13	11	11	8	14	19	1	21	11	1	10	3	7	5	4
Army	2	0	4	3	10	6	8	26	10	48	78	102	99	83	168	135	168	110	99	73	69	126	99	28

Source: Adapted from www.lib.sun.ac.za/roh.

Navy   Air Force   Army

inflict significant damage to the oil installations at Lobito and reassert control over southeast and central Angola.

The conflict intensified over the following three years and the initiative shifted away from the SADF. The South African strategy aimed at maintaining the *cordon sanitaire* in southern Angola and a succession of operations, characterised by air and mechanised attacks on Swapo bases and lines of communication deep in Angola, followed. Operation Protea (August 1981), the largest mechanised operation by the SADF since the Second World War, was aimed at a newly installed ground-to-air missile system. During Protea, two armoured columns of the SADF moved 200 kilometres into Angola; while the first bound the enemy front, the other struck at the enemy's rear. The Angolans squandered their T-34s in largely static roles, while the SADF columns occupied the bases at Xangongo and Onjiva, capturing and destroying Soviet-supplied equipment and killing more than 1 000 Swapo and Fapla troops. The equipment destroyed included newly installed radar and SAM-3 and SAM-6 anti-aircraft missile sites. Swapo's entire logistic system in southern Angola was destroyed, while Unita was assisted in defeating Fapla attacks on Mavinga in March and May 1982.[117] While this reduced Swapo's ability to infiltrate, the lessening of the insurgent threat was accompanied by an increase in the numbers of Cuban and Fapla troops in the south.[118] After Protea came Daisy (October to November 1981), Super (March 1982) and Askari (December 1983), all of which were uniformly successful.

South Africa's chief indirect instrument in Angola was Unita. With help from Pretoria, Jonas Savimbi's insurgents were able to sustain ongoing campaigns, marked by sabotage and terror, aimed at the MPLA government in Luanda. For much of the war the economically important Benguela railway, linking the copper mines of Zambia and Zaïre with the Angolan ports, was rendered inoperable.

While pursuing a counterinsurgency strategy in Namibia, the South African government continued to engage in negotiations with the international community. In the early 1980s, the introduction of 'constructive engagement' by the Reagan administration marked a shift in US policy. Washington now viewed the presence of East Bloc troops in Angola as a major security issue and linked Namibian independence to the withdrawal of these forces from the region. As a result, support for Pretoria and Savimbi's Unita grew. However, the cost of the war was rising, and was estimated to be a crushing US$1 billion per year. Moreover, there were signs that popular support for the DTA among Namibians was shrinking. The Angolan government, in turn, was spending an estimated US$1.5 billion per year on the conflict. By 1983, both parties were ready to negotiate. The Lusaka Accord was signed on 16 February 1984 and a ceasefire, as a first step to Namibian independence, was implemented.[119] The forward, offensive strategy forced the MPLA to conclude a treaty with Pretoria in 1984 involving a phased withdrawal of SADF troops from Angolan soil in exchange for an undertaking by the MPLA to cease support for Swapo.

Zimbabwe gained independence in 1980 according to the terms of the Lancaster House Agreement (1979). After failing to impose its will on the new country, South Africa employed a range of indirect methods, including economic measures and unconventional warfare. The latter took two forms. Firstly, acts of sabotage were directed at carefully selected military, economic and political targets in Zimbabwe, and there was a string of assassinations of senior ANC officials in Harare. Secondly, Pretoria supported anti-government forces in both Zimbabwe and Mozambique. The principal theatre of insurgent activity was in Mozambique, where Renamo[120] guerrillas, through a campaign of sabotage and violence, closed the strategic rail and road links through the Beira corridor, obliging Prime Minister Robert Mugabe to use South African transport and harbour facilities. The impact of these disruptions was most severe on Zimbabwe's mining industry, while the loss of export earnings led to shortages of foreign exchange and had a negative ripple effect at a time when the Zimbabwean economy was under severe pressure due to the world recession, drought and political instability.[121]

A similar approach, including incentives and disincentives, was taken with

Mozambique, a neighbour that espoused a Marxist-Leninist ideology, one as inimical to Pretoria as apartheid was to Maputo. Moreover, the increasing ANC presence and a growing number of East Bloc military advisers gave Pretoria concern. Using Rhodesian contacts, South African military intelligence developed contact with Renamo and provided weapons to the value of US$1 million by late 1979. Attacks were launched on ANC offices and 'safe houses' in Maputo. However, the primary means of influencing Maputo was through indirect strategy.[122] This Pretoria did through the exercise of economic muscle and the fostering of Renamo's campaign, which tied up Mozambican forces and enervated an already ailing economy. Following a succession of secret meetings, the two countries signed the Nkomati Accord on 16 March 1984, in terms of which Pretoria would halt support for Renamo in return for the closure of ANC offices in Maputo. The accord recognised the sovereignty and territorial integrity of both states and reaffirmed the principle of non-interference in each other's internal affairs.[123] Later in the year, 800 ANC members were expelled from Mozambique.[124] Some cadres left for Lusaka, where the new MK military headquarters was set up from 1984 under Joe Modise.[125]

Botswana, Lesotho and Swaziland, although members of the South African-dominated Southern African Customs Union (SACU), attempted to assert their independence by permitting the ANC to operate from within their borders. As a result, all were subjected to direct and indirect strategies to encourage them to expel their ANC guests, end their support for the anti-apartheid forces, tone down their criticism of Pretoria and, if possible, also bind them firmly to South Africa through formal treaty. Botswana adopted a cautious attitude, unwilling to allow the ANC to use the country as a corridor to the south and at times deploying the Botswana Defence Force to stop this. Economic pressures were applied against Lesotho and covert support was lent to an insurgent Lesotho Liberation Army (LLA). SADF raids were conducted against ANC targets in Maseru (9 December 1982) and Gaborone (14 June 1985). Swaziland conducted a friendly and open relationship with Pretoria, although giving sanctuary to the ANC and allowing Swaziland to serve as a conduit between Mozambique and South Africa. Botswana would concede nothing more than an informal agreement of non-aggression. With this South Africa was satisfied. However, with the coup against Chief Jonathan's government in Maseru and the conclusion of a Swazi-South African 'Agreement Relating to Security Matters' (17 February 1982), Pretoria had secured non-aggression pacts with practically all of its neighbours. With the expulsion of the ANC from Mozambique, Lesotho and Swaziland in the early 1980s, the front line in the armed struggle shifted decidedly to the north. Something of the *cordon sanitaire* had been re-established. However, these successes appeared to have been an illusion. In late 1984, with the introduction of a tricameral parliamentary system, part of a reform package intended to purchase consent for the maintenance of apartheid, but which excluded blacks, the black townships in South Africa rose in revolt.[126]

Believing that a direct conventional attack was an inevitability, and in view of the escalating war in Angola and growing international isolation, Pretoria moved to develop a nuclear weapons programme.[127] South Africa had acquired the technological transfer over several years; Pretoria had supplied uranium to the West since the 1950s and had benefited from long-term contacts with American, French, German and Israeli nuclear scientists. This led to the construction of two reactors in South Africa, in 1965 and 1967. Discussions about the possibility of building a nuclear bomb were conducted by the Vorster government in the late 1960s, and, in 1974, a decision was made to develop such a device. The testing site in the Kalahari, exposed in 1977, was closed after combined US-USSR pressure. Notwithstanding, at least 6, and possibly as many as 25, atomic devices were built at plants outside Pretoria, each with a power equivalent to the device that destroyed Hiroshima in 1945. Moreover, South Africa had the means for delivery, strategically by means of the Mirage and Cheetah aircraft, while smaller, tactical warheads could be delivered in a particular battlespace by means of the G6 howitzer.

The world assumed South Africa had entered the nuclear club on 22 September 1979, when an American satellite detected a flash over the Southern Ocean. The Botha government neither confirmed nor denied possession of nuclear devices. Botha hoped that such a strategy might draw Western support should the Soviet Union, with its vastly superior nuclear arsenal, ever present a direct threat to southern Africa. Through a series of carefully calibrated hints, sometimes verging on disclosure, Pretoria, while communicating its security fears, could cajole the West into muting its criticism of apartheid and possibly secure assistance in any direct struggle with the Soviet Union.[128] FW de Klerk, who succeeded the ailing Botha in 1989, announced on 24 March 1993 that six devices had been built but that these had all subsequently been dismantled.[129]

The external security policy was designed to maintain domestic stability and regional peace and foster an environment for the successful implementation of a reform programme in both Namibia and South Africa. An aggressive regional policy bore fruit. By 1984, Pretoria had secured a network of formal and informal treaties and agreements with a number of southern African states, although this fell short of the desire to create in the region a small, southern counterpart to NATO. However, while Swapo incursions into Namibia and ANC activities in South Africa remained a concern to Pretoria, it seemed that, by the mid-1980s, the environment for the implementation of Botha's reform programme had been created. As Chris Alden has noted, 'this assumption was soon to be challenged by the tide of sustained unrest sweeping the country in the months following the implementation of the government's programme for political reform'.[130]

Revolt in the townships

Following a 1983 referendum, Botha introduced a round of preliminary reforms at three levels of government (local and regional, national and supra-national). He sought to create a tricameral parliament, with separate chambers for whites, coloureds and Indians, and independent states for blacks. Moreover, it included the basis for a confederal system, comprising what was termed a Constellation of Southern African States (CONSAS). This 'constellation' was to include tricameral South Africa, the independent 'homelands' and national states, and possibly even the SACU countries. While in many respects representing a significant break from 'grand apartheid', many of the old tenets remained intact. The structures were still race-based, giving whites, coloureds and Indians each charge over 'own affairs', while the (white) House of Assembly retained power over 'general affairs' (including foreign affairs, defence and finance). But, most important of all, this round of reforms still excluded the black majority from participating in government at a national level. There was no representation for urban blacks living outside the 'homelands'. This, together with the growing centralisation of political power and the slow pace of change, further eroded moderate black support for the reform programme.[131]

Following the explosion of township violence in September 1984, Botha declared a state of emergency in 36 magisterial districts, while he continued to implement measured socio-economic and political reforms. The inadequacy of the township municipal structures established under the Black Local Authorities Act (102 of 1982) and the Black Communities Development Act (4 of 1984) and the 'problems associated with introducing an incremental reform programme in an increasingly revolutionary climate' were made worse by an economic downturn and by deprivation in the townships. Elected black officials, hamstrung by structural flaws in the local government system and unable to satisfy rising expectation, faced fierce opposition. Moreover, with the ANC banned, the election to local office of those willing to work with the apartheid system raised doubts about their legitimacy and credibility.[132]

Grievances gave rise to protests and school boycotts. New civic organisations, as a counterpoise to the new local authorities, were established in the townships. The Soweto Civic Association and the Port Elizabeth Black Civic Organisation (Pebco), both founded in 1979, were typical. The National Forum (NF), based on the Black Consciousness tradition and a rival to the UDF, was formed on 11 June 1983. The United Democratic Front (UDF), a national umbrella for over 560 anti-government organisations, was launched on 20 August 1983 and was viewed increasingly by the government as a front for the exiled ANC.

The violence that erupted in September 1984 started in the Pretoria-Witwatersrand-Vereeniging (PWV) area. Crowds of people took to the streets to protest against economic and educational poverty and the iniquities of an unjust political system. Government complacency gave way to alarm as angry mobs 'necklaced' town councillors and others associated with the system.[133] The SADF deployed with the SAP to the townships. By the end of 1984, the death toll stood at 149. Things calmed down from November, but, from March 1985, a new cycle of violence flared up in the eastern Cape, where Pebco, having declared war on the local authorities system, organised a comprehensive strike. The violence now also had more focus and better coordination. The shooting by the security forces of 19 protestors at Langa on 21 March, and the assassination of the 'Pebco Three' and the 'Cradock Four' in May and June, respectively, stoked the flames.[134] Moreover, rifts between the UDF and NF, and between the UDF and Inkatha, and other anti-apartheid organisations, introduced what was coined 'black-on-black' conflict, as all vied for local support and control of the townships across the country. Parts of Natal became a battlespace between the UDF and Inkatha from 1985.

The government's internal response took the form of emergency regulations. But dissent was fuelled by the deployment of the SAP to the townships, and later of the SADF following the declaration of a partial state of emergency in 36 districts, located mostly in the eastern Cape and the PWV area, on 21 July 1985. The limiting of the emergency regulations was later thought to be a strategic mistake. Botha had done this in the hope of mollifying international criticism. After 229 days, the emergency regulations were partially lifted.[135]

The government, through a combination of repression, socio-economic upliftment and political reform, eventually stemmed the tide.[136] While the new counterinsurgency strategy was undoubtedly drawing results, the process of political reform suffered from increasing paralysis. In the 1987 general election, the government won 123 of the 178 seats in the House of Assembly. Botha again received a mandate, but he now faced growing resistance on the far right, where the Conservative Party (CP) replaced the liberal Progressive Federal Party (PFP) as the official opposition. Botha had lost a significant portion of the NP's traditional Afrikaner support base.

Some in South Africa questioned the relevance of Parliament itself. It was not only unrepresentative of the majority of the people but also there were questions about its accountability.[137] The implementation of the NSMS had led to the presence of 'two governments'. Botha had militarised the state and politicised the security forces. But the security establishment was not part of the government, although there were small overlaps of retired personnel. On the one hand government was sited in Parliament, but on the other hand there was a militarised state entrenched in the security establishment and networked across the country through the NSMS.[138] The latter, although taking the lead in the formulation of state strategy, left the reformist function to the 'civilians' in other departments, such as Chris Heunis and the Department of Constitutional Development and Planning.[139] In effect, South Africa had become a dual state.

External security, 1984–1986

By December 1983, the international climate was favourable, for South Africa and for Pretoria's campaigns in South West Africa/Namibia. However, the collapse of understanding between Pretoria and Luanda, as laid down in the Lusaka Accord, signalled the renewal of the Border War. In May 1985 a member of the South African Special Forces was captured on a mission in Cabinda, while that September the MPLA government launched an attack against Unita in the southeast of Angola. The battle for Mavinga, Savimbi's capital, in which 4 000 Angolan-Cuban troops with air support fought against 5 500 Unita troops, was one of the most fearsome battles of the entire Angolan

Table 7.4: Incidents in South West Africa/Namibia, 1980–1988									
Incident	1980	1981	1982	1983	1984	1985	1986	1987	1988
Contacts/ ambushes	644	545	297	299	307	252	176	213	134
Mines detonated	327	349	311	188	169	170	105	103	101
Intimidation	120	121	102	92	67	98	68	60	33
Sabotage	84	37	46	41	96	136	127	107	112
Totals	**1 175**	**1 052**	**756**	**620**	**639**	**656**	**476**	**483**	**380**

Source: Leopold Scholtz, The SADF in the Border War, 1966–1989, p 202.

war.[140] Defeated on the outskirts of Mavinga, and facing a Unita insurgency spreading to almost every province, Luanda felt impelled to beef up Fapla and accept offers of more Cuban troops from an eager if cautious Castro. The Soviet Union also sent in supplies.[141]

To the south, the improved security situation in Namibia heralded the success of the SADF counterinsurgency campaign. The SADF had wrested the initiative from PLAN. The SADF were now better equipped and better trained, and relied more heavily on professional soldiers rather than national servicemen and Citizen Force call-ups. Improvements to the SWATF, the use of specialised counterinsurgency infantry battalions, such as 101 Battalion, and the use of the 'fireforce' system all combined to give the security forces a massive advantage, and 'contacts' invariably ended badly for the insurgents. Moreover, the construction of the buffer zone, or 'cutline' (*kaplyn*), slowed PLAN infiltration to a trickle, and incidents dropped off markedly (*see* Table 7.4). Furthermore, the expulsion of Swapo from Zambia in 1978, the break with Canu (the Caprivian political movement) and Unita's domination of the southeastern corner of Angola all meant that PLAN enjoyed a relatively narrow corridor of access, to Ovamboland only. The creation of the Transitional Government of National Unity in June 1985 was a major step toward a political solution in Namibia and sent a strong signal to Swapo.[142]

Incipient revolution, 1986–1989

In the meantime, South Africa moved from rebellion in the townships of the PWV in 1984 to an incipient revolution in early 1986. The ANC-in-exile called for the establishment of alternative governing structures, and the youths of the townships responded by setting up self-styled 'people's courts' and 'street committees', both linked to local civic organisations, to take up community issues, provide political direction and gather 'taxes'. Highly questionable acts were committed by the 'people's courts', which often dispensed rudimentary and instant justice, and in the harshest terms. Moreover, imbued with a sense of impending success, revolutionary groups continued to battle each other in a separate campaign for 'the hearts and the minds'. There were running street battles between 'comrades' and, on the Rand, between the 'self-defence units' (SDUs) of MK and the KwaZulu Self-Protection Force (KZSPF), the armed wing of Inkatha. In some instances, criminal elements controlled townships in the name of the revolution, terrorising people and levying 'taxes'. It became increasingly difficult for voices of moderation to be heard and, indeed, to regain authority and control of the liberation struggle. Acts of violence – public mutilations and burnings – were used to gain publicity and instil fear and insecurity in larger society. However, the UDF gradually managed to reassert itself.[143]

Following its conference at Kabwe, in Zambia, from 16 to 23 June 1985, the ANC changed strategy, moving away from the high-profile acts of sabotage of the early 1980s to the creation of a guerrilla army inside South Africa and the launching of a 'people's war'. MK insurgents, trained in the use of small arms and explosives, were infiltrated into South Africa and formed a nucleus around which it was hoped a 'people's army' could be built, as the next stage in the revolutionary war. ANC Regional Political-Military Councils (RPMCs) were established in Botswana, Lesotho, Swaziland and Zimbabwe, while three Area Political-Military Councils (APMCs) were created in the Cape Province and one in the northern Transvaal. Military activity increased during 1985 and 1986, as these structures battled both the security forces and the vigilantes of the townships, several of which had become 'ungovernable'.[144] According to Martin Legassick:

> Operation Zikomo was launched from mid-1985, sending in large numbers of combatants with and grenades to particulate as 'shock troops' in township uprisings. This led to 136 'incidents' of MK activity in 1985 ... more than double that of any previous year. Moreover, the ratio of three guerrillas captured or killed for each 13 attacks was MK's most favourable casualty rate ever.[145]

However, operations were severely curtailed following the imposition of a full state of emergency in June 1986. Confronted by precision operations by the security forces and vigilantism in the townships, the ANC risked losing control of the struggle for liberation and with it the hope of toppling the government. This gloomy assessment opened the way for dialogue, first within the ANC and the UDF, and then, as an alternative approach to power, with the government. In 1987, the National Executive Committee of the ANC announced that the organisation remained committed to 'genuine negotiations provided they are aimed at the transformation of our country into a united and non-racial democracy'.[146] This was tacit recognition that the forces for revolution could not topple the government – not in the near future, at any rate. It was a clear signal that the ANC had reduced its expectation of a military victory and, under growing pressure from an ailing Soviet Union, would seek a negotiated solution. The publication of constitutional proposals, framed in a liberal democratic mould, in mid-1988 confirmed the shift from struggle to negotiation.[147]

Endgames

The international environment posed a mix of fortune for the South African government. On the one hand, there were no immediate and direct military threats. However, on the other hand, the international campaign for sanctions continued to grow, and for this Pretoria had few answers. In Angola, hostilities returned after the collapse of the Lusaka Accord. Cuban strength inside Angola had grown to almost 50 000, and there were new Cuban and Soviet officers in command. A massive assault, including three ANC battalions totalling almost 1 000 fighters, was launched against Unita in southeastern Angola in 1986, but was halted by the SADF and Unita at the Lomba River, to the south of Cuito Cuanavale. A second assault followed in September 1987, commanded by Soviet General Konstantin Shaganovitch and supported by tens of thousands of Cuban troops and large amounts of Soviet weaponry.[148]

South Africa, not wanting to lose its ally, intervened yet again to save Unita. However, the SAAF was dealt significant losses by an Angolan air force equipped now with MiG-23s. As a result, the Cuban-Angolan forces managed to hold Cuito Cuanavale against a combined SADF-Unita counter-offensive. The battles around Cuito Cuanavale eventually ended in stalemate, and the withdrawal of the SADF in 1988 was heralded by Cuba-Angola as a much-needed victory. There was also the hope that the prestige would edge the MPLA toward negotiations. But the South African objective, of saving Unita, had been achieved. Notwithstanding, the international arms embargo had shown its effect. South Africa, unable to access the latest and most sophisticated technology, had lost air supremacy. Pretoria, faced with the task of possibly rescuing Unita again in the near future, and no longer able to guarantee relatively inexpensive military victories, looked to a diplomatic solution. Moreover, the settled state in Namibia, and the success of socio-economic and civic programmes there, pointed to a favourable outcome in the elections scheduled for November 1989. Moreover, the war was becoming increasingly unpopular in South Africa, a country more and more preoccupied with internal unrest.[149]

While international negotiations continued, Cuban and South African forces clashed in June 1988 in the Calueque area, near the Namibian border, when a Cuban mechanised battalion, supported by T-55s and SAM-6 track-mounted anti-aircraft missiles, were halted in their southward thrust by a South African mechanised battalion group supported by a squadron of Olifant tanks. This proved to be the SADF's last major operation. The Soviets, faced with enormous economic troubles of their own, were clearly tiring of their costly support, while in Cuba the number of men killed for no apparent reason was being questioned. Luanda, in turn, facing total economic collapse and the burden of the ongoing civil war and always dependent upon support from Havana and Moscow, was exposed to the dramatic policy shifts of a reforming Mikhail Gorbachev. As a result, under pressure from their superpower partners, Pretoria and Luanda moved towards a negotiated solution. A provisional agreement was signed in July 1988. The linkage between a withdrawal of Cuban forces from Angola and the implementation of UN Resolution 435 was accepted, and in December 1988 an accord was signed in New York. This provided for a ceasefire, a staged withdrawal of the Cubans from Angola, and independence and free elections in Namibia. A later protocol, signed in Geneva in August 1988, determined lines beyond which Cuban and Swapo forces were not permitted to remain and a Joint Military Monitoring Commission (JMMC) was set up. At the same time, the SADF withdrew from Angola, but US support for Unita continued while the Cubans remained in Angola. A major Unita offensive was halted by Fapla with the support of Cuban troops, in contravention of the Geneva Protocol. Moreover, it was understood that South Africa would halt support for Unita and, in turn,

Luanda would close training bases for the ANC in Angola. This effectively re-established the *cordon sanitaire* and placed South Africa well beyond the reach of MK.[150] According to Ellis and Sechaba, historians of the ANC: 'For the Soweto generation, teenagers who had left South Africa in 1976 determined to come home with guns to fight for their freedom, it was a heavy blow. They were now further from South Africa than they had been ten years earlier.'[151]

Violations of the ceasefire predictably occurred. These led to small-scale border clashes. The most serious of these was a four-pronged incursion of more than 900 Swapo insurgents into Namibia on 1 April 1989, aiming to occupy the territory ahead of the arrival of the United Nations Transition Assistance Group (Untag), the UN supervision force. This was followed by a further incursion a week later. Taken by surprise, Swapo had thought that the SADF had been largely withdrawn and the SWATF demobilised. The insurgents were severely mauled by the SADF's Ratel 90s and helicopter gunships, and more than 250 were killed.[152] Following the arrival of Untag, the Swapo leadership instructed PLAN insurgents to report to the UN military centres, while the SADF proceeded with a full withdrawal, and the SWATF was demobilised and disbanded. The 23–year-long Border War, marked by seemingly irreconcilable violence that took the widest variety of forms, was finally over.

But things were moving rapidly in South Africa too. The security situation had been brought under control, but the government's reform process had stalled. As a result, there was a growing understanding in Pretoria that reform would only succeed if the ANC was brought directly into the process. Pretoria recognised, too, that the changing international landscape, with the fall of the Iron Curtain and the collapse of the Soviet Union, presented the government with an almost unique window of opportunity. With Botha gone – he suffered a stroke and was forced to resign in 1989 – and with moderates moving to the fore in the ANC, the path was set for a negotiated settlement.

CHAPTER EIGHT

The South African National Defence Force, 1994 to circa 2000

Uncertainty and *change* are two of the most commonly used words to characterise the future of the Armed Forces and are most often coupled to demands for organisational *adjustment* and *flexibility*.[1]

— Alise Weibull, sociologist, National Defence College of Sweden, 1999

From 1989, South Africa underwent broad and systematic change as the country adjusted to a post-Cold War world and, after 1994, to a post-apartheid society. Africa, having been the playground of the superpowers for much of the latter half of the twentieth century, seemed to decline in importance. The Soviet Union, racked by economic problems of its own, was forced to re-evaluate its global stance and, with it, to redefine its national interest. Economic opportunity and growth and development now ranked ahead of ideological competition and the balance of power. This brought policy shifts with regard to Africa and the Third World. Some scholars of the former Soviet Union have even challenged the notion that internal conflict in these regions was ever ideologically motivated. Africa was no longer strategically important to the superpowers; in various ways and on different fronts, Africa had to fight against increasing marginalisation of the continent, driven by protracted internal conflict, poor leadership and governance, compromised health and struggling economies.[2]

Yet, while the United States and the Soviet Union re-evaluated their relationship, mutually and with the rest of the world, Africans, caught almost in a Cold War time warp, harboured their ideological suspicions of each other. The politicisation of the armed forces and the militarisation of politics was an unfortunate if inevitable consequence for the African states most directly influenced by the main protagonists of the Cold War.[3] Internationally, since the collapse of the Soviet Union and the ending of the Cold War the scope of change has been global. In terms of the military, as Christopher Dandeker has shown, 'the main challenge for the armed forces is that changes stemming from the external strategic context and domestic society are not occurring sequentially but simultaneously'. The continuing adjustment to international and local sources of change has brought about near-constant policy adjustments, organisational restructuring, the adjustment of equipment tables, the development of doctrine and changes in the cultural ethos of armed forces.[4]

This was perhaps nowhere more dramatically evident than in South Africa where, in a remarkable about-turn, a 'New South Africa' emerged from the democratic elections of April 1994. This chapter addresses the changing international and domestic landscape from 1989 and 1994 and some of the concomitant changes that have taken place in the South African National Defence Force during the democratic era.

Toward a post-apartheid defence policy

The Interim Constitution (1993), which established the South African National Defence Force (SANDF), called for a 'balanced, modern and technologically advanced force' but provided only a broad, yet fundamental, policy framework, which had to be further developed. Central to the transformation of the armed forces was the integration of the statutory and non-statutory forces (NSF) into the SANDF. Moreover, political oversight and democratic control over the military was instituted. Strict affirmative action and equal opportunity policies were implemented to reflect societal demographics. The post-integration processes of demobilisation and rationalisation were used to tailor the personnel in terms of race, education and training. Equally important, if somewhat neglected during the immediate post-1994 years, was the transformation of defence policy and posture, the adoption of a new force design and structure for the SANDF, and the institution of a new management framework for the Department of Defence.

The White Paper on Defence, promulgated in May 1996, established the broad policy framework and main principles of defence. This was overlapped by a comprehensive Defence Review to fill in the details of force size and design and react otherwise to the implications of a 'primarily defensive posture' for strategy and doctrine, future defence budget, efficiency improvements and the use of reserves. The Defence Review process commenced in August

1995, with the Defence Review Work Group (DRWG) comprising members of the Defence Secretariat and the SANDF, two ministerial advisors, representatives from the defence industry and the Part-Time Forces,[5] and policy analyst Laurie Nathan, who had drafted the White Paper. Their findings were opened to public scrutiny. Public hearings were held and a national consultative conference was convened, whereafter the draft Defence Review was presented to Cabinet and Parliament for ratification in April 1998. For the first time, there was a national consensus on South Africa's defence function. Moreover, strategic doctrine had been set and specific roles for the SANDF were defined.

However, the development of defence policy was hamstrung by the absence of a clear and well-coordinated national security policy, by an ambiguous foreign policy and national interest objectives, and by long-term financial stringency. The lack of strategic vision among policymakers, who had little understanding of the complexity of force development and, with an ideal vision, wished to design armed forces for the short term, did not help. The result was an unrealistic defence policy.[6] Moreover, short-term political objectives led to the rapid replacement of personnel through the three interlocking processes of integration, demobilisation and rationalisation and the affirmative action (AA) and equal opportunity (EO) programmes that followed. Within a relatively short time, a treasure-trove of experience was emptied out. Firstly, experienced long-service personnel left, enticed by attractive financial packages and by signals that there would be new ceilings and dead ends in the future. Secondly, posts were kept vacant in the hope of achieving AA and EO quotas. The first factor led to the rapid and fundamental loss of experience and capacity, while the second, over a longer term, has fundamentally undermined service delivery, force impact and force design.

The transformation of the military: integration, rationalisation and demobilisation

The South African National Defence Force (SANDF) was formed on 27 April 1994 upon the integration of no less than eight forces in terms of the 1993 Interim Constitution.[7] The largest of these were the SADF and Umkhonto we Sizwe (MK), the armed force of the African National Congress. The others were the armed forces of the independent states (the 'homelands'), namely, the Transkei Defence Force (TDF), Bophuthatswana Defence Force (BDF), Venda

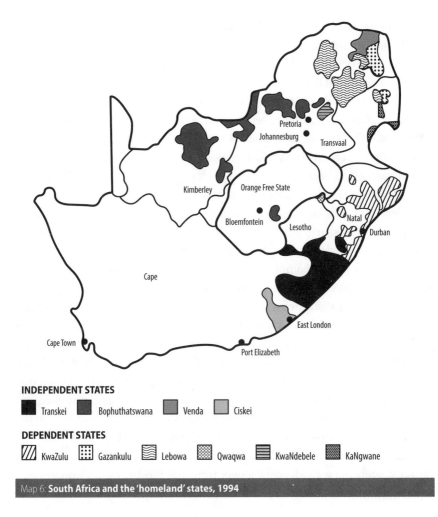

INDEPENDENT STATES

■ Transkei ■ Bophuthatswana ■ Venda ■ Ciskei

DEPENDENT STATES

▨ KwaZulu ▦ Gazankulu ▤ Lebowa ▨ Qwaqwa ▤ KwaNdebele ▨ KaNgwane

Map 6: **South Africa and the 'homeland' states, 1994**

Defence Force (VDF) and Ciskei Defence Force (CDF) – collectively known as the TBVC defence forces. The Azanian People's Liberation Army (Apla), the paramilitary wing of the Pan Africanist Congress (PAC), integrated in 1997. A late addition, too, was the KwaZulu Self-Protection Force (KZSPF), the paramilitary wing of the Inkatha Freedom Party (IFP), which opposed the ANC in Zululand and on the Rand. In fact, three processes were closely inter-linked: integration would necessarily be followed by a limited demobilisation and some rationalisation as the defence force was 'downsized' and 'right-sized'. Each of these processes, following on from the inter-force negotiations that took place in parallel to the political process, was contentious.

Negotiations

The negotiations had commenced in May 1990, when a team of 46 SADF officers met with MK representatives in Lusaka. Collectively, they recognised their
different backgrounds and traditions and called for an armed force for South
Africa that was balanced, modern and technologically advanced. However, it
seemed to the MK people present that the SADF expected MK to integrate into
the SADF, in other words through a process of absorption. In many respects,
this might have been a natural outcome, for the SADF was well established,
organisationally and technologically superior and possibly the most powerful
force on the continent. As Vyacheslav Shiryaev, a Soviet officer placed to train
MK in Angola, recalled, the SADF was 'a huge well-adjusted machine, able
through its strategy, tactics and technical capabilities to counter practically the
whole African continent'.[8] Absorption was, of course, something MK did not
want and its representatives insisted on the creation of a new force into which
all others would have to merge.[9]

However, it was soon apparent that MK faced numerous problems, and that
the pace of change set by the government had caught the ANC by surprise. All
of a sudden, the non-statutory forces (NSF, the collective noun coined for MK
and Apla members) had to confront the problems of ending the struggle and
preparing for integration into a new national defence force. There was much
disorganisation as MK headquarters relocated to South Africa. Cadres were
dispersed widely: some were in-country, others were still in exile, and many
were awaiting finalisation of their personal indemnities. There was also a 'lingering notion' while the ANC was at the negotiating table 'that MK was being
sidelined', that MK had become 'an albatross' and could now be 'conveniently
dispensed with'.[10] The sense of abandonment was greatest among the cadres
still abroad, who were particularly unhappy at the manner in which the leadership structures had relocated from Lusaka to Johannesburg, leaving those in
the frontline states seemingly to fend for themselves. As James Ngculu, deputy
chief of MK intelligence (1993), notes:

> Comrades complained that no plan or clear arrangements had been made
> for the cadres left in the rear and the other material needs of MK. The exter-
> nal and regional structures of MK were in disarray, and comrades had been
> left without clear guidance and information.[11]

These cadres had to be encouraged and exhorted, and they had to be cared for materially and otherwise. A conference held at Thohoyandou in August 1991, and the payment of a cash gratuity to MK combatants by the ANC, went some way to assuage fears and bolster endorsement of the negotiation process.

Moreover, a nucleus of well-trained, well-placed cadres was required, and the training programme had to be expanded dramatically, particularly in the regular, technical lines. Cadres received such training in Ghana, India, Uganda, Zambia and Zimbabwe, and in South Africa, from the TDF. A personnel list had to be created, and for this cadres had to register. Many were afraid to do so. But it was necessary, as precise personnel details had to be available when all forces had to declare in advance of integration.[12] New roles, if possible, had to be found for disabled comrades. And, while the negotiating process continued, MK had to remain a force in being. Ronnie Kasrils, the MK intelligence chief, who stressed the importance of 'keeping our forces intact and our powder dry', called at this time for the creation of 'self-defence units' (SDUs), which would also augment MK numbers in the future integration process.[13]

However, two matters regarding the negotiation and integration processes particularly vexed the ANC and MK at this point. Firstly, the ANC rejected outright the idea of an international peacekeeping force to supervise the transition and the elections. They felt such a force ought to be indigenous; the problem was how it would be formed. Secondly, there was already some unhappiness regarding the possible use of educational qualifications as a basis for integration. 'Comrades', Ngculu tells us,

> argued that the lack of formal education qualifications among many MK cadres was not of their own making. Everyone felt that Africans in particular had been denied education by the apartheid system. In exile, many MK members could have opted to go to school but chose to enter the ranks of MK. For these reasons, they should not be abandoned now that there were new opportunities. As one comrade argued, there is education and there is education.[14]

These two issues would arise in sequence and would threaten both the political climate and the harmony within the integrating forces.

The National Peacekeeping Force (NPKF): the first integration test

The higher-level, political negotiations took place in Kempton Park, at the Convention for a Democratic South Africa (Codesa), where it was soon obvious that the ANC had a superior negotiating team.[15] A Transitional Executive Council (TEC), to ensure a democratic transition, and a Joint Military Coordinating Committee (JMCC), to provide oversight of the security forces, were created; the JMCC included representatives from the SADF, the TBVC forces and the NSF. Ongoing violence, especially as a result of the conflict between the KZSPF and the SDUs of MK, seemed to threaten the peaceful climate needed for a free and fair election. To this end the National Peacekeeping Force (NPKF) was also created.[16]

The NPKF was the first integration test. Not only was the appointment of the commander contentious but also many and disparate forces were to be brought into the structure. The two candidates, Brigadier George Kruys of the SADF and Brigadier Derek Mgwebi of the TDF, were both found to be unacceptable, and so a compromise was reached. As a result, Brigadier Gabriel Ramushwana, a rather colourful figure, was appointed. Ramushwana was not only the president of Venda but also the commander of the VDF, and had come to power in a coup in 1990. The NPKF, with an establishment of some 400 to 500, was to comprise SADF and MK members in equal numbers, together forming some two-thirds of the force.[17] The remainder would comprise members of the South African Police and of the armed forces and police forces of the TBVC states, and the police forces of five of the six dependent 'national states'.[18] The KwaZulu Police Force, the Bophuthatswana Defence Force and the Bophuthatswana Police Force, however, remained outside of this structure.[19] In all, 13 different constituent forces jockeyed for position.

The NPKF was doomed from the start. It was not fully inclusive and had to adjust continuously to the ever-changing political game. The delays involved in Ramushwana's appointment meant that much valuable time was lost. The structures and procedures set up, in the interest of inclusivity and political balance, were cumbersome and the 'representivity charts' (ensuring representation of all forces at practically all levels and in prescribed numbers) produced an insuperable shortage of competent commanders and efficient staff officers in most areas. Problems at De Brug (near Bloemfontein), the main training base for the NPKF, did not bode well. Indiscipline and a lack of unity were compounded by politicking, as some members of the NPKF placed their political aspirations first. MK, Barnard and Swanepoel argue, operated as a force within a force. MK in turn blamed the government for not supporting the NPKF.[20] Quite simply, the NPKF was patched together too hastily, and when it deployed in April 1994 on the volatile East Rand for the first time and came under fire, some 15 people were killed. Seemingly, a member of the force panicked, wild shots were fired, and one of the casualties was the award-winning photographer Ken Oosterbroek. The SADF had to be called in to restore order.[21] Any notion that the NPKF might be developed into the new national defence force died.

The politics of integration and transformation

Hostilities ended officially with the promulgation of the Interim Constitution and the establishment of the South African National Defence Force, and South Africa again went through the process of integrating armies with diverse cultural, political and training backgrounds. General Georg Meiring (former SADF) became Chief of the SANDF, while Lieutenant General Siphiwe Nyanda (former MK) became his deputy. Born in 1951, Nyanda had enjoyed rapid advancement within MK. Trained in Eastern Europe (1975–1976), he returned to South Africa and, with the nom de guerre 'Gebhuza', became commander of MK in Swaziland (1977) and the Transvaal (1984). According to Ronnie Kasrils, Nyanda 'acquired a reputation for nerve and audacity and was responsible for many daring operations'.[22] His brother had died in a hail of bullets in 1983, in Swaziland. He and another MK operative, Mac Maharaj, had remained undercover inside South Africa after the unbanning of the ANC, and commanded Operation Vula, which was the ANC's 'insurance policy' should negotiations with the government fail. When Vula was exposed in July 1990, Nyanda was arrested, but was later released and given indemnity. He was integrated into the SANDF and succeeded Meiring in 1998, becoming the first black person to be chief of the South African armed forces.

The SANDF was, at its establishment, to consist of all of the members of the SADF, of the defence forces of 'any area forming part of the national territory', and any armed force as defined in section 1 of the Transitional Executive Council Act, 151 of 1993 – in other words, the non-statutory forces. There were, however, two provisos. The first was that the names of all of the members had to be included in a certified personnel register and, the second, that the political organisation associated with the armed force had to take part, under the Constitution, in the first elections. As a result, with the promulgation of the Interim Constitution, the SADF, the TBVC defence forces and MK were integrated into the new structure.[23] While MK met the requirements of the provisos, Apla did not. Section 224(2) was subsequently amended to allow the inclusion of Apla, and, on 4 February 1997, when the 1996 Constitution was promulgated, members of Apla, by operation of law, also became members of the SANDF.[24]

The new Defence minister, Joe Modise, and his deputy, Ronnie Kasrils, were both members of the ANC and former MK operatives. They set about shaping the SANDF, creating policy and ensuring implementation. They realised that state power was sited in the civil service they had inherited. This was an outcome of the negotiation process. The new government, contrary to the dictates of Marxist thought, had taken over the bureaucracy rather than destroying it. Here, a few mindshifts were required too. There was to be a measured transfer of power, and, as Kasrils notes, the olive branch appeared regularly along with new policy and the stick.[25]

The full-time forces presented the largest challenge, for the tension between change and stability had to be carefully managed. The ANC backbench, suspicious of former SADF officers, who were 'still seen to be in military command', had demanded a radical shake-up. But, as Kasrils explains, the ministry took their 'cue from Mandela, who often remarked to the ANC leadership that we should not behave as if we were dealing with an enemy whom we had defeated on the battlefield'.[26] Mandela remained true to the spirit of the negotiated settlement, and, in fact, even before the elections had approached Georg Meiring to serve as chief of the new defence force, which, of course, had the added benefit of calming any fears that existed within the former SADF.[27]

Some 117 000 people integrated into the SANDF. These were drawn from the SADF (82 705), MK (14 791), TBVC (11 039), Apla (6 421) and KZSPF (approximately 2 000). There were immediate fears from the NSF members that, as they were outnumbered, they would be 'absorbed by the old rather than integrated into the new'.[28] However, things changed quickly. Nine former MK officers were made generals in 1994, and by March 1997 their numbers had increased to 15. They included Themba Masuku (Surgeon General), who became the first black service chief, Gilbert Romano (Deputy Chief of Army) and Jackie Sedibe, Modise's wife, who became the first female general.

Long-term discrimination had denied blacks access to a wide range of

Table 8.1: **Racial profile of the SANDF (percentages)**			
Race	SANDF 1994 post-integration	Defence Review targets	SANDF 2009
Africans (blacks)	39.2	64.5	70.0
Coloureds	12.6	13.0	13.0
Asians	1.3	1.3	1.0
Whites	46.8	24.4	16.0

Source: Adapted from L Heinecken and N van der Waag, 'The politics of race and gender in the South African armed forces: issues, challenges, lessons', *Commonwealth & Comparative Politics*, 47(4) 2009, p 520.

employment opportunities, and had closed whole sectors of society, including the armed forces, on the basis of race. Limited numbers of blacks enlisted in the former SADF, some achieving officer rank. But the numbers remained small. This changed dramatically after 1994, with the scrapping of racial laws and the enactment of new legislation to correct historic political and socio-economic inequalities. This included assertive affirmative action (AA) and equal opportunity (EO) programmes that changed the racial, ethnic and gender profile of the South African armed forces irrevocably. The SANDF became increasingly more representative of the population. By 1997, 70 per cent of the SANDF was black, up from 37.5 per cent in the former SADF.[29] In the 1912 amalgam that produced the Union Defence Force, there had been great concern to balance three interests: language, province and former force. The 1994 integration placed a heavy emphasis on race and, to a lesser extent, gender. The Defence Review set specific race targets (*see* Table 8.1). Within 15 years these quotas were met with regard to uniformed personnel. However, amid dramatic shifts, whites are now under-represented and 'white' numbers decrease continuously.[30]

Overnight, the defence force also became multilingual. Eleven of South Africa's 17 recognised languages enjoy official status; these languages and their currency in South Africa and the SANDF are shown in Table 8.2. There are strong regional slants. The language policy is now one of situational multilingualism, with English as the 'thread' language, although only 10.3 per cent of personnel cite English as their first language (this figure is in all probability very inflated).[31] The language issue has always been problematic in the South African military. Many blacks associate Afrikaans with apartheid, but language remains an important source of power, and second- or third-level speakers find themselves at a considerable disadvantage, 'especially where

Table 8.2: **Language profile of the South African population and the SANDF/DoD compared, 2007**										
Language	isiZulu	isiXhosa	Afrikaans	Sepedi	English	Setswana	Sesotho	Xitsonga	SiSwati	Tshivenda	isiNdebele
Population (RSA)	23.8	17.6	13.3	9.4	8.2	8.2	7.9	4.4	2.7	2.3	1.6
Dept of Defence	8.3	9.0	23.6	7.5	10.3	8.3	5.7	1.6	2.1	3.0	0.5

Note: Figure represents the 11 official languages; there are a further six recognised languages.
Source: Adapted from L Heinecken, 'A diverse society, a representative military? The complexity of managing diversity in the South African armed forces', *Scientia Militaria*, 37(1) 2009, p 30.

linguistic shortcomings are construed as a sign of intellectual inferiority'.[32] Language remains in many ways a barrier, especially in conversational exclusion and education and training.

There was, and has been, little opposition to the programme of indigenisation from former SADF personnel. Guarantees for jobs and pensions were part of the negotiated settlement, and this weighed heavily in the minds of individuals; 'the essential factor uppermost in the mind of the individual officer', Kasrils tells us, 'was to retire gracefully, comfortably and hopefully with a medal and a handshake from Mandela'. An early-retirement mechanism was introduced, but, as Kasrils notes again, 'not everyone [was] willing or ready to retire and the bottom line for many [was] quite naturally a struggle to preserve job and career. And there can be nothing more bitter than such a struggle.'[33]

It is clear that all was not well at Defence Headquarters. While Meiring seemingly got on well with Modise, he and Kasrils did not get along at all. Meiring thought the new ministry not up to the job: 'We showed [Modise] around, trying to tell him what a modern army/defence force looks like. I don't think they really understood the workings of the Defence Force.'[34] That may have been true. The training MK received had focused heavily on guerrilla warfare and small-group tactics. A large, modern defence force revolves around planning and budgeting cycles. Kasrils, in turn, did not like Meiring, did not trust him. 'The deputy minister', Meiring admits, 'really worked on my tits.'[35] Meiring was shuffled out of office, somewhat controversially, in 1998.

Integration

The integration process was contested. This is not surprising, given the history of conflict and polarisation in South Africa and the fact that, to all intents and purposes, the integrating forces had been in a state of war. The regulatory framework for the integration process was established by the JMCC of the Sub-council on Defence of the Transitional Executive Council (TEC). The entire integration was to have been completed by the end of 1994. However, difficulties, some political, some military, led to an extension for three more years. The JMCC determined that the statutory forces, that is, the former SADF and TBVC defence forces, had the requisite training and rank qualifications. The non-statutory forces, on the other hand, were subjected to processes of course accreditation and training standardisation. This caused much upset; ex-cadres, feeling disadvantaged, believed the integration to be an unfair process.

Moreover, prior to the first all-race elections, the integrating forces had had to submit a full list of personnel for codification as the Certified Personnel Register (CPR), which formed the basis of the integration and the demobilisation that would follow. However, there were immediate difficulties. The non-statutory forces did not maintain detailed personnel records and the use of noms de guerre was common practice. Many of the cadres also did not qualify for the CPR: the NSF included many people with little training, and sometimes no training. MK recognised four categories of cadres: firstly, those who had left South Africa, had been trained externally, sometimes for long periods, and remained in the camps; secondly, those who had received training in South Africa, for shorter periods, with possibly a short course of one or two weeks' duration in Swaziland or Botswana; thirdly, those who had assisted and provided support for MK in South Africa through the provision of safe houses, courier work and reconnaissance; and, fourthly, those who had performed non-military tasks.[36]

A second, 'non-formal' CPR was created to accommodate a further 1 087 people. In August 1995 these were incorporated into the formal CPR. But the revised CPR satisfied neither all MK cadres nor former SADF officers. The latter were concerned that the NSF had deliberately and artificially enhanced their numbers to increase their voice in the negotiation process as well as in the new SANDF. The actual size of MK will never be known. While some scholars, including Barrel, have estimated the number of MK cadres at 12 000,[37] the ANC submitted 28 888 names for the CPR. Allegations abounded that people

Table 8.3: **The Certified Personnel Register, 1994**		
Statutory forces		
Former SADF (excluding part-time forces but including civilians)	90 000	
Former TBVC defence forces	11 039	
Subtotal		101 039
Non-statutory forces		
MK (Certified Personnel Register)	27 801	
MK ('Non-formal list')	1 087	
Apla	6 000	
Subtotal		34 888
Total		**135 927**

Source: T Motumi and A Hudson, 'Rightsizing: the challenges of demobilisation and social reintegration in South Africa', in J Cilliers, ed, *Dismissed* (IDP, Midrand, 1995), p 114.

with at best a marginal link to MK had been included, such as those who had participated in SDUs. In the end, less than 14 000 ex-NSF cadres reported for integration, a point that seemingly confirmed these suspicions.

The actual process of integration began after the finalisation of the CPR. Members of the former SADF experienced little change: their daily routines continued, the infrastructure and organisational systems of the SADF were used and, for the moment, the uniforms, rank insignia and the pantheon of medals mollified many with the fiction of business as usual. The integration of NSF personnel, mustered regionally under their former MK and Apla commanders and then sent to the assembly areas, such as Wallmansthal (Pretoria) and De Brug (Bloemfontein), was more dramatic. At the assembly areas, they were brought onto the personnel and financial systems of the new SANDF, were allotted force numbers and appeared before placement boards that comprised representatives of all of the constituent forces as well as the British Military Advisory and Training Team (BMATT). Those former NSF members without formal education and training were tested and graded. Some were not integrated. Some accepted NCO rank; others were eligible for commissioning. Various training programmes followed. There was 'bridging training' to orient former guerrillas to a conventional force, but also formation- and unit-specific training. Soldiers were then posted to units.

However, a whole range of problems surfaced with regard to the integration process. In the first place, many of the decisions reached by the TEC had not been discussed with the rank-and-file cadres, who, feeling that they had

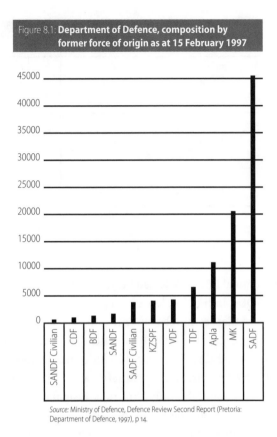

Figure 8.1: **Department of Defence, composition by former force of origin as at 15 February 1997**

Source: Ministry of Defence, Defence Review Second Report (Pretoria: Department of Defence, 1997), p 14.

been 'sold out', disagreed with some of the compromises. One MK cadre complained: 'Integration was a bit lopsided, a bit one-sided because only MK and APLA had to go before the panel and answer questions and undergo tests before they could be accepted for integration and given status. Those from the SADF remained as they were. It looked more like MK and APLA were joining the SADF and not forces being integrated as such ... I personally felt it was not a very fair exercise.'[38]

Other former combatants complained of the slowness of the process, the administrative difficulties they had to endure, the language medium for instruction, the lack of respect for cultural differences and the placement of people in ranks that were deemed lower than deserved. Discontent spilled over in September 1994 when 2 500 ex-NSF combatants walked out of Wallmansthal base; 265 never returned. Early in 1995, some 200 former MK combatants, demanding immediate incorporation into the SANDF, took to the streets in Durban, smashing windows and overturning rubbish bins. Similar protests took place in Cape Town later that year. The alleged establishment of at least five structures by disgruntled ex-NSF combatants was reported in the press. The BMATT, responsible for oversight of the integration process, admitted that there had been problems. However, they reported also that they were satisfied that the integration had been fair.[39]

This assurance did little to satisfy some former cadres, despite the resolution of initial integration difficulties. For many, the integration process meant, in effect, the absorption of MK and Apla into the SADF. Complaints persisted for some years, particularly about the composition of the SANDF, about perceived racism and harassment, the use of language, the slowness of cultural change within the new structures, the lack of respect for diversity and the appropriateness of training. Some black soldiers complained of racism and 'harsh measures' taken against them on the grounds of 'maintaining standards'. Discontent regarding the composition of the general staff, still dominated by white men in 1994, was remedied by the rapid advancement of former NSF officers.

Demobilisation

The second process, associated closely with the integration, was the reduction of the numbers of people employed by the SANDF and their successful reintroduction into wider society. Defence minister Joe Modise announced the start of the demobilisation process some 16 months into the integration. All personnel on the CPR, automatically members of the new SANDF at midnight on 26 April 1994, had to be either integrated or demobilised. The key objective was not to reduce force size, but to minimise the risks and security concerns relating to ex-combatants who were not eligible for integration or who chose not to integrate, and to guard against political and societal instability. The need for comprehensive demobilisation packages, enabling effective reintegration, was recognised. Two categories of personnel applied for demobilisation packages. First were those who were not eligible for integration on the basis of age, education level or health. A second group were those that were eligible but, for whatever reason, chose not to integrate into the SANDF, possibly because they were not satisfied with their rank or package after placement. The first group of 371 soldiers was demobilised in September 1995. They comprised mostly medically unfit veterans and those not qualifying for integration on the basis of educational level. By February 1997, 3 770 people had been demobilised.

There were suspicions about the process. Demobilisation was painted by some as an attempt to impede the integration of former guerrillas by enticing them with seemingly attractive demobilisation packages. Others argued that it was cheaper to fund a range of severance packages than to integrate the personnel involved: the average integration cost per combatant was estimated at R50 000, which was considerably more than the largest demobilisation gratuity (R40 657) and did not involve long-term personnel costs.[40]

However, as Motumi and McKenzie have argued, the demobilisation process was 'poorly planned, badly executed and wholly inadequate in meeting the needs of ex-combatants'.[41] Many ex-combatants did not have skills or appropriate experience for the civilian workplace, where they had to compete with millions of others for a limited number of places. Many ex-combatants felt disoriented on their return. They had served in exile, outside a complex cash economy, and had difficulty in dealing with money. Some, Motumi and McKenzie note, could not find a telephone number in a telephone book. Many had missed out on educational and training opportunities. Most experienced great stress and battled to reintegrate into the new South Africa.[42] Personal problems ranged from emotional conditions to matters of a social and physical nature; many suffered from post-traumatic stress disorder (PTSD). Yet, only 11 per cent of respondents in a 1993 survey reported having received some assistance in this regard. Effective and well-managed demobilisation could have reduced such risks significantly.

Ex-combatants generally received little assistance. The National Coordinating Committee for the Repatriation of South African Exiles (NCCR) offered grants, counselling, legal assistance and job placement. The Service Corps, established from 31 January 1995, was to provide for new skilling and social reintegration. However, this was located within the military and soon proved unable to provide quality training, in-service experience and concomitant employment opportunities. Its focus on NSF members led to the unfortunate perception that the Service Corps was a 'dumping ground for ex-MK and APLA soldiers'.[43]

The demobilisation process, planning for which only commenced once a crisis had developed, was inadequate and unsystematic. The top-down, standard and inflexible approach, with no allowance for differentiation or individual merit, was resented and did not foster viable, long-term productivity.[44] Some ex-combatants also qualified for additional pensions in terms of the Special Pensions Act. Some became elected representatives in the national and provincial legislatures. Yet the reports of disaffected former guerrillas involved in crime and violence, including bank robberies and cash-in-transit heists, were cause for much concern. Some former SADF soldiers, seeking greener pastures, left the SANDF to work as mercenaries, in private and government armies, in Africa (Angola, Sierra Leone, Zaïre) and Asia (Papua New Guinea) and later, after 9/11, in Iraq and Afghanistan. In all, some 3 770 personnel were demobilised. The third process, rationalisation, was thought to have affected perhaps ten times that number.

Rationalisation

Kasrils is perhaps correct regarding the 'bitter struggles' within the old SADF. But return from exile and integration into the new SANDF was also difficult for many returnees, who faced new struggles and massive disappointments. Many assumed that they would be received back into their communities as heroes, that there would be victory parades, fêtes and ample rewards, the spoils of success. But, somehow, the negotiated settlement and the piecemeal return of cadres had cheated them of this. Ngculu tells us:

> ... we did not return as we expected. We did not return home with the AK-47 on our shoulders, toyi-toying and singing 'Sizongena ngejambo' (we should enter the country toyi-toying). Instead we entered individually or in small groups to an uncertain future. We left our homes in exile to set up a new life in South Africa. We had to be integrated into this new life. We depended entirely on the ANC for accommodation, food, and clothing when we were in exile. Our children were sent to schools provided for, or paid by, the movement.[45]

There were many protests, particularly by former NSF personnel, regarding perceived racism, the continued use of Afrikaans and administrative, personnel and pay disputes. Sometimes soldiers marched on the Union Buildings or to Parliament, to present their cases to the President.[46] Sometimes these cases were heard in court. Many South Africans did not feel at ease. Max du Preez, the well-known journalist, noted in February 2008:

> I have for a very long time had the impression that our National Defence
> Force is in deep trouble. After last week I'm sure of it. My morning paper
> last Friday carried a picture of a soldier with a Jacob Zuma T-shirt on the
> front page. He was the spokesperson of the soldiers' trade union and he
> was threatening to disrupt the opening ceremony at parliament. The sol-
> diers' protest action was in support of a demand for better salaries and the
> SANDF's promotions policies. But the police had refused the soldiers per-
> mission to march in Cape Town on the day of the opening of parliament.
> The union leader then threatened revolt – that they would invade Cape
> Town in their thousands and take on the police ... In any other democracy
> this soldier would have been in detention barracks by the time the news-
> paper hit the streets and would be facing a court martial by now. Nothing
> happened to him.[47]

The case of Khululekile Chris Phike, which took the legal route, shows that
matters were not that straightforward and there was cause for some anxiety
and much disappointment. Phike trained as a member of Apla in 1983. He
infiltrated the Bophuthatswana Defence Force in the following year. During
1994, the BDF was integrated into the SANDF and Phike became a member
of the new national force, with the rank of captain. Apla, however, outside the
constitutional process at the time, instructed Phike to resign from the SANDF,
which he did with effect from 30 June 1995. Phike took up civilian employment, although he remained involved in Apla activities. On 2 July 1998, Phike
attended an induction centre for Apla members, operated by the SANDF at
Wallmannsthal, entering into an interim service agreement with the SANDF
with the provisional rank of private. However, when he appeared before the
SA Air Force Senior Staffing Board, the SANDF realised that he had previously been a member and had resigned. As a result, the SANDF terminated
Phike's contract on 28 February 1999 because, in their view, Phike had already
been integrated and could not be integrated a second time. The matter went to
the Labour Court. Judge Landman, in a landmark ruling, decided to allow the
petition. Phike was reinstated in the SANDF retrospectively, with effect from
28 February 1999, the date on which his interim service contract was terminated. But he was reinstated with the rank of private; he was hoping to become
a colonel, Apla asserted.[48]

This raises the question of education and training. Vast disparities existed, and particularly so between the integrating forces, something that bothered MK during the negotiation process. Training in South Africa for MK, and probably more so for Apla, was limited and ad hoc and available only for small numbers. During the early years of the armed struggle, ANC president Oliver Tambo had raised the question of training with the Soviets in 1963, and limited opportunities had been opened at the Military College in Odessa, at Perevalnoye in the Crimea and later at the 'Northern Training Centre' outside Moscow. The emphasis was on guerrilla warfare, until training for regular service started during the late 1980s at various centres from Minsk to Frunze.[49] Former SADF officers picked up on this during the SANDF integration process, and questioned the standard and validity of the Soviet-era courses as well as the benchmarking undertaken by the BMATT. Little was done to encourage members of the SANDF to value the diversity in education and training.

Furthermore, while the educational profile of the Department of Defence was in 2009 complete for only two-thirds of all personnel, the information captured reveals that only 4.7 per cent of staff, the bulk of them white, have accessed higher education successfully (61 per cent of staff are white, 12 per cent coloured, 2 per cent Indian and 25 per cent black African). Poor education, as Heinecken argues, often contributes to feelings of incompetence and of exclusion. Continuous training in the SANDF after 1994 brought this into dramatic relief, as course results, race and politics formed a heady mix. General Georg Meiring commented:

> What was very difficult was the fact that whenever some people on the ground didn't make the grade, almost every time they would throw in the race card. We had to go to great lengths to try to prove to the politicians, the minister, the deputy minister and the defence committee in Parliament that that was not true ... We gave [the black guys] two or three chances to pass a course – something we never did with the whites – because we felt, perhaps as a result of his background he was disadvantaged.[50]

Much of the dissatisfaction in the new SANDF has come predictably from two sources. The first of these is cited in the strong feeling among former NSF personnel that MK and Apla were *absorbed* into the SADF. There was considerable justification for this feeling. The SADF systems and procedures, structures and conventions were all taken over into the SANDF. The education and training of SADF and TBVC personnel was *verified* at integration; that of the MK and Apla was *assessed and evaluated*. Moreover, the former SADF personnel retained their force numbers; SADF uniforms and rank insignia were used in the SANDF at first; SADF discipline was enforced, as was the old SADF military justice system, code of conduct and conventions for service writing. Furthermore, the SADF's personnel system was retained and the integrating personnel from MK and Apla were brought onto this system for financial and personnel management. Some MK and Apla cadres joined the military and then, finding trouble fitting into the new system, accepted voluntary severance packages. As a former MK combatant told Wits sociologist Lepho Mashike:

> I joined the SANDF but I 'demobbed', that is I resigned. I got R9 000. The reason for 'demobbing' was that being with whites was like surrendering to the enemy and accepting defeat ... The army still resembled the apartheid army because our commanders were still white. Also it takes a bit of doing to accept whites as comrades, they were the enemy yesterday, today they are our friends – it does not make sense.[51]

Since 1997, the corporate identity of the SANDF has been changed in various ways. The uniforms have changed from the 'browns' of the old SADF to a new dispersion dress. The rank insignia has changed, several times – in 1996, 2002 and 2008 – and now incorporates some American nomenclature with Soviet visibility. The insignia instituted in 2002 reflected the new national symbols. This and a new pantheon of medals and badges point to a new, integrated identity and aspirations of cohesion and 'togetherness'. However, although there has been a break with the past, the services retain separate uniforms and, from 2002, wear distinctive rank insignia.[52]

The profile of the South African military, in terms of race, ethnicity, language and gender, has changed dramatically since 1994. Moreover, political patronage, and the heavy race/gender emphasis in the human transformation since 1994, has resulted in a new leadership dominated by former NSF members. The position regarding the senior leadership (brigadier general to general) at the end of the integration process, in April 1997, is given in Table 8.4. In 1994, former MK and former Apla members accounted, respectively, for 14 per cent and 1 per cent of general and flag ranks, the former SADF for 81 per cent. By October 2007, although forming only 20 per cent of the total force strength of the SANDF at integration, former MK and Apla officers filled 46 per cent of

	Former force 1997	Rank profile Brig Gen to Gen	Former force 2007	Rank profile Brig Gen to Gen
MK	15	14	13	37
Apla	5	1	6	9
TBVC	11	4	7	7
SADF	58	81	32	47
SANDF	11	0	42	0
%	100	100	100	100

Table 8.4: **Composition of the general staff of the SANDF in terms of former force: 1997 and 2007 compared (as percentages)**

Note: The figures given for the 'SANDF' reflect those who joined the SANDF after 1994 and who had no former, 'historic' affiliation.
Source: Adapted from L Heinecken, 'A diverse society, a representative military?' p 35

senior command positions. This trend has continued, and is increasingly connected to the battle for the history of the armed struggle and the Border War. Esterhuyse and Heinecken suggest that the 1994 transformation has offered large rewards to long-term political loyalty, which represents a strong continuity with the recent past. This is something that young soldiers, black and white, who have no previous force experience and no struggle connections to exploit, note with disdain.

A second source of dissatisfaction, albeit less far-reaching, is seated among the former members of the SADF, some of whom fear a transition from merit back to race, of a new, legalised reverse racism. Without a doubt, the AA and EO programmes, and a number of killings of white officers by black subordinates, raised tensions to new levels, at the same time there were very strong signals that there would be new ceilings and dead ends. Experienced senior staffers who took (or requested) packages have been joined by a large number of young, highly qualified, sharp-end personnel who have found alternative careers in the security sector or in the armed forces of other countries, including Australia. The posts vacated are, moreover, most often kept vacant in the hope of achieving EO quotas and finding a result on the 'representivity charts'. This has led to the rapid and fundamental loss of experience and capacity, while also, over a longer term, fundamentally undermining service delivery, force impact and force design.[53] Particularly worrying, at a time when the SANDF is called upon increasingly to take part in peace operations, is the loss of counterinsurgency skills and tactics discarded during the transition.[54]

Diversity management has become important in armed forces around the world. The reasons are many. There is, firstly, a new emphasis on human rights. Armed forces are prevented by legislation, and discouraged by NGOs and lobby groups, from discriminating in terms of race, gender and minority status. In South Africa, such discrimination is prohibited in terms of the Constitution, except for the redress of historical imbalances. Armed forces are, moreover, pressed to increase representativeness so as to preserve their legitimacy. Then armed forces encounter, as part of the move to all-volunteer forces, growing problems with regard to the recruitment and retention of personnel, which has forced recruitment from non-traditional sources of labour. Furthermore, there is an argument that greater diversity, in terms of gender and race, improves interaction with local communities and therefore enhances the general efficiency of humanitarian missions. But there is also a fifth reason why some armed forces, not all, have had to adopt policies of greater diversity. This connects to political imperatives and the integration of military structures, once in opposition and often of different ethnic and ideological background.[55] Such attempts to create new militaries after political change are not uncommon. For one country, not defeated in war, to go through three such processes within a span of some eight decades, is unique.

New roles for the armed forces

In 2013, the SANDF numbered some 78 725 full-time members, the majority of whom are distributed through four services: Army (39 642), Air Force (11 269), Navy (7 431) and Military Medical Service (8 804), with a further 11 579 in staff and support divisions.[56] In terms of role definition, the SANDF may be deployed in order to '[1] preserve life, health or property in emergency or humanitarian relief operations; [2] ensure the provision of essential services; [3] support any department of state, including support for purposes of socio-economic upliftment; and [4] effect national border control'.[57] This emphasis on humanitarian and developmental missions represents a major shift in approach away from warfighting and the harder military roles of the 1970s, 1980s and early 1990s. South Africa now occupies the tenth position on the ranking of UN peacekeeping contributions, and faces further calls to deploy forces in support of Operations Other Than War (OOTW), and especially as part of multinational peace operations.

South African peace operations started in 1996, with the posting of two officers to the UK Multinational Division in Bosnia. This was followed by the rather difficult intervention in Lesotho.[58] Codenamed Operation Boleas, some 600 South African soldiers moved into Lesotho in the early morning of 22 September 1998 to prevent a military coup d'état. The operation, launched at the request of the besieged Lesotho government, was supposed to have been a SADC operation, but the Botswana troops, numbering some 200, only arrived at nightfall on 22 September and coordination remained problematic. Things seemed to go wrong from the start, and what might have been a small, straightforward operation in a neighbouring micro-state became almost a seven-month-long operation and a milestone for the new South Africa and the transforming SANDF. The heated debate, conducted chiefly in the media, questioned the appropriateness of an intervention 'that went wrong'.[59] Moreover, difficulties regarding the interpretation of international law and the validity of the SADC mandate aside, the SANDF was severely criticised for poor planning at all levels. The invasion force, understrength, ill-prepared, lacking in supply and in operational and tactical intelligence, battled to manoeuvre in the mountain kingdom, which, although the size of Belgium, had less than 1 000 kilometres of paved roads.[60] 'Unplanned and uninvited, the South African Army thought it would be a walkover. It was anything but.'[61]

Clearly, the budget cuts and retrenchment in the armed forces after 1994 had already had a harmful effect upon training and equipment. The Strategic Defence Acquisition Programme, finalised in 1999, provided for the procurement of military hardware to the value of US$4.8 billion (more than R40 billion) to support the SANDF's new roles on the African continent. The so-called arms deal, which included the purchase of frigates and maritime helicopters, new submarines (to replace the aging Daphnes), light utility helicopters, fighter trainers and light fighter aircraft, and main battle tanks, has since been dogged by repeated, and ostensibly substantive, accusations of bribery and corruption at the highest levels.[62]

Peace deployments escalated rapidly after 1999, with deployments as part of various SADC, AU and UN operations, including those in Lesotho, Burundi, Mozambique, the Democratic Republic of Congo, the Comoros, the Central African Republic, Ethiopia and Eritrea, Uganda and Sudan (see Table 8.5). Moreover, as part of its broader goal to restore and establish peace and stability on the continent of Africa, South Africa contributes to the African Standby Force (the AU's rapid-reaction force) and the associated SADC brigade, structures that were created in 2006.[63]

Table 8.5: **South African peace missions abroad (1999–)**		
Operation	**Mission**	**Period**
Mistral	UN Organisation Mission in the Democratic Republic of Congo (MONUC)	September 1999 to date
Espresso	OAU Liaison Mission in Eritrea and Ethiopia (OLMEE) and UN Mission in Eritrea and Ethiopia (UNMEE)	November 2000 to August 2008
Fibre	Bilateral Deployment	October 2001 to April 2003
	AU Mission in Burundi – AMIB	May 2003 to May 2004
	UN operation in Burundi – ONUB	June 2004 to December 2006
Triton	Assistance to OAU Mission in Comoros (OMIC)	November 2001 to February 2002
Triton II		April to May 2002
Triton III		March to May 2004
Triton IV	AU Mission to Comoros (AMISEC)	March to July 2006
Triton V		June to July 2007
Amphibian	Assistance to the third-party verification mechanism in the Democratic Republic of Congo	August 2002 to June 2004
Sunray	Assistance to the EU Interim Emergency Multinational Force in the DRC	June to September 2003
Montego	Assistance to the UN Mission in Liberia – UNMIL	October 2003 to January 2005
Cordite	Assistance to AU Mission in Sudan – AMIS	2004 to December 2007
	UN Mission in Sudan – UNMIS	September 2006 to December 2007
	UN AU Hybrid Mission in Darfur – UNAMID	January 2004 to date
Teutonic	Bilateral Deployment of the South African Detachment Assisting with Integration and Training (SADAIT) in the DRC	January 2005 to date
Pristine	Bilateral Agreement in Support of the Peace Process in the Ivory Coast	July 2005 to December 2006
Curriculum	Assistance to the AU Special Protection Force in Burundi – AUSTF	January 2007 to June 2009
Induli	Assistance to the UN Political Mission in Nepal – UNMIN	April 2007 to 31 July 2009
Vimbezela	Security Sector Reform Assistance to the Central African Republic	March 2007 to date
Bongane	Assistance to the Peace Process in Northern Uganda and Southern Sudan	June 2007 to 31 July 2009
Copper	Maritime security in the Mozambican Channel	2010 to date

Source: Adapted and updated from Capt (SAN) CH Ross, *A Decade of Peace Missions* (Department of Defence, Pretoria, 2009), pp 1–24.

Conclusion: (Dis)Continuities

For some countries, state-making happens almost naturally, even inevitably, as part of a natural course of events. State-making in South Africa was not easy. It was certainly not automatic, but rather engineered at critical times by 'big men'. Milner brought on a war that enabled Selborne, Botha and Smuts to forge the Union, of which the Union Defence Force was a consequence. The constitutional tie to Britain, and South Africa's contested entry into the two world wars, was the focus of men like Hertzog, Smuts and Malan; under the last-mentioned a more South African defence force, albeit in a very narrow sense, was created by Erasmus and Hiemstra. De Klerk and Mandela, after a further internal struggle, but one involving the majority of South Africans, forged the second new South Africa within a hundred years of the first, of which the South African National Defence Force was a product.

Writing from the Defence ministry in 1998, Ronnie Kasrils concluded that 'our approach was in marked contrast to that of the National Party after it came to power in 1948 [which] left a legacy of bitterness … still encountered to this day'.[64] This may have been true in 1998, at the height of the 'Rainbow Nation' euphoria. However, the trends, more discernible when viewed over a longer duration, indicate several continuities and changes. In many countries, diversity management has involved the integration of minorities into the armed forces. This was also the case in South Africa in 1912 and after 1948. However, the third amalgam, associated with the first broad-based, democratic elections in 1994, entailed the accommodation of a majority. This meant, for the first time, the integration of black, coloured and Asian South Africans into a workplace that had been dominated by white South Africans since 1912. But, the third integration, like those of 1912 and 1948, has seen the infusion of political ideology and the influence of past loyalties, the shuffling out of personnel thought to be either adversarial or even reactionary, said to be in the interest of 'rightsizing and downsizing', their often-rapid replacement by the politically loyal, and the resulting compromise in efficiency. In all three cases, this was done, in differing measure, to achieve a main objective, namely, the transformation of the military within the human and political domains. The growing domination of the SANDF by former MK and former Apla cadres, the changed tenor since the Mbeki administration, and the rapid 'Africanisation' of institutions is strongly suggestive of the transformation of the Erasmus-Hiemstra era.

What South Africa requires of the SANDF, in the short term, is a thorough, unrestrained, impartial and unaffected transformation across all domains, conducted with the vigour and determination shown during the human transformation of the SANDF, and founded on the values enshrined in the Constitution. This will ensure the true, radical break that is so crucial if the South African military is to perform efficiently and professionally on the international stage.[65]

These changes necessarily affected the South African armed forces and the roles defined for them. Some commentators, particularly in the years immediately following 1994, asserted that military power had lost its vaunted Cold War importance in a new post-modern environment. Others, recognising future challenges, argued that South Africa, beset with far-reaching socio-economic crises, could no longer afford the burden of military forces. Yet most scholars agree now that these perspectives were short-sighted. While the risk of major conflict has indeed receded, the events of 9/11, for example, and its consequences, demonstrate that the continental and international landscapes are less certain, less stable and less predictable, than that for which many had hoped. South African interests are intertwined inextricably in regional and global affairs, and, if the country is to protect these interests and ensure its security, it must maintain a credible military force capable of meeting an array of contingencies.

Notes

Introduction

1 Polat Safi, 'An interview with Prof Georg G Iggers: "Every history can only present a partial reconstruction of the past"', *Kilavuz*, 52, December 2014, pp 36–49.
2 Many of these accounts are based on solely, and on a limited range of, secondary sources. See, for example, Tim Couzens, *Battles of South Africa* (David Philip, Cape Town, 2004) and *South African Battles* (Jonathan Ball, Johannesburg, 2013) as well as Greg Mills and David Williams, *Seven Battles that Shaped South Africa* (Tafelberg, Cape Town, 2006).
3 For a fine, recent example of such a study see Gary Baines, *South Africa's Border War; contested narratives and conflicting memories* (Bloomsbury, London, 2014).
4 The following need to be acknowledged specifically: Allan R Millett and Peter Maslowski, *For the Common Defense: a military history of the United States of America* (The Free Press, New York, 1994); Jeffrey Grey, *A Military History of Australia* (Cambridge University Press, Cambridge, 2008); Mesut Uyar and Edward J Erikson, *A Military History of the Ottomans: from Osman to Atatürk* (ABC Clio, Santa Barbara, CA, 2009); Allan Mallinson, *The Making of the British Army* (Bantam Books, London, 2011); and Festus B Aboagye, *Indigenous African Warfare: its concept and art in the Gold Coast, Asante and the Northern Territories up to the early 1900s* (Ulinzi African Publishing, Pretoria, 2010).
5 Michael Howard, 'The use and abuse of military history', *Journal of the Royal United Services Institution*, 107(625),1962, pp 4–10.
6 Williamson Murray, 'Innovation: past and future', in Williamson Murray and Allan R Millett, eds, *Military Innovation in the Interwar Period* (Cambridge University Press, Cambridge, 1996), pp 312–13.
7 Ian van der Waag, 'Military culture and the South African armed forces, a historical perspective', in Francois Vreÿ, Abel Esterhuyse and Thomas Mandrup, eds, *On Military Culture: theory, practice and African armed forces* (UCT Press, Cape Town, 2013).
8 RJB Bosworth, *Explaining Auschwitz and Hiroshima: history writing and the Second World War, 1945–1990* (Routledge, London and New York, 1993), p 3.

CHAPTER ONE
South Africa, 1899–1902:
The Last Gentleman's War?

1 Bill Nasson, *The War for South Africa: The Anglo-Boer War 1899–1902* (Tafelberg, Cape Town, 2010), pp 13, 15.
2 JP Fitzpatrick, *The Transvaal From Within* (William Heinemann, London, 1899), p 41.
3 J Meintjes, *De la Rey: lion of the west* (Hugh Keartland, Johannesburg, 1966), pp 26, 80–1.
4 For recent publications on the participation of the settlement dominions, see Peter Dennis and Jeffrey Grey, eds, *The Boer War: army, nation and empire* (Army History Unit, Canberra, 2000); Craig Wilcox, *Australia's Boer War: the war in South Africa, 1899–1902* (OUP, Oxford and New York, 2002), Carman Miller, *Painting the Map Red: Canada and the South African War, 1899–1902* (Canadian War Museum, Ottawa, 1998), John Crawford (with Ellen Ellis), *To Fight for the Empire: an illustrated history of New Zealand and the South African War, 1899–1902* (Reed, Auckland, 1999). Black participation is dealt with excellently by Peter Warwick, *Black People and the South African War 1899–1902* (Ravan, Johannesburg, 1983) and Bill Nasson, *Abraham Esau's War: a black South African war in the Cape, 1899–1902* (Cambridge University Press, Cambridge, 1991).
5 CR de Wet, *Three Years War, October 1899–June 1902* (Galago, Johannesburg, 1986).
6 G Nattrass and SB Spies, eds, *Jan Smuts: memoirs of the Boer War* (Jonathan Ball,

Johannesburg, 1994), p 19.

7 Anon, *The War in South Africa*, vols 1–2 (Historical Section of the Great General Staff, Berlin, 1904; reprinted Battery Press, Nashville, 1998).

8 Ian van der Waag, 'Water and the ecology of warfare in southern Africa', in JWN Tempelhoff, ed, *African Water Histories: transdisciplinary discourses* (North-West University, Vanderbijlpark, 2005), p 124.

9 Douglas Porch, *Wars of Empire* (Cassell, London, 2001), pp 110–11, 118–19, 131–32.

10 Sandra Swart, *Riding High: horses, humans and history in South Africa* (Wits University Press, Johannesburg, 2010), pp 106–14.

11 Buller to Milner, 12 November 1899, GH 39/12 Military Secretary Letters Received Miscellaneous, Western Cape Provincial Archives and Records Centre (WCPA).

12 Ivor Maxse to Violet Cecil, 2 June 1900, Violet Milner Papers, box 19, C62/15, Bodleian Library, Oxford.

13 Craig Wilcox, *Australia's Boer War: the war in South Africa, 1899–1902* (Oxford University Press, Melbourne, 2002).

14 'Als het tot vechten komen moet, zijn "onze menschen" gereed. Kost hebben wij ook in de laaste 6 of 7 weken veel opgekocht, en al duurde de oorlog 6 of 8 maanden zou er geen gebrek aan vleesch en meel zijn.' FW Reitz to Leyds, 28 August 1899 in *Leyds Correspondentie*, pp 126–27.

15 WF Butler, *The Life of Sir George Pomeroy-Colley* (John Murray, London, 1899), pp 113–39, 260–64; and WF Butler, *Sir William Butler: An Autobiography* (Constable, London, 1911), p 383.

16 Milner to Chamberlain, 28 October 1900 in Cecil Headlam, ed, *The Milner Papers: South Africa, vol II, 1899–1905* (Cassell, London, 1933), p 166.

17 Thomas Pakenham, *The Boer War* (Abacus, London, 1995), pp 77, 96, 117.

18 Notes of discussion, Molteno to Milner, November 1899, Government House archives (hereafter GH) 26/398 Draft General and Confidential Dispatches, Western Cape Provincial Archives and Records Centre (WCPA).

19 Thomas Pakenham, *The Boer War*, p 117.

20 Conyngham Greene to Milner, 11 May 1899, archives of the British Agent, Pretoria (hereafter BA) 20 Correspondence to High Commissioner, National Archives of South Africa, Pretoria (NASAP).

21 Conyngham Greene to Milner, 28 June 1899, BA 21 Correspondence to High Commissioner, NASAP.

22 ES May, *A Retrospect of the South African War* (Sampson Low Marston, London, 1901), p 3.

23 Chamberlain to Milner, 5 January 1899, BA 12 Correspondence from High Commissioner, NASAP.

24 Chamberlain to Milner, 30 March 1899, BA 12 Correspondence from High Commissioner; and Conyngham Greene to Milner, 6 May 1899, BA 20 Correspondence to High Commissioner, NASAP.

25 Conyngham Greene to Milner, 8 July 1899, BA 21 Correspondence to High Commissioner, NASAP. The total white male population for both republics (?) was estimated at 66 498. This figure is ludicrous.

26 This comparative estimate includes the approximate 10 000 *agterryers* but excludes the substantial colonial forces on which Britain could call. The number of *agterryers* varies between 7 000 and 11 000. See P Labuschagne, *Ghostriders of the Anglo-Boer War, 1899–1902: the role and contribution of Agterryers* (Unisa, Pretoria, 1999), pp ix, 1; and Fransjohan Pretorius, *Life on Commando During the Anglo-Boer War, 1899–1902* (Human & Rousseau, Cape Town, 1999), p 294.

27 Thomas Pakenham, *The Boer War*, chapters 7 and 8; MJ Grobler, *Met die Vrystaaters onder die Wapen: Generaal Prinsloo en die Bethlehem-Kommando* (Nasionale Pers, Bloemfontein, 1937), pp 33–34; and numerous items in the *Leyds Correspondentie*.

28 GHL le May, *British Supremacy in South Africa, 1899–1907* (Clarendon, Oxford, 1965), p 10.

29 Conyngham Greene to Milner, 8 July 1899, BA 21 Correspondence to High Commissioner, NASAP; and Thomas Pakenham, *The Boer War*, pp 77, 96, 117.

30 GHL le May, *British Supremacy in South Africa, 1899–1907*, pp 35–7.

31 GFH Berkeley, 'Sir Harry Smith: a reminiscence of the Boer War in 1848', *The Fortnightly Review*, 1 December 1899.

32 Hew Strachan, *European Armies and the Conduct of War* (Routledge, London and New York, 1993), pp 77–78.

33 ES May, *A Retrospect of the South African War*, p 24.

34 Ian van der Waag, 'Boer generalship and the politics of command', *War in History*, 12(1), 2005, pp 15–43.

35 See the case of Jan du Preez in J Taitz, K

Gillings and A Davey, eds, *The War Memoirs of Commandant Ludwig Krause, 1899–1900* (Van Riebeeck Society, Cape Town, 1996), p 100 *passim*.

36 G Nattrass and SB Spies, eds, *Jan Smuts*, p 70; and CR de Wet, *Three Years War*, pp 30, 32, 38.

37 G Nattrass and SB Spies, eds, *Jan Smuts*, p 71.

38 S Marks and A Atmore, eds, *Economy and Society in Pre-industrial South Africa* (Longman, London & New York, 1980), pp 33–34.

39 Deneys Reitz, *Commando: a Boer journal of the Boer War* (Jonathan Ball, Johannesburg, 2009), pp 15–6.

40 MJ Grobler, *Met die Vrystaaters Onder die Wapen*, pp 14–15.

41 See CR de Wet, *Three Years War*: 'real discipline did not exist among the burghers' (p 15); 'they were quite unaccustomed to being under orders' (p 16); 'devoid of all military discipline' (p 64); and in conversation with General Piet Joubert '… they don't know what discipline means' (p 63).

42 MJ Grobler, *Met die Vrystaaters Onder die Wapen*, p 31.

43 See, for example, the entry for FWG König, f.782, KG 1089, Staatsartillerie Strafboek, NASAP.

44 CW de Kiewiet, *A History of South Africa, Social and Economic* (Clarendon Press, Oxford, 1941), p 19.

45 C Townshend, 'People's War' in C Townshend, ed, *The Oxford Illustrated History of Modern War* (Oxford University Press, Oxford and New York, 1997), p 159.

46 C Townshend, 'People's War', p 159. [Townshend's parenthesis.]

47 RA Preston, A Roland and SF Wise, *Men In Arms: A history of warfare and its interrelationships with Western society* (Harcourt Brace Jovanovich College Publishers, Orlando, 1991), pp 228–229.

48 Many were prepared to travel to South Africa at own cost. See Leyds to Regeering Pretoria, 30 August 1899; Regeering Pretoria to Leyds, 31 August 1899; Leyds to Regeering Pretoria, 22 September 1899; Regeering Pretoria to Leyds, 28 September 1899; Leyds to Regeering Pretoria, 30 September 1899; and Regeering Pretoria to Leyds, 2 October 1899 in *Leyds Correspondentie*, pp 130, 173, 177, 180.

49 Schiel to Commandant General, 15 September 1899, archives of the Commandant General, ZAR (KG) 1139 Briewen Boek van Kommandant van die Duitse Korps, NASAP.

50 EA Schmidl, 'Adolph Zboril: an Austrian officer in the Transvaal artillery', *Militaria*, 18(2) 1988, pp 49–50.

51 Schiel to Commandant General, 20 September 1899, archives of the Commandant General, ZAR (KG) 1139 Briewen Boek van Kommandant van die Duitse Korps, NASAP.

52 EA Schmidl, 'Adolph Zboril', pp 53–54; and M van Niekerk, 'Adolf Schiel en die Duitse Kommando', *Argiefjaarboek vir Suid-Afrikaanse Geskiedenis*, 1951/II.

53 Ian Hamilton, Majuba veteran and student of military history and strategy, was again an exception.

54 JP Fitzpatrick, *The Transvaal From Within*, p 41.

55 For example, Halifax (pop 105 000), Southampton (pop 105 000) and South Shields (pop 101 000).

56 Edward Spiers, 'The Late Victorian Army 1868–1914', in David Chandler and Ian Beckett, *The Oxford History of the British Army* (OUP, Oxford, 1996), p 196.

57 MJ Grobler, *Met die Vrystaaters Onder die Wapen*, p 14.

58 '… wat is dan rede dat Commdt Genl geen Mausers en patronen wil zenden burghers hier weigert nieuwe M. H. geweren te ontvangen…' Myncoms, Krugersdorp to Dieperink, 12 August 1899, KG 457 Ammunisie Anglo-Boereoorlog, NASAP.

59 JH Breytenbach, *Die Geskiedenis van die Tweede Vryheidsoorlog in Suid-Afrika, I* (Staatsdrukker, Pretoria, 1978), pp 79–80.

60 MJ Grobler, *Met die Vrystaaters Onder die Wapen*, pp 15–16.

61 Thomas Pakenham, *The Boer War*, p 105; and JE Ellis, 'Musketry: the Anglo-Boer War experience' (paper delivered at the Second Anglo-Boer War conference, Bloemfontein, October 1999).

62 KG 1038 tot 1041 Skyfskietverslae, 1893–95, NASAP.

63 Various folios, archives of the 'Subkomitee van die Kommissariaat, Dundee' (SCD) 1, Krijgs Commissariaat Dundee Order briefjes, 1899–1900, NASAP. The approach of the German Commando was quite different: requests for arms, ammunition, horses and information on the disposition of the guns. See Schiel to Commandant General, 25 Sept 1899 (f.51); Schiel to Commandant General,

25 Sept 1899 (f.52); Schiel to Staatssecretaris, 25 Sept 1899 (f.54); Schiel to Commandant General, 30 Sept 1899 (f.110); and Schiel to Staatssecretaris, 1 Oct 1899 (f.168), KG 1139 Briewen Boek van Kommandant van die Duitse Korps, NASAP.

64 Thomas Pakenham, *The Boer War*, p 77.

65 D Porch, 'Imperial wars: from the Seven Years War to the First World War' in C Townshend, ed, *The Oxford Illustrated History of Modern War*, pp 84–85, 90.

66 MJ Grobler, *Met die Vrystaaters Onder die Wapen*, pp 30–31.

67 *The Standard and Diggers' News*, 18 August 1899. Conyngham Greene to Milner, 18 August 1899 and 19 August 1899, BA 22 Correspondence to High Commissioner, NASAP.

68 Leyds to Regeering Pretoria, 23 August 1899; Leyds to Portugeeschen Gezant de Tovar, 24 August 1899; Leyds to Max Winterfeldt, Consul-Generaal der ZAR, Berlijn, 24 August 1899; Reitz to Leyds, 28 August 1899; Leyds to Regeering Pretoria, 29 August 1899; Regeering Pretoria to Leyds, 30 August 1899; Leyds to Regeering Pretoria, 31 August 1899; PGW Grobler to Leyds, 3 September 1899 in *Leyds Correspondentie*, pp 122–7, 130–2, 153.

69 F Pretorius, 'The Second Anglo-Boer War: an overview', *Scientia Militaria*, 30(2), 2000, pp 111–25.

70 P Hopkins and H Dugmore, *The Boy: Baden-Powell and the siege of Mafeking* (Zebra, Rivonia, 1999), p 81.

71 G Nattrass and SB Spies, eds, *Jan Smuts*, p 71.

72 D Reitz, *Commando*, p 22.

73 D Reitz, *Commando*, p 28.

74 D Reitz, *Commando*, pp 30, 35–6.

75 P Warwick, *Black People and the South African War 1899–1902*, p 38 *passim*.

76 Lord Selborne to Lord Curzon, 23 December 1899, in DG Boyce, ed, *The Crisis of British Power: the imperial and naval papers of the Second Earl of Selborne, 1895–1910* (The Historians' Press, London, 1990), p 98.

77 Military Council of 12 March 1900, NJ de Wet Collection, vol 1, Notule van Krygsraad te velde, NASAP.

78 For the example of the Battle of Vegkop (October 1836), see P Becker, *Path of Blood: the rise and conquests of Mzilikazi, founder of the Matabele tribe of southern Africa* (Longmans, London, 1962), p 166.

79 FI Maxse to Violet Cecil, 3 June 1900, Violet Milner papers, box 19, Bodleian Library, Oxford.

80 Notes on discussion between Molteno and Milner, November 1899, GH 26/398 Draft General and Confidential Dispatches, WCPA.

81 F Pretorius, *Life on Commando*, pp 84–85.

82 'Als het tot vechten komen moet, zijn "onze menschen" gereed. Kost hebben wij ook in de laaste 6 of 7 weken veel opgekocht, en al duurde de oorlog 6 of 8 maanden zou er geen gebrek aan vleesch en meel zijn. Ik zie dat de Jingo-couranten van 31.500 man spreken die ons zou moeten komen aanvallen. Zij zullen meer troepen noodig hebben dan dat!': FW Reitz to Leyds, 28 August 1899 in *Leyds Correspondentie*, pp 126–7.

83 JA Mouton, 'Genl Piet Joubert in die Transvaalse Geskiedenis' (*Argiefjaarboek vir Suid-Afrikaanse Geskiedenis* 1957/I), verskeie hoofstukke; and F Pretorius, *Life on Commando*, chapter 1.

84 See archives of the 'Sekretaris van die Hoofkomitee van die Kommissariaat in die ZAR' (hereafter HCC) 2: HCC 610/99 Hoofd Comite Commissariaat seint aan Assistant Generaal Meyers en Burgers op klacht over tekort aan beschuit, 3 Nov 1899, NASAP.

85 Station Master, Belmont to Chief Traffic Manager, Cape Town, 16 October 1899, GH 26/398 Draft General and Confidential Dispatches, NASAP.

86 JP Fitzpatrick, *The Transvaal From Within*. p 41.

87 See for example CM Bakkes, 'Die Boer as berede skutter gedurende die Tweede Vryheidsoorlog' in RJ Bouch, ed, *Infantry in South Africa, 1652–1976* (Documentation Service SADF, Pretoria, 1977), pp 29–45; as well as a chapter by the same writer, 'Die kommandostelsel met spesiale verwysing na die historiese ontwikkeling van sy rangstruktuur' in PG Nel, ed, *Die Kultuurontlooiing van die Afrikaner* (HAUM, Pretoria en Kaapstad, 1979), pp 294–311.

88 S Trapido, 'Reflections on land, office and wealth in the South African Republic', in S Marks and A Atmore, eds, *Economy and Society in Pre-Industrial South Africa*, pp 350–68.

89 KG 465 Veldkornette Openbare Verkiesings, NASAP. Each burgher had to publicly declare his vote and these were recorded and sent to the office of the Commandant General. See also the example of the relationship between Coetzee and Dauth in F Pretorius, *Life on Commando*, p 253.

90 F Pretorius, *Life on Commando*, pp 252–55: 'ranging from leave to horseshoes and lost

horses'.

91 S Trapido, 'Reflections on land, office and wealth in the South African Republic', p 361.

92 The term 'bywoner' is difficult to define, but has been loosely defined as carpetbagger or peasant, a landless person working the estate of a patron, often a powerful relative.

93 S Trapido, 'Reflections on land, office and wealth in the South African Republic', p 359.

94 Rex Pope, *War and Society in Britain, 1899–1948* (Longman, Harlow, 1991), p 19.

95 J Taitz et al, eds, *The War Memoirs of Commandant Ludwig Krause*, p 5.

96 G Nattrass and SB Spies, eds, *Jan Smuts*, p 71.

97 C Townshend, 'People's War' in C Townshend, ed, *The Oxford Illustrated History of Modern War*, p 159.

98 CR de Wet, *Three Years War*, p 64.

99 Conyngham Greene to Milner, 7 June 1899, BA 21 Correspondence to High Commissioner, NASAP.

100 F Pretorius, *Life on Commando*, p 248.

101 See, for example, MCE van Schoor, *'n Bittereinder aan die Woord: geskrifte en toesprake van Mathinus Theunis Steyn* (Oorlogsmuseum van die Boererepublieke, Bloemfontein, 1997), p 21.

102 F Pretorius, *Life on Commando*, p 247. A number of contemporary observers have questioned the moral fibre of certain leaders, whose exploits were public knowledge. See, for example, J Taitz et al, eds, *The War Memoirs of Ludwig Krause*, pp 6–7. An adequate case has already been made against the simple idea that Boer society was rustic, wholesome and corruption-free.

103 F Pretorius, *Life on Commando*, p 247.

104 Schiel's Germans inquired after arms, ammunition and horses. Compare, for example, the requisitions made by the Boer commandos: extra bedding, cutlery and crockery (SCD 1, Krijgs Commissariaat Dundee Order briefjes, NASAP) with the requests made by the German Commando (KG 1139 Briewen Boek van Kommandant van die Duitse Korps, NASAP) during the same period.

105 Maud Lyttelton to a cousin, 2 January 1901, HHA 5/2/1, Hagley Hall Archives (HHA), Worcestershire.

106 See, for example, PJ Joubert, Commandant General, Hoofd Lager, Blauw Berg, to Commandant Erasmus, Pretoria Lager, 30 June 1894, Preller Collection, vol 128, ff.4–7, NASAP.

107 See CR de Wet, *Three Years War*.

108 F Pretorius, *Life on Commando*, pp 86–95.

109 See A Jones, *The Art of War in the Western World* (OUP, New York and Oxford 1987), p 67.

110 Field Marshal Lord Montgomery, *A History of Warfare* (Rainbird, London, 1982), p 452.

111 Diary, 13–15 June 1900, in P Lewsen, ed, *Selections from the Correspondence of John X Merriman 1899–1905* (VRS, Cape Town, 1966), p 211. From the entry for 15 June: 'Confused rumours of fighting, as far as one can gather of a guerrilla kind.'

112 Jack Lyttelton to Maud Lyttelton, 2 February 1902, HHA 2/6/10.

113 President Kruger to General Schoeman, 28 April 1900, Schoeman Papers, W.125/6, NASAP: 'U moet de menschen des noods met geweld keeren want daarvoor heb ik u aangesteld en zeg niet zy willen niet hooren.'

114 G Nattrass and SB Spies, eds, *Jan Smuts*, pp 146–61.

115 Diary, 25 January 1901, Mss Dawson 7, Bodleian Library, Oxford.

116 G Nattrass and SB Spies, eds, *Jan Smuts*, pp 69, 82 and chapter 3: 'Reorganisation' in general.

117 D Porch, *Wars of Empire*, pp 131–32; B Vandervort, *Wars of Imperial Conquest in Africa, 1830–1914* (UCL Press, London, 1998), p 209.

118 Beresford Gibbs to Maud Lyttelton, 5 June 1901, HHA 5/2/37.

119 Milner to Lady Edward Cecil, 28 March 1901, in C Headlam, ed, *The Milner Papers: South Africa, vol II, 1899–1905*, p 238.

120 C Headlam, ed, *The Milner Papers: South Africa, vol II, 1899–1905*, p 163.

121 Chamberlain to Milner, 22 December 1900, in C Headlam, ed, *The Milner Papers: South Africa, vol II, 1899–1905*, p 181.

122 Kitchener to Broderick, 27 September 1901, Kitchener Papers (M722), NASAP.

123 Milner to Chamberlain, 17 January 1901, in C Headlam, ed, *The Milner Papers: South Africa, vol II, 1899–1905*, pp 183–84.

124 Milner to Chamberlain, 17 January 1901, in C Headlam, ed, *The Milner Papers: South Africa, vol II, 1899–1905*, p 184.

125 Ivor Maxse to Violet Cecil, 8 April 1900, Violet Milner Papers 19, C62/14, Bodleian Library, Oxford.

126 Milner to Chamberlain, 6 February 1901, in C Headlam, ed, *The Milner Papers: South Africa, vol II, 1899–1905*, p 193.

127 These women and children included Boers and blacks, indeed all those who rendered (or

were suspected of rendering) assistance of any kind to the commandos in the field.

128 Quoted by H Strachan, *European Armies and the Conduct of War*, p 78.

129 P Warwick, *Black People and the South African War 1899–1902*, p 151. See also SV Kessler, 'The black and coloured concentration camps of the Anglo-Boer War 1899–1902: Shifting the paradigm from sole martyrdom to mutual suffering', *Historia*, 44(1) 1999, pp 110–47; and JA du Pisani and BE Mongalo, 'Victims of a white man's war: blacks in concentration camps during the South African War 1899–1902', *Historia*, 44(1), 1999, pp 148–82; Elizabeth van Heyningen, *The Concentration Camps of the Anglo-Boer War: a social history* (Jacana, Auckland Park, 2013).

130 Confidential Instruction, 7 December 1900, archives of the Military Governor (MG) 24, Free State Provincial Archives, Bloemfontein (FSPA).

131 A Jones, *The Art of War in the Western World*, pp 418–9.

132 Maud Lyttelton to a cousin, 2 January 1901, HHA 5/2/1.

133 See AM Grundlingh, *Die 'Hendsoppers' en 'Joiners': die rasionaal en verskynsel van verraad* (HAUM, Pretoria, 1999), chapters 5 and 6.

134 Thomas Pakenham, *The Boer War*, pp 497–99.

135 D Porch, *Wars of Empire*, pp 112–13.

136 Thomas Pakenham, *The Boer War*, pp 510, 512.

137 Thomas Pakenham, *The Boer War*, pp 534–37.

138 Jack Lyttelton to Maud Lyttelton, 4 April 1902, HHA 2/6/8.

139 Jack Lyttelton to Maud Lyttelton, 2 February 1902, HHA 2/6/10.

140 Jack Lyttelton to Maud Lyttelton, 4 April 1902, HHA 2/6/8.

141 Jack Lyttelton to Maud Lyttelton, 5 March [1902], HHA 2/6/3.

142 Jack Lyttelton to Maud Lyttelton, 14 March [1902], HHA 2/6/4.

143 Jack Lyttelton to Maud Lyttelton, 19 April 1902, HHA 2/6/9. On Sunday 29 December 1901, four of Milner's staff (Robinson, Perry, Rodwell and Buchan) rode from Johannesburg to Pretoria. The latter two, however, failed them 'in the veld being timorous of blockhouses & desirous of breakfast'. See Robinson's diary, 29 December 1901, Mss Dawson 7, Bodleian Library, Oxford.

144 Jack Lyttelton to Maud Lyttelton, 5 March [1902], HHA 2/6/3.

145 Jack Lyttelton to Maud Lyttelton, 14 January 1902 (HHA 5/2/41), 2 February 1902 (HHA 2/6/10) and 5 May 1902 (HHA 2/31/17).

146 Milner to Lady Edward Cecil, 26 October 1900, Milner Adds c.687, f.106, Bodleian Library, Oxford. Milner's emphasis.

147 Kitchener to St John Broderick, 3 November 1900, and Broderick to Kitchener, 9 November 1900, Kitchener Papers (M722), NASAP.

148 Beresford Gibbs to Maud Lyttelton, 5 June 1901, HHA 5/2/37; Jack Lyttelton to Maud Lyttelton, 2 February 1902, HHA 2/6/10.

149 Jack Lyttelton to Maud Lyttelton, 14 February 1902, HHA 2/6/1.

150 Hugh Wyndham to Mary Maxse, 21 June 1902, Maxse Papers 50, WSRO.

151 Goschen to Milner, 6 June 1902, Milner Adds c.688, ff.81–82, Bodleian Library, Oxford.

152 Milner to Chamberlain, 22 September 1902, CO 291/42, No 43292, The National Archives of the United Kingdom, Kew, London (TNA).

153 Lord Milner to Lord Selborne, 31 January 1900, in DG Boyce, ed, *The Crisis of British Power*, p 100. On the importance of the political dimension, see S Metz and R Millen, *Insurgency and Counterinsurgency in the 21st century: reconceptualizing threat and response* (SSI, Carlisle, PA, 2004), p 2.

154 Curtis to Owen Fleming, 8 February 1901, Ms Curtis 1, ff.70–75, Bodleian Library, Oxford.

155 Director of Agriculture, Transvaal, to Assistant Private Secretary to Governor, Transvaal, 30 October 1902, British Parliamentary Papers (BPP): Cd.1463–1903. No 13.

156 Milner to Chamberlain, 30 December 1901, BPP: Cd.1163–1902. No 20.

157 Milner to Hanbury-Williams, 27 December 1900, Milner Adds c.687, ff.175–82, Bodleian Library, Oxford. Milner's emphasis.

158 Patrick Duncan to Leo Amery, 4 January 1903, BC294 Duncan Papers, E.41.1.1, University of Cape Town (UCT); and Milner to Curtis, 17 September 1903, Ms Curtis 1, ff.143–46, Bodleian Library, Oxford.

159 Milner to Chamberlain, 25 January 1902, BPP: Cd.1163–1902. No 22.

160 Milner to Chamberlain, 30 December 1901, BPP: Cd.1163–1902. No 20.

161 Joseph Chamberlain in May 1896, quoted in FA van Jaarsveld, *The Afrikaner's Interpretation of South African History* (Simondium Publishers, Cape Town, 1964), p 94.

162 Roberts to Milner, 4 July 1900, in C Headlam,

ed., *Milner Papers II*, pp 162–63.

163 Milner to Roberts, 21 Jun 1900, in C Headlam, ed., *Milner Papers II*, pp 161–62.

164 Milner to Alfred Lyttelton, 20 Jul 1904, in C Headlam, ed, *The Milner Papers II*, p 507. The South African Military Command was reduced gradually from approximately 30 000 in March 1903 to 10 500 in 1909. See J Ploeger, 'Uit die voorgeskiedenis van die SAW, 1902–1910', *Militaria*, 1(3), 1969, p 2.

165 Milner to Field Marshal Lord Roberts, 10 October 1904, *Milner Papers II*, pp 507–508.

166 Jack Lyttelton to Maud Lyttelton, undated, HHA 2/31/28.

167 High Commissioner to Secretary of State, 5 June 1902, GOV 592, file P.S.323 Volunteer Forces in Transvaal, NASAP.

168 Richard Gabriel and Karen Metz, *A History of Military Medicine* (Greenwood, New York and London, 1992), p 217 *passim*.

169 The term 'colonial troops' refers to the troops from the Cape Colony and the Natal Colony, the volunteers raised in these colonies from Transvaal and Free State refugees, as well as the troops from Newfoundland, Canada, Australia, New Zealand and India. This is intended to differentiate these forces from the 'imperial troops' of the British Army.

170 Casualty Returns 1901, GH 40/8, WCPA.

171 D Porch, *Wars of Empire*, pp 110–11, 118–19, 131–32; H Bailes, 'Technology and imperialism: a case study of the Victorian army in Africa', *Victorian Studies*, 24(1), 1980, pp 82–104.

172 Patrick Duncan to Leo Amery, 10 January 1904, BC294 Duncan Papers E41.1.2, UCT. [Duncan's emphasis.]

CHAPTER TWO
Integration and Union, 1902–1914

1 DW Krüger, *The Making of a Nation: a history of the Union of South Africa, 1910–1961* (Macmillan, Johannesburg and London, 1982), p 3.

2 William Carter to Algernon Lawley, 6 March 1909, AB186 Archbishop Carter Letters, William Cullen Library, University of the Witwatersrand (Wits).

3 Olive Schreiner to Patrick Duncan, 27 June 1912, BC294 Sir Patrick Duncan Collection, D1.33.2, University of Cape Town Libraries, Archives and Manuscripts (UCT).

4 A major obstacle, as Milner informed the Colonial Secretary, was 'the tendency of Boer owners to hold on to enormous estates, which they [were] unable to develop.' Milner to Chamberlain, 30 December 1901, Cd.1163–1902, No 20, British Parliamentary Papers (BPP).

5 Lord Milner to Alfred Lyttelton, 30 May 1904, Cd.2104–1904, BPP. Correspondence Relating to Affairs in the Transvaal and Orange River Colony. No 13; and First Congress of Transvaal Farmers' Association, CS 447, file 2415/04, National Archives of South Africa, Pretoria (NASAP).

6 'Transvaaler' (non de plume for Geoffrey Robinson), 'Political parties of the Transvaal', *The National Review*, 45 (May 1905), pp 480–81; NG Garson, 'Het Volk: the Botha-Smuts party in the Transvaal, 1904–11', *Historical Journal*, 9 (1966), p 129.

7 Colonel CE Callwell's *Small Wars: their principles and practice*, which was first published by the War Office in 1896 (printed for HM Stationery Office by Harrison and Sons, London) and reprinted several times until 1914, became the classic primer for colonial warfare.

8 Shula Marks, *Reluctant Rebellion: the 1906–1908 disturbances in Natal* (Clarendon, Oxford, 1970); Paul Thompson, *An Historical Atlas of the Zulu Rebellion of 1906* (Pietermaritzburg, 2001).

9 Colonel HT Lukin, *Savage Warfare: hints on tactics to be adopted and precautions to be taken* (Cape Town, 1906); PA Silburn, *The Colonies and Imperial Defence* (Longman, London, 1909); HA Wyndham, 'Some aspects of South African defence', *The State*, 2(7) June 1909 and *The State*, 2(8) July 1909. George Aston, *Defence of a United South Africa as a Part of the British Empire* (John Murray, London, 1911). They were informed by, *inter alia*, William Fox's *The War in New Zealand* (London, 1866).

10 Chief of the General Staff to Minister of Defence, 8 April 1933, archives of the Secretary for Defence (DC), Box 1098, file 4/58X South African Naval History, Department of Defence Archives, SANDF Documentation Centre, Pretoria. See also BPP: Cd.4948–1909. Imperial Conference. Correspondence and Papers relating to a Conference with Representatives of the Self-Governing Dominions on the Naval and Military Defence of the Empire, 1909.

11 Charles Crewe to Patrick Duncan, 21 June 1908, BC294 Duncan Papers, A20.2.2, UCT.

12 Hugh Wyndham to Mary Maxse, 9 December 1914, Maxse Papers 455, West Sussex Record Office (WSRO).

13 Ian van der Waag, 'The thin edge of the wedge: Anglo-South African relations, dominion nationalism and the formation of the Seaward Defence Force in 1939–40', *Contemporary British History*, 24(4) December 2010, pp 427–49.

14 HA Wyndham, 'Some aspects of South African defence', *The State*, June 1909, pp 647–49.

15 HA Wyndham, 'Some aspects of South African defence', *The State* July 1909, p 97.

16 Secret report from Major JGW Leipoldt to the Adjutant General, 22 December 1917, DC, Box 356, DC40057 Intelligence Section, SANDF Documentation Centre, Pretoria.

17 HT Lukin, *Savage Warfare*; P Truter to Col Lukin, 10 May 1906, CO 8310, file X5114 'Savage Warfare' by Col Lukin Requisition for 300 copies to be printed in cheap pamphlet form, Western Cape Provincial Archives and Records Centre (WCPA).

18 Hugh Wyndham to Lady Leconfield, 27 August 1906, Petworth House Archives (PHA), WSRO.

19 Willem Steenkamp, *Assegais, Drums & Dragoons: a military and social history of the Cape* (Jonathan Ball, Johannesburg, 2012).

20 GB Pyrah, *Imperial Policy and South Africa, 1902–10* (Clarendon Press, Oxford, 1955), p 31.

21 Statistical Register of the Province of the Cape of Good Hope for the Year 1909 (Government Printer, Cape Town, 1910).

22 Lord Selborne to Patrick Duncan, 22 May 1906, BC294 Duncan Papers, D6.2.8, UCT.

23 Paul Thompson, 'The Natal Militia: defence of the colony, 1893–1910', *Journal of Natal and Zulu History*, 29, 2011, pp 20–65; Colony of Natal, Departmental Reports, 1899 (Government Printer, Pietermaritzburg, 1900); Robert Morrell, *From Boys to Gentlemen: settler masculinity in colonial Natal, 1880–1920* (UNISA, Pretoria, 2001), chapter 6.

24 Eben Jonker, 'Ontstaan en ontwikkeling van die Transvaalse Verdedigingsmag, 1900–1912: Transvaal Volunteers', *Militaria*, 3(3) 1972, pp 1–2. This article is based on Jonker's thesis (MA dissertation, University of Pretoria, 1971), but with the scaffolding removed. For a case study on a single regiment, see Ian van der Waag, 'Rural struggles and the politics of a colonial command: the Southern Mounted Rifles of the Transvaal Volunteers, 1905–1912',

in Stephen Miller, ed, *Soldiers and Settlers in Africa, 1850–1918* (Brill, Leiden, 2009), pp 251–85.

25 Martin Legassick, 'South Africa; capital accumulation and violence', *Economy and Society*, 3(3) 1974, p 260; J Higginson, 'Hell in small places: agrarian elites and collective violence in the Western Transvaal, 1900–1907', *Journal of Social History*, 35(1) 2001, pp 95–124. See also the evidence of Louis Botha, Cd.1891–1904, BPP. Transvaal Labour Commission, Minutes of Proceedings and Evidence.

26 P Jourdan to Lewis Michell, 12 September 1907, Sir Lewis Michell Collection, vol 1, WCPA.

27 Milner to Alfred Lyttelton, 20 July 1904, in C Headlam, ed, *The Milner Papers: South Africa, vol II, 1899–1905* (Cassell, London, 1933), p 507. The South African Military Command was reduced gradually from approximately 30 000 in March 1903 to 10 500 in 1909. Milner to Field Marshal Lord Roberts, 10 October 1904, *The Milner Papers II, 1899–1905*, pp 507–508.

28 The term 'geography of loyalism' is adopted from K Linch, 'A geography of loyalism? The local military forces of the West Riding of Yorkshire, 1794–1814', *War & Society*, 19(1) May 2001, p 2. The term 'uitlander' (foreigner) referred to the mainly English-speaking, but generally foreign, component of the pre-war Transvaal population. The *uitlander* regiments had served with and alongside British forces during the 1899–1902 war.

29 See, for example, Milner to Chamberlain, 6 November 1902, CO 291/44, No 45910, The National Archives of the United Kingdom, Kew (TNA).

30 Milner to Chamberlain, 28 October 1902, CO 291/43, No 44556, TNA.

31 K Fedorowich, *Unfit for Heroes: reconstruction and soldier settlement in the empire between the wars* (Manchester University Press, Manchester and New York, 1995), pp 4–5. See also K Fedorowich, 'Anglicisation and the politicisation of British immigration to South Africa, 1899–1929', *Journal of Imperial and Commonwealth History*, 19, 1991, pp 222–46.

32 J Ploeger, 'Suid-Afrikaanse Verdedigingskemas, 1887–1914', *Militaria*, 1(5) 1969, pp 12–13.

33 High Commissioner to Secretary of State, 5 June 1902, GOV 592, file P.S.323 Volunteer Forces in Transvaal, NASAP.

34 Milner to Colonel Charles Crewe, 27 April 1904, *The Milner Papers II*, p 508.

35 This term embraces all Britons, such as the Unionists and Liberal Imperialists, who held notions regarding a Greater Britain, as opposed to 'Little Englanders'. For some discussion, see D Armitage, 'Greater Britain: a useful category of historical analysis?', *American Historical Review*, 104, 1999.

36 Milner had hoped that at least some of the Boer leadership would leave South Africa after the war or not return from exile; none were encouraged to serve in the colonial government. Lord Milner to Lord Onslow, 29 December 1902, and Lord Onslow to General Ben Viljoen, 31 December 1902, CO 291/45, No 53336, TNA. On the emergence of the new Boer leadership after 1900, see I van der Waag, 'Boer generalship and the politics of command', *War in History*, 12(1) 2005, pp 15–43.

37 Ian van der Waag, 'Rural struggles and the politics of a colonial command', pp 251–85.

38 Enrolment Book of the Southern Mounted Rifles, archives of the Inspector of the Transvaal Volunteers (TVO) 50B, NASAP.

39 Hugh Wyndham to Lady Leconfield, 17 December 1906, PHA, WSRO.

40 Hugh Wyndham to Lady Leconfield, 31 March, 8 April and 16 June 1906, PHA, WSRO. In his memoirs, Kemp, himself born in 1872, refers disparagingly to Wyndham and other Kindergarteners as '*kêreltjies*': JCG Kemp, *Die Pad van die Veroweraar* (Nasionale Pers, Kaapstad, 1942 & 1946), p 66.

41 Mustering rolls of Standerton Commando, archives of the OC Records, Boxes 194 and 195, SANDF Documentation Centre, Pretoria.

42 Known as the Union Defence Forces (plural) from 1912 until the promulgation of the Defence Act Amendment Act.

43 The Annual Report on the Transvaal Volunteers and Cadets for the year 1910–1911, p 84. See also Hugh Wyndham to Lady Leconfield, 17 December 1906 and 3 December 1909, PHA, WSRO.

44 'Notes of a visit to the South Western and Western Districts of the Transvaal', by Patrick Duncan, Pretoria, 30 September [1903], BC294 Duncan Papers, A38.14, UCT. See also CJ Tearnan to Duke of Marlborough, Colonial Office, 19 September 1903, Colonial Treasurer (CT) 288, f.1021, NASAP.

45 EP Thompson, *The Making of the English Working Class* (Penguin, London, 1991),

pp 189–90. Thompson relied heavily in this study on the eighteenth- and nineteenth-century volunteers of the West Riding, Yorkshire.

46 Milner to Chamberlain, 25 January 1902, Cd.1163–1902, BPP.

47 This argument is well made by K Linch, 'A geography of loyalism?', pp 1–21.

48 J Ploeger, 'Die imperiale militêre beleid ten opsigte van Suid-Afrika, 1908–1910', *Militaria*, 3(2), 1972, p 19 *passim*.

49 These were the colonies of the Cape of Good Hope and of Natal, as well as the two former Boer republics that had been incorporated into the British Empire in 1900 as the Transvaal Colony and the Orange River Colony.

50 John Lambert, 'South African British? Or Dominion South Africans? The evolution of an identity in the 1910s and 1920s', *South African Historical Journal*, 43 November 2000, p 197 *passim*; John Lambert, 'An identity threatened: white English-speaking South Africans, Britishness and domestic South Africanism, 1934–1939', *Kleio*, 37, 2005, p 59 *passim*.

51 These conferences were convened, in Pretoria, Durban and Johannesburg, and were followed by the Imperial conferences of 1909 and 1911. *Debatten van de Volksraad*, 21 February 1911, cols 1263–66. See also War Office Documents, A1380 South African Defence.

52 WK Hancock, *Survey of British Commonwealth Affairs, vol 1: Problems of Nationality, 1918–1936* (OUP/RIIA, Oxford, 1937), pp 44–46; GB Pyrah, *Imperial Policy and South Africa, 1902–10*, p 13.

53 GB Pyrah, *Imperial Policy and South Africa, 1902–10*, p 15. See also Hancock, *Survey of British Commonwealth Affairs, vol 1*, p 47.

54 GB Pyrah, *Imperial Policy and South Africa, 1902–10*, p 16.

55 DW Krüger, *The Making of a Nation*, pp 3–4.

56 Bill Nasson, *Springboks on the Somme: South Africa and the Great War, 1914–1918* (Penguin, Johannesburg, 2007), p 1.

57 Field Marshal Lord Methuen and his chief of staff, Brigadier General George Aston, were also consulted and, at Smuts' request, both men remained in South Africa until the passage of the Bill through the South African Parliament. DC, Box 47, file 1063 South Africa Defence Bill, SANDF Documentation Centre, Pretoria.

58 See the comments in William Carter to Algernon Lawley, 3 August 1919, AB186

Archbishop Carter Letters, Wits. The term 'backveld' was used by the English South Africans to refer to 'the rolling countryside of the two old republics'; see Arthur G Barlow, *That We May Tread Safely* (Tafelberg, Cape Town, 1960), p 66. Barlow's definition, however, does not suggest the pejorative meaning that the term conveyed.

59 Herbert Stanley to Lord Gladstone, 7 August 1910, Sir Herbert James Stanley papers, MSS Afr s.1250, Rhodes House, Oxford (RHO). I thank Kent Fedorowich for this reference.

60 JX Merriman to MT Steyn, 16 January 1911, in AH Marais, ed, *Politieke Briewe, II: 1911–1912* (Instituut vir Eietydse Geskiedenis, Bloemfontein, 1973), p 5.

61 MT Steyn to CF Beyers, 16 February 1912, General CF Beyers Collection, col 1, ff.45–47, NASAP. See also the two petitions, Memorial of the Women of Nooitgedacht, undated (ff.104–7), and Memorial of the Women of Randjesfontein, undated (ff.108–10).

62 Hugh Wyndham to Lady Leconfield, 21 and 27 February 1912, PHA, WSRO.

63 Union of South Africa, Parliament, Select Committee Report: S.C.7–1912. On South Africa Defence Bill. Report, JC Smuts, 16 April 1912.

64 Richard Feetham to his mother, 19 April 1912, Feetham Papers, Box 3, file 1, f.134, RHO.

65 Smuts did not consider the term 'South Africa' in any way limited by the Act of Union. Smuts to Lord Gladstone, 16 November 1911, DC, Box 47, file 1063 South Africa Defence Bill, SANDF Documentation Centre, Pretoria.

66 Alan F Hattersley, *Carbineer: The History of the Royal Natal Carbineers* (Gale and Polden, Aldershot, 1950), p 50.

67 There were four defence councillors, two English and two Afrikaans, and representing the four provinces. DC, Box 109, files 2270 and 2271 Defence Council Agenda of 1st and 2nd meetings, SANDF Documentation Centre, Pretoria. See also I van der Waag, 'Smuts' generals: towards a first portrait of the South African high command, 1912–48', *War in History*, 18(1) January 2011, pp 1–29.

68 Beyers to Sir John French, 21 July 1913 ('the melting pot'), Beyers Collection, vol 1, NASAP. There are also numerous references to instances of nepotism and 'connection' support in J Kemp to Beyers, 5 April 1909; MT Steyn to Beyers, 30 September 1913; Smuts to Beyers, 27 February 1914; 'Maurits' to Beyers, 8 June 1914 (all in the Beyers

Collection, vol 1); as well as correspondence between Colonel Mike du Toit and former president MT Steyn, 1912, Col M du Toit Collection, W.77.1, NASAP.

69 GD Scholtz, *Generaal Christiaan Federik Beyers 1869–1914* (Voortrekkerpers, Johannesburg 1941); JCG Kemp, *Die Pad van die Veroweraar*; GD Scholtz, *Hertzog en Smuts en die Britse Ryk* (Randse Afrikaanse Universiteit, Johannesburg, 1975); L Jooste, 'Die politieke koerswending van 1948 besorg 'n nuwe identiteit aan die Univerdedigingsmag', *Militaria*, 26(2) 1996, pp 113–28; L Jooste, 'FC Erasmus as Minister van Verdediging, 1948–1959' (unpublished MA thesis, Unisa, 1995), pp 13–14.

70 HA Wyndham, 'Some Aspects of South African Defence', *The State*, 2(6) June 1909, p 651.

71 *Debatten van de Volksraad*, 7 March 1912, col 736; and Union of South Africa, Parliament, Select Committee Report: S.C.7–1912 On South Africa Defence Bill, ii.

72 Smuts to Beyers, 9 May 1914, and 'Maurits' to Beyers, 8 June 1914, Beyers Collection, vol 1, NASAP.

73 EW Nortier, 'Major General Sir HT Lukin, 1861–1925: the making of a South African hero' (unpublished MMil thesis, Stellenbosch University, December 2005); EW Nortier, '"A Just Devil": Major General Sir Henry Timson Lukin, 1860–1925.' Paper presented at the 4th War and Society in Africa Conference (Strategy, Generalship and Command in Southern Africa: Past, Present, Future), 4–6 September 2003.

74 Kemp to Beyers, 5 April 1909, and Steyn to Beyers, 16 February 1912, Beyers Collection, vol 1, NASAP; and Beyers to Du Toit, 23 December 1912, Du Toit Collection, NASAP; Kemp, *Die Pad van die Veroweraar*, p 109.

75 Charles Leonard to David Graaff, 17 February 1903, Charles Leonard Papers, NASAP.

76 Hugh Wyndham to Lady Leconfield, 2 November 1910, PHA, WSRO.

77 Sir William Clark to Sir Edward Harding, 8 March 1937, BC81 Papers of Sir WH Clark, Ca5, UCT.

78 For the incident of the speech given by Brigadier General Alfred Cavendish, see chapter 3.

79 Peter Clutterbuck to JE Stephenson, 29 September 1939, DO 35/1008/7 WG 429/13, TNA; Ian van der Waag, 'The thin edge of the wedge', pp 427–49.

80 Secretary for Defence to Director War Recruiting, 1 October 1914, archives of the Commandant General, SA Citizen Force, Box 4, file 61 SA Mounted Rifles, SANDF Documentation Centre, Pretoria.

81 Bourne to Smuts, 8 September 1910, Diverse Group 1, Box 15, file 199 Colonial Defence Committee Memoranda on General Defence Matters, SANDF Documentation Centre, Pretoria.

82 JX Merriman to MT Steyn, 16 January 1911, in AH Marais, ed, *Politieke Briewe, II*, pp 5–6.

83 MT Steyn to JX Merriman, 10 February 1911, in AH Marais, ed, *Politieke Briewe, II*, p 8.

84 Memorandum explanatory of the South African Defence Bill, 2, BC 294 Duncan Papers, A49, UCT.

85 Bill Nasson, *Springboks on the Somme*, p 38.

86 Staff Officer General Staff Duties to District Staff Officers, 18 February 1913, archives of the Adjutant General 1914–1921, Box 189, file 489 Coloured Men in Overseas Brigade, SANDF Documentation Centre, Pretoria. See also Ian Gleeson, *The Unknown Force: black, Indian and coloured soldiers through two world wars* (Ashanti, Rivonia, 1994), p 9.

87 Memorandum explanatory of the South African Defence Bill, 3–4, BC 294 Duncan Papers, A49, UCT.

88 'Die UVM se offsierskorps, en veral die bevelsposte, het in 1912 hoofsaaklik uit Engelssprekendes bestaan. Gedurende die daaropvolgende drie dekades het die getaaleverhouding tussen Afrikaans- en Engelssprekende offisiere meer ewewigtig geword.' L Jooste, 'Die politieke koerswending van 1948 besorg 'n nuwe identiteit aan die Unieverdedigingsmag', pp 113–14.

89 'The upper echelon of the military were overwhelmingly British in personnel and outlook …' J Lambert, 'South African British? Or Dominion South African?', p 215.

90 Report of the Staff Officer for General Staff Duties, 22 December 1913. UG 61 – 1913; Annual Reports Department of Defence and Executive Commands for the year ending 30 June 1913, p 14.

91 Piet van der Byl, *From Playgrounds to Battlefields* (Howard Timmins, Cape Town, 1971), p 81. For an alternative view, see 'Smuts's New Tangle: Trouble at Military School', *Rand Daily Mail*, 9 October 1912.

92 Diary, 7 December 1912, Major General Sir George Aston Papers, Royal Marines Archives, Eastney Barracks, Portsmouth, UK.

93 JCG Kemp, *Die Pad van die Veroweraar*,

pp 107–8.

94 DC, Box 109, files 2270 and 2271 Defence Council Agenda of 1st and 2nd meetings, SANDF Documentation Centre, Pretoria.

95 IL Walker and B Weinbren, *2000 Casualties: a history of the trade unions and the labour movement in the Union of South Africa* (Johannesburg, 1961), pp 23–24.

96 W Visser, 'The South African labour movement's responses to declarations of martial law, 1913–1922', *Scientia Militaria*, 31(2) 2003, pp 145–46; see also UG 55–1913. Report of the Witwatersrand Disturbances Commission.

97 Mary Drew to Dorothy Parish, 16 January 1914, in L Masterman, ed, *Mary Gladstone (Mrs Drew) Her Diaries and Letters* (EP Dutton, New York, 1930), p 474.

98 Autobiography, Major General Sir George Aston Papers, Royal Marines Archives, Eastney Barracks, Portsmouth, UK.

99 Piet van der Byl, *From Playgrounds to Battlefields*, pp 91–93.

100 Hugh Wyndham to Lady Leconfield, 21 and 27 February 1912, PHA, WSRO. See, for example, Memorial of the Women of Nooitgedacht, undated (ff.104–7), Beyers Collection, vol 2, NASAP.

101 Smuts to Beyers, 23 April 1914, Beyers Collection, vol 1, f.93, NASAP.

102 Smuts to Beyers, 1 May 1914, Beyers Collection, vol 1, f.94, NASAP.

103 Smuts to Beyers, 9 May 1914, Beyers Collection, vol 1, ff.95–6, NASAP.

104 D Visser, 'British influence on military training and education in South Africa: the case of the South African Military Academy and its predecessors', *South African Historical Journal*, 46 2002, p 64 *passim*.

105 Evidence of Capt Hendrik T Watkins, 9 May 1916, Diverse, Box 3, Minutes of Evidence on the Rebellion, SANDF Documentation Centre, Pretoria. [My emphasis.]

106 See H Oost, *Wie is die skuldiges?* (Johannesburg, 1958), pp 231, 238, for the case of Cmdt J Alberts of the Standerton Commando. FS Malan admitted in 1912 that he felt the waning of his personal influence ('Myn eigen persoonlikheid geldt tans minder'). Diary (f.133), vol 22, FS Malan Collection (A.583), WCPA.

107 Ian van der Waag, 'War memories, historical consciousness and nationalism: South African history writing and the Second Anglo-Boer War, 1899–1999', in John Crawford and Ian McGibbon, eds, *One Flag,*

One Queen, One Tongue: New Zealand, the British Empire and the South African War, 1899–1902 (Auckland University Press, Auckland 2003), pp 180–204. For an Afrikaner view, see O Geyser, Watershed for South Africa, London 1961 (Butterworths, Durban and Pretoria, 1983).

108 Maud Wyndham to Lord Cobham, 19 February 1912, Hagley Hall Archives (HHA) 2/34/13.

109 Hugh Wyndham to Lady Leconfield, 9 July 1914, PHA, WSRO.

110 DW Krüger, The Making of a Nation, p 79.

CHAPTER THREE
The First World War, 1914–1918

1 Archbishop William Carter to Rev Algernon Lawley, 31 July 1914, AB186 Archbishop Carter Letters, William Cullen Library, University of the Witwatersrand (Wits).

2 John Buchan, The History of the South African Forces in France (London, 1920; reprinted Battery Press, Nashville, 1992), p 13.

3 The South African Military Command closed with effect from 1 December 1921. Secretary for Defence to the Headquarters, SA Military Command, 28 September 1921, DC, Box 886, file Q.23892 Transfer South African Military Command to Union Defence, SANDF Documentation Centre, Pretoria.

4 Anon, The Union of South Africa and the Great War: official history (Government Printer, Pretoria, 1924), p 220.

5 Anon, The Union of South Africa and the Great War, p 3.

6 Michael Howard, 'The First World War Reconsidered', in J Winter, G Parker and MR Habeck, eds, The Great War and the Twentieth Century (New Haven and London, Yale University Press, 2000), p 14. De Burger, taking a surprisingly neutral line, described it too as 'De Grote Volkerenstrijd'. See, for example, De Burger, 29 February 1916, 20 March 1916 and 17 July 1916.

7 See, for example, PM 1/1/32, file 4/97/1914 War German South West Expedition & Supply of Ammunition & Guns, NASAP; and DC, Box 573, file D.9199 European Crisis General, vol 7, SANDF Documentation Centre.

8 'De Britse-Duitse Oorlog' (The Anglo-German War), diary of FS Malan, 7 August to 10 August 1914, A583 FS Malan Collection, vol 22, Western Cape Provincial Archives and Records Centre (WCPA).

9 MT Steyn to JC Smuts, 31 July 1914, in WK Hancock and J van der Poel, eds, Selections from the Smuts Papers, vol III: June 1910–November 1918 (Cambridge University Press, Cambridge, 1966), p 184.

10 Tilman Dedering, '"Avenge the Lusitania": the anti-German riots in South Africa in 1915', Immigrants & Minorities, 31(3), 2013, pp 1–33.

11 William Carter to Algernon Lawley, 6 August 1914, Archbishop Carter Letters, Wits; and Maud Wyndham to Lady Leconfield, 11 August 1914, Petworth House Archives (PHA), West Sussex Record Office (WSRO).

12 Bill Nasson, 'A great divide: popular responses to the Great War in South Africa', War & Society, 12(1), 1994; Bill Nasson, 'War opinion in South Africa, 1914', Journal of Imperial and Commonwealth History, 23(2), 1995; and LWF Grundlingh, 'Die Engelssprekende Suid-Afrikaners se reaksie op die uitbreek van die Eerste Wêreldoorlog' (MA thesis, Universiteit van die Oranje Vrystaat, 1978).

13 Tilman Dedering, '"Avenge the Lusitania"', pp 1–33.

14 SA Citizen Force, Box 28, file 29/244 Erection of Blockhouses, SANDF Documentation Centre, Pretoria.

15 Diary of FS Malan, 9 August 1914, A583 FS Malan Collection, vol 22, WCPA.

16 Albert Grundlingh, Fighting Their Own War: South African blacks and the First World War (Ravan, Johannesburg, 1987), pp 11–13.

17 Piet van der Byl, From Playgrounds to Battlefields (Howard Timmins, Cape Town, 1971), p 108.

18 Wyndham to Lady Leconfield, 13 August 1914, Hugh Wyndham Papers, PHA, WSRO.

19 Quoted by MH Park, 'German South-West African Campaign', Journal of the African Society, XX(LVIII), January 1916, p 115.

20 Smuts to CP Crewe, 11 August 1914, in WK Hancock and J van der Poel, eds, Selections from the Smuts Papers, vol III, p 186.

21 Lord Harcourt to Lord de Villiers, 8 and 23 August 1914, PM 1/1/32, file 4/97/1914 War German South West Expedition & Supply of Ammunition & Guns, National Archives of South Africa, Pretoria (NASAP). Diary of FS Malan, 7 August to 10 August 1914, A.583 FS Malan Collection, vol 22, WCPA.

22 Lord Harcourt to Lord de Villiers, 8 and 23 August 1914, PM 1/1/32, file 4/97/1914 War German South West Expedition & Supply of Ammunition & Guns, NASAP.

23 'De Britse-Duitse Oorlog' (The Anglo-German War), diary of FS Malan, 7 August

to 10 August 1914, A.583 FS Malan Collection, vol 22, WCPA; and SB Spies, 'The outbreak of the First World War and the Botha government', *South African Historical Journal*, 1, 1969, p 47.

24 Bill Nasson, 'A great divide', p 50. See also NG Garson, 'South Africa and World War One', *Journal of Imperial and Commonwealth History*, 8(1), 1979, pp 69–70. The rebellion and the often difficult position of the Loyal Afrikaners has been treated excellently by Kent Fedorowich, 'Sleeping with the Lion? The Loyal Afrikaners and the South African Rebellion of 1914–15', *South African Historical Journal*, 49(1) 2003, pp 71–95.

25 Hugh Wyndham to Lady Leconfield, 20 August 1914, PHA, WSRO.

26 Union of South Africa, *Debates of the House of Assembly*, 9–10 Sep 1914; and SB Spies, 'The outbreak of the First World War and the Botha government', pp 47–57.

27 Lord Harcourt to Lord de Villiers, 8 and 23 August 1914, PM 1/1/32, file 4/97/1914 War German South West Expedition & Supply of Ammunition & Guns, NASAP. See also Diary of FS Malan, 7 August to 10 Aug 1914, A.583 FS Malan Collection, vol 22, WCPA. For a general statement, converging much of the current debate and adding several new insights, see Hew Strachan, *The First World War in Africa* (OUP, Oxford, 2004), p 61 *passim*.

28 Inspector General Permanent Force to Secretary for Defence, 1 September 1914, AG 1914–1921, Box 152, file 21/9199 Information passed to Executive Commanders and Others, SANDF Documentation Centre, Pretoria.

29 Quoted by MH Park, 'German South-West African Campaign', pp 123–25. See also Deneys Reitz, *Trekking On: in the company of brave men* (Emslie, Edinburgh, 2012), p 42. The line was on two different gauges, see [HA Wyndham,] 'History of the German South West Campaign' (unpublished, Pretoria, 1916), pp 2–3. Some 800 miles (1 287 kilometres) of broad gauge (3 foot 6 inches) line ran from Lüderitzbucht via Keetmanshoop to Karibib and on to Windhoek, with an extension from Seeheim to Kalkfontein. A narrower, 2–foot-6–inch gauge ran the 420 miles (676 kilometres) from Swakopmund to Karibib and then northwards to Tsumeb and Grootfontein. See also WW Hoy to Secretary for Defence, 3 September 1914, f.20, Smuts Papers, Box 111, NASAP.

30 W Whittal, *With Botha and Smuts in Africa* (Cassell, London, 1917), p 4.

31 The estimated numbers of Schutztruppen in South West Africa at the outbreak of war vary according to sources. Zirkel, using primary German material, estimates their number to be 5 000, of which some 2 000 were active. This is in general agreement with South African sources in August 1914. Kirsten Zirkel, 'Military power in German colonial policy: the Schutztruppen and their leaders in East and South-West Africa, 1888–1918', in David Killingray and David Omissi, eds, *Guardians of Empire: the armed forces of the colonial powers, c 1700–1964* (MUP, Manchester, 1999), p 104. Capt EM Fisher, SAMR, to The Adjutant, 5th Regiment SAMR, 22 August 1914, AG 1914–1921, Box 152, file 21/9199 Information passed to Executive Commanders and Others, SANDF Documentation Centre. See the Minutes of Evidence before the Rebellion Commission (Diverse, Box 3, SANDF Documentation Centre) on the formation of a Boer Vrij Corps.

32 Character sketches attached to Lt Col P Skinner, General Staff, Intelligence, to Brig Gen Lukin, 29 August 1914, Diverse, Box 1, file 2493 Intelligence Reports, SANDF Documentation Centre.

33 Character sketches attached to Lt Col P. Skinner, General Staff, Intelligence, to Brig Gen Lukin, 29 August 1914, Diverse, Box 1, file 2493 Intelligence Reports, SANDF Documentation Centre.

34 [HA Wyndham,] 'History of the German South West Campaign', p 3; HF Trew, *Botha Treks* (Blackie & Son, London and Glasgow, 1936), p 94; and Brig Gen JJ Collyer, *The Campaign in German South West Africa, 1914–15* (Government Printer, Pretoria, 1937), pp 20–21.

35 Brig Gen JJ Collyer, *The Campaign in German South West Africa*, p 23 *passim*. See also 'Memorandum re Offensive Operations – G.S.W.A.' by Captain JGW Leipoldt, 25 August 1914, Diverse, Box 1, file 2493 Intelligence Reports, SANDF Documentation Centre; as well as [HA Wyndham], 'History of the German South West Campaign', pp 3–4.

36 Lt Col P Skinner, General Staff, Intelligence, to Brig Gen Lukin, 29 August 1914, Diverse, Box 1, file 2493 Intelligence Reports, SANDF Documentation Centre. See also HF Trew, *Botha Treks*, pp 94–95.

37 Smuts to Governor General, 16 July 1914, GG24, 1/864, NASAP; Louis Botha to Lord de Villiers, 17 August 1914 (Ministers' Minute 759), PM 1/1/32, file 4/97/1914, NASAP; and JGW Leipoldt, 'Memorandum re Offensive Operations G.S.W.A', Diverse, Box 1, file 2493 Intelligence Reports SWA, SANDF Documentation Centre.

38 The state of the South African artillery was questionable. The force was new and, the British thought, while not yet efficient, was equal to the essentials of the task to be faced in South West Africa. There were only four batteries of South African artillery, with only 4 000 rounds of ammunition. The immediate need was for 10 000 rounds of 13–pounder QF ammunition. This came from India. Australia promised 5 million rounds of Mark VI .303 ammunition, with the possibility of more later. Louis Botha to Lord de Villiers, 10 August 1914, Harcourt to De Villiers, 12 August 1914, Botha to De Villiers, 13 August 1914, Sir R Munro Ferguson to De Villiers, 20 August 1914, PM 1/1/32, file 4/97/1914, NASAP.

39 Harcourt to De Villiers, 8 and 23 August 1914, PM 1/1/32, file 4/97/1914, NASAP.

40 'Memorandum re Offensive Operations – G.S.W.A.' by Captain JGW Leipoldt, 25 August 1914, Diverse, Box 1, file 2493 Intelligence Reports, SANDF Documentation Centre.

41 Brig Gen JJ Collyer, *The Campaign in German South West Africa*, p 27. South African Parliamentary Papers: UG 46 – 1916. Union of South Africa. Report of the Judicial Commission of Inquiry into the Causes of and Circumstances Relating to the Recent Rebellion in South Africa, December 1916, p 7.

42 Brig Gen JJ Collyer, *The Campaign in German South West Africa*, p 29.

43 Merriman to Lady Courtney, 20 September 1914, in P Lewsen, ed, *Selections from the Correspondence of John X Merriman, 1905-1924* (VRS, Cape Town, 1969), p 264.

44 JP Kay Robinson, *With Botha's Army* (George Allen & Unwin, London, 1916), chapter 1.

45 Evidence of Brig Gen BGL Enslin, 17 April 1916, Diverse, Box 3, Minutes of Evidence of the Rebellion Commission, SANDF Documentation Centre.

46 See also the evidence of DP Rousseau, 12 February 1916, IM Botes, 21 February 1916, SJ Heyns, 22 February 1916, and ds JA van Zyl Viljoen, 26 February 1916, Diverse,

Box 3, Minutes of Evidence of the Rebellion Commission, SANDF Documentation Centre.

47 Merriman to FC Mackarness, 16 September 1914, in P Lewsen, ed, *Selections from the Correspondence of John X Merriman, 1905-1924*, pp 262–63.

48 See, for example, Kent Fedorowich, 'Sleeping with the Lion?'; and Albert Grundlingh and Sandra Swart, *Radelose Rebellie? Dinamika van die 1914-1915 Afrikanerrebellie* (Protea, Pretoria, 2009). For a fuller exploration of the early historiography, see Albert Grundlingh, 'Die Rebellie van 1914: 'n historiografiese verkenning', *Kleio*, 11 1979.

49 R Morrell, 'Competition and cooperation in Middelburg, 1900-1930', in W Beinart, P Delius and S Trapido, eds, *Putting a Plough to the Ground: accumulation and dispossession in rural South Africa, 1850-1930* (Ravan, Johannesburg, 1986), p 381.

50 JC Smuts to Lord Buxton, 15 September 1914, Ministers' Minute 3031, f.14, URU 209, NASAP.

51 William Carter to Algernon Lawley, 15 July 1917, Archbishop William Carter Papers, Wits.

52 As quoted by D Reitz, *Trekking On*, p 36.

53 These cantonments and buildings were given to the UDF on loan for the duration of the war. The Union government was to return all the property when the imperial troops returned after the war. When it became certain after the war that the imperial garrison would not return to South Africa, negotiations regarding the future ownership of these properties commenced between the British and Union governments and the properties were transferred to South African ownership with effect from 1 December 1921 under the Defence Endowment Property and Account Act (33 of 1922). The cantonments at Potchefstroom had been handed over already on 1 December 1920.

54 D Reitz, *Trekking On*, p 36. See also Anon, *The Union of South Africa and the Great War*, p 214.

55 This story is recounted by D Reitz, *Trekking On*, p 35.

56 Major C Burgess to Brig Gen CF Beyers, 15 September 1914, Beyers Collection, vol 1, ff.124–25, NASAP.

57 Diary of FS Malan, undated, A.583 FS Malan Collection, vol 23, pp 14–15, WCPA.

58 Botha was sufficiently confident not to keep the brigade in South Africa for the election that October. Unwisely, he had thought

he could afford to lose their votes. Hugh Wyndham to Lady Leconfield, 9 September 1915, PHA, WSRO.

59 Hew Strachan, *The First World War in Africa*, p 65.

60 Paul Halpern, *A Naval History of World War I* (United States Naval Institute, Annapolis, 1994). RK Massie, *Castles of Steel: Britain, Germany, and the winning of the Great War at sea* (Jonathan Cape, London, 2004).

61 Draft Government Notice, 18 October 1914, AG 1914–1921, Box 164, file 305/9199 Commander-in-Chief and Staff, SANDF Documentation Centre.

62 HF Trew, *Botha Treks*, p 64; Piet van der Byl, *From Playgrounds to Battlefields*, pp 140, 167–68; and Ian van der Waag, 'Smuts' generals: towards a first portrait of the South African High Command, 1912–1948', *War in History*, 18(1) 2011, p 45.

63 [HA Wyndham,] 'History of the German South West Campaign', pp 14–15.

64 KA Maxwell and JM Smith, *Aspera ad Astra, 1920–1970: South African Air Force Golden Jubilee Souvenir Book* (SAAF, Pretoria, 1970), p 12; and Report of Major Wallace, Officer Commanding South African Aviation Corps in the Campaign in German South West Africa 1915, 21 January 1916, AIR 1/1247/204/7/1, NAUK.

65 Botha to (Smuts?), 3 April 1915, Smuts Collection, Box 112, f.21, NASAP.

66 Report on a visit to German South West Africa by Maj Gen CW Thompson, March 1915, attached to Thompson to Smuts, 5 March 1915, Smuts Collection, Box 112, f.22, NASAP.

67 Farrar to Botha, 1 March 1915, Smuts Collection, Box 112, f.2, NASAP.

68 Farrar to Botha, 5 March 1915, Smuts Collection, Box 112, f.4, NASAP.

69 Farrar to Botha, 23 March 1915, Smuts Collection, Box 112, f.13, NASAP.

70 Defence to Lukin, 26 August 1914, and Disso to Defence, 26 August 1914, DC, Box 612, file A.138/9199 Feeding Troops while Travelling and Rations General, SANDF Documentation Centre.

71 OC Union Expeditionary Base to Quartermaster General, 13 October 1914, DC, Box 631, file 220/9199 Field Canteens established by SAGI; and Chebec to Defence, 24 September 1914, DC, Box 631, file 7/220/9199 SAGI copy of correspondence covering agreement on all points, SANDF Documentation Centre.

72 Piet van der Byl, *From Playgrounds to Battlefields*, p 152.

73 Report on the Work of Medical Department, March 1918, MD, box 111, file German South West Africa Campaign, SANDF Documentation Centre. AE van Jaarsveldt et al, *Militêre Geneeskunde in Suid-Afrika, 1913–1983* (Military Information Bureau, Pretoria, 1983), pp 169–173.

74 Ian van der Waag, 'Boer generalship and the politics of command', *War in History*, 12(1) 2005, pp 38, 43.

75 Brig Gen JJ Collyer, *The Campaign in German South West Africa*, p 165.

76 GG 586, file 9/51/52 War 1914–16: Trade. Exportation of certain forms of steel, NASAP. See also the rest of this series of files.

77 GG 667, file 9/93/1 War 1914: Imperial Army. Suggested recruiting of men in South Africa for enlistment in the 'New Army', NASAP. See also BC915 James Metcalfe Papers, A1 to A5, UCT.

78 John Buchan, *The History of the South African Forces in France*, p 15. See Dawid Graaff to Jan Smuts, 8 June 1915, and Smuts to Graaff, 14 June 1915, in WK Hancock and J van der Poel, eds, *Selections from the Smuts Papers, vol III*, pp 296, 298.

79 Smuts to Buxton, 21 June 1915, GG 667, file 9/93/7 War 1914–16: Imperial Army. South African Overseas Expeditionary Force, NASAP.

80 Smuts to Buxton, 24 June 1915, GG 667, file 9/93/7 War 1914–16: Imperial Army. South African Overseas Expeditionary Force, NASAP.

81 Lord Buxton to Jan Smuts, 9 July 1915, in WK Hancock and J van der Poel, eds, *Selections from the Smuts Papers, vol III*, p 303.

82 JX Merriman to J.C. Smuts, 6 September 1915, in WK Hancock and J van der Poel, eds, *Selections from the Smuts Papers, vol III*, p 311.

83 DP Graaff to JC Smuts, 8 June 1915, in WK Hancock and J van der Poel, eds, *Selections from the Smuts Papers, vol III*, p 296.

84 DP Graaff to JC Smuts, 8 June 1915, and, in particular, JX Merriman to JC Smuts, 6 August 1915, in WK Hancock and J van der Poel, eds, *Selections from the Smuts Papers, vol III*, pp 296, pp 307–8.

85 JC Smuts to JX Merriman, 30 August 1915, in WK Hancock and J van der Poel, eds, *Selections from the Smuts Papers, vol III*, p 310.

86 Bonar Law to Buxton, 8 November 1915, and Smuts to Buxton, 10 November 1915, GG 668, file 9/93/24 War 1914–15: Army, Imperial.

Overseas Expeditionary Force, NASAP.

87 Smuts to Buxton, 24 June 1915, and Smuts to Buxton, 19 July 1915, GG 667, file 9/93/7 War 1914–16: Imperial Army. South African Overseas Expeditionary Force, NASAP.

88 Smuts to Buxton, 14 July 1915, GG 667, file 9/93/7 War 1914–16: Imperial Army. South African Overseas Expeditionary Force, NASAP. It was also decided, to settle public uneasiness, to publish official correspondence relating to the raising and deployment of the South African contingents. See NASAP: GG 668, file 9/93/26.

89 'Fresh Call for Volunteers; Union's Second 'Little Bit'; Mostly Infantry Wanted; Details of Terms of Service', Rand Daily Mail, 21 July 1915; 'Heavy Artillery in Flanders; General Terms of Service', Rand Daily Mail, 22 July 1915; and 'Wanted in Europe; Call for Heavy Artillery, Opening for South Africans', Rand Daily Mail, 22 July 1915.

90 See the series of applications and expressions of interest in the series of files under reference DC 128/958/9199 and titled 'Applications for Overseas Contingent' in DC, Boxes 689, 690 and 691, SANDF Documentation Centre. At the first rumours, the town clerk of Grahamstown offered his 'commonage, both wooded and otherwise for a training ground' for the overseas contingent. Town Clerk, Grahamstown to Minister of Defence, 13 July 1915, DC, Box 690, file DC 128/958/9199 Applications for Overseas Contingent, SANDF Documentation Centre.

91 Louis Matthews to Nicholson, QMG's office, 25 November 1915, DC, Box 690, file DC 128/958/9199 Applications for Overseas Contingent, SANDF Documentation Centre.

92 Buchan has suggested that Botha, not wanting to 'denude the country of too many of her most loyal and vigilant citizens', could send no more than a brigade of infantry to Europe. John Buchan, The History of the South African Forces in France, p 14.

93 Bonar Law to Buxton, 24 July 1915, and Botha to Buxton, 10 August 1915, GG 667, file 9/93/7 War 1914–16: Imperial Army. South African Overseas Expeditionary Force, NASAP.

94 The infantrymen would each carry a rifle MLE with oil bottle, pull-through and sight protector, sword bayonet, pattern '88 with scabbard, and 200 rounds of Mark VI ammunition per rifle. See Botha to Buxton, 19 August 1915, GG 667, file 9/93/7 War 1914–16: Imperial Army. South African Overseas Expeditionary Force, NASAP.

95 Bonar Law to Buxton, 17 July 1915, GG 667, file 9/93/7 War 1914–16: Imperial Army. South African Overseas Expeditionary Force, NASAP.

96 John Buchan, The History of the South African Forces in France, p 16.

97 Ian Uys, Rollcall: the Delville Wood story (Uys Publishers, Johannesburg 1991), p 5.

98 John Buchan, The History of the South African Forces in France, p 15.

99 Lukin, in addition to his colonial experience, had enhanced his reputation in South West Africa in 1915 and then in Egypt in early 1916. Even De Burger, a strongly nationalist paper, broadcast Lukin's success. See, for example, 'In Egypte; Generaal Lukins Kolonne; De vijand op de vlucht'. De Burger, 29 February 1916.

100 Field Marshal Douglas Haig to The Secretary, War Office, 20 March 1918, WO 374/43230, National Archives, Kew, London (TNA).

101 Dictionary of South African Biography, vols 1–5.

102 Ross Anderson, The Battle of Tanga 1914 (Tempus, Stroud, 2002), p 127.

103 Ross Anderson, The Forgotten Front: the East African campaign, 1914–1918 (Tempus, Stroud, 2004), p 297.

104 Brig Gen JJ Collyer, The South Africans with General Smuts in German East Africa, 1916 (Government Printer, Pretoria, 1939), p 50.

105 History of 26 (South Africa) Squadron, RAF, AIR 1/690/21/20/26, TNA.

106 Brig Gen JJ Collyer, The South Africans with General Smuts in German East Africa, 1916, p 217.

107 Brig Gen JJ Collyer, The South Africans with General Smuts in German East Africa, 1916, p 277.

108 Brig Gen JJ Collyer, The South Africans with General Smuts in German East Africa, 1916, p 277.

109 LR Simes, 'The Three Campaigns First World War: West and East Africa and Overseas', Trooper Lyle Richmond Simes Collection, Natal Carbineers Archives, Pietermaritzburg.

110 Piet van der Byl, From Playgrounds to Battlefields, p 199.

111 William McPherson and Thomas J Mitchell, eds, History of the Great War, Medical Services General History, vol IV (HMSO, London, 1924).

112 WB Cohen, 'Malaria and French Imperialism', Journal of African History, 24 (1983), pp 23–36.

113 Hew Strachan, The First World War in Africa, p 131 passim.

114 Piet van der Byl, *From Playgrounds to Battlefields*, p 200.

115 JX Merriman to Lord Buxton, 5 December 1916, in P Lewsen, ed, *Selections from the Correspondence of JX Merriman 1905–1924*, pp 285–86.

116 Evelyn Crowe to Sir Louis Mallet, 6 January 1914, FO 195/2456, TNA. CAB 44/14, TNA.

117 Anon, *The Union of South Africa and the Great War*, pp 95–96.

118 The Senussi in the Western Desert, FO 371/2665, TNA. John Buchan, *The History of the South African Forces in France*, chapter 2: 'The campaign in Western Egypt'. Richard Cornwell, 'The Sanusi Campaign: Egypt, 1916', in Richard Bouch, ed, *Infantry in South Africa, 1652–1976* (Documentation Service SADF, Pretoria, 1977), pp 84–99.

119 Basil Liddell Hart, *History of the First World War* (Macmillan, London, 1997), p 247.

120 FJ Jacobs and JA Visser, 'Die Suid-Afrikaanse Artillerie tydens die Eerste Wêreldoorlog: die veldtog in Oos-Afrika en die Midde-Ooste, 1917–1918', in CJ Nöthling, ed, *Ultima Ratio Regum: artillery history of South Africa* (Military Information Bureau SADF, Pretoria, 1987), pp 109–114.

121 Ian Gleeson, *The Unknown Force: black, Indian and coloured soldiers through two world wars* (Ashanti, Rivonia, 1994), p 85.

122 ID Difford, *The Story of the 1st Cape Corps* (Hortors, Cape Town, 1920), p 253.

123 Ian Gleeson, *The Unknown Force*, p 92.

124 Jean Bou, *Australia's Palestine Campaign* (Army History Unit, Canberra, 2010), pp 6–7.

125 Lieutenant General Sir Archibald P Wavell, *The Palestine Campaigns* (Constable, London, 1941), pp 174–77.

126 Speech made by General Cavendish at a meeting of the St John's Ambulance on 2 November 1917, DC, Box 1142, file DCDB 2394/7 Suggested recall of Brigadier General Cavendish GOC South African Military Command and appointment of General Martyn, SANDF Documentation Centre.

127 Hew Strachan, *European Armies and the Conduct of War* (Routledge, London and New York, 1993), chapter 9. Tim Travers, *The Killing Ground: the British Army, the Western Front, and the emergence of modern warfare, 1900–1918* (Allen and Unwin, London, 1987) and *How the War Was Won: command and technology in the British Army on the Western Front, 1917–1918* (Routledge, London, 1992).

128 William Carter to Algernon Lawley, 19 March 1915, AB186 Archbishop Carter Letters, Wits.

129 Lt Cyril Newton-Thompson to Joyce Nettelfold, 7 July 1916, BC643 Joyce Newton-Thompson Collection, B1.43, UCT.

130 Hugh Wyndham to Lady Leconfield, 21 June 1916, PHA, WSRO.

131 NG Garson, 'South Africa and World War One', p 69.

132 Hugh Wyndham to Lady Leconfield, 21 July 1916, PHA, WSRO.

133 Diary, 20–22 April 1916, A20 Col HWM Bamford Collection, vol 1, NASAP.

134 Diary, 23 April 1916, A20 Col HWM Bamford Collection, vol 1, NASAP.

135 War diary, 11 June 1916, WW1 GSWA, box 128, war diary of 1st SA Brigade, SANDF Documentation Centre. See also 'Programme of Battalion Training', June 1916, WW1 Diverse, box 20, SANDF Documentation Centre. See also, Diary, 24 April–16 May 1916, A20 Col HWM Bamford Collection, vol 1, NASAP.

136 Diary, 20–23 May 1916, A20 Col HWM Bamford Collection, vol 1, NASAP.

137 Diary, 23 May 1916, A20 Col HWM Bamford Collection, vol 1, NASAP.

138 Diary, 28 May 1916, 30 June 1916, A20 Col HWM Bamford Collection, vol 1, NASAP.

139 PKA Digby, *Pyramids and Poppies: The 1st SA infantry Brigade in Libya, France and Flanders, 1915–1919* (Ashanti, Rivonia, 1993), p 112.

140 ES Smith, 'Die Geneeskundige Diens in die Eerste Wêreldoorlog: die oorlogsfront in Europa, 1915–1918', in AE van Jaarsveldt et al, *Militêre Geneeskunde in Suid-Afrika, 1913–1983*, p 22.

141 ES Smith, 'Die Geneeskundige Diens in die Eerste Wêreldoorlog', pp 23–24.

142 Quartermaster General to Chief Ordnance Officer, 24 August 1915, DC, Box 689, file 958/9199 Overseas Contingent. The nominal rolls are on DC 694, file A6/978/9199 General Hospitals for Europe 'Overseas Contingent', SANDF Documentation Centre.

143 Diary, Thursday 13 July 1916, A164 Sergeant Major Alex J Knox Collection, NASAP.

144 Diary, Thursday 13 July 1916, A164 Sergeant Major AJ Knox Collection, NASAP. See also the first sketch in the sketchbook of Captain WL Gordon, BC1096 William Lennox Gordon Collection, C1, UCT.

145 Diary, Saturday 15 July 1916, A164 Sergeant Major AJ Knox Collection, NASAP.

146 Diary, Sunday 16 July 1916, A164 Sergeant Major AJ Knox Collection, NASAP.

147 ES Smith, 'Die Geneeskundige Diens in die

Eerste Wêreldoorlog', p 24.

148 The Somme war diaries of the siege batteries are in WO 95/542, NAUK and WW1 Diverse, box 20, SANDF Documentation Centre.

149 'History of the 72nd Siege Battery, RGA', 1–4, WW1 Diverse, box 20, SANDF Documentation Centre.

150 Ernest Lane to Smuts, 25 November 1915, in WK Hancock and J van der Poel, eds, *Selections from the Smuts Papers, vol III*, pp 321–24.

151 '73rd Siege Battery, SA Heavy Artillery', WW1 Diverse, box 20, SANDF Documentation Centre.

152 '73rd Siege Battery, SA Heavy Artillery', WW1 Diverse, box 20, SANDF Documentation Centre.

153 Tactical news could be passed by word of mouth within the sector. However, for news of a more strategic nature and certainly pertaining to the whole front, soldiers had 'to wait for a home paper to find out what's going on'. NW Nichol to Capt T Purland, 26 October 1916, BC477 Purland Family Collection, UCT.

154 Diary, 1 July 1916, A20 Col HWM Bamford Collection, vol 1, NASAP.

155 Diary, 1 July 1916, A20 Col HWM Bamford Collection, vol 1, NASAP.

156 Diary, 1 July 1916, A20 Col HWM Bamford Collection, vol 1, NASAP.

157 Maud Wyndham to Lady Leconfield, 1 July 1916, PHA, WSRO.

158 J Ewing, *The History of the 9th (Scottish) Division* (John Murray, London, 1921), p 121.

159 PKA Digby, *Pyramids and Poppies*, pp 112–38. See also Ian Uys, *Rollcall*.

160 ES Smith, 'Die Geneeskundige Diens in die Eerste Wêreldoorlog', pp 24–25.

161 Diary, Tuesday 18 July 1916, A164 Sergeant Major AJ Knox Collection, NASAP.

162 Diary, Monday 24 July 1916, A164 Sergeant Major AJ Knox Collection, NASAP.

163 Diary, Monday 24 July 1916, A164 Sergeant Major AJ Knox Collection, NASAP.

164 Diary, Monday 24 July 1916, A164 Sergeant Major AJ Knox Collection, NASAP.

165 Diary, Sunday 23 July 1916, A164 Sergeant Major AJ Knox Collection, NASAP.

166 Diary, Tuesday 25 July 1916, A164 Sergeant Major AJ Knox Collection, NASAP.

167 Diary, Tuesday 25 July 1916, A164 Sergeant Major AJ Knox Collection, NASAP.

168 John Buchan, *The History of the South African Forces in France*, p 74.

169 Gordon to his mother, 16 August 1916, BC1096 Major WL Gordon Collection, B1, UCT.

170 EB Jamieson to Gordon, 14 June 1916, BC1096 Major WL Gordon Collection, B2, UCT.

171 Humphrey Wyndham to Mary Maxse, 7 July 1916, Maxse Papers 455, WSRO.

172 *De Burger*, 17 July 1916.

173 Maud Wyndham to Lady Leconfield, 9 July 1916, PHA, WSRO.

174 Maud Wyndham to Lady Leconfield, 22 October 1916, PHA, WSRO.

175 Maud Wyndham to Lady Leconfield, 15 July 1916, PHA, WSRO.

176 Maud Wyndham to Lady Leconfield, 1 July 1916, PHA, WSRO.

177 Maud Wyndham to Lady Leconfield, 15 July 1916, PHA, WSRO.

178 Buxton to Bonar Law, 21 August 1916, GG 671, file 9/93/68 Recruiting SA Brigade Overseas, NASAP.

179 Bonar Law to Buxton, 4 July 1916, GG 671, file 9/93/68 Recruiting SA Brigade Overseas, NASAP.

180 Buxton to Bonar Law, 10 July 1916, GG 671, file 9/93/68 Recruiting SA Brigade Overseas, NASAP.

181 Bonar Law to Buxton, 4 August 1916, GG 671, file 9/93/68 Recruiting SA Brigade Overseas, NASAP.

182 Bourne to Horsfall, 5 August 1916, GG 671, file 9/93/68 Recruiting SA Brigade Overseas, NASAP.

183 Buxton to Botha, 12 August 1916, GG 671, file 9/93/68 Recruiting SA Brigade Overseas, NASAP.

184 As quoted by the Governor General in Buxton to Bonar Law, 21 August 1916, GG 671, file 9/93/68 Recruiting SA Brigade Overseas, NASAP.

185 Buxton to Bonar Law, 21 August 1916, GG 671, file 9/93/68 Recruiting SA Brigade Overseas, NASAP. See also Minutes of a meeting of the Imperial War Cabinet, 30 March 1917, CAB 23/40, 6(9), TNA.

186 GG 668, file 9/93/36 War 1914–16: Army, Imperial. Union Overseas Contingent: protests against failure of Government to make up pay to Defence Force rates, NASAP. See also NG Garson, 'South Africa and World War One'.

187 Ministers Minute 1426, 30 September 1916, GG 671, file 9/93/68 Recruiting SA Brigade Overseas, NASAP.

188 Colonel RC Grant, Camp Commandant, to Director of War Recruiting, 27 October 1917, AG 1914–1921, box 189, file 489 Coloured men

in Overseas Brigade, SANDF Documentation Centre.

189 Smuts to Defence Pretoria, 6 September 1917, AG 1914–1921, box 189, file 489 Coloured men in Overseas Brigade, SANDF Documentation Centre.

190 Col RH Price, Director of War Recruiting, to Chief of the General Staff, 25 September 1917, AG 1914–1921, box 189, file 489 Coloured men in Overseas Brigade, SANDF Documentation Centre.

191 Anon, *The Union of South Africa and the Great War*, p 218.

192 Albert Grundlingh, *Fighting Their Own War*, pp 43–46. See also BP Willan, 'The South African Native Labour Contingent, 1916–1918', *Journal of African History*, 19(1), 1978, pp 61–86.

193 'Wail of the Native Widows', *Abantu-Batho*, 14 January 1918, as quoted in Albert Grundlingh, 'Mutating memories and the making of a myth: remembering the SS *Mendi* disaster, 1917–2007', *South African Historical Journal*, 63(1), 2011, p 21.

194 Albert Grundlingh, 'Mutating memories and the making of a myth', p 28 *passim*.

195 'Union's Roll of Honour. Deathless Deeds at Delville Wood. Musical Memorial Service in the City Hall. Mr Merriman on South Africa's Heritage', *Cape Times*, 19 July 1917, p 6. See also Programme, Delville Wood Day, PM 1/1/48, file 4/84/1917 European War, SA Brigade, Successes, NASAP.

196 'Union's Roll of Honour. Deathless Deeds at Delville Wood. Musical Memorial Service in the City Hall. Mr Merriman on South Africa's Heritage', *Cape Times*, 19 July 1917, p 6.

197 Major General William Furse, commander of the 9th (Scottish) Division, described the events around Longueval as 'one of the greatest battles in the world's history', while Rawlinson, his immediate superior, declared that 'with the capture of Delville Wood, the gallantry, perseverance and determination of the South African Brigade deserves the highest commendation'. Circular from Major General W Furse to his brigade commanders, 21 July 1916, and General H Rawlinson to Furse, 25 July 1916, WO1DA, box 5, War Diary of SA Inf Bde HQ, July 1916, SANDF Documentation Centre.

198 G Mills and D Williams, *Seven Battles that Shaped South Africa* (Tafelberg, Cape Town, 2006).

199 Of the South African aviators flying with the RFC, Andrew Beauchamp Proctor is best

known. See his interesting letter to 'Dear Sir', 29 May 1920, BCS115 Andrew Beauchamp Proctor Papers, UCT.

200 John Buchan, *The History of the South African Forces in France*, p 11.

201 John Buchan, *The History of the South African Forces in France*; Anon, *The Union of South Africa and the Great War*; Ian Uys, *Rollcall*; P Digby, *Pyramids and Poppies*. N Clothier, *Black Valour* (Pietermaritzburg, 1987) and Ian Gleeson, *The Unknown Force* explore, *inter alia*, the story of the SANLC in France.

202 Bill Nasson, 'A great divide'; Nasson, 'War opinion in South Africa, 1914'; and Nasson, 'Delville Wood and South African Great War Commemoration', *English Historical Review*, 69(480), February 2004.

203 Piet van der Byl, *From Playgrounds to Battlefields*, pp 266–67.

204 Archives of the Secretary for Defence (DC), Box 1152, file DB 2443/Z Union War Expenditure, Department of Defence Archives, SANDF Documentation Centre, Pretoria.

205 *The Nongqai* was the official periodical of the armed forces of South Africa. It became *Kommando* in the 1950s, *Paratus* in the 1970s, *Salut* in 1993, and is now *SA Soldier*.

206 WM Bisset, 'South Africa's role in the civil war in Russia, 1918–1920', *Militaria*, 15(4), 1985, pp 46–48. See also Col Sir Hugh Bousted, *The Wind of Morning* (London, 1971), 47–52; Maj Gen Sir KR van der Spuy, *Chasing the Wind* (Books of Africa, Cape Town, 1966), p 112; 'From the Arctic Circle', *The Nongqai*, November 1918, p 502; and 'Russia in Revolution', *The Nongqai*, May 1920, pp 233–34.

207 Lt Cyril Newton-Thompson to Joyce Nettelfold, 21 July 1916, BC643 Joyce Newton-Thompson Collection, B1.53, University of Cape Town Libraries, Archives and Manuscripts (UCT).

208 Lt Cyril Newton-Thompson to Joyce Nettelfold, 21 July 1916, BC643 Joyce Newton-Thompson Collection, B1.53, UCT.

209 Emily Hobhouse to Smuts, 8 August 1914, in WK Hancock and J van der Poel, eds, *Selections from the Smuts Papers, vol III*, p 186. This idea still has currency in South Africa. See, for example, Greg Mills, 'Canon fodder for man's first mechanised mass murder', *The Sunday Independent*, 13 February 2005, p 17: 'They were brave, but the war itself was a costly folly and the political leaders who caused it were callous and inept.'

210 NW Nichol to Capt T Purland, 1 August 1917, BC477 Purland Family Collection, UCT.

211 Circular from Maj Gen W Furse, 9th (Scottish) Division, to brigade commanders, 21 July 1916, WO1DA, box 5, war diary South African Infantry Brigade Headquarters, July 1916, SANDF Documentation Centre, Pretoria.

212 Brig Gen HT Lukin to Maj Gen W Furse, 3 August 1916, WO1DA, box 5, war diary South African Infantry Brigade Headquarters, July 1916, SANDF Documentation Centre, Pretoria. This has been quoted at length by Ian Uys in *Rollcall*.

213 *Abridged Annual Report of the Department of Defence for the Year ended 30 June 1921* (Government Printer, Pretoria, 1922), p 1.

CHAPTER FOUR
The Inter-war Years, 1919–1939

1 FC Erasmus, 'Die Agtergrond van Ons Verdedigingsbeleid', Dr DF Malan Collection, 1/1/2355, Special Collections, JS Gericke Library, Stellenbosch University (SU).

2 Diary, vol 10, 1 August 1919, A608 HES Fremantle Collection, Western Cape Provincial Archives and Records Centre (WCPA).

3 British Parliamentary Papers (BPP): Cmd 153 – 1919. Treaty of Peace between The Allied and Associated Powers and Germany. Signed at Versailles, 28 June 1919.

4 Lieut Gen Sir Giffard Martel, *East Versus West* (London, Museum Press, 1952), p 23.

5 Brig Gen HT Lukin to Maj Gen W Furse, 3 August 1916, WO1DA, box 5, war diary South African Infantry Brigade Headquarters, July 1916, SANDF Documentation Centre, Pretoria. This has been quoted at length by Ian Uys in *Rollcall: the Delville Wood story* (Uys Publishers, Johannesburg, 1991).

6 In 1921 'UDF Infantry Training, Part I (Drill) and Part II (Field Operations'; 'UDF Field Artillery Training'; 'UDF Musketry Regulations'; a revision of 'Mounted Riflemen Training'; 'Tactical Notes for Officers'; and 'Notes on Field Sanitation' were in the process of preparation.

7 JAI Agar-Hamilton, 'The Union of South Africa War Histories', in Robin Higham, ed, *Official Histories: essays and bibliographies from around the world* (Kansas State University Library, Manhattan, KS, 1970), p 443.

8 Ian van der Waag, 'Contested histories: official history and the South African military in the 20th century', in J Grey, ed, *The Last Word? Essays on Official History in the United States and British Commonwealth* (Praeger, Westport, CT, 2003), pp 27–52.

9 Brig Gen JJ Collyer, *The Campaign in German South West Africa, 1914–1915* (Government Printer, Pretoria, 1937) and *The South Africans with General Smuts in German East Africa, 1916* (Government Printer, Pretoria, 1939).

10 The Smuts and Hertzog premierships are treated in DW Krüger, *The Age of the Generals: a short political history of the Union of South Africa, 1910–1948* (Dagbreek, n/p, 1958) and GD Scholtz, *Hertzog en Smuts en die Britse Ryk* (Raandse Afrikaanse Universiteit, Johannesburg, 1975), a study that has unfortunately not found publication in English. The South African military during the interwar period has been addressed in I van der Waag, 'The Union Defence Force Between the Two World Wars, 1919–1940', *Scientia Militaria*, 30(2) 2000, pp 183–219.

11 The repercussions of industrialised warfare have been addressed by AR Millett and W Murray, eds, *Military Effectiveness, vol 1: The First World War* (Allen & Unwin, Boston, 1988); T Travers, *The Killing Ground: the British Army, the Western Front, and the emergence of modern warfare, 1900–1918* (Allen & Unwin, London, 1987) and *How the War Was Won: command and technology in the British Army on the Western Front, 1917–1918* (Routledge London 1992); A Ashworth, *Trench Warfare, 1914–1918: the live and let live system* (Macmillan, London 1980); and others.

12 Smuts to Wolstenholme, 29 November 1915, in WK Hancock and J van der Poel, eds, *Selections from the Smuts Papers, vol III: June 1910–November 1918* (Cambridge University Press, Cambridge, 1966), pp 324–25.

13 John Buchan, *The History of the South African Forces in France* (London, 1920; reprinted Battery Press, Nashville, 1992), p 260.

14 Merriman's speech quoted in 'Union's Roll of Honour. Deathless Deeds at Delville Wood. Musical Memorial Service in the City Hall. Mr Merriman on South Africa's Heritage', *Cape Times*, 19 July 1917, p 6.

15 Memorandum G.S.1/34285 Brief summary of reports received approximately within the last two months, on different districts relating to native unrest, DC, Box 356, DC40057 Intelligence Section, SANDF Documentation Centre, Pretoria.

16 Leipoldt to the Adjutant General, 22 December 1917, DC, Box 356, DC40057 Intelligence Section, SANDF Documentation Centre, Pretoria.

17 Leipoldt to Chief of the General Staff, 11 November 1921, CGS, Box 356, file 13/40057 Intelligence Service Scheme of Organization, SANDF Documentation Centre, Pretoria.

18 South African Defence Policy by CGS, 20 September 1933, CGS, Group 2, Box 53, file 96 Re-organization UDF, SANDF Documentation Centre, Pretoria.

19 See, for example, Fremantle to Hertzog, 12 November 1923, A608 Fremantle Collection, vol 14, WCPA.

20 Information extracted from War Office, Admiralty and RAF files by Capt FH Theron in September 1929 and report on 'Belgian Military Forces in Congo; Extract from Report of Colonial Ministry', DCS, Box 3, file SP 9 Capt Theron's attachment to War Office, SANDF Documentation Centre, Pretoria.

21 Donald Cowie, 'Union of South Africa', Journal of the Royal United Service Institution, 84, 1939, pp 262–63.

22 FW Perry, The Commonwealth Armies: manpower and organisation in two world wars (Manchester University Press, 1990), pp 191–92.

23 DC, Box 254, file 17767 Disbandment of Temporary Citizen Force Units and disposal of temporary officers, SANDF Documentation Centre, Pretoria.

24 N Orpen and HJ Martin, Salute the Sappers, I: the formation of the South African Engineer Corps and its operations in East Africa and the Middle East to the Battle of Alamein (Sappers Association, Johannesburg, 1981), p 8.

25 Director Medical Services to Secretary for Defence, 31 July 1919, DC, Box 1411, file 70038 Reorganisation of the Department (Medical Section), SANDF Documentation Centre, Pretoria.

26 DC, Box 412, file 50913 Police Force for the Protectorate SWA, Disposal of the Military Constabulary, SANDF Documentation Centre, Pretoria; and Proclamation 21, Official Gazette of the Protectorate of South-West Africa in Military Occupation of the Union Forces (No 25 of 24 December 1919).

27 Ian van der Waag, 'The origin and establishment of the South African Engineer Corps (SAEC), 1918–1939', Journal for Contemporary History, 37(2), 2012, pp 1–31.

28 Secretary for Defence to Headquarters, SA Military Command, 28 September 1921, DC, Box 886, file Q.23892 Transfer South African Military Command to Union Defence, SANDF Documentation Centre, Pretoria.

29 Report on the Cantonments Roberts Heights and Artillery Barracks, Pretoria, Archives of the Adjutant General (AG) 3, Box 97, file 213/22 Establishments SAEC (Maintenance Sections), SANDF Documentation Centre, Pretoria; and Quartermaster General to Adjutant General, 26 July 1922, file 212/23 Establishment Tables SA Engineer Corps Permanent (Fortress Engineer and Signal Sections).

30 DC, Box 1025, files DF 4/573 Native Disturbances Natal 1919; DF 5/573 Native Trouble at Rustenburg; and DF 6/573 Industrial and Native Unrest in the Transvaal, SANDF Documentation Centre, Pretoria.

31 Christopher Andrew and Vasili Mitrokhin, The Mitrokhin Archive II: the KGB and the world (Allen Lane, London, 2005), pp 4, 504; Christopher Andrew, The Defence of the Realm: the authorized history of MI5 (Allen Lane, London, 2009), pp 455–56.

32 K Grundy, Soldiers Without Politics: blacks in the South African armed forces (University of California Press, Berkeley and Los Angeles, 1983), pp 48 et seq.; and L Thompson, A History of South Africa (Yale University Press, New Haven and London, 1990), pp 170–172.

33 Superintendent of Natives to Magistrate Queenstown 23 August 1920, DC, Box 451, file 52002 Recalcitrant 'Israelite' Natives, SANDF Documentation Centre, Pretoria.

34 Brig Gen JL van Deventer to Chief of the General Staff, 7 June 1921, DC, Box 451, file 52002 Recalcitrant 'Israelite' Natives, SANDF Documentation Centre, Pretoria.

35 DC, Box 1025, file DF 7/573 Native Unrest Queenstown (Israelites) Medical Services, SANDF Documentation Centre, Pretoria.

36 Secretary for Defence to Secretary for Finance, 25 August 1921, DC, Box 451, file 52002 Recalcitrant 'Israelite' Natives, SANDF Documentation Centre, Pretoria.

37 Chief of the General Staff to Financial Under Secretary, 18 October 1920, DC, Box 378, file 40309 Reorganisation Artillery, SANDF Documentation Centre, Pretoria.

38 Issued under Section 79 of the South Africa Defence Act (13 of 1912).

39 Information extracted from War Office, Admiralty and Air Force files by Capt FH Theron during his attachment – Sept 1929; and Report on 'Belgian Military Forces in Congo; Extract from Report of Colonial Ministry.' Archives of the Deputy Chief of Staff (DCS),

Box 3, file SP 9 Capt Theron's attachment to War Office, SANDF Documentation Centre, Pretoria.

40 Abridged Annual Report of the Department of Defence, Union of South Africa, for the Year ended 30 June 1923 (Government Printer, Pretoria, 1924), p 13.

41 South African Defence Policy by CGS, 20 September 1933, archives of the Chief of the General Staff (CGS) Group 2, Box 53, file 96 Reorganisation UDF, vol II, SANDF Documentation Centre, Pretoria.

42 AH Marais, red, *Politieke Briewe, 1911–1912* (Tafelberg, Kaapstad en Johannesburg, 1973), pp 99–106.

43 Chief of the General Staff to Minister of Defence, 19 May 1921, and appendices, CGS Gp 1, Box 12, file 22 Union Force for Overseas, SANDF Documentation Centre, Pretoria.

44 M Kitchen, *The British Empire and Commonwealth: a short history* (Macmillan, Basingstoke and London, 1996), p 59.

45 Abridged Annual Report of the Department of Defence for the Year ended 30 June 1921 (Government Printer, Pretoria, 1922), p 4.

46 AM Pollock, *Pienaar of Alamein: the life story of a great South African soldier* (*Cape Times*, Cape Town, 1943), pp 15–20.

47 C Birkby, *Uncle George: the Boer boyhood, letters and battles of Lieutenant-General George Edwin Brink* (Jonathan Ball, Johannesburg, 1987), pp 65–66.

48 C Birkby, *Uncle George*, pp 71–72, 87–91.

49 Prime Ministers' Conference in London 1921, DC, Box 1929, file 335/1 Imperial Conferences, SANDF Documentation Centre, Pretoria; and 'The Empire Conference', *Cape Times*, 21 April 1921.

50 Report of a Committee appointed to make recommendations as to a training ship for preparing South African boys for a seafaring career, 19 November 1920, DC, Box 518, file 52561 SA Naval Services Training Ship General Botha, SANDF Documentation Centre, Pretoria.

51 Chief of the General Staff to Minister of Defence, 19 June 1922, CGS Gp 2, Box 311, file 437/2 SA Defence Act Amendment Act 1922 Reconstitution of Permanent Force, SANDF Documentation Centre, Pretoria.

52 DC, Box 1098, file 4/58X South African Naval History, SANDF Documentation Centre, Pretoria.

53 Major JGW Leipoldt to Chief of the General Staff, 11 November 1921, CGS Gp 1, Box 356, file 13/40057 Intelligence Service Scheme of

Organisation, SANDF Documentation Centre, Pretoria.

54 Government Notice No 17 of 1923 (*Supplement of the Union of South Africa Government Gazette* No 1289 of 26 January 1923), published in terms of section one of the South Africa Defence Act Amendment Act (22 of 1922).

55 As quoted by Michael Armitage, *The Royal Air Force: an illustrated history* (Brockhampton, London, 1996), p 27.

56 High Commissioner for United Kingdom, Pretoria to Secretary of State, London, 17 July 1935, DO119/1052, TNA.

57 M Armitage, *The Royal Air Force*, pp 50–51.

58 R Pound, *Evans of the Broke: a biography of Admiral Lord Mountevans* (OUP, London, 1963), p 225.

59 B Bond, 'The Army between the Two World Wars 1918–1939', in D Chandler and I Beckett, eds, *The Oxford History of the British Army* (OUP, Oxford and New York, 1996), p 257.

60 Sir Roland Bourne to Air Vice Marshal Higgins, 7 July 1921, DC, Box 1104, file R.B.1/040 Organisation of the Air Forces of the Self-Governing Dominions, SANDF Documentation Centre, Pretoria.

61 Chief of the General Staff to Chief of the Imperial General Staff, 28 March 1923, CGS Gp 1, Box 47, file 71 Intelligence Contré Espionage (MI5), SANDF Documentation Centre, Pretoria.

62 DC, Box 432, file 51848 Topographical Survey of Africa, SANDF Documentation Centre, Pretoria.

63 DC, Box 518, file 7/14/52561 Operations of HMSAS Protea, SANDF Documentation Centre, Pretoria. SAS Protea, SANDF Documentation Centre, Pretoria.

64 Minister of Agriculture to Administrator of Rhodesia, 6 June 1921, DC, Box 567, file 70054 Major Leipoldt's Expedition, SANDF Documentation Centre, Pretoria.

65 Commanding officers of 1st, 2nd and 3rd Permanent Batteries, SAMR to OC Troops, Roberts Heights, 3 April 1922, archives of the Officer Commanding, Northern Transvaal Command (N Tvl Comd) Gp 1, Box 23, file C/1 Formation of Artillery Brigade Headquarters, SANDF Documentation Centre, Pretoria.

66 OC Troops to Chief of the General Staff, 7 April 1922, N Tvl Comd, Box 23, file C/1 Formation of Artillery Brigade Headquarters, SANDF Documentation Centre, Pretoria.

67 Magistrate Springbok to the Provost Marshal, 15 February 1917, PMC5 Rebels, SANDF Documentation Centre.

68 Various correspondence and Colonel van Ryneveld's Report 'Air Operations Bondelzwart Revolt', CGS Gp 1, Box 12, file 23 SW Africa Native disturbance at Kalkfontein May 1922 Bondelzwart rebellion, SANDF Documentation Centre, Pretoria.

69 FJ Jacobs, 'Tussen twee wêreldoorloë', in RJ Bouch, ed, *Infantry in South Africa, 1652–1976* (Documentation Service SADF, Pretoria, 1977), p 127.

70 IJ van der Waag, 'South Africa and the war in Asia Minor, 1920–1923', *Militaria*, 24(1) 1994, pp 9–19.

71 I Jennings, *The British Commonwealth of Nations* (Hutchinson, London, 1956), p 133, as quoted by DO Rhoodie, *Suid-Afrika: van koloniale onderhorigheid tot soewereine onafhanklikheid* (Perskor, Johannesburg, 1974), p 110.

72 DO Rhoodie, *Suid-Afrika*, p 110.

73 Appendix 'D' memorandum on Estimated Manpower available in the Union for military operations Overseas, CGS Gp 1, Box 12, file 12 Union Force for Overseas, SANDF Documentation Centre, Pretoria.

74 Report by Chief of the General Staff, 19 September 1922, Diverse, Box 60, file 'War in Asia Minor', SANDF Documentation Centre, Pretoria.

75 IJ van der Waag, 'South Africa and the war in Asia Minor, 1921–1923', pp 9–19.

76 'Dr Malan en die Dardanelle', *Volkstem*, 2 September 1922.

77 'Geen man en geen pennie; Ons leier oor die wereld-krises', *Ons Vaderland*, 22 September 1922.

78 Telegram Troopers London to Defence Pretoria, 23 April 1919, World War I archive, Imperial Service Details group, Box 32, file 715/8/1 Men for Service in Russia, SANDF Documentation Centre, Pretoria.

79 BPP, Cmd 1987–1923 Imperial Conference, 1923. Summary of Proceedings, p 4.

80 BPP, Cmd 1990–1923 Imperial Economic Conference, 1923. Summary of Conclusions, p 11.

81 BPP, Cmd 1987–1923 Imperial Conference, 1923. Summary of Proceedings, pp 16–17.

82 Field Marshal Lord Carver, *The Apostles of Mobility: the theory and practice of armoured warfare* (Holmes & Meier, New York, 1979), pp 38, 48.

83 DC, Box 1910, file DC 251/6 Records Defence Department Destruction of Valueless Records, SANDF Documentation Centre, Pretoria.

84 Abridged Annual Report of the Department of Defence for the Year ended 30 June 1925 (Government Printer, Pretoria, 1926), par 10.

85 DC, Box 559, file DC 6/57205 O.C. Field Force Roberts Heights, SANDF Documentation Centre, Pretoria.

86 Financial Branch circular DF 9/573, 21 April 1925, DC, Box 1026, file DF 573/9 Rehoboth Disturbances 1925, SANDF Documentation Centre, Pretoria.

87 B Bond, 'The Army between the Two World Wars 1918–1939', pp 261–62; Jeffrey Grey, *A Military History of Australia* (Cambridge University Press, Melbourne, 2008), p 125.

88 Chief of the General Staff to Minister of Defence, 26 July 1926, CGS Gp 1, Box 12, file 22 Union Force for Overseas, SANDF Documentation Centre, Pretoria.

89 FC Erasmus, quoted in the *Debates of the House of Assembly*, 7 September 1938, col 2307.

90 Chief of the General Staff to Officer Commanding No 1 Military District, 12 August 1927, CGS Gp 2, Box 141, file CGS 242 Chap 1 Formation of the Engineer Corps General, SANDF Documentation Centre, Pretoria.

91 Annual Report of the Department of Defence for the Year ended 30 June 1926 (Government Printer, Pretoria, 1927), pp 12–17.

92 Annual Report of the Department of Defence for the Year ended 30 June 1932 (Government Printer, Pretoria 1933), p 1.

93 DC, Box 1026, file DF 573/10 Ovamboland Unrest, The Ipumbu Expedition, SANDF Documentation Centre, Pretoria.

94 W Otto, *Die Spesiale Diensbataljon* (Staatsdrukker, Pretoria 1973), pp 9–10.

95 Archives of the General Officer Commanding, Union Defence Forces (hereinafter GOC), Box 15, file GOC 60 Pioneer Battalion, SANDF Documentation Centre, Pretoria.

96 Oswald Pirow, *James Barry Munnik Hertzog* (Howard Timmins, Cape Town, 1957), p 220.

97 GOC, Box 15, file GOC 60 Pioneer Battalion, SANDF Documentation Centre, Pretoria.

98 Chief of the General Staff to Colonel Sir Vernon Kell, 26 August 1926, and MI5 to Chief of the General Staff, 25 September 1926, CGS Gp 1, Box 47, file 71 Intelligence Contré Espionage (MI5), SANDF Documentation Centre, Pretoria.

99 J Crwys-Williams, *A Country at War, 1939–1945: the mood of a nation* (Ashanti, Rivonia, 1992), p xix.

100 C Birkby, *Uncle George*, pp 65, 71.

101 P Liesching to Harding, 18 July 1934, CAB 63/69, TNA.

102 Sir Maurice Hankey to Ramsay Macdonald,

7 September 1934, CAB 63/69, TNA.

103 GOC UDF, Box 15, file GOC 52/4 Grant of assistance to Royal Navy.

104 Warwick Dorning, 'SA Forces in the Second World War', *Militaria*, 19(3) 1989, p 39. 'For the Junkers planes, fitted with American engines that were imported as a standard type for the railways, could be easily converted to bombers, and the Defence Department knew that if ever trouble arose those bombers would be available for it.' JSM Simpson, *South Africa Fights* (Hodder & Stoughton, London, 1941), p 195.

105 GOC, Box 15, file GOC 57 Report on Defence Organisation since inception of Coalition Government 1933.

106 FJ Jacobs, 'Tussen twee wêreldoorloë', p 131; and JA Brown, *The War of a Hundred Days: Springboks in Somalia and Abyssinia, 1940–41* (Ashanti, Johannesburg, 1990), p 30.

107 DC, Box 1098, file 4/58 Disposal of on Paying off HMSAS Protea. Secretary of State for Dominion Affairs – Minister of External Affairs, Pretoria, 7 December 1932; and Vice Admiral ER Evans, Commander-in-Chief Africa Station – Chief of the General Staff, 1 May 1933.

108 PRO: DO 119/1052 High Commissioner for United Kingdom, Pretoria – Secretary of State, London, 17 July 1935.

109 Evans to High Commissioner for Basutoland, Bechuanaland Protectorate and Swaziland, 10 September 1935, DO 119/1052, TNA.

110 Evans, quoted in R Pound, *Evans of the Broke*, p 219.

111 Oswald Pirow, quoted in R Pound, *Evans of the Broke*, p 237.

112 Dave Becker, *Waterkloof 50* (Pretoria, 1988), pp 1–3.

113 Brig Gen JJ Collyer, *The South Africans with General Smuts in German East Africa, 1916*, p 273.

114 Minutes of the 259th Meeting of the Committee for Imperial Defence held on 24 July 1933, and Minutes of Meeting held on 24 July 1933 to consider certain questions relating to South African Defence, CGS Gp 1, Box 62, file G.93 South African aspects of Imperial Defence, SANDF Documentation Centre, Pretoria.

115 Consul General, Sweden to Secretary for External Affairs, 30 October 1935, CGS Gp 2, Box 498, file G.898 Ethiopia, SANDF Documentation Centre, Pretoria. Following the invasion, Italy annexed Ethiopia in May 1936.

116 *Debates of the House of Assembly*, 4 February 1936, col 169.

117 *Debates of the House of Assembly*, 4 February 1936.

118 Collyer's preface to *The South Africans with General Smuts in German East Africa, 1916*.

119 JSM Simpson, *South Africa Fights*, p 91.

120 'So far as the enemy troops were concerned, aerial action did little damage and produced trifling information.' Brig Gen JJ Collyer, *The South Africans with General Smuts in German East Africa, 1916*, p 87.

121 Brig Gen JJ Collyer, *The South Africans with General Smuts in German East Africa, 1916*, pp 266–77, as well as Oswald Pirow, *James Barry Munnik Hertzog*, p 219, and PE von Lettow-Vorbeck, *My Reminiscences of East Africa* (Hurst and Blackett, London, 1920), p 50.

122 Brink relinquished the post of GOC UDF but stayed on as Secretary for Defence until 1939. FJ Jacobs, 'Tussen twee wêreldoorloë', p 131.

123 The Gesuiwerde Nasionale Party (Purified National Party) existed from 1934. The party reunified with the Hertzogites to fight the 1948 election as the Reunited (Herengide) National Party.

124 *Debates of the House of Assembly*, 7 September 1938, col 2309.

125 *Debates of the House of Assembly*, 15 August 1938, coll 944–45.

126 *Debates of the House of Assembly*, 28 July 1938, coll 221–28.

127 Introduction by Lt Gen George Brink to N Orpen, *East African and Abyssinian Campaigns* (Purnell, Cape Town and Johannesburg, 1968), p viii.

128 *Debates of the House of Assembly*, 7 September 1938, coll 2293–295.

129 CAB 63/69, TNA. Department of Defence, *The Nation On Guard: an exposition of South Africa's defence policy* (Maskew Miller, Cape Town, 1937), pp 1–70.

130 *Debates of the House of Assembly*, 7 September 1938, coll 2304–307.

131 As quoted by Newell M Stultz, *The Nationalists In Opposition, 1934–1948* (Human & Rousseau, Cape Town and Pretoria, 1974), p 47. See also GD Scholtz, *Hertzog en Smuts en die Britse Ryk*, p 49 et seq.

132 *Debates of the House of Assembly*, 7 September 1938, col 2310.

133 HJ Martin and N Orpen, *South Africa at War: military and industrial organisation and operations in connection with the conduct of the war, 1939–1945* (Purnell, Cape Town, 1979), p vi.

134 Introduction by Lt Gen GE Brink to

N Orpen, *East African and Abyssinian Campaigns*, p viii; and C Birkby, *Uncle George*, p 74 *et seq.*

135 JA Brown, *The War of a Hundred Days*, p 30.

136 C Birkby, *Uncle George*, pp 95–6.

137 *Debates of the House of Assembly*, 7 September 1938, coll 2296–300.

138 Commander-in-Chief, Africa Station to Commanding Officers, HM Ships, 9 February 1939, ADM 199/2352 Africa Station War Book, TNA.

139 EP Hartshorn, *Avenge Tobruk* (Purnell, Johannesburg, 1960).

140 Routine Order 240 of 28 May 1938.

141 Routine Order 427 of 8 July 1939.

142 N Orpen and HJ Martin, *Salute the Sappers*, I, p 12.

143 FJ Jacobs, 'Tussen twee wêreldoorloë', p 132.

144 C Birkby, *Uncle George*, pp 96–7.

145 N Orpen, *East African and Abyssinian Campaigns*, pp 5–7; and JA Brown, *The War of a Hundred Days*, pp 42, 69.

146 The archives of the Director General War Supplies comprise 147 volumes and contain a wealth of material on divergent matters, including Commonwealth cooperation in the manufacture and supply of material during the Second World War.

147 Industrial Development Act (22 of 1940). See Albert Grundlingh, 'South Africa and the Second World War', in BJ Liebenberg and SB Spies, eds, *South Africa in the 20th Century* (JL van Schaik, Pretoria, 1993), pp 285, 294.

148 Australia, for example, purchased South African armoured fighting vehicles and 3.7-inch howitzers.

149 See R Dummett, 'Africa's strategic minerals during the Second World War', *Journal of African History*, 26(4) 1985, pp 381–408.

150 JA Brown, *The War of a Hundred Days*, p 69.

151 D Hobart Houghton, *The South African Economy* (OUP, Cape Town, 1980), pp 126–27.

152 Report by Major Schoon on 'South African Engineer Corps', 28 August 1936, CGS Gp 2, Box 141, file G 242 Chap 2 Formation of the Engineer Corps General, SANDF Documentation Centre, Pretoria.

153 N Orpen and HJ Martin, *Salute the Sappers*, I, p 9.

154 Director Medical Services to Secretary for Defence, 31 July 1919, DC, Box 1411, file 70038 Reorganisation of the Department (Medical Section), SANDF Documentation Centre, Pretoria.

155 C Birkby, *Uncle George*, p 71.

156 Extract from a letter from SO(1) Cape Town to ADNI, 23 July 1935, and extracts from correspondence from Captain HD White, Cape Town re South African Affairs, and letter from Major CM Valentine, 17 April 1935, KV 2/908, TNA.

157 FS Crafford, *Jan Smuts: 'n Biografie* (Edina, Kaapstad, no date), pp 317–318 and, for a semi-autobiographical defence, see Oswald Pirow's biography of Hertzog, *James Barry Munnik Hertzog*, pp 218–20.

158 Joshua Furman, 'In short it was a horrible experience' in J Crwys-Williams, *A Country at War*, p 69.

159 Oswald Pirow, *James Barry Munnik Hertzog*, pp 218–20.

CHAPTER FIVE
The Second World War, 1939–1945

1 DW Krüger, *The Making of a Nation: a history of the Union of South Africa, 1910–1961* (Macmillan, Johannesburg and London, 1982), p 199.

2 Albert Grundlingh, 'South Africa and the Second World War', in BJ Liebenberg and SB Spies, eds, *South Africa in the 20th Century* (JL van Schaik, Pretoria, 1993), p 285.

3 Diary 4–10 September 1939, Harry Gordon Lawrence Papers (BC640), A2.2 Diary 1939, University of Cape Town Libraries, Archives and Manuscripts (UCT).

4 KG Dimbleby, *Hostilities Only* (Unie-Volkspers, Cape Town, 1944), p 1.

5 High Commissioner to Dominions Office, 13 September 1939, DO 35/1003/6, WG3/4/1, National Archives, Kew, London (TNA).

6 Lindie Koorts, *DF Malan and the Rise of Afrikaner Nationalism* (Tafelberg, Cape Town, 2014).

7 Oswald Pirow, *James Barry Munnik Hertzog* (Howard Timmins, Cape Town, 1957), p 219; J Crwys-Williams, *A Country at War, 1939–1945: the mood of a nation* (Ashanti, Rivonia, 1992), p 69.

8 Sir William Clark to Sir Edward Harding, 5 May 1939, DO 35/543/13, TNA.

9 John Keegan, *The Second World War* (Penguin, London and New York, 1989), p 320.

10 HJ Martin and ND Orpen, *South Africa at War: military and industrial organisation and operations in connection with the conduct of the war, 1939–1945* (Purnell, Cape Town, 1979), pp 101–103. FL Monama, 'Wartime Propaganda in the Union of South Africa,

1939–1945' (unpublished PhD dissertation, Stellenbosch University, January 2014), p 67. AM Pollock, *Pienaar of Alamein: the life story of a great South African soldier* (*Cape Times*, Cape Town, 1943), pp 25–26.

11 Albert Grundlingh, 'The King's Afrikaners? Enlistment and ethnic identity in the Union of South Africa's Defence Force during the Second World War, 1939–45', *Journal of African History*, 40(3), 1999. Cold statistics are still unavailable. The raw material lies in the Personnel Archive and Reserve at the SANDF Documentation Centre, where all of the personnel files generated in the Department of Defence since 1912 are kept. The task, no matter how rewarding, is a daunting one, even for several scholars with a team of postgraduate students.

12 Sir De Villiers Graaff, *Div Looks Back: the memoirs of Sir De Villiers Graaff* (Human & Rousseau, Cape Town, 1993).

13 HJ Martin and ND Orpen, *South Africa at War*, chapter 2.

14 See Herman Amersfoort and Piet Kamphuis, eds, *May 1940: The Battle for the Netherlands* (Brill, Leiden, 2010).

15 John Keegan, *The Second World War*, p 320.

16 Kent Fedorowich, 'German Espionage and British Counter-Intelligence in South Africa and Mozambique, 1939–1944', *Historical Journal*, 48, 2005, pp 209–30.

17 Herinneringe van Mnr FGT Radloff, band nrs 220–221, Ossewa-Brandwag-Argief, Ferdinand Postma Library, North-West University, Potchefstroom (NWU).

18 Oswald Pirow, *James Barry Munnik Hertzog*, p 254.

19 There has been some good recent work on the state of South Africa's internal security. See Kent Fedorowich, 'German Espionage and British Counter-Intelligence in South Africa and Mozambique, 1939–1944', pp 209–30; Patrick Furlong, 'Allies at war? Britain and the "Southern African Front" in the Second World War', *South African Historical Journal*, 54, 2005, pp 16–29; EDR Harrison, 'On secret service for the Duce: Umberto Campini in Portuguese East Africa, 1941–43', *English Historical Review*, 122, 2007, pp 1318–49.

20 Christoph Marx, *Oxwagon Sentinel: radical Afrikaner nationalism and the history of the Ossewabrandwag* (Unisa Press, Pretoria, 2008).

21 Smuts, quoted in 'The Broederbond States its Own Case', United Party Archives, Cape Head Office, Subject Files, The Broederbond, University of South Africa Libraries (Unisa). See also AN Pelzer, *Die Afrikaner-Broederbond: eerste 50 jaar* (Tafelberg, Kaapstad, 1982), pp 80–84.

22 Jan J van Rooyen, *Die Nasionale Party: sy opkoms end oorwinning – Kaapland se aandeel* (Cape National Party, Town, 1956), p 149 passim. See also NM Stultz, *The Nationalists in Opposition, 1934–1948* (Human & Rousseau, Cape Town, 1974), chapter 7.

23 Lt Gen Sir Pierre van Ryneveld to Field Marshal Sir Alan Brooke, 15 January 1942, WO 32/10204, TNA.

24 Except from the Report of Herr Hans Denk regarding his visit to South Africa, item 1711, Dr DF Malan Collection, Stellenbosch University. See also note to Sir John Stephenson, 22 May 1946, G581/87, DO 35/1119, TNA.

25 Lt Gen Sir Pierre van Ryneveld to Field Marshal Sir Alan Brooke, 15 January 1942, WO 32/10204, TNA. Zeesen, outside Berlin, was the site of a major German shortwave transmitter.

26 'Memo on counter espionage work on the Rand made at the request of Col FC Stallard following discussion with him on 22 April 1939' by Col BW Thwaites, Deputy Director of Intelligence, CGS War, 49/1, file 0200 Internal Security Measures, SANDF Documentation Centre.

27 High Commissioner in South Africa to Dominions Office, 11 December 1941, WO 106/4931 South African Intelligence Miscellaneous, TNA.

28 FL Monama, 'The Second World War and South African society, 1939–1945', in T Potgieter and I Liebenberg, eds, *Reflections on War: preparedness and consequences* (SUN Press, Stellenbosch, 2012), pp 54–56; Deborah Shackleton, 'South Africa and the High Commission Territories during the Second World War: politics and policies affecting war mobilization', *Scientia Militaria*, 30(2), 2000.

29 Lt JA Collard to M.O.2(b), 4 December 1941, WO 106/4931 South African Intelligence Miscellaneous, TNA.

30 Lt Gen Sir Pierre van Ryneveld to Field Marshal Sir Alan Brooke, 15 January 1942, WO 32/10204, TNA.

31 Memorandum on Contra-Sabotage Preparations, CGS War 49/1, file 0200 Internal Security Measures, SANDF Documentation Centre.

32 General minute no 13 of 25 June 1940 issued by the Chief Control Officer, DC, Box

58, file DC 17850/115/1 Internal Security, Departmental Committee (Intelligence Records Bureau), SANDF Documentation Centre.

33 Memorandum to accompany application for a special warrant from the Secretary for Defence, 23 September 1939, DC, Box 3836, file DF 1259 Intelligence Service – Expenditure: 1940/1941, SANDF Documentation Centre.

34 See, for example, Acting Administrative Secretary, Minister of Railways and Harbours, to Secretary for Defence, 13 May 1943, CGS War, box 38, file 8/7 Port and Docks Security Measures, SANDF Documentation Centre. There was also the earlier case of Karl Hens, picked up by Special Branch in October 1939. See also the anonymous report to Major Ransome, 21 September 1942, file Intelligence Shipping, United Party Archives, Central Head Office, UNISA.

35 Cape Area Intelligence Notes No 6, 5 February 1940, archives of the Director Seaward Defence, box 127, file SD 24 Intelligence Notes, SANDF Documentation Centre.

36 Cape Area Intelligence Notes No 9, 8 February 1940, archives of the Director Seaward Defence, box 127, file SD 24 Intelligence Notes, SANDF Documentation Centre. FL Monama, 'Wartime Propaganda in the Union of South Africa, 1939–45'.

37 Cape Area Intelligence Notes No 4, 2 February 1940, archives of the Director Seaward Defence (hereafter SD), box 127, file SD 24 Intelligence Notes, SANDF Documentation Centre.

38 Circular AG(1) 367/16, 2 December 1939, DC, Box 2641, file DC 943/7 chap 1 Reorganization UDF Military Sections at General Headquarters, SANDF Documentation Centre.

39 CGS circular, 8 February 1940, DC, Box 2641, file DC 943/7 chap 1 Reorganization UDF Military Sections at General Headquarters, SANDF Documentation Centre.

40 CGS circular, 8 February 1940, DC, Box 2641, file DC 943/7 chap 1 Reorganization UDF Military Sections at General Headquarters, SANDF Documentation Centre.

41 Chief of the General Staff to Adjutant General and the Director of Military Operations and Intelligence, 25 October 1940, CGS War, 49/15, file CGS 85/2/A Intelligence Records and Clearance Bureau; and Col HJ Lenton to Brig CH Blaine, Secretary for Defence,

26 October 1940, DC Gp 2, Box 3512, file 17926/29/3 Intelligence and Internal Security, Abolition of Post of Director of Intelligence, SANDF Documentation Centre.

42 Defence Advisory Committee to Minister of Defence, 27 September 1940, CGS War, 49/15, file CGS 85/2/A Intelligence Records and Clearance Bureau, SANDF Documentation Service.

43 Information officer, Department of External Affairs, to Secretary to the Prime Minister, 10 November 1939, Smuts Papers, vol 132, NASAP.

44 Smuts to Clarke, 27 December 1939, f.57, Smuts Papers, vol 132, NASAP.

45 FH Hinsley and CAG Simpkins, British Intelligence in the Second World War, vol 4: security and counter-intelligence (HMSO, London, 1990), pp 206–209.

46 Miss Pope-Hennessy, 'Z', undated, Plan Z Archive, box 1A, SANDF Documentation Centre.

47 Miss Pope-Hennessy, 'Z', undated, Plan Z Archive, box 1A, SANDF Documentation Centre.

48 High Commissioner in South Africa to Dominions Office, 23 October 1941, WO 106/4931 South African Intelligence Miscellaneous, TNA.

49 Christoph Marx, Oxwagon Sentinel, pp 515–25.

50 The cases of Charles Boyd and the agents associated with the Werz's Felix ring are mentioned briefly in FH Hinsley and CAG Simpkins, British Intelligence in the Second World War, vol 4, pp 168, 206–209.

51 I van der Waag, 'Hitler's Springboks: South African renegades and the politics of collaboration and treason, 1939–1948', conference paper 1944: Seventy Years On, Royal Military Academy Sandhurst, UK, 14–17 April 2014.

52 Statement of the Local Military Position on 7th September 1939 and steps taken thereafter, 8, A1 Smuts Papers, vol 132, NASAP.

53 Capt DJ Louw to Lt Col CL Engelbrecht, 1 November 1939 (f.11), A1 Smuts Papers, vol 132, NASAP.

54 Col BW Thwaites, Director of Intelligence to Military Secretary to the Prime Minister, 14 November 1939 (f.15), A1 Smuts Papers, vol 132, NASAP.

55 Memo 'Security of our own forces', undated (f.60), A1 Smuts Papers, vol 132, NASAP.

56 Clutterbuck to Stephenson, 29 September 1939, DO 35/1008/7 WG 429/13, TNA.

57 Defence Headquarters in Pretoria was, for part of the war, designated General Headquarters.

58 Price to Cranborne, 26 May 1941, DO 35/1008/7, WG 429/51, TNA.

59 Statement of the Local Military Position on 7th September 1939 and steps taken thereafter, A1 Smuts Papers, vol 132, NASAP.

60 As quoted by Clutterbuck to Stephenson, 29 September 1939, DO 35/1008/7, WG 429/13, TNA.

61 As quoted by Clutterbuck to Stephenson, 29 September 1939, DO 35/1008/7, WG 429/13, TNA.

62 Memorandum by Maj Gen Jack Collyer, c 1939 (f.66), A1 Smuts Papers, vol 132, NASAP.

63 HJ Martin and ND Orpen, *South Africa at War*, chapter 4.

64 HJ Martin and ND Orpen, *South Africa at War*, p 68.

65 J Ambrose Brown, *A Gathering of Eagles: the campaigns of the South African Air Force in Italian East Africa, June 1940–November 1941, with an Introduction, 1912–1939* (Purnell, Cape Town, 1970), p 17.

66 J Ambrose Brown, *A Gathering of Eagles*, p 17. Van Ryneveld coined the term from the Greek 'amphi' and 'gare', meaning a union of earth and air.

67 Sailor Malan, quoted in Oliver Walker, *Sailor Malan: a biography* (Cassell, London, 1953), pp 57–58. See also Bill Nasson, 'A flying Springbok of wartime British skies: A.G. "Sailor" Malan', *Kronos*, 35(1), 2009, pp 71–97.

68 As quoted by Oliver Walker, *Sailor Malan*, p 95.

69 ECR Baker, *Ace of Aces: M St J Pattle: Top Scoring Allied Fighter Pilot of World War II* (Ashanti, Rivonia, 1992), pp 7–16.

70 J Ambrose Brown, *A Gathering of Eagles*, pp 24–25.

71 Harald Busch, *U-Boats at War*, trans LPR Wilson (Putnam, London, 1950), pp 17–30. See LCF Turner, HR Gordon-Cumming and JE Betzler, *War in the Southern Oceans* (OUP, London, 1961).

72 Ian van der Waag, 'The thin edge of the wedge: Anglo-South African relations, dominion nationalism and the formation of the Seaward Defence Force in 1939–40', *Contemporary British History*, 24(4), December 2010, pp 427–49.

73 This section operated independently from the Union's domestic organisation, and on the closing of Combined Headquarters in 1946 it resumed its separate existence. Enc 37a Memorandum on the Naval Intelligence Organisation, South Atlantic, archives of the Minister of Defence, PW Botha Collection (MVB), Box 86, file MV62 Afdeling Direktoraat van die Militêre Inligtingsdiens, SANDF Documentation Centre.

74 Churchill was then First Lord of the Admiralty. Clark to Smuts, 25 November 1939, Smuts Papers, vol 132, NASAP.

75 Dechief to Oppositely London, 4 December 1939, Smuts Papers, vol 132, NASAP.

76 Smuts to Clark, 21 December 1939, Smuts Papers, vol 132, NASAP.

77 Clark to Smuts, 20 December 1939, and Smuts to Washington, 14 December 1939, Smuts Papers, vol 132, NASAP.

78 LCF Turner, HR Gordon-Cumming and JE Betzler, *War in the Southern Oceans*.

79 J Ambrose Brown, *A Gathering of Eagles*, pp 26–29.

80 CJ Harris, *War at Sea: South African Maritime Operations during World War II* (Ashanti, Rivonia, 1991), pp 34–55.

81 HJ Martin and ND Orpen, *South Africa at War*, pp 184–211.

82 HJ Martin and ND Orpen, *South Africa at War*, pp 336–37.

83 Bill Nasson, *South Africa at War, 1939–1945* (Jacana, Auckland Park, 2012), p 11.

84 Hofmeyr, as quoted by Nicoli Nattrass, 'Economic growth and transformation in the 1940s', in S Dubow and A Jeeves, eds, *South Africa's 1940s: worlds of possibilities* (Double Storey, Cape Town, 2005), p 20.

85 Nicoli Nattrass, 'Economic growth and transformation in the 1940s', p 21.

86 Secretary of the National Joint Committee of the SA Trade and Labour Council to Smuts, 25 November and 30 November 1939, Smuts Papers, vol 132, NASAP.

87 Philip Bonner, 'Eluding capture: African grass-roots struggles in 1940s Benoni', in S Dubow and A Jeeves, eds, *South Africa's 1940s: worlds of possibilities* (Double Storey, Cape Town, 2005), p 170.

88 Philip Bonner, 'Eluding capture', p 170.

89 Philip Bonner, 'Eluding capture', p 171.

90 Robert Edgar, 'Changing the old guard: AP Mda and the ANC Youth League, 1944–1949', in S Dubow and A Jeeves, eds, *South Africa's 1940s: worlds of possibilities* (Double Storey, Cape Town, 2005), p 149.

91 Anon, *A Record of the Organisation of the Director-General of War Supplies (1939–1943) and Director-General of Supplies (1943–1945)*

(LS Gray & Co, Johannesburg, c 1946), pp 4–19.

92 Anon, *A Record of the Organisation of the Director-General of War Supplies (1939–1943) and Director-General of Supplies (1943–1945)*, pp 16–33; Union Office of Census and Statistics, *The Union of South Africa and the War* (Government Printer, Pretoria, 1948), pp 30–33.

93 Evan Fraser and Andrew Rimas, *Empires of Food: feast, famine, and the rise of civilizations* (Simon & Schuster, New York, 2010), pp 3–4.

94 Yolandi Albertyn, 'Upsetting the Applecart: Government and Food Control in the Union of South Africa during World War II, c 1939–1948' (unpublished MA thesis, Stellenbosch University, 2013), pp 98–101.

95 Sir William Clarke to Jan Smuts, 22 December 1939, Smuts Papers, vol 132, NASAP.

96 Sir William Clarke to Jan Smuts, 22 December 1939, Smuts Papers, vol 132, NASAP.

97 J Ambrose Brown, *The War of a Hundred Days: Springboks in Somalia and Abyssinia, 1940–41* (Ashanti, Johannesburg, 1990), pp 51–53.

98 Ashley Jackson, *The British Empire and the Second World War* (Hambledon Continuum, London, 2006), p 243.

99 Neil Orpen, *East African and Abyssinian Campaigns* (Purnell, Cape Town and Johannesburg, 1968), chapter 4.

100 Neil Orpen, *East African and Abyssinian Campaigns*, chapter 5.

101 Sir Edward Harding to Viscount Caldecote, 31 July 1940, DO35/1008/7, WG429/40, TNA.

102 J Ambrose Brown, *The War of a Hundred Days*, pp 114–18, 122–24.

103 J Ambrose Brown, *The War of a Hundred Days*, pp 131–33, 144–45, 182–98.

104 EP Kleynhans, 'Armoured Warfare: The South African Experience in East Africa, 1940–1941' (unpublished MMil thesis, Stellenbosch University, December 2014), pp 178–82.

105 J Ambrose Brown, *A Gathering of Eagles*, pp 284–86.

106 Neil Orpen, *War in the Desert* (Purnell, Cape Town and Johannesburg, 1971), pp 1–18.

107 DB Katz, 'Sidi Rezegh and Tobruk: Two South African Military Disasters Revisited, 1941–1942' (unpublished MMil thesis, Stellenbosch University, December 2014), pp 43–95.

108 Carel Birkby, *In the Sun … I'm Rich* (Howard B Timmins, Cape Town, no date), p 17.

109 JAI Agar-Hamilton and LCF Turner, *Crisis in the Desert, May–July 1942* (OUP, Cape Town, 1952), pp 80–108.

110 Andrew Stewart, 'The Klopper Affair: Anglo-South African Relations and the surrender of the Tobruk garrison', *Twentieth Century British History*, 17(4), 2006. Andrew Stewart, 'The Atomic Despatch: Field Marshal Auchinleck, the fall of the Tobruk garrison and post-war Anglo-South African relations', *Scientia Militaria*, 36(1), 2008.

111 DB Katz, 'Sidi Rezegh and Tobruk', chapters 3 and 4.

112 JAI Agar-Hamilton and LCF Turner, *Crisis in the Desert, May–July 1942*, pp 316–28. Neil Orpen, *War in the Desert*, pp 457–76.

113 J Ambrose Brown, *Eagles Strike: the campaigns of the South African Air Force in Egypt, Cyrenaica, Libya, Tunisia, Tripolitania and Madagascar, 1941–1943* (Purnell, Cape Town, 1974), pp 143–175, 382.

114 Miss Pope-Hennessy, 'Z', undated, Plan Z Archive, box 1A, SANDF Documentation Centre.

115 Harald Busch, *U-Boats at War*, p 144.

116 Harald Busch, *U-Boats at War*, pp 144–150. See also LCF Turner, HR Gordon-Cumming and JE Betzler, *War in the Southern Oceans*.

117 FH Hinsley and CAG Simpkins, *British Intelligence in the Second World War*, vol 4, pp 206–209. See also Kent Fedorowich, 'German Espionage and British Counter-Intelligence in South Africa and Mozambique, 1939–1944', pp 209–30.

118 The best South African source on the invasion of Madagascar is a clutch of five articles published in five consecutive issues of the journal *Scientia Militaria* by JEH Grobler. They are: 'Die Geallieerde Besetting van Madagaskar met spesifieke verwysing na die role van die Unieverdedigingsmag in die operasies', *Scientia Militaria*, 7(4), 1977; 'Die Geallieerde Besetting van Madagaskar in 1942: die konsolidasietydperk, Mei-Augustus 1942', *Scientia Militaria*, 8(1), 1978; 'Die Geallieerde Besetting van Madagaskar in 1942: die toetrede van die Suid-Afrikaanse Landmagte en die besitting van Tananarive', *Scientia Militaria*, (8)2, 1978; 'Die Geallieerde Besetting van Madagaskar in 1942: Tamatave, Tulear en die oorgawe van Annet', *Scientia Militaria*, 8(3), 1978; 'Die Geallieerde Besetting van Madagaskar in 1942', *Scientia Militaria*, 8(4), 1978.

119 DW Krüger, *The Making of a Nation*, p 214.

120 Harlech to Secretary of State for Dominion Affairs, 4 June 1943, DO 35/1119, file G.581/40 Political Affairs Union, TNA.

121 Harlech to Secretary of State for Dominion Affairs, 4 June 1943, DO 35/1119, file G.581/40 Political Affairs Union, TNA.

122 Telex High Commissioner to Dominions Office, circa early 1942, WO 106/4931 South African Intelligence Miscellaneous, TNA.

123 Smuts as quoted in High Commissioner to Dominions Office, circa early 1942, WO 106/4931 South African Intelligence Miscellaneous, TNA.

124 Smuts quoted in High Commissioner to Dominions Office, circa early 1942, WO 106/4931 South African Intelligence Miscellaneous, TNA.

125 203 Military Mission, Pretoria, to the War Office, 2 April 1943, WO 32/10193 South African Army Union Defence Forces, TNA.

126 Col G Kreft, Office of the High Commissioner in South Africa, to Lt Col H. Bridge, MO2, War Office, 8 June 1943, WO 32/10193 South African Army Union Defence Forces, TNA.

127 203 Military Mission, Pretoria, to the War Office, 2 April 1943, WO 32/10193 South African Army Union Defence Forces, TNA.

128 Harlech to Cranborne, 9 June 1944, file G581/40 Political Affairs Union, DO 35/1119, TNA.

129 DW Krüger, *The Making of a Nation*, pp 215–16. See also FD Tothill, 'The 1943 General Election' (unpublished MA thesis, University of South Africa, 1987).

130 Harlech to Cranborne, 9 June 1944, DO 35/1119, file G.581/40 Political Affairs Union, TNA.

131 EP Kleynhans, 'The first South African armoured battle in Italy during the Second World War: the battle of Celleno, 10 June 1944', *Scientia Militaria*, 40(3), 2012, pp 251–52.

132 Neil Orpen, *Victory in Italy* (Purnell, Cape Town and Johannesburg, 1975), pp 22–27.

133 Carel Birkby, *In the Sun ... I'm Rich*, p 17.

134 Neil Orpen, *Victory in Italy*, pp 44–54.

135 Uys Krige, 'Difficulties the 8th Army have to face', radio broadcast c 1944, 225.RW.10, Uys Krige Collection, JS Gericke Library, Stellenbosch University.

136 His remarkable escape is told in Uys Krige, *The Way Out* (Unie-Volkspers, Cape Town and Port Elizabeth, 1946).

137 Uys Krige, 'Difficulties the 8th Army have to face'.

138 Neil Orpen, *Victory in Italy*, pp 182–99.

139 Neil Orpen, *Victory in Italy*, p 200 *passim*.

140 Neil Orpen, *Victory in Italy*, pp 307–308.

141 HJ Martin and Neil Orpen, *Eagles Victorious: the operations of the South African Forces over the Mediterranean and Europe, in Italy, the Balkans and the Aegean, and from Gibraltar and West Africa* (Purnell, Cape Town, 1977), pp 246–62.

142 There are two recent studies of the war experiences of South African soldiers: Gustav Bentz, 'Fighting Springboks: C Company, Royal Natal Carbineers: from Premier Mine to the Po Valley, 1939–1945' (unpublished MMil thesis, Stellenbosch University, 2013); James Bourhill, 'Red Tabs: Life and Death in the 6th South African Armoured Division, 1943–1945' (unpublished PhD dissertation, University of Pretoria, 2014). DR Fuchs, 'Durban During the Second World War, 1939–1945: A Study of War and Social Change' (unpublished MA thesis, University of Natal, 1990) is a study of the impact of the war on South Africa's premier port.

143 Bob Moore, 'Axis prisoners in Britain during the Second World War: a comparative analysis', in Bob Moore and Kent Fedorowich, eds, *Prisoners of War and their Captors in World War II* (Berg, Oxford and Washington, DC, 1996), p 24.

144 Bob Moore, 'Axis prisoners in Britain during the Second World War', p 27.

145 Martin Thomas, 'Captives of their countrymen: Free French and Vichy French POWs in Africa and the Middle East, 1940–3', in Bob Moore and Kent Fedorowich, eds, *Prisoners of War and their Captors in World War II* (Berg, Oxford and Washington, DC, 1996), pp 92–95, 103.

146 Bob Moore and Kent Fedorowich, *The British Empire and its Italian Prisoners of War, 1940–1947* (Palgrave, Basingstoke, 2002), pp 220–22.

147 Ian Gleeson, *The Unknown Force: black, Indian and coloured soldiers through two world wars* (Ashanti, Rivonia, 1994), pp 100–103, 188–191.

148 David Killingray, 'Africans and African Americans in enemy hands', in Bob Moore and Kent Fedorowich, eds, *Prisoners of War and their Captors in World War II* (Berg, Oxford and Washington, DC, 1996), pp 181–96.

149 Karen Horn, 'South African Prisoner-of-War Experience during and after World War II: 1939–c 1950' (unpublished PhD dissertation, Stellenbosch University, December 2012),

p 16. Maxwell Leigh, *Captives Courageous: South African prisoners of war, World War II* (Ashanti, Johannesburg, 1992).

150 MRD Foot and JM Langley, *MI9: The British secret service that fostered escape and evasion 1939–1945 and its American counterpart* (The Bodley Head, London, 1979), p 170.

151 Eric Axelson, *A Year in Italy: an observer with the South African 6th Armoured Division, 1944–1945* (EH Walton, Port Elizabeth, 2001), p 37.

152 The discharge of these 16 deserters in the CMF caused some trouble. Some of these men, during the time that they were deserters, committed civil offences and were arrested by the Italian civil authorities. In some cases, they are still in UDF uniform. They were tried by Italian civil courts and served at least part of their sentences in Italian prisons. They had to be repatriated after release. The UDF Liaison Office had closed and so this task fell to the South African Legation in Rome. POW, box 42, file 804–5, SANDF Documentation Centre.

153 Lt Col L du Toit, UDF Liaison Office, GHQ EMF Cairo, to Col Hingeston, 10 July 1946, POW, box 42, file 804–5, SANDF Documentation Centre.

154 Neil Roos, *Ordinary Springboks: white servicemen and social justice in South Africa, 1939–1961* (Ashgate, Burlington, VT, 2005), p 195.

155 Neil Roos, *Ordinary Springboks*, p 1.

156 Arthur Marwick, *War and Social Change in the Twentieth Century: a comparative study of Britain, France, Germany, Russia and the United States* (Macmillan, Basingstoke, 1974).

157 Ian Jacob to Prime Minister, 1 July 1952, PREM 11/274, TNA.

CHAPTER SIX
Change and Continuity: The Early Cold War, 1945–1966

1 FC Erasmus, 'Die Agtergrond van Ons Verdedigingsbeleid', Dr DF Malan Collection, 1/1/2355, Special Collections, JS Gericke Library, Stellenbosch University (SU).

2 Ian le Rougetel, UK High Commissioner in SA, to Commonwealth Relations Office, 13 February 1952, PREM 11/274, The National Archives of the United Kingdom, Kew, London (TNA).

3 Extract from statement made by Lieutenant General GE Brink and given wide publicity in

the South African press from 12 March 1952, Sir De Villiers Graaff Collection, Archives and Special Collections, University of South Africa Library (Unisa).

4 Christopher Andrew and Vasili Mitrokhin, *The Mitrokhin Archive II: the KGB and the world* (Allen Lane, London, 2005), chapter 1; and Robert Service, *Spies and Commissars: Bolshevik Russia and the West* (Macmillan, London, 2011). For two contemporary sources, see Lieutenant General Sir Giffard Martel, *East Versus West* (Museum, London, 1952) and General Sir Walter Walker, *The Bear at the Back Door: the Soviet threat to the West's lifeline in Africa* (Valiant, Sandton, 1978).

5 Edward Judge and John Langdon, *A Hard and Bitter Peace: a global history of the Cold War* (Prentice Hall, Upper Saddle River, NJ, 1996), p 151.

6 Christopher Andrew and Vasili Mitrokhin, *The Mitrokhin Archive II*, chapters 7, 8, 23 and 24. See also Vladimir Shubin, *The Hot 'Cold War': the USSR in southern Africa* (UKZN Press, Scottsville, 2008).

7 GF Hudson, 'How unified is the Commonwealth?', *Foreign Affairs*, 33(4), July 1955, p 681.

8 Dieter Fuchs, 'Durban during the Second World War, 1939–1945: A Study of War and Social Change' (unpublished MA thesis, University of Natal, 1990).

9 FG Brownell, *British Immigration to South Africa, 1946–1970* (Archives Yearbook for South African History, Pretoria, 1985), chapter 2.

10 Debates of the Senate, 30 January 1947.

11 As quoted by Francois Oosthuizen, 'Changes and expectations: the white Union Defence Force soldier prior to and during the Second World War', *Militaria*, 23(3), 1993, p 39.

12 Francois Oosthuizen, 'Demobilisation and the post-war employment of the white Union Defence Force soldier', *Militaria*, 23(4), 1993, p 38.

13 DB Sole, Political Secretary, to Secretary for External Affairs, 22 August 1945, CGS War 49/20 Rein Mission, Department of Defence Archives, SANDF Documentation Centre, Pretoria.

14 Secret notes for the Reich's Minister for Foreign Affairs by Karlowa, Berlin, 22 November 1940, and excerpt from the Report of Herr Hans Denk regarding his visit to South Africa, item 1711, Dr DF Malan Collection, SU. 'Dr Malan Exonerated', *The*

Cape Times, 18 June 1946.

15 *R v Mardon*, Transvaal Provincial Division, 15–17 April 1947. File 'British Free Corps', Diverse, box 22, SANDF Documentation Centre, Pretoria.

16 David Katz, 'The greatest military reversal of South African arms: the fall of Tobruk 1942, an avoidable blunder or an inevitable disaster?', *Journal for Contemporary History*, 37(2), 2012, pp 71–104.

17 RS Boulter, 'Afrikaner nationalism in action: FC Erasmus and South Africa's defence forces 1948–1959', *Nations and Nationalism*, 6(3), 2000, pp 437–59.

18 L Jooste, 'FC Erasmus as Minister van Verdediging, 1948–1959' (MA thesis, Unisa, 1995); RS Boulter, 'FC Erasmus and the Politics of South African Defence 1948–1959' (PhD, Rhodes University, 1997). Neither thesis has been published, but both scholars have produced article-length publications. Their approaches and interpretations differ vastly, and the one study is a necessary antidote to the other. L Jooste, 'Die politieke koerswending van 1948 besorg 'n nuwe identiteit aan die Univerdedigingsmag', *Militaria*, 26(2), 1996, pp 113–28; RS Boulter, 'Afrikaner nationalism in action', pp 437–59.

19 Ian le Rougetel, UK High Commissioner in SA, to Commonwealth Relations Office, 13 February 1952, PREM 11/274, TNA.

20 Erasmus, 'Die Agtergrond van Ons Verdedigingsbeleid', 1/1/2355, Dr DF Malan Collection, SU.

21 See also Leonard Guelke and Robert Shell, 'An early colonial landed gentry: land and wealth in the Cape Colony, 1682–1731', *Journal of Historical Geography*, 9(3) 1983, pp 265–86; and Robert Ross, 'The rise of the Cape gentry', *Journal of Southern African Studies*, 9(2) 1983, pp 193–217.

22 Ross Dix-Peek, 'Southern Africa's redcoat generals: South African and Rhodesian born general officers of the British Army, the Royal Air Force and the Royal Navy 1856–2007', The South African Military History Society, available at samilitaryhistory.org/ross/redcoats.html; accessed 12 April 2012.

23 RS Boulter, 'Afrikaner nationalism in action', p 437.

24 Boulter illustrates this point with numerous examples. See RS Boulter, 'Afrikaner nationalism in action', as well as Boulter, 'FC Erasmus and the Politics of South African Defence 1848–1959' for a fuller, in-depth study.

25 This observation is based upon a survey of the list presented in Ivor Wilkins and Hans Strydom, *The Super Afrikaners: inside the Afrikaner Broederbond* (Braamfontein, Jonathan Ball, 1978). See also UPA, Cape Head Office, Subject Files, The Broederbond, University of South Africa Libraries (Unisa).

26 'Who Governs South Africa? Peoples Government of the Broederbond: Lifting the Black Curtain', A United Party Publication, UPA, Cape Head Office, Subject Files, The Broederbond, Unisa.

27 It must said that there is as yet no study on the SADF officer corps comparable to RC Brown, 'Social Attitudes of American Generals, 1898–1940' (PhD thesis, University of Wisconsin, 1951) or CB Otley, 'The social origins of British Army officers', *The Sociological Review*, 18, 1970, pp 213–39. However, a broad reading of the literature and a survey of the socio-economic case files in the archives of the Ossewabrandwag (Ferdinand Postma Library, North-West University) lends strong support to this general observation.

28 Erasmus, 'Die Agtergrond van Ons Verdedigingsbeleid', 1/1/2355, Dr DF Malan Collection, SU. For a history of the South African Military Academy, see Deon Visser's magisterial doctoral study, 'Die Geskiedenis van die Suid-Afrikaanse Militere Akademie, 1950–1990', published as a Supplementa to *Scientia Militaria* (2000).

29 AN Pelzer, *Die Afrikaner-Broederbond: eerste 50 jaar* (Tafelberg, Cape Town, 1979), pp 9–12. See also Broederbond communiqués quoted in 'The Broederbond States its Own Case', UPA, Cape Head Office, Subject Files, The Broederbond, Unisa.

30 'Miles Cadman Resigns from Senate; Erasmus Appoints Him Deputy Chaplain-General to UDF', *Rand Daily Mail*, undated newsclip, BC640 Harry Gordon Lawrence Papers, Correspondence, B2.4, University of Cape Town Libraries, Archives and Manuscripts (UCT).

31 Thea Miles-Cadman to Cecil Miles-Cadman, 28 and 29 June 1949, Dr DF Malan Collection, 1/1/2486, SU.

32 Ken Anderson, *Rand Daily Mail* to HG Lawrence, 6 August 1949, BC640 Lawrence Papers, B2.1, UCT.

33 Lt Gen Len Beyers to Erasmus, 8 October 1949, 1/1/2514, Dr DF Malan Collection, SU.

34 Lt Gen Len Beyers to the editor, *Rand Daily Mail*, 17 April 1950.

35 RC Hiemstra, *Die Wilde Haf* (Human & Rousseau, Kaapstad, 2001), pp 133–34, 147, 169, 183–84.

36 Hiemstra introduced members of the armed forces, including Captain Gustav Radloff (born 1917), to Dr Hans van Rensburg, the Administrator of the Orange Free State, who became commandant-general of the OB in 1941. See Herinneringe van Mnr FGT Radloff, band nrs 220–221, Ossewa-Brandwag-Argief, Ferdinand Postma Library, North-West University, Potchefstroom (NWU).

37 JR Bowring, 'Thoughts on Defence Studies', 29 July 1964, Sir De Villiers Graaff Collection, Unisa.

38 Erasmus, 'Die Agtergrond van Ons Verdedigingsbeleid', Dr DF Malan Collection, 1/1/2355, SU.

39 This distance of 4 552 kilometres was the combination of the South African coastline (2 798 kilometres) with that of South West Africa (Namibia) (1 754 kilometres). FC Erasmus, 'Die Agtergrond van Ons Verdedigingsbeleid', 1/1/2355, Dr DF Malan Collection, SU. See also JJ van Rooyen, *Die Nasionale Party: sy opkoms en oorwinning – Kaapland se aandeel* (Hoofraad NP, Kaapstad, 1956), p 231.

40 Rodney Warwick, 'White South Africa and Defence, 1960–1968: Militarisation, Threat Perception and Counter Strategies' (unpublished PhD dissertation, University of Cape Town, 2009).

41 Appendix A to Minutes of Meeting of Defence Staff Council, 20 November 1957, attached to circular KG/GM/5/2, 18 June 1958, archives of the Secretary for Defence (DC), SANDF Documentation Centre, Pretoria.

42 Memo 'Visit by Director-General of the Security Service to South Africa', 14 November 1949, PREM 8/1283, TNA. See also Christopher Andrew, *The Defence of the Realm: the authorized history of MI5* (Allen Lane, London, 2009), p 444.

43 Erasmus, 'Die Agtergrond van Ons Verdedigingsbeleid', Dr DF Malan Collection, 1/1/2355, SU.

44 Erasmus, 'Die Agtergrond van Ons Verdedigingsbeleid', Dr DF Malan Collection, 1/1/2355, SU.

45 Erasmus, 'Die Agtergrond van Ons Verdedigingsbeleid', Dr DF Malan Collection, 1/1/2355, SU.

46 Memo 'Regional Defence in Africa', 3 March 1949, archive of the Minister of Defence, Erasmus and Fouché Collection (MVEF),

Box 1, file G.171 Discussions between UK, USA and Union Governments, SANDF Documentation Centre, Pretoria. On the search for alliance and the arrangements regarding MEDO, the ADO and the Simon's Town Agreement, see Geoffrey Berridge, *South Africa, the Colonial Powers and 'African Defence': the rise and fall of the white entente, 1948–1960* (Macmillan, London, 1992).

47 Ian le Rougetel, UK High Commissioner in SA, to Commonwealth Relations Office, 13 February 1952, PREM 11/274, TNA.

48 Annex 1 'Note on United Kingdom Policy in regard to South African Defence Policy' to Memorandum by the Secretary of State for Commonwealth Relations, 21 May 1952, PREM 11/274, TNA.

49 Republic of South Africa, Review of Defence and Armaments Production: Period 1960 to 1970 (Defence Headquarters, Pretoria, April 1971), p 5.

50 DF Malan to Sir Evelyn Baring, 28 August 1948, MVEF, Box 124, file MV93 Berlin Air Lift, SANDF Documentation Centre, Pretoria.

51 Secretary of State for Commonwealth Relations to Minister of External Affairs, Pretoria, 20 July 1949, MVEF, Box 124, file MV93 Berlin Air Lift, SANDF Documentation Centre, Pretoria. Anthony Speir, 'The Berlin Airlift, 1948–49', *South African Military History Journal*, 11(2), 1998, available at samilitaryhistory.org/vol112ts. html, accessed 3 February 2015.

52 Minutes of 59th Meeting of the National Security Council, 28 June 1950, President's Secretary Files, Truman Papers, Truman Presidential Library and Museum, Independence, Missouri.

53 State Department Overview of Korean Situation, 28 June 1950, Harry S Truman Administration File, Elsey Papers, as well as National Security Council Report 76/1, 'US Courses of Action in Event Soviet Forces Enter Korean Hostilities', 25 June 1950, President's Secretary Files, Truman Papers, Truman Presidential Library and Museum, Independence, Missouri.

54 The US State Department likened the Soviet strategy to 'the Hitler tactics of 1938–1939'. State Department Overview of Korean Situation, 28 June 1950, Harry S Truman Administration File, Elsey Papers, Truman Papers, Truman Presidential Library and Museum, Independence, Missouri.

55 Eric Louw to DF Malan, 16 July 1950, Dr DF

Malan Collection, 1/1/2568, SU.

56 Chief of the General Staff to South African Ambassador, The Hague, 12 November 1951, archives of the Chief of Staff Intelligence (AMI), Group 3, Box 1011, file GS/37 vol II Intelligence Policy, SANDF Documentation Centre, Pretoria.

57 Secretary for External Affairs to SA High Commissioner, Canberra, 1 July 1950, archives of the Military Adviser to the High Commissioner for the Union of South Africa in London (MA), Box 422, file Korea, SANDF Documentation Centre, Pretoria. Secretary for External Affairs to High Commissioners in London, Ottawa, and Canberra, and Minister of External Affairs, Wellington, 4 August 1950, archives of the Secretary for Defence (DC), Group 5, file DC17850/362/1 Korean Campaign, SANDF Documentation Centre, Pretoria. See also File 'Korean War', Division of Information and Research, United Party Archives (UPA), Unisa. 'Cabinet Decisions Deferred; No meeting this week on Korea', The Argus, 19 July 1950.

58 File 'Korean War', Division of Information and Research, United Party Archives (UPA), Unisa. 'Malan Calls Cabinet', The Argus, 4 August 1950. 'Meeting of the Cabinet lasted all day', The Argus, 5 August 1950.

59 Organisation and Administrative Instruction Part 1, 7 September 1950, archives of the Senior Air Liaison Officer (SALO), Box 7, file SALO/S/818/ORG Organisation SAAF Korea Contingent, SANDF Documentation Centre, Pretoria.

60 PMJ McGregor, 'The history of No 2 Squadron, SAAF, in the Korean War', Military History Journal, 4(3) June 1978, p 82.

61 Dermot Moore and P Bagshawe, South Africa's Flying Cheetahs in Korea (Ashanti, Johannesburg, 1991), pp 3–4.

62 D Moore and P Bagshawe, South Africa's Flying Cheetahs in Korea, p 6.

63 Director General Air Force to SALO, 27 March 1952, SALO, Box 1, file SALO/TS/23/1 Air Policy Union Employment of 2 SAAF Squadron, SANDF Documentation Centre, Pretoria.

64 Joint Chiefs of Staff to General Douglas MacArthur, 31 July 1950, Naval Aide Files, Truman Papers, Truman Presidential Library and Museum, Independence, Missouri.

65 William W Momeyer, Airpower in Three Wars: World War II, Korea and Vietnam (University Press of the Pacific, Honolulu, 2002), p 2.

66 PMJ McGregor, 'The History of No 2 Squadron, SAAF, in the Korean War', p 87.

67 UK Ministry of Defence to UK Service Liaison Staffs in Ottawa, Wellington and Pretoria, 28 June 1950, MA, Box 422, file MA/TS/1014 Korea, SANDF Documentation Centre, Pretoria.

68 War diary, SAAF Liaison Headquarters, 25 August 1952, War Diaries and Missions (WDM), Box 9, SANDF Documentation Centre, Pretoria.

69 War diary, SAAF Liaison Headquarters, 12 December 1951, WDM, Box 9, SANDF Documentation Centre, Pretoria.

70 PMJ McGregor, 'The History of No 2 Squadron, SAAF, in the Korean War', p 89.

71 D Moore and P Bagshawe, South Africa's Flying Cheetahs in Korea, p 120.

72 File 'Cartoons 1950', Division of Information and Research, UPA, Unisa.

73 Neil Roos, Ordinary Springboks: white servicemen and social justice in South Africa, 1939–1961 (Ashgate, Burlington, VT, 2005), p 129.

74 See, for example, Maj Gen HS Wakefield to Sir De Villiers Graaff, 3 August 1954, file 'Defence 1954', UPA, Unisa.

75 Maj Gen Frank Theron to Sir De Villiers Graaff, 7 October 1954, file 'Defence 1954', UPA, Unisa.

76 Maj Gen Frank Theron to Sir De Villiers Graaff, 25 October 1954, file 'Defence 1954', UPA, Unisa.

77 Extract from statement made by Lieutenant General GE Brink and given wide publicity in the South African press from 12 March 1952, Sir De Villiers Graaff Collection, Unisa.

78 Ian le Rougetel, UK High Commissioner in SA, to Commonwealth Relations Office, 13 February 1952, PREM 11/274, TNA.

79 Memorandum by the Secretary of State for Commonwealth Relations, 21 May 1952, PREM 11/274, TNA.

80 Annex 1 'Note on United Kingdom Policy in regard to South African Defence Policy' to Memorandum by the Secretary of State for Commonwealth Relations, 21 May 1952, PREM 11/274, TNA.

81 Ian le Rougetel, UK High Commissioner in SA, to Commonwealth Relations Office, 13 February 1952, PREM 11/274, TNA.

82 Ian Jacob to Prime Minister, 1 July 1952, PREM 11/274, TNA.

83 Annex 1 'Note on United Kingdom Policy in regard to South African Defence Policy' to Memorandum by the Secretary of State

for Commonwealth Relations, 21 May 1952, PREM 11/274, TNA.

84 Annex 1 'Note on United Kingdom Policy in regard to South African Defence Policy' to Memorandum by the Secretary of State for Commonwealth Relations, 21 May 1952, PREM 11/274, TNA.

85 Memorandum by the Secretary of State for Commonwealth Relations, 21 May 1952, PREM 11/274, TNA.

86 Annex 1 'Note on United Kingdom Policy in regard to South African Defence Policy' to Memorandum by the Secretary of State for Commonwealth Relations, 21 May 1952, PREM 11/274, TNA.

87 Memorandum by the Secretary of State for Commonwealth Relations, 21 May 1952, PREM 11/274, TNA.

88 Republic of South Africa, Review of Defence and Armaments Production: Period 1960 to 1970 (Defence Headquarters, Pretoria, April 1971), p 8.

89 Warwick Dorning, 'A concise history of the South African Defence Force, 1912–1987', *Militaria*, 17(2), 1987, p 19 *passim*.

90 Len Jerome to the editor of *The Star*, c March 1952, Sir De Villiers Graaff Collection, Unisa.

91 Defence Act (44 of 1957).

92 EGM Alexander, GKB Barron and AJ Bateman, *South African Orders, Decorations and Medals* (Human & Rousseau, Pretoria, 1986).

93 Williams to MO2, c August 1957, WO 32/16726, TNA.

94 See RS Boulter, 'Afrikaner nationalism in action', as well as Boulter, 'FC Erasmus and the Politics of South African Defence 1848–1959' for a fuller, in-depth study. For the impact on a key Citizen Force regiment, see Mark Coghlan, *Pro Patria: another 50 Natal Carbineer years, 1945 to 1995* (Natal Carbineers Trust, Pietermaritzburg, 2000).

95 For a revealing treatment of this process from the viewpoint of these regiments see Mark Coghlan, *Pro Patria*, chapter 7: 'The storm breaks: Republic'.

96 Republic of South Africa, Review of Defence and Armaments Production: Period 1960 to 1970 (Defence Headquarters, Pretoria, April 1971), pp 5–6.

97 Republic of South Africa, Review of Defence and Armaments Production: Period 1960 to 1970 (Defence Headquarters, Pretoria, April 1971), p 5.

98 Republic of South Africa, Review of Defence and Armaments Production: Period 1960 to 1970 (Defence Headquarters, Pretoria, April 1971), p 6.

99 For a probing treatment of the SADF in the 1960s, see Rodney Warwick, 'White South Africa and Defence, 1960–68'.

100 Republic of South Africa, Review of Defence and Armaments Production: Period 1960 to 1970 (Defence Headquarters, Pretoria, April 1971), p 6.

101 JP Waterfield to Mr Arthur, 22 May 1963, FO 371/167532, JSA 1223/10/9 UK defence interests in South Africa, TNA.

102 Roger Stevens to Sir Robert Scott, 18 June 1963, FO 371/167532, JSA 1223/12/G UK defence relationship with South Africa, TNA.

103 Victor Moukambi, 'Relations Between South Africa and France with Special Reference to Military Matters, 1960–1990' (unpublished PhD thesis, Stellenbosch University, 2008).

CHAPTER SEVEN
Hot War in Southern Africa, 1959–1989

1 Gary Baines, *South Africa's 'Border War': contested narratives and conflicting memories* (Bloomsbury, London, 2014), p 1.

2 David Williams, *On the Border: the white South African military experience, 1965–1990* (Tafelberg, Cape Town, 2008), pp 15–18.

3 Fidel Castro, *My Life*, with Ignacio Ramonet (Penguin, London, 2008), p 318.

4 Paulo Correira and Grietjie Verhoef, 'Portugal and South Africa: close allies or unwilling partners in southern Africa during the Cold War?', *Scientia Militaria*, 37(1), 2009, pp 50–72.

5 Roel van der Veen, *Afrika: van de Koude Oorlog naar de 21ste eeuw* (KIT, Amsterdam, 2002), pp 51–54. Christopher Andrew and Vasili Mitrokhin, *The Mitrokhin Archive II: the KGB and the world* (Allen Lane, London, 2005), p 429.

6 WO 106/589 German South West Africa Operations against Mandume on the Portuguese border, 1917, TNA. WS van der Waals, *Portugal's War in Angola, 1961–1974* (Ashanti, Rivonia, 1993), pp 47–50.

7 John W Turner, *Continent Ablaze: the insurgency wars in Africa 1960 to the present* (Jonathan Ball, Johannesburg, 1998), chapters 4–6. For a personal account, see Jacinto Veloso, *Memories at Low Altitude: the autobiography of a Mozambican security chief* (Zebra, Cape Town, 2012).

8 The nomenclature of the conflict, wide and

divergent, has become equally complex. Almost any descriptor raises questions on the score of accuracy or objectivity. Yet, in general terms, a distinction should be made between the 'Bush War', fought in Rhodesia (Zimbabwe) from the early 1960s until 1980, and the 'Border War', fought largely in northern Namibia and southern Angola from 1966 to 1989. Paul Moorcraft and Peter McLaughlin, *The Rhodesian War: a military history* (Jonathan Ball, Johannesburg and Cape Town, 2008), p 29.

9 MK operative Rocky Williams took the same view of a regional war. See his 'The other armies: writing the history of MK', in Ian Liebenberg et al, *The Long March: the story of the struggle for liberation in South Africa* (HAUM, Pretoria, 1994), p 31.

10 Leopold Scholtz, *The SADF in the Border War, 1966–1989* (Tafelberg, Cape Town, 2013), pp 4–5.

11 The International Court of Justice ruled that individual member states of the League of Nations had never been entitled to bring a case against a mandatory for maladministration of a mandated territory. Moreover, the League itself no longer existed. The judgment was a bombshell. G Cockram, *Vorster's Foreign Policy* (Academia, Pretoria and Cape Town, 1970), pp 19–22. See also Paul Giniewski, *Die Stryd om Suidwes-Afrika* (Nasionale Boekhandel, Kaapstad, 1966).

12 Willem Steenkamp, *South Africa's Border War, 1966–1989* (Ashanti, Gibraltar, 1989), p 22. Scholtz, *The SADF in the Border War, 1966–1989*, p 7.

13 Victor Moukambi, 'Relations Between South Africa and France with Special Reference to Military Matters, 1960–1990' (unpublished PhD thesis, Stellenbosch University, 2008).

14 Saul Dubow, *Apartheid, 1948–1994* (OUP, Oxford, 2014), pp 68–69.

15 Mokgethi Motlhabi, *The Theory and Practice of Black Resistance to Apartheid: a socio-ethical analysis* (Skotaville Publishers, Johannesburg, 1984), pp 38–47.

16 Natoo Babenia, *Memoirs of a Saboteur: reflections on my political activity in India and South Africa* (Mayibuye Books, Bellville, 1995), pp 60–74.

17 Stephen Ellis and T Sechaba, *Comrades Against Apartheid: the ANC and the South African Communist Party in exile* (James Currey, London, 1992), pp 34–38.

18 Chris Alden, *Apartheid's Last Stand: the rise and fall of the South African security

state* (Macmillan, Basingstoke and London, 1996), pp 17–18. Joel Joffe, *The Rivonia Story* (Mayibuye Books, Bellville, 1995), chapter 8.

19 Roger Riddell, 'The impact of new sanctions against South Africa', in Robert E Edgar, ed, *Sanctioning Apartheid* (Africa World Press, Trenton, NJ, 1990), pp 111–40.

20 Chris Alden, *Apartheid's Last Stand*, p 19.

21 David Scott, *Ambassador in Black and White: thirty years of changing Africa* (Weidenfeld and Nicholson, London, 1981), pp 181–82.

22 James Ngculu, *The Honour to Serve: recollections of an Umkhonto soldier* (David Philip, Claremont, 2009), p 22.

23 Chris Alden, *Apartheid's Last Stand*, p 27.

24 Chris Alden, *Apartheid's Last Stand*, pp 112–16. See also David Scott, *Ambassador in Black and White*, p 117.

25 See, for example, the report by General Sir Gerald Templar on colonial security, 23 April 1955, in CAB 21/2925, TNA. See also Lt Gen Sir Giffard Martel, *East Versus West* (Museum, London, 1952) and General Sir Walter Walker, *The Bear at the Back Door: the Soviet threat to the West's lifeline in Africa* (Valiant, Sandton, 1978).

26 Robert H Donaldson and Joseph L Nogee, *The Foreign Policy of Russia: changing systems, enduring interests* (ME Sharpe, Armonk, NY, 1998), chapter 3. See also Richard H Shultz and Roy Godson, *Dezinformatsia: active measures in Soviet strategy* (Pergamon-Brassey's, Washington, DC, 1984).

27 Eugene de Kock, *A Long Night's Damage: working for the apartheid state* (Contra Press, Johannesburg, 1998), p 89.

28 Eugene de Kock, *A Long Night's Damage*, p 91.

29 Darryl Howlett and John Simpson, 'Nuclearisation and denuclearisation in South Africa', *Survival: Global Politics and Strategy*, 35(3), 1993, p 154.

30 Chris Alden, *Apartheid's Last Stand*, p 30. Rodney Warwick, 'White South Africa and Defence, 1960–1968: Militarisation, Threat Perception and Counter Strategies' (unpublished PhD dissertation, University of Cape Town, 2009).

31 Anthony Clayton, *The Wars of French Decolonization* (Longman, London and New York, 1998), pp 117, 121, 128.

32 Chris Alden, *Apartheid's Last Stand*, pp 30–31, 44–45, 218.

33 These events must be studied in the context of the struggle between government departments, especially those of Defence and the Police, and of the Information Scandal.

See M Rees and C Day, *Muldergate: the story of the Info Scandal* (Macmillan, Johannesburg, 1980).

34 Ronald Hyam, 'The parting of ways: Britain and South Africa's departure from the Commonwealth, 1951–1961', *Journal of Imperial and Commonwealth History*, 26(2), 1998, pp 157–75; Rodney Warwick, 'White South Africa and Defence, 1960–1968'.

35 Chris Alden, *Apartheid's Last Stand*, p 39.

36 AM van Wyk, 'The USA and apartheid South Africa's nuclear weapons aspirations, 1949–1980', in Sue Onslow, ed, *Cold War in Southern Africa: white power, black liberation* (Routledge, Abingdon, 2009), pp 64–69.

37 Tom Mangold and Jeff Goldberg, *Plague Wars: a true story of biological warfare* (Macmillan, London, 1999), p 236. Stephen Burgess and Helen Purkitt, *The Rollback of South Africa's Chemical and Biological Warfare Programme* (USAF Counterproliferation Centre, Maxwell AFB, AL, 2001), p 3.

38 Republic of South Africa, *White Paper on Defence and Armaments Production* (Government Printer, Pretoria, 1977), pp 4–5.

39 Eugene de Kock, *A Long Night's Damage*, p 93.

40 Chris Alden, *Apartheid's Last Stand*, pp 52, 68 *passim*.

41 Chris Alden, *Apartheid's Last Stand*, p 43.

42 Deon Fourie, 'Decline and fall: why the South African civilian Defence Secretariat was dissolved in 1966', *Scientia Militaria*, 40(3), 2012, pp 40–70; Warwick Dorning, 'A concise history of the South African Defence Force, 1912–1987', *Militaria*, 17(2), 1987, pp 19–20.

43 Warwick Dorning, 'A concise history of the South African Defence Force, 1912–1987', p 20.

44 R von Moltke, 'Die ontstaan en ontwikkeling van die Stafafdeling Hoof van Staf Personeel', pp 46–55; SC le Grange, 'Die geskiedenis van Hoof van Staf Inligting', pp 56–58; SC le Grange, 'Die geskiedenis van Stafafdeling Operasies', pp 59–61; AC Bergh, 'Die geskiedenis van Afdeling Logistiek', pp 62–65, all in the 1912–1982 Commemorative Issue of *Militaria*, 12(2), 1982.

45 The Comptroller SADF was redesignated Chief of Staff Management Systems in November 1976. This office became Chief of Staff Finance in February 1978. AC Lillie, 'Chief of Staff Finance', *Militaria*, 12(2), 1982, pp 66–69.

46 Warwick Dorning, 'A concise history of the South African Defence Force, 1912–1987', p 20.

47 Defence Amendment Act 1967.

48 David Williams, *On the Border*, p 21. See also *South African Defence Force Review*, 1985, p 25.

49 McGill Alexander, 'The militarisation of South African white society, 1948–1990', *Scientia Militaria*, 30(2), 2000, p 285. For an area study on the Vaal Triangle region, see SM Fourie, 'Van mobilisering na transformasie: die era van Suid-Afrika se militêre hoogbloei met die Vaaldriehoekse samelewing (1974–1994) as konsentrasieveld', *Scientia Militaria*, 30(2), 2000, pp 291–308.

50 Graeme Callister, 'Patriotic duty or resented imposition? Public reactions to military conscription in white South Africa, 1952–1972', *Scientia Militaria*, 35(1), 2007, p 46.

51 McGill Alexander, 'The militarisation of South African white society, 1948–1990', p 287. Jacklyn Cock, 'Manpower and militarisation: women and the SADF', in Jacklyn Cock and Laurie Nathan, eds, *War and Society: the militarisation of South Africa* (David Philip, Cape Town, 1989), p 61.

52 CJ Nothling and L Steyn, 'The role of non-whites in the South African Defence Force', *Militaria*, 16(2), 1986, pp 47–54; CM Meyer, 'The role of blacks in the South African Defence Force, 1912–1987', in *South African Defence Force Review*, 1988, pp 293–99. Much of this literature, when viewed through a 2015 lens, is crude and patronising.

53 Willem Steenkamp, *South Africa's Border War*, p 22. Chris Alden, *Apartheid's Last Stand*, p 98. See also Leopold Scholtz, *The SADF in the Border War, 1966–1989*, chapter 2.

54 WS van der Waals, *Portugal's War in Angola, 1961–1974*, pp 46–53.

55 Fidel Castro, *My Life*, p 320.

56 Willem Steenkamp, *South Africa's Border War 1966–1989*, p 44.

57 Fapla, or Forças Armadas Populares de Libertação de Angola, originally the military wing of the MPLA, became the Angolan regular army.

58 Sophia du Preez, *Avontuur in Angola: die verhaal van Suid-Afrika se soldate in Angola 1975–1976* (JL van Schaik, Pretoria, 1989), chapter 1. See also FJ du Toit Spies, *Operasie Savannah: Angola, 1975–1976* (SADF, Pretoria, 1989).

59 Willem Steenkamp, *South Africa's Border War 1966–1989*, pp 52–53.

60 In hindsight this figure may be closer to 3 000. Warwick Dorning, 'A concise history of the South African Defence Force,

1912–1987', p 21.

61 The number of troops per square kilometre in theatre. Archer Jones, *The Art of War in the Western World* (OUP, Oxford, 1989), p 339.

62 WS van der Waals, *Portugal's War in Angola, 1961–1974*, pp 1–9.

63 Roland de Vries, *Eye of the Firestorm: strength lies in mobility* (Naledi, Tyger Valley, 2013), p 439.

64 John Stockwell, *In Search of Enemies: a CIA story* (Futura, London, 1979), p 191.

65 Jan Breytenbach, *Eagle Strike! The Story of the Controversial Airborne Assault on Cassinga, 1978* (Grove, Sandton, 2008), p 10.

66 Roland de Vries, *Mobiele Oorlogvoering: 'n perspektief vir Suider-Afrika* (FJN Harman Uitgewers, Menlopark, 1987), p xvii. 'Die primêre tema van hierdie geskrif is MOBILITEIT. Dit is opgstel in die vaste geloof en uit vurige oortuiging dat 'n Suider-Afrika-krygsmag in die toekoms slegs deur vinnige en doeltreffende optrede, sy wilsopponente op enige salgveld in Suider-Afrika sal kan verslaan.'

67 Eugene de Kock, *A Long Night's Damage*, p 65.

68 Leopold Scholtz, *The SADF in the Border War, 1966–1989*, pp 31–32.

69 International Institute for Strategic Studies, *The Military Balance, 1986–1987* (Garden City Press, Letchworth, 1986), p 136. Russ Stayanoff, 'Third World experience in counterinsurgency: Cuba's Operation Carlotta, 1975', *Small Wars Journal*, 17 May 2008, , p 1.

70 Sophia du Preez, *Avontuur in Angola*, p 11. *The Military Balance, 1977–1978*, p 43. Russ Stayanoff, 'Third World experience in counterinsurgency', p 9.

71 Russ Stayanoff, 'Third World experience in counterinsurgency', pp 4, 9–10. Piero Gleijeses, *Conflicting Missions: Havana, Washington, Pretoria* (Galago, Alberton, 2003), pp 377, 391.

72 Russ Stayanoff, 'Third World experience in counterinsurgency'; Fidel Castro, *My Life*, p 321.

73 Vladmir Shubin, *The Hot 'Cold War': the USSR in southern Africa* (UKZN Press, Scottsville, 2008), p 59.

74 General Ramon Espinosa Martin was among the severely wounded. Russ Stayanoff, 'Third World experience in counterinsurgency', pp 2, 4–8; Piero Gleijeses, *Conflicting Missions*, p 324 *passim*.

75 As quoted by Russ Stayanoff, 'Third World

experience in counterinsurgency', p 9.

76 Castro to Kurochkin quoted in Vladmir Shubin, *The Hot 'Cold War'*, p 97.

77 Vladmir Shubin, *The Hot 'Cold War'*, p 79 *passim*.

78 Raul Castro to the Soviet ambassador, as quoted in Vladmir Shubin, *The Hot 'Cold War'*, p 222.

79 General 'Polo', as quoted in Vladmir Shubin, *The Hot 'Cold War'*, p 226.

80 Leopold Scholtz, *The SADF in the Border War, 1966–1989*, pp 31–32.

81 Fidel Castro, *My Life*, p 308 *passim*.

82 Jannie Geldenhuys, *At the Front: a general's account of South Africa's Border War* (Jonathan Ball, Johannesburg and Cape Town, 2009), p 53.

83 Jannie Geldenhuys, *At the Front*, p 92.

84 General Constand Viljoen, quoted by Leopold Scholtz, *The SADF in the Border War, 1966–1989*, p 41.

85 Leopold Scholtz, *The SADF in the Border War, 1966–1989*, pp 39, 42–44.

86 Leopold Scholtz, *The SADF in the Border War, 1966–1989*, pp 42, 47.

87 Jannie Geldenhuys, *At the Front*, p 69 *passim*.

88 Other units were 101 Battalion (Ovambo), 102 Battalion (Kaokoveld), 201 and 203 (Bushmen), 202 (Okavango), 701 (Eastern Caprivi), 911 Battalion (multi-ethnic). Unit histories are scarce, and 31 Battalion is poorly served by Ian Uys, *Bushman Soldiers: their alpha and omega* (Fortress, Germiston, 1993).

89 Jan Breytenbach, *They Lived By The Sword: 32 'Buffalo' Battalion – South Africa's Foreign Legion* (Lemur, Alberton, 1990), pp 11–18; LJ Bothma, *Buffalo Battalion: South Africa's 32 Battalion – A tale of sacrifice* (Bothma, Bloemfontein, 2008), p 74. See also Marius Scheepers, *Striking Inside Angola with 32 Battalion* (30 Degrees South, Pinetown, 2012), p 21; and Piet Nortje, *The Terrible Ones: a complete history of 32 Battalion*, 2 vols (Zebra Press, Cape Town, 2012).

90 SJ du Preez and CJ Nothling, 'Die veldtog in Angola, 1975–1976', in CJ Nothling, ed, *Ultima Ration Regum: artillery history of South Africa* (Military Information Bureau, Pretoria, 1987), pp 265–85.

91 McGill Alexander, 'The militarisation of South African white society, 1948–1990', p 270. Warwick Dorning, 'A concise history of the South African Defence Force, 1912–1987', p 21; Rodney Warwick, 'Operation Savannah: a measure of SADF decline, resourcefulness and modernisation', *Scientia Militaria*, 40(3),

2012, pp 354–397; Leopold Scholtz, *The SADF in the Border War, 1966–1989*, pp 7–8; Evert Jordaan, 'The role of South African armour in South West Africa/Namibia and Angola, 1975–1989', *Journal of Contemporary History*, 31(3), 2006, p 166.

92 Rodney Warwick, 'Operation Savannah', pp 354–397; Leopold Scholtz, *The SADF in the Border War, 1966–1989*, pp 9–10; *The Military Balance, 1974–1977*, p 44.

93 Leopold Scholtz, *The SADF in the Border War, 1966–1989*, p 10.

94 Warwick Dorning, 'A concise history of the South African Defence Force, 1912–1987', p 21.

95 General Magnus Malan, as quoted by Hilton Hamman, *Days of the Generals: the untold story of South Africa's apartheid-era generals* (Zebra, Cape Town, 2001), pp 44–45.

96 Paul Moorcraft and Peter McLaughlin, *The Rhodesian War*, pp 31–33; James Ngculu, *The Honour to Serve*, p 29.

97 GC Khwela, 'The Clausewitzian and heuristic evolution of the ANC's armed struggle: a dependent pillar of the South African revolution', *Scientia Militaria*, 30(2), 2000.

98 Mokgethi Motlhabi, *The Theory and Practice of Black Resistance to Apartheid*, pp 66–71; Chris Alden, *Apartheid's Last Stand*, pp 90–93; Stephen M Davis, *Apartheid's Rebels: inside South Africa's hidden war* (Ad Donker, Craighall, 1987), pp 118–19.

99 See Martin Legassick, *Armed Struggle and Democracy: the case of South Africa* (Nordiska Afrikainstitutet, Uppsala, 2002) as well as James Ngculu, *The Honour to Serve*, p 156, and Chris Alden, *Apartheid's Last Stand*, p 92.

100 James Ngculu, *The Honour to Serve*, pp 156–59.

101 The atrocities committed in the ANC's camps of exile are addressed *inter alia* by Paul Trewhela, *Inside Quatro: uncovering the exile history of the ANC and SWAPO* (Jacana, Auckland Park, 2010) and Todd Cleveland, '"We still want the truth": the ANC's Angolan detention camps and postapartheid memory', *Comparative Studies of South Asia, Africa and the Middle East*, 25(1), 2005, p 7, and those in South Africa by Anthea Jeffery, *People's War: new light on the struggle for South Africa* (Jonathan Ball, Jeppestown, 2009). A more sympathetic view of the *Shishita* (sweeping) campaign within the ANC-in-exile is presented in James Ngculu, *The Honour to Serve*, chapter 11.

102 On the theory of farm protection and the range of physical measures, including communication and alarm systems, grenade screens and window and door protection, to the role of women and employees, see WM Leonard, *Plaasbeveiliging: 'n handleiding vir die boer* (Unibook, Pretoria, 1988).

103 AS Mathews, *Law, Order and Liberty in South Africa* (Juta, Cape Town, 1971), pp 221–30, 233–38.

104 Eugene de Kock, *A Long Night's Damage*, pp 92–96.

105 Paul Moorcraft and Peter McLaughlin, *The Rhodesian War*, pp 156, 177–79. Stephen Burgess and Helen Purkitt, *The Rollback of South Africa's Chemical and Biological Warfare Programme*, p 8.

106 Stephen Burgess and Helen Purkitt, *The Rollback of South Africa's Chemical and Biological Warfare Programme*, p 9.

107 Tom Mangold and Jeff Goldberg, *Plague Wars*, chapter 24.

108 Chris Alden, *Apartheid's Last Stand*, pp 97, 118–19.

109 Chris Alden, *Apartheid's Last Stand*, p 99.

110 PHR Snyman, *Beeld van die SWA Gebiedsmag* (Pretoria, 1989).

111 IFW Beckett, *Modern Insurgencies and Counter-Insurgencies: guerrillas and their opponents since 1750* (Routledge, London and New York, 2003), p 141. Leopold Scholtz, *The SADF in the Border War, 1966–1989*, pp 198–99.

112 AJ Venter, *The Chopper Boys: helicopter warfare in Africa* (Southern, Halfway House, 1994), pp 139–58.

113 Leopold Scholtz, *The SADF in the Border War, 1966–1989*, pp 197–98; Jannie Geldenhuys, *At the Front*, p 62.

114 Chris Alden, *Apartheid's Last Stand*, p 101.

115 Jannie Geldenhuys, *At the Front*, pp 95–96.

116 EGM Alexander, 'The Cassinga Raid' (unpublished MA thesis, Unisa, July 2003).

117 Warwick Dorning, 'A concise history of the South African Defence Force, 1912–1987', p 20; Willem Steenkamp, *South Africa's Border War*, chapter 7.

118 Chris Alden, *Apartheid's Last Stand*, p 101; Leopold Scholtz, *The SADF in the Border War, 1966–1989*, chapter 7.

119 Chris Alden, *Apartheid's Last Stand*, pp 102–103.

120 The Resistência Nacional Moçambicana (Renamo) was originally set up by the Rhodesian Central Intelligence Organisation (CIO) to oppose Mozambique's Marxist government.

121 John Dzimba, *South Africa's Destabilisation of Zimbabwe, 1980–89* (Macmillan, Basingstoke and London, 1998), pp 94–98; Chris Alden, *Apartheid's Last Stand*, pp 105–108.

122 Jacinto Veloso, *Memories at Low Altitude*, p 138.

123 The full text of the accord, and of the speeches delivered by PW Botha and Samora Machel, may be found in Department of Foreign Affairs, *The Accord of Nkomati* (Perskor, Pretoria, 1984), pp 1–35.

124 Jacinto Veloso, *Memories at Low Altitude*, pp 138–46; Chris Alden, *Apartheid's Last Stand*, pp 108–112.

125 James Ngculu, *The Honour to Serve*, p 155.

126 Chris Alden, *Apartheid's Last Stand*, pp 112–16. See also David Scott, *Ambassador in Black and White*, pp 185–86.

127 Darryl Howlett and John Simpson, 'Nuclearisation and denuclearisation in South Africa', p 154.

128 B Rabert, 'South Africa's nuclear weapons: a defused time bomb?', *Aussenpolitik*, 44(3), 1993, pp 232–42; Darryl Howlett and John Simpson, 'Nuclearisation and denuclearisation in South Africa', pp 154–73; Chris Alden, *Apartheid's Last Stand*, pp 97, 118–19.

129 Darryl Howlett and John Simpson, 'Nuclearisation and denuclearisation in South Africa', pp 154–73.

130 Chris Alden, *Apartheid's Last Stand*, p 120.

131 F van Zyl Slabbert, *The System and the Struggle: reform, revolt and reaction in South Africa*, ed Dene Smuts (Jonathan Ball, Johannesburg, 1989), pp 69–78.

132 Chris Alden, *Apartheid's Last Stand*, p 151.

133 Anthea Jeffery, *People's War*, pp 94, 99, 104, 109–113.

134 Anthea Jeffery, *People's War*, pp 89–94, 97–98.

135 Chris Alden, *Apartheid's Last Stand*, pp 170–751.

136 Chris Alden, *Apartheid's Last Stand*, p 208.

137 F van Zyl Slabbert, *The System and the Struggle*, pp 92–100.

138 Eugene de Kock, *A Long Night's Damage*, p 91.

139 Eugene de Kock, *A Long Night's Damage*, p 91.

140 Leopold Scholtz, *The SADF in the Border War, 1966–1989*, pp 238–42. Chris Alden, *Apartheid's Last Stand*, p 179.

141 Fidel Castro, *My Life*, pp 322–23. Vladimir Shubin, *The Hot 'Cold War'*, pp 72–103. Chris Alden, *Apartheid's Last Stand*, p 179.

142 Leopold Scholtz, *The SADF in the Border War, 1966–1989*, pp 194–214. Chris Alden, *Apartheid's Last Stand*, p 180.

143 Chris Alden, *Apartheid's Last Stand*, pp 211–15. Anthea Jeffery, *People's War*, pp 123–57.

144 Martin Legassick, *Armed Struggle and Democracy*, p 32 *passim*. Chris Alden, *Apartheid's Last Stand*, pp 211–15. Anthea Jeffery, *People's War*, pp 94–95, 113–16.

145 Martin Legassick, *Armed Struggle and Democracy*, p 51.

146 As quoted in Chris Alden, *Apartheid's Last Stand*, p 216.

147 Chris Alden, *Apartheid's Last Stand*, p 216.

148 Vladimir Shubin, *The Hot 'Cold War'*, pp 104–15. Leopold Scholtz, *The SADF in the Border War, 1966–1989*, pp 305–18. Helmoed-Römer Heitman, *War in Angola: the final South African phase* (Ashanti, Gibraltar, 1990), p 73 *passim*.

149 Helmoed-Römer Heitman, *War in Angola*, p 274 *passim*; Fred Bridgland, *The War for Africa: twelve months that transformed a continent* (Ashanti, Gibraltar, 1993).

150 Chris Alden, *Apartheid's Last Stand*, pp 235–37, 243–45.

151 Stephen Ellis and T Sechaba, *Comrades Against Apartheid*, p 191.

152 Peter Stiff, *Nine Days of War* (Lemur, Alberton, 1989).

CHAPTER EIGHT
The South African National Defence Force, 1994 to circa 2000

1 Foreword to Christopher Dandeker, *Facing Uncertainty: flexible forces for the twenty-first century* (National Defence College, Karlstad, 1999), p 1. [Emphasis in the original.]

2 Roel van der Veen, *Afrika: van de Koude Oorlog naar de 21ste eeuw* (KIT, Amsterdam, 2002), chapter 1. Luís B Serapião, 'African foreign policies and African unity', in Luís Serapião et al, *African Foreign Policies in the 21st century* (Africa Institute of South Africa, Pretoria, 2001), pp 6–8. Christopher Dandeker, *Facing Uncertainty*, pp 15–16. See also Vladimir Shubin, *The Hot 'Cold War': the USSR in southern Africa* (UKZN Press, Scottsville, 2008), pp 1–3.

3 Roel van der Veen, *Afrika: van de Koude Oorlog naar de 21ste eeuw*, p 52.

4 Christopher Dandeker, *Facing Uncertainty*, p 3.

5 The Part-Time Forces were the old Citizen Force, the Full-Time Forces the old Permanent Force.

6 Evert Jordaan, 'Contemporary South African

National Security Policy' (Research Paper, Faculty of Military Science, Stellenbosch University, 2001), p 1 *passim*.

7 Constitution of the Republic of South Africa, Act 200 of 1993 (Interim Constitution).

8 Vyacheslav Shiryaev ('Comrade Ivan'), quoted in Vladimir Shubin, *The Hot 'Cold War'*, p 249.

9 Philip Frankel, *Marching to the Millennium: the birth, development and transformation of the South African National Defence Force* (Department of Defence Communication Service, Pretoria, 1998), p 7 *passim*.

10 James Ngculu, *The Honour to Serve: recollections of an Umkhonto soldier* (David Philip, Cape Town, 2009), pp 224, 230.

11 James Ngculu, *The Honour to Serve*, p 228.

12 James Ngculu, *The Honour to Serve*, pp 203, 217–21, 231.

13 L Mashike, '"Blacks can win everything, but the army": the "transformation" of the South African military between 1994 and 2004', *Journal of Southern African Studies*, 33(3), 2007, p 608.

14 James Ngculu, *The Honour to Serve*, p 229.

15 Jan Heunis, *The Inner Circle: reflections on the last days of white rule* (Jonathan Ball, Johannesburg and Cape Town, 2007), p 155.

16 Philip Frankel, *Marching to the Millennium*, p 45 *passim*.

17 At the commencement of training at De Brug the numbers stood as follows: 927 SADF; 863 TDF; 440 Transkei Police Force; 256 CDF; 188 VDF; 197 SAP; 830 MK; and 29 policemen from the 'homelands'.

18 The six dependent 'national states' were KwaZulu, Gazankulu, Lebowa, Qwaqwa, KwaNdebele, KaNgwane.

19 L Barnard and S Swanepoel, 'Die Nasionale Vredesmag in miliêre perspektief', *Scientia Militaria*, 28(1) 1998, pp 64–67.

20 James Ngculu, *The Honour to Serve*, pp 232–33.

21 Douglas G Anglin, 'The life and death of South Africa's National Peacekeeping Force', *The Journal of Modern African Studies*, 33(1) 1995, pp 21–52; L Barnard and S Swanepoel, 'Die Nasionale Vredesmag in militêre perspektief', pp 85, 87. See also Stephen Ellis, 'The historical significance of South Africa's third force', *Journal of Southern African Studies*, 24(2), 1998, pp 261–90.

22 Ronnie Kasrils, *Armed and Dangerous: from undercover struggle to freedom* (Jonathan Ball, Jeppestown, 1998), p 218. On Nyanda's underground activities see also Vladimir Shubin, *The Hot 'Cold War'*; and Paul

Trewhela, *Inside Quatro: uncovering the exile history of the ANC and SWAPO* (Jacana, Auckland Park, 2009).

23 Section 224(1) of the Constitution of the Republic of South Africa Act of 1993 (Interim Constitution).

24 Item 3 of Part D of the 6th Schedule to the Constitution of the Republic of South Africa of 1996 (1996 Constitution).

25 Ronnie Kasrils, *Armed and Dangerous*, pp 380–81.

26 Ronnie Kasrils, *Armed and Dangerous*, p 385.

27 Hilton Hamann, *Days of the Generals: the untold story of South Africa's apartheid-era military generals* (Zebra, Cape Town, 2001), p 227.

28 Ronnie Kasrils, *Armed and Dangerous*, p 387.

29 L Mashike, '"Blacks can win everything, but the army"', p 606.

30 L Heinecken, 'A diverse society, a representative military? The complexity of managing diversity in the South African armed forces', *Scientia Militaria*, 37(1), 2009, p 29.

31 L Heinecken, 'A diverse society, a representative military?', pp 29–31. See also Department of Defence (DOD), Personnel Statistics (Department of Defence, Pretoria, 2007).

32 L Heinecken, 'a diverse society, a representative military?', p 31.

33 Ronnie Kasrils, *Armed and Dangerous*, p 389.

34 Hilton Hamann, *Days of the Generals*, p 228ff.

35 Quoted in Hilton Hamann, *Days of the Generals*, p 230.

36 Jacklyn Cock, *Towards a Common Society: the integration of soldiers and armies in a future South Africa* (Military Research Group, Johannesburg, 1993), p 40.

37 H Barrell, *MK: the ANC's armed struggle* (Penguin, London, 1990), p 64.

38 Interview with former MK operative, quoted in Tsepe Motumi and Penny McKenzie, 'After the War: demobilisation in South Africa', in Jacklyn Cock and Penny McKenzie, eds, *From Defence to Development: redirecting military resources in South Africa* (David Philip, Cape Town, 1998), p 191.

39 Philip Frankel, *Marching to the Millennium*, chapters 5 and 6.

40 Tsepe Motumi and A Hudson, 'Rightsizing: the challenges of demobilisation and social reintegration in South Africa', in J Cilliers, ed, *Dismissed* (IDP, Midrand, 1995), p 120.

41 Tsepe Motumi and Penny McKenzie, 'After the War', p 181.

42 Jacklyn Cock, *Towards a Common Society*, pp 16–17, 81.

43 Tsepe Motumi and Penny McKenzie, 'After the War', p 202.

44 Tsepe Motumi and Penny McKenzie, 'After the War', p 197 *passim*.

45 James Ngculu, *The Honour to Serve*, p 204.

46 Ronnie Kasrils, *Armed and Dangerous*, p 390.

47 Max du Preez, 'SADF vs SANDF – which way to go?', *Daily News*, 14 February 2008, p 20.

48 *Phike v South African National Defence Force* (Defence Special Tribunal DST-J1/00) [2001] ZALC 152 (28 September 2001). Judge Landman: 'The legal position, as I have outlined it, takes care, at least in the circumstances of this case, of the position of what one may call a double enlistment – a soldier wearing two helmets. The applicant, assuming he had an election to belong to the SANDF as a member of the BDF or APLA, could not have made the election at the relevant time. APLA members were not to be part of the new national defence force. It is true that the applicant could have remained a covert member of APLA in the SANDF and have emerged on 4 February 1997 to claim rank and privileges as an APLA member. He did not do this. He had resigned, remained a member of APLA and in 1998 he sought to rely on his APLA membership and take his place as a SANDF member. In my view, for the reasons outlined above, he was entitled to do this.'

49 Vladimir Shubin, *The Hot 'Cold War'*, pp 241, 243, 244, 251–52.

50 Quoted in Hilton Hamann, *Days of the Generals*, pp 228–29.

51 Quoted by L Mashike, '"Blacks can win everything, but the army"', p 617.

52 As Van Wijk has argued, 'the SANDF has [perhaps] missed a critical opportunity to enhancing a unified corporate identity'. C van Wijk, 'The new SANDF rank insignia: a missed opportunity for creating a common identity', *African Security Review*, 12(3), 2003, pp 105–108.

53 See, for example, Brig Gen George Kruys (rtd), 'Some major factors influencing military efficiency in the South African National Defence Force', *Strategic Review for Southern Africa*, 26, 2004, pp 1–14.

54 AM Gossmann, 'Lost in transition: the South African military and counterinsurgency', *Small Wars and Insurgencies*, 19(4), 2008, pp 541–72.

55 L Heinecken, 'A diverse society, a representative military?', pp 25–28.

56 Department of Defence and Military Veterans, Annual Report FY 2012–2013: Safeguarding South Africa for a Better Life for All (Pretoria, 2013), p 114.

57 Section 18 of the Defence Act (42 of 2002).

58 Capt (SAN) CH Ross, *A Decade of Peace Missions* (Department of Defence, Pretoria, 2009), pp 1–24.

59 *Pretoria News*, 26 September 1998, as quoted by Theo Neethling, 'Southern African military interventions in the 1990s: the case of SADC in Lesotho', in L du Plessis and M Hough, eds, *Managing African Conflicts: the challenge of military intervention* (HSRC, Pretoria, 2000), p 291.

60 Theo Neethling, 'Southern African military interventions in the 1990s', pp 287–331. AJ Venter, *War Stories* (Protea, Pretoria, 2011), pp 479–81.

61 AJ Venter, *War Stories*, p 479.

62 Andrew Feinstein, *After the Party: a personal and political journey inside the ANC* (Jonathan Ball, Johannesburg, 2007). J Sylvester and A Seegers, 'South Africa's strategic arms package: a critical analysis', *Scientia Militaria*, 36(1), 2008, pp 52–77.

63 Capt (SAN) CH Ross, *A Decade of Peace Missions*, pp 1–24.

64 Ronnie Kasrils, *Armed and Dangerous*, p 392.

65 A Esterhuyse, 'Getting the Job Done', forthcoming. I am grateful to my colleague Abel Esterhuyse for sharing his thoughts on this with me.

Sources

Archival and Unpublished Sources

Official Papers: Government Archives

Free State Provincial Archives, Bloemfontein (FSPA)
Military Governor (MG)

National Archives of South Africa, Pretoria (NASAP)
British Agent, Pretoria (ref BA)
Colonial Office Records, 1900–1903 (FK Vols 299–1063)
Colonial Secretary (CS)
Colonial Treasurer (CT)
Commandant General, ZAR (KG)
Executive Council, Transvaal (URU)
Governor of the Transvaal Colony (GOV)
Governor General of the Union (GG)
Inspector of the Transvaal Volunteers (TVO)
Prime Minister, South Africa (PM)
Sekretaris van die Hoofkomitee van die Kommissariaat in die ZAR (HCC)
Subkomitee van die Kommissariaat, Dundee (SCD)
Transvaal Volunteers (TVO)

South African National Defence Force Documentation Centre, Military Archives, Pretoria
Adjutant General 1914–1921 (AG 1914–1921)
Adjutant General (3) (AG(3))
Adjutant General – Prisoners of War (AG POW)
Chief of the General Staff, Group 1 and 2 (CGS) and War (CGS War)
Commandant General, SA Citizen Force (SACF)
Deputy Chief of Staff (DCS)
Director General War Supplies (DGWS)
Director Seaward Defence Force (SD)
Diverse Group 1

General Officer Commanding, Union Defence Force (UDF)
Medical Department (MD)
Military Adviser, London (MA)
Military Intelligence Division (AMI) Group 3
Minister of Defence – Erasmus and Fouché Collection (MVEF)
Minister of Defence – PW Botha Collection (MVB)
Northern Transvaal Command (N Tvl Comd)
Officer-in-Charge, Records (OC Records)
Personnel Files
Plan Z archive
Prisoner of War (POW)
Provost Marshal (PMK, PMC and PMP)
Rebel Commission
Senior Air Liaison Officer, Tokyo (SALO)
South African Mounted Rifles (SAMR)
Secretary for Defence (DC) Group 2
War Diaries and Missions (WDM)
World War 1 Diaries and Appendices (WO1DA)
World War 1 Diverse Papers (WW1 Diverse)
World War 1 German South West Africa (WW1 GSWA)
World War 1 Imperial Service Details (WWI ISD)

The National Archives of the United Kingdom, Kew (TNA)

Admiralty (ADM)
Air Ministry (AIR)
Cabinet (CAB)
Colonial Office (CO)
Dominions Office (DO)
Foreign Office (FO)
Prime Minister (PREM)
Security Service – MI5 (KV)
War Office (WO)

Western Cape Provincial Archives and Records Centre (WCPA)

Colonial Office (CO)
Government House Archives (GH)

Private Papers

Major General Sir George Aston Papers, Royal Marines Archives, Eastney Barracks,
    Portsmouth, UK
Col HWM Bamford Collection (A20), NASAP
Andrew Beauchamp Proctor Papers (BCS115), Archives and Manuscripts, Jagger
    Library, University of Cape Town (UCT)
General CF Beyers Collection (A414), NASAP
T Boydell Collection (A75), NASAP

Archbishop William Carter Papers (AB186), William Cullen Library, University of
    the Witwatersrand (Wits)
Sir WH Clark Papers (BC81), UCT
Lionel Curtis Papers, Bodleian Library, Oxford
Geoffrey Dawson Papers, Bodleian Library, Oxford
NJ de Wet Collection, NASAP
Sir Patrick Duncan Papers (BC294), UCT
Colonel Mike du Toit Collection (W77), NASAP
Elsey Papers, Truman Presidential Library and Museum, Independence, Missouri
Dr FV Engelenburg (A140), NASAP
Sir George Farrar Papers (Mss Afr S 2175), Rhodes House, Oxford (RHO)
Richard Feetham Papers (Mss Afr S 1793), RHO
Fremantle Collection (A608), WCPA
Sir De Villiers Graaff Collection, Unisa
Major WL Gordon Collection (BC1096), UCT
Field Marshal Earl Kitchener Papers – microfilm (M722), NASAP
Sergeant Major Alex J Knox Collection (A164), NASAP
Uys Krige Collection, JS Gericke Library, Stellenbosch University
HG Lawrence Papers (BC640), UCT
Charles Leonard Collection (M725), NASAP
Lyttelton Family Papers, Hagley Hall Archive (HHA), Hagley, West Midlands
Dr DF Malan Collection, Special Collections, JS Gericke Library, Stellenbosch
    University
FS Malan Collection (A583), WCPA
Maxse Papers, Chichester, West Sussex Record Office (WSRO)
James Metcalfe Papers (BC915), UCT
Sir Lewis Michell Collection (A540), WCPA
Milner Adds, Bodleian Library, Oxford
Violet Milner Papers, Bodleian Library, Oxford
Joyce Newton-Thompson Collection (BC643), UCT
Dr GS Preller Collection (A787), NASAP
Purland Family Collection (BC477), UCT
Schoeman Papers (W125/6), NASAP
Trooper Lyle Richmond Simes Collection, Natal Carbineers Archives,
    Pietermaritzburg
Field Marshal JC Smuts Papers (A1), NASAP
Sir Herbert James Stanley Papers (Mss Afr S 1250), RHO
Truman Papers, Truman Presidential Library and Museum, Independence, Missouri
Hugh and Maud Wyndham Papers, Petworth House Archive (PHA), WSRO

Organisational Papers

Ossewabrandwag Archives, Ferdinand Postma Library, North-West University,
    Potchefstroom
United Party Archives, Archives and Special Collections, University of South Africa

Published Sources

Newspaper and Periodical Articles

'Smuts's New Tangle: Trouble at Military School', *Rand Daily Mail*, 9 October 1912.

'Beyers' Letter: Strange Ideas of Duty and Honour; Stinging Reply from Smuts; No Lip-Loyalty in the Union', *Rand Daily Mail*, 21 September 1914.

'General Smuts and Mr Beyers', *Rand Daily Mail*, 22 September 1914.

'Fresh Call for Volunteers: Union's Second 'Little Bit'; Mostly Infantry Wanted; Details of Terms of Service', *Rand Daily Mail*, 21 July 1915.

'Heavy Artillery in Flanders: General Terms of Service', *Rand Daily Mail*, 22 July 1915.

'Wanted in Europe: Call for Heavy Artillery, Opening for South Africans', *Rand Daily Mail*, 22 July 1915.

'Generaal Botha's Reputatie wederrechtelik aangestast: maar Kragtig verdedigd', *De Volkstem*, 2 November 1915.

'In Egypte: Generaal Lukins Kolonne; De vijand op de vlucht', *De Burger*, 29 February 1916.

'Het Parlement, De Volksraad', *De Burger*, 18 March 1916.

'Was General Botha in 1900 'n verrader?', *De Spectator*, 8 April 1916.

'De Grote Volkerenstrijd', *De Burger*, 29 February 1916, 20 March 1916 and 17 July 1916.

'Union's Roll of Honour. Deathless Deeds at Delville Wood. Musical Memorial Service in the City Hall. Mr Merriman on South Africa's Heritage', *Cape Times*, 19 July 1917.

'From the Arctic Circle', *The Nongqai*, November 1918.

'Russia in Revolution', *The Nongqai*, May 1920.

'Dr Malan en die Dardanelle', *Volkstem*, 2 September 1922.

'Geen man en geen pennie; Ons leier oor die wereld-krises', *Ons Vaderland*, 22 September 1922.

'Democracy and Party Strife: Sir Patrick Duncan's Warning', *The Times*, London, 7 July 1939.

'Dr Malan Exonerated', *The Cape Times*, 18 June 1946.

Lt Gen Len Beyers to the editor, *Rand Daily Mail*, 17 April 1950.

'Malan Calls Cabinet', *The Argus*, 4 August 1950.

'Meeting of the Cabinet lasted all day', *The Argus*, 5 August 1950.

Len Jerome to The Editor of *The Star*, circa March 1952.

Mills, Greg, 'Cannon fodder for man's first mechanised mass murder', *The Sunday Independent*, 13 February 2005.

Max du Preez, 'SADF vs SANDF – which way to go?', *Daily News*, 14 February 2008, p 20.

Published Diaries, Memoirs, Speeches, Letters and Autobiographies

Axelson, Eric, *A Year in Italy: an observer with the South African 6th Armoured Division, 1944–1945* (EH Walton, Port Elizabeth, 2001).

Babenia, Natoo, *Memoirs of a Saboteur: reflections on my political activity in India and South Africa* (Mayibuye Books, Bellville, 1995).

Barlow, Arthur G, *That We May Tread Safely* (Tafelberg, Cape Town, 1960).

Birkby, Carel, *In the Sun … I'm Rich* (Howard B Timmins, Cape Town, nd).

Bothma, LJ, *Buffalo Battalion: South Africa's 32 Battalion – A tale of sacrifice* (Bothma, Bloemfontein, 2008).

Bousted, Col Sir Hugh, *The Wind of Morning* (London, 1971).

Boyce, DG, ed, *The Crisis of British Power: the Imperial and Naval Papers of the Second Earl of Selborne, 1895–1910* (The Historians' Press, London, 1990).

Breytenbach, Jan, *They Lived By The Sword: 32 'Buffalo' Battalion – South Africa's Foreign Legion* (Lemur, Alberton, 1990).

Butler, WF, *Sir William Butler: an autobiography* (Constable, London, 1911).

Castro, Fidel, *My Life* (Penguin, London, 2008).

De Kock, Eugene, *A Long Night's Damage: working for the apartheid state* (Contra Press, Johannesburg, 1998).

De Vries, Roland, *Mobiele Oorlogvoering: 'n perspektief vir Suider-Afrika* (FJN Harman Uitgewers, Menlopark, 1987).

De Wet, CR, *Three Years War, October 1899–June 1902* (Archibald Constable, London. 1902; Galago, Johannesburg, 1986).

Dimbleby, KG, *Hostilities Only* (Unie-Volkspers, Cape Town, 1944).

Fitzpatrick, JP, *The Transvaal From Within* (William Heinemann, London, 1899).

Geldenhuys, Jannie, *At the Front: a general's account of South Africa's Border War* (Jonathan Ball, Johannesburg and Cape Town, 2009).

Graaff, Sir De Villiers, *Div looks back: the memoirs of Sir De Villiers Graaff* (Human & Rousseau, Cape Town, 1993).

Grobler, MJ, *Met die Vrystaaters onder die Wapen: Generaal Prinsloo en die Bethlehem-Kommando* (Nasionale Pers, Bloemfontein, 1937).

Hancock, WK and J van der Poel, eds, *Selections from the Smuts Papers, vol III: June 1910–November 1918* (Cambridge University Press, Cambridge, 1966).

Hartshorn, EP, *Avenge Tobruk* (Purnell, Johannesburg, 1960).

Headlam, Cecil, ed, *The Milner Papers: South Africa, vol II, 1899–1905* (Cassell, London, 1933).

Heunis, Jan, *The Inner Circle: reflections on the last days of white rule* (Jonathan Ball, Johannesburg and Cape Town, 2007).

Hiemstra, RC, *Die Wilde Haf* (Human & Rousseau, Kaapstad, 2001).

Kasrils, Ronnie, *Armed and Dangerous: from undercover struggle to freedom* (Jonathan Ball, Jeppestown, 1998).

Kemp, JCG, *Die Pad van die Veroweraar* (Nasionale Pers, Kaapstad, 1942, 1946).

Krige, Uys, *The Way Out* (Unie-Volkspers, Cape Town and Port Elizabeth, 1946).

Lettow-Vorbeck, PE von, *My Reminiscences of East Africa* (Hurst and Blackett, London 1920).

Lewsen, P, ed, *Selections from the Correspondence of John X Merriman 1899–1905* (VRS, Cape Town, 1966).

Lewsen, P, ed, *Selections from the Correspondence of John X Merriman, 1905–1924* (VRS, Cape Town, 1969).

Leyds, WJ, *Leyds Correspondentie, 1899–1900* (NV Geuze & Co Drukkerij, 1930).

Marais, AH, ed, *Politieke Briewe, I: 1909–1910* (Instituut vir Eietydse Geskiedenis, Bloemfontein, 1971).

Marais, AH, ed, *Politieke Briewe, II: 1911–1912* (Instituut vir Eietydse Geskiedenis, Bloemfontein, 1973).

Masterman, L, ed, *Mary Gladstone (Mrs Drew) Her Diaries and Letters* (EP Dutton, New York, 1930).

May, ES, *A retrospect of the South African War* (Sampson Low Marston, London, 1901).

Nattrass, G and SB Spies, eds, *Jan Smuts: Memoirs of the Boer War* (Jonathan Ball, Johannesburg, 1994).

Ngculu, James, *The Honour to Serve: recollections of an Umkhonto soldier* (David Philip, Claremont, 2009).

Oost, Harm, *Wie is die skuldiges?* (Johannesburg, 1958).

Reitz, Deneys, *Commando: a Boer journal of the Boer War* (Jonathan Ball, 2009).

Reitz, Deneys, *Trekking On: in the company of brave men* (Emslie, Edinburgh, 2012).

Robinson, JP Kay, *With Botha's Army* (George Allen & Unwin, London, 1916).

Scott, Sir David, *Ambassador in Black and White: thirty years of changing Africa* (Weidenfeld and Nicholson, London, 1981).

Stockwell, John, *In Search of Enemies: a CIA story* (Futura, London, 1979).

Taitz, J and K Gillings and A Davey, eds, *The War Memoirs of Commandant Ludwig Krause, 1899–1900* (Van Riebeeck Society, Cape Town, 1996).

Trew, HF, *Botha Treks* (Blackie & Son, London and Glasgow, 1936).

Van der Byl, Piet, *From Playgrounds to Battlefields* (Howard Timmins, Cape Town, 1971).

Van der Spuy, Maj Gen Sir KR, *Chasing the Wind* (Books of Africa, Cape Town, 1966).

Van Schoor, MCE, *'n Bittereinder aan die woord: geskrifte en toesprake van Mathinus Theunis Steyn* (Oorlogsmuseum van die Boererepublieke, Bloemfontein, 1997).

Van Zyl Slabbert, F, *The System and the Struggle: reform, revolt and reaction in South Africa*, ed Dene Smuts (Jonathan Ball, Johannesburg, 1989).

Veloso, Jacinto, *Memories at Low Altitude: the autobiography of a Mozambican security chief* (Zebra, Cape Town, 2012).

Whittal, W. *With Botha and Smuts in Africa* (Cassell, London, 1917).

Government Publications

Hansard

Debatten van de Volksraad, 21 February 1911, cols 1263–66.

Debatten van de Volksraad, 7 March 1912, col 736.

Debates of the House of Assembly of the Union of South Africa, 1910–1994.

Debates of the Senate, 1947.

Acts of Parliament

Defence Act (No 44 of 1957)

Defence Act Amendment Act (22 of 1922)

Defence Endowment Property and Account Act (33 of 1922)

Industrial Development Act (22 of 1940)

South Africa Defence Act (13 of 1912)

Proclamations and Government Notices

Government Notice No 17 of 1923 (Supplement of the Union of South Africa, *Government Gazette* No 1289 of 26 Jan 1923), published in terms of section one of the South Africa Defence Act Amendment Act (No 22 of 1922).

Proclamation 21, *Official Gazette of the Protectorate of South-West Africa in Military Occupation of the Union Forces* (No 25 of 24 Dec 1919).

Transvaal Colony, 1901–1902.

South African Parliamentary Papers – blue books

Select Committees
SC 7–1912. Select Committee Report. On South Africa Defence Bill.

Papers printed by order of the Union Government
UG 55–1913. Report of the Witwatersrand Disturbances Commission.
UG 56–1913. Judicial Commission of Enquiry into Witwatersrand Disturbances June-July 1913.
UG 61–1913. Annual Reports Department of Defence and Executive Commands for the year ending 30th June 1913.
UG 10–1915. Report on the Outbreak of the Rebellion and the Policy of the Government with regard to its suppression.
UG 46–1916. Report of the Judicial Commission of Inquiry into the Causes and Circumstances relating to the Recent Rebellion in South Africa.

Miscellaneous
Index to the Manuscript Annexures and Printed papers of the House of Assembly including Select Committee Reports and Bills and also to Principal Motions and Resolutions and Commission Reports, 1910–1930 (Cape Town, 1931).
Statistical Register of the Province of the Cape of Good Hope for the Year 1909 (Government Printer, Cape Town, 1910).
Union Office of Census and Statistics, *The Union of South Africa and the War* (Government Printer, Pretoria, 1948).

Transvaal Legislative Council

Transvaal Official List of the Civil Service (Pretoria, 1903).

Colony of Natal

Departmental Reports, 1899 (Government Printer, Pietermaritzburg, 1900).

Department of Defence, Union of South Africa

Annual Reports and Policy Documents
Abridged Annual Report of the Department of Defence for the Year ended 30 June 1921 (Government Printer, Pretoria, 1922).
Abridged Annual Report of the Department of Defence, Union of South Africa, for the Year ended 30 June 1923 (Pretoria, 1924).

Abridged Annual Report of the Department of Defence for the Year ended 30 June 1921 (Government Printer, Pretoria, 1922).

Abridged Annual Report of the Department of Defence for the Year ended 30 June 1925 (Pretoria, 1926).

Annual Report of the Department of Defence for the Year ended 30 June 1926 (Pretoria, 1927).

Annual Report of the Department of Defence for the Year ended 30 June 1932 (Pretoria, 1933).

Department of Defence, *The Nation On Guard: An Exposition of South Africa's Defence Policy* (Maskew Miller, Cape Town, 1937).

Republic of South Africa, *Review of Defence and Armaments Production: Period 1960 to 1970* (Defence Headquarters, Pretoria, April 1971).

Republic of South Africa, *White Paper on Defence and Armaments Production* (Government Printer, Pretoria, 1977).

Training Manuals
Mounted Riflemen Training
Notes on Field Sanitation
Tactical Notes for Officers
UDF Field Artillery Training
UDF Infantry Training, Part I (Drill) and Part II (Field Operations)
UDF Musketry Regulations

Orders
Routine Order 240 of 28 May 1938.
Routine Order 427 of 8 July 1939.

South African Law Reports

R v Mardon. Transvaal Provincial Division. 15–17 April 1947.

British Parliamentary Papers (BPP) – Imperial blue books

Cd 1163, 1902, Further Correspondence relating to Affairs in South Africa.

Cd 1463, 1903, Further Correspondence relating to Affairs in South Africa.

Cd 1891, 1904, Transvaal Labour Commission, Minutes of Proceedings and Evidence.

Cd 2104, 1904, Correspondence Relating to Affairs in the Transvaal and Orange River Colony.

Cd 3528, 1907, Further Correspondence Relating to Affairs in the Transvaal and Orange River Colony, 1906–7.

Cd 4948, 1909, Imperial Conference. Correspondence and Papers relating to a Conference with Representatives of the Self-Governing Dominions on the Naval and Military Defence of the Empire, 1909.

Cd 6941, 1913, Correspondence Relating to Recent Disorders on the Witwatersrand and the Employment of Regular Troops.

Cd 7874, 1914–16, SA, Report on Outbreak of Rebellion.

Cmd 153, 1919, Treaty of Peace between The Allied and Associated Powers and Germany.

Signed at Versailles, June 28th, 1919.

Cmd 1987, 1923, Imperial Conference, 1923. Summary of Proceedings.

Cmd 1990, 1923, Imperial Economic Conference, 1923. Summary of Conclusions.

Secondary Sources

Books

Aboagye, Festus B, *Indigenous African Warfare: its concept and art in the Gold Coast, Asante and the Northern Territories up to the early 1900s* (Ulinzi African Publishing, Pretoria, 2010).

Agar-Hamilton, JAI and LCF Turner, *Crisis in the Desert, May–July 1942* (OUP, Cape Town, 1952).

Alden, Chris, *Apartheid's Last Stand: the rise and fall of the South African security state* (Macmillan, Basingstoke and London, 1996).

Alexander, EGM, GKB Barron and AJ Bateman, *South African Orders, Decorations and Medals* (Human and Rousseau, Pretoria, 1986).

Amersfoort, Herman and Piet Kamphuis, eds, *May 1940: the battle for the Netherlands* (Brill, Leiden, 2010).

Anderson, Ross, *The Battle of Tanga 1914* (Tempus, Stroud, 2002).

Anderson, Ross, *The Forgotten Front: the East African campaign, 1914–1918* (Tempus, Stroud, 2004).

Andrew, Christopher, *The Defence of the Realm: the authorized history of MI5* (Allen Lane, London, 2009).

Andrew, Christopher and Vasili Mitrokhin, *The Mitrokhin Archive II: the KGB and the world* (Allen Lane, London, 2005).

Anonymous, *The Union of South Africa and the Great War: official history* (Government Printer, Pretoria, 1924).

Anonymous, *A Record of the organisation of the Director-General of War Supplies (1939–1943) and Director-General of Supplies (1943–1945)* (LS Gray & Co, Johannesburg, c 1946).

Anonymous, *The War in South Africa*, vols 1–2 (Historical Section of the Great General Staff, Berlin, 1904; reprinted Battery Press, Nashville, 1998).

Armitage, Michael, *The Royal Air Force: an illustrated history* (Brockhampton, London, 1996), 27.

Aston, Brigadier GA, *Defence of a United South Africa as a part of the British Empire* (John Murray, London, 1911).

Baines, Gary, *South Africa's Border War: contested narratives and conflicting memories* (Bloomsbury, London, 2014).

Baker, ECR, *Ace of Aces: M St J Pattle: top scoring Allied fighter pilot of World War II* (Ashanti, Rivonia, 1992).

Barrell, H, *MK: The ANC's Armed Struggle* (Penguin, London, 1990).

Becker, Dave, *Waterkloof 50* (Pretoria, 1988).

Becker, P, *Path of Blood: the rise and conquests of Mzilikazi, founder of the Matabele tribe of southern Africa* (Longmans, London, 1962).

Berridge, Geoffrey, *South Africa, the Colonial Powers and 'African Defence': the rise and fall of the white entente, 1948–1960* (Macmillan, London, 1992).

Birkby, Carel, *Uncle George: the Boer boyhood, letters and battles of Lieutenant-General George Edwin Brink* (Jonathan Ball, Johannesburg, 1987).

Bosworth, RJB, *Explaining Auschwitz and Hiroshima: history writing and the Second World War, 1945–1990* (Routledge, London and New York, 1993).

Bou, Jean, *Australia's Palestine Campaign* (Army History Unit, Canberra, 2010).

Breytenbach, Jan, *Eagle Strike! The Story of the Controversial Airborne Assault on Cassinga, 1978* (Grove, Sandton, 2008).

Breytenbach, JH, *Die Geskiedenis van die Tweede Vryheidsoorlog in Suid-Afrika* (Staatsdrukker, Pretoria, 1978).

Bridgland, Fred, *The War for Africa: twelve months that transformed a continent* (Ashanti, Gibraltar, 1993).

Brown, JA, *A Gathering of Eagles: the campaigns of the South African Air Force in Italian East Africa, June 1940–November 1941, with an Introduction, 1912–1939* (Purnell, Cape Town, 1970).

Brown, JA, *Eagles Strike: the campaigns of the South African Air Force in Egypt, Cyrenaica, Libya, Tunisia, Tripolitania and Madagascar, 1941–1943* (Purnell, Cape Town, 1974).

Brown, JA, *The War of a Hundred Days: Springboks in Somalia and Abyssinia, 1940–41* (Ashanti, Johannesburg, 1990).

Brownell, FG, *British immigration to South Africa, 1946–1970* (Archives Yearbook for South African History, Pretoria, 1985).

Buchan, John, *The History of the South African Forces in France* (London, 1920; reprinted Battery Press, Nashville, 1992).

Burgess, Stephen and Helen Purkitt, *The Rollback of South Africa's Chemical and Biological Warfare Programme* (USAF Counterproliferation Centre, Maxwell AFB, AL, 2001).

Busch, Harald, *U-Boats at War*, trans LPR Wilson (Putnam, London, 1950).

Butler, WF, *The Life of Sir George Pomeroy-Colley* (John Murray, London, 1899).

Callwell, Colonel CE, *Small Wars: their principles and practice* (Harrison and Sons, London, 1896).

Carver, Field Marshal Lord, *The Apostles of Mobility: the theory and practice of armoured warfare* (Holmes & Meier: New York, 1979).

Clayton, Anthony, *The Wars of French Decolonization* (Longman, London and New York, 1998).

Clothier, N, *Black Valour* (Pietermaritzburg, 1987).

Cock, Jacklyn, *Towards a Common Society: the integration of soldiers and armies in a future South Africa* (Military Research Group, Johannesburg, 1993).

Cockram, G, *Vorster's Foreign Policy* (Academia, Pretoria and Cape Town, 1970).

Coghlan, Mark, *Pro Patria: another 50 Natal Carbineer years, 1945 to 1995* (Natal Carbineers Trust, Pietermaritzburg, 2000).

Collyer, Brig Gen JJ, *The Campaign in German South West Africa, 1914–15* (Government Printer, Pretoria, 1937).

Collyer, Brig Gen JJ, *The South Africans with General Smuts in German East Africa, 1916* (Government Printer, Pretoria, 1939).

Couzens, Tim, *Battles of South Africa* (David Philip, Cape Town, 2004).

Couzens, Tim, *South African Battles* (Jonathan Ball, Johannesburg, 2013).

Crafford, FS, *Jan Smuts: 'n Biografie* (Edina, Kaapstad, no date).

Crawford, John (with Ellen Ellis), *To Fight for the Empire: an illustrated history of New Zealand and the South African War, 1899–1902* (Reed, Auckland, 1999).

Crwys-Williams, J, *A Country at War, 1939–1945: the mood of a nation* (Ashanti, Rivonia, 1992).

Dandeker, Christopher, *Facing Uncertainty: flexible forces for the twenty-first century* (National Defence College, Karlstad, 1999).

Davis, Stephen M, *Apartheid's Rebels: inside South Africa's hidden war* (Ad Donker, Craighall, 1987).

De Kiewiet, CW, *A History of South Africa, Social and Economic* (Clarendon Press, Oxford, 1941).

Dennis, Peter and Jeffrey Grey, eds, *The Boer War: army, nation and empire* (Army History Unit, Canberra 2000).

De Vries, Roland, *Eye of the Firestorm: strength lies in mobility* (Naledi, Tyger Valley, 2013).

Dictionary of South African Biography, vols 1–5.

Difford, ID, *The Story of the 1st Cape Corps* (Hortors, Cape Town, 1920).

Digby, PKA, *Pyramids and Poppies: the 1st SA infantry Brigade in Libya, France and Flanders, 1915–1919* (Ashanti, Rivonia, 1993).

Donaldson, Robert H and Joseph L Nogee, *The Foreign Policy of Russia: changing systems, enduring interests* (ME Sharpe, Armonk, NY, 1998).

Dubow, Saul, *Apartheid, 1948–1994* (OUP, Oxford, 2014).

Du Preez, Sophia, *Avontuur in Angola: die verhaal van Suid-Afrika se soldate in Angola 1975–1976* (JL van Schaik, Pretoria, 1989).

Dzimba, John, *South Africa's Destabilisation of Zimbabwe, 1980–89* (Macmillan, Basingstoke, 1998).

Ellis, Stephen and T Sechaba, *Comrades Against Apartheid: the ANC and the South African Communist Party in exile* (James Currey, London, 1992).

Ewing, J, *The History of the 9th (Scottish) Division* (John Murray, London, 1921).

Fedorowich, Kent, *Unfit for Heroes: reconstruction and soldier settlement in the Empire between the wars* (Manchester University Press, Manchester and New York, 1995).

Feinstein, Andrew, *After the Party: a personal and political journey inside the ANC* (Jonathan Ball, Johannesburg, 2007).

Foot, MRD and JM Langley, *MI9: the British secret service that fostered escape and evasion 1939–1945 and its American counterpart* (The Bodley Head, London, 1979).

Fox, William, *The War in New Zealand* (London, 1866).

Frankel, Philip, *Marching to the Millennium: the birth, development and transformation of the South African National Defence Force* (Department of Defence Communication Service, Pretoria, 1998).

Fraser, Evan and Andrew Rimas, *Empires of Food: feast, famine, and the rise of civilizations* (Simon & Schuster, 2010).

Gabriel, Richard and Karen Metz, *A History of Military Medicine* (Greenwood, New York and London, 1992).

Geyser, O, *Watershed for South Africa, London 1961* (Butterworths, Durban and Pretoria 1983).

Giniewski, Paul, *Die Stryd om Suidwes-Afrika* (Nasionale Boekhandel, Kaapstad, 1966).

Gleeson, Ian, *The Unknown Force: black, Indian and coloured soldiers through two world wars* (Ashanti, Rivonia, 1994).

Gleijeses, Piero, *Conflicting Missions: Havana, Washington, Pretoria* (Galago, Alberton, 2003).

Grey, Jeffrey, ed, *The Last Word? Essays on Official History in the United States and British Commonwealth* (Praeger, Westport, Connecticut, 2003).

Grey, Jeffrey, *A Military History of Australia* (Cambridge University Press, Melbourne, 2008).

Grundlingh, Albert, *Fighting Their Own War: South African blacks and the First World War* (Ravan, Johannesburg, 1987).

Grundlingh, AM, *Die 'Hendsoppers' en 'Joiners': die rasionaal en verskynsel van verraad* (HAUM, Pretoria, 1999).

Grundlingh, Albert and Sandra Swart, *Radelose Rebellie? Dinamika van die 1914–1915 Afrikanerrebellie* (Protea, Pretoria, 2009).

Grundy, K, *Soldiers Without Politics: blacks in the South African armed forces* (University of California Press, Berkeley and Los Angeles, 1983).

Halpern, Paul, *A Naval History of World War I* (United States Naval Institute, Annapolis, 1994).

Hamann, Hilton, *Days of the Generals: the untold story of South Africa's apartheid-era military generals* (Zebra, Cape Town, 2001).

Hancock, WK, *Survey of British Commonwealth Affairs, Vol 1: problems of nationality, 1918–1936* (OUP/RIIA, Oxford, 1937).

Harris, CJ, *War at Sea: South African maritime operations during World War II* (Ashanti, Rivonia, 1991).

Hattersley, Alan F, *Carbineer: the history of the Royal Natal Carbineers* (Gale and Polden, Aldershot, 1950).

Hattingh, J and Wessels, A, *Britse Fortifikasies in die Anglo-Boereoorlog*. (Oorlogsmuseum van die Boererepublieke, Bloemfontein, 1997).

Heitman, Helmoed-Römer, *War in Angola: the final South African phase* (Ashanti, Gibraltar, 1990).

Hinsley, FH and CAG Simpkins, *British Intelligence in the Second World War, vol 4: security and counter-intelligence* (HMSO, London, 1990).

Hobart Houghton, D, *The South African Economy* (OUP, Cape Town, 1980).

Hopkins, P and H Dugmore, *The Boy: Baden-Powell and the siege of Mafeking* (Zebra, Rivonia, 1999).

Jackson, A, *The British Empire and the Second World War* (Hambledon Continuum, London, 2006).

Jeffery, Anthea, *People's War: new light on the struggle for South Africa* (Jonathan Ball, Jeppestown, 2009).

Joffe, Joel, *The Rivonia Story* (Mayibuye Books, Bellville, 1995).

Jones, A, *The Art of War in the Western World* (OUP, New York and Oxford, 1987).

Judge, Edward and John Langdon, *A Hard and Bitter Peace: a global history of the Cold War* (Prentice Hall, Upper Saddle River, NJ, 1996).

Keegan, J, *The Second World War* (Penguin, London and New York, 1989).

Kitchen, M, *The British Empire and Commonwealth: a short history* (Macmillan: Basingstoke and London, 1996).

Koorts, Lindie, *DF Malan and the Rise of Afrikaner Nationalism* (Tafelberg, Cape Town, 2014).

Krüger, DW, *The Age of the Generals: a short political history of the Union of South Africa, 1910–1948* (Dagbreek, 1958).

Krüger, DW, *The Making of a Nation: a history of the Union of South Africa, 1910–1961* (Macmillan, Johannesburg and London, 1982).

Labuschagne, P, *Ghostriders of the Anglo-Boer War, 1899–1902: the role and contribution of Agterryers* (Unisa, Pretoria, 1999).

Legassick, Martin, *Armed Struggle and Democracy: the case of South Africa* (Nordiska Afrikainstitutet, Uppsala, 2002).

Leigh, Maxwell, *Captives Courageous: South African prisoners of war, World War II* (Ashanti, Johannesburg, 1992).

Le May, GHL, *British supremacy in South Africa, 1899–1907* (Clarendon, Oxford, 1965).

Leonard, WM, *Plaasbeveiliging: 'n handleiding vir die boer* (Unibook, Pretoria, 1988).

Liddell Hart, BH, *History of the First World War* (Macmillan, London, 1997).

Lukin, Colonel HT, *Savage Warfare: hints on tactics to be adopted and precautions to be taken* (Cape Town, 1906).

Mallinson, Allan, *The Making of the British Army* (Bantam Books, London, 2011).

Mangold, Tom and Jeff Goldberg, *Plague Wars: a true story of biological warfare* (Macmillan, London, 1999).

Marks, Shula, *Reluctant Rebellion: the 1906–1908 Disturbances in Natal* (Oxford, Clarendon, 1970).

Marks, S and A Atmore, eds, *Economy and Society in Pre-Industrial South Africa* (Longman, London and New York, 1980).

Martel, Lieutenant General Sir Giffard, *East Versus West* (London, Museum Press, 1952).

Martin, HJ and ND Orpen, *Eagles Victorious: the operations of the South African Forces over the Mediterranean and Europe, in Italy, the Balkans and the Aegean, and from Gibraltar and West Africa* (Purnell, Cape Town, 1977).

Martin, HJ and ND Orpen, *South Africa at War: military and industrial organisation and operations in connection with the conduct of the War, 1939–1945* (Purnell, Cape Town, 1979).

Marwick, A, *War and Social Change in the Twentieth Century: a comparative study of Britain, France, Germany, Russia and the United States* (Macmillan, Basingstoke, 1974).

Marx, C, *Oxwagon Sentinel: radical Afrikaner nationalism and the history of the Ossewabrandwag* (Unisa Press, Pretoria, 2008).

Mathews, AS, *Law, Order and Liberty in South Africa* (Juta, Cape Town, 1971).

Massie, RK, *Castles of Steel: Britain, Germany, and the winning of the Great War at sea* (Jonathan Cape, London, 2004).

Maxwell, KA and Smith, JM, *Aspera ad Astra, 1920–1970: South African Air Force Golden Jubilee Souvenir Book* (SAAF, Pretoria, 1970).

McPherson, William and Thomas J Mitchell, eds, *History of the Great War, Medical Services General History*, Vol IV (HMSO, London, 1924).

Meintjes, J, *De la Rey: lion of the west* (Hugh Keartland, Johannesburg, 1966).

Metz, S and R Millen, *Insurgency and Counterinsurgency in the 21st century: reconceptualizing threat and response* (SSI, Carlisle, PA, 2004).

Miller, Carman, *Painting the Map Red: Canada and the South African War, 1899–1902* (Canadian War Museum, Ottawa, 1998).

Millett, Allan R and Peter Maslowski, *For the Common Defense: a military history of the United States of America* (The Free Press, New York, 1994).

Mills, G and D Williams, *Seven Battles that Shaped South Africa* (Tafelberg, Cape Town, 2006).

Momeyer, WW, *Airpower in Three Wars: World War II, Korea and Vietnam* (University Press of the Pacific, Honolulu, 2002).

Montgomery, Field Marshal Lord, *A History of Warfare* (Rainbird, London, 1982).

Moorcraft, Paul and Peter McLaughlin, *The Rhodesian War: a military history* (Jonathan Ball, Johannesburg and Cape Town, 2008).

Moore, Bob and Kent Fedorowich, *The British Empire and its Italian Prisoners of War, 1940–1947* (Palgrave, Basingstoke, 2002).

Moore, Dermot and P Bagshawe, *South Africa's Flying Cheetahs in Korea* (Ashanti, Johannesburg, 1991).

Morrell, Robert, *From Boys to Gentlemen: settler masculinity in colonial Natal, 1880–1920* (Unisa, Pretoria, 2001).

Motlhabi, Mokgethi, *The Theory and Practice of Black Resistance to Apartheid: a socio-ethical analysis* (Skotaville Publishers, Johannesburg, 1984).

Mouton, JA, 'Genl Piet Joubert in die Transvaalse Geskiedenis' (*Argiefjaarboek vir Suid-Afrikaanse Geskiedenis* 1957/I).

Murray, Williamson and Allan R Millett, eds, *Military Innovation in the Interwar Period* (Cambridge University Press, Cambridge, 1996).

Nasson, Bill, *Abraham Esau's War: A Black South African War in the Cape, 1899–1902* (Cambridge University Press, Cambridge, 1991).

Nasson, Bill, *Springboks on the Somme: South Africa in the Great War, 1914–1918* (Penguin, Johannesburg, 2007).

Nasson, Bill, *The War for South Africa: the Anglo-Boer War 1899–1902* (Tafelberg, Cape Town, 2010).

Nasson, Bill, *South Africa at War, 1939–1945* (Jacana, Auckland Park, 2012).

Orpen, N, *East African and Abyssinian Campaigns* (Purnell, Cape Town and Johannesburg, 1968).

Orpen, N, *War in the Desert* (Purnell, Cape Town and Johannesburg, 1971).

Orpen, N, *Victory in Italy* (Purnell, Cape Town and Johannesburg, 1975).

Orpen, N and HJ Martin, *Salute the Sappers, I: the formation of the South African Engineer Corps and its operations in East Africa and the Middle East to the Battle of Alamein* (Sappers Association, Johannesburg, 1981).

Otto, W, *Die Spesiale Diensbataljon* (Staatsdrukker, Pretoria, 1973).

Pakenham, Thomas, *The Boer War* (Abacus, London, 1995).

Pelzer, AN, *Die Afrikaner-Broederbond: eerste 50 jaar* (Tafelberg, Kaapstad, 1982).

Perry, FW, *The Commonwealth armies: manpower and organisation in two world wars* (Manchester University Press, 1990).

Pirow, Oswald, *James Barry Munnik Hertzog* (Howard Timmins, Cape Town, 1957).

Pollock, AM, *Pienaar of Alamein: the life story of a great South African soldier* (Cape Times, Cape Town, 1943).

Pope, Rex, *War and Society in Britain, 1899–1948* (Longman, Harlow, 1991).

Porch, Douglas, *Wars of Empire* (Cassell, London, 2001).

Pound, R, *Evans of the Broke: a biography of Admiral Lord Mountevans* (OUP, London, 1963).

Preston, RA, A Roland and SF Wise, *Men In Arms: a history of warfare and its interrelationships with Western society* (Harcourt Brace Jovanovich College Publishers, Orlando etc, 1991).

Pretorius, Fransjohan, *Life on commando during the Anglo-Boer War, 1899–1902* (Human & Rousseau, Cape Town, 1999).

Pyrah, GB, *Imperial Policy and South Africa, 1902–10* (Clarendon Press, Oxford, 1955).

Rhoodie, DO, *Suid-Afrika: van koloniale onderhorigheid tot soewereine onafhanklikheid* (Perskor, Johannesburg, 1974).

Roos, N, *Ordinary Springboks: white servicemen and social justice in South Africa, 1939–1961* (Ashgate, Burlington, VT, 2005).

Ross, Capt (SAN) CH, *A Decade of Peace Missions* (Department of Defence, Pretoria, 2009).

Scholtz, GD, *Generaal Christiaan Frederik Beyers 1869–1914* (Voortrekkerpers, Johannesburg, 1941).

Scholtz, GD, *Hertzog en Smuts en die Britse Ryk* (Raandse Afrikaanse Universiteit, Johannesburg, 1975).

Scholtz, L, *The SADF in the Border War, 1966–1989* (Tafelberg, Cape Town, 2013).

Scholtz, PGM, *Standerton, Gister en Vandag* (Bloemfontein, no date).

Service, Robert, *Spies and Commissars: Bolshevik Russia and the West* (Macmillan, London, 2011).

Shubin, Vladimir, *The Hot 'Cold War': the USSR in southern Africa* (UKZN Press, Scottsville, 2008).

Shultz, Richard H and Roy Godson, *Dezinformatsia: active measures in Soviet strategy* (Pergamon-Brassey's, Washington, DC, 1984).

Silburn, PA, *The Colonies and Imperial Defence* (Longman, London, 1909).

Simpson, JSM, *South Africa Fights* (Hodder & Stoughton, London, 1941).

Smith, JA, *John Buchan: a biography* (Rupert Hart-Davis, London, 1965).

Snyman, PHR, *Beeld van die SWA Gebiedsmag* (Pretoria, 1989).

Spies, FJ du Toit, *Operasie Savannah: Angola, 1975–1976* (SADF, Pretoria, 1989)

Steenkamp, Willem, *South Africa's Border War 1966–1989* (Ashanti, Gibraltar, 1989).

Steenkamp, Willem, *Assegais, Drums & Dragoons: a military and social history of the Cape* (Jonathan Ball, Johannesburg, 2012).

Stiff, Peter, *Nine Days of War* (Lemur, Alberton, 1989).

Strachan, Hew, *European Armies and the Conduct of War* (Routledge, London and New York, 1993).

Strachan, Hew, *The First World War in Africa* (OUP, Oxford, 2004).

Stultz, NM, *The Nationalists in Opposition, 1934–1948* (Human & Rousseau, Cape Town and Pretoria, 1974).

Swart, Sandra, *Riding High: horses, humans and history in South Africa* (Wits University Press, Johannesburg, 2010).

Thompson, EP, *The Making of the English Working Class* (Penguin, London, 1991).

Thompson, Leonard, *A History of South Africa* (Yale University Press, New Haven and London, 1990).

Thompson, Paul, *An Historical Atlas of the Zulu Rebellion of 1906* (Pietermaritzburg, 2001).

Travers, Tim, *The Killing Ground: the British Army, the Western Front, and the emergence of modern warfare, 1900–1918* (Allen and Unwin, London, 1987).

Travers, Tim, *How the War Was Won: command and technology in the British Army on the Western Front, 1917–1918* (Routledge, London, 1992).

Trewhela, Paul, *Inside Quatro: uncovering the exile history of the ANC and SWAPO* (Jacana, Auckland Park, 2010).

Turner, John W, *Continent Ablaze: the insurgency wars in Africa 1960 to the present* (Jonathan Ball, Johannesburg, 1998).

Turner, LCF, HR Gordon-Cumming and JE Betzler, *War in the Southern Oceans* (OUP, London, 1961).

Uyar, Mesut and Edward J Erikson, *A Military History of the Ottomans: from Osman to Atatürk* (ABC Clio, Santa Barbara, CA, 2009).

Uys, I, *Rollcall: the Delville Wood story* (Uys Publishers, Johannesburg, 1991).

Van der Merwe, HW, *Peacemaking in South Africa: A Life in Conflict Resolution* (Tafelberg, Cape Town, 2000).

Van der Veen, Roel, *Afrika: van de Koude Oorlog naar de 21ste eeuw* (KIT, Amsterdam, 2002).

Vandervort, B, *Wars of Imperial Conquest in Africa, 1830–1914* (UCL Press, London, 1998).

Van der Waals, WS, *Portugal's War in Angola, 1961–1974* (Ashanti, Rivonia, 1993).

Van Heyningen, Elizabeth, *The Concentration Camps of the Anglo-Boer War: a social history* (Jacana, Auckland Park, 2013).

Van Jaarsveld, FA, *The Afrikaner's Interpretation of South African History* (Simondium Publishers, Cape Town, 1964).

Van Jaarsveldt, AE, et al, *Militêre Geneeskunde in Suid-Afrika, 1913–1983* (Military Information Bureau, Pretoria, 1983).

Van Niekerk, M, 'Adolf Schiel en die Duitse Kommando' (*Argiefjaarboek vir Suid-Afrikaanse Geskiedenis* 1951/II).

Van Rooyen, JJ, *Die Nasionale Party: sy opkoms end oorwinning – Kaapland se aandeel* (Cape National Party, Cape Town, 1956).

Venter, AJ, *The Chopper Boys: helicopter warfare in Africa* (Southern, Halfway House, 1994).

Venter, AJ, *War Stories* (Protea, Pretoria, 2011).

Walker, IL and B Weinbren, *2000 Casualties. A History of the Trade Unions and the Labour Movement in the Union of South Africa* (Johannesburg, 1961).

Walker, Oliver, *Sailor Malan: a biography* (Cassell, London, 1953).

Walker, General Sir Walter, *The Bear at the Back Door: the Soviet threat to the West's lifeline in Africa* (Valiant, Sandton, 1978).

Warwick, Peter, *Black People and the South African War 1899–1902* (Ravan, Johannesburg, 1983).

Wavell, Lieutenant General Sir Archibald P, *The Palestine Campaigns* (Constable, London, 1941).

Wilcox, Craig, *Australia's Boer War: the war in South Africa, 1899–1902* (OUP, Oxford and New York, 2002).

Wilkins, Ivor and Hans Strydom, *The Super Afrikaners: inside the Afrikaner Broederbond* (Braamfontein, Jonathan Ball, 1978).

Williams, David, *On the Border: the white South African military experience, 1965–1990* (Tafelberg, Cape Town, 2008).

Journal Articles and Book Chapters

Agar-Hamilton, JAI, 'The Union of South Africa War Histories', in Robin Higham, ed, *Official Histories: essays and bibliographies from around the world* (Kansas State University Library, Manhattan, KS, 1970).

Alexander, McGill, 'The militarisation of South African white society, 1948–1990', *Scientia Militaria*, Vol 30, No 2, 2000.

Anglin, Douglas G, 'The life and death of South Africa's National Peacekeeping Force', *The Journal of Modern African Studies*, Vol 33, No 1, 1995.

Armitage, D, 'Greater Britain: A Useful Category of Historical Analysis?', *American Historical Review*, Vol 104, 1999.

Bailes, H, 'Technology and Imperialism: a case study of the Victorian army in Africa', *Victorian Studies*, Vol 24, No 1, 1980.

Bakkes, CM, 'Die Boer as berede skutter gedurende die Tweede Vryheidsoorlog', in RJ Bouch, ed, *Infantry in South Africa, 1652–1976* (Documentation Service SADF, Pretoria, 1977).

Bakkes, CM, 'Die kommandostelsel met spesiale verwysing na die historiese ontwikkeling van sy rangstruktuur', in PG Nel, ed, *Die Kultuurontlooiing van die Afrikaner* (HAUM, Pretoria en Kaapstad, 1979).

Barnard, L and S Swanepoel, 'Die Nasionale Vredesmag in militêre perspektief', *Scientia Militaria*, Vol 28, No 1, 1998.

Berkeley, GFH, 'Sir Harry Smith: a reminiscence of the Boer War in 1848', *The Fortnightly Review*, Vol 1, December 1899.

Bisset, WM, 'South Africa's role in the Civil War in Russia, 1918–1920', *Militaria*, Vol 15, No 4, 1985.

Bond, B, 'The Army between the Two World Wars 1918–1939', in D Chandler and I Beckett, eds, *The Oxford History of the British Army* (OUP, Oxford and New York, 1996).

Bonner, Phillip, 'Eluding capture: African grass-roots struggles in 1940s Benoni', in S Dubow and A Jeeves, eds, *South Africa's 1940s: worlds of possibilities* (Double Storey, Cape Town, 2005).

Boulter, RS, 'Afrikaner nationalism in action: FC Erasmus and South Africa's defence forces 1948–1959', *Nations and Nationalism*, Vol 6, No 3, 2000.

Callister, Graeme, 'Patriotic duty or resented imposition? Public reactions to military conscription in white South Africa, 1952–1972', *Scientia Militaria*, Vol 35, No 1, 2007.

Cleveland, Todd, '"We still want the truth": the ANC's Angolan detention camps and postapartheid memory', *Comparative Studies of South Asia, Africa and the Middle East*, Vol 25, No 1, 2005.

Cock, Jacklyn, 'Manpower and militarisation: women and the SADF', in Jacklyn Cock and Laurie Nathan, eds, *War and Society: the militarisation of South Africa* (David Philip, Cape Town, 1989).

Cohen, WB, 'Malaria and French imperialism', *Journal of African History*, Vol 24, 1983.

Cornwell, R, 'The Sanusi Campaign: Egypt, 1916', in Richard Bouch, ed, *Infantry in South Africa, 1652–1976* (Documentation Service SADF, Pretoria, 1977).

Correira, Paulo and Grietjie Verhoef, 'Portugal and South Africa: close allies or unwilling partners in southern Africa during the Cold War?', *Scientia Militaria*, Vol 37, No 1 (2009), pp 50–72.

Cowie, Donald, 'Union of South Africa', *Journal of the Royal United Service Institution*, Vol 84, 1939.

Dedering, T, '"Avenge the Lusitania": the anti-German riots in South Africa in 1915', *Immigrants & Minorities*, Vol 31, No 3, 2013.

Dix-Peek, Ross, 'Southern Africa's redcoat generals: South African and Rhodesian born general officers of the British Army, the Royal Air Force and the Royal Navy 1856–2007', The South African Military History Society, available from http://samilitaryhistory.org/ross/redcoats.html; accessed 12 April 2012.

Dorning, Warwick, 'A concise history of the South African Defence Force, 1912–1987', *Militaria*, Vol 17, No 2, 1987.

Dorning, Warwick, 'SA forces in the Second World War', *Militaria*, Vol 19, No 3, 1989.

Dummett, R, 'Africa's strategic minerals during the Second World War', *Journal of African History*, Vol 26, No 4, 1985.

Du Pisani, JA and BE Mongalo, 'Victims of a white man's war: blacks in concentration camps during the South African War 1899–1902', *Historia*, Vol 44, No 1, 1999.

Du Preez, SJ and CJ Nothling, 'Die veldtog in Angola, 1975–1976', in CJ Nothling, ed, *Ultima Ration Regum: artillery history of South Africa* (Military Information Bureau, Pretoria, 1987).

Edgar, Robert, 'Changing the old guard: AP Mda and the ANC Youth League, 1944–1949', in S Dubow and A Jeeves, eds, *South Africa's 1940s: worlds of possibilities* (Double Storey, Cape Town, 2005).

Ellis, Stephen, 'The historical significance of South Africa's third force', *Journal of Southern African Studies*, Vol 24, No 2, 1998.

Fedorowich, Kent, 'Anglicisation and the politicisation of British immigration to South Africa, 1899–1929', *Journal of Imperial and Commonwealth History*, Vol 19, 1991.

Fedorowich, Kent, 'Sleeping with the lion? The Loyal Afrikaners and the South African Rebellion of 1914–15', *South African Historical Journal*, Vol 49, No 1, 2003.

Fedorowich, Kent, 'German espionage and British counter-intelligence in South Africa and Mozambique, 1939–1944', *Historical Journal*, Vol 48, 2005.

Fourie, Deon, 'Decline and fall: why the South African civilian Defence Secretariat was dissolved in 1966', *Scientia Militaria*, Vol 40, No 3, 2012.

Fourie, SM, 'Van mobilisering na transformasie: die era van Suid-Afrika se militêre hoogbloei met die Vaaldriehoekse samelewing (1974–1994) as konsentrasieveld', *Scientia Militaria*, Vol 30, No 2, 2000.

Furlong, Patrick, 'Allies at war? Britain and the "Southern African Front" in the Second World War', *South African Historical Journal*, Vol 54, 2005.

Garson, NG, 'Het Volk: the Botha-Smuts Party in the Transvaal, 1904–11', *Historical Journal*, Vol 9, 1966.

Garson, NG, 'South Africa and World War One', *Journal of Imperial and Commonwealth History*, Vol 8, No 1, 1979.

Gossmann, AM, 'Lost in transition: the South African military and counterinsurgency', *Small Wars and Insurgencies*, Vol 19, No 4, 2008.

Grobler, JEH, 'Die Geallieerde Besetting van Madagaskar met spesifieke verwysing na die role van die Unieverdedigingsmag in die operasies', *Scientia Militaria*, Vol 7, No 4, 1977.

Grobler, JEH, 'Die Geallieerde Besetting van Madagaskar in 1942: Die Konsolidasietydperk, Mei-Augustus 1942', *Scientia Militaria*, Vol 8, No 1, 1978.

Grobler, JEH, 'Die Geallieerde Besetting van Madagaskar in 1942: Die Toetrede van die Suid-Afrikaanse Landmagte en die Besitting van Tananarive', *Scientia Militaria*, Vol 8, No 2, 1978.

Grobler, JEH, 'Die Geallieerde Besetting van Madagaskar in 1942: Tamatave, Tulear en die Oorgawe van Annet', *Scientia Militaria*, Vol 8, No 3, 1978.

Grobler, JEH, 'Die Geallieerde Besetting van Madagaskar in 1942', *Scientia Militaria*, Vol 8, No 4, 1978.

Grundlingh, Albert, 'Die Rebellie van 1914: 'n historiografiese verkenning', *Kleio*, Vol 11, 1979.

Grundlingh, Albert, 'South Africa and the Second World War', in BJ Liebenberg and SB Spies, eds, *South Africa in the 20th Century* (JL van Schaik, Pretoria, 1993).

Grundlingh, Albert, 'The King's Afrikaners? Enlistment and ethnic identity in the Union of South Africa's Defence Force during the Second World War, 1939–45', *Journal of African History*, Vol 40, No 3, 1999.

Grundlingh, Albert, 'Mutating memories and the making of a myth: remembering the SS *Mendi* disaster, 1917–2007', *South African Historical Journal*, Vol 63, No 1, 2011.

Guelke, Leonard and Robert Shell, 'An early colonial landed gentry: land and wealth in the Cape Colony, 1682–1731', *Journal of Historical Geography*, Vol 9, No 3, 1983.

Harrison, EDR, 'On secret service for the Duce: Umberto Campini in Portuguese East Africa, 1941–43', *English Historical Review*, Vol 122, 2007.

Heinecken, L, 'A diverse society, a representative military? The complexity of managing diversity in the South African armed forces', *Scientia Militaria*, Vol 37, No 1, 2009.

Heinecken, L and N van der Waag, 'The politics of race and gender in the South African armed forces: issues, challenges, lessons', *Commonwealth & Comparative Politics*, Vol 47, No 4, 2009.

Higginson, John, 'Hell in small places: agrarian elites and collective violence in the Western Transvaal, 1900–1907', *Journal of Social History*, Vol 35, No 1, 2001.

Howard, Michael, 'The use and abuse of military history', *Journal of the Royal United Services Institution*, Vol 107, No 625, 1962.

Howard, M, 'The First World War Reconsidered', in J Winter, G Parker and MR Habeck, eds, *The Great War and the Twentieth Century* (Yale University Press, New Haven and London, 2000).

Howlett, Darryl and John Simpson, 'Nuclearisation and denuclearisation in South Africa', *Survival: Global Politics and Strategy*, Vol 35, No 3, 1993.

Hudson, GF, 'How unified is the Commonwealth?', *Foreign Affairs*, Vol 33, No 4, July 1955.

Hyam, Ronald, 'The parting of ways: Britain and South Africa's departure from the Commonwealth, 1951–1961', *Journal of Imperial and Commonwealth History*, Vol 26, No 2, May 1998.

International Institute for Strategic Studies, *The Military Balance, 1986–1987* (Garden

City Press, Letchworth, 1986).

Jacobs, FJ, 'Tussen twee wêreldoorloë', in RJ Bouch, ed, *Infantry in South Africa, 1652–1976* (Pretoria, 1977).

Jacobs, FJ and JA Visser, 'Die Suid-Afrikaanse Artillerie tydens die Eerste Wêreldoorlog: die veldtog in Oos-Afrika en die Midde-Ooste, 1917–1918', in CJ Nöthling, ed, *Ultima Ratio Regum: artillery history of South Africa* (Military Information Bureau SADF, Pretoria, 1987).

Jonker, Eben, 'Ontstaan en ontwikkeling van die Transvaalse Verdedigingsmag, 1900–1912: Transvaal Volunteers', *Militaria*, Vol 3, No 3, 1972.

Jooste, L, 'Die politieke koerswending van 1948 besorg 'n nuwe identiteit aan die Univerdedigingsmag', *Militaria*, Vol 26, No 2, 1996.

Jordaan, Evert, 'Contemporary South African National Security Policy' (Research Paper, Faculty of Military Science, Stellenbosch University, 2001).

Jordaan, Evert, 'The role of South African armour in South West Africa/Namibia and Angola, 1975–1989', *Journal of Contemporary History*, Vol 31, No 3, 2006.

Katz, DB, 'The greatest military reversal of South African arms: the fall of Tobruk 1942, an avoidable blunder or an inevitable disaster?', *Journal for Contemporary History*, Vol 37, No 2, 2012.

Kessler, SV, 'The black and coloured concentration camps of the Anglo-Boer War 1899–1902: shifting the paradigm from sole martyrdom to mutual suffering', *Historia*, Vol 44, No 1, 1999.

Khwela, GC, 'The Clausewitzian and heuristic evolution of the ANC's armed struggle: a dependent pillar of the South African revolution', *Scientia Militaria*, Vol 30, No 2, 2000.

Killingray, David, 'Africans and African Americans in enemy hands', in Bob Moore and Kent Fedorowich, eds, *Prisoners of War and their Captors in World War II* (Berg, Oxford and Washington, DC, 1996).

Kleynhans, EP, 'The first South African armoured battle in Italy during the Second World War: the battle of Celleno, 10 June 1944', *Scientia Militaria*, Vol 40, No 3, 2012.

Kruys, Brig Gen George (rtd), 'Some major factors influencing military efficiency in the South African National Defence Force', *Strategic Review for Southern Africa*, Vol 26, 2004.

Lambert, John, 'South African British? Or Dominion South Africans? The evolution of an identity in the 1910s and 1920s', *South African Historical Journal*, Vol 43, November 2000.

Lambert, John, 'An identity threatened: white English-speaking South Africans, Britishness and domestic South Africanism, 1934–1939', *Kleio*, Vol 37, 2005.

Legassick, Martin, 'South Africa: capital accumulation and violence', *Economy and Society*, vol 3, no 3, 1974.

Linch, K, 'A geography of loyalism? The local military forces of the West Riding of Yorkshire, 1794–1814', *War & Society*, Vol 19, No 1, May 2001.

Mashike, L, '"Blacks can win everything, but the army": the "transformation" of the South African military between 1994 and 2004', *Journal of Southern African Studies*, Vol 33, No 3, 2007.

McGregor, PMJ, 'The history of No 2 Squadron, SAAF, in the Korean War', *Military History Journal*, Vol 4, No 3, June 1978.

Meyer, CM, 'The role of blacks in the South African Defence Force, 1912–1987', in *South African Defence Force Review*, 1988.

Möller, PL, 'The South African Air Force and the Warsaw Airlift of 1944', *Historia*, Vol 45, No 1, 2000.

Monama, FL, 'The Second World War and South African society, 1939–1945', in T Potgieter and I Liebenberg, eds, *Reflections on War: preparedness and consequences* (SUN Press, Stellenbosch, 2012).

Moore, Bob, 'Axis prisoners in Britain during the Second World War: a comparative analysis', in Bob Moore and Kent Fedorowich, eds, *Prisoners of War and their Captors in World War II* (Berg, Oxford and Washington, DC, 1996).

Morrell, R, 'Competition and cooperation in Middelburg, 1900–1930', in W Beinart, P Delius and S Trapido, eds, *Putting a Plough to the Ground: accumulation and dispossession in rural South Africa, 1850–1930* (Ravan, Johannesburg, 1986).

Motumi, Tsepe and A Hudson, 'Rightsizing: the challenges of demobilisation and social reintegration in South Africa', in J Cilliers, ed, *Dismissed* (IDP, Midrand, 1995).

Motumi, Tsepe and Penny McKenzie, 'After the war: demobilisation in South Africa', in Jacklyn Cock and Penny McKenzie, eds, *From Defence to Development: redirecting military resources in South Africa* (David Philip, Cape Town, 1998).

Nasson, Bill, 'A great divide: popular responses to the Great War in South Africa', *War & Society*, Vol 12, No 1, 1994.

Nasson, Bill, 'War opinion in South Africa, 1914', *Journal of Imperial and Commonwealth History*, Vol 23, No 2, 1995.

Nasson, Bill, 'Delville Wood and South African Great War commemoration', *English Historical Review*, Vol 69, No 480, February 2004.

Nasson, Bill, 'A flying Springbok of wartime British skies: A.G. "Sailor" Malan', *Kronos*, Vol 35, No 1, 2009.

Nattrass, Nicoli, 'Economic growth and transformation in the 1940s', in S Dubow and A Jeeves, eds, *South Africa's 1940s: worlds of possibilities* (Double Storey, Cape Town, 2005).

Neethling, Theo, 'Southern African military interventions in the 1990s: the case of SADC in Lesotho', in L du Plessis and M Hough, eds, *Managing African Conflicts: the challenge of military intervention* (HSRC, Pretoria, 2000).

Nothling CJ and L Steyn, 'The role of non-whites in the South African Defence Force', *Militaria*, Vol 16, No 2, 1986.

Oosthuizen, Francois, 'Changes and expectations: the white Union Defence Force soldier prior to and during the Second World War', *Militaria*, Vol 23, No 3, 1993.

Oosthuizen, Francois, 'Demobilisation and the post-war employment of the white Union Defence Force soldier', *Militaria*, Vol 23, No 4, 1993.

Park, MH, 'German South-West African campaign', *Journal of the African Society*, Vol 20, No 58, January 1916.

Ploeger, J, 'Uit die voorgeskiedenis van die SAW, 1902–1910', *Militaria*, Vol 1, No 3, 1969.

Ploeger, Jan, 'Suid-Afrikaanse verdedigingskemas, 1887–1914', *Militaria*, Vol 1, No 5, 1969.

Ploeger, Jan, 'Die imperiale militêre beleid ten opsigte van Suid-Afrika, 1908–1910', *Militaria*, Vol 3, No 2, 1972.

Porch, D, 'Imperial wars: from the Seven Years War to the First World War', in
C Townshend, ed, *The Oxford Illustrated History of Modern War* (Clarendon,
Oxford, 1997).

Pretorius, F, 'The Second Anglo-Boer War: an overview', *Scientia Militaria*, Vol 30,
No 2, 2000.

Rabert, B, 'South Africa's nuclear weapons: A defused time bomb?', *Aussenpolitik*,
Vol 44, No 3, 1993.

Riddell, Roger, 'The impact of new sanctions against South Africa', in Robert E Edgar,
ed, *Sanctioning Apartheid* (Africa World Press, Trenton, NJ, 1990).

Ross, Robert, 'The rise of the Cape gentry', *Journal of Southern African Studies*, Vol 9,
No 2, 1983.

Safi, Polat, 'An interview with Prof Georg G Iggers: "Every history can only present a
partial reconstruction of the past"', *Kilavuz*, Vol 52, December 2014.

Schmidl, EA, 'Adolph Zboril: an Austrian officer in the Transvaal artillery', *Militaria*,
Vol 18, No 2, 1988.

Serapião, Luís B, 'African foreign policies and African unity', in Luís Serapião et al,
African Foreign Policies in the 21st century (Africa Institute of South Africa,
Pretoria, 2001).

Shackleton, Deborah, 'South Africa and the High Commission Territories during
the Second World War: politics and policies affecting war mobilization', *Scientia
Militaria*, Vol 30, No 2, 2000.

Smith, ES, 'Die Geneeskundige Diens in die Eerste Wêreldoorlog: die oorlogsfront
in Europa, 1915–1918', in AE van Jaarsveldt et al, *Militêre Geneeskunde in Suid-
Afrika, 1913–1983* (Military Information Bureau, Pretoria, 1983).

Speir, Anthony, 'The Berlin Airlift, 1948–49', *South African Military History Journal*,
Vol 11, No 2, 1998.

Spiers, Edward, 'The late Victorian Army 1868–1914', in David Chandler and Ian
Beckett, *The Oxford History of the British Army* (OUP, Oxford, 1996).

Spies, SB, 'The outbreak of the First World War and the Botha government', *South
African Historical Journal*, Vol 1, 1969.

Stayanoff, Russ, 'Third World experience in counterinsurgency: Cuba's Operation
Carlotta, 1975', *Small Wars Journal*, 17 May 2008.

Stewart, Andrew, 'The Klopper Affair: Anglo-South African relations and the
surrender of the Tobruk garrison', *Twentieth Century British History*, Vol 17,
No 4, 2006.

Stewart, Andrew, 'The atomic despatch: Field Marshal Auchinleck, the fall of the
Tobruk garrison and post-war Anglo-South African relations', *Scientia Militaria*,
Vol 36, No 1, 2008.

Sylvester, J and A Seegers, 'South Africa's strategic arms package: a critical analysis',
Scientia Militaria, Vol 36, No 1, 2008.

Thomas, Martin, 'Captives of their countrymen: Free French and Vichy French
POWs in Africa and the Middle East, 1940–3', in Bob Moore and Kent
Fedorowich, eds, *Prisoners of War and their Captors in World War II* (Berg,
Oxford and Washington, DC, 1996).

Thompson, Paul, 'The Natal Militia: defence of the Colony, 1893–1910', *Journal of
Natal and Zulu History*, Vol 29, 2011.

Townshend, Charles, 'People's War', in C Townshend, ed, *The Oxford Illustrated*

History of Modern War (Oxford University Press, Oxford and New York, 1997).

Trapido, S, 'Reflections on land, office and wealth in the South African Republic', in S Marks and A Atmore, eds, *Economy and Society in Pre-Industrial South Africa* (Longman, London and New York, 1980).

'Transvaaler' (Geoffrey Robinson), 'Political parties of the Transvaal', *The National Review*, Vol 45, May 1905.

Van der Waag, Ian, 'The Union Defence Force between the two world wars, 1919–1940', *Scientia Militaria*, Vol 30, No 2, 2000.

Van der Waag, Ian 'War memories, historical consciousness and nationalism: South African history writing and the Second Anglo-Boer War, 1899–1999', in John Crawford and Ian McGibbon, eds, *One Flag, One Queen, One Tongue: New Zealand, the British Empire and the South African War, 1899–1902* (Auckland University Press, Auckland 2003).

Van der Waag, Ian, 'Contested histories: official history and the South African military in the 20th century', in J Grey, ed, *The Last Word? Essays on Official History in the United States and British Commonwealth* (Praeger, Westport, CT, 2003).

Van der Waag, Ian, 'Water and the ecology of warfare in southern Africa', in JWN Tempelhoff, ed, *African Water Histories: transdisciplinary discourses* (North-West University, Vanderbijlpark, 2005).

Van der Waag, Ian, 'Boer generalship and the politics of command', *War in History*, Vol 12, No 1, 2005.

Van der Waag, Ian, 'Rural struggles and the politics of a colonial command: the Southern Mounted Rifles of the Transvaal Volunteers, 1905–1912', in Stephen Miller, ed, *Soldiers and Settlers in Africa, 1850–1918* (Brill, Leiden, 2009).

Van der Waag, Ian, 'The thin edge of the wedge: Anglo-South African relations, dominion nationalism and the formation of the Seaward Defence Force in 1939–40', *Contemporary British History*, Vol 24, No 4, December 2010.

Van der Waag, Ian, 'Smuts' generals: towards a first portrait of the South African high command, 1912–48', *War in History*, Vol 18, No 1, January 2011.

Van der Waag, Ian, 'The origin and establishment of the South African Engineer Corps (SAEC), 1918–1939', *Journal for Contemporary History*, Vol 37, No 2, 2012.

Van der Waag, Ian, 'The battle of Sandfontein, 26 September 1914: South African military reform and the German South-West Africa campaign, 1914–1915', *First World War Studies*, Vol 4, No 2, October 2013.

Van der Waag, Ian, 'Military Culture and the South African armed forces, a historical perspective', in Francois Vreÿ, Abel Esterhuyse and Thomas Mandrup, eds, *On Military Culture: theory, practice and African armed forces* (UCT Press, Cape Town, 2013).

Van der Waag, IJ, 'South Africa and the war in Asia Minor, 1920–1923', *Militaria*, Vol 24, No 1, 1994.

Van Wijk, C, 'The new SANDF rank insignia: a missed opportunity for creating a common identity', *African Security Review*, Vol 12, No 3, 2003.

Van Wyk, AM, 'The USA and apartheid South Africa's nuclear weapons aspirations, 1949–1980', in Sue Onslow, ed, *Cold War in Southern Africa: white power, black liberation* (Routledge, Abingdon, 2009).

Visser, Deon, 'British influence on military training and education in South Africa:

the case of the South African Military Academy and its predecessors', *South African Historical Journal*, Vol 46, 2002.

Visser, Wessel, 'The South African labour movement's responses to declarations of martial law, 1913–1922', *Scientia Militaria*, Vol 31, No 2, 2003.

Warwick, Rodney, 'Operation Savannah: a measure of SADF decline, resourcefulness and modernisation', *Scientia Militaria*, Vol 40, No 3, 2012.

Willan, BP, 'The South African Native Labour Contingent, 1916–1918', *Journal of African History*, Vol 19, No 1, 1978.

Williams, Rocky, 'The other armies: writing the history of MK', in Ian Liebenberg et al, *The Long March: the story of the struggle for liberation in South Africa* (HAUM, Pretoria, 1994).

Wyndham, HA, 'Some aspects of South African Defence', *The State*, Vol 2, No 7, June 1909.

Wyndham, HA, 'Some aspects of South African Defence', *The State*, Vol 2, No 8, July 1909.

Zirkel, Kirsten, 'Military power in German colonial policy: the *Schütztruppen* and their leaders in East and South-West Africa, 1888–1918', in David Killingray and David Omissi, eds., *Guardians of Empire: the armed forces of the colonial powers, c 1700–1964* (MUP, Manchester, 1999).

Theses and Dissertations

Albertyn, Y, 'Upsetting the Applecart: Government and Food Control in the Union of South Africa during World War II, c 1939–1948' (MA thesis, Stellenbosch University, 2013).

Alexander, EGM, 'The Cassinga Raid' (unpublished MA thesis, Unisa, July 2003).

Bentz, G, 'Fighting Springboks: C Company, Royal Natal Carbineers: from Premier Mine to the Po Valley, 1939–1945' (MMil thesis, Stellenbosch University, 2013).

Boulter, RS, 'FC Erasmus and the Politics of South African Defence 1948–1959' (PhD dissertation, Rhodes University, 1997).

Bourhill, J, 'Red Tabs: Life and Death in the 6th South African Armoured Division, 1943–1945' (PhD dissertation, University of Pretoria, 2014).

Fuchs, DR, 'Durban During the Second World War, 1939–1945: A Study of War and Social Change' (MA thesis, University of Natal, 1990).

Grundlingh, LWF, 'Die Engelssprekende Suid-Afrikaners se reaksie op die uitbreek van die Eerste Wêreldoorlog' (MA thesis, Universiteit van die Oranje Vrystaat, 1978).

Horn, K, 'South African Prisoner-of-War Experience during and after World War II: 1939–c. 1950' (PhD dissertation, Stellenbosch University, December 2012).

Jooste, L, 'FC Erasmus as Minister van Verdediging, 1948–1959' (MA thesis, Unisa, 1995).

Katz, DB, 'Sidi Rezegh and Tobruk: Two South African Military Disasters Revisited, 1941–1942' (MMil thesis, Stellenbosch University, December 2014).

Kleynhans, EP, 'Armoured Warfare: The South African Experience in East Africa, 1940–1941' (MMil thesis, Stellenbosch University, December 2014).

Monama, FL, 'Wartime Propaganda in the Union of South Africa, 1939–1945' (PhD dissertation, Stellenbosch University, Jan 2014).

Moukambi, V, 'Relations Between South Africa and France with Special Reference to Military Matters, 1960–1990' (PhD, Stellenbosch University, 2008).

Nortier, EW, 'Major General Sir HT Lukin, 1861–1925: the making of a South African hero' (MMil thesis, Stellenbosch University, December 2005).

Tothill, FD, 'The 1943 General Election' (MA thesis, University of South Africa, 1987).

Visser, GE, 'Die Geskiedenis van die Suid-Afrikaanse Militêre Akademie, 1950–1990' (published as Supplementa I to *Scientia Militaria*, 2000).

Warwick, R, 'White South Africa and Defence, 1960–1968: Militarisation, Threat Perception and Counter Strategies' (PhD dissertation, UCT, 2009).

Conference and Seminar Papers

Ellis, JE, 'Musketry: the Anglo-Boer War experience'. Paper delivered at the Second Anglo-Boer War conference, Bloemfontein, October 1999.

Nortier, EW, '"A Just Devil": Major General Sir Henry Timson Lukin, 1860–1925'. Paper presented at the 4th War and Society in Africa Conference. 'Strategy, Generalship and Command in Southern Africa: Past, Present, Future', 4–6 September 2003.

Van der Waag, I, 'Hitler's Springboks: South African renegades and the politics of collaboration and treason, 1939–1948'. Conference paper, '1944: Seventy Years On', Royal Military Academy Sandhurst, UK, 14–17 April 2014.

Index